1998

INTERNATIONAL RELATIONS

INTERNATIONAL RELATIONS

Second Edition

JOSHUA S. GOLDSTEIN

American University, Washington, D.C.

HarperCollins*CollegePublishers*

Acquisitions Editor: Leo A. W. Wiegman
Developmental Editor: Ann Marie Kirby
Project Editor: Susan Goldfarb
Text and Cover Designer: Alice Fernandes-Brown
Art Studio: Ed Smith Design/Burmar
Photo Researcher: Rosemary Hunter
Electronic Production Manager: Alexandra Odulak
Manufacturing Manager: Hilda Koparanian
Electronic Page Makeup: Americomp
Printer and Binder: RR Donnelley & Sons Company
Color Map Insert Printer: The Lehigh Press, Inc.
Cover Printer: Phoenix Color Corp.

Cover Photos: *Beijing McDonald's:* Jeffrey Aaronson/Network Aspen. *Fleeing woman and armored car, Sniper's Alley, Sarajevo:* Chris Pfuhl/Agence France-Presse Photo. *Child with rifle, Sarajevo:* Senad Gubelic/93-1149/Reprinted with permission of UNICEF.

Source for color insert maps: Central Intelligence Agency.

Text photo credits appear on pp. 563–564.

International Relations, Second Edition

Library of Congress Cataloging-in-Publication Data

Goldstein, Joshua S. (date)
    International relations / Joshua S. Goldstein. — 2nd ed.
        p.   cm.
    Includes bibliographical references and indexes.
    ISBN 0-673-99758-8
    1. International relations.   I. Title.
    JX1391.G593   1996
    327—dc20
                                                                    95–34892
                                                                    CIP

96 97 98 99 9 8 7 6 5 4 3 2 1

To Andra
❖

BRIEF CONTENTS

DETAILED CONTENTS

PART TWO
INTERNATIONAL POLITICAL
ECONOMY   309

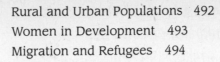

PREFACE

International relations is a compelling subject. The rich complexity of international relationships—political, economic, and cultural—provides a fascinating puzzle to try to understand. The puzzle is not just intellectually challenging; it is also emotionally powerful. It contains numerous human-scale stories in which the subject's grand themes—war and peace, tragedy and triumph, intergroup conflict and community—are played out. International relations is also relevant to our daily lives as never before; today's students will graduate into a global economy in which no nation stands alone.

Above all, the substance of international relations is changing profoundly in the 1990s, right before our eyes. The rules of world politics are being rewritten daily in large and small ways as global society races toward the millennium. Both the Cold War and its end are history. Students, professors, and policy makers alike are rethinking the subject of international relations. They are hungry for information about the New World Order and for explanations of how it works.

Power still matters, but economic forms of power now rival military ones. Nuclear weapons are still important, but now because of proliferation rather than the superpower arms race. Relations among states remain central to the rules of world politics, but there are substate and supranational actors and processes as well. Global telecommunications, multinational business networks, and transnational ethnic communities are undermining state sovereignty from within, while the nascent supranational authority of the United Nations and the European Union is doing the same from without. The most important global division is now the North-South gap between the world's rich and poor regions, not the East-West cleavage of the Cold War.

At the same time, scholarship in IR has moved in new directions as well—expanding the scope of the field and often creating uncertain boundaries and a jumble of divergent approaches to the subject. Unfortunately for people first approaching the subject, the tangle of ideas, theories, and ever-changing facts is confusing—a problem made worse when old textbooks are "updated" by tacking on chapters to cover new topics. Such was the motivation for a new textbook born in the 1990s.

❖ Changes in the Second Edition

The new synthesis laid out in the first edition of this book has held up well to the challenges of the post–Cold War era as it has unfolded over the past few years. Its reception by students has been gratifying. Therefore, the changes in this second edition are not radical. The overall organization of the text has been adjusted in one way in order to better present the various theories with which IR scholars attempt to explain world events: the chapter on alternatives to realism has been moved up front, following the chapter on realism. This chapter, now Chapter 3, presents more fully the main liberal and revolutionary critiques of traditional power politics, including neoliberal institutionalism, feminist theory, postmodernism, and peace studies.

To reinforce the importance of theoretical explanations and to help students think about episodes and cases in a more general and theoretical way, a series of new text boxes has been added under the title "Thinking Theoretically." Each box shows how a particular issue or case discussed in a chapter can be explained by different theoretical approaches. The boxes link back to the overview of conservative, liberal, and revolutionary theoretical traditions now laid out in Chapter 1. (The previous edition's boxes, titled "Theory in Practice," have been incorporated into this edition's text, where they better contribute to the sequence of ideas presented on each subject.)

World political events have continued to unfold in the past few years, and this second edition updates the examples, cases, photos, and descriptions accordingly. In a world of rapid change, students demand and deserve to learn the status of today's conflicts, organizations, treaties, and other aspects of international relations. An emphasis on the Gulf War—a key defining event of the post–Cold War era—is retained in this edition. But the conflict in Bosnia has been added as a second recurring example—one that contrasts with the Gulf War in many ways, notably in the efficacy of collective security. This contrast is used (especially in the first few "Thinking Theoretically" boxes) to explore how different theories explain puzzling outcomes. The Bosnia case is especially suitable for exploring the predictive power of theories, since the ultimate outcome of the conflict is still unknown at the time of this writing.

Another kind of updating has been undertaken for this edition: all quantitative data have been revised, using the latest available numbers. The author believes that data, presented simply and appropriately, allow students to form their own judgments and to reason through the implications of different policies and theories. Since the data are changing rapidly in the 1990s—be they numbers of military forces, regional inflation rates, or currency exchange rates—students deserve to have access to the most recent available numbers. This edition also adopts the new method of calculating internationally comparable GDP data based on purchasing-power parity.

❖ Pedagogical Elements

This book's aim is to present the current state of knowledge in IR in a comprehensive and accessible way—to provide a map of the subject covering its various research communities in a logical order.

The map is organized around the subfields of international security and international political economy. These subfields, although separated physically in this book, are integrated conceptually and overlap in many ways. No longer does one set of principles apply to military affairs and another set to economic relations, as was sometimes argued during the Cold War. Using the concepts of power and bargaining to bridge the two subfields, this book connects both subfields to the real world by using concrete examples to illustrate theories.

Many people in the television generation find information—especially abstract theories—easier to grasp when linked with pictures. Thus the book uses photographs extensively to illustrate important points.

In a subject like IR, where knowledge is tentative and empirical developments can overtake theories, critical thinking is a key skill for college students to develop. Narratives and boxes present what is known but leave conclusions open-ended in order to encourage critical thinking. The questions at the end of each chapter are designed to engage students in thinking critically about the contents of the chapter. The role of data in encouraging critical thinking by students has been mentioned. In presenting quantitative information, the text uses global-level data (showing the whole picture), rounds off numbers to highlight what is important, and conveys information graphically where appropriate.

Many people come to the study of IR with little background in world geography and history. The first chapter of this book presents background material on these topics. A historical perspective places recent decades in the context of the evolution of the modern international system. The global orientation of the book reflects the diversity of IR experiences for different actors, especially those in the global South.

Three levels of analysis—individual, domestic, and interstate—have often been used to sort out the multiple influences operating in international relations. This book adds a fourth, the global level. Global-level phenomena such as the United Nations, the world environment, and global telecommunications and culture receive special attention.

IR is a large subject that offers many directions for further exploration. The footnotes in this book, keyed to areas of the text and updated for this second edition, suggest further reading on various topics. Unless otherwise noted, they are not traditional sourcenotes.

❖ Structure of the Book

The overall structure of this book follows substantive topics, first in international security (Part One) and then in international political economy (Part Two).

Chapter 1 introduces the study of IR and provides some of the geographical and historical context of the subject. Chapters 2 and 3 lay out the various theoretical approaches to the subject, focusing primarily on international security but laying the groundwork for later treatments of international political economy as well. The concepts of power and bargaining, developed in Chapter 2, remain central to later discussions. They are augmented, in Chapter 3, by the important concepts of interdependence and collective goods, and by feminist (and other) critiques of realism.

The remaining four chapters of Part One move generally from the individual to the global level of analysis. Chapter 4 examines the foreign policy process, with special attention to U.S. foreign policy. Chapter 5 introduces the main sources of international conflict, including ethnic, territorial, and economic conflicts. The conditions and manner in which such conflicts lead to the use of violence are discussed in Chapter 6, on military force. Chapter 7 shows how international organizations and law, especially the United Nations, have evolved to become major influences in security relations.

The second part of the book similarly moves upward through levels of analysis, from microeconomic principles and national economies through trade and monetary relations, international integration, the environment, and North-South relations. Chapter 8 introduces theoretical concepts in political economy (showing how theories of international security translate into new issue areas), and discusses the most important topic in international political economy, namely, trade relations. Chapter 9 describes the politics of international money, banking, and multinational business operations. Chapter 10 explores the processes of international integration, telecommunications, and cultural exchange on both a regional scale—the European Union—and a global one. Chapter 11 shows how environmental politics expands international bargaining and interdependence both regionally and globally. Chapter 12 addresses global North-South relations, with particular attention to poverty in the third world. Chapter 13 then considers alternatives for third-world economic development in the context of international business, debt, and foreign aid. Chapter 14—a postscript set fifty years in the future—serves as a vehicle for reflection and critical thinking.

❖ Home Page

Faculty and students are invited to visit this book's home page on the World Wide Web, housed within the behavioral and social science site at http://www.harpercollins.com/college. The home page offers useful teaching tips and content-related web links for each chapter of *International Relations*, Second Edition.

❖ Acknowledgments

Many scholars, colleagues, and friends have contributed ideas that ultimately influenced both editions of this book. I owe a special debt to Robert North, who suggested more than a decade ago that the concepts of bargaining and leverage could be used to integrate IR theory across four levels of analysis. This second edition benefited from the superb assistance of Burcu Akan and from the suggestions of Jerry Bender, Maria Green Cowles, Randy Forsberg, David Gibbs, Louis Klarevas, Andrew Moravcsik, my colleagues at American University, and the students and section leaders in my World Politics classes.

The following reviewers made many useful suggestions:

Philip Baumann, *Moorhead State University*

Robert E. Breckinridge, *St. Francis College*

Gregory A. Cline, *Michigan State University*

Cynthia Combs, *University of North Carolina at Charlotte*

Patricia Davis, *University of Notre Dame*

Jonathan Galloway, *Lake Forest College*

Marc Genest, *University of Rhode Island*

Emily O. Goldman, *University of California, Davis*

Vicki Golich, *California State University, San Marcos*

Robert Gregg, *School of International Service, American University*

Wolfgang Hirczy, *University of Houston*

Piper Hodson, *University of Illinois, Urbana-Champaign*

Steven W. Hook, *University of Missouri*

Ted Hopf, *University of Michigan*

Akira Ichikawa, *University of Lethbridge*

Joyce Kaufman, *University of Maryland at College Park*

John Keeler, *University of Washington*

Michael Kelley, *University of Central Arkansas*

Mark Lagon, *Georgetown University*

William Lamkin, *Glendale Community College*

Renée Marlin-Bennett, *School of International Service, American University*

James Meernick, *University of North Texas*

Karen Mingst, *University of Kentucky*

Richard Moore, *Lewis-Clark State College*

John W. Outland, *University of Richmond*

Salvatore Prisco, *Stevens Institute of Technology*

David Rapkin, *University of Nebraska at Lincoln*

Edward Rhodes, *Rutgers University*

Leonard Riley, *Pikes Peak Community College*

Henry Schockley, *Boston University*

David Wilsford, *School of International Affairs, Georgia Institute of Technology*

The errors, of course, remain my own responsibility.

For editorial, production, and marketing work at HarperCollins, I thank Leo Wiegman, Ann Kirby, Susan Goldfarb, and Suzanne Daghlian.

JOSHUA S. GOLDSTEIN

TO THE STUDENT

The topics studied by scholars are like a landscape with many varied locations and terrains. This textbook is a map that can orient you to the main topics, debates, and issue areas in international relations. This map divides international relations into two main territories: international security and international political economy. However, these territories overlap and interconnect in many ways. Also, the principles that apply to the interactions of states in security affairs are similar to those that apply to economic relations.

Scholars use specialized language to talk about their subjects. This text is a phrase book that can translate such lingo and explain the terms and concepts that scholars use to talk about international relations. However, IR is filled with many voices speaking many tongues. The text translates some of those voices—of presidents and professors, free-traders and feminists—to help you sort out the contours of the subject and the state of knowledge about its various topics. But ultimately the synthesis presented in this book is the author's own. Both you and your professor may disagree with many points. Thus, this book is only a starting point for conversations and debates.

With map and phrase book in hand, you are ready to explore a fascinating world. The great changes in world politics in the past few years have made the writing of this textbook an exciting project. May you enjoy your own explorations of this realm.

J.S.G.

A Note on Nomenclature

In international relations, names are politically sensitive; different actors may call a territory or an event by different names. This book cannot resolve such conflicts; it has adopted the following naming conventions for the sake of consistency. The United Kingdom of Great Britain (England, Scotland, Wales) and Northern Ireland is called Britain. Burma, renamed Myanmar by its military government, is referred to as Burma. Cambodia, renamed Kampuchea by the Khmer Rouge in the 1970s, is called Cambodia. The 1991 U.S.-led multinational military campaign that retook Kuwait after Iraq's 1990 invasion is called the Gulf War. The war between Iraq and Iran in the 1980s is called the Iran-Iraq War (not the "Gulf War," as some called it at the time). The Republic of Bosnia and Herzegovina is generally shortened to "Bosnia" (with apologies to the residents of Herzegovina). The "Former Yugoslav Republic of Macedonia" is called Macedonia (despite Greek objections). The People's Republic of China, formally including breakaway Taiwan island, is referred to as China. Elsewhere, country names follow common usage, dropping formal designations such as "Republic of."

The World from South Perspective

North
America

Latin
America

Western
Europe

Africa

Middle East

Russia/Eastern Europe

South
Asia

China

Japan/
Pacific

World States and Territories

Inset map (upper left) labels

U.S.A.
BAHAMAS
CUBA
HAITI
DOMINICAN REPUBLIC
PUERTO RICO
VIRGIN ISLANDS
JAMAICA
BARBUDA
ANTIGUA
MEXICO
BELIZE
HONDURAS
ST. KITTS AND NEVIS
NICARAGUA
DOMINICA
MARTINIQUE
BARBADOS
GUATEMALA
NETHERLANDS ANTILLES
ST. VINCENT AND THE GRENADINES
ST. LUCIA
EL SALVADOR
GRENADA
COSTA RICA
PANAMA
COLOMBIA
VENEZUELA
TRINIDAD AND TOBAGO

Main map labels

ARCTIC OCEAN
GREENLAND (DANISH)
ICELAND
U.S.
CANADA
ATLANTIC OCEAN
MOROCCO
WESTERN SAHARA
PACIFIC OCEAN
UNITED STATES
BERMUDA
SENEGAL
CAPE VERDE
MAURITANIA
GAMBIA
GUINEA BISSAU
MEXICO
GUINEA
SIERRA LEONE
LIBERIA
SURINAME
FRENCH GUIANA
COLOMBIA
ECUADOR
GUYANA
PERU
BRAZIL
BOLIVIA
PARAGUAY
ATLANTIC OCEAN
CHILE
PACIFIC OCEAN
URUGUAY
ARGENTINA

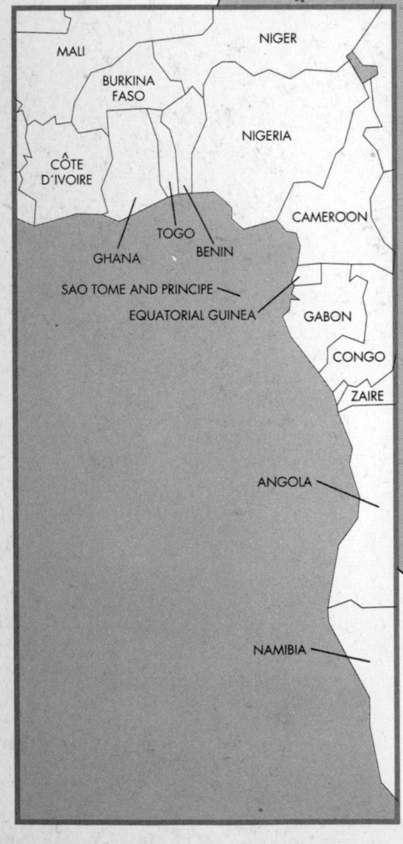

Inset map (lower left) labels

U.S.
MALI
NIGER
BURKINA FASO
NIGERIA
CÔTE D'IVOIRE
CAMEROON
GHANA
TOGO
BENIN
SAO TOME AND PRINCIPE
EQUATORIAL GUINEA
GABON
CONGO
ZAIRE
ANGOLA
NAMIBIA

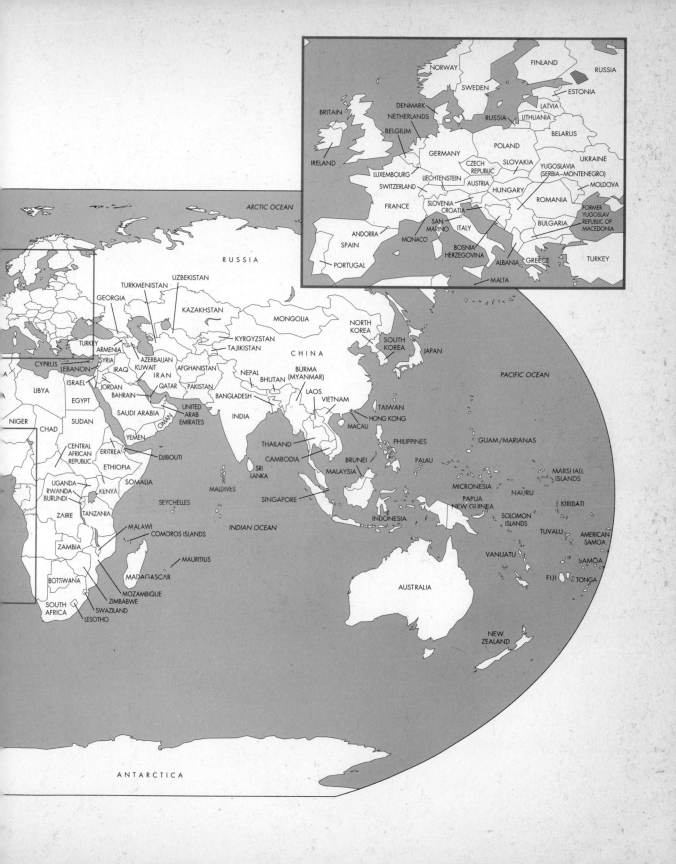

Wars in Progress, Late 1995

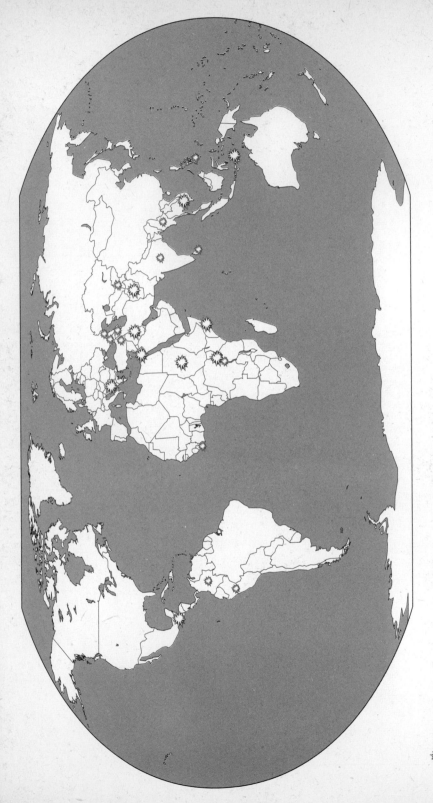

Source: Based on data from Center for Defense Information, Washington, D.C.

⊛ Estimated deaths to date over 100,000

⊙ Estimated deaths to date under 100,000

Nine Regions of the World

North America

Scale 1:38,700,000

Lambert Conformal Conic Projection,
standard parallels 37° N and 65° N

0   500 Kilometers

0   500 Nautical Miles

Boundary representation is
not necessarily authoritative.

802374 (B01267) 5-95

Central America and the Caribbean

United States

New Orleans •
Miami •

Gulf of Mexico

Straits of Florida

Tropic of Cancer

North Atlantic Ocean

Tropic of Cancer

THE BAHAMAS

Nassau ★

Havana ★

Cancún •
Isla Cozumel

Isla de la Juventud

CUBA

George Town ★
Cayman Islands (U.K.)

Swan Islands (HONDURAS)

MEXICO

Belmopan ★
BELIZE

San Pedro Sula •
GUATEMALA
Guatemala ★
Tegucigalpa •
HONDURAS

San Salvador ★
EL SALVADOR

Managua ★
NICARAGUA

Cayos Miskitos (NICARAGUA)

Isla de Providencia (COLOMBIA)

Islas del Maíz (NICARAGUA)

Puerto Limón •
San José ★
COSTA RICA

Isla del Coco (COSTA RICA)

North Pacific Ocean

Galapagos Islands (ECUADOR)

Equator

Scale 1:21,500,000

Lambert Conformal Conic Projection, standard parallels 7N and 19N

300 Nautical Miles
300 Kilometers

PANAMA
Panamá ★
Colón •
Panama Canal

Isla de San Andrés (COLOMBIA)

JAMAICA
Kingston ★

GREATER ANTILLES

Turks and Caicos Islands (U.K.)
Grand Turk ★

DOMINICAN REPUBLIC
Santo Domingo ★

HAITI
Port-au-Prince ★

Guantánamo Bay (U.S. NAVAL BASE)

Caribbean Sea

A N T I L L E S

Puerto Rico (U.S.)
San Juan ★

Virgin Islands (U.S.)
Charlotte Amalie ★

British Virgin Islands (U.K.)
Road Town ★

Anguilla (U.K.)
The Valley ★

Basseterre ★
ST. KITTS AND NEVIS

Montserrat (U.K.)
Plymouth ★

ANTIGUA AND BARBUDA
St. John's ★

Basse-Terre ★
Guadeloupe (FRANCE)

DOMINICA
Roseau ★

Fort-de-France ★
Martinique (FRANCE)

Castries ★
ST. LUCIA

Bridgetown ★
BARBADOS

Kingstown ★
ST. VINCENT AND THE GRENADINES

St. George's ★
GRENADA

Leeward Islands
Windward Islands

LESSER ANTILLES

Netherlands Antilles (NETHERLANDS)
Bonaire
Curaçao
Willemstad ★

Aruba (NETH.)
Oranjestad ★

Maracaibo •
Caracas ★
San Cristóbal •

Port-of-Spain ★
TRINIDAD AND TOBAGO

Ciudad Guayana •

VENEZUELA

Barranquilla •
Cartagena •
Medellín •
Cali •
Bogotá ★
COLOMBIA

Magdalena

ECUADOR

Georgetown ★
GUYANA

Paramaribo ★
SURINAME

Cayenne ★
French Guiana (FRANCE)

Boa Vista •

B R A Z I L

Equator

Boundary representation is not necessarily authoritative.

802107 (R00769) 8-93

South America

Caribbean Sea

Guadeloupe (FRANCE)
DOMINICA
Martinique (FRANCE)
ST. LUCIA
ST. VINCENT AND THE GRENADINES
GRENADA
BARBADOS

North Atlantic Ocean

HONDURAS
Tegucigalpa
Puerto Lempira
Puerto Cabezas
NICARAGUA
Managua
Liberia
San José
COSTA RICA
David
Colón
PANAMA
Panamá

Isla de San Andrés (COLOMBIA)
Barranquilla
Maracaibo
Caracas
Port-of-Spain
TRINIDAD AND TOBAGO
San Cristóbal
VENEZUELA
Ciudad Guayana
Medellín
GUYANA
Georgetown
Paramaribo
SURINAME
French Guiana (FRANCE)
Cayenne
Bogotá
COLOMBIA
Boa Vista
Cali
Isla de Malpelo (COLOMBIA)
Mitú
Macapá
Belém
São Luís

Equator

Quito
ECUADOR
Guayaquil
Fonte Boa
Manaus
Santarém
Amazon
Río Negro
Amazon
Fortaleza
Teresina
Natal

Iquitos
Piura
Río Marañón
Río Ucayali
Rio Branco
Pôrto Velho
BRAZIL
Recife

Trujillo
Huánuco
PERU
Palmas
Aracaju
Lima
Cusco
Trinidad
Cuiabá
Salvador
Ica
Lago Titicaca
BOLIVIA
Río Xingu
Río Tocantins
Río São Francisco
Arequipa
La Paz
Cochabamba
Santa Cruz
Goiânia
Brasília

South Pacific Ocean

Arica
Potosí
Sucre
Belo Horizonte
Tropic of Capricorn
Antofagasta
PARAGUAY
Vitória
Río Paraguai
Rio de Janeiro
Asunción
São Paulo
San Miguel de Tucumán
Resistencia
Curitiba
Isla San Félix (CHILE)
Isla San Ambrosio (CHILE)
Florianópolis

South Atlantic Ocean

CHILE
Córdoba
Río Paraná
Pôrto Alegre
Salto
URUGUAY
Valparaíso
Mendoza
Rosario
Archipiélago Juan Fernandez (CHILE)
Santiago
Buenos Aires
Montevideo
ARGENTINA
Concepción
Bahía Blanca
Mar del Plata
San Carlos de Bariloche
Puerto Montt
Comodoro Rivadavia

Scale 1:35,000,000

Azimuthal Equal-Area Projection

0   250   500 Kilometers
0   250   500 Nautical Miles

Boundary representation is not necessarily authoritative.

Strait of Magellan
Punta Arenas
Ushuaia
Stanley
Falkland Islands (Islas Malvinas) (administered by U.K., claimed by Argentina)

South Georgia and the South Sandwich Islands (administered by U.K., claimed by Argentina)

802376 (545528) 5-95

Africa

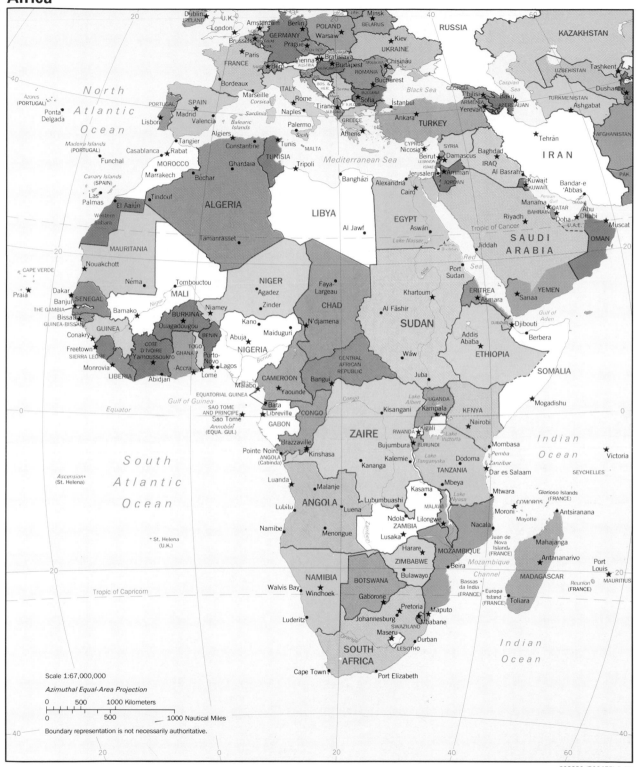

Scale 1:67,000,000

Azimuthal Equal-Area Projection

0   500   1000 Kilometers

0   500   1000 Nautical Miles

Boundary representation is not necessarily authoritative.

802380 (R00475) 5-95

Northern Africa and the Middle East

North Atlantic Ocean

Azores (PORT.)

Madeira Islands (PORT.)

Canary Islands (SP.)

PORTUGAL
Lisbon ★

SPAIN
Madrid ★

GIBRALTAR (U.K.)

Rabat ★
MOROCCO

El Aaiún ●
Western Sahara

MAURITANIA
Nouakchott ★

Dakar ★
SENEGAL
Banjul ★
THE GAMBIA
GUINEA-BISSAU
Bissau ★
Conakry ★
GUINEA
SIERRA LEONE
Freetown ★
Monrovia ★
LIBERIA

MALI
Bamako ★

CÔTE D'IVOIRE
Yamoussoukro ★

BURKINA
Ouagadougou ★

GHANA
Accra ★

TOGO
Lomé ★

BENIN
Porto-Novo ★

NIGER
Niamey ★

NIGERIA
Abuja ★

ALGERIA

Algiers ★

FRANCE

Balearic Islands

Corsica

Sardinia

ITALY
Rome ★

Tunis ★
TUNISIA

Tripoli ★
LIBYA

Sicily

MALTA
Valletta ★

Mediterranean Sea

Tropic of Cancer

Niger

Gulf of Guinea

CAMEROON
Yaoundé ★
Malabo ★
EQUATORIAL GUINEA
SAO TOME AND PRINCIPE
São Tomé ★
GABON
Libreville ★
CONGO

EGYPT
Cairo ★

Nile

CHAD
N'Djamena ★

CENTRAL AFRICAN REPUBLIC
Bangui ★

ZAIRE

SUDAN
Khartoum ★

Blue Nile

White Nile

Benue

UGANDA
Kampala ★
Lake Victoria

KENYA

Equator

Indian Ocean

SOMALIA
Mogadishu ★

ETHIOPIA
Addis Ababa ★

DJIBOUTI
Djibouti ★

ERITREA
Asmara ★

YEMEN
Sanna ★

Gulf of Aden

Socotra (YEMEN)

Gulf of Oman

OMAN
Muscat ★

U.A.E.
Abu Dhabi ★
QATAR
Doha ★
Dhabi

BAHRAIN
Manama ★

Persian Gulf

KUWAIT
Kuwait ★

SAUDI ARABIA
Riyadh ★

Red Sea

OMAN

Gulf of Oman

IRAN
Tehrān ★

AFGHANISTAN
Kabul ★

PAKISTAN

TAJIKISTAN
Dushanbe ★

UZBEKISTAN

TURKMENISTAN
Ashgabat ★

KAZAKHSTAN

RUSSIA

Baku ★
AZERBAIJAN
ARMENIA
Yerevan ★
Tbilisi ★
GEORGIA

Caspian Sea

Black Sea

TURKEY
Ankara ★

Tigris
Euphrates

IRAQ
Baghdad ★

SYRIA
Damascus ★

LEBANON
Beirut ★
ISRAEL
Jerusalem ★
JORDAN
Amman ★

CYPRUS
Nicosia ★

GREECE
Athens ★

Crete

ALBANIA
Tiranë ★

BULGARIA
Sofia ★

ROMANIA
Bucharest ★

SERBIA
Belgrade ★

Zagreb ★

MONT.
Podgorica ★

BOS. & HERZ.
Sarajevo ★
CRO.
SLO.

UKRAINE

Adriatic Sea

MAC.
Skopje ★

Scale 1:42,300,000

500 Nautical Miles

500 Kilometers

Azimuthal Equal-Area Projection

Boundary representation is not necessarily authoritative.

802095 (546325) 9-93

Europe

Greenland
(DENMARK)

Jan Mayen
(NORWAY)

Serbia and Montenegro have asserted the formation
of a joint independent state, but this entity has
not been formally recognized as a state by the
United States.

F.Y.R.O.M. - The Former Yugoslav Republic of
Macedonia

Greenland Sea

Barents Sea

Hammerfest

Murmansk

Norwegian Sea

Navik

Kiruna

White Sea

Arkhangel'sk

Arctic Circle

Reykjavik

ICELAND

NORWAY

Oulu

Lake Onega

FINLAND

Trondheim

Umeå

Tampere

Lake Ladoga

Tórshavn   Faroe Islands
(DENMARK)

Shetland Islands

Bergen

Oslo

SWEDEN

Gävle

Helsinki

St. Petersburg

Rockall
(U.K.)

Orkney Islands

Göteborg

Stockholm

Åland Islands

Gulf of Finland

Tallinn

ESTONIA

RUSSIA

Hebrides

Aberdeen

Gotland

Riga

LATVIA

Smolensk

North Atlantic Ocean

Edinburgh

Isle
of
Man
(U.K.)

Newcastle

North Sea

DENMARK

Copenhagen

Baltic Sea

Oland

LITHUANIA

Vilnius

Minsk

Belfast

UNITED

Bornholm

Kaliningrad

RUSSIA

BELARUS

Dublin

Irish Sea

Liverpool

Rostock

Gdańsk

IRELAND

Cardiff

KINGDOM

Amsterdam

Hamburg

Berlin

Poznań

Warsaw

Brest

Kiev

London

NETHERLANDS

Hannover

POLAND

English Channel

Brussels

GERMANY

Leipzig

Wrocław

Kraków

U K R A I N E

Guernsey (U.K.)
Jersey (U.K.)

BELGIUM

Bonn

Frankfurt

Prague

CZECH REPUBLIC

Kiev

Le Havre

LUX.

Luxembourg

SLOVAKIA

MOLDOVA

Paris

Stuttgart

Bratislava

Budapest

Chişinău

Nantes

Strasbourg

Munich

Vienna

Odesa

Loire

FRANCE

SWITZ.

AUSTRIA

HUNGARY

Cluj-Napoca

ROMANIA

Geneva

LIECH.

Graz

Pécs

Bern

Danube

Lyon

Milan

SLOVENIA

Zagreb

Belgrade

Bucharest

Black Sea

Bay of Biscay

Bordeaux

Turin

Genoa

Venice

Ljubljana

CROATIA

BOSNIA AND HERZEGOVINA

Constanța

Varna

MONACO

SAN MARINO

Florence

Sarajevo

Serbia

BULGARIA

Bilbao

Marseille

Adriatic Sea

Podgorica

Sofia

Istanbul

PORTUGAL

ANDORRA

ITALY

Rome

Montenegro

Skopje

Thessaloniki

TURKEY

Porto

SPAIN

Barcelona

Corsica

VATICAN CITY

Tiranê

F.Y.R.O.M.

Madrid

ALB.

Icánnina

Valencia

Naples

Aegean Sea

Sevilla

Sardinia

Tyrrhenian Sea

GREECE

Lisbon

Balearic Islands

Ionian Sea

Athens

Málaga

Rhodes

Strait of Gibraltar

Gibraltar
(U.K.)

Ceuta
(SPAIN)

Palermo

Sicily

Peloponnisos

Crete

Melilla
(SPAIN)

Mediterranean Sea

Tunis

Scale 1:19,500,000

Rabat

MOROCCO

ALGERIA

Algiers

TUNISIA

Valletta

MALTA

Lambert Conformal Conic Projection,
standart parallels 40°N and 56°N

0   300 Kilometers

0   300 Nautical Miles

20

802377 (R01083) 5-95

Asia

802382 (R01813) 5-95

PART ONE

INTERNATIONAL SECURITY

Afghanistan, 1995

Sarajevo father, 1994.

UNDERSTANDING INTERNATIONAL RELATIONS

❖ THE STUDY OF IR

Our world is large and complex. International relations is a fascinating topic because it concerns peoples and cultures throughout the world. The scope and complexity of these groups' interactions make international relations a challenging subject to master. There is always more to learn. This book is only the beginning of the story.

Strictly defined, the field of **international relations (IR)** concerns the relationships among the world's national governments. But these political relations cannot be understood in isolation. They are closely connected with other actors (such as the United Nations, multinational corporations, and individuals); with other social relationships (including economics, culture, and domestic politics); and with geographic and historical influences. IR is a large subject that overlaps several other fields.

This book's purpose is to introduce the field of IR, to organize what is known and theorized about IR in a logical way, and to convey the key concepts used by political scientists to discuss relations among nations. This first chapter defines IR as a field of study, introduces the actors of interest, and reviews the geographical and historical contexts within which IR occurs.

IR and Daily Life

Sometimes international relations is portrayed as a distant and abstract ritual conducted by a small group of people such as presidents, generals, and diplomats. This is not accurate. Although leaders do play a major role in international affairs, many other people participate as well. College students and other citizens participate in international relations every time they vote in an election or work on a political campaign; every time they buy a product or service traded on world markets; and every time they watch the news. The choices we make in our daily lives ultimately affect the world we live in. Each person contributes a small bit to the flow of history, and each faces unique choices as an individ-

IR touches our lives in many ways. The Vietnam Veterans Memorial, 1982.

ual human being. Through those choices, every person makes a unique contribution, however small, to the world of international relations.

In turn, IR profoundly affects the daily lives of college students and other citizens. The prospects for college students' getting jobs after graduation depend on the global economy and international economic competition. Those jobs also are more likely than ever to entail international travel or communication. And the rules of the world trading system affect the goods that students consume, from television sets to gasoline.

Although international economics affects daily life all the time, war dominates daily life only infrequently. In major wars, of course, students and their friends and loved ones go off to war and their lives change irreversibly. But even in peacetime, war is among the most pervasive international influences in daily life. Children play with war toys; young people go into military service; TV and films reproduce and multiply the images of war; and a sizable sector of the world economy is structured around military production.

The internationalization of daily life is increasing rapidly. Better communication and transportation capabilities are constantly expanding the ordinary person's contact with people, products, and ideas from other countries. As technology advances, the world is thus shrinking year by year.

IR as a Field of Study

As a field of study, IR has uncertain boundaries.[1] As a part of political science, IR is about *international politics*—the decisions of governments concerning their actions toward other governments. To some extent, however, the field is interdisciplinary, relating international politics to economics, history, sociology, and other disciplines. Some universities offer separate degrees or departments for IR. Most, however, teach IR in political science classes. The focus is on the *politics* of economic relationships, or the *politics* of environmental management.

Political relations among nations cover a range of activities—diplomacy, war, trade relations, alliances, cultural exchanges, participation in international organizations, and so forth. Particular activities within one of these spheres make up distinct **issue areas** on which scholars and foreign policy makers focus attention. Examples of issue areas include global trade negotiations, or specific ethnic conflicts such as the India-Pakistan or Arab-Israeli conflicts. Within each issue area, and across the range of issues of concern in any international relationship, policy makers of one nation can behave in a **cooperative** manner or a **conflictual** manner—extending either friendly and helpful behavior or hostile and harmful behavior toward the other nation. IR scholars often look at international relations in terms of the mix of conflict and cooperation in a relationship between two nations.

One kind of politics that has an international character is not generally included in the field of IR: the domestic politics of foreign countries. That is a separate field of political science: *comparative politics*. Comparative politics overlaps with IR to the considerable extent that domestic politics influences foreign policy in many countries. (In the case of U.S. foreign policy, IR overlaps with the field of American government.) Furthermore, the scholars who know about IR and foreign policies in a certain country or region often are the same people who know the most about domestic politics within that country or region. Despite these overlaps, IR as a field tends to avoid issues that concern domestic politics in the United States or other countries *except* to the extent that they affect international politics.

The scope of the field of IR may also be defined by the *subfields* it encompasses. Traditionally, the study of IR has focused on questions of war and peace—the subfield of **international security** studies. The movements of armies and of diplomats, the crafting of treaties and alliances, the development and deployment of military capabilities—these are the subjects that dominated the study of IR in the past, especially in the 1950s and 1960s, and they continue to hold a central position in the field. In the early 1990s, as the Cold War ended, the subfield of security studies broadened beyond its traditional focus on military forces and the superpower arms race. Regional conflicts began to receive more attention, and ethnic conflicts became more prominent. Scholars of foreign-policy

---

[1]Howell, Llewellyn D., ed. International Studies: The State of the Discipline [special issue]. *International Studies Notes* 16 (3), 1991. Holsti, K. J. *The Dividing Discipline: Hegemony and Diversity in International Theory.* Boston: Allen & Unwin, 1985. Hoffmann, Stanley. An American Social Science: International Relations. *Daedalus* 106 (3), 1977: 41–60. Lynch, Allen. *The Soviet Study of International Relations.* New York: Cambridge University Press, 1987.

processes increasingly saw themselves as part of this broader security studies community. Meanwhile, interdisciplinary peace studies programs, which emerged in the 1980s at many universities, sought to broaden concepts of "security" further—as did feminist scholars. While the study of war, weapons, and military forces continues to be the core concern of international security studies, these trends have expanded the boundaries of the subfield.[2]

In the 1970s and 1980s, as economics became increasingly central to international relations, the subfield of **international political economy (IPE)** grew and became the counterpoint to international security studies as a second main subfield of IR. Scholars of IPE study trade relations and financial relations among nations, and try to understand how nations have cooperated politically to create and maintain institutions that regulate the flow of international economic and financial transactions. These topics mainly relate to relations among the world's richer nations. But in the 1990s, growing attention is being paid to global North-South relations between rich and poor nations (see pp. 19–23), including such topics as economic dependency, debt, foreign aid, and technology transfer. As the East-West confrontation of the Cold War recedes into history, North-South problems are becoming more salient. So are problems of international environmental management and of global telecommunications. The subfield of IPE is expanding accordingly. There are, of course, other ways that the scope and structure of the field of IR can be organized. Each professor probably has her or his own mental map of the field.

Increasingly, IR scholars are recognizing the close connections of IPE with security (after decades of treating them as separate and different). The same principles and theories that help us understand international security (in the first half of this book) also help us to understand IPE (in the second half).

Theories and Methods

IR scholars want to understand why international events occur in the way they do. Why did a certain war break out? Why did a certain trade agreement benefit one nation more than another? Why are some countries so much richer than others? These "why" questions can be answered in several ways. One kind of answer results from tracing the immediate, short-term sequences of events and decisions that led to a particular outcome. For instance, the outbreak of war might be traced to a critical decision made by a particular leader. This kind of answer is largely *descriptive*—it seeks to describe how particular forces and actors operate to bring about a particular outcome.

Another kind of answer to "why" questions results from seeking general explanations and longer-term, more indirect causes. For example, a war outbreak might be seen as an instance of a general pattern in which arms races lead to war (or some such hypothesis).

[2]Walt, Stephen M. The Renaissance of Security Studies. *International Studies Quarterly* 35 (2), 1991: 211–40. Haftendorn, Helga. The Security Puzzle: Theory-Building and Discipline-Building in International Security. *International Studies Quarterly* 35 (1), 1991: 3–18. Buzan, Barry. *People, States and Fear: An Agenda for International Security Studies in the Post–Cold War Era.* 2nd ed. Boulder, CO: Lynne Rienner, 1991. Klare, Michael T., and Daniel C. Thomas, eds. *World Security: Challenges for a New Century.* New York: St. Martin's Press, 1994.

This kind of answer is *theoretical* because it places the particular event in the context of a more general pattern applicable across many cases.

Understanding IR requires both descriptive and theoretical knowledge. It would do little good to only describe events without being able to generalize or draw lessons from them. Nor would it do much good to formulate purely abstract theories without being able to apply them to the finely detailed and complex real world in which we live.

Ultimately, IR is a rather practical discipline. There is a close connection between scholars in colleges, universities, or think tanks and the policy-making community working in the government—especially in the United States. Some professors serve in the government (for instance, Professor Henry Kissinger was secretary of state in the 1970s), and sometimes professors publicize their ideas about foreign policy through newspaper columns or TV interviews. Influencing their government's foreign policy gives these scholars a laboratory to test their ideas in practice. Diplomats, bureaucrats, and politicians can benefit from both the descriptive and the theoretical knowledge produced by IR scholars.

Different IR scholars emphasize different mixes of descriptive and theoretical work. Like other disciplines, IR includes both basic and applied research. Generally speaking, scholars closer to the policy process are more interested in descriptive and short-term explanations that are useful for managing a particular issue area or region—information like who the individual players are, their backgrounds and past behavior patterns, the various interests at stake to various participants, and so forth. Scholars closer to the academic ivory tower tend to be interested in more abstract, more generalizable, and longer-term explanations.

A parallel (though not a perfect one) can be drawn when it comes to the *methods* to use in developing and testing various theories. The methodological approaches can be arrayed roughly along an empirical versus theoretical axis. At one end, many scholars seek knowledge about IR by interviewing people in various places and piecing together their stories (or their memoirs, archival documents, etc.)—a method well suited to descriptive explanation or to induction (building theories from facts). At the other end, some researchers create abstract mathematical models of relationships which are all theory with no real grounding in the empirical reality of international politics—a method suited to deduction (predicting facts from a theory). Between these approaches are others that mix theory and empirical evidence in various ways. Many IR scholars try to make quantitative measurements of things like international conflict or trade, and use statistical methods to make inferences about the relationships among those variables. All of these methods of learning about IR can be useful in different ways, though they yield different kinds of knowledge.

IR is an unpredictable realm of turbulent processes and events that catch all the experts by surprise. Most IR scholars are modest about their ability to make accurate predictions—and with good reason. The best theories provide at best only a rough guide to understanding what actually occurs in IR or predicting what will happen next.

Perhaps because of this complexity and unpredictability, IR scholars do not agree on a single set of theories to explain IR or even on a single set of concepts with which to discuss the field. Traditionally, the most widely accepted theories—though never unchallenged by critics—have explained international outcomes in terms of power politics or "realism."[3] But there are many theoretical disagreements—different answers to the "why" questions—both within realism and between realists and their critics. Throughout these discussions, no single theoretical framework has the support of all IR scholars.[4]

One way to order the variety of theories scholars use to explain IR is to distinguish three broad theoretical perspectives which may be called the *conservative, liberal, and revolutionary world views*. In some sense, each is a lens through which the world looks different and different things seem important. At the same time, the three perspectives can complement each other, and most theories draw on all three, though in different proportions. Furthermore, there is not just one conservative approach or one revolutionary approach. Each world view encompasses a variety of distinct theoretical approaches.

A *conservative* world view generally values maintenance of the status quo and discounts the element of change in IR. These perpectives focus on the laws of power politics, which are considered timeless and universal. Conservative perspectives find their most fertile ground in the subfield of international security with its logic of military power. They see states as the most important actors (largely because states control the biggest armies). Relative position with regard to other states is more important than the absolute condition of a state, because in the anarchic world with its ever present possibility of war, winning and losing matters above all. Conservative approaches tend to value *order*. Their advocates are prudent and not eager for change, especially rapid change or change that upsets the hierarchy of power in the international system. These perspectives tend to see war as the natural order of things, a sometimes necessary evil for which one should always be prepared. They see international trade as a potential source of national power, a view expressed in IPE as *mercantilism* (the accumulation of national war chests, or the equivalent, through control of trade).

A *liberal* world view values reform of the status quo through an evolutionary process of incremental change. Theories that build on the liberal tradition often focus on the mutual benefits to be gained in IR through interdependence and reciprocity. Gaining wealth in absolute terms is more important from this perspective than gaining power relative to other countries. Liberal approaches find their most fertile ground in the international-political-economy subfield because of the potentials for mutual gain in trade and exchange, with each nation exploiting its comparative advantage in particular products and services. Liberal approaches tend to value *freedom*, especially free trade and free exchange of ideas. They tend to see war not as a natural tendency but as a tragic mistake, to be prevented or at least minimized by international agreements and organizations.

---

[3]Shafritz, Jay M., and Phil Williams. *International Relations: The Classic Readings.* Belmont, CA: Wadsworth, 1993. Vasquez, John A. *Classics of International Relations.* Englewood Cliffs, NJ: Prentice Hall, 1986. Knutsen, Torbjörn L. *The History of International Relations Theory: An Introduction.* Manchester, England: Manchester University Press, 1992. Rothstein, Robert L., ed. *The Evolution of Theory in International Relations: Essays in Honor of William T. R. Fox.* Columbia: University of South Carolina Press, 1991.

[4]Groom, A. J. R., and Margot Light. *Contemporary International Relations: A Guide to Theory.* New York: St. Martin's Press, 1994. Art, Robert J., and Robert Jervis, eds. *International Politics: Enduring Concepts and Contemporary Issues.* 3rd ed. New York: HarperCollins, 1992. Dougherty, James E., Jr., and Robert L. Pfaltzgraff. *Contending Theories of International Relations: A Comprehensive Survey.* 3rd ed. New York: HarperCollins, 1990. Palan, Ronen P., and Barry Gills, eds. *Transcending the State-Global Divide: A Neostructuralist Agenda in International Relations.* Boulder, CO: Lynne Rienner, 1994.

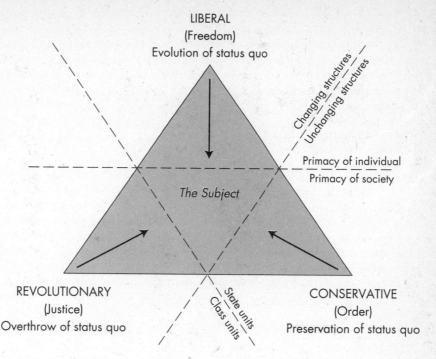

FIGURE 1.1 Conservative, Liberal, and Revolutionary World Views
Source: Adapted from J. S. Goldstein, *Long Cycles: Prosperity and War in the Modern Age.* New Haven: Yale University Press, 1988.

A *revolutionary* world view values transformation of the status quo through revolutionary and rapid change. These perspectives often focus on the unfair and exploitive aspects of international relationships, and on efforts to radically change those relationships. Revolutionary approaches have found resonance in those areas of IR scholarship dealing with North-South relations and third-world development because of the evident injustice of grinding poverty suffered by a majority of the world's people. Revolutionary approaches tend to value *justice*. They often see war as a product of underlying exploitive economic relationships, and see changes in those economic relationships as the key to solving the problem of war.

Real-world politics mixes these three perspectives in various ways. For instance, President Reagan was quite conservative in most matters, including military policy, but favored a classically liberal position when it came to free trade (like the more liberal President Clinton). Similarly, no theory or scholar in IR is purely conservative, liberal, or revolutionary.

In *international security*, a conservative world view strongly influences the contours of "realism" or power politics (taken up in Chapter 2), which holds that a nation rationally uses power to pursue its self-interest. The latest incarnation of realism is "neorealism," which has attempted to make realist principles simpler and more formal. The liberal counterpoint to realism, originally called "idealism" (taken up in Chapter 3), has been less influential in IR scholarship and policy making regarding international security. Its

Theories provide possible explanations for events in IR. These boxes on "thinking theoretically" will encourage you to think of possible theoretical (generalizable) explanations for several prominent cases. For example, consider the two biggest tests of response to aggression in the post–Cold War era—Kuwait and Bosnia. As you read about these cases (on pp. 43–46 at the end of this chapter), ask yourself: What accounts for the different outcomes, one a success for great-power intervention and the other a failure? Can you think of one or more (relatively) conservative, liberal, and revolutionary theoretical explanations? This example will be taken up again in the next several boxes.

Theoretical knowledge accumulates by a repeated cycle of generalizing and then testing. For a given puzzle, such as the difference in outcomes in Kuwait and Bosnia, various theories can explain the result (though none perfectly) as a case of a more general principle or category. Each theory also logically predicts other outcomes as well, and these can be tested empirically. A laboratory science, controlling all but one variable, can test theoretical predictions efficiently. Obviously IR does not have this luxury and must untangle many variables that operate simultaneously. Since knowledge of IR is tenuous in this way, it is especially important to think critically about IR events and consider several different theoretical explanations before deciding which (if any) provides the best explanation.

latest version is called "neoliberal institutionalism"; it grants some assumptions of neorealists but claims that the neorealists' pessimistic conclusions about international cooperation do not follow. Several new and more radical critical perspectives have emerged in recent years as serious alternatives to realism as well—peace studies, feminism, and postmodernism (also discussed in Chapter 3).

In *international political economy*, as opposed to international security, it is the liberal world view that dominates scholarship (and often policy). More conservative approaches such as mercantilism have been less influential than those based on liberal "free-market" economics. The theoretical contrast of liberalism and mercantilism, and their connection with the collective goods problem, are laid out in Chapter 8 at the beginning of Part Two of the book. More revolutionary theories of IPE—notably those influenced by Marxism—are taken up in Chapter 12 ("The North-South Gap"), where they find greatest resonance.

The theoretical debates in the field of IR are fundamental, but unresolved. They leave IR scholarship in a turbulent condition, racing to try to make sense of a rapidly changing world in which old ideas work poorly. It will be up to the next generation of IR scholars—today's college students—to achieve a better understanding of how world politics works. This book tries to lay out the current state of knowledge without exaggerating the successes of the discipline.

❖ ACTORS AND INFLUENCES

Who are the actors in IR? In one sense, this is easy to answer. The actors in IR are nations—or specifically, their governments. It is the decisions and acts of those governments, in relation to other such governments, that scholars of IR study.

But in reality, the international stage is crowded with actors large and small who are intimately interwoven with the decisions of governments. These actors are individual leaders and citizens. They are bureaucratic agencies in foreign ministries. They are multinational corporations and terrorist groups. The main contours of the drama are defined by the interactions of large conglomerate characters—nations—while other actors weave in and out of that drama.

State Actors

The most important actors in IR are states. A **state** is a territorial entity controlled by a government and inhabited by a population. A state government answers to no higher authority; it exercises *sovereignty* on its territory (to make and enforce laws, to collect taxes, and so forth). This sovereignty is recognized (acknowledged) by other states through diplomatic relations and usually by membership in the the United Nations (UN). (The concepts of state sovereignty and territoriality are elaborated in Chapter 2.) The population inhabiting a state forms a *civil society* to the extent it has developed participatory institutions of social life. All or part of the population which shares a group identity may consider itself a *nation* (see "Nationalism, 1500–2000" later in this chapter). The state's government is a *democracy* to the extent that the government is controlled by the population rather than imposed on them.[5] (Note that the word *state* in IR does not mean a state in the United States.)

In political life, and to some extent in IR scholarship, the terms *state*, *nation*, and *country* are used imprecisely, usually to refer to the decisions of state governments. It is common to discuss states as if they were people, as in "France supports the UN resolution" or "Iraq invaded Kuwait." In reality, states take such actions as the result of complex internal processes and the alliances of various domestic groups and interests. Ultimately, only individual human beings are true actors making conscious decisions. But treating states like people makes it easier to describe and explain the relations among them. It is convenient to use such language metaphorically, though it is only a mental construction.

With few exceptions, each state has a capital city—the seat of government from which it administers its territory—and often a single individual who acts in the name of the state. We may refer to this person simply as the "state leader." Often he or she is the *head of government* (such as a prime minister), or the *head of state* (such as a president, or a king or queen). In some countries, such as the United States, the same person is head of state and government. In other countries the president or royalty has become a figurehead symbolic position; elsewhere the prime minister might be a figurehead. In any case the most powerful political figure is the one we mean by "state leader," and these figures are the key individual actors in IR, ever since the days when kings or queens ruled territories by decree. The state actor includes the individual leader as well as bureaucratic organizations (such as foreign ministries) that act in the name of the state.

The **international system** is the set of relationships among the world's states, structured according to certain rules and patterns of interaction. Some such rules are explicit, some implicit. They include who is considered a member of the system, what rights and

[5]Poggi, Gianfranco. *The State: Its Nature, Development, and Prospects.* Stanford: Stanford University Press, 1991. Spruyt, Hendrik. *The Sovereign State and Its Competitors: An Analysis of Systems Change.* Princeton: Princeton University Press, 1994.

States are the most important actors in IR. The U.S. president, here meeting Russian president Yeltsin in Rome in June 1994, leads the world's most powerful state. Yeltsin's state is also a very important actor in world politics, but no longer a second superpower.

responsibilities the members have, and what kinds of actions and responses normally occur between states. The international system is discussed in more detail in Chapter 2.

The modern international system has existed for less than 500 years. Before that, people were organized into more mixed and overlapping political units such as city-states, empires, and feudal fiefs. In the last two hundred years the idea has spread that nations—groups of people who share a sense of national identity, usually including a language and culture—should have their own states (see "Nationalism, 1500–2000" on pp. 31–33). Most large states today are such **nation-states.** But since World War II, the decolonization process in much of Asia and Africa has added many new states, not all of which can be considered nation-states. A major source of conflict and war at present is the frequent mismatch between perceived nations and actual state borders. When people identify with a nationality that their state government does not represent, they may fight to form their own state and thus to gain sovereignty over their territory and affairs.

The independence of former colonies and, more recently, the breakup into smaller states of large multinational states (the Soviet Union, Yugoslavia, and Czechoslovakia) have increased the number of states in the world. The exact total depends on the status of a number of quasi-state political entities, and it keeps changing as political units split apart or merge. There were 185 members of the UN in 1995. In addition, one independent state (Switzerland) was a nonmember.

Some other political entities are often referred to as states or countries although they are not strictly states and are not recognized as such. Taiwan island is considered an integral part of China, although it is independent in practice; its current status is ambiguous. The status of the Vatican (Holy See) in Rome is also ambiguous. Hong Kong is a British colony (due to formally become part of China in 1997). Other colonies and possessions still exist as well; their status may change in the future. They include Puerto Rico (U.S.), Bermuda (British), Martinique (French), French Guiana, the Netherlands Antilles, the Falkland Islands (British), Macau (Portuguese), and Guam (U.S.). Including these territorial entities with states brings the world total to about 200 state-type units.

There are also several would-be states (such as Palestine, Kurdistan, and East Timor) that do not fully control the territory they claim and are not universally recognized. Since smaller states may continue to split away from larger ones (for instance, Quebec from Canada), the number of states is likely to grow (though perhaps not as dramatically as during decolonization in the 1960s and 1970s).

The size of the world's states varies dramatically, from China with over 1 billion people to tiny states (sometimes called microstates) with populations of less than 100,000. With the creation of many small states in recent decades, the majority of states now have fewer than 10 million people each, and more than half of the rest have 10 to 50 million each. Only 23 of the world's 200 states have more than 50 million people each. These 23 states contain 75 percent of the world's people. In decreasing order of population, they are China, India, the United States, Indonesia, Brazil, Russia, Japan, Pakistan, Bangladesh, Nigeria, Mexico, Germany, Vietnam, the Philippines, Iran, Turkey, Thailand, Britain, Italy, France, Egypt, Ukraine, and Ethiopia. These are important international actors.

States also differ tremendously in the size of their total annual economic activity— **Gross Domestic Product (GDP)**[6]—from the $6 trillion U.S. economy to the economies of tiny states like the Pacific island of Vanuatu ($100 million). The world economy is dominated by a few states, just as world population is. The United States alone accounts for one-fifth of the world economy; together with six other great powers it accounts for nearly half (see p. 77). The world's 15 largest economies—which together make up three-quarters of the world economy—are the United States, Japan, China, India, Germany, Russia, France, Britain, Italy, Brazil, Mexico, Canada, Indonesia, Spain, and South Korea. All of these are important international actors.

A few of these large states possess especially great military and economic strength and influence, and are called *great powers*. They are defined and discussed in Chapter 2. The *great-power system* may be defined as the set of relationships among great powers, with their rules and patterns of interaction (a subset of the international system). Great powers have special ways of behaving and of treating each other that do not apply to other states. The most powerful of great powers, those with truly global influence, have been called *superpowers*. This term generally meant the United States and the Soviet

---

[6]GDP is the total of goods and services produced by a nation; it is very close to the Gross National Product (GNP). Such data are difficult to compare across nations with different currencies, economic systems, and levels of development. In particular, comparisons of GDP in capitalist and socialist economies, or in rich and poor countries, should be treated cautiously. GDP data used in this book are mostly from the International Comparison Project (PWT 5.6); GDPs are adjusted through time and across countries for "purchasing power parity" (how much a given amount of money can buy). See Summers, Robert, and Alan Heston. The Penn World Table (Mark 5): An Expanded Set of International Comparisons, 1950–1988. *Quarterly Journal of Economics* 106 (2), 1991: 327–68. GDP and population data are for 1992 unless otherwise noted.

Union during the Cold War, but most IR scholars now consider the United States to be the world's only superpower (if indeed it still is one). The great powers and other *major states* (those that have large populations or play important roles in international affairs) are the most important of the state actors in IR. Smaller and weaker states also are important in IR, but taken singly most of them do not affect the outcomes in IR nearly as much as the major states do.

Nonstate Actors

National governments may be the most important actors in IR, but they are strongly conditioned, constrained, and influenced by a variety of actors that are not states. These **nonstate actors** may be grouped in several categories. First there are groups and interests within states that influence the state's foreign policy. These are *substate actors*. For instance, the American automobile industry and tobacco industry have distinct interests in American foreign economic policy (to sell cars or cigarettes abroad; to reduce imports of competing products made abroad). They are politically mobilized to influence those policies through political action committees, lobbying, and other means. Similarly the Greek-American community has an interest in U.S. government actions toward Greece with regard to the Greek-Turkish dispute over the divided island of Cyprus. And farmers in Europe, Japan, and America have all organized themselves politically and influenced their governments' positions in negotiations concerning agricultural trade.

The actions of substate economic actors—companies, consumers, workers, investors—help to create the context of economic activity against which international political events play out, and within which governments must operate. Day in and day out, people extract natural resources, produce and consume goods, buy and sell products and services. These activities of substate actors take place in what is now clearly a world economy—a global exchange of goods and services woven together by a worldwide network of communication and culture.

Increasingly, then, actors operating below the state level also operate across state borders, becoming *transnational actors*. Businesses that buy, sell, or invest in a variety of countries are a good example. The decision of a company to do business with or in another state changes the relationship between the two states, making them more interdependent and creating a new context for the decisions the governments make about each other.[7]

The thousands of multinational corporations (MNCs) are important transnational actors. The interests of a large company doing business globally do not correspond with any one state's interests. Such a company may sometimes even act against its home government's policies, as when the U.S.-based oil company Conoco signed (but then backed out of) a $1 billion deal in 1995 to develop Iranian oil fields while the U.S. government was trying to isolate Iran. MNCs often control greater resources, and operate internationally with greater efficiency, than many small nation-states. MNCs may prop up (or even create) friendly foreign governments, as the United Fruit Company did in the banana republics of Central America earlier this century. But MNCs also provide poor states with

[7]Alger, Chadwick F. The World Relations of Cities: Closing the Gap Between Social Science Paradigms and Everyday Human Experience. *International Studies Quarterly* 34 (4), 1990: 493–518. Huntington, Samuel P. Transnational Organizations in World Politics. *World Politics* 25 (3), 1973: 333–68.

Nonstate actors are important participants in IR. In Bosnia, for example, they include citizens like this woman in besieged Gorazde in 1993, and multinational UN forces sent on a problematical mission to try to protect them.

much-needed foreign investment and tax revenues. MNCs in turn depend on states to provide protection, well-regulated markets, and a stable political environment. MNCs as international actors receive special attention in Chapters 9 and 13.

Another type of transnational actor is the **nongovernmental organization (NGO)**, thousands of which pull and tug at international relations every day. These private organizations, some of considerable size and resources, interact with states, MNCs, and other NGOs. Increasingly NGOs are being recognized, in the UN and other forums, as legitimate actors along with states, though not equal to them. Examples of NGOs include the Catholic Church, Greenpeace, the International Olympic Committee, and the International Studies Association. Some of these groups have a political purpose, some a humanitarian one, some an economic or technical one. There is no single pattern to NGOs that describes their origins, purposes, or effects on IR.

Finally, states often take actions through, within, or in the context of **intergovernmental organizations (IGOs)**—organizations whose members are national governments. The UN and its agencies are IGOs. So are most of the world's economic coordinating institutions such as the World Bank and the International Monetary Fund (IMF). IGOs fulfill a variety of functions, and they vary in size from just a few states to virtually the whole

UN membership. For example, the Organization of Petroleum Exporting Countries (OPEC) seeks to coordinate the production and pricing policies of its twelve member states. The International Atomic Energy Agency seeks to regulate the flow of nuclear technology to poor states. The General Agreement on Tariffs and Trade (GATT) serves as a forum for negotiations on lowering trade barriers worldwide.

Military alliances such as NATO and political groupings such as the Arab League, the Organization of African Unity (OAU), and the British Commonwealth are also IGOs. The hundreds of IGOs now operating on the world scene (several times more than the number of states) all have been created by their member states to provide some function that those states find useful.

Together, IGOs and NGOs are referred to simply as international organizations (IOs). In this world of interlaced connections, of substate actors and transnational actors, states are still important. But to some extent they are being gradually pushed aside as companies, groups, and individuals deal ever more directly with each other across borders, and as the world economy becomes globally integrated (see Chapter 10). Now more than ever, IR extends beyond the interactions of national governments.

Levels of Analysis

The many actors involved at once in IR contribute to the complexity of competing explanations and theories. One way scholars of IR have sorted out this multiplicity of influences, actors, and processes is to categorize them into different *levels of analysis* (see Table 1.1). A level of analysis is a perspective on IR based on a set of similar actors or processes that suggests possible explanations to "why" questions. The lowest levels focus on small, disaggregated units like individual people, while the highest levels focus on macro processes like global trends. IR scholars have proposed various level-of-analysis schemes, most often with three main levels (and sometimes a few sublevels between).[8]

The *individual* level of analysis concerns the perceptions, choices, and actions of individual human beings. Great leaders influence the course of history, as do individual citizens, thinkers, soldiers, voters. Without Lenin, it is said, there might well have been no Soviet Union. If the assassin of Archduke Ferdinand in 1914 had bungled the job, World War I might not have broken out when it did. If a few more college students had voted for Nixon rather than Kennedy in the razor-close 1960 election, the Cuban Missile Crisis might have ended differently. The study of foreign policy decision making, which is discussed in Chapter 4, pays special attention to individual-level explanations of IR outcomes because of the importance of psychological factors in the decision-making process.

The *domestic* (or *state* or *societal*) level of analysis concerns the aggregations of individuals within states that influence state actions in the international arena. Such aggregations include interest groups, political organizations, and government agencies. These groups operate differently (with different international effects) in different kinds of societies and states. For instance, democracies may act differently than dictatorships do, and democracies may act differently in an election year than at other times. The politics of ethnic conflict and nationalism, bubbling up from within states, plays an increasingly important role in the relations among states. Economic sectors within states, including the

---

[8]Singer, J. David. The Level-of-Analysis Problem in International Relations. *World Politics* 14 (1), 1961: 77–92. Waltz, Kenneth. *Man, the State and War*. New York: Columbia University Press, 1959.

TABLE 1.1 LEVELS OF ANALYSIS

Many influences affect the course of international relations. Levels of analysis provide a framework for categorizing these influences and thus for suggesting various explanations of international events. Examples include:

I. Global Level
- North-South gap
- World regions
- European imperialism
- Technological change
- Global telecommunications
- World environment
- Worldwide scientific and business communities
- UN

II. Interstate Level
- Power
- Balance of power
- Alliance formation and dissolution
- Wars
- Treaties
- Trade agreements
- IGOs
- Diplomacy
- Summit meetings
- Bargaining
- Reciprocity

III. Domestic Level
- Nationalism
- Ethnic conflict
- Type of government
- Democracy
- Dictatorship
- Domestic coalitions
- Political parties
- Election campaigns
- Public opinion
- Economic sectors and industries
- Military-industrial complex
- Foreign-policy bureaucracies

IV. Individual Level
- Great leaders
- Crazy leaders
- Decision making in crises
- Psychology of perception and decision
- Learning
- Assassinations, accidents of history
- Citizens' participation (voting, rebelling, going to war, etc.)

military-industrial sector, can influence their governments to take actions in the international arena that are good for business. Within governments, foreign policy agencies often fight bureaucratic battles over policy decisions.

The *interstate* (or *international* or *systemic*) level of analysis concerns the influence of the international system upon outcomes. This level of analysis therefore focuses on the interactions of states themselves, without regard to their internal makeup or the particular individuals who lead them. This level pays attention to states' geographic locations and their relative power positions in the international system. It has been traditionally the most important of the levels of analysis.

To these three levels can be added a fourth, the *global* level of analysis.[9] It seeks to explain international outcomes in terms of global trends and forces that transcend the interactions of states themselves. This level of analysis deserves particular attention because of the growing importance of global-level processes. The evolution of human technology, of

[9]North, Robert C. *War, Peace, Survival: Global Politics and Conceptual Synthesis.* Boulder, CO: Westview, 1990.

certain worldwide beliefs, and of humans' relationship to the natural environment are all processes at the global level that permeate down to influence international relations. The global level is also increasingly the focus of IR scholars studying transnational integration through worldwide scientific, technical, and business communities (see Chapter 10). Another pervasive global influence is the lingering effect of historical European imperialism—Europe's conquest of Latin America, Asia, and Africa (see "Imperialism, 1500–2000" later in this chapter).

Levels of analysis offer different sorts of explanations for international events. For example, there are many possible explanations for the Gulf War in 1991 between Iraq and a U.S.-led coalition of states from around the world. At the individual level, the war might be attributed to the irrational gambles and mistaken judgments of Iraq's leader, Saddam Hussein—or to U.S. president George Bush's efforts to disprove critics who had called him a "wimp." At the domestic level, the war might be attributed to the kind of society and government that Iraq had—a dictatorship in which public opinion could not check a leader's unwise aggression. At the interstate level, the war might be attributed to the end of the U.S.-Soviet bipolar order (which had often restrained client states such as Iraq): the sudden shift in the distribution of power in the international system may have led Iraq to try to exploit a perceived power vacuum. At the global level, the war might be attributed to British imperialism, which had established Kuwait as a state separate from Iraq decades earlier, or to the dependence of the world's rich states on oil imports from the Middle East.

While IR scholars often focus their study mainly on one level of analysis, other levels bear on a problem simultaneously. There is no single correct level for a given "why" question. Rather, levels of analysis help to suggest multiple explanations and approaches to consider in trying to explain a given event. They remind scholars and students to look beyond the immediate and superficial aspects of an event to explore the possible influences of more distant causes. IR is such a complex process that there is rarely any single cause that completely explains an outcome. Table 1.1 lists some of the processes operating on each level of analysis. Note that the processes at higher levels tend to operate more slowly than those on the lower levels. Individuals go in and out of office often; the structure of the international system changes rarely.

An analogy can be drawn with scholars who seek to understand a disease or a pattern of automobile accidents. In the case of the disease, a careful study would consider processes operating at several levels of analysis—DNA molecules, cells, organs, the entire organism, and whole species and ecosystems. In the case of traffic accidents, a serious attempt to understand their causes could consider such factors as the individual drivers (were they drunk?), the kinds of vehicles (mechanically unsound or unsafe?), and the road system (poorly designed?). Just as different individuals would drive the same car differently, so would different national leaders drive the same state into different international outcomes. And just as the same driver would drive a subcompact differently than a bus, so would the same individual behave differently as president of Iraq than as president of Russia.

Geography

International relations takes place in the fixed context of geography (as well as history)—an important context to master in order to understand IR. To highlight the insights afforded by a global level of analysis, this book uses a division of the world into nine regions. These *world regions* differ from each other in the number of states they contain and in each region's particular mix of cultures, geographical realities, and languages. But each represents a geographical corner of the world, and together they reflect the overall macro-level divisions of world regions. Later chapters refer back to these regions, especially in discussing the North-South gap (Chapters 12 and 13).

The global **North-South gap** between the industrialized, relatively rich countries of the North and the relatively poor countries of the South is the most important geographical element at the global level of analysis. The regions used in this book have been drawn so as to separate (with a few exceptions) the rich countries from the poor ones. The North includes both the West (the rich countries of North America, Western Europe, and Japan) and the old East (the former Soviet Union and its bloc of allies).[10] The South includes Latin America, Africa, the Middle East, and much of Asia. The South is often called the "third world" (third after the West and East)—a term that is still widely used despite the second world's collapse. Countries in the South are also referred to as "developing" countries or "less-developed" countries (LDCs), in contrast to the "developed" countries of the North.

In grouping the world's states into nine regions, several criteria were applied in addition to the effort to separate rich from poor states. The regions are geographically contiguous. Countries with similar economic levels, cultures, and languages have been kept together where possible. States with a history of interaction, including historical empires or trading zones, are also placed together in a region. Finally, countries that have declared an intention to unify in the future—notably South Korea with North Korea, and China with Hong Kong and Taiwan—are kept in the same region. Of course, no scheme works perfectly, and some states are pulled toward two regions.

The overall world regions are shown on the first map of the map section preceding the text; reference maps for each region follow. (Names of countries are listed on the map on the inside front cover.) The global North is divided into *North America* (the United States and Canada); *Western Europe* (mainly European Union members); *Japan/Pacific* (mainly Japan, the Koreas, Australia, and New Zealand); and *Russia and Eastern Europe* (mainly the former Soviet bloc). The South is divided into *China* (including Hong Kong and Taiwan); the *Middle East* (from North Africa through Turkey and Iran); *Latin America* (Mexico, Central America, the Caribbean, and South America); *South Asia* (Pakistan through Indonesia and the Philippines); and *Africa* (below the Sahara desert).

Using the nine world regions as an organizing framework, the world's states and territories are listed in Table 1.2, with an estimate of the total size of each state's economy (aggregate GDP). Most of these regions correspond with commonly used geographical names, but a few notes may help. East Asia refers to China, Japan, and Korea. Southeast Asia refers to countries from Burma through Indonesia and the Philippines. Russia is considered a European state, although a large section (Siberia) is in Asia. The Pacific Rim usually means East Asia, Southeast Asia, and Siberia—linked with the west coast of

---

[10]Note that geographical designations like the "West" and the "Middle East" are European-centered. From Korea, for example, China and Russia are to the west and Japan and the United States are to the east. On world-level geography, see Kidron, Michael, and Ronald Segal. *The New State of the World Atlas.* 2nd ed. New York: Simon & Schuster, 1987; Boyd, Andrew. *An Atlas of World Affairs.* 9th ed. New York: Routledge, 1994.

TABLE 1.2 STATES AND TERRITORIES WITH ESTIMATED TOTAL 1992 GDP (IN BILLIONS OF 1995 U.S. DOLLARS)

North America

United States 6406	Canada 629	Bahamas 4

Western Europe

Germany 1502	Switzerland[a] 154	Luxembourg 9
France 1118	Austria 143	Iceland 5
Britain 1030	Portugal 108	Malta 4
Italy 1030	Denmark 102	Andorra 0
Spain 536	Greece 99	Monaco 0
Netherlands 282	Norway 93	Liechtenstein 0
Belgium 190	Finland 85	San Marino 0
Sweden 170	Ireland 48	

Japan/Pacific

Japan 2622	Fiji 4	Marshall Islands 0
South Korea 461	Solomon Islands 1	Micronesia 0
Australia 354	Samoa 0.5	Nauru[a] 0
New Zealand 55	Vanuatu 0.4	Palau 0
North Korea 22	Tonga[a] 0.3	Tuvalu[a] 0
Papua New Guinea 9	American Samoa[b] 0	
Guam/Marianas[b] 4	Kiribati[a] 0	

Russia and Eastern Europe

Russia[c] 1400	Yugoslavia (Serbia-Montenegro) 25	Estonia 15
Ukraine[c] 400	Slovakia 22	Georgia[c] 15
Poland 205	Azerbaijan[c] 20	Kyrgyzstan[c] 15
Belarus[c] 100	Croatia 20	Slovenia 15
Kazakhstan[c] 100	Latvia 20	Armenia[c] 10
Uzbekistan[c] 90	Lithuania 20	Tajikistan[c] 10
Hungary 67	Moldova[c] 20	Macedonia 7
Bulgaria 62	Turkmenistan[c] 20	Albania 5
Czech Republic 50	Bosnia and Herzegovina 15	Mongolia 5
Romania 46		

China

China 2429	Hong Kong[b] 134	Macau[b] 3
Taiwan[b] 248		

The Middle East

Turkey 312	Israel 71	Oman 20
Iran 308	United Arab Emirates 46	Kuwait 18
Saudi Arabia 162	Tunisia 36	Jordan 16
Egypt 143	Yemen 31	Qatar 10
Algeria 100	Libya 25	Cyprus 9
Morocco/W. Sahara 80	Iraq 24	Bahrain 7
Syria 73		Lebanon 5

[a]Nonmember of UN (independent state). [b]Nonmember of UN (colony or territory). [c]Commonwealth of Independent States (former USSR).

Latin America

Brazil 837
Mexico 744
Argentina 258
Venezuela 201
Colombia 158
Chile 93
Peru 66
Ecuador 44
Puerto Rico[b] 44
Guatemala 31
Dominican Republic 23
Uruguay 23
Cuba 20

Bolivia 18
Costa Rica 16
El Salvador 14
Paraguay 14
Trinidad & Tobago 14
Panama 12
Honduras 11
Jamaica 8
Haiti 6
Nicaragua 6
Netherlands Antilles[b] 3
Barbados 2
Bermuda[b] 2

Guyana 2
Martinique[b] 2
Suriname 2
Virgin Islands[b] 2
Belize 1
St. Lucia 0.6
St. Vincent & Grenadines 0.5
Dominica 0.4
Grenada 0.4
St. Kitts & Nevis 0.3
Antigua & Barbuda 0
French Guiana[b] 0

South Asia

India 1587
Indonesia 541
Thailand 320
Bangladesh 241
Pakistan 239
Philippines 152

Malaysia 150
Vietnam 132
Sri Lanka 54
Singapore 50
Burma (Myanmar) 39
Nepal 31

Cambodia 18
Laos 9
Afghanistan 6
Brunei 3
Bhutan 2
Maldives 0

Africa

South Africa 171
Nigeria 140
Kenya 33
Sudan 30
Zaire 22
Ghana 21
Côte d'Ivoire
 (Ivory Coast) 20
Tanzania 20
Cameroon 18
Zimbabwe 17
Mozambique 16
Uganda 13
Senegal 12
Madagascar 11
Angola 10
Ethiopia 10

Mauritius 9
Congo 8
Rwanda 8
Zambia 8
Benin 7
Burkina Faso 7
Mali 7
Gabon 6
Guinea 6
Malawi 6
Namibia 6
Botswana 5
Burundi 5
Eritrea 5
Niger 5
Sierra Leone 4
Somalia 4

Chad 3
Swaziland 3
Togo 3
Central African Republic 2
Lesotho 2
Liberia 2
Mauritania 2
Reunion[b] 2
Gambia 1
Guinea-Bissau 0.9
Djibouti 0.8
Cape Verde 0.6
Comoros Islands 0.4
Seychelles 0.4
Equatorial Guinea 0
São Tomé & Principe 0

Note: GDP data are inexact by nature. Estimates for Russia and Eastern Europe, China, North Korea, and other nonmarket or transitional economies are particularly suspect and should be used cautiously. Numbers below 0.1 are listed as 0.
Sources: Data are author's estimates based on Penn World Table 5.6. See footnote 6 on p. 13.

TABLE 1.3 COMPARISON OF WORLD REGIONS

Region	Population (Millions)	GDP (Trillion $)	GDP per Capita (Dollars)
The North			
North America	300	$7.0	$25,000
Western Europe	400	6.7	18,000
Japan/Pacific	200	3.5	16,000
Russia & E. Europe	400	2.8	7,000
The South			
China	1,200	2.8	2,400
Middle East	300	1.5	4,600
Latin America	500	2.7	5,800
South Asia	1,600	3.6	2,200
Africa	600	0.7	1,300
Total North	1,300 (24%)	20.0 (64%)	15,000
Total South	4,200 (76%)	11.2 (36%)	2,700
World Total	5,500	31.2	5,800

Note: Data adjusted for purchasing-power parity. 1992 GDP estimates (in 1995 dollars) are from Table 1.2; those for Russia and Eastern Europe, and for China, should be treated especially cautiously.

North America and Latin America.[11] South Asia only sometimes includes parts of Southeast Asia. Narrow definitions of the Middle East exclude both North Africa and Turkey. The Balkans are the states of southeastern Europe, bounded by Slovenia, Romania, and Greece.

Table 1.3 shows the approximate population and economic size (GDP) of each region in relation to the world as a whole. As the table shows, income levels per capita are, overall, about five times higher in the North than in the South.

The North contains one-quarter of the world's people but two-thirds of its goods and services. The other three-quarters of the world's people, in the South, have one-third of the goods and services.

Within the global North, Russia and Eastern Europe lag behind in income levels and have suffered declines in recent years. In the global South, the Middle East, Latin America, and (more recently) China have achieved somewhat higher income levels than have Africa and South Asia, which remain extremely poor. Even in the somewhat higher income regions, income is distributed quite unevenly and many people remain very poor. Note that more than half the world's population lives in the densely populated regions of South Asia and China.

IR scholars have no single explanation of the tremendous North-South gap in wealth and poverty (see Chapter 12). Some see it as part of a natural process of uneven growth in

---

[11]Hsiung, James C., ed. *Asia Pacific in the New World Politics*. Boulder, CO: Lynne Rienner, 1993. Segal, Gerald. *Rethinking the Pacific*. New York: Oxford University Press, 1991. Gourevitch, Peter A., ed. The Pacific Region: Challenges to Policy and Theory [special issue]. *Annals of the American Academy of Political and Social Science* 505, 1989.

the world economy. Others tie it to the history of imperialism by European states (as well as by Russia, the United States, and Japan). Some see the North-South gap as a reflection of racism—most of the North is predominantly white whereas most of the South is non-white.

Although geography provides one fixed context in which IR takes place, history provides another. The world as we know it developed over many years, step by step. Of special interest in IR are the past five hundred years, known as the "modern age." This has been the age of the international system as we know it (sovereign states). The remainder of this chapter briefly reviews the historical development of that system and its context. Special attention is given to the relations between Europe and the rest of the world, in which are found the roots of the present North-South gap.

❖ HISTORY

The turn of the present century and of the millennium finds the world breaking free of the logic of the two World Wars and the Cold War that dominated the twentieth century. New possibilities are emerging everywhere, some good and some bad. With so much change occurring, one might wonder whether history is still relevant to understanding the world. It is. The basic structures and principles of international relations, even in the current era, are deeply rooted in historical developments. Our discussion of these developments—necessarily only a series of brief sketches—begins with a long-term perspective and gradually focuses in on more recent history.

World Civilizations, 1000–2000

The present-day international system is the product of a particular civilization—Western civilization, centered in Europe. The international system as we know it developed among the European states of 300 to 500 years ago, was exported to the rest of the world over several centuries, and has in the last century subsumed virtually all of the world's territory into sovereign states. It is important to recognize the special importance of the European tradition to IR. It is also important to keep in mind that other civilizations existed in other world regions for centuries before Europeans ever arrived. These cultural traditions continue to exert an influence on IR, especially when the styles and expectations of these cultures come into play in international interactions.[12]

North American students should note that much of the world differs from North America in this regard. Before Europeans arrived, native cultures in North America did not have extensive agriculture, cities, irrigation, armies, and the other trappings of civilization. Native cultures were exterminated or pushed aside by European settlers. Today's

---

[12]Asimov, Isaac. *Asimov's Chronology of the World: The History of the World from the Big Bang to Modern Times.* New York: HarperCollins, 1991. Barraclough, Geoffrey, ed. *The Times Atlas of World History.* Maplewood, NJ: Hammond, 1978. McNeill, William Hardy. *The Pursuit of Power.* Chicago: University of Chicago Press, 1982. Abu-Lughod, Janet. *Before European Hegemony: The World System,* A.D. *1250–1350.* New York: Oxford University Press, 1989. Hodgson, Marshall G. S. *The Venture of Islam: Conscience and History in a World Civilization.* Chicago: University of Chicago Press, 1974. Bozeman, Adda. *Politics and Culture in International History.* Princeton: Princeton University Press, 1960.

WORLD CIVILIZATIONS, 1000–2000

	Before A.D. 1000	A.D. 1000	1250	1500	1750	2000
Japan	Korean and Chinese influences	samurai → shoguns		Tokugawa isolation	Meiji restoration → WW II → prosperity	
China	Dynasties; Great Wall built; Taoism; Buddhism; paper, gunpowder	Sung dynasty	Mongol dynasty	Ming dynasty	Manchu dynasty → European dominance → People's Republic	
S. Asia	Emergence of Hinduism, Buddhism; Ancient India; Arab conquest	Turkish period		Taj Mahal built	European colonialism → independence	
Africa	Kingdom of Ghana	Yoruba, Mali, Benin (kingdoms)	Congo	Zimbabwe; slave trade; Buganda	Ashanti; European colonialism → independence	
Middle East	Mesopotamia, Egypt, Persia; Jews, Christians; Greeks/Romans; Islam	Crusades — Arab empire		Ottoman Empire	Arab nationalism → Islamic rev.	
W. Europe	Ancient Greece; Roman Empire; Vikings; Feudalism	"Dark Ages"	Venice	Renaissance; Protestantism; Empires	French Revolution; German/Italian unifications → WW I/II → loss of empires	
Russia & E. Europe	Khazars		Genghis Khan	Ivan the Terrible — czars	Lenin → USSR → WW II → CIS	
N. America	(Preagricultural)			Columbus; European colonization	American Revolution; U.S. Civil War; westward expansion → WW II → Cold War	
Latin America	Mayans	Aztec & Inca Empires		Portuguese & Spanish conquest	colonialism; European & U.S. interventions; independence → wars, debts, dictators, revolutions	

North American population is overwhelmingly descended from immigrants. In other regions, however, the European conquest followed many centuries of advanced civilization—more advanced than that of Europe in the case of China, India, Japan, the Middle East, and Central America. In most of the world (especially in Africa and Asia), European empires incorporated rather than push aside native populations. Today's populations are descended primarily from native inhabitants, not immigrants. These populations are therefore more strongly rooted in their own cultural traditions and history than are most Americans.

European civilization evolved from roots in the Eastern Mediterranean—Egypt, Mesopotamia (Iraq), and especially Greece. Of special importance for IR is the classical period of Greek city-states around 400 B.C., which exemplified some of the fundamental principles of interstate power politics. Thucydides' account of the Peloponnesian Wars between Athens and Sparta is still popular reading in IR. By that time states were carrying out sophisticated trade relations and warfare with each other in a broad swath of the world from the Mediterranean through India to East Asia. Much of this area came under Greek influence with the conquests of Alexander the Great (around 300 B.C.), then under the Roman Empire (around A.D. 1), and then under the Arab empire (around A.D. 600).

China remained an independent civilization during all this time. In the "warring states" period, at about the same time as the Greek city-states, sophisticated states (organized as territorial political units) first used warfare as an instrument of power politics; this is described in the classic work *The Art of War*, by Sun Tzu.[13] By about A.D. 800, when Europe was in its "dark ages" and Arab civilization in its golden age, China under the T'ang dynasty was a highly advanced civilization quite independent of Western influence. Japan, strongly influenced by Chinese civilization, flowered on its own in the centuries leading up to the Shoguns (around A.D. 1200). Japan isolated itself from Western influence under the Tokugawa shogunate for several centuries, ending after 1850 when the Meiji restoration began Japanese industrialization and international trade. Latin America also had flourishing civilizations—the Mayans around A.D. 100 to 900 and the Aztecs and Incas around 1200—independent of Western influence until conquered by Spain around 1500. In Africa, the great kingdoms flowered after about A.D. 1000 (as early as A.D. 600 in Ghana) and were highly developed when the European slave traders arrived on the scene around 1500.

The great Arab empire of about A.D. 600 to 1200 plays a special role in the international relations of the Middle East. Almost the whole of the region was once united in this empire, which arose and spread with the religion of Islam. European invasions—the Crusades—were driven out. In the sixteenth to nineteenth centuries the eastern Mediterranean came under the Turkish-based Ottoman Empire, which gave relative autonomy to local cultures if they paid tribute. This history of empires continues to influence the region in the twentieth century. For example, *Pan-Arabism* (or Arab nationalism), especially strong in the 1950s and 1960s, saw the region as potentially one nation again, with a single religion, language, and identity. Iraq's Saddam Hussein in 1991 likened himself to the Arab ruler who drove away Crusaders a thousand years ago. The strength of Islamic fundamentalism throughout the region today, as well as the emotions attached to the Arab-Israeli conflict, reflect the continuing importance of the historic Arab empire.

---

[13]Sun Tzu. *The Art of War*. Translated by Samuel B. Griffith. New York: Oxford University Press, 1963.

Europe itself began its rise to world dominance around 1500, after the Renaissance (when the Greek and Roman classics were rediscovered). The Italian city-states of the period also rediscovered the rules of interstate power politics, as described by an advisor to Renaissance princes named Machiavelli. Feudal units began to merge into large territorial nation-states under single authoritarian rulers (monarchs). The military revolution of the period created the first modern armies.[14] European monarchs put cannons on sailing ships and began to "discover" the world. The development of the international system, of imperialism, of trade and war, were all greatly accelerated by the *Industrial Revolution* after about 1750. Ultimately the European conquest of the world brought about a single world civilization, albeit with regional variants and subcultures.[15]

In recent decades, the world regions formerly dominated by Europe have gained independence, with their own sovereign states participating in the international system. Independence came earlier in the Americas (around 1800). In Latin America most of the nineteenth century was absorbed with wars, border changes, the rise and fall of dictatorships and republics, a chronic foreign debt problem, revolutions, and recurrent military incursions by European powers and the United States to recover debts.

The Great-Power System, 1500–2000

The modern international system is often dated from the *Treaty of Westphalia* in 1648, which established the principles of independent, sovereign states that continue to shape the international system today. These rules of state relations did not, however, materialize at Westphalia from scratch; they took form in Europe in the sixteenth century. Key to this system was the ability of one state, or a coalition, to balance the power of another state so that it could not gobble up smaller units and create a universal empire (as had happened in China after the "warring states" period).

This power-balancing system placed special importance on the handful of great powers with strong military capabilities, global interests and outlooks, and intense interactions with each other. (Great powers are defined and discussed on pp. 76–78.) A system of great-power relations has existed since around A.D. 1500, and the structure and rules of that system have remained fairly stable through time, although the particular members change. The structure is a balance of power among the six or so most powerful states, who form and break alliances, fight wars, and make peace, letting no single state conquer the others.

---

[14]Howard, Michael. *War in European History.* Oxford: Oxford University Press, 1976. Parker, Geoffrey. *The Military Revolution: Military Innovation and the Rise of the West, 1500–1800.* New York: Cambridge University Press, 1988. Black, Jeremy, ed. *The Origins of War in Early Modern Europe.* Edinburgh: J. Donald, 1987. Thomson, Janice E. *Mercenaries, Pirates, and Sovereigns: State-Building and Extraterritorial Violence in Early Modern Europe.* Princeton: Princeton University Press, 1994.

[15]Barraclough, Geoffrey. *An Introduction to Contemporary History.* New York: Penguin Books, 1964. Cipolla, Carlo M. *Guns, Sails and Empires.* New York: Pantheon Books, 1965. Parry, J. H. *The Establishment of the European Hegemony, 1415–1715.* 3rd ed. New York: Harper & Row, 1966. Anderson, Perry. *Lineages of the Absolutist State.* London: N.L.B., 1974. Braudel, Fernand. *Civilization and Capitalism, 15th–18th Century* [3 volumes]. New York: Harper & Row, 1984.

The most powerful states in sixteenth-century Europe were Britain (England), France, Austria-Hungary, and Spain. The Ottoman Empire (Turkey) recurrently fought with the European powers, especially with Austria-Hungary. Today, that historical conflict between the (Islamic) Ottoman Empire and (Christian) Austria-Hungary is a source of ethnic conflict in the former Yugoslavia (the edge of the old Ottoman Empire).

Within Europe, Austria-Hungary and Spain were allied under control of the Hapsburg family, which also owned the territory of the Netherlands. The Hapsburg countries (which were Catholic) were defeated by Protestant countries in northern Europe—France, Britain, Sweden, and the newly independent Netherlands—in the *Thirty Years' War* of 1618–1648.[16] The 1648 Treaty of Westphalia established the basic rules that have defined the international system ever since—the sovereignty and territorial integrity of states as equal and independent members of an international system. Since then, states defeated in war might be stripped of some territories but were generally allowed to continue as independent states rather than being subsumed into the victorious state.

In the eighteenth century, the power of Britain increased as it industrialized, and Britain's great rival was France. Sweden, the Netherlands, and the Ottoman Empire all declined in power, but Russia and later Prussia (the forerunner of modern-day Germany) emerged as major players. In the *Napoleonic Wars* (1803–1815), which followed the French Revolution, France was defeated by a coalition of Britain, the Netherlands, Austria-Hungary, Spain, Russia, and Prussia. The *Congress of Vienna* (1815) ending this war reasserted the principles of state sovereignty in reaction to the challenges of the French Revolution and Napoleon's empire.[17] In the *Concert of Europe* that dominated the following decades, the five most powerful states tried, with some success, to cooperate on major issues to prevent war—a possible precedent for today's UN Security Council. In this period Britain became a balancer, joining alliances against whatever state emerged as the most powerful in Europe.

By the outset of the twentieth century, three new rising powers had appeared on the scene: the United States (which had become the world's largest economy), Japan, and Italy. The great-power system became globalized instead of European. Powerful states were industrializing, extending the scope of their world activities and the might of their militaries. After Prussia defeated Austria and France in wars, a larger Germany emerged to challenge Britain's position.[18] In *World War I* (1914–1918), Germany and Austria-Hungary were defeated by a coalition that included Britain, France, Russia, Italy, and the United States; Japan was neutral. After a twenty-year lull, Germany, Italy, and Japan were defeated in World War II (1939–1945) by a coalition of the United States, Britain, France, Russia (the Soviet Union), and China. Those five winners of World War II make up the permanent membership of today's UN Security Council.

After World War II, the United States and the Soviet Union, who had been allies in the war against Germany, became adversaries for forty years in the Cold War. Europe was

---

[16]Rabb, Theodore K., ed. *The Thirty Years' War*. New York: University Press of America, 1981.

[17]Kissinger, Henry A. *A World Restored*. Boston: Houghton Mifflin, 1973.

[18]Langer, William L. *European Alliances and Alignments, 1871–1890*. New York: Knopf, 1931.

THE GREAT-POWER SYSTEM, 1500–2000

	1500	1600	1700	1800	1900	2000
Wars	Spain conquers Portugal; Spanish Armada	30 Years' War	War of the Spanish Succession; 7 Years' War	Napoleonic Wars	Franco-Prussian War; World War I	World War II; Cold War
Major Alliances	Turkey (Muslim) vs. Europe (Christian)	Hapsburgs (Austria-Spain) vs. France, Britain, Netherlands, Sweden	France vs. Britain, Spain	France vs. Britain, Netherlands		Germany (& Japan) vs. Britain, France, Russia, United States, China; Russia vs. U.S., W. Eur., Japan
Rules & Norms	Nation-states (France, Austria); Grotius on int'l law	Dutch independence; **Treaty of Westphalia 1648**	Treaty of Utrecht 1713	Kant on peace; Congress of Vienna 1815; **Concert of Europe**	League of Nations; Geneva conventions; Communism	UN Security Council 1945–; Human rights
Rising Powers	Britain, France	Netherlands	Russia	Prussia → United States, Germany, Japan, Italy		China
Declining Powers	Venice	Spain	Netherlands; Sweden; Ottoman Empire		Britain, France, Austria, Italy	Russia; U.S.?

Hegemony periods: **Netherlands hegemony** (c. 1600–1700) → **British hegemony** (c. 1700–1900) → **U.S. hegemony** (c. 1900–2000)

split into rival blocs—East and West—with Germany itself split into two states. The rest of the world became contested terrain where each bloc tried to gain allies or influence, often by sponsoring opposing sides in regional and civil wars. The end of the Cold War around 1990, when the Soviet Union collapsed, returned the international system to a more cooperative arrangement of the great powers somewhat similar to the Concert of Europe in the nineteenth century. However, new strains emerged among the European-American-Japanese "allies" once they no longer faced a common threat from the Soviet Union.[19]

Imperialism, 1500–2000

European imperialism (described more fully in Chapter 12) got its start in the fifteenth century with the development of oceangoing sailing ships in which a small crew could transport a sizable cargo over a long distance. Portugal pioneered the first voyages of exploration beyond Europe. Spain, France, and Britain soon followed. With superior military technology, Europeans gained control of coastal cities and of resupply outposts along major trade routes. Gradually this control extended further inland, first in Latin America, then in North America, and later throughout Asia and Africa.

In the sixteenth century Spain and Portugal had extensive empires in Central America and Brazil, respectively. Britain and France had colonies in North America and the Caribbean. The imperialists bought slaves in Africa and shipped them to Mexico and Brazil, where they worked in tropical agriculture and in mining silver and gold. The wealth produced was exported to Europe, where monarchs used it to buy armies and build states.

These empires decimated native populations and cultures, causing immense suffering. Over time, the economies of colonies developed with the creation of basic transportation and communication infrastructure, factories, and so forth. But these economies were often molded to the needs of the colonizers, not the local populations.

Decolonization began with the British colonists in the United States who declared independence in 1776. Most of Latin America gained independence a few decades later. The new states in North America and Latin America were, of course, still run by the descendants of Europeans, to the disadvantage of Native Americans and African slaves.

Meanwhile, new colonies were still being acquired by Europe through the end of the nineteenth century, culminating in a scramble for colonies in Africa in the 1890s (resulting in arbitrary territorial divisions as competing European armies rushed inland from all sides). Latecomers such as Germany and Italy were frustrated to find few attractive territories remaining in the world when they tried to build overseas empires in the late nineteenth century. India became Britain's largest and most important colony in the nineteenth century. With possessions stretching from Africa to South Asia to Australia to Canada, Britain could boast that "the sun never sets on the British Empire." Ultimately, only a few non-European areas of the world retained their independence: Japan, most of China, Iran, Turkey, and a few other areas. Japan began building its own empire,

---

[19]Unger, Daniel, and Paul Blackburn, eds. *Japan's Emerging Global Role*. Boulder, CO: Lynne Rienner, 1993. Akaha, Tsuneo, and Frank Langdon, eds. *Japan in the Posthegemonic World*. Boulder, CO: Lynne Rienner, 1993. Inoguchi, Takashi, and Daniel I. Okimoto, eds. *The Political Economy of Japan*. Volume 2: *The Changing International Context*. Stanford: Stanford University Press, 1988.

IMPERIALISM, 1500–2000

	1500	1600	1700	1800	1900	2000
North America	Columbus	British & French colonization		U.S. independence	War of 1812	Canada →
Latin America	Brazil (Portuguese) Central & S. America (Spanish)			Independence		
East Asia		Russian conquest of Siberia			European & U.S. interventions Mexican Revolution T'ai P'ing Rebellion Opium Wars (China) Taiwan & Korea (Japanese) Boxer Rebellion Japanese empire Korea split Taiwan autonomous Communist China Hong Kong to China	
South Asia	Dutch East Indies Company	Indonesia (Dutch) →			India (British) Philippines (U.S.) Indian independence Vietnam War	
Africa	Slave trade Angola, Mozambique (Portuguese)			Scramble for colonies (Brit., Fr., Ger.)	Independence	
Middle East	Ottoman Empire				British & French mandates (Palestine) Algerian independence	

European explorers

as did the United States, at the end of the nineteenth century. China became weaker and its coastal regions fell under the domination, if not the formal control, of European powers.

In the wave of decolonization after World War II, it was not local colonists (as in the Americas) but native populations in Asia and Africa who won independence. Decolonization continued through the mid-1970s until almost no European colonies remained. Most of the newly independent states have faced tremendous challenges and difficulties in the postcolonial era. Because long-established economic patterns continue despite political independence, some refer to the postcolonial era as being *neocolonial*. Although the global North no longer imports slave labor from the South, it continues to rely on the South for cheap labor, for energy and minerals, and for the products of tropical agriculture. However, the North in turn makes vital contributions to the South in capital investment, technology transfer, and foreign assistance (see Chapter 13).

The collapse of the Soviet Union and its bloc, which reduced Russia to its size of a century earlier, can be seen as an extension of the post–World War II wave of decolonization and self-determination. There, as in much of the third world, imperialism has left ethnic conflict in its wake, as new political units come to terms with territorial divisions created in distant imperial capitals.

Nationalism, 1500–2000

Many people consider **nationalism**—devotion to the interests of one's nation—to be the most important force in world politics in the last two centuries. A nation is a population that shares an identity, usually including a language and culture. For instance, most of the 60 million inhabitants of France speak French, eat French cuisine, learned French history in school, and are represented (for better or worse) by the national government in Paris. But nationality is a difficult concept to define precisely. To some extent, the extension of political control over large territories like France created the commonality necessary for nationhood—states created nations. At the same time, however, the perceived existence of a nation has often led to the creation of a corresponding state as a people win sovereignty over their own affairs—nations created states.

Around A.D. 1500, countries like France and Austria began to bring entire nations together into single states. These new nation-states were very large and powerful; they overran smaller neighbors. Over time, many small territorial units were conquered and incorporated into nation-states.[20] Eventually the idea of nationalism itself became a powerful force and ultimately contributed to the disintegration of large, multinational states like Austria-Hungary (in World War I), the Soviet Union, and Yugoslavia.

The principle of *self-determination* implies that people who identify as a nation should have the right to form a state and exercise sovereignty over their affairs. Self-determination is a widely praised principle in international affairs today (not historically). But it is gen-

---

[20]Tilly, Charles, ed. *The Formation of National States in Western Europe.* Princeton: Princeton University Press, 1975. Hobsbawm, E. J. *Nations and Nationalism Since 1780: Programme, Myth, Reality.* New York: Cambridge University Press, 1990. Mayall, James. *Nationalism and International Society.* New York: Cambridge University Press, 1990. Greenfeld, Liah. *Nationalism: Five Roads to Modernity.* Cambridge, MA: Harvard University Press, 1992.

erally secondary to the principles of sovereignty (noninterference in other states' internal affairs) and territorial integrity, with which it frequently conflicts. Self-determination does not give groups the right to change international borders, even those imposed arbitrarily by colonialism, in order to unify a group with a common national identity. Generally, though not always, self-determination has been achieved by violence. When the borders of (perceived) nations do not match those of states, conflicts almost inevitably arise. Today such conflicts are widespread—in Northern Ireland, Quebec, Israel-Palestine, India-Pakistan, Sri Lanka, Tibet, and many other places.[21]

The Netherlands helped to establish the principle of self-determination when it broke free of Spanish ownership around 1600 and set up a self-governing Dutch republic. The struggle over control of the Netherlands was a leading cause of the Thirty Years' War (1618–1648), and in that war states mobilized their populations for war in new ways. For instance, Sweden drafted one man out of ten for long-term military service, while the Netherlands used the wealth derived from global trade to finance a standing professional army.

This process of popular mobilization intensified greatly in the French Revolution and the subsequent Napoleonic Wars, when France instituted a universal draft and a centrally run "command" economy. People participated in part because they were patriotic. Their nation-state embodied their aspirations, and brought them together in a common national identity.

The United States meanwhile had followed the example of the Netherlands by declaring independence from Britain in 1776. The U.S. nation held together in the Civil War of the 1860s and developed a surprisingly strong sense of nationalism, considering how large and diverse the country was. Latin American states gained independence early in the nineteenth century, and Germany and Italy unified their nations out of multiple political units (through war) later in that century.

Before World War I, socialist workers from different European countries had banded together *as* workers to fight for workers' rights. In that war, however, most abandoned such solidarity and instead fought for their own nation; nationalism proved a stronger force than socialism. Before World War II, nationalism helped Germany, Italy, and Japan to build political orders based on *fascism*—an extreme authoritarianism undergirded by national chauvinism. And in World War II it was nationalism and patriotism (not communism) that rallied the Soviet people to sacrifice themselves by the millions to turn back Germany's invasion.

In the past fifty years, third-world nations by the dozens have gained independence and statehood. Jews worked persistently in the first half of the twentieth century to create the state of Israel, and Palestinians have aspired in the second half to create a Palestinian state. While multinational states such as the Soviet Union and Yugoslavia have fragmented in recent years, ethnic and territorial units such as Ukraine and Slovenia have established themselves as independent nation-states. The continuing influence of nationalism in today's world is evident.

National identity is psychologically reinforced on a daily basis by symbols such as the national flag, by rituals such as pledges of allegiance, and by other practices designed to reinforce the identification of a population with its nation and government. In truth,

---

[21]Alexander, Yonah, and Robert A. Friedlander, eds. *Self-Determination: National, Regional, and Global Dimensions*. Boulder, CO: Westview, 1980.

people have multiple identities, belonging to various circles from their immediate family through their town, ethnic or religious group, nation or state, and species (see pp. 202–205). Nationalism has been remarkably successful in establishing national identity as a people's primary affiliation in much of the world. (In many places a sense of local affiliation remains important, however.)

Nationalism harnesses the energies of large populations based on their patriotic feelings toward their nation. The feeling of "we the people" is hard to sustain if the people are excluded from participating in their government. This participation is so important that even authoritarian governments often go through the motions of holding elections (with one candidate or party). Democracy can be a force for peace, constraining the power of state leaders to commit their nations to war. But popular influence over governments can also increase conflict with other nations, especially when ethnic tensions erupt.

Over time, democratic participation has broadened to more countries and more people within those countries (nonlandowners, women, etc.). The trend toward democracy seems to be continuing in most regions of the world in recent years—in Russia and Eastern Europe, Africa, Latin America, and Asia. Both nationalism and democracy remain great historical forces exerting strong influences in IR.

The World Economy, 1750–2000

In 1750, before the Industrial Revolution, the world's most advanced economy, Britain, had a GDP of about $1200 per capita (in today's dollars). That is less than the present level of most of the global South. However, today Britain produces more than ten times this much per person (and with a much larger population than in 1750). This accomplishment was due to **industrialization**—the use of energy to drive machinery and the accumulation of such machinery along with the products created by it. The Industrial Revolution started in Britain in the eighteenth century (notably with the invention of a new steam engine in 1769, a mechanized thread-spinner in 1770, and the cotton gin in America in 1794). It was tied to Britain's emerging leadership role in the world economy (such as the cotton and textile trades). Industrialization—a process at the world level of analysis—spread to the other advanced economies.[22]

By around 1850 the wooden sailing ships of earlier centuries had been replaced by larger and faster coal-powered iron steamships. Coal-fueled steam engines also drove factories producing textiles and other commodities. The great age of railroad building—of steam and steel—was taking off. These developments not only increased the volume of world production and trade, but also tied distant locations more closely together economically. The day trip across France by railroad contrasted with the same route a hundred years earlier, when it took three weeks to complete. In this period of mechanization, however, factory conditions were extremely harsh, especially for women and children operating machines.

---

[22]North, Douglass C., and Robert Paul Thomas. *The Rise of the Western World: A New Economic History*. New York: Cambridge University Press, 1973. Hobsbawm, E. J. *Industry and Empire: From 1750 to the Present Day*. Harmondsworth, U.K.: Penguin-Pelican, 1969. Tracy, James D., ed. *The Political Economy of Merchant Empires: State Power and World Trade, 1350–1750*. New York: Cambridge University Press, 1991.

THE WORLD ECONOMY, 1750–2000

Timeline axis: 1750 — 1800 — 1850 — 1900 — 1950 — 2000

Production: industrialization; WW I; world depression; Soviet industrialization; WW II; postwar prosperity; Cold War arms race; Japanese & German growth; world recession; Soviet collapse

Energy: coal; steam engine; oil; nuclear power; nat. gas

Leading Sectors: cotton gin; iron & steam; textiles; steel; electricity; motor vehicles; electronics; plastics; computers; biotech

Transportation: (wooden sailing ships); iron steamships; railroads; Suez Canal; airplanes; Trans-Siberian Railroad; Panama Canal; automobiles; jets; freeways; high-speed rail

Trade: British dominance; (free trade); protectionism; U.S. dominance; GATT; European integration; NAFTA

Money: sterling (British) as world currency; post-WWI inflation; Keynes; Bretton Woods; Marshall Plan; IMF; U.S. dollar as world currency; U.S. drops gold standard; debt crises; Russia joins IMF

Communication: telegraph; telephone invented; transoceanic cables; radio; information revolution; communication satellites; fax, modem, cellular, etc.

Britain dominated world trade in this period. Because Britain's economy was the most technologically advanced in the world, its products were competitive worldwide. Thus British policy favored **free trade.** In addition to its central role in world trade, Britain served as the financial capital of the world, managing an increasingly complex world market in goods and services in the nineteenth century. The British currency, pounds sterling (silver), became the world standard. International monetary relations were still based on the value of precious metals, as they had been in the sixteenth century when Spain bought its armies with Mexican silver and gold.

By the outset of the twentieth century, however, the world's largest and most advanced economy was no longer Britain but the United States. The industrialization of the U.S. economy was fueled by territorial expansion throughout the nineteenth century, drawing in vast natural resources. The U.S. economy was attracting huge pools of immigrant labor from the poorer fringes of Europe as well. The United States led the world in converting from coal to oil and from horse-drawn transportation to motor vehicles. New technical innovations, from electricity to airplanes, also helped push the U.S. economy into a dominant world position. For instance, the telephone and light bulb were both invented in the United States in the late 1870s.

In the 1930s, the U.S. and world economies suffered a severe setback in the Great Depression. The protectionist Hawley-Smoot Act adopted by the United States in 1930, which imposed tariffs on imports, contributed to the severity of this depression by provoking retaliation and reducing world trade. Adopting the principles of *Keynesian economics*, the U.S. government used deficit spending to stimulate the economy, paying itself back from new wealth generated by economic recovery. The government role in the economy intensified during World War II.

Following World War II the capitalist world economy was restructured under U.S. leadership. Today's international economic institutions, such as the World Bank, International Monetary Fund (IMF), and General Agreement on Tariffs and Trade (GATT), date from this period. The United States provided massive assistance to resuscitate the Western European economies (through the Marshall Plan) as well as Japan's economy. World trade greatly expanded, and the world market became ever more closely woven together through air transportation and telecommunications. Electronics emerged as a new leading sector, and technological progress accelerated throughout the twentieth century.

Standing apart from this world capitalist economy in the years after World War II were the economies of the Soviet Union and Eastern Europe, organized on communist principles of central planning and state ownership. The Soviet economy had some notable successes in rapidly industrializing the country in the 1930s, surviving the German assault in the 1940s, and developing world-class aerospace and military production capability in the 1950s and 1960s. The Soviet Union launched the world's first satellite (*Sputnik*) in 1957, and in the early 1960s Premier (Prime Minister) Khrushchev boasted that communist economies would outperform capitalist ones within decades. Instead, the Soviet bloc economies stagnated under the weight of bureaucracy, ideological rigidity, environmental destruction, corruption, and extremely high military spending. By the early 1990s the former Soviet republics and their Eastern European neighbors were almost all trying to make a transition to some form of capitalist market economy.

Today there is a single integrated world economy that almost no country can resist joining. At the same time, the imperfections and problems of that world economy were

THE TWO WORLD WARS, 1900–1950

World War I (c. 1914–1918) · **World War II** (c. 1939–1945)

	1900	1910	1920	1930	1940	1950
Europe	mobilization plans developed	Balkan crises; Sarajevo; U.S. enters war		Italy invades Ethiopia; Munich Agreement	U.S. enters war; D Day	
Germany	naval arms race with Britain		Defeat; Weimar Republic; hyperinflation	Hitler wins power; rearmament; invasion of Poland; occupation of Austria, Czech.	The Holocaust; strategic bombing; Defeat; occupied by Allied forces	
Russia		Russian Revolution	USSR formed; (civil war)	(industrialization)	pact with Hitler; German invasion; Victory	
Asia	U.S. in Philippines; Russo-Japanese War	Japan neutral in WW I		Japan occupies Manchuria (China); Japan invades China	Pearl Harbor; Japan occupies S.E. Asia; island battles; Hiroshima; Occupied by U.S.	
International Norms & Law	Hague Peace Conferences		Versailles treaty; League of Nations →; Washington Naval Treaty	U.S. isolationism; Japan quits League of Nations	Nuremberg Tribunal; United Nations →	
Technology	destroyers	submarines; chemical weapons; trench warfare; tanks		mechanized armor	air war; radar; nuclear weapons	

evident in the world recession of the early 1990s, which hit Russia and Eastern Europe hardest but also affected the United States, Japan, and Western Europe. Just as the world economy climbed out of previous depressions in the 1890s and 1930s, it is likely that a new wave of technological innovation will pull the advanced industrialized countries into a new phase of growth—probably one that is more information-intensive and resource-efficient. Much less clear is how the global South will fare in the coming years (see Chapters 12 and 13).

The Two World Wars, 1900–1950

World Wars I (1914–1918) and II (1939–1945) occupied only ten years of the twentieth century. But they have shaped the character of the century. Nothing like these wars has happened since, and they remain a key reference point for the world in which we live today. With perhaps just two other cases in history—the Thirty Years' War and the Napoleonic Wars—the two world wars were global or hegemonic wars in which almost all major states participated in an all-out struggle over the future of the international system.[23]

For many people, World War I symbolizes the tragic irrationality of war. It fascinates scholars of IR because it was a catastrophic war that seems unnecessary and perhaps even accidental (as some Cold War scholars imagined a nuclear war might be). After a century of relative peace, the great powers marched off to battle for no good reason. There was even a popular feeling that Europe would be uplifted and reinvigorated by a war—that young men could once again prove their manhood on the battlefield in a glorious adventure. Such ideas were soon crushed by the immense pain and evident pointlessness of the war.

The previous major war had been the Franco-Prussian war of 1870–1871, when Germany executed a swift offensive using railroads to rush forces to the front. That war had ended quickly, decisively, and with a clear winner (Germany). People expected that a new war would follow the same pattern. All the great powers made plans for a quick railroad-borne offensive and rapid victory—what has been called the *cult of the offensive*. Under these doctrines, one country's mobilization for war virtually forced its enemies to mobilize as well. The one to strike first would win, it was believed. Thus, when a Serbian nationalist assassinated Archduke Ferdinand of Austria in 1914 in Sarajevo, a minor crisis escalated and the mobilization plans pushed Europe to all-out war.[24]

Contrary to expectations, the war was neither short nor decisive, and certainly not glorious. It bogged down in *trench warfare* along a fixed front—in the mud, under artillery bombardment, with occasional charges over the top into the enemy machine guns. For

---

[23]Dockrill, Michael. *Atlas of Twentieth Century World History*. New York: HarperCollins, 1991. Keegan, John, ed. *The Times Atlas of the Second World War*. New York: HarperCollins, 1989. Taylor, A. J. P. *The Origins of the Second World War*. New York: Atheneum, 1966.

[24]Van Evera, Stephen. The Cult of the Offensive and the Origins of the First World War. *International Security* 9, 1984: 58–107. Snyder, Jack Lewis. *The Ideology of the Offensive: Military Decision Making and the Disasters of 1914*. Ithaca: Cornell University Press, 1984. Kahler, Miles. Rumors of War: The 1914 Analogy. *Foreign Affairs* 58 (2), 1979/80: 374–96.

example, in 1917 at the Battle of Passchendaele (Belgium) the British in three months fired five tons of artillery shells per yard of front line, over an 11-mile-wide front, and then lost 400,000 men in a failed ground attack. These horrific conditions were worsened by chemical weapons and by the attempts of Britain and Germany to starve each other's population into surrender.

Russia was the first state to crumble. Revolution at home removed Russia from the war in 1917 (and led to the founding of the Soviet Union). But the entry of the United States into the war on the anti-German side that year quickly turned the tide. In the *Treaty of Versailles* of 1919, Germany was forced to give up territory, pay reparations, and limit its future armaments. German resentment against the harsh terms of Versailles would contribute to Hitler's rise to power in the 1930s. After World War I, U.S. president Woodrow Wilson led the effort to create the **League of Nations,** a forerunner of today's UN. But the U.S. Senate would not approve U.S. participation, and the League did not prove effective. U.S. isolationism between the world wars, along with declining British power and Russia's withdrawal into revolution, left a power vacuum in world politics.

In the 1930s Germany and Japan stepped into that vacuum, embarking on aggressive expansionism that ultimately led to a second world war. Japan had already occupied Taiwan and Korea, after defeating China in 1895 and Russia in 1905. In World War I Japan was neutral but gained some German colonies in Asia. In 1931 Japan occupied Manchuria (northeast China) and set up a puppet regime there. In 1937 Japan invaded the rest of China and began a brutal occupation that continues to haunt Chinese-Japanese relations. Japanese leaders planned a *coprosperity sphere* in which an industrialized Japan would control the natural resources of East and Southeast Asia.

In Europe, meanwhile, Nazi Germany under Hitler in the 1930s had rearmed, intervened to help fascists win the Spanish Civil War, and grabbed territory from its neighbors under the rationale of reuniting ethnic Germans in those territories with their homeland. Hitler learned from the weak response of the international community and League of Nations to aggression by fascist regimes in Italy and Spain. In an effort to appease German ambitions, Britain agreed in the **Munich Agreement** of 1938 to let Germany occupy part of Czechoslovakia. Appeasement has since had a negative connotation in IR, because the Munich Agreement seemed only to embolden Hitler for further conquest.

In 1939 Germany invaded Poland, and Britain joined the war against Germany in response. Hitler signed a nonaggression pact with his archenemy Stalin of the Soviet Union and threw his full army against France, occupying most of it quickly. Unlike World War I, the rapid offensive of mechanized armored units (tanks) worked this time for Germany. Hitler then double-crossed Stalin and invaded the Soviet Union in 1941. This offensive ultimately bogged down and was turned back after several years. But the Soviet Union took the brunt of the German attack and suffered by far the greatest share of the 60 million deaths caused by World War II. This trauma continues to be a powerful memory that shapes views of IR in Russia and Eastern Europe.

The United States joined World War II against Germany in 1942. The U.S. economy produced critically important weapons and supplies for allied armies. The United States played an important role with Britain in the strategic bombing of German cities—including the firebombing of Dresden in February 1945, which caused

100,000 civilian deaths. In 1944, after crossing the British Channel on June 6 (*D Day*), British-American forces pushed into Germany from the west while the Soviets pushed from the east. A ruined Germany surrendered and was occupied by the allied powers.

At its peak, Nazi Germany and its allies occupied virtually all of Europe, except for Britain and part of Russia. Under its fanatical policies of racial purity, Germany rounded up and exterminated six million Jews and millions of others, including homosexuals, Gypsies, communists, and others. These mass murders, now known as the Holocaust, along with the sheer scale of war unleashed by Nazi aggression, are considered among the greatest *crimes against humanity* in history. Responsible German officials faced justice in the *Nuremberg Tribunal* after the war (see pp. 299–300). The pledges of world leaders after that experience to "never again" allow genocide—the systematic extermination of a racial or religious group—have been found wanting as genocide recurred in the post–Cold War era in Bosnia and Rwanda.

While the war in Europe was raging, Japan fought a war over control of Southeast Asia with the United States and its allies. Japan's expansionism in the 1930s had only underscored the dependence on foreign resources that it was intended to solve: the United States punished Japan by cutting off U.S. oil exports. Japan then destroyed much of the U.S. Navy in a surprise attack at *Pearl Harbor* (Hawaii) in 1941 and seized desired territories (including Indonesia, whose oil replaced that of the United States). The United States, however, built vast new military forces and retook a series of Pacific islands in subsequent years. The strategic bombing of Japanese cities by the United States culminated in the only historical use of nuclear weapons in war—the destruction of the cities of *Hiroshima* and *Nagasaki* in August 1945—which triggered Japan's quick surrender.

The lessons of the two world wars seem contradictory. From the failure of the Munich Agreement in 1938 to appease Hitler, many people have concluded that only a hard-line foreign policy with preparedness for war will deter aggression and prevent war. Yet in 1914 it was just such hard-line policies that apparently led Europe into a disastrous war, which might have been avoided by appeasement. Evidently the best policy would be sometimes harsh and at other times conciliatory, but IR scholars have not discovered a simple formula for choosing (see "The Causes of War" in Chapter 5).

The Cold War, 1945–1990

The United States and the Soviet Union became the two superpowers of the post–World War II era.[25] Each had its ideological mission (capitalist democracy versus communism), its networks of alliances and third-world clients, and its deadly arsenal of nuclear weapons. Europe was divided, with massive military forces of the United States and its

---

[25]Gaddis, John Lewis. *The Long Peace: Inquiries into the History of the Cold War.* New York: Oxford University Press, 1987. Cohen, Stephen F. *Sovieticus: American Perceptions and Soviet Realities.* New York: W. W. Norton, 1985. Garthoff, Raymond. *Détente and Confrontation: American-Soviet Relations from Nixon to Reagan.* Washington, DC: The Brookings Institution, 1985. Nogee, Joseph L., and John W. Spanier. *Peace Impossible—War Unlikely: The Cold War Between the United States and the Soviet Union.* New York: HarperCollins, 1988.

THE COLD WAR, 1945–1990

Timeline axis: 1940 — 1950 — 1960 — 1970 — 1980 — 1990

Soviet Union
- Stalin | Khrushchev | Brezhnev | Andropov | Chernenko | Gorbachev
- (WW II alliance)
- A-bomb
- Warsaw Pact →
- Sputnik
- nuclear parity with U.S.
- nuclear arms race
- military buildup
- reforms (perestroika, glasnost)

United States
- F. D. Roosevelt | Truman | Eisenhower | Kennedy | Johnson | Nixon | Ford | Carter | Reagan | Bush
- NATO
- containment policy →
- (nuclear superiority over USSR)
- human rights
- (Iran crisis)
- "Star Wars" (SDI)
- student protests

China
- civil war (Nationalists-Communists)
- Sino-Soviet alliance
- People's Republic → (Taiwan nationalist)
- Taiwan Straits crises (vs. U.S.)
- Sino-Soviet split
- A-bomb
- Cultural Revolution
- U.S.-China rapprochement
- death of Mao
- joins UN
- neutral to pro-U.S.

Confrontations
- Korean War
- Soviet invasion of Hungary
- U-2 incident
- Berlin Wall
- Berlin crisis
- Cuban Missile Crisis
- Vietnam War
- USSR invades Czechoslovakia
- Afghanistan War
- U.S. invasion of Grenada

Proxy Wars
- Berlin crisis
- Greek civil war
- Cuban revolution
- Suez crisis
- Indonesia
- Chile coup
- Arab-Israeli wars
- Somalia vs. Ethiopia
- Cambodia
- Nicaragua
- El Salvador
- Angola

Co-operation
- Yalta summit
- Geneva summit
- Limited Test Ban Treaty
- Non-Proliferation Treaty
- détente
- SALT I
- SALT II
- Paris summit (CFE)
- INF treaty
- START talks

North Atlantic Treaty Organization (NATO) allies on one side and massive forces of the Soviet Union and its *Warsaw Pact* allies on the other. Germany itself was split, with three-quarters of the country—and three-quarters of the capital city of Berlin—occupied by the United States, Britain, and France. The remainder, surrounding West Berlin, was occupied by the Soviet Union. Crises in Berlin in 1948 and 1961 led to armed confrontations but not war. In 1961 East Germany built the Berlin Wall separating East from West Berlin. It symbolized the division of Europe by what Winston Churchill had called the "iron curtain."

Despite the hostility of East-West relations during the Cold War, a relatively stable framework of relations emerged, and conflicts never escalated to all-out war. At a U.S.-Soviet-British meeting at *Yalta* in 1945, when the defeat of Germany was imminent, the Western powers acknowledged the fact of the Soviet army's presence in Eastern Europe, allowing that area to remain under Soviet influence. While the Soviet bloc did not join Western economic institutions such as the IMF, all the world's major states joined the UN. The UN (unlike the ill-fated League of Nations) managed to maintain almost universal membership and adherence to basic structures and rules throughout the Cold War era.

The central concern of the West during the Cold War was that the Soviet Union might gain control of Western Europe—either through outright invasion or through communists' taking power in war-weary and impoverished countries of Western Europe. This could have put the entire industrial base of the Eurasian land mass (from Europe to Siberia) under one state. The *Marshall Plan*—U.S. financial aid to rebuild European economies—responded to these fears, as did the creation of the NATO alliance. Half of the entire world's military spending was devoted to the European standoff. Much spending was also devoted to a superpower nuclear arms race, in which each superpower produced tens of thousands of nuclear weapons (see pp. 259–262).

Through the policy of **containment,** adopted in the late 1940s, the United States sought to halt the expansion of Soviet influence globally on several levels at once—military, political, ideological, economic. The United States maintained an extensive network of military bases and alliances worldwide. Virtually all of U.S. foreign policy in subsequent decades, from foreign aid and technology transfer to military intervention and diplomacy, came to serve the goal of containment.

The *Chinese communist revolution* in 1949 led to a Sino-Soviet alliance ("Sino" means Chinese). But China became fiercely independent in the 1960s following the **Sino-Soviet split,** when China opposed Soviet moves toward *peaceful coexistence* with the United States.[26] In the late 1960s young radicals, opposed to both superpowers, ran China during the chaotic and destructive *Cultural Revolution*. But feeling threatened by Soviet power, China's leaders developed a growing affiliation with the United States during the 1970s, starting with a dramatic visit by U.S. president Nixon in 1972. During the Cold War, China generally tried to play a balancer role against whichever superpower seemed most threatening at the time.

In 1950 the *Korean War* broke out when communist North Korea attacked and overran most of U.S.-allied South Korea. The United States and its allies (under UN

---

[26]Mayers, David Allan. *Cracking the Monolith: U.S. Policy Against the Sino-Soviet Alliance, 1949–1955.* Baton Rouge: Louisiana State University Press, 1986. Kim, Ilpyong J., ed. *Beyond the Strategic Triangle.* New York: Paragon, 1992.

authority obtained after the Soviets walked out of the Security Council in protest) counterattacked and overran most of North Korea. China sent masses of "volunteers" to help North Korea, and the war bogged down near the original border until a 1953 truce ended the fighting. The Korean War hardened U.S. attitudes toward communism and set a negative tone for future East-West relations, especially for U.S.-Chinese relations in the 1950s. U.S. leaders considered using nuclear weapons during the Korean War, but decided not to do so.

The Cold War thawed temporarily after Stalin died in 1953. The first **summit meeting** between superpower leaders took place in Geneva in 1955. But the Soviet Union sent tanks to crush a popular uprising in Hungary in 1956 (an action it repeated in 1968 in Czechoslovakia), and the Soviet missile program that orbited *Sputnik* in 1957 alarmed the United States. The shooting down of a U.S. spy plane (the *U-2*) over the Soviet Union in 1960 scuttled a summit meeting between superpower leaders Khrushchev and Eisenhower. Meanwhile in Cuba, after Fidel Castro's communist revolution in 1959, the United States attempted a counterrevolution in the botched 1961 *Bay of Pigs* invasion.

These hostilities culminated in the **Cuban Missile Crisis** of 1962, when the Soviet Union installed medium-range nuclear missiles in Cuba (to reduce the Soviet Union's strategic nuclear inferiority and deter a new U.S. invasion of Cuba). U.S. president John F. Kennedy imposed a naval blockade to force their removal. The Soviet Union backed down on the missiles, and the United States promised not to invade Cuba in the future. Leaders on both sides were shaken by the possibility of nuclear war (which, as historical documents have now revealed, was all too possible).[27] They signed the *Limited Test Ban Treaty* in 1963, prohibiting atmospheric nuclear tests, and began to cooperate in cultural exchanges, space exploration, aviation, and other such issues.

The two superpowers often jockeyed for position in the third world, supporting **proxy wars** in which they typically supplied and advised opposing factions in civil wars. The alignments were often arbitrary. For instance, the United States backed the Ethiopian government and the Soviets backed next-door rival Somalia in the 1970s; when an Ethiopian revolution caused the new government to seek Soviet help, the United States switched to support Somalia instead.

One flaw of U.S. policy in the Cold War period was to see such regional conflicts through East-West lenses. Its preoccupation with communism led the United States to support unpopular pro-Western governments in a number of poor countries, nowhere more disastrously than in the *Vietnam War* in the 1960s. The war in Vietnam divided U.S. citizens and ultimately failed to prevent a communist takeover. The fall of South Vietnam in 1975 appeared to signal U.S. weakness, especially combined with U.S. setbacks in the Middle East—the 1973 Arab oil embargo against the United States and the 1979 overthrow of the U.S.-backed Shah of Iran by Islamic fundamentalists.

Perhaps tempted by this apparent U.S. weakness, the Soviet Union invaded Afghanistan in 1979. But, like the United States in Vietnam, the Soviet Union could not suppress rebel armies supplied by the opposing superpower. The Soviets ultimately withdrew after almost a decade of war that considerably weakened the Soviet Union. Meanwhile President Reagan built up U.S. military forces to record levels and supported rebel armies in the Soviet-allied states of Nicaragua and Angola (and one faction in Cambo-

---

[27]Nathan, James A., ed. *The Cuban Missile Crisis Revisited*. New York: St. Martin's Press, 1992.

dia) as well as Afghanistan. Superpower relations slowly improved after Mikhail Gorbachev, a reformer, took power in 1985. But some of the third-world battlegrounds (notably Afghanistan and Angola) continued to suffer from brutal civil wars (fought with leftover Cold War arms) into the mid-1990s.

In retrospect, it seems that both superpowers exaggerated Soviet strength. In the early years of the nuclear arms race, U.S. military superiority was absolute, especially in nuclear weapons. The Soviets managed to match the United States over time, from A-bombs to H-bombs to multiple-warhead missiles. By the 1970s the Soviets had achieved strategic parity, meaning that neither side could prevent its own destruction in a nuclear war. But behind this military parity lay a Soviet Union lagging far behind the West in everything else—sheer wealth, technology, infrastructure, and citizen/worker motivation.

In June 1989, massive pro-democracy demonstrations in China's capital of Beijing—touched off by a visit from Gorbachev—were put down violently by the Communist government. Hundreds or more were shot dead in the streets. Around 1990, as the Soviet Union stood by, one after another Eastern European country replaced its communist government under pressure of mass demonstrations. The toppling of the Berlin Wall in late 1989 symbolized the end of the Cold War division of Europe. Germany formally reunified in 1990. The Soviet leader, Gorbachev, allowed these losses of external power (and more) in hopes of concentrating on Soviet domestic restructuring under his policies of *perestroika* (economic reform) and *glasnost* (openness in political discussion). In 1991, however, the Soviet Union itself broke apart.

Scholars do not agree on the important question of why the Cold War ended. One line of argument holds that U.S. military strength under President Reagan forced the Soviet Union into bankruptcy as it tried to keep up in the arms race. Another argument holds that the Soviet Union suffered from internal stagnation over a number of decades and ultimately imploded because of weaknesses in its system of governance that had little to do with external pressure. Indeed, some scholars think the Soviet Union might have fallen apart earlier without the United States as a foreign enemy to bolster the Soviet government's legitimacy with its own people.

The Early Post–Cold War Era, 1990–1995

In 1990, perhaps believing that the end of the Cold War had left a power vacuum in its region, Iraq occupied its neighbor Kuwait in an aggressive grab for control of Middle East oil. Western powers were alarmed—both about the example that such aggression could set in a new era, if unpunished, and about the direct threat to energy supplies for the world economy. The United States mobilized a coalition of the world's major countries (with almost no opposition) to oppose Iraq. Working through the UN, the U.S.-led coalition applied escalating sanctions against Iraq—from condemnation, to embargoing Iraq's oil exports, to threats and ultimatums. President Bush received from the U.S. Congress authorization to use force against Iraq.

When Iraq did not withdraw from Kuwait by the UN's deadline, the United States and its allies easily smashed Iraq's military and evicted its army from Kuwait in the *Gulf War*. But the coalition did not occupy Iraq or overthrow its government. (Ironically, Saddam Hussein outlasted George Bush in office.) The costs of the Gulf War were shared among the participants in the coalition, with Britain and France making military commitments while Japan and Germany made substantial financial contributions. The pass-the-hat financing for this war was a new innovation, one that worked fairly well.[28]

The final collapse of the Soviet Union followed only months after the Gulf War. The 15 republics of the Union—of which Russia under President Boris Yeltsin was just one—had begun taking power from a weakened central government, declaring themselves as sovereign states. This process, which is still working itself out fully, raised complex problems ranging from issues of national self-determination to the reallocation of property. The Baltic republics (Estonia, Latvia, and Lithuania), which had been incorporated into the Soviet Union only in the 1940s, were leaders in breaking away. The others held long negotiations under Gorbachev's leadership to restructure their confederation, with stronger republics and a weaker center.

The *Union Treaty* outlining this new structure provoked hard-liners in the old central government to try to seize control of the Soviet Union in a military coup in 1991.[29] The failure of the coup—and the prominent role of Russian president Yeltsin in opposing it—accelerated the collapse of the Soviet Union. The Communist party was banned, and soon both capitalism and democracy were adopted as the basis of the economies and political systems of the former Soviet states. (In reality the daily workings of society change somewhat more slowly; the old guard tends to retain power wearing new hats.) The republics became independent states and formed a loose coordinating structure—the **Commonwealth of Independent States (CIS)**—whose future is still unclear. Of the former Soviet republics, only the three small Baltic States are nonmembers.

Western relations with Russia and the other republics were not trouble-free after 1991. Because of their own economic problems, Western countries provided only limited aid for the region's harsh economic transition, which had drastically reduced living standards. Russia's brutal suppression of its secessionist province of Chechnya in 1995 provoked Western fears of an expansionist, aggressive Russian nationalism, especially after the earlier success of ultranationalists in Russian parliamentary elections. Russian leaders feared that NATO expansion into Eastern Europe would place threatening Western military forces on Russia's borders, creating a new division of Europe. Russian president Yeltsin warned of a "Cold Peace." Meanwhile, Japan had a lingering (mostly symbolic) territorial dispute with Russia.[30]

---

[28]Freedman, Lawrence, and Efraim Karsh. *The Gulf Conflict: 1990–1991*. Princeton: Princeton University Press, 1993.

[29]Colton, Timothy, and Robert Legvold. *After the Soviet Union: From Empire to Nations*. New York: W. W. Norton, 1992. Billington, James H. *Russia Transformed: Breakthrough to Hope: Moscow, August 1991*. New York: Free Press, 1992. Goldman, Marshall I. *What Went Wrong with Perestroika*. New York: W. W. Norton, 1994.

[30]Garthoff, Raymond L. *The Great Transition: American-Soviet Relations and the End of the Cold War*. Washington, DC: The Brookings Institution, 1994. Gaddis, John Lewis. *The United States and the End of the Cold War: Implications, Reconsiderations, Provocations*. New York: Oxford University Press, 1992. Jervis, Robert, and Seweryn Bialer, eds. *Soviet-American Relations After the Cold War*. Durham: Duke University Press, 1991. Ramberg, Bennett, ed. *Arms Control Without Negotiation: From the Cold War to the New World Order*. Boulder, CO: Lynne Rienner, 1993. Fukuyama, Francis. *The End of History and the Last Man*. New York: Free Press, 1992.

Despite these problems, overall the world's great powers increased their cooperation after the Cold War. Russia was accepted as the successor state to the Soviet Union and took its seat on the Security Council. Russia and the United States agreed to radical reductions in their nuclear weapons, to be carried out in the 1990s. The UN helped end several of the festering regional conflicts of the 1980s—in Afghanistan, Cambodia, Iraq-Iran, and Central America—with mixed success. The number, scope, and expense of UN peacekeeping missions grew rapidly in the early 1990s.

U.S. leaders had hoped that the Gulf War would set valuable precedents for the future—the punishment of aggression, the reaffirmation of sovereignty and territorial integrity (of both Kuwait and Iraq), the utility of the UN Security Council, and the willingness of the United States to lead the post–Cold War order, which President Bush named the "New World Order." The prime architect of the "New World Order" of the early 1990s was, in many ways, Franklin D. Roosevelt—the U.S. president during most of World War II in the 1940s. His vision was of a great power collaboration through a new United Nations after the defeat of Germany and Japan in the war. Included would be the winners of the war—the United States, the Soviet Union, and Britain, along with France and (for the first time) China. These five would hold permanent seats on the UN Security Council. Germany and Japan would be reconstructed as democracies, and the United States would take a strong leadership role in world affairs. Roosevelt's vision was delayed by forty years while the Soviet Union and United States contested the world order. But then, surprisingly, it came into existence in the early 1990s in something close to its original form.

Hopes for a "New World Order" after the Gulf War quickly collided with less pleasant realities, however. Nowhere was this more evident than in Bosnia-Herzegovina (hereafter called Bosnia for short), where the UN came to have its largest peacekeeping mission and where the gap between the international community's words and deeds was most striking. Just after the Gulf War in 1991, the former Yugoslavia broke apart, with several of its republics declaring independence. Ethnic Serbs, who were minorities in Croatia and Bosnia, seized about a third of Croatia and two-thirds of Bosnia as territory to form a "Greater Serbia" with the neighboring republic of Serbia. In those territories, with help from Serbia, which controlled the Yugoslav army, the Serb forces massacred hundreds of thousands of non-Serb Bosnians and Croatians and expelled millions more, to create an ethnically pure state.

The international community recognized the independence of Croatia and Bosnia, admitting them to the UN and passing dozens of Security Council resolutions to protect their territorial integrity and their civilian populations. But in contrast to the Gulf War, no great power showed willingness to bear major costs to protect Bosnia. Instead they tried to contain the conflict by appeasing Serb forces and assuming a neutral role as peacekeepers and intermediaries, offering a variety of peace plans, economic sanctions and rewards, and other inducements, none of which convinced Serb forces to withdraw from the territory they occupied. This neutrality included an arms embargo imposed on unarmed Bosnia and heavily armed Serbia alike, despite the UN resolutions declaring Serbia the aggressor. The UN sent almost 40,000 peacekeepers to Bosnia and Croatia, at a cost of over $1 billion per year. NATO threatened military strikes (and carried out a few symbolic ones) to deter Serb forces from attacking UN personnel and UN-declared "safe havens" for Bosnian civilians. But these threats turned out to be bluffs when tested.[31]

By 1995, the international community's Bosnia policy was in shambles and the Clinton administration felt heavy pressure from Congress (and an approaching presidential election) to come up with a solution. The Serbian forces overran two of three UN-designated "safe areas" in eastern Bosnia, expelling the women and slaughtering the men, but then lost most of their Croatian territory and a fifth of Bosnia on the battlefield, resulting in movements of Serbian populations from those areas. Two weeks of NATO air strikes (the first serious, though limited, use of Western military leverage) meanwhile restored a measure of credibility to Western threats and induced Serb forces to ease the seige of the Bosnian capital, Sarajevo. All of these actions received tacit approval from the Western great powers, because they "cleaned up" the map of Bosnia, created a more equal balance of power, and thus set the stage for an ethnic partition plan. U.S. negotiators pushed through the "Dayton agreement," to be enforced by 60,000 NATO troops. Its fate is unclear at this writing. It upholds Bosnia's multiethnic society on paper but leaves half the country, ethnically "cleansed" of non-Serbs, in the hands of the Serbian forces (whose leaders have been indicted for genocide by an international tribunal). While the hope of peace glimmered for Bosnia's people, the war severely damaged the United Nations, the Western alliance, and the idea of collective security.

Thus, the "New World Order" passed its first major test (the Gulf War) but failed the second (Bosnia). Other less critical cases also called into question the new world order. In Somalia, a U.S.-led coalition sent tens of thousands of troops to suppress factional fighting and deliver relief supplies to a large population that was starving. However, when those forces were drawn into the fighting and sustained casualties, the United States abruptly pulled out, with the UN following by 1995.[32] In Rwanda in 1994 a horrendous case of genocide—half a million civilians massacred in a matter of weeks—was virtually ignored by the international community. The great powers, burned by failures in Somalia and Bosnia, decided their vital interests were not at stake. The one successful U.S. military intervention, in Haiti to restore the elected president, was a backyard action by a great power, as were Russian interventions in the former Soviet Union. Such cases usually do not set precedents for world order. Furthermore, by 1995 there were signs of U.S. retreat from world leadership (including a weakened U.S. financial position, President Clinton's focus on domestic policy, and isolationist sentiments in the new Republican-controlled Congress).

The post–Cold War era has barely begun. The transition into that era has been a turbulent time, full of international changes and new possibilities (both good and bad). Whether these rapid changes will settle down as a "New World Order" emerges, or whether the new order will be an ever more chaotic one, we do not know.[33] It is likely,

---

[31]Rieff, David. *Slaughterhouse: Bosnia and the Failure of the West.* New York: Simon & Schuster, 1995. Malcolm, Noel. *Bosnia: A Short History.* New York: New York University Press, 1994. Gjelten, Tom. *Sarajevo Daily: A City and Its Newspaper Under Siege.* New York: HarperCollins, 1995. Gutman, Roy. *A Witness to Genocide.* New York: Macmillan, 1993. Ali, Rabia, and Lawrence Lifschultz, eds. *Why Bosnia? Writings on the Balkan War.* Stony Creek, CT: The Pamphleteer's Press, Inc., 1993.

[32]Makinda, Samuel M. *Seeking Peace from Chaos: Humanitarian Intervention in Somalia.* Boulder, CO: Lynne Rienner, 1993.

[33]Mearsheimer, John J. Back to the Future: Instability in Europe After the Cold War. *International Security* 15 (1), 1990: 5–56.

however, that basic rules and principles of IR—those that scholars have long struggled to understand—will continue to apply even though their contexts and outcomes may change in the new era that has begun to unfold. Most central to those rules and principles in traditional IR scholarship is the concept of power, to which we now turn.

❖ CHAPTER SUMMARY

- ◆ IR affects daily life profoundly; we all participate in IR.
- ◆ IR is a field of political science, concerned mainly with explaining political outcomes in international security affairs and international political economy.
- ◆ Theories complement descriptive narratives in explaining international events and outcomes, but scholars do not agree on a single set of theories or methods to use in studying IR.
- ◆ States are the most important actors in IR; the international system is based on the sovereignty of (about 200) independent territorial states.
- ◆ States vary greatly in size of population and economy, from tiny microstates to great powers.
- ◆ Nonstate actors such as multinational corporations (MNCs), nongovernmental organizations (NGOs), and intergovernmental organizations (IGOs) exert a growing influence on international relations.
- ◆ Four levels of analysis—individual, domestic, interstate, and global—suggest multiple explanations (operating simultaneously) for outcomes observed in IR.
- ◆ The global level of analysis—a recent addition—draws attention especially to the global gap in wealth and well-being between the industrialized North and the poor South.
- ◆ A variety of world civilizations were conquered by Europeans over several centuries and forcefully absorbed into a single global international system initially centered in Europe.
- ◆ The great-power system is made up of about half a dozen states (membership changing over time as state power rises and falls).
- ◆ Great powers have restructured world order through recurrent wars, alliances, and the reign of hegemons (states that temporarily gain a preponderance of power in the international system). The most important wars are the Thirty Years' War (1618–1648), the Napoleonic Wars (1803–1815), World War I (1914–1918), and World War II (1939–1945). Periods of hegemony include the United States after World War II and Britain in the nineteenth century.
- ◆ European states colonized most of the rest of the world during the past five centuries. Latin American countries gained independence shortly after the United States did (about two hundred years ago), while those in Africa, Asia, and the Middle East became independent states only in the decades after World War II.
- ◆ Nationalism strongly influences IR; conflict often results from the perception of nationhood leading to demands for statehood or for the adjustment of state borders.
- ◆ Democracy is a force of growing importance: more states are becoming democratically governed, and democracies rarely fight each other in wars.

◆ The world economy has generated wealth at an accelerating pace in the past two centuries and is increasingly integrated on a global scale.

◆ World Wars I and II have dominated the character of the twentieth century, yet they seem to offer contradictory lessons about the utility of hard-line or conciliatory foreign policies.

◆ For most of the fifty years since World War II, world politics revolved around the East-West rivalry of the Cold War. This bipolar standoff created stability and avoided great-power wars, including nuclear war, but it had harmful consequences for third-world states that became proxy battlegrounds.

◆ The post–Cold War era that has just begun holds hope of general great-power cooperation despite an upsurge of ethnic and regional conflicts.

❖ THINKING CRITICALLY

1. Pick a current area in which interesting international events are taking place. Can you think of possible explanations for those events from each of the four levels of analysis? Do explanations from different levels provide insights into different aspects of the events?

2. For a given nation-state that was once a *colony*, can you think of ways in which the state's current foreign policies might be influenced by its history of having been a colony?

3. For a state that was once a *colonizer*, can you think of ways in which its experience as colonizer might influence its current foreign policies?

4. Given the contradictory lessons of World Wars I and II, can you think of situations in today's world where appeasement (a conciliatory policy) would be the best course? Situations where hard-line containment policies would be best? Why?

5. What do you expect will be the character of the post–Cold War era that has begun in the 1990s? Peaceful? War-prone? Orderly? Chaotic? Why do you have the expectations you do, and what clues from the unfolding of events in the world might tell you whether your guesses were correct?

❖ KEY TERMS

international relations (IR)
issue areas
cooperation and conflict
international security
international political economy (IPE)
state
international system
nation-state

Gross Domestic Product (GDP)
nonstate actors
nongovernmental organization (NGO)
intergovernmental organization (IGO)
North-South gap
nationalism

industrialization
free trade
League of Nations
Munich Agreement
containment
Sino-Soviet split

summit meeting
Cuban Missile Crisis
proxy wars
Commonwealth of Independent States
  (CIS)

Iraqi soldier during the occupation of Kuwait, September 1990.

POWER POLITICS

❖ REALISM

There is no single theory that reliably explains the wide range of international interactions, both conflictual and cooperative. But there is a theoretical framework that has traditionally held a central position in the study of IR. This approach, called realism, is favored by some IR scholars and vigorously contested by others, but almost all take it into account. It is a relatively conservative theoretical approach; liberal and revolutionary alternatives will be reviewed in Chapter 3.

Realism (or *political realism*) is a school of thought that explains international relations in terms of power (see "Defining Power" on pp. 53–55). The exercise of power by states toward each other is sometimes called *realpolitik*, or just *power politics*. Realism has a long history, and it dominated the study of IR in the United States during the Cold War.

Realism as we know it developed in reaction to a liberal tradition that realists called **idealism** (of course, idealists themselves do not consider their approach unrealistic). Idealism emphasizes international law, morality, and international organization, rather than power alone, as key influences on international events. Idealists think that human nature is basically good and that with good habits, education, and appropriate international structures, human nature can become the basis of peaceful and cooperative international relationships. Idealists see the international system as one based on a community of states that have the potential to work together to overcome mutual problems, just as neighbors in a small town might do (see Chapter 3).

For idealists, the principles of IR must flow from morality. The logic of this position was laid out over 2000 years ago by a Chinese writer, Mo Ti. He pointed out that everyone "knows that [murder] is unrighteous," yet "when murder is committed in attacking a country it is not considered wrong; it is applauded and called righteous." For Mo Ti, this made no sense. "If a man calls black black if it is seen on a small scale, but calls black white when it is seen on a large scale, then he is one who cannot tell black from white."[1]

---

[1]Sun Tzu. *The Art of War*. Translated by Samuel B. Griffith. New York: Oxford University Press, 1963: 22.

Idealists were particularly active in the period between World Wars I and II, following the painful experience of World War I. U.S. president Woodrow Wilson and other idealists placed their hopes for peace in the League of Nations as a formal structure for the community of nations.

These hopes were dashed when that structure proved helpless to stop German and Japanese aggression in the 1930s. After World War II, realists blamed idealists for looking too much at how the world *ought to be* instead of how it *really is*. Sobered by the experiences of World War II, realists set out to understand the principles of power politics without succumbing to wishful thinking. Realism provided a theoretical foundation for the Cold War policies of containment and the determination of U.S. policy makers not to appease the Soviet Union and China.

Realists ground themselves in a long tradition. The Chinese strategist *Sun Tzu*, who lived at the time of Mo Ti, advised the rulers of states how to survive in an era when war had become a systematic instrument of power for the first time (the "warring states" period). Sun Tzu argued that the moral reasoning of scholars like Mo Ti was not very useful to the state rulers of the day, faced with armed and dangerous neighbors. Sun Tzu by contrast showed rulers how to use power to advance their interests and protect their survival.

At roughly the same time, in Greece, *Thucydides* wrote an account of the Peloponnesian War (431–415 B.C.) focusing on relative power among the Greek city-states. He wrote that "the strong do what they have the power to do and the weak accept what they have to accept."[2] Much later, in Renaissance Italy (around 1500), *Niccolò Machiavelli* advised Italian princes whose dangerous environment resembled that faced by Sun Tzu's clients. Machiavelli urged princes to concentrate on expedient actions to stay in power and to pay attention to war above all else. Today the adjective "Machiavellian" refers to excessively manipulative power maneuvers.[3]

English philosopher *Thomas Hobbes* in the seventeenth century discussed the free-for-all that exists when government is absent and people seek their own self-interest. He called it the "state of war"—what we would now call the "law of the jungle" in contrast to the rule of law. Hobbes favored a strong monarchy to prevent this condition, but in international affairs there is no such central authority (see pp. 72–74).

In the nineteenth century, the German military strategist *Karl von Clausewitz* said that "war is a continuation of politics by other means." U.S. admiral *Alfred Mahan* promoted naval power as the key means of achieving national political and economic interests. Realists see in these historical figures evidence that the importance of power politics is timeless and cross-cultural.

After World War II, scholar *Hans Morgenthau* argued that international politics is governed by objective, universal laws based on national interest defined as power (not on psychological motives of decision makers). He reasoned that no nation had "God on its side" (a universal morality) and that all nations had to base their actions on prudence and practicality.

Realists tend to treat political power as separate from, and predominant over, morality, ideology, and other social and economic aspects of life. For realists ideologies do not

---

[2]Thucydides. *History of The Peloponnesian War.* Translated by R. Warner. New York: Penguin, 1972:402.

[3]Machiavelli, Niccolò. *The Prince, and The Discourses.* Translated by Luigi Ricci. Revised by E. R. P. Vincent. New York: Modern Library, 1950. Meinecke, Friedrich. *Machiavellism: The Doctrine of Raison d'État and Its Place in Modern History.* New Haven: Yale University Press, 1957.

TABLE 2.1 ASSUMPTIONS OF REALISM AND IDEALISM

Issue	Realism	Idealism
Human Nature	Selfish	Altruistic
Most Important Actors	States	States and others including individuals
Causes of State Behavior	Rational pursuit of self-interest	Psychological motives of decision makers
Nature of International System	Anarchy	Community

matter much, nor do religions or other cultural factors with which states may explain their actions. Realists see states with very different religions or ideologies or economic systems as quite similar in their actions with regard to national power.[4]

Today realists share several assumptions about how IR works. They assume that IR can be best (though not exclusively) explained by the choices of states operating as autonomous actors rationally pursuing their own interests in a system of sovereign states. Sometimes the realist framework is summarized in three propositions: (1) *states* are the most important actors (the state-centric assumption); (2) they act like *rational* individuals in pursuing national interests (the unitary rational-actor assumption); and (3) they act in the context of an international system lacking central government (the *anarchy* assumption).

Table 2.1 summarizes some major differences between the assumptions of realism and idealism. We will return to the realism-liberalism debate at the start of Chapter 3.

❖ POWER

Power is a central concept in international relations—*the* central one for realists—but one that is surprisingly difficult to define or measure.

Defining Power

Power is often defined as *the ability to get another actor to do what it would not otherwise have done* (or not to do what it *would* have done).[5] A variation on this idea is that actors are powerful to the extent that they affect others more than others affect them.[6] These definitions treat *power as influence*. If actors get their way a lot, they must be powerful.

One problem with this definition is that we seldom know what a second actor would have done in the absence of the first actor's power. There is a danger of circular logic: power explains influence, and influence measures power. This makes it hard to use power to explain why international events occur (the aim of realism). A related problem is that common usage treats power as a thing rather than a process: states "have" power.

These problems are resolved by recalling that power is not influence itself, but the ability or potential to influence others. IR scholars believe that such potential is based on specific (tangible and intangible) characteristics or possessions of states—such as their

---

[4]Morgenthau, Hans J., and Kenneth W. Thompson. *Politics Among Nations: The Struggle for Power and Peace.* 6th ed. New York, Knopf, 1985. Carr, Edward Hallett. *The Twenty Years' Crisis 1919–1939: An Introduction to the Study of International Relations.* London: Macmillan Press, 1974. Aron, Raymond. *Peace and War: A Theory of International Relations.* Translated by R. Howard and A. B. Fox. New York: Doubleday, 1966.

[5]Dahl, Robert A. *Modern Political Analysis.* 2nd ed. Englewood Cliffs, NJ: Prentice Hall, 1970.

[6]Waltz, Kenneth. *Theory of International Politics.* Reading, MA: Addison-Wesley, 1979.

sizes, levels of income, armed forces, and so forth. This is *power as capability.* Capabilities are easier to measure than influence and less circular in logic.

Measuring capabilities, in order to use them to explain how one nation influenced another, is not simple, however. It requires summing up various kinds of potentials—like adding apples and oranges. States possess varying amounts of population, territory, military forces, and so forth. *The best single indicator of a state's power may be its total GDP,* which combines overall size, technological level, and wealth. But even GDP is at best a rough indicator. An alternative method of estimating GDP, compared to the method followed in this book, gives GDP estimates that are on average about 50 percent higher for countries in the global North and about 50 percent lower for the global South (see Chapter 1, footnote 6). So GDP is a very useful estimator of material capabilities but not a precise one.

Furthermore, beyond the tangible capabilities, such as a country's GDP, power depends on intangible elements. Capabilities give a state the potential to influence others only to the extent that political leaders can mobilize and deploy those capabilities effectively and strategically. This depends on national will, on diplomatic skill, on popular support for the government (its legitimacy), and so forth. Some scholars emphasize the *power of ideas*—the ability to maximize the influence of capabilities through a psychological process. This process includes the domestic mobilization of capabilities—often through religion, ideology, or (especially) nationalism. International influence is also gained by being the one to set agendas, to form rules of behavior, to change how others

Power is the ability to influence the behavior of others. Military force and economic sanctions are among the various means states use to try to influence each other. Here a U.S. warship enforces economic sanctions against Serbia and an arms embargo against Bosnia, 1993.

see their own national interests. If a state's own values become widely shared among other states, it will easily influence others to follow its lead. For example, the United States has influenced many other states to accept the value of free markets and free trade. This has been called *soft power*.[7]

A state can have power only relative to other states. *Relative power* is the ratio of the power that two states can bring to bear against each other. In terms of power as capability, it matters little to realists whether a state's capabilities are rising or declining in absolute terms, only whether they are falling behind or overtaking the capabilities of rival states.

Even realists recognize the limits to explanations based on power. At best, power provides a general understanding of typical or average outcomes. In actual IR there are many other elements at work, including an element of accident or luck (Machiavelli called it "fortune"). The more powerful actor does not always prevail. Power provides only a partial explanation.[8]

Estimating Power

In Sun Tzu's first chapter, called "Estimates," his advice is to accurately estimate one's own power—ranging from money to territory to popular domestic support—and that of one's potential enemies. "Know the enemy and know yourself; in a hundred battles you will never be in peril," he wrote. Any estimate of an actor's overall power must combine diverse elements and will therefore be inexact. But such estimates are nonetheless very useful.

Consider two examples in which states went to war: Iraq and Iran in 1979, and Iraq and the United States in 1990. The logic of power suggests that in wars the more powerful state will generally prevail. Thus, estimates of the relative power of the two antagonists should help explain the outcome of each war. These estimates could take into account the nations' relative military capabilities and the popular support for each one's government, among other factors. But most important in terms of overall potential power is the total size of each nation's economy—the total GDP—which reflects both population size and the level of income per person (per capita). With a healthy enough economy, a state can buy a large army, it can buy popular support (by providing consumer goods), and it can even buy allies.

When Iraq attacked its neighbor Iran in 1979, the two countries appeared roughly equal in power. Both were oil-producing countries with middle-range income levels. Both could use oil income to buy arms on world markets, and both had relatively large and advanced military forces (by third-world standards). Iran's military had been developed under the Shah in alliance with the United States; Iraq's had been largely supplied by the Soviet Union. Iran's population of 38 million was three times as large as Iraq's but its total GDP was less than double Iraq's.

---

[7]Nye, Joseph S., Jr. *Bound to Lead: The Changing Nature of American Power.* New York: Basic Books, 1990.

[8]Rothgeb, John M., Jr. *Defining Power: Influence and Force in the Contemporary International System.* New York: St. Martin's Press, 1992. Pettman, Ralph. *International Politics: Balance of Power, Balance of Productivity, Balance of Ideologies.* Boulder, CO: Lynne Rienner, 1991. Cox, Robert W. *Production, Power, and World Order: Social Forces in the Making of History.* New York: Columbia University Press, 1987. Liska, George. *The Ways of Power: Patterns and Meaning in World Politics.* Cambridge, U.K.: Basil Blackwell, 1990. Stoll, Richard, and Michael D. Ward, eds. *Power in World Politics.* Boulder, CO: Lynne Rienner, 1988. Sullivan, Michael P. *Power in Contemporary International Politics.* Columbia: University of South Carolina Press, 1990.

Counterbalancing Iran's modest advantage in GDP was its short-term internal disorder. The Shah had been overthrown. Much of the military could be expected to offer little support, and perhaps active opposition, to Ayatollah Khomeini and the other new leaders who had overthrown the Shah. It seemed that the new government would be unable to mobilize its potential power. By contrast, Saddam Hussein (also known as just Saddam) had recently taken absolute power as leader of Iraq and could count on a loyal military. He invaded Iran, hoping for a quick victory and the installation of a friendly government there.

The key element on which Saddam's plan depended was Iran's low internal cohesion, which would counteract Iran's advantage in size. As it turned out, Saddam miscalculated this element. The Iranian military pulled together under Khomeini to put up a spirited defense, and the population proved more willing to die for its cause than were Iraq's soldiers for theirs. The tide soon turned against Iraq. Saddam then looked to allies in the Arab world. These, with the tacit support of all the great powers, provided him enough aid to keep from losing (which would expand Iran's power) but not enough to win (which would expand Iraq's power). Thus the two sides were roughly equal in the power they could bring to bear. The war dragged on for ten years, killing a million people, before its end was negotiated with no winner.

The second example could hardly be more different. When Iraq seized and annexed its small and rich neighbor Kuwait, it came into a confrontation with the United States (which was determined not to let Iraq control the oil of the Persian Gulf). The power disparity was striking. In GDP the United States held an advantage of nearly a hundred to one, in population more than ten to one. The U.S. armed forces were much larger than Iraq's and much more capable technologically. The United States also enjoyed a power advantage in the moral legitimacy stamped upon its cause by the UN Security Council. All of this power was augmented by the active participation of a broad alliance coalition against Iraq that included the most powerful states both regionally and globally. Iraq had few allies of any kind and no strong ones.

Iraq had the advantage in one important element, geography: Kuwait was right next to Iraq and was occupied by its dug-in troops, whereas the United States was halfway around the world and had few military forces in the Middle East region at the outset. Saddam also looked to the internal-cohesion dimension, where (as with Iran) he expected domestic politics in the United States to sap its will to fight. Again this was a miscalculation. The U.S. political leadership and citizenry rallied behind the war.

Overall, in this situation, the GDP ratio—nearly one hundred to one—provided a good estimate of the power imbalance between Iraq and the United States. (In the short term, of course, other factors ranging from political strategies to military forces to weather played a role.) When the war began, the U.S.-led coalition established its dominance within the first few hours of the war and went on to systematically crush Iraq's military power over six weeks and evict its forces from Kuwait. Thus, despite its lack of precision, GDP is probably the best single indicator of power.

Elements of Power

National power is a mix of many ingredients, such as natural resources, industrial capacity, moral legitimacy, military preparedness, popular support of government, and so forth.

Military power such as tanks rests on economic strength, roughly measured by GDP. Here a U.S. tank arrives in a Saudi port shortly after Iraq's invasion of Kuwait, July 1990. The large U.S. economy produced the military might that defeated Iraq.

All these elements contribute to an actor's power. The mix varies from one actor to another, making it hard to compare them, but overall power *does* relate to the rough quantities of the elements on which that power is based.

Power resources are elements that an actor can draw on over the *long term* to develop particular capabilities, plans, and actions. The power measure used earlier—total GDP—is in this category. So are population, territory, geography, and natural resources. These attributes change only slowly. Less tangible long-term power resources include political culture, patriotism, education of the population, and strength of the scientific and technological base. The credibility of its commitments (reputation for keeping its word) is also a power resource that a state can nurture over time. So is the ability of one state's culture and values to consistently shape the thinking of other states (the power of ideas). Power resources shape an actor's potential power.

The importance of long-term power resources was illustrated after the Japanese surprise attack on the U.S. fleet at Pearl Harbor in 1941, which decimated U.S. naval capabilities in the Pacific. In the short term, Japan had superior military power and was able to occupy territories in Southeast Asia while driving U.S. forces from the region. U.S. general Douglas MacArthur left the Philippines under Japanese attack, vowing "I shall return." In the longer term, the United States had greater power resources due to its underlying economic potential. It built up military capabilities over the next few years that gradually matched and then overwhelmed those of Japan in the Pacific. After Japan's defeat, MacArthur became the top authority in Japan under U.S. occupation.

Power capabilities allow actors to exercise influence in the *short term*. Military forces are such a capability—perhaps the most important kind. The size, composition, and preparedness of two states' military forces matter more in a short-term military confrontation than do their respective economies or natural resources. Another capability is the military-industrial capacity to quickly produce tanks, fighter planes, bullets, and so forth. The quality of a state's bureaucracy is another type of capability, allowing the state to gather information, regulate international trade, attend international conferences, and so on.

As with power resources, some power capabilities are intangible. The *support* and legitimacy that an actor commands in the short term from constituents and allies are capabilities that the actor can use to gain influence. The *loyalty* of a nation's army and politicians to its leader (in the short term) is in effect a capability available to the leader.

While capabilities come into play more quickly than power resources, they are narrower in scope. In particular, military capabilities are useful only when military power can be effective in gaining influence. They are of little use, for example, in U.S. trade negotiations with the European Community. Likewise, economic capabilities, such as OPEC's influence on world oil markets, are of little use in situations dominated by a military component, such as Iraq's invasion of Kuwait.

Given the limited resources that any actor commands, there are always trade-offs among the capabilities that could be developed. Building up military forces will divert resources that could have been put into foreign aid, for instance. Or buying a population's loyalty with consumer goods could reduce the resources available for building up military capabilities. To the extent that one element of power can be converted into another, it is called *fungible*. Generally money is the most fungible capability because it can buy other capabilities.

Realists tend to see *military force* as the most important element of national power in the short term, and they see other elements like economic strength or diplomatic skill or moral legitimacy as being important to the extent that they are fungible into military power. Such fungibility of nonmilitary elements of power into military ones is considerable, at least in the long term. Well-paid soldiers fight better, as do soldiers imbued with moral fervor for their cause, or soldiers using higher-technology weapons. Skilled diplomats can avoid unfavorable military confrontations or provoke favorable ones. Moral foreign policies can help sway public opinion in foreign countries and cement alliances that increase military strength. Realists tend to treat these dimensions of power as important mainly because of their potential military impact. Incidentally, realists share this emphasis on military power with revolutionaries such as communist leaders during the Cold War. Chairman Mao of China said: "All power grows out of the barrel of a gun." And Stalin once dismissed the opinion of the pope with the retort: "How many divisions [armies] does the pope have?"

The different types of power capabilities can be contrasted by considering the choice to possess tanks or gold. One standard power capability that states want is battle tanks. In land warfare to control territory, the tank is arguably the most powerful instrument available, and the leading defense against it is another tank. One can assess power on this dimension by counting the size and quality of a state's tank force (an imprecise but not impossible exercise). A different power capability of time-honored value is the stockpile of *gold* (or its modern-day equivalent in hard currency reserves; see Chapter 9). Gold represents economic power and is a power resource, whereas tanks represent military power and are a power capability.

Over the long term, the gold is better because one can always turn gold into tanks (it is fungible), but it might be hard to turn tanks into gold (especially after they lose a battle). However, over the short term the tanks might be better because if an enemy tank force invades one's territory, gold will not stop them; indeed they will soon take the gold for themselves. For example, in 1990 Iraq (which had gone for tanks) invaded its neighbor Kuwait (which had gone for gold). In the short term, Iraq proved much more powerful: it occupied Kuwait and plundered it.

Morality can contribute to power, by increasing the will to use power and by attracting allies. States have long clothed their actions, however aggressive, in rhetoric about their peaceful and defensive intentions. For instance, the U.S. War Department was renamed the Defense Department; the U.S. invasion of Panama was named "Operation Just Cause." This is because military capabilities are most effective in the context of justifications that make state actions seem moral.

The use of geography as an element of power is called *geopolitics*. It is often tied to the logistical requirements of military forces (see Chapter 6). Frequently, state leaders use maps in thinking about international power positions and alignments. In geopolitics, as in real estate, the three most important considerations are location, location, location. States increase their power to the extent they can use geography to enhance their military capabilities, such as by securing allies and bases in locations close to a rival power, or along strategic trade routes, or by controlling key natural resources. In general, power declines as a function of distance from a home state.[9]

A recurrent geopolitical theme for centrally located, largely land-locked states like Germany and Russia is the threat of being surrounded. German expansionists before World War I clamored for "living room"—more territory and resources for Germany's expanding population. In the 1840s, British politician Lord Palmerston warned that "Russia has a basic drive for warm water ports" (free of ice year-round). The 1979 Soviet invasion of Afghanistan was seen by some Western leaders as a step toward Soviet expansion southward to the Indian Ocean, driven by such a geopolitical drive.

Central states like Germany and Russia face a related military problem called the *two-front problem*. Germany had to fight France to the west and Russia to the east simultaneously in World War I—a problem reduced in World War II by Hitler's pact with Stalin. During the Cold War, the Western allies forced the Soviet Union to confront a two-front problem by stationing military forces both in Western Europe and in Japan and Asia. China in the late 1960s likewise faced Soviet troops to the north and American ones to the south (in Vietnam).

For states less centrally located, like Britain or the United States, different geopolitical problems appear. These states have been called "insular" in that bodies of water protect them against land attacks.[10] Their geopolitical problem in the event of war is to move soldiers and supplies over long distances to reach the scene of battle. This capability

---

[9]Boulding, Kenneth E. *Conflict and Defense*. New York: Harper & Row, 1962. Dalby, Simon. American Security Discourse: The Persistence of Geopolitics. *Political Geography* 9 (2), 1990: 171–88.

[10]Dehio, Ludwig. *The Precarious Balance: Four Centuries of the European Power Struggle*. Translated by Charles Fullman. New York: Vintage Books, 1962. [From the German version of 1948.] Modelski, George, and William R. Thompson. *Seapower in Global Politics, 1494–1993*. Seattle: University of Washington Press, 1988. Goldstein, Joshua S., and David P. Rapkin. After Insularity: Hegemony and the Future World Order. *Futures* 23 (9), 1991: 935–59.

was demonstrated in the U.S. participation in the world wars, the Cold War, and the Gulf War. The extensive British empire in the nineteenth century and the present-day worldwide network of U.S. bases, facilities, and alliances both maintained supply routes to support military operations at great distances (see p. 240).

❖ BARGAINING

The exercise of power involves two or more parties, each trying to influence the other more than it is itself influenced.

Bargaining and Leverage

Bargaining may be defined as tacit or direct communication in an attempt to reach agreement on an exchange of value—that is, of tangible or intangible items that one or both parties value. Bargaining need not be explicit. Sometimes the content is communicated through actions rather than an exchange of words.[11]

A bargaining process has two or more *participants* and sometimes has *mediators* whose participation is nominally neutral with respect to the outcome. Participants have a direct stake in the outcome; mediators do not. There are one or more *issues* on which each participant hopes to reach agreement on terms favorable to itself, but the participants' *interests* diverge on these issues, creating conflicts. These conflicts define a *bargaining space*—one or more dimensions each of which represents a distance between the positions of two participants concerning their preferred outcomes on an issue. The bargaining process disposes of these conflicts by achieving agreement on the distribution of the various items of value that are at stake. The end result is a position arrived at in the bargaining space.

Such agreements do not necessarily represent a *fair* exchange of value; many agreements are manifestly one-sided and unfair (much closer to one participant's preferred position in the bargaining space). But in a broad sense, bargains whether fair or unfair contain an element of *mutual gain*. This is possible because the items of value being exchanged have different value to the different parties. To take a clearly unfair example, an armed robber values a victim's wallet more than the victim does, and the victim values his or her own life more than the robber does. The robber "gives" the victim life and the victim "gives" the robber money, so both gain. As this example illustrates, the mutual gains in bargaining are relative to other possible outcomes, not necessarily to the status quo before the bargain.

Participants bring different means of *leverage* to the bargaining process.[12] Leverage derives from power capabilities that allow one actor to influence the other to reach agree-

[11]Synder, Glenn H., and Paul Diesing. *Conflict Among Nations: Bargaining, Decision Making, and System Structure in International Crises*. Princeton: Princeton University Press, 1977. Morgan, T. Clifton. *Untying the Knot of War: A Bargaining Theory of International Crises*. Ann Arbor: University of Michigan Press, 1994. Telhami, Shibley. *Power and Leadership in International Bargaining: The Path to the Camp David Accords*. New York: Columbia University Press, 1990. Habeeb, William Mark. *Power and Tactics in International Negotiation: How Weak Nations Bargain with Strong Nations*. Baltimore: Johns Hopkins University Press, 1988. Zartman, I. William, ed. *The 50% Solution: How to Bargain Successfully with Hijackers, Strikers, Bosses, Oil Magnates, Arabs, Russians, and Other Worthy Opponents in This Modern World*. New Haven: Yale University Press, 1987.

[12]North, Robert C. *War, Peace, Survival: Global Politics and Conceptual Synthesis*. Boulder, CO: Westview, 1990.

ments more favorable to the first actor's interests. Leverage may operate on any of three dimensions of power: the *promise* of positive sanctions (rewards) if the other actor gives one what one wants; the *threat* of negative sanctions (damage to valued items) if not; or an *appeal* to the other's feeling of love, friendship, sympathy, or respect for oneself.[13] For instance, Cuba during the Cold War could obtain Soviet oil by purchasing the oil with hard currency, by threatening to cut its alliance with the Soviet Union unless given the oil at subsidized prices, or by appealing to the Soviet leaders' sense of socialist solidarity.

Bringing a bargaining leverage into play generally opens up a new dimension in the bargaining space, allowing outcomes along this new dimension to be traded off against those on the original dimension (the main issue at stake). Leverage thus helps to get deals done—albeit not always fair ones. One-sided agreements typically result when one side has a preponderance of leverage relative to the other.

The use of violence can be a means of settling conflicts. The application of violent negative leverage can force an agreement that ends a conflict. (Again, the agreement may not be fair.) Such violence may also create new sources of conflict—hatred, desire for revenge, etc.—so agreements reached through violence may not last. Nonetheless, from a realist perspective violence is just another leverage—an extension of politics by other means as Clausewitz said. Politics itself has been described as the process of deciding "who gets what, when, how."[14]

The same principles of bargaining apply to both international security affairs and international political economy. In both cases power and leverage matter. Also in both cases structures and institutions have been designed to facilitate the bargaining process. Economic markets serve this purpose, from the New York Stock Exchange to the local supermarket. In international security such institutions as diplomatic missions and international organizations help to facilitate the bargaining process. Realists studying international security focus on political-military bargaining more than economic bargaining because they consider it more important. The economic framework will be fleshed out in Chapter 8.

When bargaining takes place formally—usually sitting at a table talking back and forth—it is called **negotiation.** Because the issues in IR are important and the actors are usually sophisticated players in a game with long-established rules and traditions, most issues of contention find their way to a negotiating table sooner or later. Often bargaining takes place simultaneously at the negotiating table and in the world (often on the battlefield). The participants talk in the negotiation hall while manipulating instruments of leverage outside it.

Negotiating styles vary from one culture or individual to another. For instance, in a Middle Eastern marketplace the negotiating tradition may call for the seller to start with an extreme price, which the buyer would be foolish to accept. But in a U.S. department store it would be pointless to offer a sales clerk $50 for an item marked at $150. In international negotiations on major political and military issues, problems of cultural difference may become serious obstacles. For example, Western negotiators sometimes have difficulty understanding Japanese and Chinese negotiating styles. A good negotiator will

---

[13]Boulding, Kenneth E. *Three Faces of Power.* Newbury Park, CA: Sage, 1990.
[14]Lasswell, Harold D. *Politics: Who Gets What, When, How.* New York: Meridian, 1958.

Bargaining includes both indirect moves and explicit negotiations. Palestinians got a seat at the table in formal Arab-Israeli peace negotiations only in 1991, and the Israeli and PLO leaders first shook hands in September 1993. But for decades Israel and the PLO used various power capabilities as leverage in implicit bargaining with each other.

take time to understand the other party's culture and bargaining style, as well as its interests and available means of leverage.

Strategies

Power strategies are plans actors use to develop and deploy power capabilities to achieve goals. A key aspect of strategy is choosing the kinds of capabilities to develop, given limited resources, in order to maximize international influence. This requires foresight because the particular situations may not yet exist when the capabilities to manage them would have to be developed. Yet the capabilities chosen often will not be fungible in the short term. Central to this dilemma is what kind of standing military forces to maintain in peacetime—enough to prevent a quick defeat if war breaks out, but not so much as to overburden one's economy (see pp. 224–231).

Strategies also include choices about how capabilities are used in situations—sequences of actions designed for maximum effect; the use of deception to influence others' perceptions of a situation; the creation of alliances; the use of contingency plans for rapid responses to various circumstances; and so forth. Most power strategies mix economic instruments (trade, aid, loans, investment, boycotts) with military ones depending on the situation. (In the short term, within a given situation such plans are called *tactics*.)

Strategies include whether (and in what situations) a state is willing to use its power capabilities.[15] For example, in the Vietnam War the United States had overall power capabilities far superior to those of the Vietnamese communists but lost the war because it was unwilling or unable to commit the resources necessary or use them effectively. The *will* of a nation or leader is hard to estimate. Even if leaders make explicit their intention to fight over an issue, they might be bluffing.

Some actors are better than others at using the capabilities they have. For instance, U.S. president Jimmy Carter in the 1970s had great-power capabilities available, but his own strategic and tactical skill seems to have been the key to success in the Camp David agreements (which achieved the U.S. foreign-policy goal of an Egyptian-Israeli treaty). Good strategies bring together power capabilities for maximum effect, but poor strategies make inefficient use of available capabilities. Of course, an actor's skill at strategy and tactics is hard to measure or estimate, but it often plays an important role in the outcome of power struggles, especially when a weaker actor manages to outfox a stronger one. Even the most skillful leader never has total control of an international situation, but can make best use of the opportunities available while minimizing the effects of bad luck.

In the context of bargaining, actors use various strategies to employ leverage in an effort to move the final agreement point closer to their own positions. One common bargaining strategy is to start with extreme demands and then gradually compromise them in an effort to end up close to one's true (but concealed) position. Another strategy is to "drive a hard bargain" by sticking closely to one's original position in the belief that the other participant will eventually accept it. Henry Kissinger in the 1970s, however, used a policy of preemptive concessions to induce movement on the other side and get to a middle-ground agreement quickly in few steps.[16]

Another common bargaining strategy is *fractionation*—splitting up a complex issue into a number of small components so that progress may be sought on solvable pieces. For instance, the Arab-Israeli negotiations that began in 1991 had many sets of talks concurrently working on various pieces of the problem. The opposite approach, which some bargainers prefer, is to lump together diverse issues—called *linkage*—so that compromises on one can be traded off against another in a grand deal. This was the case, for instance, in the Yalta negotiations of 1945 among the United States, Britain, and the Soviet Union. On the table simultaneously were such matters as the terms of occupation of Germany, the Soviet presence in Eastern Europe, the strategy for defeating Japan, and the creation of the United Nations.

Reciprocity, Deterrence, and Arms Races

To have the best effect, strategic bargaining over IR outcomes should take into account the other actor's own goals and strategies. Only then can one predict which forms of leverage may induce the other actor to take the actions one desires. But this is

---

[15]Kennedy, Paul, ed. *Grand Strategies in War and Peace.* New Haven: Yale University Press, 1991.

[16]Kissinger, Henry. *White House Years.* Boston: Little, Brown, 1979.

a problem—because often states do not know each others' true intentions but can only observe each others' actions and statements (which may be lies). For example, just days before Saddam Hussein's invasion of Kuwait, both U.S. leaders and those in Kuwait interpreted Saddam's actions as intended to threaten an attack but not actually carry one out.

One very effective strategy for influencing another actor whose plans are not known is reciprocity—a response in kind to the other's actions.[17] A strategy of reciprocity uses positive forms of leverage as promises of rewards (if the actor does what one wants); simultaneously it uses negative forms of leverage as threats of punishment (if the actor does not refrain from doing what one does not want). Reciprocity is effective because it is easy to understand. After one has demonstrated one's ability and willingness to reciprocate—gaining a reputation for consistency of response—the other actor can easily calculate the costs of failing to cooperate or the benefits of cooperating.

Reciprocity can be an effective strategy for achieving cooperation in a situation of conflicting interests. If one side expresses willingness to cooperate and promises to reciprocate the other's cooperative and conflictual actions, the other side has great incentive to work out a cooperative bargain. And because reciprocity is relatively easy to interpret, the vow of future reciprocity often need not be stated explicitly.[18] For example, in 1969, China's antiforeigner Cultural Revolution was in its fourth year and relations with the United States had been on ice for twenty years. A total U.S. economic embargo against China was holding back the latter's economic development. China's support of North Vietnam was costing many American lives. The two states were not on speaking terms. President Nixon (and advisor Kissinger) decided to try a signal to China in hopes of improving relations (splitting China away from North Vietnam and further away from the Soviet Union). He slightly relaxed the U.S. trade embargo against China. Three days later, with no explicit connection to the U.S. move, China released three U.S. citizens whose boat had earlier drifted into Chinese waters. Nixon and Kissinger concluded that "Peking [China] had understood."[19] China reciprocated other U.S. initiatives in the following months, and the two states resumed formal talks within six months. By 1972 Nixon visited China in a spirit of rapprochement.

Reciprocity can also help achieve cooperation in the sense of refraining from an undesired action. This is the intent of the strategy of deterrence—the threat to punish another actor if it takes a certain negative action (especially attacking one's own state or one's allies). The slogan "peace through strength" reflects this approach. If deterrence

---

[17]Keohane, Robert O. Reciprocity in International Relations. *International Organization* 40 (1), 1986: 1–27. Larson, Deborah Welch. The Psychology of Reciprocity in International Relations. *Negotiation Journal* 4, 1988: 281–301. Jervis, Robert. Security Regimes. In Stephen D. Krasner, ed. *International Regimes*. Ithaca: Cornell University Press, 1983. Downs, George W., and David M. Rocke. *Tacit Bargaining, Arms Races, and Arms Control*. Ann Arbor: University of Michigan Press, 1990. Rock, Stephen R. *Why Peace Breaks Out: Great Power Rapprochement in Historical Perspective*. Chapel Hill: University of North Carolina Press, 1989.

[18]Goldstein, Joshua S., and John R. Freeman. *Three-Way Street: Strategic Reciprocity in World Politics*. Chicago: University of Chicago Press, 1990. George, Alexander L., Philip J. Farley, and Alexander Dallin, eds. *U.S.-Soviet Security Cooperation: Achievements, Failures, Lessons*. New York: Oxford University Press, 1988.

[19]Kissinger, Henry. *White House Years*, pp. 179–80.

works, its effects are almost invisible; its success is measured in attacks that did not oc-cur.[20] Nuclear deterrence is the threat to use nuclear weapons if another state does so.

Generally, advocates of deterrence believe that conflicts are more likely to escalate into war when one party to the conflict is weak. In this view, building up military capabilities usually convinces the stronger party that a resort to military leverage would not succeed, so conflicts are less likely to escalate into violence. A strategy of **compellence,** sometimes used after deterrence fails, refers to the use of force to make another actor take some action (rather than refrain from taking an action).[21] Generally it is harder to get another state to change course (the purpose of compellence) than it is to get it to refrain from changing course (the purpose of deterrence).

One strategy used to try to compel compliance by another state is *escalation*—a series of negative sanctions of increasing severity applied in order to induce another actor to take some action. In theory the less severe actions establish credibility—showing the first actor's willingness to exert its power on the issue—and the pattern of escalation establishes the high costs of future sanctions if the second actor does not cooperate. This should induce the second actor to comply, assuming that it finds the potential costs of the escalating punishments to be greater than the costs of compliance.

U.S. actions against Saddam Hussein prior to the Gulf War illustrate the strategy of escalation. First came statements of condemnation, then UN resolutions, then the formation of an alliance with power clearly superior to Iraq's. Next came the application of economic sanctions, then a military buildup with an implicit threat to use force, then explicit threats of force, and finally ultimatums threatening force after a specific deadline. This strategy did not induce compliance, and in this case only military defeat induced Iraq to accept U.S. terms.

Escalation can be quite dangerous (especially when dealing with an adversary not as easily defeated as Iraq was). During the Cold War, many IR scholars worried that a conventional war could lead to nuclear war if the superpowers tried to apply escalation strategies. In fact, side by side with the potential for eliciting cooperation, reciprocity in general contains a danger of runaway hostility. When two sides both reciprocate but never manage to put relations on a cooperative footing, the result can be a drawn-out, nasty, tit-for-tat exchange of punishments. This characterizes Israeli relations with Islamic guerrillas in southern Lebanon, for instance.

An **arms race** is a reciprocal process in which two (or more) states build up military capabilities in response to each other. Since each wants to act prudently against a threat (often a bit overblown in the leaders' perceptions), the attempt to reciprocate leads to a runaway production of weapons by both sides. The mutual escalation of threat erodes confidence, reduces cooperation in the relationship, and makes it more

---

[20]Hopf, Ted. *Peripheral Visions: Deterrence Theory and American Foreign Policy in the Third World, 1965–1990.* Ann Arbor: University of Michigan Press, 1994. Huth, Paul K. *Extended Deterrence and the Prevention of War.* New Haven: Yale University Press, 1988. Zagare, Frank. *The Dynamics of Deterrence.* Chicago: University of Chicago Press, 1987. Jervis, Robert, Richard Ned Lebow, and Janice Gross Stein. *Psychology and Deterrence.* Baltimore: Johns Hopkins University Press, 1985. George, Alexander L., and Richard Smoke. *Deterrence in American Foreign Policy: Theory and Practice.* New York: Columbia University Press, 1974.

[21]Leng, Russell, and S. G. Walker. Comparing Two Studies of Crisis Bargaining: Confrontation, Coercion, and Reciprocity. *Journal of Conflict Resolution* 26, 1982: 571–91.

likely that a crisis (or accident) could cause one side to strike first and start a war rather than wait for the other side to strike. The arms race process was illustrated vividly in the U.S.-Soviet nuclear arms race, which created arsenals of tens of thousands of nuclear weapons on each side.[22]

Rationality

Consistent with the bargaining framework just outlined, most realists (and many nonrealists) assume that those who wield power behave as **rational actors** in their efforts to influence others.[23] This means first of all that the actor exercising power is a single entity that can "think" about its actions coherently and make choices. This is called the *unitary actor* assumption, or sometimes the strong leader assumption, and it is used to describe the nature of states as international actors. Although useful, this simplification does not capture the complexity of how states actually arrive at decisions (see Chapter 4).

Second, the assumption of rationality implies that states and other international actors can identify their interests and put priorities on various interests. Rationality implies that a state's actions seek to advance its interests. Again, the assumption is a simplification, because the interests of particular politicians, parties, economic sectors, or regions of a country often conflict. Yet realists assume that the exercise of power attempts to advance the **national interest**—the interests of the state itself. President Kennedy, for instance, said that "every nation determines its policies in terms of its own interests."[24]

But national interest can be hard to define. What are the interests of a state? Are they the interests of domestic groups (see Chapter 4)? The need to prevail in conflicts with other states (see Chapter 5)? Does the national interest demand cooperation with the international community for mutual benefit (see Chapter 7)? There is no simple answer. Some realists, including Morgenthau, simply define the national interest as maximizing power—a debatable assumption.

Third, rationality implies that actors are able to perform **cost-benefit analysis**—calculating the costs incurred by a possible action and the benefits it is likely to bring. Applying power incurs costs and should produce commensurate gains. As in the problem of estimating power, one has to add up different dimensions in such a calculation. For instance, states presumably do not initiate wars that they expect to lose, except in cases where they stand to gain political benefits, domestic or international, that outweigh the costs of losing the war. But it is not easy to tally intangible political benefits against the

[22]Isard, Walter, and Charles H. Anderton. Arms Race Models: A Survey and Synthesis. *Conflict Management and Peace Science* 8, 1985: 27–98. Allan, Pierre. *Crisis Bargaining and the Arms Race: A Theoretical Model*. Cambridge, MA: Ballinger, 1983. Plous, S. Perceptual Illusions and Military Realities: The Nuclear Arms Race. *The Journal of Conflict Resolution* 29 (3), 1985: 363–90. McGinnis, Michael D., and John T. Williams. Stability and Change in Superpower Rivalry. *American Political Science Review* 83, 1989: 1101–24.

[23]Nicholson, Michael. *Rationality and the Analysis of International Conflict*. New York: Cambridge University Press, 1992. Green, Donald P., and Ian Shapiro. *Pathologies of Rational Choice Theory: A Critique of Applications in Political Science*. New Haven: Yale University Press, 1994. Bueno de Mesquita, Bruce. *The War Trap*. New Haven: Yale University Press, 1981.

[24]Address at Mormon Tabernacle, Salt Lake City, UT, September 26, 1963.

The unitary actor assumption holds that states make important decisions as though they were single individuals able to act in the national interest. For example, Pakistan's decision to build nuclear weapons would reflect decisions of Pakistan's leadership as a unitary entity, rather than conflicting pressure of factions and organizations with differing interests. In truth, Pakistan's prime minister, Benazir Bhutto, here assuming power in 1988, struggled frequently with her country's military leadership about national policies.

tangible costs of a war. Even in a winning war, it is not easy to say whether the victory was worth the costs paid. Of course, even a rational actor can miscalculate costs or benefits, or calculate on the basis of faulty information. And, again, human behavior and fortune (luck) are unpredictable.

The ancient realist Sun Tzu insisted on cost-benefit calculations in wielding power: he prohibited the use of superstitious rituals of prediction in preparing for battle, instead ordering rational appraisals of power. The best general in his view was not the most courageous or aggressive one, but the one who could coolly calculate the costs and benefits of alternative courses. Because wars consume economic resources, Sun Tzu advised that wars must be short to be worthwhile. The best policy in his view was to take another state intact without fighting—by intimidation, deception, and the disruption of enemy alliances. Capturing an enemy army was better than fighting it. If fighting was necessary, it should occur on another state's territory so the army could live off the land to reduce costs. Attacking cities was too costly and reduced the benefits of war by destroying one of the main prizes.

In the 1980s Sun Tzu's book was added to the required reading list for officers in the U.S. Marines: the idea was to get the Marines to "fight smart" with an eye to costs and benefits, rather than use the traditional Marine attack strategy of "hey diddle diddle, right

What theories could account for the puzzle of different outcomes in the cases of Kuwait and Bosnia—one a success for world order and the other a failure (see box, p. 10)? Realism portrays states' actions—such as sending military forces to turn back aggression—as being based on national interests, narrowly defined. Military intervention to turn back aggression by a rogue regional power (Iraq or Serbia) is expensive—perhaps as much as $100 billion in the case of the Gulf War. The cost of the UN Protection Force (UNPROFOR) in Bosnia and Croatia was only about a billion dollars per year, and perhaps not surprisingly the force was ineffective if not counterproductive. A tougher "peace enforcement" operation for Bosnia was proposed, but for three years the great powers balked at the cost of $3 billion annually (and fear that the cost could go higher if it failed).

So by this logic something about the Kuwait case made it in the national interest to pay a high cost to reverse the aggression, something absent in the Bosnia case. One answer, clearly, is the threat to Persian Gulf oil exports, which are extremely important to the economies of Europe, Japan, and North America.

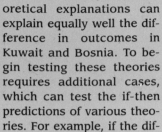

As we shall see in later boxes, other theoretical explanations can explain equally well the difference in outcomes in Kuwait and Bosnia. To begin testing these theories requires additional cases, which can test the if-then predictions of various theories. For example, if the different outcomes in Kuwait and Bosnia are explained by a cost-benefit calculation of national interest based on economic gain (such as access to cheap natural resources), then in other cases of aggression the response of great powers should be predictable from the economic stakes involved and the costs of effectively turning back the aggression. Can you make a list of other cases of aggression, the costs and economic benefits of response, and the effectiveness of the international response? Try to include cases of both effective and ineffective response, and cases of high and low economic stakes. How well does national interest explain the response?

up the middle." The rational cost-benefit approach to the exercise of power was evident in the subsequent war with Iraq and the low U.S. casualties it produced.

These three assumptions about rationality—that states are unitary actors, that they have coherent interests, and that they can make cost-benefit calculations—are simplifications that not all IR scholars accept. But realists consider these simplifications quite useful because they allow scholars to explain in a general way the actions of diverse actors. The rational-actor model is parallel to *microeconomics*, with its laws of supply and demand that govern the functioning of markets. Power in IR has been compared with money in economics, as a universal measure. In this view, just as firms compete for money in economic markets, states compete for power in the international system.[25]

In order to provide a general explanation of state actions, realism makes a fourth assumption, implicit in the parallel to economics. This is the assumption that all states (or their leaders) have basically the same values and interests—*intersubjective preferences*.

---

[25]Waltz, *Theory of International Politics*. (See footnote 6 in this chapter.)

(The outcomes valued by an actor are called preferences or *utility*.) Economists assume that everyone prefers more money to less. Realists assume that all states prefer more power to less.

This assumption has been criticized. If a state leader prefers upholding his or her honor by fighting a losing war rather than being dictated to, such an action is rational in terms of the leader's own preferences—even though a U.S. college student or European prime minister might find it inexplicable in terms of Western cultural norms. Similarly, the suicidal charges of Iranian teenagers against Iraqi positions in the Iran-Iraq war were rational for the teenagers, who believed that as martyrs they would go directly to heaven. But such preferences are hardly universal.

Despite these criticisms, realists argue that rational-actor models capture not all but the most important aspects of IR. These simplified models provide the foundations for a large body of IR research that represents international bargaining relationships mathematically. By accepting the limitations of the four assumptions of rationality, IR scholars can build very general and abstract models of international relationships.

Game Theory

Game theory is a branch of mathematics concerned with predicting bargaining outcomes. A game is a setting in which two or more players choose among alternative moves, either once or repeatedly. Each combination of moves (by all players) results in a set of payoffs (utility) to each player. The payoffs can be tangible items like money or any intangible items of value. Game theory aims to deduce likely outcomes (what moves players will make), given the players' preferences and the possible moves open to them. Games are sometimes called *formal models*.

Game theory was first used extensively in IR in the 1950s and 1960s by scholars trying to understand U.S.-Soviet nuclear war contingencies. Moves were decisions to use nuclear weapons in certain ways, and payoffs were outcomes of the war. The use of game theory to study international interactions has become more extensive among IR scholars in recent years, especially among realists, who accept the assumptions about rationality. To analyze a game mathematically, one assumes that each player chooses a move rationally, to maximize its payoff.

Different kinds of situations are represented by different classes of games, as defined by the number of players and the structure of the payoffs. One basic distinction is between **zero-sum games,** in which one player's gain is by definition equal to the other's loss, and *non-zero-sum games*, in which it is possible for both players to gain (or lose). In a zero-sum game there is no point in communication or cooperation between the players because their interests are diametrically opposed. But in a non-zero-sum game, coordination of moves can maximize the total payoff to the players, although each may still maneuver to gain a greater share of that total payoff.

A *two-person game* has only two players; because it is simple and easy to analyze mathematically, this is the most common type of game studied. An *N-person* game has more than two players, and the moves typically result in coalitions of players, with the winning coalition dividing the payoff among themselves in some manner. In most games, all the players make a move simultaneously. They may do so repeatedly, which is called a *repeated game* (or an *iterated game,* a *sequential game,* or a *supergame*). In a few games the players alternate moves so each knows the other's move before deciding on its own.

Analysis of a game entails searching for a *solution*—a set of moves by all the players such that no player can increase its payoff by changing its move. It is the outcome that rational players will arrive at. Some simple games have one solution, but many games have multiple solutions or no stable solution.

A category of games with a given structure—in terms of the relationships between moves and payoffs—is sometimes given a name that evokes a story or metaphor representing the nature of the game. Each such game yields an insight or lesson regarding a category of international bargaining situation.[26]

The game called *Prisoner's Dilemma (PD)* is the one most commonly studied. It is a situation in which rational players will choose moves that produce an outcome in which all players are worse off than under a different set of moves. They all could do better, but as individual rational actors they are unable to achieve this outcome. How can this be?

The original story tells of two prisoners questioned separately by a prosecutor. The prosecutor knows they committed a bank robbery but has only enough evidence to convict them of illegal possession of a gun unless one of them confesses. The prosecutor tells each prisoner that if he confesses and his partner doesn't confess, he will go free. If his partner confesses and he doesn't, he will get a long prison term for bank robbery (while the partner goes free). If both confess, they will get a somewhat reduced term. If neither confesses, they will be convicted on the gun charge and serve a short sentence. The story assumes that neither prisoner will have a chance to retaliate later, that only the immediate outcomes matter, and that each prisoner cares only about himself.

This game has a single solution: both prisoners will confess. Each will reason as follows: "If my partner is going to confess, then I should confess too, because I will get a slightly shorter sentence that way. If my partner is not going to confess, then I should still confess because I will go free that way instead of serving a short sentence." The other prisoner follows the same reasoning. The dilemma is that by following their individually rational choices both prisoners will end up serving a fairly long sentence when they could have both served a short one by cooperating (keeping their mouths shut).

In IR, the PD game has been used to gain insight into arms races. Consider the decision of India and Pakistan about whether to build nuclear weapons arsenals. Both have the ability, and it is hard to keep either from doing so secretly (unless they reach an arms control agreement with strict verification provisions). To analyze the game one must assign values to each possible outcome—often called a *preference ordering*—for each player. This is not simple: if one misjudges the value a player puts on a particular outcome, one may draw wrong conclusions from the game.

The following preferences regarding possible outcomes are plausible: the best outcome would be that oneself but not the other had a nuclear arsenal (the expense of build-

[26]O'Neill, Barry. A Survey of Game Theory Models on Peace and War. In R. Aumann and S. Hart, eds. *Handbook of Game Theory.* Volume 2. Amsterdam: North-Holland, 1994. Morrow, James D. *Game Theory for Political Scientists.* Princeton: Princeton University Press, 1995. Myerson, Roger B. *Game Theory: Analysis of Conflict.* Cambridge, MA: Harvard University Press, 1991. Brams, Steven J. *Superpower Games: Applying Game Theory to Superpower Conflict.* New Haven: Yale University Press, 1985.

TABLE 2.2 PAYOFF MATRIX IN INDIA-PAKISTAN PD GAME

		Pakistan	
		Cooperate	Defect
India	Cooperate	(3,3)	(1,4)
	Defect	(4,1)	(2,2)

Note: First number in each group is India's payoff, second is Pakistan's. The number 4 is highest payoff, 1 lowest.

ing nuclear weapons would be worth it because one could then use them as leverage); second best would be for neither to go nuclear (no leverage, but no expense); third best would be for both to develop nuclear arsenals (a major expense without gaining leverage); worst would be to forgo nuclear weapons oneself while the other developed them (and thus be subject to blackmail).

The game can be summarized in a *payoff matrix* (see Table 2.2). The first number in each cell is India's payoff, and the second number is Pakistan's. To keep things simple, we may use 4 to indicate the highest payoff, down to 1 for the lowest. As is conventional, a decision to refrain from building nuclear weapons will be called "cooperation," and a decision to proceed with nuclear weapons will be called "defection."

The dilemma here parallels that of the prisoners just discussed. Each state's leader reasons: "If they go nuclear, we must; if they don't, we'd be crazy not to." The model seems to predict an inevitable Indian-Pakistani nuclear arms race, even though both states would do better to avoid one.

But the model can be made more realistic by allowing the players to play the game repeatedly; as in most IR contexts, the same actors will bargain over this issue repeatedly over a sustained time period. Game theorists have shown that in a *repeated* PD game, the possibility of reciprocity can make it rational to cooperate. Now the state leader reasons: "If we defect now, they will respond by defecting and both of us will lose; if we cooperate they might cooperate too; and if we are suckered once we can defect in the future." The keys to cooperation are the non-zero-sum nature of the PD game and the ability of each player to respond in the future to present moves.[27]

PD is the most popular game among IR scholars, but many others have been analyzed. For example, *Chicken* takes its name from the story of two male teenagers driving stolen cars at high speed toward a head-on collision. The first to swerve is "chicken." Each reasons: "If he doesn't swerve, I must; but if he swerves, I won't." The player who first commits irrevocably to not swerve (throws the steering wheel out the window) will win. This game has been used to study international crises such as the 1962 Cuban Missile Crisis, where it seemed that President Kennedy "won" by seeming ready to risk nuclear war if Premier Khrushchev did not back down and remove Soviet missiles from Cuba. (Note: there are alternative explanations of the outcome.)

---

[27]Majeski, Stephen J. Arms Races as Iterated Prisoner's Dilemma Games. *Mathematical Social Sciences* 7, 1984: 253–66. Snidal, Duncan. Coordination vs. Prisoner's Dilemma: Implications for International Cooperation and Regimes. *American Political Science Review* 79, 1985: 923–42.

Through analysis of these and other games, IR researchers try to predict what rational actors would do in various situations that may resemble those occurring in world or regional politics. Games can capture and simplify the fundamental dynamics of various bargaining situations. However, a game-theoretic analysis is only as good as the assumptions that go into it. In particular, the results of the analysis depend on the preferences that players are assumed to have about outcomes. And it is difficult to test empirically either the assumptions or the predictions of a formal model against the realities of IR, which are so much more complex in practice.

❖ THE INTERNATIONAL SYSTEM

States interact within a set of well-defined and long-established "rules of the game" governing what is considered a state and how states treat each other. Together these rules shape the international system as we know it.[28]

Anarchy and Sovereignty

Realists emphasize that the rules of the international system create **anarchy**—a term that implies not complete chaos or absence of structure and rules, but rather the lack of a central government that can enforce rules.[29] In domestic society within states, governments can enforce contracts, deter participants from breaking rules, and use their monopoly on legally sanctioned violence to enforce a system of law. This is true in both democracies and dictatorships: both provide central government enforcement of a system of rules. The lack of such a government among states is what realists mean by anarchy. There is no central authority to enforce rules and ensure compliance with norms of conduct. The power of one state can be countered only by the power of other states. States must rely on *self-help*, which they supplement with alliances and the (sometimes) constraining power of international norms.

Some people think that only a world government can solve this problem. Others think that adequate order can be provided by international organizations and agreements, short of world government (see Chapter 7). But most realists think that IR cannot escape from a state of anarchy and will continue to be dangerous as a result. In this anarchic world, realists emphasize *prudence* as a great virtue in foreign policy. States should pay attention not to the *intentions* of other states but rather to their *capabilities*. Sun Tzu made this point two thousand years ago in advising heads of state not to assume that other states would not attack but rather to be ready to meet them if they did.

Despite its anarchy, the international system is far from chaotic. The great majority of state interactions closely adhere to **norms** of behavior—shared expectations about

---

[28]Luard, Evan. *Conflict and Peace in the Modern International System: A Study of the Principles of International Order.* London: Macmillan, 1988. Wight, Martin. *Systems of States.* Leicester, U.K.: Leicester University Press, 1977. Kaplan, Morton A. *System and Process in International Politics.* New York: Wiley, 1957.

[29]Bull, Hedley. *The Anarchical Society: A Study of Order in World Politics.* New York: Columbia University Press, 1977. Taylor, Michael. *Anarchy and Cooperation.* New York: Wiley, 1976.

what behavior is considered proper.[30] Norms change over time, slowly, but the most basic norms of the international system have changed little in recent centuries.

Sovereignty—traditionally the most important norm—means that a government has the right, at least in principle, to do whatever it wants in its own territory. States are separate, are autonomous, and answer to no higher authority (due to anarchy). In principle, all states are equal in status if not in power. Sovereignty also means that states are not supposed to *interfere in the internal affairs* of other states. Although states do try to influence each other (exert power) on matters of trade, alliances, war, and so on, they are not supposed to meddle in the internal politics and decision processes of other states. For example, it would be considered inappropriate for Russia or Britain to endorse a candidate for U.S. president.[31]

The principles of state sovereignty are exemplified in the 1972 Shanghai Communiqué, signed during President Nixon's visit to China. The United States recognized the reality that the Communist government (not the government on Taiwan) controlled mainland China. Both sides agreed to uphold respect for the sovereignty and territorial integrity of all states, nonaggression against other states, and noninterference in the internal affairs of other states. In recent years, China has vigorously protested U.S. efforts to improve China's human rights record as "meddling in China's internal affairs."

In practice, states have a harder and harder time warding off interference in their affairs. Such "internal" matters as human rights or self-determination are, increasingly, concerns for the international community. For example, in the Helsinki agreements that codified East-West détente in the Cold War, the Soviet Union and Eastern Europe promised to respect human rights within their own borders (an internal affair). Also, the integration of global economic markets and telecommunications makes it easier than ever for ideas to penetrate state borders.

States are based on territory. Respect for the *territorial integrity* of all states, within recognized *borders*, is a very important principle of IR. Many of today's borders are the result of past wars (in which winners took territory from losers), or were imposed arbitrarily by third parties such as colonizers. These borders therefore create many problems—the splitting of nations or ethnic groups into different states, the creation of oddly shaped states that may lack resources or access to ports, and so forth (see pp. 185–191). Despite these imperfections, the international system places the highest value on respect for internationally recognized borders. Almost all of the world's land territory falls under the sovereign control of existing states; very little is considered "up for grabs" (high seas are outside any state's territory; see Chapter 11).

Membership in the international system rests on general *recognition* (by other states) of a government's sovereignty within its territory. This recognition is extended formally through diplomatic relations and by membership in the UN. It does not imply that a gov-

---

[30]Jones, Dorothy. *Code of Peace: Ethics and Security in the World of the Warlord States*. Chicago: University of Chicago Press, 1991. Franck, Thomas M. *The Power of Legitimacy Among Nations*. New York: Oxford University Press, 1990. Goertz, Gary, and Paul F. Diehl. Toward a Theory of International Norms: Some Conceptual and Measurement Issues. *Journal of Conflict Resolution* 36 (4), 1992: 634–64.

[31]Heiberg, Marianne, ed. *Subduing Sovereignty: Sovereignty and the Right to Intervene*. New York: St. Martin's Press, 1994.

ernment has popular support but only that it controls the state's territory and agrees to assume its obligations in the international system—to accept internationally recognized borders, to assume the international debts of the previous government, and to refrain from interfering in other states' internal affairs.

States have developed norms of *diplomacy* to facilitate their interactions. An *embassy* is considered to be territory of the home state, not the country where it is located (see pp. 296–298). The U.S. embassy in China, for instance, harbored a wanted Chinese dissident for two years after the Tiananmen Square crackdown of 1989, and Chinese troops did not simply come in and take him away. To do so would have been a violation of U.S. territorial integrity.

Realists acknowledge that the rules of IR often create a **security dilemma**—a situation in which states' actions taken to assure their own security (such as deploying more military forces) tend to threaten the security of other states.[32] The responses of those other states (such as deploying more of their own military forces) in turn threaten the first state. The dilemma parallels the Prisoner's Dilemma game discussed earlier; it is a prime cause of arms races in which states waste large sums of money on mutually threatening weapons that do not ultimately provide security. The security dilemma is a negative consequence of anarchy in the international system. Realists tend to see the dilemma as unsolvable, while liberals think it can be solved through the development of norms and institutions (see Chapters 3 and 7).

As we shall see in future chapters, changes in technology and in norms are undermining the traditional principles of territorial integrity and state autonomy in IR. Some IR scholars find states to be practically obsolete as the main actors in world politics, as some integrate into larger entities and others fragment into smaller units.[33] Other scholars find the international system quite enduring in its structure and state units.[34] One of its most enduring features is the balance of power.

Balance of Power

In the anarchy of the international system, the most reliable brake on the power of one state is the power of other states. The term **balance of power** refers to the general concept of one or more states' power being used to balance that of another state or group of states. The term is used in several ways and is imprecisely defined. Balance of power can refer to any ratio of power capabilities between states or alliances; or it can mean only a relatively equal ratio. Alternatively, balance of power can refer to the process by which counterbalancing coalitions have repeatedly formed in history to prevent one state from conquering an entire region.[35]

---

[32]Jervis, Robert. Cooperation Under the Security Dilemma. *World Politics* 30 (2), 1978: 167–214.

[33]Haas, Ernst B. *Beyond the Nation-State: Functionalism and International Organization.* Stanford: Stanford University Press, 1964.

[34]Gilpin, Robert. *War and Change in World Politics.* New York: Cambridge University Press, 1981.

[35]Gulick, Edward V. *Europe's Classical Balance of Power.* Ithaca, NY: Cornell University Press, 1955. Niou, Emerson M. S., Peter C. Ordeshook, and Gregory F. Rose. *The Balance of Power: Stability and Instability in International Systems.* New York: Cambridge University Press, 1989. Cusack, Thomas R., and Richard J. Stoll. *Exploring Realpolitik: Probing International Relations Theory with Computer Simulation.* Boulder, CO: Lynne Rienner, 1990.

Realists emphasize relative power as an explanation of war and peace. The modernization of China's military—symbolized here by new missiles on old trucks in a 1984 military parade in Beijing—is increasing China's power. Some observers fear instability in Asia if the overall balance of power among states in the region shifts rapidly.

The *theory of balance of power* basically argues that such counterbalancing occurs regularly and maintains the stability of the international system. The system itself is stable in that its rules and principles stay the same: state sovereignty does not collapse into a universal empire. This stability does not, however, imply peace; it is rather a stability maintained by means of recurring wars that adjust power relations.

Alliances (to be discussed shortly) play a key role in the balance of power. Building up one's own capabilities against a rival is a form of power balancing, but forming an alliance against a threatening state is often quicker, cheaper, and more effective. When such a counterbalancing coalition has a geopolitical element—physically hemming in the threatening state—the power-balancing strategy is called *containment*. In the Cold War, the United States encircled the Soviet Union with military and political alliances to prevent Soviet territorial expansion.[36]

Sometimes a particular state deliberately becomes a *balancer* (in its region or the world), shifting its support to oppose whatever state or alliance is strongest at the moment. Britain played this role on the European continent for centuries, and China played it in the Cold War. But states do not always balance against the strongest actor. Sometimes smaller states "jump on the bandwagon" of the most powerful state; this has been called *bandwagoning* as opposed to balancing. For instance, after World War II a broad

---

[36]Kennan, George F. Containment Then and Now. *Foreign Affairs* 65 (4), 1987: 885–90.

coalition did not form to contain U.S. power; rather most major states joined the U.S. bloc. States may seek to balance *threats* rather than raw power; U.S. power was greater than Soviet power but was less threatening to Europe and Japan (and later to China as well).[37] Furthermore, small states create variations on power-balancing themes when they play off rival great powers against each other. For instance, Cuba during the Cold War received massive Soviet subsidies by putting itself in the middle of U.S.-Soviet rivalry.

Great Powers and Middle Powers

Power, of course, varies greatly from one state to another. The *most powerful* states in the system exert most of the influence on international events and therefore get the most attention from IR scholars. By almost any measure of power, a handful of states possess the majority of the world's power resources. At most a few dozen states have any real influence beyond their immediate locality. These are called the great powers and middle powers in the international system.

Although there is no firm dividing line, **great powers** are generally considered the half dozen or so most powerful states. Until the past century the great power club was exclusively European. Sometimes great powers' status is formally recognized in an international structure such as the nineteenth-century Concert of Europe or the UN Security Council. In general, great powers may also be distinguished by the criterion that they can be defeated militarily only by another great power. Great powers also tend to share a global outlook based on national interests far from their home territories.[38]

The great powers generally have the world's strongest military forces and the strongest economies to pay for military forces and for other power capabilities. These large economies in turn rest on some combination of large populations, plentiful natural resources, advanced technology, and educated labor forces. Because power is based on these underlying resources, membership in the great-power system changes only slowly. Only rarely does a great power—even one defeated in a massive war—lose its status as a great power, because its size and long-term economic potential change slowly. This helps explain why Germany and Japan, decimated in World War II, are today so powerful and why Russia, after gaining and then losing the rest of the Soviet Union, is still considered a great power.

What states are great powers today? Although definitions vary, seven states appear to meet the criteria. Certainly the *United States* is one. In total GDP, a measure of potential power, the United States ranks highest by far at almost $7 trillion per year. *Japan* ranks next with less than $3 trillion. Along with *Germany* (under $2 trillion GDP), Japan is an economic great power, but both countries' military roles in international security affairs have been curtailed since World War II. Nonetheless, both Japan and Germany have very large and capable military forces, and both have been edging toward using military forces beyond their own territories or regions.

[37]Walt, Stephen M. *The Origins of Alliances*. Ithaca: Cornell University Press, 1987.

[38]Rasler, Karen A., and William R. Thompson. *The Great Powers and Global Struggle, 1490–1990*. Lexington: University Press of Kentucky, 1994. Levy, Jack S. *War in the Modern Great Power System, 1495–1975*. Lexington: University Press of Kentucky, 1983.

China, with a total GDP of over $2 trillion, is the world's third largest economy; however, China's GDP is especially hard to estimate, and another method would put it well under $1 trillion. In any case, China's sheer size (over 1 billion people) and its rapid economic growth (around 10 percent annually in the early 1990s), make it a powerful state. China has a large military but not a very modern one, and its orientation appears to be regional more often than global. But with a credible nuclear arsenal and a seat on the UN Security Council, China qualifies as a great power.

Russia, even after the breakup of the Soviet Union, has a GDP of nearly $2 trillion, fourth largest in the world (but again a hard one to estimate), and very large military forces including a massive nuclear arsenal. *France* and *Britain* finish out the list at just over $1 trillion GDP each. With Russia, they were winners in World War II and have been active military powers since then. Although much reduced in stature from their colonial heyday, they still qualify as great powers by most standards.

The great powers thus include the five permanent members of the UN Security Council—the United States, the Soviet Union (now Russia), France, Britain, and China. The same five states are also the members of the "club" possessing large nuclear weapons arsenals (there are also a few recent small-scale nuclear states). In world political and economic affairs, Germany and Japan are also great powers (they would like Security Council seats too; see p. 279).

These seven great powers account for about half of the world's total GDP—and hence, presumably, about half of the total power in the world. This concentration of power is even stronger in practice because the remaining half of the world's power is split up among 183 other states (see Figure 2.1).

The slow change in great-power status is evident. Britain and France have been great powers for 500 years, Russia and Germany for over 250 years, the United States and Japan

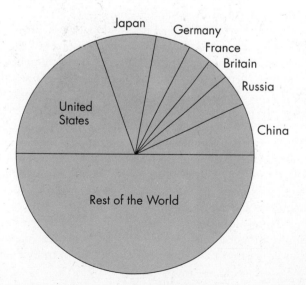

FIGURE 2.1 Great-Power Shares of World GDP

for about 100 years, and China for 50 years. Only six other states were ever (but no longer are) considered great powers: Italy, Austria (Austria-Hungary), Spain, Turkey (the Ottoman Empire), Sweden, and the Netherlands.

Middle powers rank somewhat below the great powers in terms of their influence on world affairs. Some are large but not highly industrialized; others have specialized capabilities but are small. Some aspire to regional dominance, and many have considerable influence in their regions. Even more than with great powers, it is hard to establish a bottom criterion for distinguishing middle powers.

The top rungs of middle powers are easier to identify. *Brazil* ($800 billion), and *India* ($1.5 trillion) are both regional giants that some scholars see as rising powers and possible new great powers in the coming century. In terms of total GDP, *Italy* and *Canada* are just below the range of France and Britain. Both states belong to the Group of Seven (G7) economic powers (along with the United States, Germany, Japan, France, and Britain). Some would consider them great powers. *Mexico* ($700 billion) is emerging as an important middle power. Below this level, GDP estimates become more closely bunched and the order of national economies becomes much harder to sort out.

A list of middle powers (not everyone would agree on it) might include the following states. The first tier would include large states with substantial economic activity, fairly strong military forces, and considerable regional political influence: Canada, Italy, India, Brazil, Mexico, South Korea, Iran, and Turkey. A second tier could include important regional actors with somewhat smaller economies or with strong capabilities on specific dimensions of power: Taiwan, Indonesia, Australia, Spain, Ukraine, Argentina, Israel, Saudi Arabia, Egypt, Pakistan, South Africa, and Kazakhstan. A third tier might include smaller rich states along with middle-sized, middle-income ones and regional "activists" that exercise power beyond their size: the Netherlands, Belgium, Sweden, Greece, Poland, Nigeria, Venezuela, Vietnam, Syria, Iraq, Serbia, and North Korea.

Middle powers have not received as much attention in IR as have great powers. These states do, however, often come into play in the specific regional conflicts that dominate the day-to-day flow of international news. Smaller, weaker states (not even of middle-power strength) also are often at the center of specific conflicts and crises. But their own actions have only minor influence on world politics; the actions of great powers and middle powers in those conflicts and crises have more impact.

Power Distribution

With each state's power balanced by other states, the most important characteristic of an international system in the view of many realists is the *distribution* of power among states in an international system. Power distribution as a concept can apply to all the states in the world or to just one region, but most often it refers to the great power-system (with most of the world's total power capabilities).

Neorealists (so called because they have adopted and refined realism) try to explain international events in terms of the *system structure*—the international distribution of power—rather than the internal makeup of individual states.[39] *Neorealism* is thus also

---

[39]Waltz, *Theory of International Politics*. (See footnote 6 in this chapter.)

called *structural realism*. Neorealists often use game theory and related models in such analyses.[40] Compared to traditional realism, neorealism is more scientific in the sense of proposing general laws to explain events, but neorealism has lost some of the richness of traditional realists who weighed in many complex elements (geography, willpower, diplomacy, etc.).

Sometimes an international power distribution (world or regional) is described in terms of *polarity* (a term adopted from physics), which refers to the number of independent power centers in the system. This concept encompasses both the underlying power of various participants and their alliance groupings.[41]

In a **multipolar** system there are typically five or six centers of power, which are not grouped into alliances. Each state participates independently and on relatively equal terms with the others. They may form a *coalition of the whole* for mutual security through coordination of efforts. Some IR researchers think that multipolarity provides a context for smooth interaction, rather like a market with efficient competition. There are always enough actors present to prevent one from predominating. But to other IR scholars a multipolar system is particularly dangerous, lacking the discipline that predominant states or alliance blocs impose. In a sense, both are correct: in the classical multipolar balance of power, the great-power system itself was stable but wars were frequently used as power-adjusting mechanisms.

At the other extreme, a *unipolar* system has a single center of power around which all others revolve. This is called hegemony, and will be discussed shortly. The predominance of a single state tends to reduce the incidence of war; the hegemonic state performs some of the functions of a government, somewhat reducing anarchy in the international system.

A *bipolar* system has two predominant states or two great rival alliance blocs. This was the structure of world politics during the Cold War. *Tight bipolar* systems, such as the East-West standoff in the 1950s, may be distinguished from looser ones such as developed when China and (to a lesser extent) France split off from their alliance blocs. IR scholars do not agree about whether bipolar systems are relatively peaceful or warlike. The U.S.-Soviet standoff seemed to provide stability and peace to great-power relations (although an icy one). But rival blocs in Europe before World War I did not prove stable or peaceful.

In a *tripolar* system there are three great centers of power. Such a configuration is fairly rare; there is a tendency for a two-against-one alliance to form (creating bipolarity). Aspects of tripolarity can be found in the "strategic triangle" of the United States, the Soviet Union, and China around the 1960s and 1970s.[42] Some scholars imagine that the

[40]Keohane, Robert O., ed. *Neorealism and Its Critics*. New York: Columbia University Press, 1986. Nye, Joseph S., Jr. Neorealism and Neoliberalism [review article]. *World Politics* 40 (2), 1988: 235–51. Buzan, Barry, Charles Jones, and Richard Little. *The Logic of Anarchy: Rethinking Neorealism*. New York: Columbia University Press, 1993. Wayman, Frank W., and Paul F. Diehl, eds. *Reconstructing Realpolitik*. Ann Arbor: University of Michigan Press, 1994. Buzan, Barry, Charles Jones, and Richard Little. *The Logic of Anarchy: Neorealism to Structural Realism*. New York: Columbia University Press, 1993.

[41]Sabrosky, Alan Ned, ed. *Polarity and War: The Changing Structure of International Conflict*. Boulder, CO: Westview, 1985.

[42]Segal, Gerald. *The Great Power Triangle*. New York: St. Martin's Press, 1982.

coming decades could see a tripolar world emerge, with rival power centers in North America, Europe, and East Asia.

These various polarities can be conceptually combined in the idea of a *pyramid* or *hierarchy* of power in an international system. At the top is the most powerful state, with the other great powers and middle powers arrayed below. Such a pyramid is similar to the dominance (or status) hierarchies that many animal species use to regulate access to valuable resources such as food (we often call this a "pecking order"). A multipolar system, then, is one with a relatively flat pyramid—relative equality of status among actors. A unipolar system has a relatively steep pyramid with unequal status. The steepness of the pyramid represents the concentration of power in the international system.

Some IR scholars have argued that peace is best preserved by a relatively equal power distribution (multipolarity) because then no country has an opportunity to win easily. The empirical evidence for this theory, however, is not strong. The opposite proposition has more support: peace is best preserved by hegemony, and next best by bipolarity.

Such is the thrust of *power transition* theory.[43] This theory holds that the largest wars result from challenges to the top position in the status hierarchy, when a rising power is surpassing (or threatening to surpass) the most powerful state. At such times power is relatively equally distributed, and these are the most dangerous times for major wars. *Status quo powers* who are doing well under the old rules will try to maintain them, while *challengers* who feel locked out by the old rules may try to change them.[44] *Status disequilibrium* refers to a difference between a rising power's status (formal position in the hierarchy) and its actual power. In such a situation the rising power may suffer from *relative deprivation*—the feeling that it is not doing as well as others or as well as it deserves, even though its position may be improving in absolute terms. The classic example is Germany's rise in the nineteenth century, which gave it great-power capabilities even though it was left out of colonial territories and other signs of status.

If the challenger does not start a war to displace the top power, the latter may provoke a war to stop the rise of the challenger before it becomes too great a threat (this is called *preventive war*).[45] In the case of Germany, an intensive arms race with Britain (the top power) led to increasing hostility and ultimately the outbreak of World War I. After World War I there was again a disparity between Germany's actual power (still considerable) and its harsh treatment under the terms of the Versailles treaty. This disparity may have contributed to World War II.

According to power transition theory, then, peace among great powers results from having one state firmly in the top position, and the positions of others in the status hierarchy clearly defined and corresponding with their actual underlying power. Such a situation usually results only from a great war, when one state predominates in power because

---

[43]Organski, A. F. K. *World Politics*. New York: Knopf, 1958. Organski, A. F. K., and Jacek Kugler. *The War Ledger*. Chicago: University of Chicago Press, 1980.

[44]Mansfield, Edward D. The Concentration of Capabilities and the Onset of War. *Journal of Conflict Resolution* 36 (1), 1992: 3–24. Thompson, William R., and Karen Rasler. War and Systemic Capability Reconcentration. *Journal of Conflict Resolution* 32 (2), 1988: 335–66. Doran, Charles F. *Systems in Crisis: New Imperatives of High Politics at Century's End*. New York: Cambridge University Press, 1991.

[45]Levy, Jack S. Declining Power and the Preventive Motivation for War. *World Politics* 40 (1), 1987: 82–107.

its rivals and allies alike have been drained. Even then, over time the different rates of growth among great powers lead to a slow equalization of power and eventually the emergence of challengers: the system becomes more multipolar. For example, the U.S. predominance right after World War II gave way to the bipolar Cold War and perhaps now to a multipolar power structure (with the rising power of Europe, Japan, and China). But the end of the Cold War also brought a return toward unipolarity—with the U.S. as the only superpower—so the outcome is complex.

Hegemony

Hegemony is the holding by one state of a preponderance of power in the international system, so that it can single-handedly dominate the rules and arrangements by which international political and economic relations are conducted.[46] Such a state is called a *hegemon*. (Usually hegemony means domination of the world, but sometimes it refers to regional domination.) Sometimes the term is used (as it was by the Italian Marxist theorist Antonio Gramsci earlier this century) to refer to the complex of ideas that rulers use to gain consent for their legitimacy and keep subjects in line.[47] By extension, such a meaning in IR refers to the hegemony of ideas such as democracy and capitalism, and to the global predominance of U.S. culture (see pp. 418–419).

Most studies of hegemony point to two examples: Britain in the nineteenth century, and the United States after World War II. Britain's predominance followed the defeat of its archrival France in the Napoleonic Wars. Both world trade and naval capabilities were firmly in British hands, as "Britannia ruled the waves." U.S. predominance followed the defeat of Germany and Japan (and the exhaustion of the Soviet Union, France, Britain, and China in the effort). In the late 1940s the U.S. GDP was over half the world's total; U.S. vessels carried the majority of the world's shipping; the U.S. military could single-handedly defeat any other state or combination of states; and only the United States had nuclear weapons. U.S. industry led the world in technology and productivity, and U.S. citizens enjoyed the world's highest standard of living.

As the extreme power disparities resulting from major wars slowly diminish (states rebuild over years and decades), *hegemonic decline* may occur, particularly when hegemons have overextended themselves with costly military commitments. IR scholars do not agree about how far or fast U.S. hegemonic decline has proceeded, if at all, and whether international instability will result from such a decline.[48] And beyond the U.S. and

---

[46]Rupert, Mark. *Producing Hegemony: The Politics of Mass Production and American Global Power.* New York: Cambridge University Press, 1995. Brilmayer, Lea. *American Hegemony: Political Morality in a One-Superpower World.* New Haven: Yale University Press, 1994. Rapkin, David P., ed. *World Leadership and Hegemony.* Boulder, CO: Lynne Rienner, 1990.

[47]Gramsci, Antonio. *The Modern Prince and Other Writings.* New York: International Publishers, 1959.

[48]Kennedy, Paul. *The Rise and Fall of the Great Powers: Economic Change and Military Conflict from 1500–2000.* New York: Random House, 1987. Mead, W. R. *Mortal Splendor: The American Empire in Transition.* Boston: Houghton Mifflin, 1987. Russett, Bruce. The Mysterious Case of Vanishing Hegemony. *International Organization* 39 (2), 1985: 207–31.

In the 1990s the United States is the most powerful single actor in world politics, but whether it can (or is willing to) resume a hegemonic role as after World War II is questionable. President Clinton, said to be uninterested in foreign policy, reduced the U.S. leadership profile in the international system from what it was in the time of President Bush. Here Clinton attends a European summit meeting, December 1994.

British cases, IR scholars do not agree on what historical cases were instances of hegemony. Some see the Netherlands in the early seventeenth century, or Spain in the sixteenth, as cases of hegemony.

The theory of *hegemonic stability* (see pp. 103–104) holds that hegemony provides some order in the international system, reducing anarchy, and provides some functions similar to a central government—deterring aggression, promoting free trade, and providing a hard currency that can be used as a world standard. Hegemons can help to resolve or at least keep in check conflicts among middle powers or small states.

From the perspective of less powerful states, of course, such hegemony may seem an infringement of state sovereignty, and the order it creates may seem unjust or illegitimate. For instance, China chafed under U.S.-imposed economic sanctions for twenty years after 1949, feeling itself encircled by U.S. military bases and hostile alliances led by the United States. To this day, Chinese leaders use the term hegemony as an insult, and the theory of hegemonic stability does not impress them.

❖ ALLIANCES

An *alliance* is a coalition of states that coordinate their actions to accomplish some end. But not every such coalition can properly be considered an alliance. Alliances are such coalitions that are *formalized* in written treaties, that concern issues of international security, and that *endure* across a range of issues and a period of time (not just for one issue at one time). If actors' purposes in banding together were shorter-term, less formal, or more issue-specific, the association might be called a *coalition* rather than an alliance. But all these terms are somewhat ambiguous. Two countries may have a formal alliance and yet be bitter enemies, such as the Soviet Union and China in the 1960s or NATO members Greece and Turkey today. Or two countries may create the practical equivalent of an alliance without a formal treaty, as did the United States and Israel in the 1970s.

Purposes of Alliances

Alliances generally have the purpose of augmenting their members' power relative to other states. By pooling their power capabilities, two or more states can exert greater leverage in their bargaining with other states. For smaller states, alliances can be their most important power element, and for great powers the structure of alliances shapes the configuration of power in the system. Sun Tzu, in the "warring states" period marked by ever changing alliances, saw that disrupting the alliances of enemy states was the most cost-effective way to win a power struggle. Of all the elements of power, none can change as quickly and decisively as alliances.

Most alliances form in response to a perceived threat. When a state's power grows and threatens to overmatch that of its rivals, the latter often form an alliance to limit that power. Thucydides attributed the outbreak of the Peleponnesian Wars over 2000 years ago to the growing power of Athens, and to the fear this caused in Sparta. Sparta turned to its neighbors in the Peleponnesian League, and this alliance managed to defeat Athens.

The importance of alliances in a state's overall power is illustrated by Saddam Hussein's situation when his 1979 invasion of Iran went sour. As we have seen, Iran's economy was somewhat larger than Iraq's and both armies were well equipped. So there was a real chance that Iran's counterattack would topple Saddam's government. What capabilities could he draw on to stop Iranian power from rolling over him? Only the capabilities of other states, added to his own, could counterbalance Iran's power. Saddam convinced other Arab states—especially his rich neighbors Saudi Arabia and Kuwait—to support his cause. Their money bought Iraq the foreign weapons to stop Iran's army and the consumer goods to keep Iraqis satisfied while doing so.

Iraq's neighbors decided to help not out of sympathy for their Iraqi brothers but because they thought it was in their own interest to do so. They feared the new radical Islamic government in Iran, which could stir up fundamentalist movements throughout the region that might threaten their own domestic rule. The nearby states such as Kuwait also feared a potential direct attack from Iran itself. The Gulf states had small armies themselves, and the only large army between themselves and Iran was that of Iraq. As in any bargain, the formation of an alliance created benefits through an exchange of value (Iraq had lots of soldiers but lacked money; Kuwait and Saudi Arabia had lots of money but lacked soldiers).

Alliances are an important component of the balance of power. Except in the rare circumstance of hegemony, every state is weaker than some combination of other states. If states overstep norms of international conduct they may face a powerful alliance of opposing states. This happened to Iraq when it invaded Kuwait in 1990, as it had to Hitler's Germany in the 1940s and to Napoleon's France in the 1800s.

Realists emphasize the *fluidity of alliances*. Because of the autonomy of states, alliances can be made or broken fairly easily. Alliances are not marriages of love; they are marriages of convenience. Alliances are based on national interests, and can shift as national interests change. This fluidity helps the balance-of-power process to operate effectively.

As critics of realism point out, it is not simple or costless to break an alliance: one's reputation may suffer and future alliances may be harder to enter into. There is an important norm that says that written treaties should be honored—in Latin, *pacta sunt servanda*. So states often do adhere to alliance terms even when it is not in their short-term interest to do so.

Alliances, such as that between Kuwait and the United States, generally result from a convergence of practical interests, not sentimental or ideological reasons. U.S. general Norman Schwarzkopf meets with the emir of Kuwait, April 1991.

Nonetheless, because of the nature of international anarchy, there is no mechanism to enforce contracts in IR, so the possibility of turning against a friend is always present. Realists would agree with the statement of French president Charles de Gaulle (under whom France withdrew militarily from NATO and developed its own nuclear weapons in the 1960s): "France has no permanent friends, only permanent interests." He also said, "Treaties are like roses and young girls. They last while they last."[49] One hears echoes of Napoleon, 150 years earlier: "Treaties are observed as long as they are in harmony with interests."[50]

Examples are many. Anticommunist president Nixon could cooperate with communist Mao Zedong because it was in both nations' interests to do so. Stalin could sign a nonaggression pact with a fascist, Hitler, and then cooperate with the capitalist West against Hitler. Every time history brings another such reversal in international alignments, many people are surprised or even shocked. Realists are not so surprised.

The fluidity of alliances deepens the security dilemma in a world of multiple actors. Recall that the dilemma is that one state's efforts to ensure its own security (building up military capabilities) reduce the security of another state. With only two states, it is possible to match their capabilities so that both have adequate defense but cannot attack. But if one adds a third state, free to ally with either side, then each state has to build adequate defenses against the potential alliance of its enemy with the third state. The threat is greater and the security dilemma is harder to escape.

The nightmare of being overpowered looms large when a state faces a potential hostile alliance that could form overnight. For example, in a war Israel could defeat any of its neighbors alone. But to Israel it is only prudent to arm against the worst contingency. Israelis do not feel secure unless they could defeat all their neighbors together. Because the neighbors are not very together (and the most important, Egypt and Jordan, are at peace with Israel), Israel's military capabilities appear excessive to them.

Alliance cohesion is the ease with which the members hold together an alliance.[51] Cohesion tends to be high when national interests converge and when cooperation within the alliance becomes institutionalized and habitual. When states with divergent interests form an alliance against a common enemy—"the enemy of my enemy is my friend"—the alliance may come apart if the threat subsides. This happened, for instance, with the World War II U.S.-Soviet alliance. Even when alliance cohesion is high, as in NATO during the Cold War, conflicts may arise over who bears the costs of the alliance (**burden sharing**).[52]

The *credibility* with which an alliance can deter an enemy depends on the alliance's cohesion as well as its total power capabilities. If an alliance is successful at displaying a

---

[49]*Time* magazine, July 12, 1963.

[50]Napoleon. *Maxims, 1804–1815*. See Tripp, Rhoda Thomas. *The International Thesaurus of Quotations*. New York: Thomas Y. Crowell, 1970.

[51]Kegley, Charles W., and Gregory A. Raymond. *When Trust Breaks Down: Alliance Norms and World Politics*. Columbia: University of South Carolina Press, 1990.

[52]Oneal, John R. The Theory of Collective Action and Burden Sharing in NATO. *International Organization* 44 (3), 1990: 379–402. Palmer, Glenn. Corralling the Free Rider: Deterrence and the Western Alliance. *International Studies Quarterly* 34 (2), 1990: 147–64.

common front and taking a unified line on issues, a potential enemy is more likely to believe that members will honor their *alliance commitments* (such as their promise to fight if an ally is attacked). An enemy may try to split the alliance (as Sun Tzu recommended) by finding issues on which the interests of the members diverge. For instance, the United States subtly encouraged the Sino-Soviet split, and the Soviet Union subtly tried to wedge European states in NATO away from the United States.

Great powers often form alliances with smaller states, sometimes called *client states*.[53] In the Cold War, each superpower extended a security umbrella over its allies. Germany did the same with Austria-Hungary and Italy earlier in the century. The issue of credibility in such an alliance is whether (and under what circumstances) the great power will assist its clients in a war. *Extended deterrence* refers to a strong state's use of threats to deter attacks on weaker clients—such as the U.S. threat to attack the Soviet Union if it invaded Western Europe.

Great powers face a real danger of being dragged into wars with each other over relatively unimportant regional issues if their respective clients go to war. If the great powers do not come to their clients' protection, they may lose credibility with other clients, but if they do, they may end up fighting a costly war.[54] This happened to Germany when Austria-Hungary helped drag it into World War I. The Soviet Union worried that its commitments to China in the 1950s, to Cuba in the 1960s, and to Syria and Egypt in the 1970s (among others) could result in a disastrous war with the United States.

NATO, the U.S.-Japanese Security Treaty, and the CIS

At present, there are three very important formal alliances that dominate the international security scene. First, and by far the most powerful (although with a somewhat uncertain future in the post–Cold War era), is the *North Atlantic Treaty Organization (NATO)*, which encompasses Western Europe and North America. Using GDP as a measure of power, the 16 NATO members possess nearly half the world total (roughly twice the power of the United States alone). The members are the United States, Canada, Britain, France, Germany, Italy, Belgium, the Netherlands, Luxembourg, Denmark, Norway, Iceland, Spain, Portugal, Greece, and Turkey. NATO headquarters is in Brussels (Belgium), where military staffs from the member countries coordinate plans and periodically direct exercises in the field. The NATO "allied supreme commander" has always been a U.S. general. In NATO each state contributes its own military units—with its own national culture, language, and equipment specifications.

NATO was founded in 1949 to oppose and deter Soviet power in Europe. Its counterpart in Eastern Europe during the Cold War, the Soviet-led *Warsaw Pact*, was founded in 1955 and disbanded in 1991. During the Cold War, the United States maintained over 300,000 troops in Europe, with advanced planes, tanks, and other equipment. After the Cold War ended, these forces were cut to about 100,000. But NATO stayed together

---

[53]David, Steven R. *Choosing Sides: Alignment and Realignment in the Third World.* Baltimore: Johns Hopkins University Press, 1991.

[54]Siverson, Randolph M., and Michael R. Tennefoss. Power, Alliance, and the Escalation of International Conflict, 1815–1965. *American Political Science Review* 78 (4), 1984: 1057–69.

The NATO alliance has been the world's strongest military force since 1949; its mission in the post–Cold War era is somewhat uncertain. President Kennedy reviews U.S. forces in Germany, June 1963.

because its members felt that NATO provided useful stability even though its mission was unclear.[55]

The first actual use of force by NATO was in Bosnia in 1994, in support of the UN mission there. A "dual key" arrangement gave the UN control of NATO's actions in Bosnia, and the UN feared retaliation against its lightly armed peacekeepers if NATO attacked the Serbian forces to protect Bosnian civilians. As a result, NATO made threats, underlined by symbolic pinprick air strikes, but then backed down due to UN qualms; this undermined NATO credibility. More extensive NATO air strikes in 1995, however, alarmed Russian leaders already concerned by NATO's expansion plans. These problems, along with tensions between the American and European NATO members over Bosnia policy, dogged the first major NATO mission of the post–Cold War era.

In the 1990s Germany began forming a joint military corps with France (which does not participate in NATO military operations) and other smaller neighbors. This French-German experiment could eventually contribute to an alternative multinational security

[55]Stuart, Douglas, and William Tow. *The Limits of Alliance: NATO Out-of-Area Problems Since 1949.* Baltimore: Johns Hopkins University Press, 1990.

framework in Europe that excluded NATO (and the United States). So could the newly reinvigorated *Western European Union*, a military alliance to which the United States does not belong. But as of 1995 NATO still dominated European security.

NATO also faced the question of eastward expansion following the Cold War's end. Several countries in Eastern Europe, such as Poland, asked to join NATO as protection against a possible future attempt by Russia to reassert control of Eastern Europe. Russian leaders for their part saw NATO's possible expansion into Eastern Europe as aggressive and anti-Russian. A compromise category of premembership, with no certain date of admission to NATO, was created—the *Partnership for Peace*—and most of the Eastern European and former Soviet states including Russia joined it.

The *U.S.-Japanese Security Treaty* is a bilateral alliance that, in sheer capability, is the world's second most powerful after NATO (of course, the United States overlaps both). Under this alliance the United States maintained about 45,000 troops in Japan as of 1994 (with weapons, equipment, and logistical support). Japan pays the United States several billion dollars annually to offset about half the cost of maintaining these troops. The alliance was created in 1951 against the potential Soviet threat to Japan.

Because of its roots in the U.S. military occupation of Japan after World War II, the alliance is very *asymmetrical*, like a patron-client relationship. The United States is committed to defend Japan if it is attacked, but Japan is not similarly obligated to defend the United States. The United States maintains troops in Japan, but not vice versa. The United States belongs to several other alliances, but Japan's only major alliance is with the United States. The U.S. share of the total military power in this alliance is also far greater than its share in NATO.

Japan's constitution (written by U.S. general MacArthur after World War II) renounces the right to make war and maintain military forces, although interpretation has loosened this prohibition over time. Japan maintains military forces, called the *Self-Defense Forces*, strong enough for territorial defense but not for aggression. It is a powerful army by world standards but much smaller than Japan's economic strength could support. Japanese public opinion restrains militarism in general and precludes the development of nuclear weapons in particular (a "nuclear allergy" acquired when Japanese cities were destroyed by nuclear weapons in World War II). Even the dispatch of unarmed Japanese troops on a UN peacekeeping mission to Cambodia was barely approved in 1992 after a vigorous debate. Japan has little reason to alter its low profile in military affairs because low military spending has contributed to Japan's past economic successes.

In military and security affairs, Japan often adopts the stance of a junior partner to the United States. But Japan has gradually created its own concept of international security as well, which links security with economic relations (trade and investment) and foreign aid. Japan is as dependent as ever on natural resources from foreign countries, but Japanese leaders now believe that military capabilities are not useful for obtaining such resources. Instead, economic and diplomatic capabilities assure a smooth flow of resources to Japan and export markets for Japanese goods. The security alliance with the United States—Japan's largest trading partner—provides a stable security framework conducive to business. Japan need not worry that in a dispute over trade barriers the U.S. Navy will arrive to pry Japan's doors open (as it did in 1854). Nonetheless, some Japanese leaders feel that Japan's formal security role should now expand commensurate with its economic power: they call for a Japanese seat on the UN Security Council. The UN in turn is pressing Japan to participate fully in peacekeeping missions.

For its part, the United States has used the alliance with Japan as a base to project U.S. power in Asia, especially during the wars in Korea (1950–1953) and Vietnam (1965–1975) when Japan was a key staging area for U.S. war efforts. The continued U.S. military presence in Japan (as in Europe) symbolizes the U.S. commitment to remain engaged in Asian security affairs.[56] However, the high cost of maintaining U.S. troops in both Japan and Europe has been criticized by some U.S. political leaders.

The third major alliance—which is more economic and political in nature than military—is the *Commonwealth of Independent States (CIS)*. Its 12 members comprise the former Soviet republics except the Baltic States (Estonia, Latvia, and Lithuania). Russia is the leading member and Ukraine the second largest. Officially, CIS headquarters is in the city of Minsk, in Belarus, but in practice there is no strong center and meetings rotate around. The future of the CIS was still unclear by 1995, but any military component appeared less and less central to its purpose.

When the Soviet Union disintegrated in 1991, a chaotic situation emerged. Power for several years had been shifting from the center in Moscow to the 15 constituent Soviet republics. The Warsaw Pact had collapsed. The Soviet army itself began to break up, and several republics began forming their own military forces using Soviet forces, bases, and equipment located on their territory. At the same time, other former Soviet forces located outside Russia remained in a chain of command centered in Moscow, effectively under Russian control. Russia and Ukraine debated ownership of the Black Sea fleet, whose port was in Ukraine but whose history was distinctly Russian.

One reason for forming the CIS was simply to speed the death of the old Soviet Union and ease the transition to full independence for its republics. After the formation of the CIS at the end of 1991, the Soviet Union quickly dissolved; its last president, Gorbachev, resigned. The extensive property of the Union (including state-owned industry and military forces) went to the individual republics, especially to Russia, which became the USSR's successor state. For instance, when Gorbachev returned a few days after resigning to clear out his office in the Kremlin (the Soviet headquarters), he found Russian president Boris Yeltsin already sitting at his desk.

The disposition of the Union's property and armed forces was negotiated by CIS members. Although some military coordination takes place through the CIS, plans for a joint military force instead of 12 independent armies did not succeed. Among the largest CIS members, Kazakhstan and Belarus are the most closely aligned with Russia, while Ukraine is the most independent.

It is to the CIS's credit that in the post-Soviet chaos no major war erupted between major CIS member states. Substantial warfare did occur between some of the smaller members (notably Armenia and Azerbaijan), and there was civil violence within several other CIS states (Tajikistan, Moldova, Russia); CIS forces were drawn into a few small

---

[56]Mochizuki, Mike M. To Change or to Contain: Dilemmas of American Policy Toward Japan. In Oye, Kenneth A., Robert J. Lieber, and Donald Rothchild, eds. *Eagle in a New World: American Grand Strategy in the Post–Cold War Era*. New York: HarperCollins, 1992, pp. 335–59.

clashes. But the large members were not drawn into large wars. The outcome could have been much worse.

The most important relationship within the CIS is between its two largest members, *Russia* and *Ukraine*. They distrust each other somewhat but have managed to cooperate fairly effectively since becoming independent. Disputes over issues such as ownership of the Black Sea fleet have been negotiated step by step, often painfully but productively in the end.

One of the first problems facing CIS military forces was what position to take in inter-republic warfare, such as that between Armenia and Azerbaijan, secessionist wars as in Georgia, or civil wars to control republics' governments as in Tajikistan. In some cases CIS troops from the former Soviet army were stationed close to the fighting, and sometimes they were drawn in or took sides. More often they stood clear or played a peace-keeping role in such conflicts. As of 1994, the CIS operated a 24,000-person peacekeeping force in Tajikistan, generally supporting the government in a civil war there. A 1,500-person force in Moldova and a 500-person force in Georgia, both acting as buffer forces to monitor ceasefires, operated under joint commands of Russia and the governments and rebel forces in each of those countries.

Another pressing military problem for the CIS was the disposition of the tens of thousands of nuclear weapons of the former Soviet Union. As the Soviet successor state, Russia assumed control of the weapons and within a year moved all the *tactical* nuclear weapons out of the other republics and into Russian territory. This was a very touchy operation because of the danger of theft or accident while so many weapons were in transit. The United States provided specially designed railroad cars for use in moving the weapons. Still, there were reports that nuclear materials (or perhaps even warheads) had been stolen and sold on the international market by corrupt CIS officers or officials (see the discussion of proliferation in Chapter 6).

The *strategic* nuclear weapons—those on long-range missiles—presented another kind of problem. These weapons were located in four republics—Russia, Ukraine, Belarus, and Kazakhstan—under control of Russian commanders. They were not easily moved, and the three republic leaders expressed some ambivalence about losing them to Russia. At a minimum they wanted assurances that the nuclear weapons would be destroyed, not retargeted on their own republics. Ukraine in particular toyed with using the missiles as bargaining chips in negotiations with Russia or with the Western powers. But in the end all the former Soviet republics except Russia agreed to become non-nuclear states.

Overall, the CIS is an unusual alliance and a fractious one. It has no external enemy to hold it together, and its internal cohesion suffers from some long-standing feuds and resentments. It is a marriage of convenience. For now the members find it a necessary marriage—especially because of the tight economic integration of the member states—if not always a happy one.

Regional Alignments

Beyond the three alliances just discussed and the regional IGOs mentioned earlier, most international alignments and coalitions are not formalized in alliances. Among the great powers, a close working relationship (through the UN) developed among the United States, Western European powers, Japan, and Russia after the Cold War. By the mid-1990s new strains had appeared in great-power relations, including economic conflicts among the former Western allies, differences over policy in Bosnia, and Western alarm at Russia's war in secession-minded Chechnya province. Of the great powers, China continues to be the most independent, but prudently avoids conflict with the others unless China's immediate security interests are at stake.

In the third world, many states joined a *nonaligned movement* during the Cold War, standing apart from the U.S.-Soviet rivalry. This movement, led by India and Yugoslavia, was undermined by the membership of states like Cuba that were clearly clients of one superpower. In 1992 the nonaligned movement agreed to stay in business, though its future is unclear. One vestige from the empires of past centuries is the *British Commonwealth*—a group of former British colonies (including Canada and Australia) working together for mutual economic and cultural benefit. France also maintains ties (including regular summit meetings) with its former colonies in Africa.

In Asia, *China* has had frictions with most of its major neighbors. Between 1940 and 1979 it engaged in military hostilities with Japan, South Korea, the United States, India, Russia, and Vietnam. In 1965, China lost its only major regional ally (Indonesia) after a violent change of government there. China has long been loosely aligned with *Pakistan* in opposition to *India* (which was aligned with the Soviet Union). The United States tended to favor the Pakistani side as well (for instance, U.S. aid to Afghan rebels in the 1980s mostly went through Pakistan). But U.S.-Indian relations have improved a bit since the Cold War ended, and U.S.-Pakistani relations have been strained by Pakistan's nuclear weapons program. *Vietnam* is slowly normalizing relations with the United States now that the wars in Vietnam and Cambodia are over. The United States has 35,000 troops stationed in *South Korea* under terms of a formal bilateral alliance dating to the Korean War (North Korea is loosely aligned with China). Other long-standing U.S. friends in Asia include the Philippines, the Chinese Nationalists on Taiwan (only informally since the 1970s), Singapore, and Thailand. With Australia and New Zealand the United States has had since 1951 a formal military alliance called *ANZUS*.

In the Middle East the *Arab-Israeli* conflict created a general anti-Israel alignment of the Arab countries, but this alignment has broken down as Egypt in 1978 and then the Palestine Liberation Organization (PLO) and Jordan in 1993–1994 made peace with Israel. Despite its small size, Israel has been the largest recipient of U.S. foreign aid since the 1980s (about $3 billion per year). On the Arab side the United States has very close relations with Kuwait and Saudi Arabia (cemented by the 1991 Gulf War), with Turkey (a NATO member), with Egypt (a major U.S. foreign aid recipient since 1978), and with Morocco. The Gulf War and the Soviet collapse caused U.S. relations with Syria to improve around 1991. But U.S.-Iranian relations remained frosty 15 years after the 1979 revolution. The United States has very hostile relations with Libya and Iraq as well.

It is unclear what new international alignments may emerge in the years to come. The fluidity of alliances makes them something of a wild card for scholars to understand, just as they are for policy makers to deal with. This is doubly true in the uncertain atmosphere following the end of the Cold War. For the present, international alignments center on the United States; although several independence-minded states such as China and Iran are going their own way, there is little sign of a rival power alignment emerging to challenge the United States. However, the United States has offered only weak leadership since the Gulf War, and may be in transition to a role as "just another great power." This question will be central to the course of world politics in the remaining years of the twentieth century.

This chapter has focused on the concerns of realists—the interests of states, distributions of power among states, bargaining between states, and alliances of states. Consistent with the realist framework, the chapter has treated states as unitary actors, much as one would analyze the interactions of individual people. The actions of state leaders have been treated as more or less rational in terms of pursuing definable interests through coherent bargaining strategies.

But realism is not the only way to frame the major issues of international security. In Chapter 3 we reexamine these themes critically, from more liberal and more revolutionary theoretical perspectives.

❖ CHAPTER SUMMARY

- ◆ Realism explains international relations in terms of power.
- ◆ Realists and idealists differ in their assumptions about human nature, international order, and the potential for peace.
- ◆ Power can be conceptualized as influence or as capabilities that can create influence.
- ◆ The most important single indicator of a state's power is its GDP.
- ◆ Short-term power capabilities depend on long-term resources, both tangible and intangible.
- ◆ Realists consider military force the most important power capability.
- ◆ International affairs can be seen as a series of bargaining interactions in which states use power capabilities as leverage to influence the outcomes.
- ◆ Bargaining outcomes depend not only on raw power but also on strategies and luck.
- ◆ Reciprocity can be an effective strategy for reaching cooperation in ongoing relationships but carries a danger of turning into runaway hostility or arms races.
- ◆ Rational-actor approaches treat states as though they were individuals acting to maximize their own interests. These simplifications are debatable but allow realists to develop concise and general models and explanations.
- ◆ Game theory draws insights from simplified models of bargaining situations. In the Prisoner's Dilemma model, selfish participants cannot achieve mutually beneficial cooperation (except over time in some circumstances).
- ◆ International anarchy—the absence of world government—means that each state is a sovereign and autonomous actor pursuing its own national interests.
- ◆ The international system traditionally places great emphasis on the sovereignty of states, their right to control affairs in their own territory, and their responsibility to respect internationally recognized borders.
- ◆ Seven great powers account for half of the world's GDP as well as the great majority of military forces and other power capabilities.
- ◆ Power transition theory says that wars often result from shifts in relative power distribution in the international system.

◆ Hegemony—the predominance of one state in the international system—can help provide stability and peace in international relations, but with some drawbacks.

◆ States form alliances to increase their effective power relative to another state or alliance.

◆ Alliances can shift rapidly, with major effects on power relations.

◆ The world's three most powerful alliances, all of which face an uncertain future, are NATO, the U.S.-Japanese alliance, and the CIS (former Soviet republics).

❖ THINKING CRITICALLY

1. Using Table 1.2 on pp. 20–21 (with GDP as a measure of power) and the map at the front of the book, pick a state and speculate about what coalition of nearby states might form with sufficient power to oppose it if it became aggressive.

2. Pick a recent international event and list the power capabilities that participants used as leverage in the episode. Which capabilities were effective, and which were not? Why?

3. Given the distinction between zero-sum and non-zero-sum games, can you think of a current international situation that is a zero-sum conflict? One that is non-zero-sum?

4. If you were the leader of a small state in Africa, bargaining with a great power about an issue where your interests diverged, what leverage and strategies could you bring into play to improve the outcome for your state?

5. Given recent changes in international power distribution and the end of the Cold War order, where do you think the threats to peace will come from in the future? Through what means—unilateral actions, alliances, collective security—could states respond to those threats?

6. The modern international system came into being at a time when agrarian societies relied primarily on farm land to create wealth. Now that most wealth is no longer created through farming, is the territorial nature of states obsolete? How might the diminishing economic value of territory change the ways in which states interact?

❖ KEY TERMS

realism and idealism	zero-sum games
power	anarchy
bargaining	norms (of behavior)
negotiation	sovereignty
reciprocity	security dilemma
deterrence	balance of power
compellence	great powers and middle powers
arms race	multipolar (system)
rational actor	hegemony
national interest	alliance cohesion
cost-benefit analysis	burden sharing

*Remains of an Egyptian
soldier, Sinai desert, 1967.*

ALTERNATIVES TO POWER POLITICS

❖ LIBERALISM

How well do the assumptions of realism capture what is important about IR? Where are the problems in the realist framework—the places where abstractions diverge too much from the reality of IR, where realism is "unrealistic" in its portrayal?[1]

This chapter revisits the realism-idealism debate, discusses current liberal approaches to international security, and then considers three broader and more interdisciplinary alternatives to the realist framework—feminism, postmodernism, and peace studies. Each of these three research communities seeks to radically recast the terms of reference in which we see IR—discarding realism altogether. These are more revolutionary streams of thought among IR scholars than are the more limited criticisms directed at realism by liberals.

Traditional Liberal Critiques

Since the time of Mo Ti and Sun Tzu in ancient China, idealism has provided a counterpoint to realism. This long tradition of idealism in IR holds that morality, law, and international organization can form the basis for relations among states; that human nature is not evil; that peaceful and cooperative relations among states are possible; and that states can operate as a community rather than merely as autonomous self-interested agents.[2]

To recapitulate the core concepts of realism, states (which are the central actors in IR) use power to pursue their own interests in the context of an anarchic system lacking central enforcement mechanisms. Power capabilities come into play as leverage in bargaining among states over the outcomes of conflicts. Leverage can be positive (rewards)

---

[1]Vasquez, John A. *The Power of Politics: A Critique*. New Brunswick: Rutgers University Press, 1983.

[2]Nardin, Terry, and David R. Mapel, eds. *Traditions of International Ethics*. New York: Cambridge University Press, 1992. Holmes, Robert L. *On War and Morality*. Princeton: Princeton University Press, 1989.

or negative (punishments), but in both cases the purpose is to influence the rational decisions and actions of another state so as to bring about a more favorable outcome for the actor using the leverage. Military force is an important form of leverage—emphasized by realists over all other forms—because of the inherent insecurity of living in an anarchic world.

Traditionally, liberals have offered four major lines of criticism against these assumptions of realism. First, the key assumption of international *anarchy* is no more than a partial truth. International interactions are highly structured in several ways. Of course, they are structured by power relations, by the distribution of power in the international system—whether a predominant power in the system (hegemony) or a multipolar "concert" of great powers. Realists can accept that anarchy includes international order structured by power. But order also evolves through norms and institutions based on reciprocity and cooperation, even on law. Realists have a harder time reconciling the ever expanding scope of international interdependence and cooperation with the assumptions of anarchy, of the inevitability of security dilemmas, and of the primacy of military leverage.

Second, liberals criticize the notion of states as *unitary actors*, each with a single set of coherent interests. As the study of foreign policy reveals (Chapter 4), state actions often do not reflect a single individual set of preferences. Rather, state behavior is shaped by internal bargaining among and within bureaucracies, interest groups, and other actors with divergent goals and interests. Nonstate actors—individuals, NGOs, IGOs, and ethnic groups, among others—further confound the idea that IR can be reduced to interactions of a small number of well-defined state actors pursuing national interests.

Third, the concept of *rationality* is problematical. If states are single actors with coherent interests, they often seem to do a poor job in maximizing those interests. Of course, it is hard to tell from an actor's unexpected behavior whether the actor was irrational or merely pursued a goal, interest, or value that *we* would not consider normal or productive. But at the least the notion of rationality as the pursuit of objective, universal interests (applicable to various actors) draws criticism from liberals. And the evident importance in ethnic conflicts of emotions like hatred (see Chapter 5) also calls into question the more simplistic realist interpretations of such conflicts as rational bargaining moves by the participating actors.

Finally, *military force* as a form of leverage does not seem nearly as all-important as realism implies. It is a costly way to influence other actors (see Chapter 6), as compared with diplomacy, conflict resolution, peacekeeping, and other nonmilitary means. International organizations, laws, and norms create stable contexts for bargaining, making nonmilitary leverage increasingly effective as international organization develops (see Chapter 7). This criticism of realism applies even more to international political economy (Chapters 8 through 13) than to security affairs.

In addition to these general criticisms of realism, some liberals have argued that changes in the way IR works have made realist assumptions obsolete. Realism may once have been realistic, when European kings and queens played war and traded territories as property. But the world has changed dramatically since then. States are now interconnected, contradicting the assumptions of autonomy and sovereignty. Borders are becoming fluid, making territorial integrity increasingly untenable. The evolution of norms regarding the use of force have substantially changed the ways in which military force contributes to international power. This line of argument has been prominent in liberal interdependence approaches to IR since the 1970s.

What Is Rationality?

At the core of the liberal approach is a concept of *rationality* that differs sharply from the realist concept. Realists see rationality as an individual actor's attempt to maximize its own short-term interests. Liberals believe that rational actors are capable of forgoing short-term individual interests in order to further the long-term well-being of a community to which they belong. Such actions are rational because they contribute to the actor's individual well-being, indirectly or over the long term. Thus Kant could argue that states, although autonomous, could join a worldwide federation like today's UN and respect its principles even at the cost of forgoing certain short-term individual gains. To Kant, international cooperation was a more rational option for states than resort to war.

Thus, in realist conceptions of rationality, war and violence appear rational (because they often advance short-term state interests), but liberals tend to see war and violence as irrational deviations that result from defective reasoning and harm the (collective, long-term) well-being of states.[3]

This disagreement is particularly acute when it comes to nuclear weapons.[4] Liberals find it absurd to spend money building weapons that could destroy the world or to claim (as realists do) that there is a rational logic behind their deployment. Furthermore, many realists argue that nuclear deterrence will *prevent* the world from being destroyed—because the state actors owning nuclear weapons are rational. But liberals consider this a dangerous illusion. Because they see war as a breakdown in rationality generally, they fear that a similar breakdown could cause nuclear weapons to be used, with tragic consequences.

Liberal and realist approaches to *power* reflect the distinction between rationality as seeking narrow self-interest and rationality as seeking to share in long-term collective benefits. Realists define power as the ability to get another actor to do something—or as the capabilities required to so influence an actor (see pp. 53–55). This is *power over* others—a concept that some liberals consider inherently oppressive, rooted in a need to control or dominate other people. The definition assumes conflicting interests among actors, such that one actor achieves better outcomes only by making another actor do what it would not naturally want to do. This is the power of the bully, to make others do his bidding. But are bullies really the most powerful actors? Do they achieve the best outcomes? And do we really live in an international world populated by bullies?

An alternative definition of power is based not on power over others but on power to accomplish desirable ends. This kind of power often derives from finding and capitalizing on common interests rather than gaining an edge in bargaining over conflicting interests. Such empowerment often entails the formation of coalitions and partnerships, or the mobilization of the resources of multiple actors for a common purpose. For many liberals, this is a truer and more useful concept of power.

---

[3]Angell, Norman. *The Foundations of International Polity*. London: William Heinemann, 1914.

[4]Scott D. Sagan, and Kenneth N. Waltz. *The Spread of Nuclear Weapons: A Debate*. New York: W. W. Norton, 1995. Lifton, Robert Jay, and Richard Falk. *Indefensible Weapons: The Political and Psychological Case Against Nuclearism*. New York: Basic Books, 1982.

Liberals emphasize the potential for rivalries to evolve into cooperative relationships as states recognize that achieving mutual benefits is most cost-effective in the long run. The emergence of cooperation between U.S. and Soviet/Russian space program is an example. Russian cosmonaut joined U.S. space shuttle crew in February 1995 as a step toward a joint space station.

cooperation is possible

Neoliberalism

In the 1980s a new liberal critique of realism emerged. This approach stressed the importance of international institutions in reducing the inherent conflict that realists assume in an international system. The reasoning is based on the core liberal idea that seeking long-term mutual gains is often more rational than maximizing individual short-term gains. The approach became known as "neoliberal institutionalism" or **neoliberalism** for short.

The neoliberal approach differs from earlier liberal approaches in that it concedes to realism several important assumptions—among them, that states are unitary actors rationally pursuing their self-interests. Neoliberals say to realists, "Even if we grant your assumptions about the nature of states and their motives, your pessimistic conclusions still do not follow." States will be able to achieve cooperation fairly often because it is in their interest to do so, and they can learn to use institutions to facilitate the pursuit of mutual gains and the reduction of possibilities for cheating or taking advantage of another state.

Despite the many sources of conflict in IR, states do find their way to cooperation most of the time. Neoliberal scholars ask how this is possible in an anarchic world.[5] Neoliberals try to show that even in a world of unitary rational states, the neorealists' pessimism regarding international cooperation is not valid. This is because states can create mutual rules, expectations, and institutions to promote behavior that enhances (or at least doesn't destroy) the possibilities for mutual gain.

Neoliberals use the *Prisoner's Dilemma (PD)* game (see pp. 70–71) to illustrate their argument that cooperation is possible. Each actor can gain by individually defecting, but both lose out when both defect. The narrow, self-serving behavior of each player leads to a bad outcome for both players, one they could have improved by cooperating with each other. This reflects the common situation in IR in which states have a mix of conflicting interests and mutual interests. The dilemma can be resolved if the game is played over and over again—an accurate model of IR, where states deal with each other in repeated interactions.

A strategy of strict reciprocity after an initial cooperative move (nicknamed **tit for tat**) can bring about mutual cooperation in a PD game, because the other player must conclude that any defection will merely provoke a like defection in response.[6] The strategy parallels just war doctrine (see pp. 301–302), which calls for states to never initiate war but to use war in response to war. In international trade, such a strategy calls for opening one's markets but selectively closing them in response to another state's closing of its markets (see pp. 336–338).

Reciprocity is an important principle in IR that helps international cooperation emerge despite the absence of central authority. Through reciprocity, not a world government, norms and rules are enforced. In international security, reciprocity underlies the gradual improvement of relations sought by arms control agreements and peacekeeping missions. In IPE, where cooperation can create great benefits through trade, the threat to restrict trade in retaliation for unfair practices is a strong incentive to comply with rules and norms.

Although reciprocity is an important norm it is just one among many norms that mediate states' interactions. For example, diplomatic practices, participation in international organizations (IOs), and the symbolic trappings of statehood (flags, anthems) are all strongly governed by shared expectations about the rules of correct behavior. As dilemmas like the PD crop up in IR, states rely on a context of rules, norms, habits, and institutions that make it rational for all sides to avoid the self-defeating outcomes that would come from following narrow short-term self-interest. Neoliberals study historical and contempo-

---

[5]Baldwin, David A., ed. *Neorealism and Neoliberalism: The Contemporary Debate*. New York: Columbia University Press, 1993. Ruggie, John Gerard, ed. *Multilateralism Matters: The Theory and Praxis of an Institutional Form*. New York: Columbia University Press, 1993. Milner, Helen. International Theories of Cooperation Among Nations: Strengths and Weaknesses. *World Politics* 44 (3), 1992: 466–94. Oye, Kenneth A., ed. *Cooperation Under Anarchy*. Princeton: Princeton University Press, 1986.

[6]Axelrod, Robert. *The Evolution of Cooperation*. New York: Basic Books, 1984. Axelrod, Robert, and Robert O. Keohane. Achieving Cooperation Under Anarchy: Strategies and Institutions. In Oye, ed. *Cooperation Under Anarchy*. Princeton: Princeton University Press, 1986. Gowa, Joanne. Anarchy, Egoism and Third Images: The Evolution of Cooperation and International Relations. *International Organization* 40, 1986: 167–86.

rary cases in IR to see how institutions and norms affected the possibilities for overcoming dilemmas and achieving international cooperation. Thus, for neoliberals the emergence of international institutions is key to understanding how states achieve a superior type of rationality that includes long-term self-interest and not just immediate self-interest.

Collective Goods

The problem of the security dilemma (p. 74), which helps explain costly arms races, is an example of a PD-like dilemma in international security. Such examples are even more common in IPE, where protectionism and other forms of economic nationalism attempt to increase national wealth (relative to other states), at some cost to global wealth (see Chapter 8). The overall efficiency of the world economy is reduced, but the distribution of gains from trade shifts toward one's own state. The problem is that if other states take similar actions, global efficiency decreases and the distribution of benefits remains about the same. So all states end up worse off than they could be.

All of these situations are examples of what is called the **collective goods problem.** A collective good is a tangible or intangible good, created by the members of a group, that is available to all group members, regardless of their individual contributions. As in the security dilemma or Prisoner's Dilemma, participants can gain by lowering their own contribution to the collective good, yet if too many participants do so, the good cannot be provided.

For example, it is cheaper to drive a polluting car than pay for emission controls, and the air that the car owner breathes is hardly affected by his or her own car. The air quality is a collective good. If too many car owners pollute, all will breathe dirty air. But if just a few pollute, they will breathe fairly clean air; the few who pollute are then termed **free riders,** because they benefit from someone else's provision of the collective good. These concepts are very important in IPE and come up again in later chapters, especially in discussions of the global environment (Chapter 11). They are also important concepts in international organization and law (Chapter 7).

Within domestic society, many collective goods problems are solved by governments, which enforce rules in the common good. Governments can punish free riders who are tempted to avoid contributing. Governments can pass laws against polluting cars or force citizens to pay taxes to support collective goods such as national defense, highways, or schools. In the anarchic international system, the absence of central government sharpens the difficulties created by collective goods. It is difficult to maintain multilateral cooperation when each government is tempted by its own possibility of free riding.

In general, collective goods are easier to provide in small groups than in large ones.[7] In a small group the defection (free riding) of one member is harder to conceal, has a greater impact on the overall collective good, and is easier to punish. The advantage of small groups helps explain the importance of the great-power system in international security affairs. And it is one reason why the G7 industrialized countries have frequent meetings to try to coordinate their economic policies, instead of relying only on groups like the World Bank or GATT (each of which has over a hundred member states). But

---

[7]Olson, Mancur. *The Logic of Collective Action.* Cambridge, MA: Harvard University Press, 1971 [1965].

Collective goods are provided to all members of a group regardless of their individual contributions, just as these Vietnamese boat people (1984) will sink or float together. Liberal theorists see the community of nations as similarly interdependent. Individual states have conflicting interests over limited resources (as do the boat people) but strong incentives to find ways to maintain collective goods such as peace and stability.

whether in small groups or large, without a government to enforce contributions to collective goods, states must look to other means of enforcement.

Regimes and Institutions

Because of the conflicting interpretations that parties to a conflict usually have, it is difficult to resolve such conflicts without a third party to arbitrate or an overall framework to set common expectations of all parties regarding the rules and standards to be followed. These considerations underlie the creation of IOs in the international security field (see Chapter 7). In international economics, norms of behavior are at least as important as in international security because of the large volume of economic transactions that occur and the great gains to be realized from maintaining a stable framework for smoothly carrying on those transactions.

An **international regime** is a set of rules, norms, and procedures around which the expectations of actors converge in a certain issue area (whether arms control, international trade, or Antarctic exploration).[8] The convergence of expectations means that participants in the international system have similar ideas about what rules will govern their mutual participation: everyone expects to play by the same rules. (Note that this meaning of regime is not the same as when the word refers to the domestic governments of states, especially to governments considered illegitimate or in power for only a short time—such as a military regime after a coup.)

Regimes are an important and widespread phenomenon in IR. Several will be discussed in the remaining chapters on international security. The Ballistic Missile Control Regime (see p. 256) is a set of rules and expectations governing the international trade in missiles. The Concert of Europe after 1815 and the "New World Order" in the 1990s have been described as security regimes in which the great powers develop common expectations about the rules for their behavior (see pp. 27, 45). In IPE, regimes are even more central. The frameworks within which states carry on trade, monetary relations, communications, and environmental protection policies—among other issues—are key to realizing the benefits of mutual cooperation in these areas.

IR scholars conceive of regimes in several different ways, and the concept has been criticized as too vague. But the most common conception of regimes combines elements of realism and liberalism. States are considered the important actors, and states are seen as autonomous units maximizing their own interests in an anarchic context. Regimes do not play a role in issues where states can realize their interests directly through unilateral applications of leverage. Rather, regimes come into existence to overcome collective goods dilemmas by coordinating the behaviors of individual states. Although states continue to seek their own interests, they create frameworks to coordinate their actions with those of other states if and when such coordination is necessary to realize self-interest (that is, in collective goods dilemmas). Thus, regimes help make cooperation possible even within an international system based on anarchy—exactly the point neoliberals focus on.

Regimes do not substitute for the basic calculations of costs and benefits by states; they just open up new possibilities with more favorable benefit-cost ratios. Regimes do not constrain states, except in a very narrow and short-term sense. Rather they facilitate and empower national governments faced with issues where collective goods problems would otherwise prevent governments from achieving their ends. Regimes can be seen as *intervening variables* between the basic causal forces at work in IR—for realists, the relative power of state actors—and the outcomes such as international cooperation (or lack thereof). Working through a regime does not nullify the power factors in a bargaining situation, but it does modify them.

Regimes do not negate the effects of power: more often they codify and normalize existing power relations. For example, the ballistic missile regime (Chapter 6) protects the status quo in which only a few states have such missiles. If the regime works, it will keep less-powerful states from gaining leverage they could use against more-powerful states.

---

[8]Krasner, Stephen D., ed. *International Regimes*. Ithaca: Cornell University Press, 1983. Rittberger, Volker, and Peter Mayer, eds. *Regime Theory and International Relations*. New York: Oxford University Press, 1993. Lipson, Charles. Why Are Some International Agreements Informal? *International Organization* 45 (4), 1991: 495–538.

Hegemonic Stability

Since regimes depend on state power for their enforcement, some IR scholars argue that regimes are most effective when power in the international system is most concentrated—when there is a hegemon to keep order (see "Hegemony" on pp. 81–82). This theory is known as **hegemonic stability theory.**[9] When one state's power is predominant, it can enforce rules and norms unilaterally, avoiding the collective goods problem. In particular, hegemons can maintain global free trade and promote world economic growth, in this view.

This theory attributes the peace and prosperity of the decades after World War II to U.S. hegemony, which created and maintained a global framework of economic relations supporting relatively stable and free international trade, as well as a security framework that prevented great-power wars. In the nineteenth century, prosperity was promoted by the similar role of Britain. By contrast, the Great Depression of the 1930s and the outbreak of World War II have been attributed to the power vacuum in the international system at that time—Britain was no longer able to act as hegemon, and the United States was unwilling to begin doing so.[10]

Why should a hegemon care about enforcing rules for the international economy that are in the common good? According to hegemonic stability theory, a hegemon basically has the same interests as the common good of all states. Hegemons as the largest international traders have an inherent interest in the promotion of integrated world markets (where the hegemon will tend to dominate). As the most advanced state in productivity and technology, a hegemon does not fear competition from industries in other states; it fears only that its own superior goods will be excluded from competing in other states. Thus hegemons favor free trade and use their power to achieve free trade. Hegemony, then, provides both the ability and the motivation to maintain regimes that provide a stable political framework for free international trade, according to hegemonic stability theory. This theory is not, however, accepted by all IR scholars.[11]

What happens to regimes when hegemons lose power and decline? The case of the 1930s suggests that Britain's loss of power destabilized international regimes and contributed to the Great Depression and World War II. But this happened after quite a few decades of British decline, and only under the added uncertainties in world politics that resulted from World War I, the Russian Revolution, German ascent, and the unusual role of the United States (see p. 38).[12]

---

[9]Keohane, Robert O. The Theory of Hegemonic Stability and Change in International Economic Regimes, 1967–1977. In Ole R. Holsti, R. M. Siverson, and A. L. George, eds. *Change in the International System.* Boulder, CO: Westview, 1980. McKeown, Timothy J. Hegemonic Stability Theory and 19th Century Tariff Levels in Europe. *International Organization* 37 (1), 1983: 73–91.

[10]Kindleberger, Charles P. *The World in Depression, 1929–1939.* Berkeley: University of California Press, 1973.

[11]Gowa, Joanne. Rational Hegemons, Excludable Goods, and Small Groups: An Epitaph for Hegemonic Stability Theory? *World Politics* 41 (3), 1989: 307–24. Grunberg, Isabelle. Exploring the "Myth" of Hegemonic Stability. *International Organization* 44 (4), 1990: 431–78. Snidal, Duncan. The Limits of Hegemonic Stability Theory. *International Organization* 39 (4), 1985: 580–614.

[12]Lake, David A. *Power, Protection, and Free Trade: International Sources of U.S. Commercial Strategy, 1887–1939.* Ithaca: Cornell University Press, 1988.

Regimes do not always decline with the power of hegemons that created them. Rather, they may take on a life of their own. Although hegemony may be crucial in *establishing* regimes in the first place, it is not necessary for *maintaining* them.[13] Once actors' expectations converge around the rules embodied in a regime, the actors come to realize that the regime serves their own interests. Working through the regime becomes a habit, and national leaders may not even give serious consideration to breaking out of the established rules.

This persistence of regimes was demonstrated in the 1970s, when U.S. power declined following the decades of U.S. hegemony since 1945. Diminished U.S. power was evident in the loss of the Vietnam War, the rise of OPEC, and the malaise of the U.S. economy (with simultaneous stagnation and inflation). Some IR scholars expected that the entire framework of international trade and monetary relations established after World War II would collapse once the United States was no longer able to enforce the rules of that regime. But this did not happen. The international economic regimes adjusted somewhat and survived.

In part, that survival is attributable to the embedding of regimes in permanent *institutions* such as the UN, NATO, or the International Monetary Fund. As the rules of the game persist over time and become habitual, institutions develop around them. These institutions become the tangible manifestation of shared expectations as well as the machinery for coordinating international actions based on those expectations. In international security affairs, the UN and other IOs provide a stable framework for resolving disputes (Chapter 7). IPE is even more institutionalized, again because of the heavier volume of activity and the wealth that can be realized from cooperation.[14]

Institutions gain greater stability and weight than do noninstitutionalized regimes. With a staff and headquarters, an international institution can actively intervene to promote adherence to the rules in its particular area of political or economic life. The most important institutions in international security and IPE are discussed in Chapters 7 and 8 respectively.

Collective Security

A major application of liberal conceptions of international security affairs is the concept of **collective security**—the formation of a broad alliance of most major actors in an international system for the purpose of jointly opposing aggression by any actor. The rationale for this approach was laid out by the philosopher Immanuel Kant in Germany over two hundred years ago. Since past treaties ending great-power wars had never lasted permanently, Kant proposed a *federation* (league) of the world's states. Through such a federation, Kant proposed, the majority of states could unite to punish any one state that committed aggression. This would safeguard the collective interests of all the nations together

---

[13]Keohane, Robert O. *After Hegemony: Cooperation and Discord in the World Political Economy*. Princeton: Princeton University Press, 1984. Gowa, Joanne. Bipolarity, Multipolarity, and Free Trade. *American Political Science Review* 83 (4), 1989: 1227–44.

[14]Taylor, Paul, and A. J. R. Groom, eds. *International Institutions at Work*. New York: St. Martin's Press, 1988. Ruggie, John Gerard, ed. *Multilateralism Matters: The Theory and Praxis of an Institutional Form*. New York: Columbia University Press, 1993. Keohane, Robert O. International Institutions: Two Approaches. *International Studies Quarterly* 32 (4), 1988: 379–96.

against the narrow self-interest of one nation that might otherwise profit from aggression. The federation would also protect the self-determination of small nations that all too easily became pawns in great-power games.[15]

After the horrors of World War I, a *League of Nations* was actually formed. But it was flawed in two ways. Its membership did not include all the great powers (nor the most powerful one, the United States). And its members proved unwilling to bear the costs of collective action to oppose aggression when it occurred (in the 1930s, starting with Japan and Italy).

After World War II the UN was created as the League's successor to promote collective security (see Chapter 7). Several regional IGOs also currently perform collective security functions (deterring aggression) as well as economic and cultural ones. In Latin America and the United States there is the *Organization of American States (OAS)*. In the Middle East (including North Africa) there is the *Arab League*. In Africa (also including North Africa) there is the *Organization of African Unity (OAU)*. All these organizations serve to mediate security issues among their members.

The success of collective security depends on two points. First, the members must keep their alliance commitments to the group. When a powerful state commits aggression against a weaker one, it often is not in the immediate interest of other powerful states to go to war over the issue. It can be very costly to suppress a determined aggressor.

A second requisite for collective security is that enough members must agree on what constitutes aggression. When the United States sent an army half a million strong to try to put down a rebellion in South Vietnam in the 1960s, was that aggression? Or was it aggression for North Vietnam to infiltrate its army into the south in support of the rebellion? The UN Security Council is structured so that aggression is defined by what all five permanent members, plus at least four of the other ten members, can agree on (see "The Security Council" on pp. 276–279). This collective security system does not work against aggression by a great power. When the Soviet Union invaded Afghanistan, or the United States mined the harbors of Nicaragua, or France blew up the Greenpeace ship *Rainbow Warrior*, the UN could do nothing—because those states can veto Security Council resolutions.[16]

Both requirements were met in the case of Kuwait in 1990–1991. The aggressor, Iraq, was a member of the UN, as was the victim, Kuwait. The invasion was so blatant a violation of Kuwaiti sovereignty and territorial integrity that the Security Council had little trouble agreeing to label it aggression. It was the first case since the founding of the UN that one member had invaded, occupied, and annexed another member—attempting to erase it as a sovereign state. The Security Council took a keen interest in reversing Iraq's aggression for three reasons: the aggression was flagrant, the rules of world order were being redefined as the Cold War ended, and of course there was the threat to the oil supply of the West.

In a series of resolutions, the Council condemned Iraq, applied mandatory economic sanctions (requiring all UN members to stop trading with Iraq), and ultimately authorized the use of force by a multinational coalition. With vigorous efforts by President Bush, a

[15]Kant, Immanuel. *Perpetual Peace*. Lewis White Beck, ed. Indianapolis: Bobbs-Merrill, 1957 [1795].

[16]Downs, George W., ed. *Collective Security Beyond the Cold War*. Ann Arbor: The University of Michigan Press, 1994. Weiss, Thomas G., ed. *Collective Security in a Changing World*. Boulder, CO: Lynne Rienner, 1993.

sufficient number of countries was induced to contribute enough money to pay for the war. After the war, the Security Council imposed cease-fire terms that required Iraq to give up its most threatening weapons. Collective security worked in the Iraqi case because the conquest of Kuwait brought all the great powers together and because they were willing to bear the costs of confronting Iraq. (China abstained on the resolution authorizing force and did not contribute to the coalition, but it did not veto the resolution.)

In the case of Bosnia, the aggression was somewhat less clear-cut, since it followed on the disintegration of what had been a single state, Yugoslavia. What would have been an internal affair became an international one when Serbia and Bosnia became separate states. Also the conquest of two-thirds of Bosnia was done in the name of Bosnia's minority Serbian population and its political party, though supported from Serbia itself. And traditional ties between Serbia and three Security Council members (Russia, France, and Britain) made these great powers reluctant to punish Serbia.

But the Serb forces' use of genocide and other war crimes demanded a response. And having recognized Bosnia's independence and admitted it to the UN, the Security Council members had some obligation to oppose the conquest and dismemberment of Bosnia. The Security Council was able to agree that Serbia and Bosnian Serb forces were the primary aggressors. Dozens of resolutions were then passed, demanding a halt to the aggression and imposing economic sanctions on Serbia. The resolutions also authorized UNPROFOR peacekeepers and proclaimed various no-fly zones, humanitarian "safe areas" and the like; few of these resolutions had success.

On one major question, however, the great powers equivocated on distinguishing between aggressor and victim in Bosnia. An *arms embargo*, which had been imposed on the former Yugoslavia in hopes of preventing its disintegration, was applied to the Bosnians and Serbs alike. Since Serbian forces were heavily armed and Bosnia practically disarmed, this arms embargo locked in the aggressor's advantage and became a subject of great controversy, pitting the great powers against the majority of UN members and the U.S. Congress. Ironically, such an arms embargo against both sides had been tried before, in the 1930s against Italy and Ethiopia, and had only contributed to the breakdown of collective security in that decade.

But ultimately, the sticking point for collective security in Bosnia was not identifying the aggressor; it was cost. Members of the UN (especially the great powers) were not willing to pay the price to turn back aggression. Collective security was thus a collective good, and in this case norms and institutions failed to get all the members to contribute to provide that good.

The concept of collective security has been broadened in recent years. Toward the end of the Cold War, the liberal premises of international community and mutual state interests provided the foundations for a new idea called *common security* (or "mutual security").[17] This is the notion that the security of all states, enemies as well as friends, is interdependent, so the insecurity of one state makes all states less secure. A local dispute in one part of the world can threaten another part; economic and ethnic rivalries can spill

[17]Palme Commission [Independent Commission on Disarmament and Security Issues]. *Common Security: A Programme for Disarmament*. London: Pan Books, 1982. Stephenson, Carolyn M., ed. *Alternative Methods for International Security*. Washington: University Press of America, 1982. Forsberg, Randall. Creating a Cooperative Security System. *Boston Review* 17 (6), 1992.

How can neoliberals explain the failure to provide the collective good of collective security in the case of Bosnia? Where a realist might argue simply that the cost was too high relative to the importance of turning back aggression, a neoliberal might say that the overall costs were not too high but the problem of dividing those costs was too difficult. It is because the outcome was less than what might have been achieved that the international response was considered a failure. So why was the problem of dividing costs too difficult in the Bosnia case but not in the Kuwait case?

Neoliberals could offer this explanation: The norms and institutions of the post–Cold War era are still young, and are developing slowly through practice and learning. Kuwait was an easier case because of the clear economic stakes and because Western armies had long prepared for possible military action to turn back a Soviet attack on Gulf oil supplies. Bosnia was a harder case in which to reach consensus on expectations of what norms should apply—what is the right thing to do in a case like this—because it was a new type of conflict in a new era. The UN took on a bigger and tougher mission in the former Yugoslavia, without much experience and without enough money or a clear enough consensus on what the mission was. Indeed, the whole UN collective security system is only fifty years old, and was paralyzed by the Cold War standoff for almost all of those years, so it is still immature.

Over time, a neoliberal might argue, as the post–Cold War era proceeds through a series of cases like Bosnia, the norms and institutions will mature so that future cases will be handled better. Indeed, policy makers spent much effort analyzing what went

THINKING THEORETICALLY
❖

wrong in Bosnia and trying to enunciate new policy guidelines for a new era. And in the Bosnia case itself, there was an increase over time in both the strength of international response and the cohesion of the great powers. Liberals believe in incremental progress, the slow change that moves in little steps as groups and individuals learn and adapt.

Another factor might also be relevant to neoliberals. The presence of hegemony in the international system has been extremely helpful in creating new regimes. The sudden end of the Cold War called for such new regimes—a new consensus among countries about what to expect in the new era. At first, under President Bush, the United States appeared to be moving into a hegemonic role and helping form those new rules of the game. But after Bush was defeated for reelection and President Clinton promised to focus on domestic policy, the United States appeared to retreat suddenly from the role of world leadership. This shift would make it harder for new regimes to solidify in the post–Cold War era. However, this explanation is problematical because the failure of response in Bosnia began in 1991–1992 under President Bush, right after the Gulf War triumph that seemed to demonstrate U.S. hegemony.

Thus, neoliberals could accept a neorealist framework in which the cases of Kuwait and Bosnia are analyzed in terms of rational calculations by unitary states in an anarchic international system. But neoliberals would draw more optimistic conclusions about the viability of collective security in future cases, since they would predict that over time states will develop solutions to the Bosnia-type collective goods problems that arise in the post–Cold War era.

over into violent conflicts; the costs of preparing for war can bankrupt great powers even in peacetime. Security itself can be seen in a new way, not so much as a set of individual national interests but more as a seamless web. This new reality—if state leaders recognized it—would resolve the security dilemma (see p. 74), because a state's own security interests would be (indirectly) *diminished* if it threatened another state.

The theory and practice of common security were promoted during the late 1980s by Soviet president Gorbachev, who won the Nobel peace prize for his accomplishments (although he was swept from office when the Soviet Union collapsed). Gorbachev and his foreign minister, Eduard Shevardnadze (now the leader of independent but war-torn Georgia), spoke of a "common European house" in which East and West both had to live under the same roof. They argued that as states became more closely connected economically and culturally, it was futile and wasteful to arm against each other, especially with nuclear weapons. Of course, domestic economic stagnation was a major factor in Gorbachev's realization that the Soviet Union could no longer afford the Cold War.

From Mo Ti to Kant to Gorbachev, liberals have sought to reform rather than radically reshape the international system as we know it. They have tried to overhaul the realist model but not to reject its terms of reference entirely (this is one reason that realists and liberals can continue to debate and to understand each other's argument even while disagreeing). Liberal scholars and liberal state leaders alike have argued that international cooperation and the avoidance of violence are ultimately better for states themselves and more rational for state leaders to pursue.

In the remainder of this chapter, we consider more revolutionary critiques of realism. These approaches broadly reject the terms of reference—issues, assumptions, language—that realists use to discuss IR. As a result, there has not been much productive debate between realism and these schools of thought. Yet, with growing numbers of IR scholars taking these critiques seriously, they provide valuable new perspectives which compete with realist and liberal approaches.

❖ FEMINISM

Feminist scholarship has cut a broad swath across academic disciplines, from literature to psychology to history. In recent years it has made inroads in international relations, which was considered one of the fields most resistant to feminist arguments. Such resistance perhaps stems from the heavily male composition of the major actors studied in IR—political decision makers, diplomats, and soldiers. Resistance may also derive from the fact that most IR scholars are themselves male—but not all female scholars are feminists nor do all male scholars reject feminist arguments. Nonetheless, feminist scholarship in IR has received increasing interest in the 1990s and has produced a rapidly growing literature.[18]

---

[18]Sylvester, Christine. *Feminist Theory and International Relations in a Postmodern Era.* New York: Cambridge University Press, 1994. Whitworth, Sandra. *Feminism and International Relations.* New York: St. Martin's Press, 1994. Tickner, J. Ann. *Gender in International Relations: Feminist Perspectives on Achieving Global Security.* New York: Columbia University Press, 1992. Grant, Rebecca, and Kathleen Newland, eds. *Gender and International Relations.* Bloomington: Indiana University Press, 1991.

Why Gender Matters

Feminist scholarship encompasses a variety of strands of work, but all have in common the insight that *gender matters* in understanding how IR works—especially in issues relating to war and international security. Feminist scholarship in various disciplines seeks to *uncover hidden assumptions about gender* in how we study a subject such as IR. What scholars traditionally claim to be universal often turns out to be true only of males. For instance, in other fields, feminists criticize medical studies that include only male patients or studies of developmental psychology that look only at boys.

Feminists have argued that the core assumptions of realism—especially of anarchy and sovereignty—reflect the ways in which *males* tend to interact and to see the world. In this view, the realist approach simply assumes male participants when discussing foreign policy decision making, state sovereignty, or the use of military force.

This is a somewhat complex critique, because in fact the vast majority of heads of state, of diplomats, and of soldiers *are* male, so it may be realistic to study them as males. What feminists ask is that scholars explicitly recognize the gendered nature of their subject (rather than implicitly assuming all actors are male). In this view, traditional male actors in IR can be better understood by analyzing how their gender affects their views and decision processes. And females also influence IR (more often through nonstate channels than males do)—influences often ignored by realism.

Beyond revealing the hidden assumptions about gender in a field of scholarship, feminists often *challenge traditional concepts of gender* as well. In IR, these traditional concepts revolve around the assumptions that males fight wars and run states, whereas females are basically irrelevant to IR. Such gender roles are based in the broader construction of masculinity as suitable to *public* and political spaces, whereas femininity is associated with the sphere of the *private* and domestic. An example of this gendered construction was provided by White House chief of staff Donald Regan's comment at a 1985 Reagan-Gorbachev summit meeting that women do not care about throw weights of ICBMs (see p. 248) and would rather watch Nancy Reagan. Later he said that U.S. women would not support sanctions against white-ruled South Africa because they would not want to lose their diamonds (a South African export). Feminists call into question, at a minimum, the stereotypes of women as caring more about jewelry and fashion than apartheid and arms control.

Beyond a basic agreement that gender is important, there is no single feminist approach to IR but several such approaches—*strands* of scholarship and theory. Each moves forward on its own terms, and although they are interwoven (all paying attention to gender and to the status of women) they often run in different directions. On some core issues concerning critiques of realism, the different strands of feminism have conflicting views, creating interesting debates *within* feminism.

One strand, **essentialist feminism,** focuses on valorizing the feminine—that is, valuing the unique contributions of women *as* women. Essentialist feminists do not think women do all things as well as men or vice versa. Because of their greater experience with nurturing and human relations, women are seen as potentially more effective than men (on average) in conflict resolution as well as in group decision making. Essentialist feminists believe there are *real* differences between the genders that are not just social constructions and cultural indoctrination (although these contribute to gender roles too). In

Feminist scholars emphasize the importance of gender roles in IR, especially the traditional distinction between males in the political-military roles and females in the domestic-family roles. Here in Sarajevo, UN soldier participates in protection force as a Bosnian citizen runs along "sniper's alley" (August 1994). Realities often diverge from stereotypes, however. In Bosnia, the UN force mainly protected itself, while ethnic cleansing and siege killed over a hundred thousand women and children (note that only the male has helmet, bulletproof vest, and armored vehicle; the female is exposed).

other words, there is a core biological *essence* to being male or female. This view is supported by recent research showing differences in how male and female brains process language. Some essentialist feminists argue that feminine perspectives create a standpoint from which to observe, analyze, and criticize the traditional perspectives on IR.[19]

Another strand, **liberal feminism,** rejects these claims as being based on stereotyped gender roles. Liberal feminists see the "essential" differences in men's and women's abilities or perspectives as trivial or nonexistent. They see men and women as equal. They deplore the exclusion of women from positions of power in IR but do not believe that including women would fundamentally change the nature of the international system. Liberal feminists seek to include women more often as subjects of study—such as women state leaders, women soldiers, and other women operating outside the traditional gender roles in IR.

---

[19]Keohane, Robert O. International Relations Theory: Contributions of a Feminist Standpoint. *Millennium* 18 (2), 1989: 245–53.

A third approach combines feminism with postmodernism, which is discussed later in this chapter. **Postmodern feminism** tends to reject the assumptions about gender made by both essentialists and liberal feminists.

To some extent the differences between feminist strands—essentialist, liberal, and postmodern—reflect more general themes of conservative, liberal, and revolutionary world views, respectively. But these distinctions are among approaches that collectively are closer to the revolutionary world view than are either realism or liberalism as discussed thus far.

The Masculinity of Realism

Essentialist feminism provides a standpoint from which to reexamine the core assumptions of realism—especially the assumption of *autonomy*, from which flow the concepts of sovereignty and anarchy. According to realists, the international system consists of separate, autonomous actors (states) that control their own territory and have no right to infringe on another's territory. Do these concepts rest on a "masculine" view of the world? If so, what would a feminist approach to international security look like? Some essentialist feminists have argued that realism emphasizes autonomy and separation because men find separation easier to deal with than interconnection.

This view rests on psychological research showing that boys and girls grow up from a young age with different views of separateness and connection.[20] In this view, because a child's primary caretaker is almost always female in the early years, *girls* form their gender identity around the perception of *similarity* with their caretaker (and by extension the environment in which they live), but *boys* perceive their *difference* from the caretaker. From this experience, boys develop social relations based on individual *autonomy*, but girls' relations are based on *connection*. As a result, women are held to be more likely than men to fear abandonment whereas men are more likely to fear intimacy.

In *moral* reasoning, according to this research, boys tend to apply abstract rules and stress individual rights (reflecting their sense of separation from the situation) but girls pay more attention to the concrete contexts of different situations and to the responsibility of group members for each other. In playing *games*, boys resolve disputes through arguments about the rules and then keep playing, but girls are more likely to abandon a game rather than argue over the rules and risk the social cohesion of their group. In *social relations*, boys form and dissolve friendships more readily than girls, who are more likely to stick loyally with friends. All these gender differences in children reflect the basic concept that for girls connection matters more than independence, but for boys the reverse is true. (In addition to its masculine nature, individual autonomy is a *Western* construction that is not as important in many non-Western cultures; it is unclear how many of these gender roles are specific to Western culture.)[21]

---

[20]Gilligan, Carol. *In a Different Voice: Psychological Theory and Women's Development*. Cambridge, MA: Harvard University Press, 1982. Hirschmann, Nancy J. Freedom, Recognition, and Obligation: A Feminist Approach to Political Theory. *American Political Science Review* 83 (4), 1989: 1227–44. Chodorow, Nancy. *The Reproduction of Mothering*. Berkeley: University of California Press 1978.

[21]Sampson, Edward E. The Debate on Individualism: Indigenous Psychologies of the Individual and Their Role in Personal and Societal Functioning. *American Psychologist* 43 (1), 1988: 15–22.

Realism, of course, rests on the concept of states as separate, autonomous actors that make and break alliances freely while pursuing their own interests (but not interfering in each other's internal affairs). Such a conception of autonomy reflects the male psychology just described. Thus, some feminists find in realism a hidden assumption of masculinity. Furthermore, the sharp distinction that realists draw between international politics (anarchic) and domestic politics (ordered) parallels the distinction in gender roles between the public (masculine) and private (feminine) spheres. Thus, realism constructs IR as a man's world, above and beyond the fact that most participants are male.

By contrast, an international system based on *feminine* principles might give greater importance to the *interdependence* of states than to their autonomy. It would stress the responsibility of people to care for each other with less regard for the abstractions called borders and states. In the struggle between the principles of human rights and of sovereignty (noninterference in internal affairs), human rights would clearly receive priority. In the choice of forms of leverage when conflicts arise between states, violence might be less prevalent. The concept of national security might be based on common security (see pp. 104–108) rather than narrow self-interest.

An essentialist feminist reconceptualization of IR also calls into question the realist preoccupation with the interstate level of analysis. The interstate level presumes that the logic of war itself is autonomous and can be separated from other social relationships such as economics, domestic politics, sexism, racism, and so forth. A feminist standpoint, however, reveals the *connections* of these phenomena with war. It suggests new avenues for understanding war at the domestic and individual levels—underlying causes that realists largely ignore.

At the domestic level of analysis, gender relations within a society (both cross-gender and same-gender relationships among both adults and children) may be a cause of war. For example, the psychological theory just discussed suggests that societies in which fathers participate more in child rearing would produce adult males less enamored of autonomy (sovereignty). This is because more boys would grow up seeing themselves as similar to their caregiver. In fact there is some anthropological evidence that in cultures where fathers are distant from their young sons and not affectionate toward them, males are more aggressive and go to war more frequently.[22]

From this feminist standpoint, neoliberalism has gone backward from traditional liberalism, by accepting the realist assumption of separate unitary states as the important actors, and downplaying substate and transnational actors including women.

Gender in War and Peace

In addition to its emphasis on autonomy and anarchy, realism stresses military force as the key form of leverage in IR. Here, too, many essentialist feminists see in realism a hidden assumption of masculinity. They see war as not only a male occupation, but the quintessentially male occupation. In this view, men are inherently the more warlike sex and

---

[22]West, Mary Maxwell, and Melvin J. Konner. The Role of the Father: An Anthropological Perspective. In Michael E. Lamb, ed. *The Role of the Father in Child Development*. New York: Wiley-Interscience, 1976, pp. 185–216. Adorno, T. W., et al. *The Authoritarian Personality*. New York: Wiley, 1950. Alcorta, Candace Storey. Paternal Behavior and Group Competition. *Behavior Science Research* 17, 1982: 3–23. See also footnote 53 in this chapter.

Feminist theories provide explanations that often differ from both realist and liberal theories. In the case of response to aggression, such as in Kuwait and Bosnia, feminists might call attention to the importance of gender roles such as the need for state leaders to prove their manhood by standing up to the bad guys. This is connected with the male role as protector of the orderly domestic sphere (home, family, country) against the dangerous and anarchic outside world.

In the case of Kuwait, President Bush had long been criticized as being a "wimp" (an insult to his manhood), and his determination to respond to Iraq's aggression became a very personal battle with Saddam Hussein. A key moment in Bush's decision process was said to be when Britain's prime minister, Margaret Thatcher—a woman—urged him to act firmly, saying, "Don't go all wobbly on us, George." Perhaps, by this line of reasoning, the key difference in the response to Bosnia versus Kuwait was that by the time of the Bosnian war, Thatcher was no longer the British prime minister. Thus Bush did not have to prove his manhood.

women the more peaceful. Thus, although realism may accurately portray the importance of war and military force in IR as we now know it, this merely reflects the male domination of the international sphere to date—not a necessary, eternal, or inescapable logic of relations among states.[23]

Essentialist feminists find plenty of evidence to support the idea of war as a masculine pursuit. Anthropologists have found that in virtually all hunter-gatherer cultures it is the males who engage in warfare, despite the enormous diversity of those cultures in so many other ways. Historically, as well, warfare in agrarian and industrial societies has continued as an almost exclusively male pursuit. (Of course, so were voting and participation in domestic politics for most of history, yet feminists would hardly call those activities essentially masculine.)

One strong piece of evidence linking war to masculinity is that levels of male sex hormones (primarily testosterone) are correlated with aggressive behavior. Biologists have found this correlation in rats, apes, humans, and other animals. (Some recent studies have suggested that aggressive behavior and social relations also "feed back" to affect hormones.) Although complex behaviors such as aggression and war cannot be said to be biologically *driven* in any simple sense, it appears that males more than females may be biologically (not just culturally) *adapted* to engage in such behaviors under certain circumstances (and when they choose to do so).

Even for some feminists who see gender differences as strictly cultural and not biological at all, war has been seen as an essentially masculine construction. In one theory, for example, war may fill a void left for men by their inability to give birth; war provides a

---

[23]Elshtain, Jean Bethke, and Sheila Tobias, eds. *Women, Militarism, and War: Essays in History, Politics, and Social Theory.* Lanham, MD: University Press of America, 1989. Cock, Jacklyn. *Colonels and Cadres: War and Gender in South Africa.* New York: Oxford University Press, 1992.

meaning to life and gives men an opportunity through heroism to transcend their individual isolation and overcome their fear of death.[24]

By contrast, women are usually portrayed by essentialist feminists as more peaceful creatures than men—whether because of biology, culture, or (most likely) both. These feminists emphasize women's unique abilities and contributions as *peacemakers*. They stress women's roles as *mothers* and potential mothers. Because of such caregiving roles, women are presumed to be more likely than men to oppose war and more likely to find alternatives to violence in resolving conflicts.[25]

Biologically, there is no firm evidence connecting women's caregiving functions (pregnancy and nursing) with any particular kinds of behavior such as reconciliation or nonviolence. (Perhaps biologists have studied female hormones less intensively than male ones.) The strongest biological basis for a peacemaking role would seem to be women's low levels of testosterone. In anthropology, too, the evidence on women's role as peacemakers in hunter-gatherer societies is also less clear than that on men as warmakers. The role of women varies considerably from one society to another. Although they rarely take part in combat, women sometimes provide logistical support to male warriors and sometimes help to drive the men into a war frenzy by dancing, singing, and other activities supportive of a war effort. Yet in other hunter-gatherer societies, women restrain the men from war or play special roles as mediators in bringing wars to an end. For instance, women may walk in front of the men to an enemy village to show that the men intend to make peace.

The idea of women as peacemakers has a long history (or as some prefer to say, "herstory"). In ancient Athens the playwright Aristophanes speculated about how women might end the unpopular Peloponnesian War with Sparta, then in progress.[26] In the play, a young woman named Lysistrata organizes the Athenian and Spartan women to withhold sex from the men until the latter stop the war. In short order, the men come to their senses and make peace.

Women have formed their own organizations to work for peace on many occasions. In 1852, *Sisterly Voices* was published as a newsletter for women's peace societies. Bertha von Suttner, the author of *Lay Down Your Arms!* in 1892, persuaded Alfred Nobel to create the Nobel peace prize (which Suttner won in 1905). During World War I, in 1915, Jane Addams and other feminists convened an international women's peace conference at the Hague. The Women's Peace Party (now called the Women's International League for Peace and Freedom) was founded there.[27]

After World War I, the *suffrage* movement won the right for women to vote. Essentialist feminists thought that women would vote for peace and against war, changing the

---

[24]Hartsock, Nancy C. M. Masculinity, Heroism, and the Making of War. In Adrienne Harris and Ynestra King, eds. *Rocking the Ship of State: Toward a Feminist Peace Politics*. Boulder, CO: Westview, 1989, pp. 133–52.

[25]Woolf, Virginia. *Three Guineas*. London: Hogarth, 1977 [1938]. Pierson, Ruth Roach. *Women and Peace: Theoretical, Historical and Practical Perspectives*. London: Croom Helm, 1987. Burguier, M. K. Feminist Approaches to Peace: Another Step for Peace Studies. *Millennium* 19 (1), 1990: 1–18. Brock-Utne, Birgit. *Educating for Peace: A Feminist Perspective*. New York: Pergamon Press, 1985. Reardon, Betty. *Sexism and the War System*. New York: Teachers College Press, 1985. Di Leonardo, Micaela. Morals, Mothers, and Militarism: Antimilitarism and Feminist Theory [review essay]. *Feminist Studies* 11, 1985: 599–617.

[26]Aristophanes. *Lysistrata*. Edited by Jeffrey Henderson. New York: Oxford University Press, 1987.

[27]Degen, Marie Louise. *The History of the Woman's Peace Party*. New York: Burt Franklin Reprints [1939 edition, Johns Hopkins University Press], 1974.

Mother demonstrates against U.S. intervention in the Persian Gulf, 1990. Essentialist feminists see women as inherently less warlike than men and more adept at making peace.

nature of foreign policy. But this did not happen; women generally voted like their husbands. Similarly, decades later when women participated in liberation struggles against colonialism in the third world, some feminists thought such participation would lead to different kinds of foreign policies in the newly independent countries, but in general such changes did not materialize (partly because women were often pushed aside from political power after the revolutions).

Recently, however, U.S. public opinion on foreign policy issues has partially vindicated essentialist feminists. A **gender gap** in polls shows women to be about ten percentage points lower than men on average in their support for military actions (including the Gulf War). This gender gap has been growing over time and has begun to translate into distinctly different average female and male voting patterns.

Meanwhile, feminists in recent decades have continued to organize women's peace organizations. In the 1960s, groups like Women Strike for Peace and Another Mother for Peace opposed nuclear testing and the Vietnam War.[28] The United Nations Decade for Women in the 1970s developed the theme of women and peace.[29] In the 1980s, Women's Action for Nuclear Disarmament (WAND) opposed the nuclear arms buildup.

[28]Swerdlow, Amy. Pure Milk, Not Poison: Women Strike for Peace and the Test Ban Treaty of 1963. In Harris and King, eds. *Rocking the Ship of State* (see footnote 24 in this chapter), pp. 225–37.

[29]Stephenson, Carolyn M. Feminism, Pacifism, Nationalism, and the United Nations Decade for Women. In Judith Stiehm, ed. *Women and Men's Wars*. Oxford: Pergamon Press, 1983, pp. 341–48.

In the 1980s, British women besieged the **Greenham Common** air base, where U.S. nuclear cruise missiles were being deployed.[30] The Greenham women created feminist symbolism designed to contrast with the masculine war-culture of the air base. For instance, they wove into the base perimeter fence various objects representing things they would lose in a nuclear war (such as pictures of loved ones). These creative tactics captured public attention and led to a similar (but smaller) encampment in Seneca Falls, New York. Through such actions, essentialist feminists have tried to begin developing a feminist theory and practice of international relations that would provide an alternative to the masculine theory and practice of realism.

The motto of UNESCO is "Since war begins in the minds of men, it is in the minds of men that the foundations for peace should be sought." For essentialist feminists, war does indeed begin in the minds of men but the foundations for peace would better be sought in the minds of women.

Women in IR

Liberal feminists are skeptical of these essentialist critiques of realism. They believe that when women are allowed to participate in IR, they play the game basically the same way men do, and with similar results. They think that women can practice realism—based on autonomy, sovereignty, anarchy, territory, military force, and all the rest—just as well as men can. Liberal feminists therefore tend to reject the critique of realism as masculine. (In practice many feminists draw on both essentialist and liberal views in various proportions.)

Liberal feminism focuses on the integration of women into the overwhelmingly male preserves of foreign policy making and the military. In most states these occupations are typically at least 90 percent male. For instance, in the 1980s the world's diplomatic missions to the UN overall were 91 percent male. The U.S. military, even with one of the highest proportions of women anywhere in the world, is still almost 90 percent male.

For liberal feminists, the main effect of this gender imbalance on the nature of IR—that is, apart from the effects that such discrimination has on the status of women—is to waste talent. Inasmuch as liberal feminists think that women have the same capabilities as men, the inclusion of women in traditionally male occupations (from state leader to foot soldier) would bring additional capable individuals into those areas. Gender equality would thus increase national capabilities by giving the state a better overall pool of diplomats, generals, soldiers, and politicians.

In support of their argument that, on average, women handle power just as men do, liberal feminists point to the many examples of women who have served in such positions. There is no distinctly feminine feature of their behavior in office that distinguishes these leaders from their male counterparts. Rather, they have been quite diverse in character and policy. Of course, there is an unavoidable weakness in this line of argument, in that women in traditionally male roles may have been selected (or self-selected) on the basis of their suitability to such roles: they may not act the way "average" women would act.

---

[30]Kirk, Gwyn. Our Greenham Common: Feminism and Nonviolence. In Harris and King, eds. *Rocking the Ship of State* (see footnote 24 in this chapter), pp. 115–30.

Even with this caveat, it is notable that *female state leaders* do not appear to be any more peaceful, any more oriented to nonviolent leverage in international conflicts, or any less committed to state sovereignty and territorial integrity than are male leaders. It has even been suggested that women in power tend to be more masculine in policy—in particular, *more* warlike—to compensate for being females in traditionally male roles. However, liberal feminists might dispute this assertion as well as the claim that women leaders are *less* warlike.

Only one female has been the top leader of a great power this century—Britain's Margaret Thatcher in the 1980s. She went to war in 1982 to recover the Falkland Islands from Argentina (at issue were sovereignty and territorial integrity). Among middle powers, Indira Gandhi likewise led India in war against Pakistan in 1971, as did Israel's Golda Meir against Egypt and Syria in 1973. But Benazir Bhutto of Pakistan and Corazón Aquino of the Philippines both struggled to control their own military forces in the late 1980s (Aquino survived seven coup attempts). Turkey's Tansu Çiller prosecuted a harsh war to suppress Kurdish rebels in the mid-1990s. But Violetta Chamorro of Nicaragua kept the peace between factions that had fought a brutal civil war in the 1980s. The president of Sri Lanka and her mother, the prime minister, tried to make peace with separatist rebels, but with mixed success. Other states, such as Norway and Iceland, have had female leaders at times when war and peace were not major political issues in those countries. Overall, women state leaders, like men, seem capable of leading in war or in peace as circumstances demand.[31]

Within the United States foreign policy establishment, the record of women leaders similarly does not show any particular soft or hard tendency relative to their male counterparts. For example, U.N. ambassador Madeleine Albright was considered one of the tougher foreign policy makers in the Clinton administration, as was her predecessor Jeane Kirkpatrick in the Reagan administration (both women are IR professors when not in government). U.S. trade representative Carla Hills (in the Bush administration) was a pragmatic negotiator who struck complex trade deals with other states. Senator Nancy Kassebaum (also a Republican) was considered a voice for compassion, as she led efforts to increase humanitarian aid to Somalia in 1992.

In the U.S. Congress, it is hard to compare men's and women's voting records on foreign policy issues because there have been so few women. The U.S. Senate (which approves treaties and foreign policy appointments) was 98 to 99 percent male until 1992, when it dropped to 94 percent male. Women have never chaired the key foreign policy committees (Armed Services and Foreign Relations) in the Senate or House—although Patricia Schroeder was the second-ranking member of the House Armed Services Committee in 1993–1994 and played a major (avowedly feminist) role in Congress on military policy.

In addition to women state leaders and other female foreign policy makers, *women in military forces* also break from traditional gender roles in IR. Liberal feminists believe that women soldiers, like women politicians, have a range of skills and abilities comparable to

[31]Nelson, Barbara J., and Najma Chowdhury, eds. *Women and Politics Worldwide*. New Haven: Yale University Press, 1994. Genovese, Michael A., ed. *Women as National Leaders: The Political Performance of Women as Heads of Government*. Thousand Oaks, CA: SAGE Publications, Inc., 1993. McGlen, Nancy E., and Meredith Reid Sarkees. *Women in Foreign Policy: The Insiders*. New York: Routledge, 1993.

men's. Again the main effect of including more women would be to improve the overall quality of military forces.[32]

The evidence on women soldiers, like that on women political leaders, seems to support liberal feminists. In the U.S. military in the early 1990s there were about 200,000 women soldiers (11 percent of the total) and over 1 million women veterans. Pentagon studies have concluded that women perform comparably to men in a variety of military roles from logistical and medical support to training and command. Women have had similar success in other countries that have allowed them into the military (or, in a few cases, drafted them into it).

However, although women have served with distinction in military forces, they have been excluded from *combat roles* in almost all those forces. (There is a myth that women in the Israeli army serve in combat infantry roles; this is not true, although women *are* drafted in Israel.) In some countries military women are limited to traditional female roles such as nurses and typists. Even where women are allowed into nontraditional positions such as mechanics and pilots (as in the United States), most women remain in the traditional roles. And certain jobs still remain off-limits; for instance, women cannot serve on U.S. submarines or in combat infantry. Because of these exclusions, there are only a few cases from which to judge women's abilities in combat.

Those cases include historical examples of individual women who served in combat (sometimes disguised as men, sometimes not). In the fifteenth century, Joan of Arc rallied French soldiers to defeat England, turning the tide of the Hundred Years' War. (The English burned her at the stake as a witch after capturing her.) More recent experiences include several in which U.S. women soldiers found themselves in combat (present-day mobile tactics and fluid front lines make it hard to separate combat from support roles). Female U.S. soldiers were drawn into a battle during the Panama invasion of 1989. Women helicopter pilots flew in combat zones during the Gulf War of 1991, in which tens of thousands of U.S. women served, 13 were killed, and 2 were captured as POWs. In 1995 women began serving aboard one U.S. aircraft carrier and began flying in some combat roles in the navy. Women have also repeatedly served in combat in rebel forces fighting *guerrilla* wars in Vietnam, Nicaragua, and elsewhere. The Peruvian "Shining Path" movement included women fighters, as did terrorist factions in Germany and Italy in recent decades. All these cases suggest that (at least some) women are able to hold their own in combat.

In fact, the main reason that military forces exclude women from combat has nothing to do with their performance. Rather, it is fear about what effect their presence might have on the male soldiers, whose discipline and loyalty have traditionally been thought to depend on male bonding. (A similar rationale was given for racial segregation in U.S. military forces before 1948 and for the exclusion of gay men and lesbians in the 1980s and 1990s.) Liberal feminists reject such arguments, and argue that group bonding in military units does not depend on gender segregation. However, it is clear that all-male traditions

---

[32]Addis, Elisabetta, Valerie E. Russo, and Lorenza Ebesta, eds. *Women Soldiers: Images and Realities*. New York: St. Martin's Press, 1994. Howes, Ruth, and Michael Stevenson, eds. *Women and the Use of Military Force*. Boulder, CO: Lynne Rienner, 1993. Schneider, Dorothy, and Carl J. Schneider. *Sound Off! American Military Women Speak Out*. New York: Paragon, 1992. Stiehm, Judith Hicks. *Arms and the Enlisted Woman*. Philadelphia: Temple University Press, 1989. Stiehm, Judith, ed. *Women and Men's Wars*. Oxford: Pergamon Press, 1983. Isaksson, Eva, ed. *Women and the Military System*. New York: St. Martin's Press, 1988.

Women soldiers have performed as well as men in military tasks, as predicted by liberal feminists. But in state armies, women are barred from almost all infantry combat units worldwide. These Kurdish guerrillas from Turkey (August 1991) are the exception.

in military forces will not adapt painlessly to the presence of women. Female soldiers do face sexual harassment from males. The U.S. secretary of the navy had to resign after male navy pilots sexually assaulted passing women at the 1991 "Tailhook" aviators' convention in Las Vegas. A 1992 Pentagon survey reported that about one-third of women soldiers experience some form of verbal or physical sexual harassment or abuse. (Such figures do not show, however, whether sexual harassment is more common in the military than in other sectors of society.)

Another reason given for excluding women from combat is that they are more vulnerable if taken as POWs (a point underscored by Joan of Arc's fate). Again liberal feminists disagree. All POWs are vulnerable, and both men and women POWs can be sexually abused. In the Gulf War, the two U.S. female POWs were sexually abused whereas the 19 male POWs apparently were not. But the male POWs, and not the females, received severe electric shocks, beatings, and other physical abuse.

Thus, liberal feminists reject the argument that women bring uniquely feminine assets or liabilities to foreign and military affairs. They do not critique realism as essentially masculine in nature but do criticize state practices that exclude women from participation in international politics and war.

Balancing the Arguments

The arguments of essentialist and liberal feminists may seem totally at odds. Essentialist feminists argue that realism reflects a masculine perception of social relations, whereas liberal feminists think that women can be just as realist as men. Liberal feminists believe that female participation in foreign policy and the military would enhance state capabilities, but essentialists think women's unique abilities can be put to better use in transforming (feminizing) the entire system of international relations rather than in trying to play men's games.

The evidence in favor of both positions can be reconciled to a large extent by bearing in mind that the character and ability of an individual is not the same as that of his or her group. Rather, the qualities of individuals follow a bell curve distribution, with many people clustered in the middle and fewer people very high or low on some dimension. (Relevant dimensions include warlike tendencies or the value placed on autonomy and sovereignty, for example.)

Gender differences posited by essentialists mean that one bell curve is shifted from the other, even though the two may still overlap quite a bit (see Figure 3.1). To take a simple example, a few women are physically larger than almost all men, and a few men smaller than almost all women. But on average men are somewhat larger than women. On different dimensions of capability, the women's curve is above the men's on average, but there is still much overlap.

Liberal feminist arguments emphasize the overlap of the two bell curves. They are right to say that individual women—*most* women on most relevant dimensions—are well within the male curve and thus can perform equally with the men. Indeed, it is likely that women in nontraditional gender roles will perform better than their male counterparts, because presumably women who self-select into such roles (like joining the military) are near the high end of the female bell curve, whereas the men are closer to the middle of the male curve (because more of them join).

Similarly, women who become state leaders are presumably more adept at foreign policy making than most women (or men), whether or not the foreign policy process as we know it (and as realists describe it) is more compatible with the average man's way of

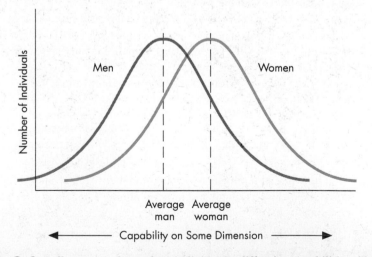

FIGURE 3.1 Bell curves show that individuals differ in capabilities like physical strength or peacemaking ability. Although the genders differ on average, for most individuals (in the area of overlap) such differences do not come into play. Liberal feminists emphasize the area where the curves overlap; essentialist feminists emphasize the overall group differences.

thinking than with the average woman's. Political processes probably tend to select women at the high end of the curve for foreign policy skills.

Essentialist feminists are more interested in the shift in the two bell curves, not their overlap. On average, in this perspective, women tend to see international relations somewhat differently than men do. So, although *individuals* selected to participate in foreign policy and the military may not differ from their male counterparts, women as a group differ. Women voters display different concerns regarding IR than men (the gender gap in opinion polls and voting patterns).

By this logic, then, profound differences in IR—and a shift away from the utility of realism in explaining state behavior—would occur only if many women participated in key foreign policy positions. That is, a *few* women politicians or women soldiers do not change the masculine foundations of IR, according to this view. Women foreign policy makers today are surrounded by males (advisors, military officers, political leaders, and foreign state leaders).

But a world in which *most* politicians or soldiers were female might be a different story. Then, instead of women being selected for their ability to fit into men's games, the rules of the game might themselves change to reflect the fact that "average" women would be the main actors in IR roles. Of course, these theories of essentialist feminists have never been tested, because women have never attained predominance in foreign policy making in any country—much less in the international system as a whole.

Overall, then, the essentialist feminist critique of realism is intriguing but hard to demonstrate empirically. It may be, as this critique claims, that realism and neoliberalism alike put too much emphasis on the aspects of IR that fit a typical masculine view of the world—particularly autonomy, sovereignty, and anarchy. If so, realism and neoliberalism miss many important aspects that could help provide fuller and more accurate explanations of why events occur the way they do in IR. But it is hard to test feminist theories against realism and neoliberalism because the empirical reality is that the international arena is populated predominantly by males (a poor experimental design for testing gender effects).

In addition to liberal and essentialist strands of feminism, the third strand, postmodern feminism, is connected with the rise of postmodernism in the social sciences.

❖ POSTMODERNISM

Postmodernism, like feminism, is a broad approach to scholarship that has left its mark on various academic disciplines, especially the study of literature. Because of their literary roots, postmodernists pay special attention to *texts* and to *discourses*—how people talk and write about their subject (IR).[33] Postmodern critiques of realism thus center on analyzing realists' words and arguments.[34]

---

[33]Rosenau, Pauline Marie. *Post-Modernism and the Social Sciences: Insights, Inroads, and Intrusions.* Princeton: Princeton University Press, 1992.

[34]Ashley, Richard K., and R. B. J. Walker. Speaking the Language of Exile: Dissident Thought in International Studies [Introduction to special issue]. *International Studies Quarterly* 34 (3), 1990: 259–68. Wendt, Alexander. Anarchy Is What States Make of It: The Social Construction of Power Politics. *International Organization* 46 (2), 1992: 391–426. Lapid, Yosef. The Third Debate: On the Prospects of International Theory in a Post-Positivist Era. *International Studies Quarterly* 33 (3), 1989: 235–54. Der Derian, James. *On Diplomacy: A Geneology of Western Estrangement.* New York: Basil Blackwell, 1987.

Deconstructing Realism

A central idea of postmodernism is that there is no single, objective reality but a multiplicity of experiences and perspectives that defy easy categorization. For this reason, postmodernism itself is difficult to present in a simple or categorical way. This section will merely convey some important postmodern themes, necessarily oversimplified, and show how postmodernism can help illuminate some problems of realism.

From a postmodern perspective, realism cannot justify its claim that states are the central actors in IR and that states operate as unitary actors with coherent sets of objective interests (which they pursue through international power politics). Postmodern critics of realism see nothing objective about state interests, and certainly nothing universal (in that one set of values or interests applies to all states).

More fundamentally, postmodernism calls into question the whole notion of states as actors. As was mentioned in Chapter 1, states have no tangible reality; they are "fictions" that we (as scholars and citizens) construct to make sense of the actions of large numbers of individuals. For postmodernists, the stories told about the actions and policies of states are just that—stories. From this perspective, it is an arbitrary distinction that leads bookstores to put spy novels on the fiction shelf whereas biographies and histories go on the nonfiction shelf. All are forms of discourse, none are objective realities, and all are filtered through an interpretive process that distorts the actual experiences of those involved.[35]

Contrary to realism's claim that states are unitary actors, postmodernists see multiple realities and experiences lurking below the surface of the fictional entities that realists construct (states). The Soviet Union, for example, was treated by realists as a single actor with a single set of objective interests. Indeed, it was considered the second most important actor in the world. Realists were amazed and embarrassed when the Soviet Union split into 15 pieces, each containing its own fractious groups and elements. It became clear that the "unitary state" called the Soviet Union had masked (and let realists ignore) the divergent experiences of constituent republics, ethnic groups, and individuals.

Postmodernists seek to "deconstruct" such constructions as states, the international system, and the associated stories and arguments (texts and discourses) with which realists portray the nature of international relations. To *deconstruct* a text—a term borrowed from literary criticism—means to tease apart the words in order to reveal hidden meanings, looking especially for what might be omitted from the text, or included only implicitly. The hidden meanings not explicitly addressed in the text are often called the **subtext** (written "between the lines").[36]

What are the hidden assumptions and meanings (subtext) in the stories realists tell about IR? What does realism omit from its accounts of IR? We have just discussed one major omission—women and gender. Furthermore, in its emphasis on states, realism omits the roles of individuals, domestic politics, economic classes, MNCs, and other non-

[35]Onuf, Nicholas Greenwood. *World of Our Making: Rules and Rule in Social Theory and International Relations.* Columbia: University of South Carolina Press, 1989.

[36]Campbell, David. *Politics Without Principle: Sovereignty, Ethics, and the Narratives of the Gulf War.* Boulder, CO: Lynne Rienner, 1993. Stephanson, Anders. *Kennan and the Art of Foreign Policy.* Cambridge, MA: Harvard University Press, 1992. Chaloupka, William. *Knowing Nukes: The Politics and Culture of the Atom.* Minneapolis: University of Minnesota Press, 1992.

state actors. In its focus on the great powers, realism omits the experiences of third-world countries. In its attention to military forms of leverage, it omits the roles of various non-military forms of leverage.

Realism focuses so narrowly because its aim is to reduce IR down to a simple, coherent model. The model is claimed to be objective, universal, and accurate. To postmodernists the realist model is none of these things: it is a biased model that creates a narrow and one-sided story for the purpose of promoting the interests of powerful actors. Postmodernists seek to destroy this model along with any other model (including neoliberalism) that tries to represent IR in simple objective categories. Postmodernists instead want to celebrate the diversity of experiences that make up IR without needing to make sense of them by simplifying and categorizing.[37]

Postmodern Feminism

One line of criticism directed at realism combines feminism and postmodernism.[38] This approach seeks to deconstruct realism with the specific aim of uncovering the pervasive hidden influences of gender in IR while showing how arbitrary the construction of gender roles is. Feminist postmodernists agree with essentialists that realism carries hidden meanings about gender roles but deny that there is any fixed inherent meaning (essence) in either male or female genders. Rather, feminist postmodernists seek to look at the interplay of gender and power in a more open-ended way. Postmodern feminists criticize liberal feminists for trying merely to integrate women into traditional structures of war and foreign policy. They criticize essentialists as well, for glorifying traditional feminine virtues.

In studying war, postmodern feminists have challenged the archetypes of the (male) "just warrior" and the (female) "beautiful soul." They argue that women are not just passive bystanders or victims in war, but active participants in a system of warfare tied to both male and female identities. In that system women act not only as nurses and journalists at the "front" but as mothers, wives, and girlfriends on the "home front." World War II is the story of women back home in Colorado as much as of men on the front lines in Europe.[39] Stories of military forces should not omit the roles of prostitutes living near military bases, nor should stories of diplomacy omit the roles of diplomats' wives.[40]

---

[37]Walker, R. B. J., and Saul H. Mendlovitz, eds. Contending Sovereignties: Redefining Political Community. Boulder, CO: Lynne Rienner, 1990. Walker, R. B. J. Inside/Outside: International Relations as Political Theory. New York: Cambridge University Press, 1992. Weber, Cynthia. Simulating Sovereignty: Intervention, the State and Symbolic Exchange. New York: Cambridge University Press, 1995. Sjolander, Claire Turenne, and Wayne S. Cox, eds. Beyond Positivism: Critical Reflections on International Relations. Boulder, CO: Lynne Rienner, 1994. George, Jim. Discourses of Global Politics: A Critical (Re)Introduction to International Relations. Boulder, CO: Lynne Rienner, 1994.

[38]Peterson, V. Spike, ed. Gendered States: Feminist (Re)Visions of International Relations Theory. Boulder, CO: Lynne Rienner, 1992. Sylvester, Christine. Feminist Theory and International Relations in a Postmodern Era. New York: Cambridge University Press. 1994.

[39]Elshtain, Jean Bethke. Women and War. New York: Basic Books: 1987. Braybon, Gail, and Penny Summerfield. Out of the Cage: Women's Experiences in Two World Wars. New York: Pandora, 1987.

[40]Enloe, Cynthia. Bananas, Beaches, and Bases: Making Feminist Sense of International Politics. Berkeley: University of California Press, 1989. Enloe, Cynthia. Does Khaki Become You?: The Militarization of Women's Lives. Boston: South End Press, 1983.

Postmodern feminists reject not only realism but also some of the alternative approaches—such as the just war doctrine (see pp. 301–302), which emphasizes the protection of women and other noncombatants. This doctrine is considered too abstract—a set of concepts and rules that does not do justice to the richness of each historical context and the varied roles of individual men and women within it.[41]

Postmodern feminists have tried to deconstruct the language of realism, especially where it reflects influences of gender and sex. For instance, the first atomic bombs had male gender (they were named "Fat Man" and "Little Boy"); the coded telegram informing Washington, DC, that the first test bomb had worked said simply, "It's a boy" (presumably being born a girl would have indicated a failure). The plane that dropped the atomic bomb on Hiroshima (the *Enola Gay*) had female gender; it was named after the pilot's mother. Likewise the French atom-bomb test sites in the South Pacific were all given women's names.[42] Similarly, pilots have pasted pinup photos of nude women onto conventional bombs before dropping them.

Realism and liberalism ignore these sexual images in weaponry, limiting themselves to such issues as a weapon's explosive power, its range, and other technical information about its use as state leverage. But if sexual drives enter (perhaps unconsciously) into decisions about whether and when to use bombs or other military forces, then realism and liberalism cannot adequately explain those decisions.[43] Postmodernism thus reveals another reality (the sexual gratification of male politicians and soldiers), which competes with the realities of realism and neoliberalism, with their focus on maximizing national interests (narrowly or broadly construed). By radically shifting the focus and approach of IR scholarship, postmodernists thus hope to increase our understanding of IR in general and of the notion of rationality in particular.

These efforts find sex and gender all over the subtext of realism. For example, the terms *power* and *potency* refer to both state capability and male virility. Military force depends on phallic objects—weapons designed to shoot projectiles, penetrate targets, and explode. In basic training, men chant: "This is my rifle [holding up rifle], this is my gun [pointing to crotch]; one's for killing, the other's for fun."[44] Female models are hired to market tanks, helicopter missiles, and other "potent" weapons to male procurement officers at international military trade shows.[45] The phallic character of weapons has seemingly persisted even as technology has evolved—from spears to guns to missiles. Nuclear weapons are also repeatedly spoken of in sexual terms, perhaps due to their great "potency."

An example of how such hidden sexual meanings can affect foreign policy decision making is given by peace activist Helen Caldicott in her book *Missile Envy*.[46] She tells how Pentagon officials got Congress to approve bigger military budgets during the Cold

---

[41]Elshtain. *Women and War* (see footnote 39 in this chapter). Ruddick, Sara. *Maternal Thinking: Towards a Politics of Peace*. London: The Women's Press, 1989.

[42]Cohn, Carol. Sex and Death in the Rational World of Defense Intellectuals. *Signs* 12, 1987: 687–718.

[43]Mansfield, Sue. *The Gestalts of War: An Inquiry into Its Origins and Meanings as a Social Institution*. New York: Dial, 1982.

[44]Dyer, Gwynne. *War*. New York: Crown, 1985.

[45]Center for Defense Information [Washington, DC]. "Weapons Bazaar" [slide show], mid-1980s.

[46]Caldicott, Helen. *Missile Envy: The Arms Race and Nuclear War*. Revised edition. New York: Bantam, 1986.

Feminist postmodernists try to reveal hidden subtexts connecting gender with IR, such as the roles of sex and death in the constructions of masculinity by U.S. airmen in England, April 1944.

War. They painted scale models of missiles—red for the Soviet Red Army and blue for the U.S. Air Force—and brought them along to congressional hearings. Although the Soviet missiles were larger and carried heavier payloads, the smaller U.S. missiles were more accurate. But the subtext of the painted scale models seemed to be: "Look! Their red ones are bigger than our blue ones!" Certainly realism and neoliberalism—with their emphasis on the rational pursuit of state interests—do not even *try* to understand such effects on the foreign policy decisions of male congressional committee members.

In sum, through these various deconstructions, postmodernists deliberately *undermine* the realist foundations of IR. They seek to replace an orderly picture with a hall of mirrors in which multiple realities coexist—realities of rationality and power side by side with those of love and interdependence and those of gender and sexuality. They seek to better understand IR by listening to voices silenced by power—the voices of women, of oppressed ethnic minorities, and of others whose interests and actions are not done justice by states or by theories of IR that focus exclusively on states. These postmodern efforts are controversial among IR scholars.

❖ PEACE STUDIES

Another approach of growing importance which challenges some fundamental concepts behind both realism and liberalism is peace studies. Many colleges have recently created interdisciplinary peace studies programs through which scholars and students organize discussions and courses about peace.[47] Typically such programs include not only political scientists but psychologists who have studied conflict, physicists who have studied nuclear weapons, religious scholars who have studied practical morality, and so forth. With these various disciplinary backgrounds, scholars of peace studies tend to be more eclectic than political scientists and much more broad-ranging in the topics they consider worthy of study in international security affairs. Since peace studies approaches differ more from realism than from liberalism, the focus here will be on critiques of realism.

Broadening the Focus

In particular, peace studies seeks to shift the focus of IR away from the interstate level of analysis and toward a broad conception of social relations (at the individual, domestic, and global levels of analysis). Peace studies connects war and peace with individual responsibility, with economic inequality, with gender relations, with cross-cultural understanding, and with other aspects of social relationships. Peace studies seeks the potentials for peace not in the transactions of state leaders but in the transformation of entire societies (through social revolution) and in transnational communities (bypassing states to connect people and groups globally, ignoring borders).[48]

Another way in which peace studies seeks to broaden the focus of inquiry is to reject the supposed objectivity of traditional (realist and liberal) approaches. Most scholars of peace studies think that a good way to gain knowledge is to participate in action—not just to sit back and observe objectively. For example, many scholars in peace studies have a theory that peace movements can influence the propensity of governments for war. And many of those scholars find that becoming participants and even leaders in such peace movements enhances their knowledge about that theory. This approach seeks to integrate theory with practice.

In addition to gaining better knowledge about their theories, peace studies scholars participate in the practice of seeking peace because they want to use their theories and knowledge to influence the world they live in. They are not interested just in describing the world as it is, but in exploring how it *should*, or could, be, and helping make it that way. The main reason for studying war and peace, in this view, is to lessen war and promote the chances for peace. This lack of objectivity is called a **normative bias** because

---

[47]Barash, David P. *Introduction to Peace Studies*. Belmont, CA: Wadsworth, 1991. Klare, Michael T., ed. *Peace and World Security Studies: A Curriculum Guide*. 6th ed. Boulder, CO: Lynne Rienner, 1994. Smoker, Paul, Ruth Davies, and Barbara Munske, eds. *A Reader in Peace Studies*. New York: Pergamon, 1990. Lopez, George A., ed. *Peace Studies: Past and Future. Annals of the American Academy of Political and Social Science*, Number 504. Newbury Park, CA: Sage, 1989.

[48]Cancian, Francesca M., and James William Gibson. *Making War/Making Peace: The Social Foundations of Violent Conflict*. Belmont, CA: Wadsworth, 1990. Galtung, Johan. *The True Worlds: A Transnational Perspective*. New York: Free Press, 1980. Rapoport, Anatol. *Peace: An Idea Whose Time Has Come*. Ann Arbor: University of Michigan Press, 1992.

scholars impose their personal norms and values on the subject.[49] Some political scientists (especially realists) dismiss peace studies because it lacks scientific objectivity about outcomes.

Scholars in peace studies are quick to respond, however, that realism itself has normative biases and makes policy prescriptions. Realists (from Sun Tzu to Henry Kissinger) even take jobs as advisors to state leaders, urging them to follow the principles of realism. Because realism's assumptions—that actors pursue only their own interests, that violence is a normal and acceptable way to achieve ends, that order is more important than justice—are debatable as objective statements of fact, they might better be seen as value statements. Realism, then, becomes more of an ideology than a theory.

Thus scholars in peace studies defend both their broader approach to the subject and their willingness to bring their own values into play when studying that subject. These characteristics of peace studies can be seen in its approach to war—the central topic in international security affairs.

War and Militarism

Most scholars in peace studies reject realism's willingness to treat war as normal, or its willingness to be objective about the merits of war or peace. Peace studies resonates with Benjamin Franklin's observation that "there never was a good war or a bad peace."[50] In particular, peace studies scholars object to realism's willingness to treat nuclear weapons as just another instrument of state military power. In general, peace studies tries to call into question the nature of war and its role in society.

Peace studies scholars argue that war is not just a natural expression of power, but one closely tied to militarism in (some) cultures.[51] **Militarism** is the glorification of war, military force, and violence through TV, films, books, political speeches, toys, games, sports, and other such avenues. Militarism also refers to the structuring of society around war—for example, the dominant role of a military-industrial complex in a national economy, the dominance of national security issues in domestic politics, and so forth. Militarism is thought to underlie the propensity of political leaders to use military force.

Historically, militarism has had a profound influence on the evolution of societies. War has often been glorified as a "manly" enterprise that refreshes and ennobles the human spirit (especially before World War I, which changed that perspective). Even Mahatma Gandhi (discussed later) conceded that "war is an unmitigated evil. But it certainly does one good thing. It drives away fear and brings bravery to the surface."[52] Not only evil acts but also exemplary acts of humanity are brought forth by war—sacrifice, honor, courage, altruism on behalf of loved ones, and bonding with a community larger than oneself.

[49]Brown, Chris. *International Relations Theory: New Normative Approaches*. New York: Columbia University Press, 1993.

[50]Letter to Josiah Quincy, Sept. 11, 1773.

[51]Boulding, Elise, ed. *New Agendas for Peace Research: Conflict and Security Reexamined*. Boulder, CO: Lynne Rienner, 1992.

[52]Gandhi, Mohandas K. *Non-Violence in Peace and War*. Volume 1. New York: Garland, 1972 [1942], p. 270.

Militarism in a culture, or the lack thereof, can influence foreign policy. In Japan, a deeply antimilitaristic culture since World War II, even the deployment of these peacekeeping troops to Cambodia in 1992 aroused public suspicion.

The culture of modern states—and of realism—celebrates and rewards these qualities of soldiers, just as hunter-gatherer cultures create rituals and rewards to induce participation in warfare. We have holidays in honor of warriors, provide them (or their survivors) with veterans' benefits, and bury them in special cemeteries where their individual identities are symbolically submerged into a larger collective identity. Because militarism seems so pervasive and so strongly associated with the state, many scholars in peace studies question whether the nature of states themselves must change before lasting peace will be possible. In this regard peace studies differs from both realism and neoliberalism.

Even in the United States—generally sheltered from the world's wars—the militarization of culture is pervasive. In the 1950s children hid under school desks to practice for a nuclear attack. In the 1960s and 1970s, the Vietnam War dominated the experiences of young people. In the 1980s fear of nuclear war returned, and in 1991 came the Gulf War. Scholars in peace studies have made a connection between U.S. uses of military force and the American gun mania, high murder rate, Wild West myths, television violence, and other aspects of American life indicating that violence is socially acceptable.

Peace studies seeks examples of less-militarized cultures, to show that realism's emphasis on military force is not universal or necessary. For instance, Costa Rica has no army (just lightly armed police) despite the presence of military conflicts in both of Costa Rica's neighbors (Nicaragua and Panama) in the 1980s. Japanese culture since World War II has developed strong norms against war and violence. Public opinion, even more than

Japan's constitution, prevents political leaders from considering military force a viable instrument of foreign policy.

Anthropologists have tried to connect the domestic characteristics of hunter-gatherer societies with their external propensity to engage in warfare. There is some evidence that war occurs more frequently in societies with internal inequalities (especially gender inequality), with harsh childrearing practices, and with fathers who are absent from child rearing. By contrast, relatively peaceful societies are more likely to have open decision-making processes, relative gender equality, and permissive and affectionate child-rearing practices.[53] But all these societal attributes could as well be *effects* of war as causes. And as will be noted in Chapter 5, virtually all kinds of society seem to have the potential for warfare under some conditions, so distinctions such as "warlike" are only relative.

Positive Peace

Just as war is seen in peace studies as a pervasive aspect of society as a whole, so can peace be reconceptualized in a broader way.[54] According to peace studies scholars, peace should be defined as more than just the absence of war. The mere absence of war does not guarantee that war will not recur. As Kant pointed out, each peace treaty ending a European great-power war in the sixteenth through eighteenth centuries merely set the stage for the next war. Nor can the absence of great-power war in the Cold War be considered true peace: third-world proxy wars killed millions of people while a relentless arms race wasted vast resources. Because realism assumes the normalcy of military conflicts, it recognizes only a negative kind of peace—the temporary absence of war.

By contrast, **positive peace** refers to a peace that resolves the underlying reasons for war—peace that is not just a cease-fire but a transformation of relationships. Under positive peace, not only do state armies stop fighting each other, but they stop arming, stop forming death squads against internal protest, and reverse the economic exploitation and political oppression that scholars in peace studies believe are responsible for social conflicts that lead to war.

Proponents of the positive peace approach see broad social and economic issues—assumed by realists to be relatively unimportant—as inextricably linked with positive peace. Some scholars define poverty, hunger, and oppression as forms of violence—which they call **structural violence** because it is caused by the structure of social relations rather than by direct actions like shooting people. Structural violence in this definition kills and harms many more people each year than do war and other forms of direct political violence. Positive peace is usually defined to include the elimination of structural violence because it is considered a source of conflict and war.

In this view, negative peace that merely prevents violence may actually lock in place an unjust status quo. That injustice is epitomized in the global North-South disparity (see

---

[53]Ross, Marc Howard. A Cross-Cultural Theory of Political Conflict and Violence. *Political Psychology* 7, 1986: 427–69. Ember, Carol R. A Cross-Cultural Perspective on Sex Differences. In Ruth H. Munroe et al., eds. *Handbook of Cross-Cultural Human Development*. New York: Garland, 1980, pp. 531–80. Whiting, Beatrice B., and John W. M. Whiting. *Children of Six Cultures: A Psycho-Cultural Analysis*. Cambridge, MA: Harvard University Press, 1975.

[54]Elias, Robert, and Jennifer Turpin, eds. *Rethinking Peace*. Boulder, CO: Lynne Rienner, 1994. Forcey, Linda Rennie, ed. *Peace: Meanings, Politics, Strategies*. New York: Praeger, 1989. Kende, Istvan. The History of Peace: Concept and Organizations from the Late Middle Ages to the 1870s. *Journal of Peace Research* 26 (3), 1989: 233–47. Boulding, Kenneth E. *Stable Peace*. Austin: University of Texas Press, 1978.

Chapter 12) with its massive structural violence against the South. Thus, a narrow, negative definition of peace is seen as inadequate because it conflicts with the achievement of justice, which in turn is necessary for positive peace.

Advocates of positive peace also criticize militaristic culture. The "social construction of war"—a complex system of rules and relations that ultimately supports the existence of war—touches our lives in many ways: from children's war toys to patriotic rituals in schools; from teenagers' gender roles to military training for young men; from the taxes we pay to the sports we play. The positive peace approach seeks to change the whole system, not just one piece of it.

Positive peace encompasses a variety of approaches to social change. These include alternative mechanisms for conflict resolution to take the place of war; popular pressure on governments through peace movements and political activism; strengthening of norms against the use of violence (including the philosophy of nonviolence); the development of international or global identity transcending national, ethnic, and religious divisions; and egalitarian relations within societies in the economic, social, and political realms (including changes in gender roles). All these topics—not considered legitimate subjects of study by realists—are put on the table for discussion by peace studies.

Many people think that positive peace would depend on overcoming ethnic conflict, racism, xenophobia, and other sources of tension between groups with different cultures, languages, and religions—tensions that may contribute to war and violence (see "Ethnic Conflict" on pp. 198–204). One approach explores travel, tourism, cultural exchanges (concerts, films), and citizen diplomacy as means of overcoming intergroup conflicts. Some decades ago, a world language called *Esperanto* was created in hopes of encouraging worldwide communication and global identity; the results have been disappointing overall. But the UN General Assembly with its simultaneous translation does serve as a kind of global town hall. It is a powerful symbol of respect for (and communication across) world cultures—at least those with statehood and a seat in the hall.

Another approach to intergroup conflict is reform in the educational system. For example, Western European countries revised textbooks after World War II to remove nationalistic excesses and promote respect for neighboring countries (see p. 202).

Positive peace is usually defined to include political equality and human rights as well. When a small ruling group or dictator holds political power, fewer checks on government violence operate than when democratic institutions exist (see pp. 161–163). And when avenues of legitimate political participation are open, citizens are less likely to turn to violence.

More controversial within peace studies is the question of whether positive peace requires that states' authority be subordinated to a **world government.**[55] The creation of a world government has long been debated by scholars and pursued by activists; many plans have been drawn up, though none have yet succeeded. Some scholars believe progress is being made (through the UN) toward the eventual emergence of a world government. Others think the idea is impractical or even undesirable (merely adding another layer of centralized control, when peace demands decentralization and freedom).

---

[55]Wooley, Wesley T. *Alternatives to Anarchy: American Supranationalism Since World War II.* Bloomington: Indiana University Press, 1988.

Peace Movements

Scholars in peace studies also study how to achieve the conditions for positive peace. Approaches vary, from building a world government to strengthening democratic governance, from redistributing wealth to strengthening spiritual communities (whether the Catholic Church or transcendental meditation). But most in peace studies share a skepticism that state leaders left to themselves would ever achieve positive peace. Rather, the practice of IR will change only as a result of pressures from individuals and groups.

The most commonly studied method of exerting such pressure is through **peace movements**—people taking to the streets in protest against war and militarism.[56] Such protests occur in many, though not all, states involved in wars. In peace studies it is believed that people all over the world want peace more than governments do. As U.S. president Eisenhower once said, "People want peace so much that one of these days governments had better get out of their way and let them have it."[57]

In addition to mass demonstrations, common *tactics* of peace movements include getting antiwar messages into the media, participating in civil disobedience (nonviolently breaking laws and inviting arrest to show one's beliefs), and occasionally organizing consumer boycotts. Favorite *targets* of peace movements include the draft, government buildings, taxes, and nuclear test sites. Like other interest groups, peace movements also participate in elections and lobbying (see pp. 153–154). And peace movements try to educate the public by spreading information about a war or arms race that the government may be suppressing or downplaying. One accomplishment of the U.S. "nuclear freeze" movement of the 1980s, for example, was to educate the public about nuclear weapons and help demystify the nuclear arms race as an issue area.

Peace activists often disagree on goals. In the U.S. peace movement since World War I an *internationalist* wing has seen international organizations (today, the UN) as the best hope for peace and has supported wars against aggression. A *pacifist* wing has opposed all wars, distrusted international organizations whose members are state governments, and favored more-radical social change to achieve positive peace.[58]

In other countries, peace movements vary greatly in their goals and character. In Japan, peace movements are extremely broad-based (enjoying wide popular support) and are pacifist in orientation (as a result of reaction against militarism before and during World War II). In Western Europe, large movements developed in the 1980s against new nuclear missiles on the continent, in Germany, Britain, and the Netherlands. In the Soviet Union and Eastern Europe during the Cold War, official state-sponsored peace groups linked international peace to the struggle against Western imperialism while unofficial peace groups linked peace to the struggle for human rights and democracy at home.

These divergent tendencies in peace movements come together at peak times in opposition to particular wars or arms races. But beyond this reactive mode of politics, peace

---

[56]Carter, April. *Peace Movements: International Protest and World Politics Since 1945.* White Plains, NY: Longman, 1992. Solo, Pam. *From Protest to Policy: Beyond the Freeze to Common Security.* Cambridge, MA: Ballinger, 1988.

[57]Eisenhower, Dwight D. *Ike's Letters to a Friend, 1941–1958.* Edited by Robert Griffith. Lawrence: University Press of Kansas, 1984.

[58]De Benedetti, Charles. *Origins of the Modern American Peace Movement, 1915–1929.* Milwood, NY: KTO Press, 1978.

Peace demonstrators play a role in many international conflicts. Here citizens of the Russian republic of Chechnya form a human chain across the republic to protest Russian army's invasion.

movements often have had trouble defining a long-term direction and agenda. Scholars of peace studies are interested in studying the successes and failures of peace movements to understand how popular influence on foreign policy can affect state decisions.

Nonviolence

A philosophy of **nonviolence,** or **pacifism,** is based on a unilateral commitment to refrain from using any violent forms of leverage in bargaining. No state today follows such a strategy; indeed, it is widely believed that in the international system as it exists a state that adopted a nonviolent philosophy would risk exploitation or conquest.[59]

Pacifism nonetheless figures prominently in debates concerning the peaceful solution of conflicts and the achievement of positive peace. Many states contain substantial numbers of citizens, often organized into popular movements, who believe that only pacifism—an ironclad commitment to renounce violence—can change the nature of IR so as to avoid future wars. As British pacifist A. J. Muste put it: "There is no way to peace. Peace is the way." Japan has a sizable pacifist movement, and pacifists have historically formed the hard core of the peace movement in the United States and Western Europe as well. Prominent U.S. pacifist groups—such as the Women's International League for Peace and Freedom (WILPF), the Fellowship of Reconciliation (FOR), and the War Resisters League—date from World War I, the "war to end all wars" that didn't.

The term *pacifism* has fallen into disfavor because it has been taken to imply passivity in the face of aggression (a charge leveled at U.S. isolationists in the 1930s). The more

[59]Miller, Richard B. *Interpretations of Conflict: Ethics, Pacifism, and the Just-War Tradition.* Chicago: University of Chicago Press, 1991.

popular term, nonviolence, reflects especially the philosophy and practice of *Mahatma Gandhi,* who led India's struggle for independence from the British Empire before 1948. Gandhi emphasized that nonviolence must be *active* in seeking to prevent violence, to resolve conflicts without violence, and especially to stand up against injustice enforced violently. Gandhi organized Indians to resist the British colonial occupation without resorting to violence, even when British troops shot down unarmed Indian protesters.

Can a party to a conflict ever gain by renouncing potential means of leverage because they are violent? Proponents of nonviolence think so. They emphasize the *practical side* of nonviolence in addition to its morality. As a tactic in bargaining, it uses moral norms as leverage. That is, by renouncing one kind of leverage (violent force) it gains other kinds of leverage (popular support and the force of a just cause). Furthermore, reassuring the other side that one will not employ violent leverage makes it easier for the other side to put such options aside as well (by eliminating the security dilemma).

As a tool of the *powerless* standing up against injustices by the powerful, nonviolence is often the most cost-effective approach—because the costs of violent resistance would be prohibitive.[60] Thus, nonviolence has traditionally been promulgated by people with the greatest stake in social change but the least access to the instruments of large-scale violence. In the United States, the philosophy of nonviolence spread widely in the 1960s in the civil rights movement, especially through the work of Martin Luther King, Jr. The powerful, unfortunately, have fewer practical incentives to adopt nonviolence because they have greater access to types of leverage that rely on violence.

The dilemma of nonviolence is how to respond to violence.[61] Gandhi believed that there was always a third alternative to passivity or response in kind. Nonviolence does not always succeed when faced with violence, but then neither does violent response. However, political leaders may feel they have done their duty if they respond violently without success, but not if they respond nonviolently without success.

Ironically, in order to be effective as a strategy, nonviolence must not appear too strategic—being used only as a practical means to achieve a bargaining advantage. Rather, successful mobilization of the moral leverage implicit in nonviolence depends on its being perceived as steadfast whatever the cost. Gandhi said that "non-violence is not a garment to be put on or off at will. Its seat is in the heart, and it must be an inseparable part of our very being."[62]

Nonviolence overlaps in many ways with the other subjects of interest to the peace studies community, such as peace movements and positive peace. Yet within peace studies there are also substantial differences among scholars who emphasize different aspects of peace and how to achieve it. These differences are deepened by the multidisciplinary nature of peace studies (sociologists, political scientists, psychologists, anthropologists, etc.). Peace studies tends to be inclusive and tolerant, hoping that different scholars (and activists) can find a core of agreement on the meaning of peace. This tolerance can mask

---

[60]Ackerman, Peter, and Christopher Kruegler. *Strategic Nonviolent Conflict: The Dynamics of People Power in the Twentieth Century.* Westport, CT: Praeger, 1993. Wehr, Paul, Heidi Burgess, and Guy Burgess, eds. *Justice Without Violence.* Boulder: Lynne Rienner, 1994. Crow, Ralph, Philip Grant, and Saad E. Ibrahim, eds. *Arab Nonviolent Political Struggle in the Middle East.* Boulder, CO: Lynne Rienner, 1990.

[61]Sharp, Gene. *Civilian-Based Defense: A Post-Military Weapons System.* Princeton: Princeton University Press, 1990.

[62]Gandhi, Mohandas K. *Non-Violence in Peace and War.* Volume 1. New York: Garland, 1972 [1942], p. 61.

incompatibilities within peace studies, however. Those who think that war can be ended through international mediation may find they have little common ground with those who think that individual meditation is the way to end war.

With this chapter and the previous one as theoretical background, the next five chapters will cover the major topics in international security studies, broadly defined. These chapters move through all four levels of analysis, from foreign policy processes (individual and domestic levels) through conflict and military force (domestic and interstate levels), to international law and organization (interstate and global levels).

Beginning at the bottom levels of analysis means turning now to what happens inside the state. How do states decide on actions? What kinds of bargaining go on within a state that is engaged in international bargaining? How do individual and group psychology affect the decision process, pulling it away from rationality? These questions are the domain of foreign policy studies, which are the subject of Chapter 4.

❖ CHAPTER SUMMARY

- ◆ The central claims of realism—regarding anarchy, state actors, rationality, and the utility of military force—have been challenged on a variety of grounds.
- ◆ Liberals dispute the realist notion that narrow self-interest is more rational than mutually beneficial cooperation.
- ◆ Neoliberalism argues that even in an anarchic system of autonomous rational states, cooperation can emerge through the building of norms, regimes, and institutions.
- ◆ Collective goods are benefits received by all members of a group regardless of their individual contribution. Shared norms and rules are important in getting members to pay for collective goods.
- ◆ International regimes—convergent expectations of state leaders about the rules for issue areas in IR help provide stability in the absence of a world government.
- ◆ Hegemonic stability theory suggests that the holding of predominant power by one state lends stability to international relations and helps create regimes.
- ◆ In a collective security arrangement, a group of states agrees to respond together to aggression by any participating state; the UN and other IGOs perform this function.
- ◆ Feminist scholars of IR agree that gender is important in understanding IR but diverge into several strands regarding their conception of the role of gender.
- ◆ Essentialist feminists argue that real (not arbitrary) differences between men and women exist. Men think about social relations more often in terms of autonomy (as do realists), but women think in terms of connection.
- ◆ Essentialist feminists argue that men are more warlike on average than women. Although individual women participants (such as state leaders) may not reflect this difference, the participation of large numbers of women would change the character of the international system, making it more peaceful.
- ◆ Liberal feminists disagree that women have substantially different capabilities or tendencies as participants in IR. They argue that women are equivalent to men in virtually all IR roles. As evidence, liberal feminists point to historical and present-day women leaders and women soldiers.
- ◆ Postmodern critics reject the entire framework and language of realism, with its unitary state actors. Postmodernists argue that no simple categories can capture the multiple realities experienced by participants in IR.

◆ Postmodern feminists seek to uncover gender-related subtexts implicit in realist discourse, including sexual themes connected with the concept of power.

◆ Peace studies programs are interdisciplinary and seek to broaden the study of international security to include social and economic factors ignored by realism.

◆ Peace studies acknowledges a normative bias—that peace is good and war is bad—and a willingness to put theory into practice by participating in politics.

◆ For scholars in peace studies, militarism in many cultures contributes to states' propensity to resort to force in international bargaining.

◆ Positive peace implies not just the absence of war but addressing conditions that scholars in peace studies connect with violence—especially injustice and poverty.

◆ Peace movements try to influence state foreign policies regarding military force; such movements are of great interest in peace studies.

◆ Nonviolence—the renunciation of force—can be an effective means of leverage, especially for poor or oppressed people with few other means available.

❖ THINKING CRITICALLY

1. U.S.-Canadian relations seem better explained by liberalism than realism. What other (one or more) interstate relationships have this quality? Discuss the contrasting tenets of realism and liberalism, showing how each applies to the relationship(s).

2. Would IR operate differently if most leaders of states were women? What would the differences be? What evidence (beyond gender stereotypes) supports your suppositions?

3. Deconstruct this book by identifying implicit themes, subjects not covered, and hidden biases.

4. Peace studies claims that internal characteristics of states (at the domestic level of analysis) strongly affect the propensity for war or potential for lasting peace. For one society, show how internal characteristics—social, economic, and/or cultural—influence that society's external behavior.

5. Write your own critical-thinking question concerning the topics discussed in this chapter. What are the merits of your question? How would you go about answering it?

❖ KEY TERMS

neoliberalism
tit for tat
collective goods problem
free riders
international regime
hegemonic stability theory
collective security
essentialist feminism
liberal feminism
postmodern feminism
gender gap

Greenham Common
postmodernism
subtext
normative bias
militarism
positive peace
structural violence
world government
peace movements
nonviolence, pacifism

MAKING FOREIGN POLICY

DECISION MAKING

Models of Decision Making
Individual Decision Makers
Group Dynamics
Crisis Management

SUBSTATE ACTORS

Bureaucracies
Interest Groups
The Military-Industrial
 Complex
Public Opinion
Democracy

U.S. FOREIGN POLICY

The President
Federal Agencies
Congress and Domestic
 Politics
U.S. Views of the World

Mothers of drafted soldiers protest government's military policies, Moscow, October 1990.

FOREIGN POLICY

❖ MAKING FOREIGN POLICY

Looking at states as though they were unitary actors is useful up to a point, but not very accurate. A state is not a single conscious being; its actions are a composite of individual human choices—by its citizenry, its political leaders, its diplomats and bureaucrats—aggregated through the state's internal structures. This chapter looks at the state from inside out, trying to understand the processes and structures *within* states that make them take the actions they do toward other states. The chapter concludes with a brief overview of the foreign policy process in the United States.

Foreign policies are the strategies used by governments to guide their actions in the international arena (various alternative definitions have been proposed). Foreign policies spell out the objectives state leaders have decided to pursue in a given relationship or situation as well as the general means by which they intend to pursue those objectives. Day-to-day decisions made by various arms of government are guided by the goal of implementing foreign policies.

Every day, states take actions in international affairs. Diplomats are appointed to posts, given instructions for their negotiations, or recalled home. Trade negotiators agree to reduce their demands by a few percent. Military forces are moved around and occasionally sent into battle. Behind each of these actions are decisions by foreign policy bureaucrats in national capitals (including but not limited to the top state leaders). These decisions in turn generally reflect the overall policies states have developed to govern their relationships with other states.

The study of foreign policies includes studying the substance of various states' policies—for instance, what are France's aims with regard to the European Community, or Iran's plans regarding the spread of Islamic revolution in the Middle East? The end of this chapter touches on the substantive policies of the United States (as the most powerful actor). But in general IR scholars are more interested in the **foreign policy process**—how policies are arrived at, and implemented, in various states.[1]

---

[1]Gerner, Deborah J. Foreign Policy Analysis: Exhilarating Eclecticism, Intriguing Enigmas. *International Studies Notes* 16 (3), 1991: 4–19. Macridis, Roy C., ed. *Foreign Policy in World Politics: States and Regions.* 7th ed. Englewood Cliffs, NJ: Prentice Hall, 1989. Hermann, Charles F., Charles W. Kegley, Jr., and James N. Rosenau, eds. *New Directions in the Study of Foreign Policy.* Boston: Allen & Unwin, 1987.

States establish various organizational structures and functional relationships to create and carry out foreign policies. Officials and agencies (such as the foreign ministry) collect information about a situation through various channels; they write memoranda outlining possible options for action; they hold meetings to discuss the matter; some of them meet privately outside these meetings to decide how to steer the meetings in certain directions. Such activities, broadly defined, are what is meant by "the foreign policy process." IR scholars are especially interested in exploring whether certain kinds of policy processes lead to certain kinds of decisions—whether certain processes produce better outcomes (for the state's self-defined interests) than do others.

Foreign policy outcomes result from multiple forces working at once on the various levels of analysis. The outcomes depend on individual decision makers, on the type of society and government they are working within, and on the international and global context of their actions. Since the study of foreign policy concentrates on forces within the state, its main emphasis is on the individual and domestic levels of analysis.

Comparative foreign policy is the study of foreign policy in various states in order to discover whether similar types of societies or governments consistently have similar types of foreign policies (comparing across states or across different time periods for a single state). Such studies have focused on three characteristics in particular: size (large states versus small ones); wealth (rich societies versus poor ones); and degree of participation in government (states with democratic governments versus authoritarian ones in which only a few people participate).[2] An alternative approach categorizes societies according to their relative populations, natural resources, and levels of technology.[3]

A major focus of such studies is whether certain characteristics of a state or society predispose it to be more warlike or aggressive. In particular, during the Cold War scholars debated whether communism or capitalism was inherently more warlike in nature. However, no simple rule has been found to predict a state's warlike tendencies based on attributes such as size, wealth, and type of government. There is great variation among states, and even within a single state over time. Both capitalist and communist states have proven capable of naked aggression or peaceful behavior, depending on circumstances.

Some political scientists have tried to interpret particular states' foreign policies in terms of each one's *political culture and history*. For example, both superpowers in the Cold War had been shaped by long periods of geographical expansion, which reached limits only in the twentieth century. This may help explain the global, expansionist foreign policies of both superpowers during the Cold War. But the Soviet Union (Russia) had experienced repeated devastating land invasions over the centuries (culminating in World War II) while the United States had experienced two centuries of safety behind great oceans. Thus the military might of the Soviet Union, and its control of buffer states in Eastern Europe, seemed defensive in nature to Soviet leaders but appeared aggressive to U.S. leaders.

Most studies of foreign policy have not focused on the comparison of policies of different states, however; they have instead concentrated on understanding in a more general

---

[2]Rosenau, James N. *The Scientific Study of Foreign Policy*. 2nd ed. London: Frances Pinter, 1980.

[3]North, Robert C. *The World That Could Be*. Stanford: Stanford Alumni Association, 1976.

Foreign policy outcomes result from processes at several levels of analysis. The influence of Soviet president Mikhail Gorbachev on history was tremendous for one individual. Yet he was overtaken by larger social forces, such as the rise of nationalism, that split his multinational state into pieces. Here Gorbachev pleads in vain with Lithuanian nationalists not to leave the Soviet Union (Vilnius, January 1989).

way the kinds of processes used in various states to reach (and implement) foreign policies. Scholars have tried to probe the effects of these processes on the resulting outcomes.

❖ DECISION MAKING

The foreign policy process is a process of *decision making*. States take actions because people in governments choose those actions. People whose job it is to make decisions about international relations—*decision makers*—have to go through the same kinds of processes, in one way or another, that anyone would go through in picking a college to attend or deciding what to eat for dinner.

Decision making is a *steering* process in which adjustments are made as a result of feedback from the outside world. Decisions are carried out by *actions* taken to change the world, and then information from the world is *monitored* to evaluate the effects of actions.

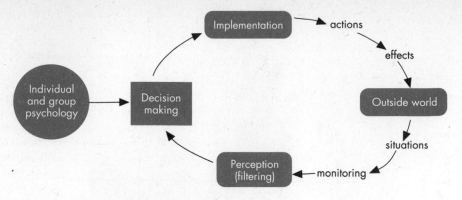

FIGURE 4.1 Decision Making as Steering

These evaluations—along with information about other, independent changes in the environment—go into the next round of decisions (see Figure 4.1).

This steering process with external feedback is based on the *goals* of the decision maker—where she or he is trying to steer to. Along the way to these goals, decision makers set *objectives* as discrete steps to be reached. Objectives fall along a spectrum from core, long-term objectives to very short-term, practical objectives.

Models of Decision Making

A common starting point for studying the decision-making process is the **rational model.**[4] In this model of the process, decision makers calculate the costs and benefits of each possible course of action, then choose the one with the highest benefits and lowest costs. This is done through a sequence of steps:

1. *Clarify goals* in the situation.
2. *Order them* by importance (in case different goals conflict).
3. *List the alternatives* available to achieve the goals.
4. *Investigate the consequences* (probable and possible outcomes) of those alternatives.
5. *Choose* the course of action that will produce the best outcome (in terms of reaching one's goals).

The choice may be complicated by *uncertainty* about the costs and benefits of various actions. In such cases, decision makers must attach probabilities to each possible outcome of an action. Some decision makers are relatively *accepting of risk*, whereas others are *averse to risk*. These factors affect the importance that decision makers place on various alterna-

---

[4]It, along with the organizational process and bureaucratic politics models discussed later, derives from Allison, Graham T. *Essence of Decision: Explaining the Cuban Missile Crisis*. New York: Harper & Row, 1971. Bendor, Jonathan, and Thomas H. Hammond. Rethinking Allison's Models. *American Political Science Review* 86 (2), 1992: 301–22.

tive outcomes that could result from an action. For example, Saddam Hussein's decision to invade Kuwait showed high acceptance of risk. The potential benefits were great (seizing Kuwait's wealth to solve Iraq's economic problems), and Saddam was willing to risk failure on the chance that such a gamble might pay off.

The rational model may imply that decision making is simpler than is actually the case. A decision maker may hold different conflicting goals simultaneously. The goals of different individuals involved in making a decision may diverge, as may the goals of different state agencies. For example, a leader's decision to use military force could be made as a means to win reelection, not in pursuit of any *national* interests. The rational model of decision making thus is somewhat complicated by uncertainty and the multiple goals of decision makers.

An alternative to the rational model of decision making is the **organizational process** model. In this model, foreign policy decision makers generally skip the labor-intensive process of identifying goals and alternative actions, relying instead for most decisions on standardized responses or *standard operating procedures*. For example, in the Cold War the Soviet Foreign Ministry did not have to go through an involved decision process for each situation because it had a party line to guide it; any use of military force by the United States, Britain, or France, for instance, was opposed as imperialist aggression.

The U.S. State Department every day receives over a thousand cables with reports or inquiries from its embassies around the world and sends out over a thousand cables to those embassies with instructions or responses. The vast majority of those cables are never seen by the top decision makers (the secretary of state or the president); instead they are handled by low-level decision makers who apply general principles—or simply try to make the least controversial, most standardized decision, one that will not get them into trouble with their superiors. These low-level decisions may not even reflect the high-level policies adopted by top leaders, but rather have a life of their own. The organizational process model implies that much of foreign policy results from "management by muddling through."[5]

Another alternative to the rational model is the **government bargaining** (or *bureaucratic politics*) model, in which foreign policy decisions result from the bargaining process among various government agencies that have somewhat divergent interests in the outcome.[6] For example, in 1992 the Japanese government had to decide whether to allow sushi manufactured in California to be imported—a weakening of Japan's traditional ban on importing rice (to maintain self-sufficiency in its staple food). The Agriculture Ministry, with an interest in the well-being of Japanese farmers, opposed the imports. The Foreign Ministry, with an interest in smooth relations with the United States, wanted to allow the imports. The final decision to allow imported sushi resulted from the tug-of-war between the ministries. Thus, according to the government bargaining model, foreign policy decisions reflect (a mix of) the interests of state agencies.

---

[5]Avant, Deborah D. *Political Institutions and Military Change: Lessons from Peripheral Wars*. Ithaca: Cornell University Press, 1995. Levy, Jack S. Organizational Routines and the Causes of War. *International Studies Quarterly* 30 (2), 1986: 193–222.

[6]Welch, David A. The Organizational Process and Bureaucratic Politics Paradigms: Retrospect and Prospect. *International Security* 17 (2), 1992: 112–46.

Although the rational model is the usual starting point for thinking about foreign policy decision making, there are many reasons to question whether decisions arrived at can be considered rational, above and beyond the influences of organizational inertia and government bargaining. These nonrational elements in decision making are best understood from a *psychological* analysis of individual and group decision processes.[7]

Individual Decision Makers

Individuals are the only true actors in IR. Every international event is the result, intended or unintended, of decisions made by individuals. IR does not just happen. President Harry Truman, who made the decision to drop U.S. nuclear bombs on two Japanese cities in 1945, understood this. He had a sign on his desk: "The buck stops here." As leader of the world's greatest power, he had nobody to pass the buck to. If he chose to use the bomb (as he did), 200,000 civilians would die. If he chose not to, the war might drag on with potentially many more deaths. Truman had to choose. Some people applaud his decision; others condemn it. But for better or worse, Truman as an individual human being had to decide, and to take responsibility for the consequences. Similarly at the other end of the spectrum of power, the decisions of individual citizens, although they may not seem important when taken one by one, are what create the great forces of world history.

The study of individual decision making revolves around the question of rationality. To what extent are national leaders (or citizens) able to make rational decisions in the national interest—if indeed such an interest can be defined—and thus to conform to a realist view of IR? Individual rationality is not equivalent to state rationality: states might filter individuals' irrational decisions so as to arrive at rational choices, or states might distort individually rational decisions and end up with irrational state choices. But realists tend to assume that both states and individuals are rational and that the goals or interests of states correlate with those of leaders. Partly this assumption reflects the role of strong individuals such as monarchs and dictators in many states, where the rationality and interests of the leader determine those of the state.

The most simplified rational-actor models go so far as to assume that interests are the same from one actor to another (see pp. 70–71). If this were so, individuals could be substituted for each other in various roles without changing history very much. And states would all behave similarly to each other (or rather, the differences between them would reflect different resources, geography, and similar features, not differences in the nature of national interests). This is at best a great oversimplification.[8]

In truth, individual decisions reflect the *values* and *beliefs* of the decision maker. For example, in 1990–1991 Iraqi leader Saddam Hussein had radically different values from those of the Western leaders opposing him, making it hard for each to predict the effect that an action would have on the other. Each may have appeared irrational to the other, and this may have contributed to their inability to resolve the conflict short of war. The

---

[7]Tetlock, Philip E. Psychological Advice on Foreign Policy: What Do We Have to Contribute? *American Psychologist* 41, 1986: 557–67.

[8]Goldgeier, James M. *Leadership Style and Soviet Foreign Policy: Stalin, Khrushchev, Brezhnev, Gorbachev.* Baltimore: Johns Hopkins University Press, 1994. Bunçe, Valerie. *Do New Leaders Make a Difference? Executive Succession and Public Policy Under Capitalism and Socialism.* Princeton: Princeton University Press, 1981.

belief systems of political leaders influence how they interpret information (for instance, interpretations may depend on beliefs about who are the "good guys" and "bad guys").

How can IR scholars characterize an individual's values and beliefs? Sometimes beliefs and values are spelled out in ideological autobiographies such as Hitler's *Mein Kampf*. Other times, IR researchers try to infer beliefs through a method called *content analysis*— analyzing speeches or other documents to count the number of times key words or phrases are repeated, and in what contexts. Scholars of IR have also described *operational codes*— routines and methods that mediate between beliefs and practical actions. They have traced out such operational codes, for example, for Soviet Communist leaders.[9] Other scholars have created computer-based models of beliefs.[10]

Not only do individuals' goals differ, how they pursue those goals also varies. Individual decision makers not only have differing values and beliefs, but also have unique personalities—their personal experiences, intellectual capabilities, and personal styles of making decisions. Some IR scholars study individual psychology in order to understand how personality affects decision making. *Psychoanalytic approaches* hold that personalities reflect the subconscious influences of childhood experiences. For instance, U.S. president Woodrow Wilson's desire for power may have resulted from a feeling of insecurity due to an abusive father; this insecurity led to his greatest failure, when he could not compromise with Congress to achieve ratification of the Versailles treaty.[11]

Beyond individual *idiosyncracies* in goals or decision processes, there are at least three *systematic* ways in which individual decision making diverges from the rational model. First, decision makers suffer from **misperceptions** and **selective perceptions** (taking in only some kinds of information) when they compile information on the likely consequences of their choices.[12] Decision processes must by necessity reduce and filter the incoming information on which a decision is based; the problem is that such filtration often is biased. **Information screens** are subconscious filters through which people put the information coming in about the world around them. Often they simply ignore any information that does not fit their expectations. Information is also screened out as it passes from one person to another in the decision process. For example, in 1990 Kuwaiti leaders paid little attention to information suggesting that Iraq was about to invade, because such an idea did not fit their expectations. The same kind of selective perception caused Israeli leaders in 1973 and Soviet leaders in 1941 to ignore evidence of a pending invasion of their country.

---

[9]George, Alexander L. The "Operational Code": A Neglected Approach to the Study of Political Leaders and Decision-Making. *International Studies Quarterly* 13 (2), 1969: 199–222.

[10]Taber, Charles S. POLI: An Expert System Model of U.S. Foreign Policy Belief Systems. *American Political Science Review* 86 (4), 1992. Hudson, Valerie M., ed. *Artificial Intelligence and International Politics*. Boulder, CO: Westview, 1991.

[11]George, Alexander L., and Juliette L. George. *Woodrow Wilson and Colonel House: A Personality Study*. New York: J. Day, 1956. Lasswell, Harold. *World Politics and Personal Insecurity*. New York: Free Press, 1965 [1935]. Waite, Robert G. L. Leadership Pathologies: The Kaiser and the Führer and the Decisions for War in 1914 and 1939. In Betty Glad, ed. *Psychological Dimensions of War*. Newbury Park, CA: Sage, 1990: 143–68.

[12]Jervis, Robert. *Perception and Misperception in International Politics*. Princeton: Princeton University Press, 1976. Jervis, Robert. *The Logic of Images in International Relations*. New York: Columbia University Press, 1989.

Misperceptions can affect the implementation of policy by low-level officials as well as its formulation by high-level officials. For example, in 1983 Soviet military officers ordered pilots to shoot down a civilian Korean Air Lines jet that they thought to be on a spy mission over Soviet territory (it wasn't). In 1988, officers on a U.S. warship in the Persian Gulf shot down a civilian Iranian jet that they believed to be a military jet attacking them. In both cases the officers were trying to carry out policies established by national leaders, but due to misperceptions their actions instead caused serious embarrassment to their state and damage to its international standing.

Second, the rationality of individual cost-benefit calculations is undermined by emotions that decision makers feel while thinking about the consequences of their actions—an effect referred to as *affective bias*. (Positive and negative affect refer to feelings of liking or disliking someone). As hard as a decision maker tries to be rational in making a decision—calculating what effect a choice will have on his or her goals—the decision process is bound to be influenced by strong feelings held about the person or state toward which a decision is directed. (Affective biases can also contribute to information screening, as positive information about disliked people or negative information about liked people is screened out.)

Third, *cognitive biases* are systematic distortions of rational calculations based not on emotional feelings but simply on the limitations of the human brain in making choices. The most important seems to be the attempt to produce *cognitive balance*—or to reduce *cognitive dissonance*. These terms refer to the tendency people have to try to maintain mental models of the world that are logically consistent (this seldom succeeds entirely). When models contain contradictory elements, a person may ignore certain knowledge that he or she possesses or may change how important an item of information is judged to be. For instance, after deciding whether to intervene militarily in a conflict, a state leader will very likely adjust his or her mental model to downplay the risks and exaggerate the gains of the chosen course of action. (Cognitive biases are yet another source of information screens in incoming information.)[13]

One implication of cognitive balance is that decision makers place greater value on goals that they have put great effort into achieving—the *justification of effort*. "If I've worked so hard for this, it must be really important!" This is especially true in a democracy where politicians must face their citizens' judgment at the polls and so do not want to admit failures. The Vietnam War trapped U.S. decision makers in this way in the 1960s. After sending half a million troops halfway around the world it was difficult for U.S. leaders to admit to themselves that the costs of the war were greater than the benefits. Often in protracted regional conflicts, such as the Iran-Iraq War in the 1980s, it is hard to bring a long, costly war to an end because neither side wants to settle for less than total victory after expending so much effort.

Another way decision makers achieve cognitive balance is through *wishful thinking*—that is, an overestimate of the probability of a desired outcome. A variation of wishful

---

[13]Herrmann, Richard. The Empirical Challenge of the Cognitive Revolution: A Strategy for Drawing Inferences About Perceptions. *International Studies Quarterly* 32 (2), 1988: 175–204. Vertzberger, Yaacov Y. I. *The World in Their Minds: Information Processing, Cognition, and Perception in Foreign Policy Decisionmaking.* Stanford: Stanford University Press, 1990. Cottam, Martha L. *Foreign Policy Decision Making: The Influence of Cognition.* Boulder, CO: Westview, 1986.

thinking is to assume that an event with a *low probability* of occurring will definitely *not* occur. This could be a dangerous way to think about catastrophic events such as accidental nuclear war.

Cognitive balance often leads decision makers to maintain a hardened image of an *enemy* and to interpret all the enemy's actions in a negative light (since the idea of bad people doing good things would create cognitive dissonance).[14] Obviously this cognitive bias overlaps with the affective bias felt toward such enemies. The enemy-image problem is especially important today in ethnic conflicts (see pp. 202–203).

A *mirror image* refers to two sides in a conflict maintaining very similar enemy images of each other ("we are defensive, they are aggressive," etc.). This occurred between the superpowers in the Cold War and happens frequently in ethnic conflicts. A decision maker may experience psychological *projection* of his or her own feelings onto another actor. For instance, if (hypothetically) Indian leaders wanted to gain nuclear superiority over Pakistan but found that goal inconsistent with their image of themselves as peaceful and defensive, the resulting cognitive dissonance might be resolved by believing that Pakistan was trying to gain nuclear superiority (the example works as well with the states reversed).

Another form of cognitive bias, related to cognitive balance, is the use of *historical analogies* to structure one's thinking about a decision. This can be quite useful or quite misleading, depending on whether the analogy is appropriate.[15] Each historical situation is unique in some way, so when a decision maker latches onto an analogy and uses it as a shortcut to a decision, the rational calculation of costs and benefits may be cut short as well. For example, U.S. leaders used the analogy of Munich in 1938 to convince themselves that appeasement of communism in the Vietnam War would lead to increased communist aggression in Asia. In retrospect, the differences between North Vietnam and Nazi Germany made this a poor analogy. Vietnam then itself became a potent analogy which helped convince U.S. leaders to avoid involvement in certain overseas conflicts, including Bosnia; this was called the "Vietnam syndrome" in U.S. foreign policy.

All these psychological processes—misperception, affective biases, and cognitive biases—interfere with the rational assessment of costs and benefits in making a decision.[16] Two specific modifications to the rational model of decision making have been proposed to accommodate psychological realities.

First, the model of *bounded rationality* takes into account the costs of seeking and processing information. Nobody thinks about every single possible course of action when making a decision. So instead of **optimizing,** which means picking the very best option, people usually work on the problem until they come up with a "good enough" option that meets some minimal criteria; this is called **satisficing** (finding a satisfactory solution).[17] The time constraints faced by top decision makers in IR—who are constantly besieged

---

[14]Keen, Sam. *Faces of the Enemy: Reflections of the Hostile Imagination*. San Francisco: Harper & Row, 1986.

[15]Breslauer, George W., and Philip E. Tetlock, eds. *Learning in U.S. and Soviet Foreign Policy*. Boulder, CO: Westview, 1991.

[16]Tuchman, Barbara W. *The March of Folly: From Troy to Vietnam*. New York: Knopf/Random House, 1984. Parker, Richard B. *The Politics of Miscalculation in the Middle East*. Bloomington: Indiana University Press, 1993.

[17]Simon, Herbert A. *Models of Bounded Rationality*. Cambridge, MA: MIT Press, 1982.

with problems, crises, and situations requiring their attention—generally preclude their finding the very best response to a situation.

Second, *prospect theory* provides an alternative explanation (rather than simple rational optimization) of decisions made under risk or uncertainty.[18] According to this theory decision makers go through two phases. In the editing phase they frame the options available and the probabilities of various outcomes associated with each option. Then in the evaluation phase they assess the options and choose one. Prospect theory holds that evaluations take place by comparison with a *reference point*, which is often the status quo but might be some past or expected situation. (In extreme cases the reference point may be a centuries-old moment of glory for a nation or ethnic group; see "irredentism" on p. 185.) The decision maker asks if she or he can do better than that reference point, but the value placed on outcomes depends on how far from the reference point they are. The theory also holds that individuals *fear losses* more than they relish gains. Decision makers are therefore often willing to forgo opportunities rather than risk a setback.

Individual decision making thus follows an imperfect and partial kind of rationality at best. Not only do the goals of different individuals vary, but decision makers face a series of obstacles in receiving accurate information, constructing accurate models of the world, and reaching decisions that further their own goals. The rational model is only a simplification at best and must be supplemented by an understanding of individual psychological processes that affect decision making.

Not even an absolute dictator, however, makes decisions all alone. State decisions result from the interactions of groups of people. Leaders surround themselves with advisors to help them think about decisions. Decision-making bodies—from committees and agency task forces to legislatures and political parties—all rely on the interactions of relatively small groups of people reasoning or arguing together. The psychology of group dynamics thus has great influence on the way foreign policy is formulated.

Group Dynamics

What are the implications of group psychology for foreign policy decision making? In one respect, groups promote rationality by balancing out the blind spots and biases of any individual. Advisors or legislative committees may force a state leader to reconsider a rash decision. And the interactions of different individuals in a group may result in the formulation of goals that more closely reflect state interests rather than individual idiosyncrasies.

However, group dynamics also introduce new sources of irrationality into the decision process.[19] These fall into two general categories: the psychological dynamics that occur within groups, and the ways that the structure of group decision processes can bias the outcomes.

---

[18]Farnham, Barbara, ed. *Avoiding Losses/Taking Risks: Prospect Theory and International Conflict*. Ann Arbor: University of Michigan Press, 1994. Levy, Jack. Prospect Theory and International Relations: Theoretical Applications and Analytical Problems. *Political Psychology* 13 (2), 1992: 283–310.

[19]Maoz, Zeev. Framing the National Interest: The Manipulation of Foreign Policy Decisions in Group Settings. *World Politics* 43 (1), 1990: 77–110. Maoz, Zeev. *National Choices and International Processes*. New York: Cambridge University Press, 1990.

Both individual and group psychology are important in understanding the formation of foreign policy. Here President Clinton consults with foreign policy advisors, fall 1994. Clinton picked a consensual team with no strong leader, and he himself focused on a domestic agenda in his first two years. This, combined with the president's inexperience in foreign policy and his party's lack of recent experience in the White House, produced an unsteady foreign policy widely criticized in Clinton's first years.

Group Psychology The most important psychological problem is the tendency for groups to validate wrong decisions, convincing each other that a wrong idea is right. This is called **groupthink**.[20] The basic phenomenon is illustrated by a simple psychology experiment. A group of six people is asked to compare the lengths of two lines projected onto a screen. When five of the people are accomplices instructed to say that line A is longer—when anyone can see that line B is actually longer—the sixth person is likely to agree with the group rather than believe her or his own eyes.

Unlike individuals, groups tend to be overly optimistic about the chances of success and are thus more willing to take risks. Doubts about dubious undertakings are suppressed by participants because everyone else seems to think an idea will work. For example, in the Iran-Contra affair of the late 1980s, a group of U.S. foreign policy makers thought it would be a good idea to secretly send arms to Iran in exchange for the release of U.S.

[20]Janis, Irving L. *Victims of Groupthink: A Psychological Study of Foreign-Policy Decisions and Fiascoes*. Boston: Houghton Mifflin, 1972.

hostages held in Lebanon and to use the Iranian arms payments to fund a covert war in Nicaragua at a time when Congress had banned U.S. engagement there. Because the operation was secret, the small group involved was cut off from skeptical views, and they seem to have talked themselves into thinking that the operation was a smart idea. They discounted risks like being discovered and exaggerated the benefits of opening channels to Iranian moderates. The involvement of a top authority figure—the head of the U.S. Central Intelligence Agency (CIA), who was a close friend of the president—surely reassured other participants that the idea was sound. When the operation came to light it did tremendous damage to the interests of the United States and of President Reagan, and it wrecked the careers of many of those involved.

Decision Structure The *structure of a decision process*—the rules for who is involved in making the decision, how voting is conducted, and so forth—can affect the outcome. This is especially true when a group has *indeterminate preferences* because no single alternative appeals to a majority of participants. Experienced participants in foreign policy formation are familiar with various techniques for manipulating decision processes to favor outcomes they prefer.

A common technique is to control a group's formal *decision rules*. These rules include what items of business the group discusses and the order in which proposals are considered (especially important when participants are satisficing). Probably most important is the ability to *control the agenda* and thereby structure the terms of debate. A group's voting procedures—for instance, whether a proposal needs a majority to be adopted, or a plurality, or a two-thirds majority, or total consensus—also affect the choices it makes. Procedures requiring more votes for adoption tend to favor conservative approaches to policy, whereas those allowing adoption with a mere plurality of votes tend to allow more frequent changes in policy.

The structure of decision making also reflects the composition of a decision group. Who is represented? Often the group is composed of individuals cast in particular *roles* in the group. (Some IR scholars treat role as a distinct level of analysis between the individual and domestic levels.) Roles can be institutional—a participant representing a viewpoint shared by her or his particular agency. For example, the representative of an intelligence agency might speak up at an interagency meeting to emphasize the importance of accurate intelligence in reaching a decision. Different sorts of roles within particular groups can be based on factions, mediators, swing voters, and so forth. For instance, one advisor might often play the role of introducing new ideas while another might play the role of defending the status quo and another the role of staying neutral so as to gain the leader's ear last.

Another aspect of a group's decision structure is the tendency of participants to rely on *informal* consultations in addition to formal meetings. Informal conversations such as chats over lunch or at a party play an important part in decision making, though it is hard to measure. Some leaders create a "kitchen cabinet"—a trusted group of friends who discuss policy issues with the leader even though they have no formal positions in government. For instance, Israel's Golda Meir held many such discussions at her home, sometimes literally in the kitchen. Russian president Boris Yeltsin relied on the advice of his bodyguard, who was a trusted friend.

Informal settings may be used in another way—to shake up formal decision groups and draw participants away from their usual bureaucratic roles. For example, Soviet premier Brezhnev in 1972 took President Nixon on a speedboat ride before settling down for discussions at Brezhnev's dacha (villa) in the countryside. Likewise, President Jimmy Carter brought Israeli and Egyptian leaders to the U.S. government's Camp David retreat in 1978 to hammer out a peace agreement.

Crisis Management

The difficulties in reaching rational decisions, both for individuals and for groups, are heightened during a crisis.[21] *Crises* are foreign policy situations in which outcomes are very important and time frames are quite compressed. There is no firm boundary between crises and more routine policy making. But if a situation drags on for months or loses the dedicated attention of the top political leaders, it is not considered a crisis anymore. (In the United States it has been suggested that foreign policy crises are reliably indicated by a sharp increase in pizza deliveries to certain government agencies, as decision makers work through mealtimes.) Crisis decision making is harder to understand and predict than is normal foreign policy making.

In a crisis, decision makers operate under tremendous time constraints. The normal checks on unwise decisions may not operate. Communications become shorter and more stereotyped, and information that does not fit a decision maker's expectations is more likely to be discarded simply because there is no time to consider it. In framing options there is a tendency to restrict the choices, again to save time, and a tendency to overlook creative options while focusing on the most obvious ones.

Groupthink occurs easily during crises. During the 1962 Cuban Missile Crisis, President Kennedy created a small, closed group of advisors who worked together intensively for days on end, virtually cut off from outside discussion and contact. Even the president's channel of communication to Soviet leader Khrushchev was rerouted through Kennedy's brother Robert and the Soviet ambassador, cutting out the State Department. Recognizing the danger of groupthink, Kennedy made a practice of leaving the room from time to time—removing the authority figure from the group—to encourage free discussion. Through this and other means, the group managed to identify a third option (a naval blockade) beyond their first two choices (bombing the missile sites or doing nothing).

Participants in crisis decision making are not only rushed, they experience severe psychological *stress*. As most of us have experienced personally, people usually do not make decisions wisely when under stress. Stress amplifies the biases just discussed. Decision makers tend to overestimate the hostility of adversaries and to underestimate their own hostility toward those adversaries. Dislike easily turns to hatred, anxiety to fear. More and more information is screened out in order to come to terms with decisions being made and to restore cognitive balance.

---

[21]Brecher, Michael. *Crises in World Politics: Theory and Reality.* New York: Pergamon Press, 1993. Richardson, James L. *Crisis Diplomacy: The Great Powers Since the Mid-Nineteenth Century.* New York: Cambridge University Press, 1994. Lebow, Richard Ned. *Between Peace and War: The Nature of International Crisis.* Baltimore: Johns Hopkins University Press, 1981.

Crisis decision making also leads to physical exhaustion. *Sleep deprivation* sets in within days as decision makers use every hour to stay on top of the crisis. College students who have "pulled an all-nighter"—or several in a row—know that within days people deprived of sleep lose touch with reality, experience everything as exaggerated, and suffer from depression and even hallucinations. Unless decision makers are careful about getting enough sleep, these are the conditions under which vital foreign policy decisions may be made. In addition to sleep deprivation, physiological stress comes from drugs used by top policy makers—usually nicotine and caffeine in high doses, and sometimes alcohol.

Because of the importance of sound decision making during crises, voters pay great attention to the psychological stability of their leaders. For instance, before Israeli prime minister Yitzhak Rabin won election in 1992, he faced charges that he had suffered a one-day nervous breakdown when he headed the armed forces just before the 1967 war. Not so, he responded; he was just smart enough to realize that the crisis had caused both exhaustion and acute nicotine poisoning; he needed to rest up for a day in order to go on and make good decisions.

Whether in crisis mode or normal routines, individual decision makers do not operate alone. Their decisions are shaped by the government and society in which they work.

Crisis management takes a high toll psychologically and physiologically. President Eduard Shevardnadze of Georgia seems to show this strain in 1992—just the beginning of several years of civil war and perpetual crisis in that country. Shevardnadze, formerly Gorbachev's foreign minister, returned to lead his native Georgia when the Soviet Union dissolved.

Foreign policy is constrained and shaped by substate actors ranging from government agencies to political interest groups and industries.

❖ SUBSTATE ACTORS

Foreign policy is shaped not only by the internal dynamics of individual and group decision making but by the states and societies within which decision makers operate.

Bureaucracies

The substate actors closest to the foreign policy process are the state's bureaucratic agencies maintained for developing and carrying out foreign policy. Different states maintain different foreign policy bureaucracies, but there are some common elements across states.

Diplomats Virtually all states maintain a *diplomatic corps*, or *foreign service*, of diplomats working in *embassies* in foreign capitals (and in *consulates* located in noncapital foreign cities), as well as diplomats who remain at home to help coordinate foreign policy. States appoint *ambassadors* as their official representatives to other states and to international organizations. Diplomatic activities are organized through a *foreign ministry* or the equivalent (e.g., the U.S. State Department).

In many democracies, some diplomats are *political appointees* who come and go with changes in government leaders (often as patronage for past political support). Others are *career diplomats*, who come up through the ranks of the foreign service and tend to outlast changes in administration. Skilled diplomats are assets that increase a state's power.

Diplomats provide much of the information that goes into making foreign policies, but their main role is to carry out policies rather than create them. Nonetheless, foreign ministry bureaucrats can often make foreign relations so routine that top leaders and political appointees can come and go without greatly altering the country's relations.

Tension is common between state leaders and foreign policy bureaucrats. Both try to tame the other. Career diplomats try to orient new leaders and their appointees, and to control the flow of information they receive (creating information screens). Often, state leaders appoint a close friend or key advisor to manage the foreign policy bureaucracy. President Nixon did this with his trusted national security advisor, Henry Kissinger, as did President Bush with his closest friend, James Baker. Chinese leader Mao Zedong put his loyal ally, Zhou Enlai, in charge of foreign policy, and Soviet president Gorbachev had his close ally Shevardnadze running the foreign ministry.

Interagency Tensions Tensions between top political leaders and foreign policy bureaucracies are only one form of *interagency* tension in the formulation of foreign policy. Certain agencies traditionally clash, and an endless tug-of-war shapes the foreign policies that emerge. In an extreme example of interagency rivalry, the U.S. State Department and the CIA backed opposite sides in a civil war in Laos in 1960. In the United States and the Soviet Union during the Cold War, the defense ministry was usually more hawkish (favoring military strength) and the foreign ministry or State Department more dovish (favoring diplomacy), with the top leader holding the balance. (But more recently,

As a candidate for president, Bill Clinton promised to support Bosnia with arms and air strikes. As president, Clinton gave up that idea after meeting resistance from European leaders. What theories might help explain Clinton's switch?

THINKING THEORETICALLY

❖

The organizational process model holds that government bureaucracies churn out policy in a routine manner, with only incremental change as political leaders come and go. By this reasoning, continuity in U.S. policy toward Bosnia was to be expected even when new individuals appear as leaders with new policy ideas. The State Department and Pentagon "educated" Clinton on Bosnia, and policy remained relatively unchanged despite a few backs-and-forths as Clinton tried unsuccessfully to find a policy that worked.

A different theoretical approach would attribute Clinton's switch to a personality trait, his weakness in standing on principle and his readiness to compromise—a trait (real or imagined) to which many Clinton problems were attributed in his first years in office. Other individual personality factors include his youth (not having experienced World War II as had previous presidents) and his uneasy relations with the military due to his avoidance of military service during the Vietnam War.

How could we begin testing these theories against each other? Here is an "experiment" in which the two theories would make different predictions. Imagine that Robert Dole was elected president in 1996 and that the war in Bosnia was still going on then. (This is written in 1995, so the outcome of the experiment will not be known until after this book has been published.) Dole as senator led the fight to lift the U.S. arms embargo on Bosnia (as Clinton had done before becoming president). What would Dole do as president? The organizational process model suggests that Dole, like Clinton, would more or less stay the course on Bosnia. But the personality approach makes the opposite prediction: since Dole is older and was a military hero in World War II, his personality should lead to a significant change toward a tougher policy of countering Serbian aggression. A good experiment will test two contradictory hypotheses by setting up a situation in which certain factors remain the same (e.g., the nature of the U.S. foreign policy bureaucracy) while others change (e.g., the personality of the president). Then the influence of each factor on the outcome can be assessed.

Here is another "experiment." Suppose that President Clinton himself decided (after the publication of this book) to get tough and lead the international community in an effective response to aggression in Bosnia. Such an outcome would contradict both the "weak personality" theory and the organizational process theory. We would need to find new candidate theories, such as a learning model in which policy makers learn from mistakes and achieve incremental progress. (Like the other two theories, this one is generally liberal in approach.)

on Bosnia for instance, the U.S. State Department has often been more hawkish and the Pentagon more dovish.) In general, bureaucracies promote policies in which their own capabilities would be effective and their power would increase.

Generally, representatives of bureaucratic agencies promote the interests of their own bureaucracy. This is not always true, especially because heads of agencies try to appear loyal to the state leader by occasionally forgoing the interests of their own agencies. But in general it is said that "where you stand [on an issue] depends on where you sit" (in what agency). Again the individuals are somewhat interchangeable. One can often predict just from the job titles of participants how they will argue on a policy issue. The government bargaining model pays special attention to the interagency negotiations that result from conflicts of interest between agencies of the same government. The conflicting and overlapping interests of agencies can be quite complex, especially in large governments such as those of the great powers, which have dozens of agencies that deal with international relations.

Units within agencies have similar tensions. In many countries the different military services (army, navy, air force) pull in somewhat different directions, even if they ultimately unite to battle the foreign ministry. Bureaucrats working in particular units or projects become attached to them. Officials responsible for a new weapon system will lose bureaucratic turf, and perhaps their jobs, if the weapon's development is canceled.

Of special concern in many poor states is the institutional interest that military officers have in maintaining a strong military. If civilian state leaders allow officers' salaries to fall or the size of the military forces to be cut for budgetary reasons, they may well face institutional resistance from the military—in the extreme case a military takeover of the government (see pp. 234–236). These issues were factors in attempted military coups in the Philippines, Venezuela, and other states in the early 1990s. Similarly, the reduction of El Salvador's military forces (and firing of some high-ranking officers) called for under a UN peace plan required delicate maneuvering by the country's president even though he had traditionally been an ally of the military.

Different states develop different institutional capabilities, in terms of both size (of budget and personnel) and specialization. These differences in institutions help explain differences in states' foreign policies.

In general, bureaucratic rivalry as an influence on foreign policy challenges the notion of states as unitary actors in the international system. Such rivalries suggest that a state does not have any single set of goals—a national interest—but that its actions may result from the bargaining of subunits, each with its own set of goals.[22] Furthermore, such a perspective extends far beyond bureaucratic agencies because other substate actors have their own goals, which they seek to advance by influencing foreign policy.

Interest Groups

Foreign policy makers do not work in a political vacuum. They operate in the context of the political debates in their society. In all states there are societal pressures that influence foreign policy, although these are aggregated and made effective through different channels in different societies. In pluralistic democracies, interested parties influence foreign policy through interest groups and political parties. Generally in dictatorships similar

---

[22]Anderson, Richard D., Jr., Margaret G. Hermann, and Charles F. Hermann. Explaining Self-Defeating Foreign Policy Decisions: Interpreting Soviet Arms for Egypt in 1973 Through Process or Domestic Bargaining Models? [Comment and Response]. *American Political Science Review* 86 (3), 1992: 759–67.

influences occur but less visibly. Thus foreign policies adopted by states generally reflect some kind of process of domestic coalition formation.[23] Of course, international factors also have strong effects on domestic politics.[24]

Interest groups are coalitions of people who share a common interest in the outcome of some political issue and who organize themselves to try to influence the outcome. For instance, French farmers have a big stake in international negotiations on the European Community (which subsidizes agriculture) and in world trade talks (which set agricultural tariffs). The farmers exert political pressure on the French government through long-established and politically sophisticated associations and organizations. They lobby for desired legislation and contribute to politicians' campaigns. More dramatically, when their interests are threatened—as during a U.S.-European trade dispute in 1992—French farmers have turned out in large numbers across the country to block roads, stage violent street demonstrations, and threaten to grind the national economy to a halt if the government does not adopt their position.

Similarly (but often less dramatically), interest groups form around businesses, labor unions, churches, veterans, senior citizens, members of an occupation, or citizens concerned about an issue such as the environment.

Lobbying is the process of talking with legislators or officials to influence their decisions on some set of issues. Three important elements that go into successful lobbying are the ability to gain a hearing with busy officials, the ability to present cogent arguments for one's case, and the ability to trade favors in return for positive action on an issue. These favors—legal and illegal—range from campaign contributions through dinners at nice restaurants and trips to golf resorts, to securing illicit sexual liaisons and paying bribes. In many states corruption is a major problem in governmental decision making (see pp. 525–527), and interest groups may induce government officials by illegal means to take certain actions. The effectiveness of different techniques (such as providing information versus bribes) varies from one country or situation to another.

In numerous cases ethnic groups within one state become interest groups concerned about their ancestral nation outside that state. Members of ethnic groups often feel strong emotional ties to their relatives in other countries, but the rest of the population generally does not care about such issues one way or the other, so even a small ethnic group can have considerable influence on policy toward a particular country. Such ethnic ties are emerging as a powerful foreign policy influence in the former Soviet republics—for instance, Russians living in Ukraine are very interested in relations with Russia—and in various ethnic conflicts in poor regions. The effect is especially strong in the United States, which is ethnically mixed and has a pluralistic, interest-group form of democracy.

---

[23]Evans, Peter B., Harold K. Jacobson and Robert D. Putnam, eds. *Double-Edged Diplomacy: International Bargaining and Domestic Politics*. Berkeley, California: University of California Press, 1993. Bueno de Mesquita, Bruce, and David Lalman. *War and Reason: Domestic and International Imperatives*. New Haven: Yale University Press, 1992. Zakaria, Fareed. Realism and Domestic Politics: A Review Essay. *International Security* 17 (1), 1992: 177–98. Snyder, Jack. *Myths of Empire: Domestic Politics and International Ambition*. Ithaca: Cornell University Press, 1991. Barnett, M. High Politics Is Low Politics: The Domestic and Systemic Sources of Israeli Security Policy, 1967–1977. *World Politics* 42 (4), 1990: 529–62.

[24]Gourevitch, Peter. The Second Image Reversed: International Sources of Domestic Politics. *International Organization* 32 (4), 1978: 881–911.

Foreign policies are affected by the pulling and tugging of various domestic interest groups. French farmers tried to influence France's foreign policy by repeatedly blocking rail and road traffic throughout the country, including the entrance to Euro Disney in June 1992.

For example, Cuban Americans organize to influence U.S. policy toward Cuba, as do Greek Americans on Greece, Jewish Americans on Israel, and African-Americans on South Africa.

Interest groups have goals and interests that may or may not coincide with the national interest as a whole (if indeed such an interest can be identified). As with bureaucratic agencies, the view of the state as a unitary actor can be questioned. The head of General Motors once said that "what's good for General Motors is good for the country, and vice versa." This is not self-evident. Nonetheless, defenders of interest group politics argue that various interest groups tend to push and pull in different directions, with the ultimate decisions generally reflecting the interests of society as a whole.

According to *Marxist* theories of international relations (which are discussed in Chapter 12), the key domestic influences on foreign policy in capitalist countries are rich owners of big businesses; in this view state policies and actions serve the interests of these owners rather than the national interest or the interests of ordinary workers and citizens. For instance, European imperialism benefited banks and big business, which made huge profits from exploiting cheap labor and resources in overseas colonies. This is the official view (if not always the operative one) of the Chinese government (and the former Soviet

Union) toward Western industrialized states.[25] During the Cold War, Marxists argued that U.S. foreign policy and that of its Western allies were driven by the profit motive of arms manufacturers.[26]

The Military-Industrial Complex

A **military-industrial complex** is a huge interlocking network of governmental agencies, industrial corporations, and research institutes, all working together to supply their nation's military forces. Because of the domestic political clout of these actors, it was a very powerful influence on foreign policy in *both* the United States and the Soviet Union during the Cold War. Some of that influence remains, though it has diminished greatly. During the Cold War, both superpowers developed military-industrial complexes, though their structures differed somewhat (state-owned industries in the Soviet Union and private corporations filling government contracts in the United States). The military-industrial complex was a response to the growing importance of technology (nuclear weapons, electronics, and others) and of logistics in Cold War military planning.

States at war have long harnessed their economic and technological might for the war effort. But during the Cold War military procurement occurred on a massive scale in "peacetime," as the superpowers raced to develop new high-technology weapons. This race created a special role for scientists and engineers in addition to the more traditional role of industries that produce war materials. In response to the Soviet satellite *Sputnik* in 1957, the United States increased spending on research and development and created new science education programs.

But by 1961, President Eisenhower warned in his farewell speech that the military-industrial complex (a term he coined) was gaining "unwarranted influence" in U.S. society and that militarization could erode democracy in the United States. The influence Eisenhower referred to was similar to that of any domestic interest group with its own goals for foreign policy, but magnified by the vast scale of the military effort. The threat to democracy was that the interest of the military-industrial complex in the arms race conflicted with the interest of ordinary citizens in peace, while the size of the complex gave it more political clout than ordinary citizens could muster.

The complex encompasses a variety of constituencies, each of which has an interest in military spending. *Corporations* that produce goods for the military profit from government contracts. So do military *officers* whose careers advance by building bureaucratic empires around new weapons systems. And so do universities and scientific institutes that receive military research contracts—a major source of funding for scientists in Russia and the United States.

When big weapons projects are developed, subcontractors and parts suppliers are usually spread around many states and congressional districts in the United States (or around equivalent constituencies in the old Soviet Union), so that local citizens and politicians join the list of constituents benefiting from military spending. Recently, a similar phenomenon has emerged in the European Community, where weapons development programs have been parceled out to several European states. A new fighter jet is less likely to

---

[25]Shih, Chih-yu. *China's Just World: The Morality of Chinese Foreign Policy.* Boulder, CO: Lynne Rienner, 1992.

[26]Konobeyev, V. The Capitalist Economy and the Arms Race. *International Affairs* [Moscow] 8, 1982: 28–48.

In the post–Cold War era, the military-industrial complex has been hit hard in the United States and harder in the former Soviet Union by cuts in military spending. Here, B-2 long-range stealth bombers (which survived the end of the Cold War despite their enormous cost) are on the assembly line at the Northrop Corporation in southern California, 1988. Companies like Northrop have an interest in high military spending—one link in the military-industrial complex.

be canceled if one country gets the contract for the wings, another for the engines, and so forth.

Executives in military industries; as the people who best understand their industries, are often appointed as government officials responsible for military procurement decisions and then return to their companies again—a practice called the *revolving door*. In democracies, military industries also try to influence public opinion through *advertising* that ties their products to patriotic themes. Finally, U.S. military industries give generous *campaign contributions* to national politicians who vote on military budgets, and sometimes bribes to Pentagon officials as well. Military industry became an important source of *political action committee (PAC)* money raised by members of Congress during the Cold War.

When the Cold War ended, the military-industrial complex in both superpowers endured cutbacks in military budgets. In Russia after the Soviet Union collapsed, military industries formed the backbone of a political faction seeking to slow down economic reforms and continue government subsidies to state-owned industries. They succeeded in replacing Russia's reformist prime minister with an industrial manager in late 1992. In the

United States, meanwhile, the lingering influence of the military-industrial complex may help to explain why Congress kept funding certain Cold War weapons (such as the Seawolf submarine and B-2 bomber) after their purpose seemingly disappeared.

Public Opinion

Military industries and other substate actors seek to influence **public opinion**—the range of views on foreign policy issues held by the citizens of a state. Public opinion has greater influence on foreign policy in democracies than in authoritarian governments. But even dictators must pay attention to what citizens think. No government can rule by force alone: it needs legitimacy to survive. It must convince people to accept (if not to like) its policies, because in the end policies are carried out by ordinary people—soldiers, workers, petty bureaucrats. Unpopular wars are hard to wage successfully. For instance, Saddam Hussein's Iraq would have been a more formidable adversary in the Gulf War if Iraqi soldiers had believed in the cause and been willing to die for it (generally they were not). In some cases, governments that are not warlike *enough* for their own people can also lose domestic support (as happened in Azerbaijan in 1992 when the government was seen as too weak in confronting Armenia).

Because of the need for public support, even authoritarian governments spend great effort on *propaganda*—the public promotion of their official line—to win support for foreign policies. States use television, newspapers, and other information media in this effort. For instance, when China invited President Nixon to visit in 1972, the Chinese government, after decades of opposing "U.S. imperialism," mounted a major propaganda campaign to explain to its people that the United States was not so bad after all.

In democracies, where governments must stand for election, public opinion is even more important. An unpopular war can force a leader or party from office, as happened to U.S. president Johnson in 1968 during the Vietnam War. Or a popular war can help secure a government's mandate to continue in power, as happened to Margaret Thatcher in Britain after the 1982 Falkland Islands War.

In democracies, where the flow of information and opinions is not tightly restricted by the state, it is possible to accurately measure public opinion through *polling*—analyzing the responses of a sample group to questionnaires in order to infer the opinions of a larger population. This is impossible to do in societies where secret police monitor any expressions of opposition to state policies. But in societies where individuals feel free to speak out, public opinion polling has developed into an important part of the foreign policy making process.

Occasionally a foreign policy issue is decided directly by a referendum of the entire citizenry (the United States lacks such a tradition, which is strong in Switzerland and Denmark, for example).[27] In 1992 the Maastricht Treaty on closer European political union (see pp. 400–401) was narrowly defeated in a popular referendum in Denmark, despite the support of the government, all major political parties, labor unions, and other political groups. (A later referendum narrowly approved the treaty.) In France, the treaty

---

[27]Rourke, John T., Richard P. Hiskes, and Cyrus Ernesto Zirakzadeh. *Direct Democracy and International Politics: Deciding International Issues Through Referendums.* Boulder, CO: Lynne Rienner, 1992.

barely squeaked through. Because of these signs of public opposition to the Maastricht Treaty, European leaders were forced to reconsider the pace of European integration.

However, even in the most open democracies, states do not merely *respond* to public opinion. Decision makers enjoy some autonomy to make their own choices, and they are also pulled in various directions by bureaucracies and interest groups, whose views often conflict with the direction favored by public opinion at large. Furthermore, public opinion is seldom unified on any policy, and sophisticated polling can show that particular segments of the population (regions of the country, genders, income groups, races, etc.) often differ in their perceptions of foreign policy issues. So a politician may respond to the opinion of one constituency rather than the whole population. Public opinion varies considerably over time on many foreign policy issues. States use propaganda (in dictatorships) or try to manipulate the media (in democracies) to keep public opinion from diverging too much from state policies.

In democracies, public opinion generally has *less effect on foreign policy than on domestic policy*. In addition to their power to shape opinion on all issues (by making televised speeches, for instance), national leaders traditionally have additional latitude to make decisions in the international realm. This derives from the special need of states to act in a unified way in order to function effectively in the international system, as well as from the traditions of secrecy and diplomacy that remove IR from the realm of ordinary domestic politics. In the nuclear age, IR was further distanced from everyday political life in the nuclear states by the public's willingness to trust experts and officials to deal with the technical and frightening issues of nuclear strategy. Over time, however, peace movements have sometimes pushed governments toward disarmament (see "Peace Movements" on pp. 131–132).

In the case of Japan, public opinion is a major political force restraining the military spending of the government, its commitment of military forces beyond Japan's borders, and especially the development of nuclear weapons (which are within Japan's technical abilities). The ruling party—under pressure from the United States to share the burden of defense and to shoulder its responsibilities as a great power—has slowly but steadily pushed to increase Japan's military spending and allow Japanese military forces to expand their role modestly (in the 1980s, to patrol Asian sea lanes vital to Japanese trade; in the 1990s to participate in UN peacekeeping operations). Repeatedly, these efforts have been slowed or rebuffed by strong public opinion against the military. In Japan people remember the horrible consequences of militarism in the 1930s and World War II, culminating in the nuclear bombings of 1945. They are suspicious of any increase in the size or role of military forces, and dead set against Japan's having nuclear weapons. In this case public opinion strongly constrains the state's conduct of foreign policy.

The *attentive public* in a democracy is that minority of the population that stays informed about international issues. This segment varies somewhat from one issue to another—for instance, ethnic groups may be informed about foreign policies that affect their ancestral countries—but there is also a core of people who care in general about foreign affairs and follow them closely. The most active members of the attentive public on foreign affairs constitute a foreign policy *elite*—people with power and influence who affect foreign policy. This elite includes people within governments as well as outsiders such as business people, journalists, lobbyists, professors of political science, and so forth. Public opinion polls show that elite opinions sometimes (but not always) differ considerably from those of the general population, and sometimes from those of the government as well.[28]

Governments sometimes adopt foreign policies for the specific purpose of generating public approval and hence gaining domestic legitimacy.[29] This is the case when a government undertakes a war or foreign military intervention at a time of domestic difficulty, to distract attention and gain public support—taking advantage of the **rally 'round the flag syndrome** (the public's increased support for government leaders during wartime, at least in the short term). Citizens who would not hesitate to criticize their government's policies on education or health care will often refrain from criticism when the government is at war and the lives of the nation's soldiers are on the line. Britain's prime minister, Margaret Thatcher, enjoyed high popularity ratings during the 1982 Falkland Islands War, as did President Bush in the 1989 Panama and 1991 Gulf wars.

However, wars that go on too long, or are not successful, can turn public opinion against the government and even lead to a popular uprising to overthrow the government. In Argentina, the military government in 1982 led the country into war with Britain over the Falkland Islands. At first Argentineans rallied around the flag, but after losing the war they rallied around the cause of getting rid of the military government, and they replaced it with a new civilian government that prosecuted the former leaders. So public opinion with regard to wars can be a two-edged sword.

Democracy

Overall, the differences in the foreign policy process from one state to another are more influenced by a state's type of government than by the particular constellation of bureaucracies, interest groups, or individuals within it. Government types include military dictatorship, communist party rule, one-party (noncommunist) rule, and various forms of multiparty democracy. Relatively democratic states tend to share values and interests, and hence to get along better with each other than with nondemocracies.

Nondemocratic governments are often called **authoritarian.** This means that the government rules without the need to stand for free elections, to respect civil and political rights, to allow freedom of the press, and so forth. By contrast, a **democracy** is a government of the people, usually through elected representatives, and usually with a respect for individual rights in society (especially rights to hold political ideas differing from those of the government).

In practice, most states lie along a spectrum with some mix of democratic and authoritarian elements. For example, because of campaign contributions, even democracies in North America and Japan (and elsewhere) give greater influence to rich people than to poor people. In many states, governments control TV and radio stations, putting opposition politicians at a disadvantage in elections. In Angola, relatively fair elections were

---

[28]Holsti, Ole R. Public Opinion and Foreign Policy: Challenges to the Almond-Lippmann Consensus. *International Studies Quarterly* 36 (4), 1992: 439–66. Nincic, Miroslav. A Sensible Public: New Perspectives on Popular Opinion and Foreign Policy. *Journal of Conflict Resolution* 36 (4), 1992: 772–89. Brace, Paul, and Barbara Hinckley. *Follow the Leader.* New York: Basic Books, 1993.

[29]Morgan, T. Clifton, and Kenneth N. Bickers. Domestic Discontent and the External Use of Force. *Journal of Conflict Resolution* 36 (1), 1992: 25–52. Bueno de Mesquita, Bruce, Randolph M. Siverson, and Gary Woller. War and the Fate of Regimes: A Comparative Analysis. *American Political Science Review* 86 (3), 1992: 638–46.

held in 1992, but the losing side rejected the results and resorted to military attacks. In Burma, a military government held elections, lost them, and then simply refused to step aside or allow the newly elected parliament to meet. In Algeria the military canceled elections midway as Islamic parties were winning.

How do the foreign policies of democracies differ from those of authoritarian governments? We have already referred to a number of differences in the nature of internal decision making, the effects of interest groups, and the importance of public opinion. Although public opinion and interest group activism operate in some form in virtually all states, they are more influential in democracies.

Some two hundred years ago, Kant argued that lasting peace would depend on states' becoming republics, with legislatures to check the power of monarchs (or presidents) to make war. He thought that checks and balances in government would act as a brake on the use of military force—as compared to autocratic governments where a single individual (or small ruling group) could make war without regard for the effect on the population.

IR scholars have examined the empirical evidence for the idea that democracy is associated with a fundamentally different kind of foreign policy than is authoritarianism.[30] One theory they considered was that democracies are generally *more peaceful* than authoritarian governments (fighting fewer, or smaller, wars). This turned out to be *not true*. Democracies fight as many wars as do authoritarian states. Indeed, the three most war-prone states of the past two centuries (according to political scientists who count wars) were France, Russia, and Britain. Britain was a democracy throughout, France for part of the period, and Russia not at all.

What *is* true about democracies is that although they fight wars against authoritarian states, *democracies almost never fight each other*. No major historical cases contradict this generalization. Why this is so is not entirely clear. There have not been many democracies for very long, so the generalization could be just a coincidence, though this seems unlikely. It may be that democracies do not tend to have severe conflicts with each other, as they tend to be capitalist states whose trade relations create strong interdependence (war would be costly since it would disrupt trade). Or, citizens of democratic societies (whose support is necessary for wars to be waged) may simply not see the citizens of other democracies as enemies. By contrast, authoritarian governments of other states can be seen as enemies. Note that the peace among democracies gives empirical support to a long-standing liberal claim which, because it is rooted in the domestic level of analysis, contradicts a fundamental premise of realism (that the most important explanations are to be found at the interstate level).

Over the last two centuries, democracy has become more and more widespread as a form of government, and this is changing the nature of the foreign policy process worldwide. Many states do not yet have democratic governments (the most important of these

---

[30]Russett, Bruce. *Grasping the Democratic Peace: Principles for a Post–Cold War World.* Princeton: Princeton University Press, 1993. Russett, Bruce. *Controlling the Sword: The Democratic Governance of National Security.* Cambridge, MA: Harvard University Press, 1990. Ember, Carol R., Melvin Ember, and Bruce M. Russett. Peace Between Participatory Polities: A Cross-Cultural Test of the "Democracies Rarely Fight Each Other" Hypothesis. *World Politics* 44 (4), 1992: 573–99. Nincic, Miroslav. *Democracy and Foreign Policy: The Fallacy of Political Realism.* New York: Columbia University Press, 1992. Bueno de Mesquita, Bruce J., Robert W. Jackman, and Randolph M. Siverson, eds. Democracy and Foreign Policy: Community and Constraint [special issue]. *Journal of Conflict Resolution* 35 (2), 1991.

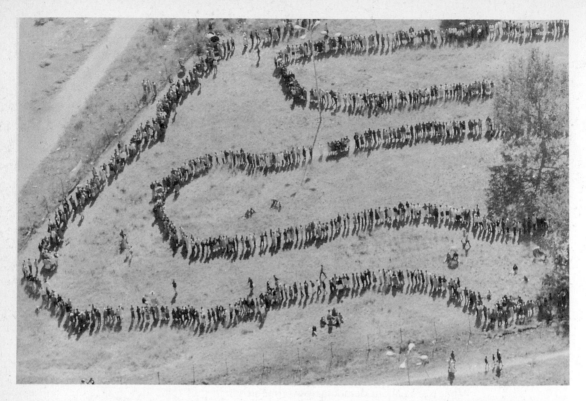

Upsurges of democratic movements throughout the world in recent years testify to the power of the idea of democracy. Since democracies rarely fight each other, worldwide democratization might lead to lasting peace. Here South Africans line up to vote in that country's first all-race elections, which ended apartheid and elected Nelson Mandela as president, April 1994.

is China). And existing democracies are imperfect in various ways—from political apathy in the United States and corruption in Japan to autocratic traditions in Russia. Nonetheless, the trend is toward democratization in most of the world's regions.

In the past decade this trend accelerated in several ways. New democracies emerged in several (though not all) states of the old Soviet bloc. Military governments were replaced with democratically elected civilian ones throughout most of Latin America as well as in several African and Asian countries. South Africa, the last white-ruled African country, adopted majority rule in 1994. In several of these cases (for instance, in the Philippines in 1986), long-standing dictatorships were ended by nonviolent popular movements. Elsewhere (for instance, in Nicaragua) civil wars ended with internationally supervised democratic elections. Finally, in several other authoritarian states such as China, public pressures for greater democratic participation in government became evident in the past decade. We do not know where these trends toward democracy will lead, but it is now conceivable that someday all or most of the world's states will be democratically governed.

As the trend toward democratization continues, wars may become less and less frequent. As Kant envisaged, an international community based on peaceful relations may emerge. Perhaps the initial burst of cooperation among the great powers after the Cold War could be seen as a halting step toward Kant's vision.[31]

A caution is in order, however. The generalization about democracies not fighting each other is historically valid but not necessarily applicable in the future. By way of analogy, there was a generalization during the Cold War to the effect that communist governments never yield power peacefully. That generalization held up beautifully until suddenly a series of communist governments did just that around 1990.

As is evident in the preceding discussion, the attempt to explain foreign policy in a general and *theoretical* way has met only limited success. This is one reason why realists continued to find simple unitary actor models of the state useful; the domestic and individual elements of the foreign policy process add much complexity and unpredictability. One area of foreign policy where knowledge stands on a somewhat firmer basis is the *descriptive* effort to understand how particular mechanisms of foreign policy formation operate in various states. This chapter has largely bypassed such approaches until now (they belong properly to the field of comparative politics). But an exception will be made in the case of the United States, because its foreign policies have such importance for world politics as a whole.

❖ U.S. FOREIGN POLICY

The remainder of this chapter discusses the foreign policy of the United States, which is the most influential actor in the world and (coincidentally) the home of most readers of this book. These sections revisit some of the main concepts of the chapter with reference to concrete situations in one country. The discussion begins with the most important individual decision maker (the president), then examines the foreign policy bureaucracy, and then moves to the influence of domestic politics and public opinion on U.S. foreign policy.[32]

The President

The hub of foreign policy in the United States is the *president*. The U.S. Constitution establishes the president as commander in chief of the military, chief executive of the diplomatic and policy bureaucracies, head of state, and spokesperson for the nation in the international arena (for instance, in negotiating treaties).

---

[31]Doyle, Michael W. Liberalism and World Politics. *American Political Science Review* 80 (4), 1986: 1151–70.

[32]Nathan, James A., and James K. Oliver. *Foreign Policy Making and the American Political System.* 3rd ed. Baltimore: Johns Hopkins University Press, 1994. Michalak, Stanley J., Jr., ed. *Competing Conceptions of American Foreign Policy: Worldviews in Conflict.* New York: HarperCollins, 1992. Ambrose, Stephen E. *Rise to Globalism: American Foreign Policy Since 1938.* 6th ed. New York: Penguin, 1991. Ikenberry, G. John, ed. *American Foreign Policy: Theoretical Essays.* New York: Harper & Row, 1989.

Formally, the president administers most of the foreign policy bureaucracy through the *cabinet*, which consists of the heads of the major departments (Defense, State, Treasury, etc.), who are called *secretaries*. In many countries, major foreign policies must be approved by the cabinet, whose ministers often represent different political parties in a coalition government. The U.S. cabinet has less power, and the president's inner circle of advisors (which may include particular secretaries) has more. Increasingly important are the dozens of independent (noncabinet) agencies, such as the CIA, which report directly to the president. Table 4.1 summarizes the executive branch agencies involved in U.S. foreign policy.

The *Executive Office*—headed by the president's *chief of staff*—coordinates the president's immediate circle of advisors and the independent federal agencies; it controls access to the president and the president's schedule; and through the Office of Management and Budget (OMB) it tries to tame the vast federal bureaucracy and integrate the budget requests of various agencies. Within the Executive Office are two small but powerful agencies—the *Office of the U.S. Trade Representative (USTR)* and the **National Security Council (NSC).** The USTR negotiates trade agreements with other states and monitors compliance (see Chapter 8). The NSC advises the president on international security affairs. (In 1993 President Clinton created a new National Economic Council parallel to the NSC, reflecting the view that economics now matters as much as military affairs in national security.) The USTR staff of under 200 people compares to about 5,000 people with international responsibilities in the Commerce Department, and the NSC staff of fewer than 100 compares to about 20,000 in the State Department. But the power of these agencies is multiplied by their proximity to the president. The NSC headquarters is in the White House basement, which also has a situation room where the president can follow international crises or events. (Further below is a bomb shelter for use in a nuclear attack.)

The NSC itself is a committee on which the president, vice president, and secretaries of state and defense sit. It is supported by the *NSC staff*, which is headed by the *assistant for national security affairs (ANSA)*, who traditionally briefs the president every morning on international security issues. (President Bush complained during the tumultuous period at the end of the Cold War that although the briefing was up-to-date in the morning, it was often obsolete by the end of the day.) The NSC staff is supposed to be neutral and give the president options and information. It can integrate policy objectives into a coherent whole, as it did in the *NSC-68* document of 1950, which laid out U.S. goals in the Cold War. However, critics accuse the NSC of narrowing, not expanding, the options that reach the president.

Increasingly, presidents have used the NSC to actively develop foreign policy rather than just integrate information and identify options. Since the 1970s this has created chronic tensions between the NSC (White House) and the State Department; the secretaries of state under Presidents Carter and Reagan both resigned in part because they felt robbed of power by the ANSA.

Presidents have also used the NSC several times for covert operations because it is small and close at hand. In the most spectacular case, President Reagan's close friend and CIA director, William Casey, bypassed his own agency and ran covert operations spanning three continents using the NSC staff in the White House basement. These operations, managed by an obscure NSC aide named Oliver North, led to the **Iran-Contra**

TABLE 4.1 U.S. EXECUTIVE BRANCH AGENCIES INVOLVED IN FOREIGN POLICY[a]

President/Executive Office

Office of Management and Budget (OMB)—administers bureaucracy, integrates budgets

National Security Council (NSC)—monitors and advises president on security affairs

U.S. Trade Representative (USTR)—negotiates trade agreements, monitors compliance

National Economic Council—advises president on international economic policy

Cabinet Departments

State—operates embassies, conducts diplomacy

Defense—operates military forces

Commerce—regulates international trade

Treasury—coordinates economic policy with the other major industrialized nations

Justice—international law enforcement including drug trafficking and terrorism

Agriculture—agricultural trade policies

Energy—nuclear weapons production

Others—Veterans' Affairs, Transportation, Education, Health and Human Services, etc.

Cabinet-status officials—representative to the UN, CIA director

Agencies Working in International Security Areas

Central Intelligence Agency (CIA)—intelligence gathering and covert operations

Arms Control and Disarmament Agency (ACDA)—statistics and advice on arms control

Federal Emergency Management Agency (FEMA)—civil defense in wartime

U.S. Information Agency (USIA)—Voice of America and other broadcast media

Agencies Working in International Political Economy Areas

U.S. Agency for International Development—administers foreign aid

Export-Import Bank—administers loans and credits to support U.S. trade

Federal Maritime Commission—regulates shipping by sea in and out of U.S. ports

Panama Canal Commission—administers the canal pending its return to Panama

Securities and Exchange Commission (SEC)—regulates financial markets

Environmental Protection Agency (EPA)—international environmental policy

National Aeronautics and Space Administration (NASA)—coordinates space activities

National Science Foundation (NSF)—funds and oversees international scientific collaboration

Peace Corps—sends U.S. volunteers to poor countries

U.S. International Development Cooperation Agency—coordinates development policy

Inter-American Foundation—promotes good relations with Latin America

African Development Foundation—promotes economic development in Africa

[a]Many of these agencies also have other responsibilities.

scandal when the public learned that the NSC had sold weapons to Iran in exchange for the freedom of U.S. hostages held in Lebanon, and had then used the Iranian payments to illegally fund Nicaraguan Contra rebels. Since this scandal, the NSC has returned to a traditional advisory role and the ANSA has not challenged the secretary of state for foreign policy leadership.

Presidents rely on an *inner circle of advisors* (including the ANSA) in making foreign policy decisions. The composition and operation of the inner circle varies from one president to the next. For instance, President Johnson had "Tuesday lunches" to discuss national security policy with the secretaries of state and of defense, the ANSA, the head of the CIA, the chairman of the Joint Chiefs of Staff (the top military officer), and Johnson's press secretary. President Carter had weekly breakfast meetings for the same purpose. Presidents also create *interagency groups* to coordinate policy across the various bureaucratic agencies—again outside the formal cabinet. Usually these groups are organized by topic (trade, terrorism, arms control, etc.).

At times, frustration with the bureaucracy has led presidents to bypass normal channels of diplomacy altogether. During the 1962 Cuban Missile Crisis, President Kennedy used an ad hoc circle of 13 advisors and negotiated through his brother Robert (the attorney general). President Nixon's ANSA, Henry Kissinger, secretly negotiated with China, the Soviet Union, and North Vietnam outside of the State Department or other formal bureaucratic structures.

Federal Agencies

Presidents struggle so hard to exercise power over the formal bureaucratic agencies because the latter are so huge and bureaucratic (cumbersome, routinized, conservative) that presidents cannot easily control them. Also, these agencies are staffed mostly by career officials who do not share the loyalty to the president of political appointees.

The *State Department*, for example, has about 20,000 employees and sends over 1,000 cables a day to its embassies. Most decisions made on a daily basis never reach the secretary of state (much less the president). The top levels of the department are staffed by political appointees whose term coincides with the president who appointed them. But the middle and lower ranks of the bureaucracy are filled with career professionals owing little loyalty to any particular president. From these bureaucrats' perspective, presidents come and go, but foreign policy is ongoing. The national interest is served, they believe, by the stability of overall U.S. goals and positions in international affairs.

The State Department is organized by regions, with a superstructure of overall policy officials at the top, managing programs and policies that are not regionally based. The *U.S. Agency for International Development (USAID)* employs more than a quarter of State Department personnel and provides nonmilitary U.S. foreign aid worldwide (see Chapter 13, p. 541). USAID operates with autonomy, but was being considered by Congress in the mid-1990s for possible merger with other agencies into the State Department. State Department task forces consider issues such as terrorism or specific crises such as the Iraq-Kuwait crisis in 1990. The main lines of authority, however, follow world *regions* (similar but not identical to those used in this book). Each region has a *bureau* headed by an *assistant secretary* that coordinates U.S. policy in the region. Regional bureaus try to interpret data from the region and develop coherent responses. Within regions, each country is represented by a *country desk* at which a desk officer stays abreast of developments in that

The president is the center of U.S. foreign policy. His power is symbolized by the constant presence of an aide with a briefcase containing codes required for a nuclear strike. Here President Bush descends the steps of the Hungarian parliament, July 1989.

country and communicates with the embassy there. U.S. embassy staffs abroad conduct negotiations, facilitate travel by U.S. citizens, provide information and U.S. visas to foreign nationals, gather intelligence, and coordinate all U.S. government activities in the country.

The *Department of Defense (DOD)*—or *Pentagon* (after its five-sided headquarters)—is the most important foreign policy agency other than the State Department. It is also the State Department's traditional rival in courting the president's support. DOD is headed by the *secretary of defense*—a civilian presidential appointee. It is mainly organized by military branch—the Departments of the Army, of the Navy (including the Marine Corps), and of the Air Force. Each has a civilian secretary and a military chief of staff (or the equivalent), under whom are the officers and soldiers, commands and agencies, within that branch of the military. But the branch secretaries have lost power over time as military operations have become more integrated across branches. Branch commanders meet together as the **Joint Chiefs of Staff (JCS),** headed by the *chairman of the Joint Chiefs of Staff,* who is the nation's top military officer.

Specific *commands*—both functional ones such as military airlift and regional ones such as the Pacific command—integrate resources from all the military branches. A regional command has a field commander in chief heading the chain of command for all forces in the region. As in the State Department, DOD has a *policy superstructure* to formulate overall policies. Civilian professionals intermingle with military officers to deal with policy areas such as humanitarian assistance or special forces and operations (commandos, hostage rescues, etc.). Attached to the policy bureaucracy are *defense agencies* with functions ranging from auditing contracts to planning logistics.

After the Vietnam War the policy preferences of the DOD changed. Top military officers became more reluctant to send U.S. forces into combat. The Pentagon now generally supports using military force only when there is a clear goal that can be achieved militarily, when the public supports the action, and when military forces can be used massively for a quick victory. Panama in 1989 and Kuwait in 1991 fit these new conditions. Intervention in Bosnia was generally opposed by military officers as not meeting the criteria. Military officers also demand greater autonomy of decision once force is committed, in order to avoid the problems created in the Vietnam War when President Johnson sat in the White House situation room daily picking targets for bombing raids. (Worse yet, in Bosnia it was French, British, or Japanese UN officials who held decision power over each bombing attack by U.S. planes in NATO forces.)

The *Central Intelligence Agency (CIA)* was established in 1947 to consolidate intelligence activities under a single, civilian director. However, several other U.S. intelligence agencies continue to operate, mostly in the military. Together these agencies are known as the *intelligence community*.

The CIA has two distinct functions. The more important one is to *gather intelligence* about other countries using various means—a role it shares with the other intelligence agencies. The second function is to undertake *covert operations* aimed at influencing events in foreign countries. These operations can range from funding a political party in a foreign election to assassinating a foreign state leader (now illegal under U.S. law). Covert operations are supposed to be the sole domain of the CIA (despite occasional forays by others such as the NSC).

Intelligence gathering relies on various sources, including satellite photos, electronic monitoring of telephone lines and other communications, reports from embassies, and information in the open press. Some kinds of information are obtained by sending agents into foreign countries as *spies*. They use ingenuity (plus money and technology) to penetrate walls of secrecy that foreign governments have constructed around their plans and capabilities. In the 1991 Gulf War, a lack of U.S. spies within Iraq reportedly hindered efforts to locate Iraq's nuclear weapons complex. During that war the U.S. secretary of defense said he was getting his information about the war from CNN like everyone else (including Saddam Hussein).

The DOD has its own intelligence-gathering agencies, especially for information relevant to battlefield deployments and other tactical matters. The *Defense Intelligence Agency (DIA)* coordinates these military intelligence activities. Satellite reconnaissance is now so important and so massive (with huge numbers of photos to be analyzed every day) that a separate agency attends solely to the task—the *National Reconnaissance Office (NRO)* operated by the Air Force. The largest intelligence agency of all, also within DOD, is the *National Security Agency (NSA)*, whose mission is encoding U.S. communications and breaking the codes for foreign communications. The size and complexity of this mission speaks to the increasing importance of information in war (see pp. 233–234). The NSA is believed to have the most powerful computer facility in the world.

The budgets of U.S. intelligence agencies are secret, but have been estimated at around $28 billion in 1995—including $3 billion for the CIA, $4 billion for NSA, $7 billion for NRO, $0.5 billion for the DIA, and $12 billion for other Pentagon agencies. Clearly these operations taken together are very large.

The CIA's *covert operations* in foreign countries are the dagger part of the "cloak and dagger" spy business. Several thousand such operations were mounted during the Cold War, when the CIA and its Soviet counterpart, the *KGB*, waged an ongoing worldwide secret war. CIA covert operations in the 1950s overthrew unfriendly foreign governments—in Iran and Guatemala—by organizing coups against them. The CIA-organized Bay of Pigs invasion in Cuba in 1961 was its first big failure, followed by other failed efforts against the Castro government (including eight assassination attempts).

CIA covert activities were sharply scaled back after congressional hearings in the 1970s revealed scandals. CIA covert operations now must be reported to special congressional *oversight* committees through an elaborate set of procedures. The difficulties of the oversight process were summarized by a member of the House Intelligence Committee (Norman Mineta), who said in the 1980s, "We are like mushrooms. They keep us in the dark and feed us a lot of manure."

In the post–Cold War era, fewer CIA resources are devoted to counting Soviet missile factories and more to counting Japanese computer factories. In 1995 France and the United States had an unusual public dispute when France accused four Americans of spying—on French trade deals. U.S. analysts after the Cold War also pored over information in Russia and Eastern Europe after the fall of communism there. For instance, the East German secret police archives held information about international terrorists.

Congress and Domestic Politics

Tension between the Congress and the executive branch is rooted in the checks and balances of the Constitution.[33] The Constitution grants Congress extensive foreign policy powers, the most important being the ability to *allocate funds* for foreign policy purposes and for the military. Sometimes presidents make promises to other states only to find that Congress refuses to fund them. Presidents try to induce Congress to allocate the funds they need, through lobbying, public pressure, "horse trading," and so forth.

A second congressional power in foreign policy is the ability to *legislate* the foreign policy behavior of the executive branch—or at least set limits on that behavior. For instance, after the Vietnam War, Congress temporarily barred the president from involvement in civil wars in Angola and Nicaragua. Congress is also explicitly authorized by the Constitution to regulate international commerce and to punish international crimes such as piracy (today, terrorism) and violations of international law.

Through both its control of funding and its legislative powers, Congress controls the size and shape of U.S. military forces. The *military budget* goes through a long and complex cycle each year as it moves through Congress. Detailed allocations of funds and the procurement of specific weapons must be worked out by congressional committees in the House and Senate, starting from proposals submitted by the president.

---

[33]Hinckley, Barbara. *Less Than Meets the Eye: Foreign Policy Making and the Myth of the Assertive Congress.* Chicago: The University of Chicago Press, 1994. Blechman, Barry M. *The Politics of National Security: Congress and U.S. Defense Policy.* New York: Oxford University Press, 1990. Warburg, Gerald Felix. *Conflict and Consensus: The Struggle Between Congress and the President over Foreign Policymaking.* New York: Harper & Row, 1989.

A third power of Congress is to *declare war*. This has become less important because the United States has not formally declared war in fifty years. However, Congress passed the equivalent of such a declaration when it narrowly voted, before the Gulf War, to authorize the president to use force there. Congress and the president have struggled over the power to use force, especially when control of the White House and Congress have rested with different parties, as has been true most often in the 1980s and 1990s.

The Senate must *ratify treaties* (by a two-thirds vote). To avoid the need for ratification, presidents have frequently used *executive agreements* instead of treaties when concluding deals with foreign states. The Senate also has the power to confirm or block *presidential appointments* to top foreign policy positions. For example, the Senate rejected President Bush's first nominee for secretary of defense in 1989.

During the 1950s and 1960s, Congress gave over much foreign policy power to the president, who seemed to need extraordinary freedom of action in a world of superpower rivalry and potential nuclear war. Congressional resolutions from 1949 to 1964 gave the president broad latitude in handling U.S. military and political activities in a variety of regions—Europe, China, the Middle East, Cuba, Berlin, and Vietnam.

Since the 1970s, the failures of U.S. policy in Vietnam, along with revelations about CIA activities, have led to a more assertive Congress on foreign policy. The **War Powers Act,** passed in 1973 over President Nixon's veto, strictly limits the president's authority to commit U.S. military forces to combat. Under the act, Congress must be notified promptly and operations cannot continue beyond 60 days without congressional approval. Presidents since 1973 have accommodated, evaded, or ignored the War Powers Act to various degrees.

Congress is limited by its need to rely on the executive branch for much expertise and information regarding complex international issues. Congress does have *committees* to work on foreign policy issues—each with its skilled and knowledgeable *committee staff*—but these are no match for the executive branch bureaucracies. Committee staffs often organize *hearings* where witnesses, including agency officials (but not the president) are called to testify about policies. The Senate and House have separate and generally parallel sets of committees. The most important committees for foreign policy are the Senate *Foreign Relations* and House *International Relations* Committees, the Senate and House *Armed Services* Committees, the *Intelligence* Committees, the *Budget* and *Appropriations* Committees, the *Judiciary* Committees (immigration policy), *Commerce* and *Finance* (*Ways and Means*) Committees, and related committees on energy, science and technology, banking, and agriculture.

Unlike the president, members of Congress are elected by small geographical units with particular *parochial interests*, such as a local defense factory or military base, an industry seeking protection from international competition, or an ethnic group with foreign policy interests.[34] Although Congress can patch together legislation through the process of compromise among these diverse interests, it seems that only the president can give a coherent direction to U.S. foreign policy.

U.S. public opinion is generally less concerned with foreign affairs than domestic

---

[34]Kegley, Charles W., Jr., and Eugene R. Wittkopf, eds. *Domestic Sources of American Foreign Policy: Insights and Evidence*. New York: St. Martin's Press, 1988.

Congress often struggles with the president over foreign policy, especially over the use of force. President Bush won Senate approval for the Gulf War by just one vote. Here, Senator Robert Dole (R-KS) visits troops deployed to the Gulf (1991). As Senate majority leader in 1995, Dole pushed legislation to overturn President Clinton's Bosnia policy.

ones.[35] But the public does become engaged with foreign policy issues at certain times. One such time is when dangers to the nation appear to be high or foreign affairs impinge on the public's everyday life—as when the United States is at war, or when U.S. citizens faced gasoline shortages in the 1970s. Another time is when the decisions involve big issues such as the Vietnam War or (at times) the nuclear arms race. A key influence on public opinion is the content of scenes appearing on TV: U.S. soldiers were sent to Somalia to assist in relief efforts in 1992 after TV news showed the heart-rending results of civil war and famine there. But after TV news showed pictures of an American soldier's body being dragged through the streets by members of a Somali faction, after a deadly firefight that killed 18 U.S. soldiers, public opinion shifted quickly against the Somalia operation. In the case of Bosnia, officials in the U.S. State Department said privately that the main goal of U.S. policy was often just to keep the conflict there off of the front pages of newspapers (an elusive goal, as it turned out).

---

[35]Holsti, Ole R., and James N. Rosenau. Consensus Lost. Consensus Regained? Foreign Policy Beliefs of American Leaders, 1976–1980. *International Studies Quarterly* 30 (4), 1986: 375–410. Wittkopf, Eugene R. *Faces of Internationalism: Public Opinion and American Foreign Policy.* Durham: Duke University Press, 1990. Hartley, Thomas, and Bruce Russett. Public Opinion and the Common Defense: Who Governs Military Spending in the United States? *American Political Science Review* 86 (4), 1992: 905–15.

Presidential elections can also focus public attention on foreign policy. Although international issues seldom dominate elections, they often receive increased attention during the campaign. Incumbent presidents can use to advantage their power to manipulate international events—from getting into a war to holding a summit meeting. Challengers fear that an incumbent will create an "October surprise" in international affairs that dominates the news just before the election. Reagan's campaign in 1980, for instance, feared that President Carter would win the release of U.S. hostages in Iran just before the election.

Most foreign policy is made without great pressure from public opinion. A foreign policy elite—decision makers in the State Department, the other executive agencies, and Congress, along with some prominent journalists, some university professors, and some business people and interest group leaders—has relatively high autonomy. This elite foreign policy process gives policy greater stability and continuity, protecting it from the turbulence of domestic politics. But it also makes the foreign policy process less democratic and gives a greater voice to powerful interests such as the military-industrial complex. Members of the foreign policy elite are *unrepresentative* of the U.S. population in character, values, and outlook, according to critics. Its members are predominantly male, upper class, white, Anglo-Saxon, and Protestant. Most went to prestigious schools such as Ivy League universities and pursued careers in law, business, or academia.

An important wing of the foreign policy elite, and its link to the population, is made up of the *mass media* (or "press"). Journalists serve as the gatekeepers of information passing from the foreign policy elite to the public. And, through public opinion polls, the media collect information from the public and pass it to the elite. The media and government often conflict, because of the traditional role of the press as a watchdog and critic of government actions and powers. The media try to uncover and publicize that which the government wants to hide, especially in situations like the Iran-Contra scandal.

The press has great power over government because people in the foreign policy elite rely on the media for information about foreign affairs. It is said that State Department officers read the *New York Times* every morning so they know what is going on in the world as they write their reports that day. Reportedly, President Kennedy ordered his own subscription to the *New York Times* so that he could anticipate by a day the reports coming to him from the State Department. Foreign policy elites also get information from (among other places) the *Washington Post* and the *Wall Street Journal,* and from in-depth television news shows such as the *MacNeil/Lehrer Newshour,* Sunday morning interview shows, and the Cable News Network (CNN). Nonelite citizens increasingly turned to talk shows in the 1990s, a new element for political leaders to contend with. The media can define the *terms of political debate* about foreign policy issues, boxing the government into a corner or giving it a clear path.

Yet the *media also depend on government* for information; the size and resources of the foreign policy bureaucracies dwarf those of the press. This gives the government great power to *manipulate* journalists by feeding them information, in order to shape the news and influence public opinion. Government decision makers can create dramatic stories in foreign relations—through summit meetings, crises, actions, and so forth. Bureaucrats can also *leak* secret information to the press in order to support their own point of view and win bureaucratic battles. Finally, the military and the press have a running battle about journalists' access to military operations; for instance, in the invasion of Grenada and the

Gulf War, U.S. military censors limited media coverage. A *Doonesbury* cartoon during the 1983 U.S. invasion of Grenada exaggerated the relationship slightly:

Soldier: Who goes there? Friend or Foe?

Journalist: Press!

Soldier: BLAM! BLAM!

U.S. Views of the World

All of the struggles just described—between the public and the elite, the media and government, the Congress and the executive branch, the State Department and the Pentagon—produce U.S. foreign policy. One might expect policies formed in such a manner to be unstable or even incoherent. Instead, one finds a consistency in the themes and directions that shape U.S. foreign policy, especially national security policy.[36] This has allowed the United States to maintain a *bipartisan foreign policy* on many important international issues. When President Clinton replaced President Bush, for instance, the change in party control of the White House did not lead to sudden, dramatic changes in the direction of U.S. foreign policy. Even on issues where Clinton as a candidate had criticized Bush, such as on Bosnia and China, the ultimate directions of Clinton's policies diverged little from Bush's. Indeed, while the particular issues change over the years and decades, several key themes in U.S. foreign policy repeatedly appear.[37]

One such theme is the alternation of *internationalist* and *isolationist* moods in U.S. foreign policy.[38] The United States has never quite come to terms with its role as the world's most powerful state. It was founded as a breakaway from the European-based international system, and its growth in the nineteenth century was based on industrialization and expansion within North America. The United States acquired overseas colonies in the Philippines and Puerto Rico but did not relish a role as imperial power. In World War I, the country waited three years to weigh in and refused to join the League of Nations afterwards. U.S. isolationism peaked in the 1930s; public opinion polls late in that decade showed 95 percent of the U.S. public opposed to participation in a future great European war, and about 70 percent opposed to joining the League of Nations or joining with other nations to stop aggression.[39]

Internationalists, such as presidents Theodore Roosevelt and Woodrow Wilson, favored U.S. leadership and activism in world affairs. These views seemed vindicated by the failure of isolationism to prevent World War II (or to allow the United States to stay out

---

[36]Sarkesian, Sam C. *U.S. National Security: Policymakers, Processes, and Politics.* 2nd ed. Boulder, CO: Lynne Rienner, 1994. Jordan, Amos A., William J. Taylor, Jr., and Lawrence J. Korb. *American National Security: Policy and Process.* 3rd ed. Baltimore: Johns Hopkins University Press, 1989. Perret, Geoffrey. *A Country Made by War: From the Revolution to Vietnam: The Story of America's Rise to Power.* New York: Random House, 1989.

[37]Oye, Kenneth A., Robert J. Lieber, and Donald Rothchild, eds. *Eagle in a New World: American Grand Strategy in the Post–Cold War Era.* New York: HarperCollins, 1992. Lynn-Jones, Sean M., and Steven E. Miller, eds. *America's Strategy in a Changing World: An "International Security" Reader.* Cambridge, MA: MIT Press, 1992.

[38]Klingberg, Frank L. The Historical Alternation of Moods in American Foreign Policy. *World Politics* 4 (2), 1952: 239–73.

[39]Free, Lloyd A., and Hadley Cantril. *The Political Beliefs of Americans.* New Brunswick: Rutgers University Press, 1967.

of it). U.S. leaders after the war became alarmed by the threat of Soviet (and then Chinese) communism and drummed up U.S. public opinion to favor a strong internationalism during the Cold War. The United States became an activist, global superpower. Despite an inward-looking period after the Vietnam War, the United States has largely continued this internationalist stance ever since. However, in the post–Cold War era U.S. internationalism is tempered by a new cost consciousness and a willingness to work through the UN to attain U.S. goals. For instance, over 80 percent of U.S. citizens in a 1991 poll favored joint action of the United States and UN to stop dictators who sponsor terrorism, get nuclear weapons, violate human rights, invade their neighbors, or build up offensive armed forces.[40] However, by the mid-1990s U.S. and UN failures in Somalia, Bosnia, and elsewhere—as well as new strains in America's traditional alliances with Europe and Japan—seemed to be fueling a new isolationism.

A second recurrent theme in U.S. foreign policy is that of *morality versus realism* as the basis of U.S. actions toward other states. Should the United States be a moral guiding light for the world—pursuing goals such as democracy and human rights—or should it concentrate on pursuing its own national interests, such as natural resources and geostrategic position? Most of the U.S. public does not want to be "the world's policeman" and resents paying for the security of allies such as Japan and Europe. After the collapse of the Soviet Union, efforts to win congressional approval of foreign aid for Russia had to be couched in terms of U.S. interests (avoiding a return to costly Russian aggression), not humanitarian assistance or a moral obligation to help a nation achieve freedom and democracy. Yet the U.S. people also think of themselves as a caring nation and a beacon of hope for the world. Presidents continue to say things like "where people are hungry, we will help. We are the United States!"[41]

The tension between morality and self-interest in U.S. foreign policy was evident during the Iraq-Kuwait crisis of 1990–1991. Secretary of State Baker roamed the globe stitching together an impressive coalition dedicated to moral principles—stopping aggression and building a "New World Order." Then he told U.S. reporters to tell the American people that "it's about jobs" because cheap Middle East oil would stimulate U.S. economic growth. Perhaps U.S. public opinion supported the administration's policy in this case because it was both moral *and* in the national interest—achieving both the reversal of aggression and cheap Middle East oil. In Bosnia, the tension between morality and self-interest played out in a zigzag U.S. policy that seemed unable to find its bearings.

Beyond these broad themes concerning the basis of U.S. involvement in international affairs, U.S. foreign policy toward world *regions* also shows a certain continuity. U.S. interests and experiences, however, differ from one region to another.[42]

---

[40]*Americans Talk Issues.* Surveys 16 & 17. Washington, DC: The Americans Talk Issues Foundation, 1991.

[41]President George Bush, June 1992, speech on Sarajevo. McElroy, Robert W. *Morality and American Foreign Policy: The Role of Ethics in International Affairs.* Princeton: Princeton University Press, 1992. Smith, Tony. *America's Mission: The United States and the Worldwide Struggle for Democracy in the Twentieth Century.* Princeton: Princeton University Press, 1994. Korey, William. *The Promises We Keep: Human Rights, The Helsinki Process and American Foreign Policy.* New York: St. Martin's Press, 1994.

[42]Schraeder, Peter J., ed. *Intervention in the 1990s: U.S. Foreign Policy in the Third World.* 2nd ed. Boulder, CO: Lynne Rienner, 1992. Macdonald, Douglas J. *Adventures in Chaos: American Intervention for Reform in the Third World.* Cambridge, MA: Harvard University Press, 1992. Haass, Richard N. *Conflicts Unending: The United States and Regional Disputes.* New Haven: Yale University Press, 1990. Kolko, Gabriel. *Confronting the Third World: United States Foreign Policy, 1945–1980.* New York: Random/Pantheon, 1991.

Because of its nearby location, *Latin America* has historically preoccupied U.S. policy makers. The *Monroe Doctrine* of 1823 sought to limit European states' power in the region and establish a U.S. sphere of influence there. The United States built and owned (until recently) the Panama Canal. Over the years, the United States has used armed intervention more times in Latin America than anywhere else (most recently in the 1989 invasion of Panama). Some of the most intense conflicts of the Cold War occurred there (the Cuban Missile Crisis, the Nicaraguan civil war, and U.S. invasions of the Dominican Republic and of Grenada). In the 1990s, Latin America's importance to the United States revolves around newer issues: drug trafficking, immigration, and the U.S.-Canadian-Mexican free-trade area (see pp. 196–198, 494–498, and 343, respectively).[43]

Europe was the central concern of U.S. foreign policy during the Cold War. Half of U.S. military spending in those decades went for the defense of Western Europe. Europe is the most important trading partner for the United States overall, and NATO partners continue to be among the closest U.S. allies. In the 1990s, the economic integration of Western Europe and the troubled efforts to incorporate Russia and Eastern Europe into the Western economic system are shaping the context of U.S. foreign policy.[44]

U.S. activity has expanded westward into *Asia and the Pacific* ever since the United States forced open Japan's ports to trade in 1854 and advocated an "open door" for trade in China. Various Asian-Pacific territories fell under U.S. control after wars with Spain in 1898 and Japan in 1941–1945. Historically, U.S. leaders have seen the Pacific as an "American lake." The Korean and Vietnam Wars took place in Asia, and Japan emerged in recent decades as one of the most important U.S. trading partners and political allies. China is becoming more important in U.S. security and trade concerns alike, and the newly industrializing countries (NICs) of Asia are becoming more important to U.S. economic policy.[45]

Finally, the *Middle East* is of special interest in U.S. foreign policy, especially since the United States became a net importer of energy in the 1970s. The region's conflicts figured in Cold War strategy and in post–Cold War realignments. The *Truman Doctrine* (1947), *Eisenhower Doctrine* (1957), and *Carter Doctrine* (1980) all extended U.S. commitments in the region, as did President Bush's "New World Order" (1990).[46] The United States played a key role as mediator in the Arab-Israeli peace agreements (with Egypt in the 1970s and with the PLO and Jordan in the 1990s).

---

[43]Lowenthal, Abraham F., ed. *Exporting Democracy: The United States and Latin America*. Baltimore: Johns Hopkins University Press, 1991. Lowenthal, Abraham F. *Partners in Conflict: The United States and Latin America in the 1990s*. Revised edition. Baltimore: Johns Hopkins University Press, 1990. LaFeber, Walter. *Inevitable Revolutions: The United States in Central America*. 2nd ed. New York: W. W. Norton, 1993. Pastor, Robert A. *Whirlpool: U.S. Foreign Policy Toward Latin America and the Caribbean*. Princeton: Princeton University Press, 1992. Pastor, Robert A., and Jorge Castañeda. *Limits to Friendship: The United States and Mexico*. New York: Random/Vintage, 1991.

[44]Kelleher McArdle, Catherine. *The Future of European Security: An Interim Assessment*. Washington, DC: The Brookings Institution, 1995. Harper, John Lamberton. *American Visions of Europe: Franklin D. Roosevelt, George F. Kennan, and Dean G. Acheson*. New York: Cambridge University Press, 1994.

[45]Harding, Harry. *A Fragile Relationship: The United States and China Since 1972*. Washington, DC: The Brookings Institution, 1992. Rotter, Andrew J., ed. *Light at the End of the Tunnel: A Vietnam War Anthology*. New York: St. Martin's Press, 1991.

[46]Herrmann, Richard K. The Middle East and the New World Order: Rethinking U.S. Political Strategy After the Gulf War. *International Security* 16 (2), 1991: 42–75.

In each of these regions, U.S. foreign policy contains a mixture of pragmatic interests (such as Middle East oil), global ideals (such as promoting democracy), and the influence of domestic political groups (such as ethnic groups tied to various regions).

Both regionally and globally, U.S. foreign policy is a complex outcome of a complex process. It results from the struggle of competing themes, competing domestic interests, and competing government agencies. No single individual, agency, or guiding principle determines the outcome.

Yet foreign policy—in the United States and in other countries—does achieve a certain overall coherence. States do form foreign policy on an issue or toward a region; it is not just an incoherent collection of decisions and actions taken from time to time. Out of the turbulent internal processes of foreign policy formation come relatively coherent interests and policies that states pursue.

Of course, those aggregate state interests and policies frequently come into conflict with the interests and policies of other states. Such conflicts are the subject of the next chapter.

❖ CHAPTER SUMMARY

- ◆ Foreign policies are strategies governments use to guide their actions toward other states. The foreign policy process is the set of procedures and structures that states use to arrive at foreign policy decisions and to implement them.

- ◆ In the rational model of decision making, officials choose the action whose consequences best help to meet the state's established goals. By contrast, in the organizational process model, decisions result from routine administrative procedures, and in the government bargaining (or bureaucratic politics) model, decisions result from negotiations among governmental agencies with different interests in the outcome.

- ◆ The actions of individual decision makers are influenced by their personalities, values, and beliefs as well as by common psychological factors that diverge from rationality. These factors include misperception, selective perception, emotional biases, and cognitive biases (including the effort to reduce cognitive dissonance).

- ◆ Foreign policy decisions are also influenced by the psychology of groups (including "groupthink"), the procedures used to reach decisions, and the roles of participants.

- ◆ During crises, the potentials for misperception and error are amplified.

- ◆ Struggles over the direction of foreign policy are common between professional bureaucrats and politicians, as well as between different government agencies.

- ◆ Domestic constituencies (interest groups) have distinct interests in foreign policies and often organize politically to promote those interests.

- ◆ Prominent among such constituencies—especially in the United States and Russia, and especially during the Cold War—have been military-industrial complexes consisting of military industries and others with an interest in high military spending.

- ◆ Public opinion influences governments' foreign policy decisions (more so in democracies than in authoritarian states), but governments also manipulate public opinion.

- ◆ Democracies have historically fought as many wars as authoritarian states, but democracies have not fought wars against other democracies.

- ◆ U.S. foreign policy making is dominated by the president, who often struggles to control the State and Defense Departments and other large agencies.

◆ The U.S. Congress has important foreign policy roles, and checks the power of the president and executive branch.

◆ Public opinion affects U.S. foreign policy indirectly, but in day-to-day policy making a small elite operates with relative freedom.

◆ U.S. foreign policy revolves around several consistent themes, including isolationism versus internationalism and morality versus realism.

❖ THINKING CRITICALLY

1. India and Pakistan are neighbors and enemies. Given the problems of misperception and bias in foreign policy decision making, what steps could you propose each government to adopt to help ensure that policies adopted toward the other succeed in achieving goals established by national leaders?

2. Sometimes aggressive international actions are attributed to a "madman" such as Iraq's Saddam Hussein or Nazi Germany's Adolf Hitler. Do you agree that such leaders (each of whose actions severely damaged his state's well-being) must be "mad"? What other factors could account for their actions? How do you think such people achieve and maintain national leadership?

3. Imagine a sudden, unexpected crisis caused by an event like the explosion of a nuclear weapon (of unknown origin) in Moscow. Given the dangers inherent in crisis decision making, what steps could the leaders of affected states take to prevent the situation from spinning out of control? Which of these steps might be taken *before* any crisis occurred, to prepare for a future crisis?

4. Inasmuch as democracies do not seem to fight wars with each other, do existing democracies have a national security interest in seeing democratization spread to today's authoritarian states? If so, how can that interest be reconciled with the long-standing norm of noninterference in the internal affairs of other sovereign states?

5. Traditionally the U.S. foreign policy elite has faced only occasional pressure from mass public opinion. Is the role of television changing this relationship? If you were a top U.S. foreign policy maker, what steps could you take to keep TV news from shaping the foreign policy agenda before you could define your own goals and directions?

❖ KEY TERMS

foreign policy process
rational model
organizational process
   (model)
government bargaining
   (model)
misperceptions, selective
   perceptions
information screens
optimizing
satisficing

groupthink
interest groups
military-industrial complex
public opinion
rally 'round the flag syndrome
authoritarian (government)
democracy
National Security Council (NSC)
Iran-Contra scandal
Joint Chiefs of Staff (JCS)
War Powers Act

*Palestinian youth slings
stone at Israeli police,
February 1994.*

CHAPTER 5

INTERNATIONAL CONFLICT

❖ THE CAUSES OF WAR

The Roman writer Seneca said nearly two thousand years ago: "Of war men ask the outcome, not the cause."[1] This is not true of political scientists. They ask two fundamental questions: Why do international actors (states and nonstate actors alike) come into conflict with each other? And why do those conflicts sometimes lead to violence and war? (War will be formally defined a bit later.) This chapter addresses both questions.

Conflict among states is not an unusual condition but an ordinary one. **Conflict** may be defined as a difference in preferred outcomes in a bargaining situation. International conflicts will always exist. In such conflict bargaining, states develop capabilities that give them leverage to obtain more favorable outcomes than they could obtain without such leverage. Whether fair or unfair, the ultimate outcome of the bargaining process is a **settlement** of the particular conflict.

Violence is an effective form of leverage in some bargaining situations (see p. 61). So states develop capabilities for using violence in international conflicts (these military capabilities are discussed in Chapter 6). But these capabilities only sometimes come into play in international conflicts. In fact, the great majority of international conflicts do not lead to war, but are resolved in other ways. The study of the causes of war, then, is really an effort to understand the *outbreak* of war—the resort to violence as a means of leverage in international conflicts. But understanding the outbreak of war requires studying the underlying conflicts as well.

The question of why war breaks out can be approached in different ways. More descriptive approaches, favored by historians, tend to focus narrowly on specific direct causes of the outbreak of war, which vary from one war to another.[2] For example, one could say that the assassination of Archduke Ferdinand in 1914 "caused" World War I.

---

[1]Seneca. Hercules Furens. In *Seneca's Tragedies*. Volume 1. Translated by Frank Justus Miller. London: Heinemann, 1917.

[2]Howard, Michael. *The Causes of Wars, and Other Essays*. 2nd ed. Cambridge, MA: Harvard University Press, 1984. Rotberg, Robert I., and Theodore K. Rabb, eds. *The Origin and Prevention of Major Wars*. New York: Cambridge University Press, 1989.

More general, theoretical approaches, favored by many political scientists, tend to focus on the search for general explanations, applicable to a variety of contexts, about why wars break out.[3] For example, one can see World War I as caused by shifts in the balance of power among European states, with the assassination being only a catalyst.

Theories About War

Broad generalizations about the causes of war have been elusive. Wars do not have a single or simple cause. Many theories about war have been put forward, but few have universal validity. As a way of organizing these theories (types of explanations of war) we may again use levels of analysis.[4] Wars have been viewed as resulting from forces and processes operating on all the levels.

The Individual Level On the *individual* level of analysis, the question of why conflicts turn violent revolves around the familiar issue of rationality. One theory, consistent with realism, holds that the use of war and other violent means of leverage in international conflicts is normal and reflects *rational* decisions of national leaders: that "wars begin with conscious and reasoned decisions based on the calculation, made by *both* parties, that they can achieve more by going to war than by remaining at peace."[5]

An opposite theory holds that conflicts often escalate to war because of *deviations from rationality* in the individual decision-making processes of national leaders. These potentials were discussed in Chapter 4—information screens, cognitive biases, groupthink, and so forth. A related theory holds that the education and mentality of whole populations of individuals determines whether conflicts become violent. In this view, public nationalism or ethnic hatred may put pressure on leaders to solve conflicts violently. Some IR researchers and activists alike believe that the reeducation of populations can result in fewer conflicts turning violent.

Neither of these theories holds up very well. Some wars clearly reflect rational calculations of national leaders, whereas others clearly were mistakes and cannot be considered rational. Certainly some individual leaders seem more prone to turn to military force to try to settle conflicts on favorable terms. But no reliable guide has been discovered that predicts what kind of person will be a more warlike or more peaceful leader. A man of war can become a man of peace, as did Egypt's Anwar Sadat, for example. Individuals of many

---

[3]Vasquez, John A. *The War Puzzle*. New York: Cambridge University Press, 1993. Brown, Seyom. *The Causes and Prevention of War*. New York: St. Martin's Press, 1987. Dessler, David. Beyond Correlations: Toward a Causal Theory of War. *International Studies Quarterly* 35 (3), 1991: 337–55. Holsti, Kalevi J. *Peace and War: Armed Conflicts and International Order*. New York: Cambridge University Press, 1991. Siverson, Randolph M., and Harvey Starr. *The Diffusion of War: A Study of Opportunity and Willingness*. Ann Arbor: University of Michigan Press, 1991. Thompson, W. Scott, and Kenneth M. Jensen, with Richard N. Smith and Kimber M. Schrauh, eds. *Approaches to Peace: An Intellectual Map*. Washington: United States Institute of Peace Press, 1991. Beer, Francis. *Peace Against War*. San Francisco: W. H. Freeman, 1981. Blainey, Geoffrey. *The Causes of War*. London: Macmillan, 1973.

[4]Levy, Jack S. The Causes of War: A Review of Theories and Evidence. In P. E. Tetlock et al., eds. *Behavior, Society, and Nuclear War*. Volume 1. New York: Oxford University Press, 1989.

[5]Howard. *Causes of Wars* (see footnote 2 in this chapter), p. 22. Emphasis in original.

cultural backgrounds and religions lead their states into war, as do both male and female leaders.

The Domestic Level The *domestic* level of analysis draws attention to the characteristics of states or societies that may make them more or less prone to use violence in resolving conflicts. During the Cold War, Marxists frequently said that the aggressive and greedy *capitalist* states were prone to use violence in international conflicts while Western leaders claimed that the expansionist, ideological, and totalitarian nature of communist states made them especially prone to using violence. In truth, both types of society have used violence regularly in international conflicts.

Likewise, we have seen (in Chapter 4) that both democracies and authoritarian states fight wars (though democracies do not fight other democracies). Rich industrialized states and poor agrarian ones both use war at times. In fact, anthropologists have found that a wide range of *preagricultural* hunting-gathering societies are also prone to warfare under certain circumstances.[6] Thus the potential for warfare seems to be universal across cultures, types of society, and time periods—although the importance and frequency of war varies greatly from case to case.

Few useful generalizations can be made about what kinds of domestic society are more prone or less prone to war (given that all are war-prone to some extent). The same society may change greatly in this regard over time. For example, Japan was prone to using violence in international conflicts before World War II, but averse to such violence since then. Likewise the !Kung bush people in Angola and Namibia—a hunting-gathering society—were observed by anthropologists in the 1960s to be extremely peaceful. Yet anthropologists in the 1930s had observed them engaging in murderous intergroup violence.[7] If there are general principles to explain why some societies at some times are more peaceful than others and why they change under different conditions, political scientists have not yet identified them.

The Interstate Level The theories at the *interstate* level explain wars in terms of power relations among major actors in the international system. Some of these theories are discussed in Chapter 2. For example, power transition theory holds that conflicts generate large wars at times when power is relatively equally distributed and a rising power is threatening to overtake a declining hegemon in overall position.

At this level, too, there are competing theories that seem incompatible. Deterrence, as we have seen, is supposed to stop wars by building up power and threatening its use. But the theory of arms races holds that wars are caused, not prevented, by such actions.

---

[6]Ember, Carol R., and Melvin Ember. Resource Unpredictability, Mistrust, and War: A Cross-Cultural Study. *Journal of Conflict Resolution* 36 (2), 1992: 242–62. Turner, Paul R., and David Pitt, eds. *The Anthropology of War and Peace: Perspectives on the Nuclear Age.* Granby, MA: Bergin and Garvey, 1989. Rubinstein, Robert A., and Mary LeCron Foster, eds. *The Social Dynamics of Peace and Conflict: Culture in International Security.* Boulder, CO: Westview, 1988. Ross, Marc Howard. A Cross-Cultural Theory of Political Conflict and Violence. *Political Psychology* 7, 1986: 427–69. Fabbro, David. Peaceful Societies: An Introduction. *Journal of Peace Research* 15, 1978: 67–83.

[7]Eibl-Eibesfeldt, Irenaus. *The Biology of Peace and War: Men, Animals, and Aggression.* New York: Viking, 1979.

As is noted in Chapter 2, no general formula has been discovered to tell us in what circumstances each of these principles holds true.

Lacking a reliable method for predicting what power configurations among states will lead to war, some political scientists have tried to estimate by statistical means the *probabilities* that one or another type of interstate relationship might lead to war.[8] A major research effort along these lines is the *Correlates of War* project. Even though this project has focused fairly narrowly on nineteenth- and twentieth-century interstate wars, it has not yet accounted for the outbreak of war in a general way. And once again the results seem to change over time. For instance, researchers found that a tight system of alliances was associated with a higher probability of war in the nineteenth century but a lower probability in the twentieth century. Such a finding hardly tells us what to expect in the twenty-first century.[9]

Scholars use quantitative and statistical methods to test various ideas about international conflict, such as by analyzing data about wars, weapons, and arms races.[10] For example, researchers are analyzing conflicts between democracies to see why they almost never escalate to war (see "Democracy" on pp. 160–163). The quality of data, however, is a major problem for statistical studies of infrequent occurrences such as wars.

The Global Level At the *global* level of analysis a number of theories of war have been proposed. There are several variations on the idea that major warfare in the international system is *cyclical*. One such approach links large wars with *long economic waves* (also called *Kondratieff cycles*) in the world economy, of about fifty years' duration. Another approach links the largest wars with a one hundred-year cycle based on the creation and decay of world orders (see "Hegemony" on pp. 81–82). These cycle theories at best can explain only general tendencies toward war in the international system over time.[11]

An opposite approach in some ways is the theory of linear long-term change in the propensity for war in the international system. In this theory, war as an outcome of conflict is becoming less likely over time due to the worldwide development of both technology and international norms. Some IR scholars argue that war and military force are becoming *obsolete* as a leverage in international conflicts because these means of influence are not very effective in today's highly complex, interdependent world. A parallel line of argument holds that military technology has developed so far that it is too powerful to use in most conflicts; this is especially applicable to nuclear weapons.

---

[8]Wright, Quincy. *A Study of War*. Chicago: University of Chicago Press, 1965 [1942]. Richardson, Lewis F. *Arms and Insecurity*. Pittsburgh: Boxwood Press, 1960. Midlarsky, Manus I., ed. *Handbook of War Studies*. Ann Arbor: The University of Michigan Press, 1993. Cioffi-Revilla, Claudio. *The Scientific Measurement of International Conflict: Handbook of Datasets on Crises and War, 1495–1988 A.D.* Boulder, CO: Lynne Rienner, 1990.

[9]Singer, J. David, and Paul F. Diehl, eds. *Measuring the Correlates of War*. Ann Arbor: University of Michigan Press, 1990. Vasquez, John A. The Steps to War: Toward a Scientific Explanation of Correlates of War Findings [review article]. *World Politics* 40 (1), 1987: 108–44. Leng, Russell J., and J. David Singer. Militarized Interstate Crises: The BCOW Typology and Its Applications. *International Studies Quarterly* 32 (2), 1988: 155–74. Small, Melvin, and J. David Singer. *Resort to Arms: International and Civil Wars, 1816–1980*. Beverly Hills: Sage, 1982.

[10]Wallensteen, Peter, ed. *Peace Research: Achievements and Challenges*. Boulder, CO: Westview, 1988. Van Den Dungen, Peter. Jean De Bloch: A 19th Century Peace Researcher. *Peace Research* 15 (3), 1983: 21–27.

[11]Goldstein, Joshua S. *Long Cycles: Prosperity and War in the Modern Age*. New Haven: Yale University Press, 1988. Modelski, George. *Long Cycles in World Politics*. Seattle: University of Washington Press, 1987.

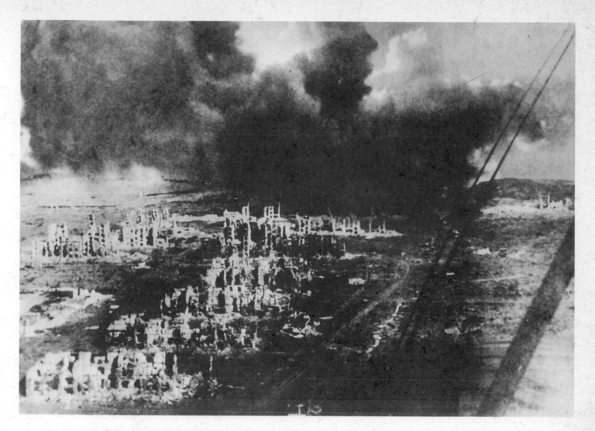

Political scientists do not agree on a theory of why great wars like World War II occur, and cannot predict whether it could happen again. The city of Stalingrad (Volgograd) was decimated during Germany's invasion of the Soviet Union, 1943.

A possibly complementary theory traces the obsolescence of war to the evolution of international norms against the use of force. War once was seen as a normal way to resolve disputes but now is considered distasteful. An analogy has been drawn to the practices of slavery and dueling—once considered normal but now obsolete.[12] However, all these arguments about the linear evolution of warfare in the international system rest on mixed empirical evidence. In truth, although major wars have become shorter and less frequent, they are more destructive than ever when they occur. And even in the absence of major wars, smaller wars around the world have not yet evolved out of existence. War may be obsolete, but it still occurs with great frequency.[13]

Thus, although the levels of analysis suggest many explanations for why conflicts lead to war, few such generalizations hold up. On all the levels of analysis, competing theories offer very different explanations for why some conflicts become violent and others do not. Empirical evidence is not strong enough to decide definitively among these vari-

---

[12]Mueller, John. *Retreat from Doomsday: The Obsolescence of Major War.* New York: Basic Books, 1989.

[13]Brogan, Patrick. *The Fighting Never Stopped: A Comprehensive Guide to World Conflict Since 1945.* New York: Random/Vintage, 1991.

ous explanations; rather, each seems to work some of the time. For these reasons, political scientists cannot yet predict with any confidence which of the world's many international conflicts will lead to war.

What can be done is to study various types of conflicts to understand better what it is that states are fighting about. We can also examine some of the alternative forms of leverage, violent and nonviolent, that states use in conflicts.

❖ CONFLICTS OF INTEREST

One way of looking at international conflicts is to assume that all states want maximum power relative to other states. Conflict then becomes a universal condition among states, and they fight about power, status, and alliances in the international system. This realist approach does offer insights into power rivalries that sometimes become rather detached from any specific underlying conflict over territory, religion, or other specific causes. For example, China attacked Vietnam in 1979 to "teach Vietnam a lesson" after Vietnam invaded Cambodia and overthrew the Chinese-aligned Khmer Rouge government there. China did not want Vietnamese territory; it just wanted to administer punishment for an act it disapproved of. In such cases the struggle for power in an abstract sense takes on its own logic.

But why do states want power? Power gives states specific benefits—the ability to gain better outcomes in bargaining over particular issues that matter to their well-being. Most international conflicts—including those behind the dozens of wars going on at present—are disputes about concrete grievances and demands. They are about territorial borders, ethnic hatreds, revolutions, and so forth. To understand the nature of international conflicts, including their potential for becoming violent, one must study the underlying interests and goals of the actors involved.

The following sections discuss six types of international conflict. Three are conflicts over tangible material interests:

1. Territorial border disputes, including secession attempts
2. Conflicts over who controls national governments
3. Economic conflicts over trade, money, natural resources, drug trafficking, and other such economic transactions

The other three types of conflict concern less-tangible clashes of ideas:

4. Ethnic conflicts
5. Religious conflicts
6. Ideological conflicts

These six types of conflict are not mutually exclusive categories, and they overlap considerably in practice. For example, the conflicts between Russia and Ukraine after the 1991 Soviet breakup were quite complex. The two new states had a *territorial* dispute over the Crimean peninsula, which Soviet premier Khrushchev had transferred to Ukraine in the 1950s. There and elsewhere, *ethnic* Russians living in Ukraine, and Ukrainians in Russia, experienced ethnic conflict. There are *religious* differences between Ukrainian and Russian forms of Christianity. The two states also had *economic* conflicts over trade and money, such as Russian fears that Ukraine, after printing its own currency, would flood Russia with old rubles (thereby fueling inflation in Russia).

These multiple conflicts did not lead to the use of military force or violence, however, in the first five years after the Soviet breakup. This is a reminder that conflict is not the same as war—that most conflicts do not entail the use of violence. Conflicts of interest lie at the heart of all international bargaining, from trade negotiations to arms control. Only sometimes do they turn violent.

Territorial Disputes

Among the international conflicts that concern tangible "goods," those about territory have special importance because of the territorial nature of the state (see "Anarchy and Sovereignty" on pp. 72–74). Conflicts over control of territory are really of two varieties: territorial disputes (about where borders are drawn) and conflicts over control of entire states within existing borders (discussed next under "Control of Governments"). Consider first differences over where borders between two states should be drawn—that is, about which state should control disputed territory.[14]

Because states value home territory with an almost fanatical devotion, border disputes tend to be among the most intractable in IR. States will seldom yield territory in exchange for money or any other positive reward. Nor do states quickly forget territory that they lose involuntarily. For example, after defeating France in 1871, Germany took the French provinces of Alsace and Lorraine. French indignation over the loss and French nationalism among the inhabitants of the province made Germany's possession of the territory difficult; ultimately it was returned after Germany lost World War I. The goal of regaining territory lost to another state ("redeeming" it) is called **irredentism.** It is a form of nationalism that leads directly to serious interstate conflicts.[15]

Because of their association with the integrity of states, territories are valued far beyond any inherent economic or strategic value they hold. For example, after Israel and Egypt made peace in 1978, it took them a decade to settle a border dispute at Taba, a tiny plot of beach front on which Israeli developers had built a hotel just slightly across the old border. The two states finally submitted the issue for binding arbitration, and Egypt ended up in possession. For Egypt, regaining every inch of territory was a matter of national honor and a symbol of the sovereignty and territorial integrity that defined Egyptian statehood. French leaders felt the same way about Alsace-Lorraine.

An exception to this attitude toward territories used to be found with regard to colonies and other territorial possessions of states. Because these were not part of the home territory or associated with the idea of the nation, they were valued only as property that could be won, lost, sold, or traded in political deals and wars. For example, France and Russia sold their territories in Louisiana and Alaska, respectively, to the United States. Such territories are valued for the natural resources they contain or for their geopolitical location. For example, Britain has since 1704 possessed the tiny Rock of

---

[14]Diehl, Paul F., and Gary Goertz. *Territorial Changes and International Conflict*. New York: Routledge, 1992.

[15]Chazan, Naomi, ed. *Irredentism and International Politics*. Boulder, CO: Lynne Rienner, 1991.

Gibraltar commanding the entrance to the Mediterranean; the United States has since 1898 owned the Pacific island of Guam, used for military bases. But today, with few colonies remaining, most of the world's territory is home territory to some state.

The value states place on home territory seems undiminished despite the apparent reduction in the inherent value of territory over time as technology has developed. Historically, territory was the basis of economic production—agriculture and the extraction of raw materials. Even in Sun Tzu's time, it was said that "land is the foundation of the state." It was in these agrarian societies that the international system developed. Winning and losing wars meant gaining or losing territory, with which came wealth and hence long-term power. Today, however, much more wealth derives from trade and technology than from agriculture. The costs of most territorial disputes appear to outweigh any economic benefits that the territory in question could provide.

Means of Controlling Territory Historically, military means have been the most effective leverage for controlling territory, and wars have often redrawn the borders of states. Military forces can seize control on the ground in a way that is hard to contest by any means except other military forces. For example, when Saddam Hussein redrew the borders of Iraq to include Kuwait, his opponents found no better means to dislodge him (economic sanctions, diplomatic isolation, negotiations, and so on) than to use military force themselves.

Since World War II, however, there has been a strong norm in the international system *against* attempting to alter borders by force. Such attempts are considered grave matters by the international community. That is why when Iraq annexed Kuwait and erased its borders, most states treated the act as not merely distasteful but intolerable. The war against Iraq was intended to underline the message that even after the Cold War international borders are inviolable. By contrast, it is considered a lesser offense for one state merely to topple another's government and install a puppet regime, even if done violently, because although that state's *sovereignty* has clearly been violated its *territorial integrity* has not. The principle is: governments come and go; borders remain.

The norm of territorial integrity was illustrated in 1992 when a group of Pakistani nationalists tried to march across the border into a part of India populated by fellow Muslims. Pakistani police fired on their own nationalists to keep them from reaching the border (and possibly triggering a war with India). Because the Pakistani action upheld the integrity of the border, Western democracies did not disapprove of Pakistan's use of force against the demonstrators.

Secession Efforts by a province or region to secede from an existing state are a special type of conflict over borders—not the borders of two existing states but the efforts by a substate area to draw international borders around itself as a new state. Dozens of secession movements exist around the world, of varying sizes and political effectiveness, but they succeed in seceding only rarely. The existing state almost always tries to hold onto the area in question.

For example, the oil-rich and mainly Muslim republic of Chechnya, one of the republics of Russia (the Russian Federation), tried to split away from Russia in the early 1990s after the Soviet Union collapsed. In 1994–1995 Russia sent in a huge armed force which destroyed the Chechen capital, but faced fierce resistance from Chechen national-

Efforts by a region to secede from a state are a frequent source of current international conflict. But international norms generally treat such conflicts as internal matters unless they spill over borders. Russia in 1995 violently asserted control of its oil-rich, mainly Muslim republic of Chechnya. Here Chechen rebels stand in the rubble of the presidential palace in the capital, Grozny, after weeks of Russian bombardment (January 1995).

ist guerrillas. Similarly, Kurdish separatists in Turkey and Iraq have sought a Kurdish state carved out of those two states; in 1995 Turkey sent a large military force into northern Iraq to destroy Kurdish guerrilla bases.

As these examples suggest, wars of secession can be large and deadly, and they can easily spill over international borders or draw in other countries. This cross-border spillover is particularly likely if members of an ethnic or religious group span two sides of a border, constituting the majority group in one state and a majority in a nearby region of another state, but a minority in the other state as a whole. This pattern is found in such cases as Bosnia-Serbia, Moldova-Russia, Iraq-Iran, and India-Pakistan. In some cases the secessionists wish to merge their territories with the neighboring state (as in the effort to carve out a "greater Serbia"), which amounts to redrawing the international border. International norms frown on such an outcome. (Ethnic and religious conflict are discussed later in this chapter.)

The strong international norms of sovereignty and territorial integrity treat secession movements as domestic problems that are of little concern to other states. In the case of Chechnya, the Western governments objected not to Russia's goal of maintaining control of the republic, but only to Russia's methods of waging the war—which included indiscriminate bombing and shelling of civilian areas. These actions violated standards of human rights, which are however a weaker set of norms than those promoting state sovereignty. Thus, the international community expressed concern over Russia's treatment of

Chechen civilians, but President Clinton went to Moscow for a summit meeting while the Russian military was still fighting in Chechnya. Even when secession conflicts occasionally spill over international borders, as with Turkey's incursion into Iraq in 1995, the international community tends to treat the matter lightly as long as the cross-border incursion is temporary. The general principle is something like "We existing states all have our own domestic problems and disaffected groups or regions, so we must stick together behind sovereignty and territorial integrity."

Messy border problems have been created in some recent cases in which multinational states broke up into pieces. In such cases, borders which had been internal become international, and since these borders are new they may be more vulnerable to challenge. Certainly this is the case in the former Yugoslavia, where ethnic groups had intermingled and intermarried, leaving mixed populations in most of the Yugoslav republics. When Yugoslavia broke up in 1991–1992, several republics declared their independence as separate states. Two of these, Croatia and Bosnia, contained minority populations of ethnic Serbs. Serbia seized effective control (through local Serbian militias with the support of the Serbian-dominated Yugoslav federal army) of significant areas of Croatia and Bosnia that contained Serbian communities or linked such populations geographically. Non-Serbian populations in these areas were driven out or massacred—"ethnic cleansing." Then, when Croatia reconquered most of its territory in 1995, Serbian populations there in turn fled from Croatia. Ethnic nationalism proved stronger than multiethnic tolerance in both Serbia and Croatia, making borders problematical.

The breakup of a state need not lead to violence, however. Czechoslovakia split into the Czech Republic and Slovakia in a cooperative and civil manner. And the breakup of the Soviet Union did not lead to violent territorial disputes between republics in *most* cases, even where ethnic groups were split across new international borders (such as Ukraine-Russia).

The norm against forceful redrawing of borders does not apply to cases of colonial liberation. It is only the territorial integrity of existing, intact states that the international system respects. For example, when the Portuguese relinquished control of their Asian colony of East Timor in 1975, neighboring Indonesia invaded and annexed it. Because East Timor had never gained status as an independent state, Indonesia's action drew little opposition from other states. As with Chechnya, the problem was treated as one of human rights. Similarly, when Spain withdrew from its colony of Western Sahara (in North Africa), neighboring Morocco sought to incorporate the phosphate-rich territory, over the objections of a guerrilla group that wanted to establish an independent state. Neighboring Mauritania also claimed part of the territory for a while. The international community showed little interest in the outcome of this conflict. (Morocco apparently had prevailed by the mid-1990s.)

Interstate Borders Border disputes between existing states are taken more seriously by the international community, but are less common than secessionist conflicts. Because of the norm of territorial integrity, few important border conflicts remain among long-established states. At one time, huge chunks of territory were passed between states at the stroke of a pen (on a peace treaty or marriage contract). For instance, after the Soviet Union defeated Germany in World War II, Soviet borders expanded to take in the eastern part of Poland while Germany's borders with Poland contracted westward to compensate; it was said that Poland had taken a step sideways. This kind of wholesale redrawing of borders has not occurred among established states for fifty years.

Since 1945, only a minuscule amount of territory has changed hands between established states through force. Such efforts have been made, but have failed. For instance, when Iraq attacked Iran in 1980, one objective was to control the Shatt-al-Arab waterway (with access to the Persian Gulf) because of its commercial and strategic value. But ten years and a million deaths later, the Iran-Iraq border was back where it started. Bits of land have changed hands in recent decades through war, but it is remarkable how small those bits have been. (Again, this does not apply to the formation of new states and the fragmenting of old ones.)

Furthermore, when territorial disputes do occur between established states, they *can* sometimes be settled peacefully, especially when the territory involved is small compared with the states disputing it. The Soviet Union simply agreed to China's boundary preferences in 1986 after the two states had disputed ownership of some minor river islands for years. El Salvador and Honduras got the World Court to adjudicate their border disputes in 1992. And in 1994 a panel of Latin American judges settled a century-long border dispute between Argentina and Chile over some mountainous terrain that both claimed. The 3-2 ruling, after the countries submitted the dispute for judicial arbitration, awarded the territory to Argentina and provoked howls of protest from Chile—even a hair-pulling fight between the Chilean and Argentine contestants in the Miss World beauty contest two months later. But despite the strong feelings evoked by the loss of territory, Argentina and Chile had settled 22 of 24 remaining border disputes peacefully over the previous ten years (after nearly going to war in 1978 over disputed islands).

Lingering Disputes Today, only a few of the world's interstate borders are disputed. Nonetheless, those that persist are important sources of international conflict. Among the most difficult are the borders of *Israel*, which have never been firmly defined and recognized by its neighbors. The 1948 cease-fire lines resulting from Israel's war of independence expanded in the 1967 war, then contracted again on the Egyptian border with the Camp David peace treaty of 1978. The remaining pieces of territory occupied in 1967—the *West Bank* near Jordan, the *Gaza Strip* near Egypt, and the *Golan Heights* of Syria—are central to the Arab-Israeli conflict. The Israeli-Palestinian agreements of 1993–1995 tried to move toward Palestinian autonomy in Gaza and parts of the West Bank, but the borders of this Palestinian entity were not resolved as of 1995.

Another major border dispute is in the *Kashmir* area where India, Pakistan, and China intersect. Among the former Soviet republics, the most serious border dispute is over *Nagorno-Karabakh*, an Armenian-populated territory within neighboring Azerbaijan, which both republics want to control. Russia and Ukraine had some conflicts over the Crimean peninsula, which had been part of Russia until Soviet leader Khrushchev gave it to Ukraine as a birthday present in the 1950s (when Ukraine and Russia were both part of the Soviet Union).

Peru and Ecuador fought border skirmishes in early 1995 over a nearly inaccessible stretch of mountainous terrain, part of a sizable area signed over to Peru following its victory in a brief war with Ecuador in 1941. The conflict, which involved no tangible assets worth fighting over, illustrated once again the almost mystical power of territory as a symbol of national honor, and the continuing usefulness of nationalism in generating political support for state leaders (the popularity of both presidents increased as the conflict heated up). International mediation cooled off the dispute after a month of fighting.

Many of the world's other remaining interstate territorial disputes—and often the most serious ones—concern the control of small islands, which may provide strategic advantages, natural resources (such as offshore oil), or fishing rights. Perhaps the most serious of these in the mid-1990s was China's effort to assert control over the tiny disputed *Spratly Islands* in the South China Sea—which are closer to Vietnam, the Philippines, Malaysia, and Brunei than to China, and are claimed in part or in full by all five countries and by Taiwan (see Figure 5.1). The islands and surrounding waters may hold substantial oil reserves. In 1992 the countries agreed to refrain from destabilizing activities and work for a peaceful resolution (a small Chinese-Vietnamese naval battle had been fought there in 1988). But in 1995 China took over a small reef close to the Philippines, building what it called shelters for fishermen there, and hoisting the Chinese flag. The Philippines then dismantled the shelters. The conflict was considered dangerous since it could involve expansionism by a rising great power (China), and a possible power vacuum left by U.S. military withdrawal from the Philippines.

Another notable island dispute is in the Middle East, where Iran and the United Arab Emirates dispute ownership of small islands near the mouth of the Persian Gulf. In 1995 Iran was reported to have moved military forces, including antiaircraft missiles and

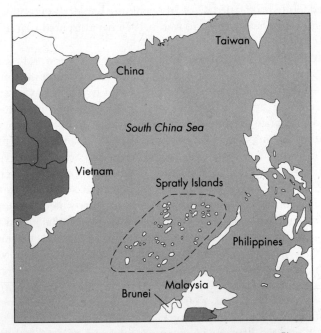

FIGURE 5.1 The Spratly Islands exemplify contemporary conflicts over territory and natural resources around islands. All or part of the Spratlys are claimed by China, Vietnam, Malaysia, Brunei, the Philippines, and Taiwan.

possibly chemical weapons, to the disputed islands, from which they could block shipping of Persian Gulf oil to Europe and Japan. However, the Iranian intent may have been defensive (a forward line of air defense for Iran), or economic (claims to offshore oil deposits).

In South America, Argentina and Britain still dispute control of the *Falkland Islands* (*Islas Malvinas*), over which they fought a war in 1982. And the major bone of contention in Russian-Japanese relations is the ownership of the small *Kuril Islands* occupied by the Soviet Union in 1945. With islands now bringing control of surrounding economic zones, international conflicts over islands will undoubtedly continue in the coming years.

Territorial Waters States treat **territorial waters** near their shores as part of their national territory. Definitions of such waters vary by type of use and are not universally agreed upon, but norms have developed in recent years, especially with the *UN Convention on the Law of the Sea (UNCLOS)* coming into effect (see pp. 437–440). Waters within three miles of shore have traditionally been recognized as territorial, but beyond that there are disputes about how far out national sovereignty extends and for what purposes. UNCLOS generally allows a 12-mile limit for shipping, and a 200-mile *exclusive economic zone* (EEZ) covering fishing and mineral rights (but allowing for free navigation by all). The EEZs together cover a third of the world's oceans. It is because of the EEZs that sovereignty over a single tiny island can now bring with it rights to as much as 100,000 square miles of surrounding ocean. But these zones overlap greatly, and shorelines do not run in straight lines, so numerous questions of interpretation arise about how to delineate territorial and economic waters. For example, Libya claims ownership of the entire Gulf of Sidra, treating it as a bay; the United States treats it as a curvature in the shoreline and insists that most of it is international waters. In 1986 the United States sent warships into the Gulf of Sidra to make its point. In a brief encounter, U.S. planes shot down two Libyan jets that challenged the U.S. maneuvers. Less dramatically, Canada in 1994–1995 sent its navy to seize Spanish fishing boats that were allegedly violating Canadian economic rights in the North Atlantic, just beyond the 200-mile zone. In the Sea of Okhotsk, Russia's EEZ includes all but a small "doughnut hole" of international waters in the middle (see p. 438).

Airspace Airspace above a state is considered the territory of the state. Any airplane that wants to fly over a state's territory must have the state's permission. For example, in a raid on Libya, U.S. bombers based in Britain had to fly a long detour over the Atlantic Ocean because France (between Britain and Libya) would not grant permission for U.S. planes to use its airspace during the mission.

Orbital space (starting about 60 miles up), however, is considered to be international territory like the oceans. This is based on three practical considerations: First, satellites move very fast and cannot easily change direction to avoid overflying a country. Second, with a few exceptions states can shoot down airplanes over their territory but lack the technical means to shoot down satellites. Third, satellites have become useful to all the great powers as intelligence-gathering tools. No state has ever shot down the satellite of another, and doing so would be considered a severe provocation.

Control of Governments

Despite the many minor border disputes that continue to plague the world, most of the struggles to control territory do not involve changing borders. Rather, they are conflicts over which governments will control entire states.

In theory, states do not interfere in each other's governance. In practice, states often have strong interests in the governments of other states and use a variety of means of leverage to influence who holds power in those states. When one state wants to alter or replace the government of a second state, a conflict always exists between the two governments. In addition, the first state may come into conflict with other parties that oppose changing the second state's government. These conflicts over governments take many forms, some mild and some severe, some deeply entwined with third parties and some more or less bilateral. Sometimes a state merely exerts subtle influences in another state's elections; at other times a state supports rebel elements seeking to overthrow the second state's constitutional order altogether.

A severe conflict over government composition arose after the 1991 Gulf War. The U.S. side won the war but the architect of Iraq's aggression—Saddam Hussein—was still in power. Under the official terms of the UN cease-fire, Iraq had to take certain measures before UN economic sanctions on Iraq would be lifted. In conformity with international norms, the UN conditions did not demand changes in the Iraqi government, only in its behavior. However, the United States used its power on the Security Council to prevent sanctions from being lifted while Saddam was still in power, even several years later when Iraq had generally complied with the UN conditions. The United States also repeatedly expressed hope that the Iraqi military would overthrow Saddam.

During the Cold War, both superpowers actively promoted changes of government in third-world countries through covert operations and support of rebel armies. Such involvement of outside parties raises the stakes in a conflict, and U.S.-Soviet rivalry often magnified the importance of changes of government in the third world. Wherever two parties contested a civil war—or sometimes even an election—they often sought backing from one of the superpowers. The civil wars in Nicaragua and Angola are good examples. Both superpowers poured in weapons, money, military advisors, and so forth—all in hopes of influencing the composition of the country's government.

Occasionally one state invades another in order to change its government. The Soviet Union did this in Czechoslovakia in 1968; the United States did it in Grenada in 1983 but refrained from doing so in Iraq in 1991. It is sometimes hard for new governments created in this way to gain legitimacy both domestically and internationally. People generally resent having foreigners choose their government for them—even if they didn't like the old government—and the international community frowns on such overt violations of national sovereignty. For instance, the government installed in Afghanistan after the Soviet invasion of 1979 was seen as a Soviet puppet and was finally toppled after a dozen years of rule marked by constant war.

Even in Cambodia—where the Khmer Rouge government's atrocities led many people inside and outside the country to welcome the Vietnamese invasion that installed a new Cambodian government in 1978—the new government could not consolidate its international position for over a decade. It did not gain Cambodia's seat in the UN, and the United States and China sent assistance to rebel groups that fought a long and bloody

Control of the national government was at issue in the long civil war following the Soviet invasion of Afghanistan in 1979, and in the years of factional warfare that followed the fall of the capital, Kabul, in 1992. Rebels here approach Kabul to take power (April 1992).

civil war against the Vietnamese-backed Cambodian government. (In the 1990s the UN mediated a cease-fire and implemented a peace plan under which the UN basically ran the government while organizing elections.)

International conflicts over the control of governments are—along with territorial disputes—likely types of conflict to lead to the use of violence. They involve core issues of the status and integrity of states, the stakes tend to be high, and the interests of involved actors are often diametrically opposed. Other types of conflict are both more widespread and less likely to lead to violence. Chief among these are economic conflicts among states.

Economic Conflict

Economic competition is the most pervasive form of conflict in international relations because economic transactions are pervasive. Every sale made and every deal reached across international borders entails a resolution of conflicting interests. Costa Rica wants the price of coffee, which it exports, to go up; Canada, which imports coffee, wants the price to go down. Angola wants foreign producers of Angolan oil to receive less of the profits from oil sales; those companies' home states want them to take home more profits. In a global capitalist market, all economic exchanges involve some conflict of interest.

However, such economic transactions also contain a strong element of mutual economic gain in addition to the element of conflicting interests (see Chapters 3 and 8). These mutual gains provide the most useful leverage in bargaining over economic exchanges: States and companies enter into economic transactions because they profit from doing so. The use of violence would for the most part interrupt and diminish such profit by more than could be gained as a result of the use of violence. Thus, economic conflicts do not usually lead to military force and war. The U.S. Navy will not be called upon to sink Japanese freighters carrying automobiles for sale in the United States because, although this might help the U.S. automobile industry in the short term, it would disrupt U.S.-Japanese trade, which is valuable to both countries. Even in the extreme case where a government nationalizes the property of a U.S.-based corporation, the U.S. Marines do not storm ashore to recover the company's assets, as they might have done some decades ago.

This has not always been so. In the sixteenth century, England's Sir Francis Drake intercepted Spanish ships bringing gold and silver from Central America and took the loot in the name of queen and country—a practice known as *privateering*. In the seventeenth century England fought several naval wars against the Netherlands. An English general, when asked the reason for England's declaration of war in 1652, replied, "What matters this or that reason? What we want is more of the trade the Dutch now have."[16] And in 1861 France, Britain, and Spain invaded Mexico when it failed to pay its international debts.

Economic conflict seldom leads to violence today because military forms of leverage are no longer very effective in economic conflicts. With the tight integration of the world economy and the high cost of military actions, the use of force is seldom justified by the stakes of any given economic issue.

Most economic conflicts therefore are not issues in international security; they receive their own discussion in Chapters 8 through 13 on international political economy. But economic conflicts do still bear on international security in some ways.

First, many states' foreign policies are influenced by *mercantilism*—a practice of centuries past in which trade and foreign economic policies were manipulated to build up a monetary surplus that could be used to finance war (see "Liberalism and Mercantilism" on pp. 312–315). Because a trade surplus confers an advantage in international security affairs over the long run, trade conflicts have implications for international security relations.

Second, the theory of **lateral pressure** also connects economic competition with security concerns. This theory holds that the economic growth of states leads to geographic expansion as they seek natural resources beyond their borders (by various means peaceful and violent). As great powers expand their economic activities outward, their

---

[16]Howard, Michael. *War in European History*. Oxford: Oxford University Press, 1976, p. 47.

competition leads to conflicts and sometimes to war. The theory has been used to help explain both World War I and the expansion of Japan prior to World War II.[17]

Another kind of economic conflict that affects international security concerns *military industry*—the capacity to produce military equipment, especially high-technology weapons like fighter aircraft or missiles. There is a world trade in such items, but national governments try (not always successfully) to keep control of such production—to try to ensure that national interests take priority over those of companies involved and that the state is militarily self-sufficient in case of war. Economic competition (over who profits from such sales) is interwoven with security concerns (over who gets access to the weapons). The transfer to potentially hostile states of knowledge about high-tech weaponry and military technologies is a related concern.

Economic competition also becomes a security issue when it concerns trade in *strategic materials* needed for military purposes, such as special minerals or alloys for aircraft production, uranium for atomic weapons, and so forth. Few countries are entirely self-sufficient in these materials: the United States imports about half of the strategic materials it uses.

Thus, economic competition as a source of international conflict has important implications for international security. Nonetheless, military force plays a diminishing role in resolving such economic conflicts.

A different kind of economic conflict revolves around the distribution of wealth within and among states. As discussed in depth in Chapter 12, there are tremendous disparities in wealth in our world, disparities that create a variety of international security problems with the potential for violence. These include conflicts over issues like migration and trade, but chief among them is the issue of revolutions in poor countries. Such revolutions are often fueled by disparities of wealth within the country as well as its poverty relative to other countries. These revolutions in turn frequently draw in other states as supporters of one side or the other in a civil war. If successful, revolutions can abruptly change a state's foreign policy, leading to new alliances and power alignments.

Marxist approaches to international relations, which are discussed in Chapter 12, treat class struggle between rich and poor people as the basis of interstate relations. According to these approaches, capitalist states adopt foreign policies that serve the interests of the rich owners of companies. Conflicts and wars between the global North and South—rich states versus poor states—are seen as reflections of the domination and exploitation of the poor by the rich—imperialism whether in direct or indirect form. For example, most Marxists saw the Vietnam War as a U.S. effort to suppress revolution in order to secure continued U.S. access to cheap labor and raw materials in Southeast Asia. The Gulf War was seen in similar terms. Many Marxists portray conflicts among capitalist states as competition over the right to exploit poor areas. For instance, Soviet founder V. I. Lenin portrayed World War I as a fight over the imperialists' division of the world.

---

[17]Choucri, Nazli, and Robert C. North. *Nations in Conflict: National Growth and International Violence*. San Francisco: W. H. Freeman, 1975. Ashley, Richard K. *The Political Economy of War and Peace: The Sino-Soviet-American Triangle and the Modern Security Problematique*. London: Frances Pinter, 1980. Choucri, Nazli, Robert C. North, and Susumu Yamakage. *The Challenge of Japan: Before World War II and After*. New York: Routledge, 1993.

Recent events in *Haiti*, the poorest country in Latin America, illustrate how disparities of wealth can create international security conflicts. For decades the country was ruled by an absolute dictator, "Papa Doc" Duvalier, backed by a ruthless secret police agency. The dictator and his associates got very rich while the population remained very poor (producing export crops to earn cash for the rich). When the dictator died, his son "Baby Doc" took over. During most of the Cold War, the United States backed the dictatorship because it provided a reliable ally next door to Soviet-allied Cuba (a U.S. enemy after its 1959 revolution). Finally a popular uprising forced Baby Doc to flee in 1986; a Catholic priest who had organized on behalf of the poor, Jean-Bertrand Aristide, was elected president of Haiti. But within a year the military seized power in a coup d'état and began to enrich itself again. This, along with international sanctions against the Haitian economy, led tens of thousands of people to flee on rickety boats heading for the prosperous United States. These boat people were intercepted by the U.S. Navy, and most were sent back to Haiti because they were labelled "economic" refugees (see "Migration and Refugees" on pp. 494–498)—but the issue caused problems in U.S. domestic politics, forcing a response. The United States sent an invasion force, intimidated the military leaders into leaving, and restored Aristide as president. Then the U.S. military occupation was converted into a UN peacekeeping operation. Thus, the disparities of wealth in Haiti had ramifications for global alliances (in the Cold War), for regional containment (of Cuba), and for international norms concerning military intervention.

Drug Trafficking As a form of illegal trade across international borders, drug trafficking is smuggling. Smuggling deprives states of revenue and violates states' legal control of their borders. But smuggling in general is an economic issue rather than a security one (see "Illicit Trade" on pp. 335–336). Unlike other smuggled goods, however, drug trafficking supplies illegal products whose very presence has been considered a security threat because of their effect on national (and military) morale and efficiency. Drug trafficking also has become linked with security concerns because military forces participate regularly in operations against the heavily armed drug traffickers.[18]

Conflicts over drugs generally concern states on one side and nonstate actors on the other. But other states are easily drawn in because the activities in question cross national borders and may involve corrupt state officials.

These international ramifications are evident in the efforts of the U.S. government to prevent *cocaine cartels* based in Colombia from supplying cocaine to U.S. cities. Such cocaine derives mostly from coca plants grown by peasants in mountainous areas of Peru and Bolivia. Processed in simple laboratories in the jungle, the cocaine moves across the border into Colombia and is transported through other countries such as Panama before arriving in the United States. In each of these states (yes, even the United States), the drug smugglers have bribed some corrupt officials, including military or police officers, to stay clear. But other state officials in each country are working with U.S. law enforcement agencies and the U.S. military to crack down on the cocaine trade.

---

[18] Tullis, LaMond. *Unintended Consequences: Illegal Drugs and Drug Policies in Nine Countries.* Boulder, CO: Lynne Rienner, 1995. Thoumi, Francisco E. *Political Economy and Illegal Drugs in Colombia.* Boulder, CO: Lynne Rienner, 1994. Toro, Celia. *Mexico's "War" on Drugs: Causes and Consequences.* Boulder, CO: Lynne Rienner, 1995.

U.S. forces in Panama, 1989. Because drug trafficking crosses national borders and involves lots of guns and money, it is a source of interstate conflict. The United States invaded Panama to stop dictator Manuel Noriega's collusion with traffickers shipping illegal drugs to the United States. Ironically, a billboard advertises the United States's own drug export to Panama (tobacco).

The truth is that the populations in several of these countries, especially in cocaine-producing regions, benefit substantially from the drug trade. For poor peasants in Bolivia or for residents of the Colombian cocaine cartels' home provinces, the cocaine trade may be their only access to a decent income. Benefits to corrupt state officials are also substantial. In rural Peru and Colombia, leftist guerrillas have funded their operations by controlling peasants' production of coca.

The cocaine trade thus creates some conflicts between the United States and the states of the region. Most such interstate conflicts are resolved through positive forms of leverage such as U.S. financial or military aid. State officials are also often willing to make common cause with the United States because they are threatened by the drug traffickers, who control great wealth and power, and who, being outlaws, have few incentives against using violence.

Because of the long history of U.S. military intervention in Latin America, state cooperation with U.S. military forces is a sensitive political issue. Governments in the region must respect a delicate balance between the need for U.S. help and the need to uphold national sovereignty. In some countries, governments have faced popular criticism for allowing the "Yankees" to "invade" in the drug war.

In one case, the U.S. military literally invaded. In 1989 U.S. forces invaded Panama and arrested its leader, dictator Manuel Noriega. He was taken to the United States, and convicted in U.S. courts of complicity in drug trafficking through Panama. A new president of Panama—from whom Noriega had stolen a recent election—was sworn into office in a U.S. military base in Panama. Through this use of power, the United States influenced Panama to change its behavior, although some drug shipments have continued in spite of new enforcement efforts.

Conflicts arising from cocaine trafficking have thus had ramifications for U.S. foreign aid, Latin American sovereignty, the economic well-being of populations in poor countries, guerrilla war in Peru, a military invasion in Panama, and other interstate tensions in the region. (The world trade in heroin creates some similar conflicts, though they are less concentrated in one region.)

Like the other sources of international conflict discussed so far, conflicts over drug trafficking arise from conflicting interests regarding tangible items like money, territory, or control of governments. More difficult to understand, in some ways, are international conflicts rooted in clashes of ideas. Of course, the two overlap—especially around the material and intangible aspects of nationalism—but conflicts of ideas also require special attention in their own right.

❖ CONFLICTS OF IDEAS

If all international conflicts were strictly material in nature, it might be easier to settle them. Given a large enough positive leverage—a payment in some form—any state would agree to another state's terms on a disputed issue. More difficult are the types of conflict in which intangible elements like ethnic hatred, religious fervor, or ideology come into play.

Ethnic Conflict

Ethnic conflict is quite possibly the most important source of conflict in the numerous wars now occurring throughout the world.[19] **Ethnic groups** are large groups of people who share ancestral, language, cultural, or religious ties and a common *identity* (individuals identify with the group). Although conflicts between ethnic groups often have material aspects—notably over territory and government control—ethnic conflict itself stems from a dislike or hatred that members of one ethnic group systematically feel toward another ethnic group. Ethnic conflict is thus not based on tangible causes (what someone does) but on intangible ones (who someone is).

Ethnic groups often form the basis for *nationalist* sentiments. Not all ethnic groups identify as nations; for instance, within the United States various ethnic groups coexist (albeit uneasily) with a common *national* identity as Americans. But in locations where millions of members of a single ethnic group live as the majority population in their ancestors' land, they usually think of themselves as a nation. In most such cases they aspire to have their own state with its formal international status and territorial boundaries.[20]

---

[19]Esman, Milton J. *Ethnic Politics*. Ithaca: Cornell University Press, 1995. Griffiths, Stephen Iwan. *Nationalism and Ethnic Conflict*. New York: Oxford University Press, 1993. Gurr, Ted Robert. *Minorities at Risk: A Global View of Ethnopolitical Conflicts*. Washington, DC: United States Institute of Peace Press, 1993. Horowitz, Donald L. *Ethnic Groups in Conflict*. Berkeley: University of California Press, 1985. Ryan, Stephen. *Ethnic Conflict and International Relations*. Brookfield, VT: Dartmouth University Press, 1990.

[20]Bertelsen, Judy S., ed. *Nonstate Nations in International Politics: Comparative Systems Analyses*. New York: Praeger, 1977.

Territorial control is closely tied to the aspirations of ethnic groups for statehood. Any state's borders will deviate to some extent (sometimes substantially) from the actual location of ethnic communities. Members of the ethnic group will be left outside its state's borders, and members of other ethnic groups will be located within the state's borders. The resulting situation can be dangerous, with part of an ethnic group controlling a state and another part living as a minority within another state controlled by a rival ethnic group. Frequently the minority group suffers discrimination in the other state and the "home" state tries to rescue or avenge them.

Other ethnic groups lack any home state. Kurds, for example, speak a common language and share a culture, and many of them aspire to create a state of Kurdistan. However, Kurds are distributed across four states—Turkey, Iraq, Iran, and Syria—all of which strongly oppose giving up control of part of their own territory to create a Kurdish state (see Figure 5.2). In recent years, rival Kurdish guerrilla armies have fought both Iraqi and Turkish military forces, and each other.

In ethnic conflicts there are often pressures to redraw borders by force. For example, the former Soviet republic of Moldova is inhabited mostly by ethnic Romanians but also by quite a few ethnic Russians, who are concentrated at the eastern end of Moldova (furthest from Romania). A river separates a strip of land at the east end from the rest of Moldova, and ethnic Russians make up the majority in that strip of territory. When Moldova became independent in 1991 and began asserting its Romanian identity—even considering merging into Romania—the Russians living in the eastern strip of land sought to break away and make the river a new international border. Armed conflict ensued, and both Russia and Romania threatened to intervene. Eventually a ceasefire and peacekeeping arrangement were implemented, with no formal change in borders.

When ethnic populations are minorities in territories controlled by rival ethnic groups, they may even be driven from their land or (in very rare cases) systematically exterminated. By driving out the minority ethnic group, a majority group can assemble a more unified, more contiguous, and larger territory for its nation-state, as ethnic Serbs did through "ethnic cleansing" after the breakup of Yugoslavia.

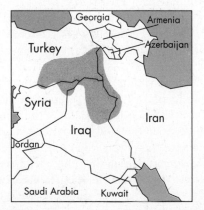

FIGURE 5.2 Ethnic populations often span international borders. Shaded region shows the approximate area of Kurdish settlements.

Outside states often worry about the fate of "their people" living as minorities in neighboring states. For instance, Albania is concerned about ethnic Albanians who are the majority population in the Serbian province of Kosovo. But if Kosovo became independent of Serbia (or merged with Albania), then Serbia would worry about the minority of ethnic Serbs living in Kosovo. Similar problems have fueled wars between Armenia and Azerbaijan (in the former Soviet Union) and between India and Pakistan. Before World War II, Hitler used the fate of ethnic German communities in Poland and Czechoslovakia to justify German territorial expansion into those neighboring states. It appears likely that the dangerous combination of ethnic conflict and territorial disputes will lead to more wars in the future.

In extreme cases such as Hitler's Germany, governments use genocide—systematic extermination based on ethnic or religious group—to try to destroy scapegoated groups or political rivals. In Rwanda, where the Hutu group are the majority and the Tutsi group the minority, a Hutu-nationalist government in 1994 slaughtered roughly half a million Tutsis (and Hutus opposed to the government) in a matter of weeks. The weak international response to this atrocity reveals how frail are international norms of human rights compared to norms of noninterference in other states' internal affairs. (It also reveals how little the world cares about Africa, but this is another story.) The Hutu ultranationalists quickly lost power, however, when Tutsi rebels defeated the government militarily.

The Cold War, with its tight system of alliances and authoritarian communist governments in Eastern Europe, seems to have helped to keep ethnic conflicts in check. In the Soviet Union and Yugoslavia—multinational states—the existence of a single strong state (willing to oppress local communities) kept the lid on ethnic tensions and enforced peace between neighboring communities. The breakup of these states allowed ethnic and regional conflicts to come to center stage, sometimes bringing violence and war. These cases may indicate a dilemma in that freedom comes at the expense of order and vice versa. Of course, not all ethnic groups get along so poorly together, and even in the former Soviet Union most of the numerous ethnic rivalries did not lead to warfare (and in Czechoslovakia and elsewhere ethnic relations were relatively peaceful after the fall of communism).

Causes of Ethnic Hostility Why do ethnic groups often dislike each other? Often there are long-standing historical conflicts over specific territories or natural resources, or over one ethnic group's economic exploitation or political domination of another. Over time ethnic conflicts may transcend these concrete historical causes and take on a life of their own. They become driven not by tangible grievances (though these may well persist as irritants) but by the kinds of processes described by social psychology that are set in motion when one group of people has a prolonged conflict with another and experiences violence at the hands of the other group.[21]

The ethnic group is a kind of extended *kinship* group—a group of related individuals sharing some ancestors. Even when kinship relations are not very close, a *group identity* makes a person act as though the other members of the ethnic group were family. For instance, African-American men who call each other "brother" express group identity as kinship. Likewise Jews around the world treat each other as family even though each

---

[21]Glad, Betty, ed. *Psychological Dimensions of War*. Newbury Park, CA: Sage, 1990.

Ethnocentrism based on an in-group bias can promote intolerance and ultimately dehumanization of an out-group, as in Bosnian and Rwandan genocide, South African apartheid, the persecution of Jews and other minorities in Nazi Germany, and slavery in the United States. Ethnic conflicts play a role in many international conflicts. Americans, as part of a multiethnic society, view such conflicts somewhat differently than citizens of more homogeneous great powers. U.S. student protests (1985) created pressure that helped end South African apartheid.

community has intermarried over time and may have more ancestors in common with local non-Jews than with distant Jews.

Ethnocentrism, or *in-group bias*, is the tendency to see one's own group in favorable terms and an *out-group* in unfavorable terms. Some scholars believe that ethnocentrism has roots in a biological propensity to protect closely related individuals, but this idea is quite controversial.[22] More often in-group bias is understood in terms of social psychology.

There is *no minimum criterion* of similarity or kin relationship that is needed to evoke the group identity process, including in-group bias. In psychological experiments, even trivial differentiations can evoke these processes. If people are assigned to groups based on a known but unimportant characteristic (such as preferring, say, circles to triangles), be-

---

[22]Shaw, Paul, and Yuwa Wong. *Genetic Seeds of Warfare: Evolution, Nationalism, and Patriotism*. Boston: Unwin Hyman, 1989. Groebel, J., and R. A. Hinde, eds. *Aggression and War: Their Biological and Social Bases*. New York: Cambridge University Press, 1989. Somit, Albert. Humans, Chimps, and Bonobos: The Biological Bases of Aggression, War, and Peacemaking [review essay]. *Journal of Conflict Resolution* 34 (3), 1990: 553–82. McGuinness, Diane, ed. *Dominance, Aggression, and War*. New York: Paragon, 1987.

fore long the people in each group show in-group bias and find they don't much care for the other group's members.[23]

In-group biases are far stronger when the other group looks different, speaks a different language, or worships in a different way (or all three). All too easily, an out-group can be **dehumanized** and stripped of all human rights. This dehumanization includes the common use of animal names—"pigs," "dogs," and so forth—for members of the out-group. U.S. propaganda in World War II depicted Japanese people as apes. Especially in wartime, when people see members of an out-group killing members of their in-group, dehumanization can be extreme. The restraints on war that have evolved in regular interstate warfare, such as not massacring civilians (see "War Crimes" on pp. 298–300), are easily discarded in interethnic warfare.

Experience in Western Europe shows that education over time can overcome ethnic animosities between traditionally hostile nations, such as the French and Germans. After World War II, governments undertook to rewrite the textbooks with which a new generation would learn its peoples' histories. Previously each state's textbooks had glorified its own past deeds, played down its misdeeds, and portrayed its traditional enemies in unflattering terms. In a continentwide project, new textbooks that gave a more objective and fair rendition were created. This project helped pave the way for European integration in subsequent decades.

The existence of a threat from an out-group promotes the cohesion of an in-group, thereby creating a somewhat self-reinforcing process of ethnic division. Yet although ethnocentrism creates in-group cohesion, it often causes members of a group to view themselves as disunited (because they see their own divisions up close) and the out-group as monolithic (because they see it only from outside). This usually reflects a group's sense of vulnerability. Furthermore, overstating the threat posed by an enemy is a common way for political leaders to bolster their own position within an in-group. For example, in the Arab-Israeli conflict, Israelis tended to see themselves as fragmented into dozens of political parties and diverse immigrant communities all pulling in different directions, while they saw the Arabs as a monolithic bloc united against them. Meanwhile, Arab Palestinians saw themselves as fragmented into factions and weakened by divisions in the Arab states, while the Israelis appeared monolithic to them.

Over time, rival ethnic groups may develop a pattern of *feuding*. Each side retaliates for actions of the other in a seemingly unending circle of violence. Usually each side believes it is acting defensively and that the other side "started it." This reflects in-group bias on one or both sides.

Ethnic conflicts are hard to resolve because they are not about "who gets what" but about "I don't like you." To cast the conflict in terms of a bargaining situation, each side places value on the other's loss of value, making it like a zero-sum game in which one side's gains are always losses for the other side (see p. 69). A person inflamed with hatred of an enemy is willing to *lose* value in absolute terms—to lose money, the support of allies, or even his or her life—in order to deprive the enemy of value as well. Almost all the means of leverage used in such conflicts are negative, and bargains are very hard to reach. So ethnic conflicts tend to drag on without resolution for generations.

---

[23]Tajfel, H., and J. C. Turner. The Social Identity Theory of Intergroup Behavior. In S. Worchel and W. Austin, eds. *Psychology of Intergroup Relations*. 2nd ed. Chicago: Nelson-Hall, 1986, pp. 7–24.

Ethnic Hutu extremists in the government of Rwanda in 1994 carried out an organized genocide, giving orders throughout the country to kill ethnic Tutsis and those Hutus who had opposed the government. In short order, about 500,000 men, women, and children were massacred, mostly by machete, and their bodies dumped into rivers; thousands at a time washed up on lakeshores in neighboring Uganda. What theories could help explain this event?

THINKING THEORETICALLY

❖

Hutu hatred toward Tutsis could reflect concrete interests and experiences of the two groups, especially since the minority Tutsis had earlier held power over the Hutu, and Belgian colonialism had exploited local rivalries. Realists might try to explain how the interests of Hutu extremists were served by their actions in exterminating rivals for power. This explanation is undermined, however, by the outcome in this case: the Hutu extremists lost power as a result of the episode.

We might instead view Hutu-Tutsi hatred as part of a pattern of age-old ethnic hatreds that are cropping up in the post–Cold War era, especially in "backward" areas like Africa. This theory was often articulated by Western politicians in the Bosnia case, to justify their inaction. In that case, the Balkans are treated with the same attitude as Africa ("backward, primitive"). However, this theory holds up even worse than the realist explanation, since one of the world's most civilized, "advanced" states, Germany, exterminated its Jews even more efficiently than Rwanda did its Tutsis—the difference being simply that the "advanced" society could kill with industrial chemicals instead of at knifepoint.

Social psychology theories would tend to view the Rwandan genocide as entirely pathological—a deviation from both rationality and social norms. In-group biases based on fairly arbitrary group characteristics become amplified by a perceived threat from an out-group, exaggerated by history, myth, and propaganda (including schooling). A key threshold is crossed when the out-group is dehumanized; norms of social interaction such as not slitting children's throats can then be disregarded.

Ethnic groups are only one point along a spectrum of kinship relations—from nuclear families through extended families, villages, provinces, and nations, up to the entire human race. Loyalties fall at different points along the spectrum. Again there is no minimum criterion for in-group identity. For instance, experts said that of all the African countries, Somalia was surely immune from ethnic conflicts because Somalis were all from the same ethnic group and spoke the same language. Then in 1991–1992 a ruinous civil war erupted between members of different clans (based on extended families), leading to mass starvation and the intervention of foreign military forces (which by 1995 had to withdraw after a humiliating failure to tame the violence).

It is unclear why people identify most strongly at one level of group identity.[24] In Somalia, loyalties are to clans; in Serbia, they are to the ethnic group; in the United States and elsewhere, multiethnic states have managed to gain people's primary loyalty. States

---

[24]Bloom, William. *Personal Identity, National Identity, and International Relations.* New York: Cambridge University Press, 1990.

reinforce their citizens' identification with the state through flags, anthems, pledges of allegiance, patriotic speeches, and so forth. Perhaps someday people will shift loyalties even further, developing a *global identity* as humans first and members of states and ethnic groups second.

Religious Conflict

One reason why ethnic conflicts often transcend material grievances is that they find expression as *religious* conflicts. Since religion is the core of a community's value system in much of the world, those whose religious practices differ are easily disdained and treated as unworthy or even inhuman.

When overlaid on ethnic and territorial conflicts, religion often surfaces as the central and most visible division between groups. For instance, most Indians are Hindus and most Pakistanis are Muslims. People in Azerbaijan are Muslims; Armenians are Christians. Most Croats are Roman Catholic Christians, whereas most Serbs are Orthodox Christians and most Albanians are Muslims. This is a very common pattern in ethnic conflicts.

There is nothing inherent in religion that must create conflicts—in many places members of different religious groups coexist peacefully. But religious differences hold the potential for conflict, and for making existing conflicts more intractable, because religions involve core values, defining what is good and bad, which are held as absolute truth. This is increasingly true as *fundamentalist* movements have gained strength in recent decades. (The reasons for fundamentalism are unclear, but it is clearly a global-level phenomenon). Members of these movements organize their lives and communities around their religious beliefs, and many are willing to sacrifice and even die for those beliefs. Fundamentalist movements have become larger and more powerful in recent decades in Islam, Christianity, Judaism, Hinduism, and other religions. Such movements challenge the values and practices of **secular** political organizations—those created apart from religious establishments (the separation of church and state). Often, outside value systems—both competing religions and secular politics—are cast by fundamentalists as devils with whom no compromise is possible.

Among the secular practices threatened by fundamentalist movements are the rules of the international system, whereby states are treated as formally equal and sovereign whether they are "believers" or "infidels." As transnational belief systems, religions often are taken as a higher law than state laws and international treaties. Iranian "revolutionary guards" train and support Islamic fundamentalists in other states such as Algeria, Egypt, Jordan, and Lebanon. Jewish fundamentalists build settlements in Israeli-occupied territories and vow to cling to the land even if their government evacuates it. Christian fundamentalists in the United States convince their government to withdraw from the UN Population Fund. All these actions in one way or another run counter to the norms of the international system, and to the assumptions of realism.[25]

Islam, the religion practiced by **Muslims** (or Moslems), deserves special attention since it has played a role in a number of recent ethnic conflicts. Islam is not inherently

---

[25]Juergensmeyer, Mark. *The New Cold War? Religious Nationalism Confronts the Secular State.* Berkeley: University of California Press, 1993.

Religious intolerance can exacerbate tensions between groups, sometimes crossing the line to violence. Here Hindus destroy Muslim mosque at Ayodhya, India (December 1992). This incident provoked days of civil violence in India, mostly directed against Muslims, in which thousands died. Hindu-Muslim conflict affects India's relations with its Muslim neighbors like Pakistan, Bangladesh, and Indonesia.

warlike as compared with other religions. Terrible atrocities and wonderful works alike have been created in the name of most of the world's religions. Nor is Islam a single monolithic religion, any more than Christianity is. Sunni Muslims, Shiite Muslims, and many smaller branches and sects are rivals within Islam. The areas of the world that are predominantly Islamic stretch from Nigeria to Indonesia, centered in the Middle East (see Figure 5.3).

The area where most Muslims live—the Middle East—may be geographically prone to conflict. For centuries it has connected other regions (Europe, Asia, Africa), and armies have swarmed across it. It continues to be geopolitically central, between the global North and South. Competition over vast oil resources in the region also contributes to international conflict.

In some, but by no means all, religious conflicts involving Muslims, the rise of Islamic fundamentalism has created new tensions. These fundamentalists reject Western-oriented secular states in favor of governments more explicitly oriented to Islamic values.[26] These movements reflect long-standing *anti-Western* sentiment in these countries—against the old European colonizers who were Christian—and are in many ways *nationalist* movements expressed through religious channels. In Middle Eastern countries with authoritarian governments, religious institutions (mosques) have often been the only available avenue for political opposition. Religion has therefore become a means for expressing opposition to the status quo in both politics and culture.

Islamic fundamentalism has gained strength in recent years. In 1979 an Islamic republic was created in Iran. An Islamic government was established in Afghanistan in 1992 after a civil war, though rival Islamic factions then continued the war with even greater intensity for several years. Pakistan and Sudan adopted the rhetoric of fundamentalist Islam without a revolution. In Algeria the Islamic movement was winning democratic elections for a new Parliament in 1991 when the military intervened to take power and stop the elections. The Islamic rebels went underground and the ensuing violence had killed an estimated 30,000 people by 1995. The rebels targeted foreigners as well as intellectuals, journalists, outspoken women, and of course military and political authorities. The government waged a brutal war of repression on its part. In Jordan, however, Islamic parties won the largest bloc of seats in Parliament several years ago but violence has not ensued.

Fundamentalist movements not only threaten some existing governments—especially those tied to the West—they undermine norms of state sovereignty (for better or worse). They are creating new transnational ties among Muslims in various countries. They reject Western political conceptions of the state (based on individual autonomy) in favor of a more traditional Islamic orientation based on community. Some aspire to create a single political state encompassing most of the Middle East, as existed in A.D. 600–1200.

For better or worse, such a development would create a profound challenge to the present international system—and in particular to its current status quo powers—and would therefore be opposed at every turn by the world's most powerful states. From the perspective of some outsiders, the religious conflicts boiling and simmering around the edges of the Islamic world look like an expansionist threat to be contained. The view from within the region looks more like being surrounded and repressed from several directions—a view reinforced by massacres of Muslims in Bosnia and in India in recent years.

Overall, Islamic fundamentalism (and the opposition to it) is more complex than simply a religious conflict; it concerns power, economic relations, ethnic chauvinism, and historical empires as well.

Recently it has been proposed that international conflicts in the coming years may

---

[26]Johnson, James Turner, and John Kelsay. *Cross, Crescent, and Sword: The Justification and Limitation of War in Western and Islamic Tradition.* New York: Greenwood, 1990. Piscatori, James. *Islam in a World of Nation-States.* New York: Cambridge University Press, 1984. Esposito, John L. *The Islamic Threat: Myth or Reality?* New York: Oxford University Press, 1992. Binder, Leonard. *Islamic Liberalism: A Critique of Development Ideologies.* Chicago: University of Chicago Press, 1988.

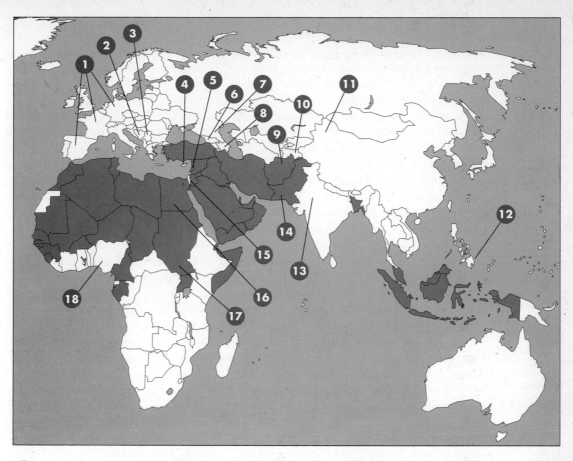

1	Germany, France, Spain	6	Georgia	11	Western China	16	Egypt
2	Bosnia-Herzegovina	7	Southern Russia/Chechnya	12	Philippines	17	Sudan
3	Serbia	8	Armenia, Azerbaijan	13	India	18	Nigeria
4	Cyprus	9	Afghanistan	14	Pakistan		
5	Lebanon	10	Tajikistan	15	Israel/Palestine		

FIGURE 5.3 Members of the Islamic Conference
Shaded countries are members of the conference; numbered regions are areas of conflict between Islamic and non-Islamic groups.

be generated by a clash of civilizations—based on the differences between the world's major cultural groupings, which overlap quite a bit with religious communities.[27] The idea has been criticized for being overly general, and for assuming that cultural differences naturally create conflict.

---

[27]Huntington, Samuel P. The Clash of Civilizations? *Foreign Affairs* 72 (summer), 1993: 21–49.

Ideological Conflict

To a large extent, ideology is like religion: it intensifies and symbolizes conflicts between groups and states more than it causes them. Ideologies have a somewhat weaker hold on core values and absolute truth than religions do, so they pose somewhat fewer problems for the international system.

For realists, ideological differences among states do not matter much, because all members of the international system pursue their national interests in the context of relatively fluid alliances. For example, during the Cold War there was a global ideological struggle between capitalist democracy and communism. But the alliances and military competitions in that struggle were fairly detached from ideological factors. The two communist giants—the Soviet Union and China—did not stay together very long. And even the two great rival superpowers managed to live within the rules of the international system for the most part (such as both remaining UN members).

Over the long run, even countries that experience revolutions based on strong ideologies tend to lose their ideological fervor—be it Iran's Islamic fundamentalism in 1979, China's Maoist communism in 1949, Russia's Leninist communism in 1917, or even U.S. democracy in 1776. In each case the revolutionaries expected that their assumption of power would dramatically alter their state's foreign policy, because in each case their ideology had profound international implications. The first foreign minister of the Soviet Union, Leon Trotsky, believed in spreading revolution to the world's working class with no respect for state borders or governments. Upon taking office he declared he would "issue a few proclamations and then close up shop."

Yet, within a few decades, each of these revolutionary governments turned to the pursuit of national interests above ideological ones. The Soviet Union soon became in many ways just another great power on the European scene—building up its own armed forces, expanding its territory at the expense of Poland, making alliances with enemies (the Stalin-Hitler pact in 1939 and the alliance with the West during World War II), and so forth. Likewise, China's Chairman Mao wanted to spread a "prairie fire" of revolution through the third world to liberate it from U.S. imperialism, but within a few decades Mao was welcoming the very embodiment of U.S. imperialism, President Nixon, to pursue mutual national interests.

Sometimes even self-proclaimed ideological struggles are not as ideological as they appear. In Angola in the 1980s the United States backed a rebel army called UNITA against a Soviet-aligned government—supposedly a struggle of democracy against Marxism. In truth, the ideological differences between the two sides were quite arbitrary. The government mouthed Marxist rhetoric to get the Soviet Union to give it aid (a policy that was reversed as soon as Soviet aid dried up). After years of this "Marxism" the official radio announcer at a big government parade could not identify the pictures of Marx, Lenin, and Stalin adorning the square. The "democratic" rebels meanwhile adopted democratic rhetoric to get U.S. support but practiced nothing of the sort. In fact, they had earlier received Chinese support and had mouthed Maoist rhetoric. When UN-sponsored elections were won by the government, the "democratic" UNITA refused to accept the results and resumed fighting. This conflict really had nothing to do with ideology. If the Soviet Union had one day switched its allegiance to UNITA, the United States might well have rushed to rescue the "democratic" Angolan government from the "Marxist"

Ideology plays only a limited role in most international conflicts. After revolutions, such as Iran's in 1979, ideologies such as the Ayatollah Khomeini's teachings may come into play in foreign policy (here, Khomeini supporters outside U.S. embassy where hostages were held, 1979). But over ten or twenty years such countries typically revert to a foreign policy based more on national interests (for Iran, exporting oil and developing the economy) than ideology (exporting Islamic revolution).

rebels, and Thomas Jefferson's picture might have been hanging in the main square of the capital, still unrecognized!

In the short term, revolutions *do* change international relations—they make wars more likely—but not because of ideology. Rather, the sudden change of governments can alter alliances and change the balance of power. With calculations of power being revised by all parties, it is easy to miscalculate or to exaggerate threats on both sides. Saddam Hussein, for example, miscalculated Iran's power after its revolution (see "Estimating Power" on pp. 55–56). But ideology itself plays little role in this postrevolutionary propensity for wars: revolutions are seldom exported to other states.[28]

All of this does not mean that ideology and political philosophies play no role at all in international politics. Ideologies can help to *mobilize* national populations to support a state in its international dealings, such as war. For instance, fascism (the Nazi ideology) inflamed German nationalism before World War II, legitimizing German aggression by placing it in an ideological framework. And ideology can sharpen and intensify the conflict between two rivals, as happened to the superpowers during the Cold War. In some third-world proxy wars of that era—for instance, in Vietnam in the 1960s or Nicaragua in

---

[28]Walt, Stephen M. Revolution and War. *World Politics* 44 (3), 1992: 321–68.

the 1980s—the rebels and governments had real ideological differences that resonated with the Cold War rivalry.

If one considers political democracy to be an ideology, it may be the exception to the rule that ideology does not affect IR much. Democracy has become a global-level force in world politics, transcending the interests of particular states. A commitment to democracy does not yet outweigh a commitment to national interest in states' foreign policies, and perhaps never will, but global democracy is slowly emerging as a norm that states increasingly are pursuing in their dealings with other states (see "Democracy" on pp. 160–163). Democracies and nondemocracies may increasingly find themselves in conflict with each other if this trend continues. Because democracies do not fight wars with each other (although they still have conflicts), the spread of democratic ideology may have great implications for future prospects for peace.

All six types of conflict just discussed have potentials for being pursued through peaceful or violent means. We can better understand conflict by examining the types of leverage, violent and otherwise, that are typically brought into play in international conflicts.

❖ MEANS OF LEVERAGE

Conflicts are settled when some explicit or implicit bargaining process arrives at an outcome acceptable to both parties (see "Bargaining" on pp. 60–62). Acceptable does not mean that both parties are happy or that the outcome is fair, but only that neither party thinks it would be worth the effort to try to change the outcome. That may occur because both parties are satisfied that they have struck a beneficial or fair deal, or it may happen because one party has been stripped of its leverage (in the extreme case, destroyed altogether) and has no prospect of improving a bad outcome through further bargaining.

War and other violent actions taken in international conflicts are aimed at settling conflicts on favorable terms by inflicting violence as a negative form of leverage. States also have available to them alternative means of leverage and strategies that often work better than war in resolving conflicts (ending them on mutually acceptable terms).[29]

Types of War

War has been defined in various ways. For present purposes, we may define *war* as sustained intergroup violence (deliberately inflicting death and injury) in which state military forces participate on at least one side—on both sides in the case of *interstate war* and generally on only one side in the case of civil war. Around this definition are gray areas. In a world of standing military forces it is hard to say exactly where peace ends and war begins. A military battle that is not sustained over time may or may not be considered a war. The brief Chinese-Soviet border clashes in March and July 1969, for example, entailed several small battles at a few points along the border, in which some hundreds of people were killed. Similarly ambiguous is a long-term violent struggle involving irregular

---

[29]Bar-Tal, Daniel, Arie W. Kruglanski, and Yechiel Klar. Conflict Termination: An Epistemological Analysis of International Cases. *Political Psychology* 10 (2), 1989: 233–55.

(substate) forces, such as in Northern Ireland. There, uniformed British military forces waged a sustained violent struggle with a nonstate "army," the Irish Republican Army (IRA), until a 1995 ceasefire.

Gang violence in American inner cities is not considered war by most definitions, unlike the gang-type violence in the former Yugoslavia. One difference is a question of scale ("only" thousands of deaths in the case of U.S. gangs versus hundreds of thousands in Yugoslavia). But the main reason the latter case is generally considered war is the involvement of state military units (and quasi-state military forces created out of pieces of state armies that disintegrated).

Thus, many different activities are covered by the general term *war*. Consequently, it is not easy to say how many wars are going on in the world at the moment. Political scientists can count the number of militarized disputes or the number of international conflicts that regularly entail violence. But most lists of wars set some minimum criteria—for instance, a minimum of a thousand battle deaths—to distinguish the large-scale violence implied by war from the more common lower-level violence that occurs in many international conflicts. Criteria that are not often used include formal declarations of war (now largely obsolete) or other legal standards. For example, Japan and the Soviet Union never signed a treaty ending World War II but are not considered to be at war.

The map of wars in progress at the front of the book shows the locations of the 23 wars in progress in late 1995. Those that have cost the most lives (though some have now reached lower levels of violence) are in Cambodia, Afghanistan, Iraq, Rwanda, Somalia, Sudan, Bosnia, Guatemala, Indonesia (East Timor), and the Middle East (the Arab-Israeli conflict). Of the 23 wars, none is in North America, Japan or the Pacific, or Western Europe. Five are in Russia and Eastern Europe. Eighteen are in the global South—seven in South Asia, five in Africa, three in the Middle East, and three in Latin America. Since the end of the Cold War, the levels of violence in the world's wars have generally decreased, and in the past few years several serious wars have ended—in Angola, Mozambique, South Africa, and Northern Ireland (and in Bosnia, at least temporarily).

Wars are very diverse. We may distinguish several types of war that tend to arise from different situations and play different sorts of roles in bargaining over conflicts. Starting from the largest wars (which most obviously meet the criteria), we may distinguish the following main categories.

Hegemonic war is a war over control of the entire *world order*—the rules of the international system as a whole, including the role of world hegemony (see "Hegemony" pp. 81–82). This class of wars (with some variations in definition and conception) is also known as *world war, global war, general war, or systemic war.*[30] The last case of hegemonic war was World War II. Quite possibly this kind of war cannot occur any longer without destroying civilization.

Total war is warfare by one state waged to conquer and occupy another. The goal is to reach the capital city and force the surrender of the government, which can then be replaced with one of the victor's choosing (see pp. 192–193). In rare cases the victor may annex the loser into its own state, as Iraq tried to do with Kuwait. Total war as we know it

---

[30]Levy, Jack S. Theories of General War. *World Politics* 37 (3), 1985: 344–74. Thompson, William R. *On Global War: Historical-Structural Approaches to World Politics*. Columbia: University of South Carolina Press, 1988.

originated in the mass destruction of the Napoleonic Wars, which introduced conscription on a large scale and geared the entire French national economy toward the war effort. The practice of total war evolved with industrialization, which further integrated all of society and economy into the practice of war. The last total war among great powers was World War II, which ended with Germany and Japan in ruins and occupied by the Western alliance.

In total war, with the entire society mobilized for the struggle, the entire society of the enemy is considered a legitimate target. For instance, in World War II Germany attacked British civilians with V-2 rockets, while British and U.S. strategic bombing killed 600,000 German civilians (and hundreds of thousands more Japanese) in an effort to weaken morale.

Limited war includes military actions carried out to gain some objective short of the surrender and occupation of the enemy. For instance, the U.S.-led war against Iraq in 1991 retook the territory of Kuwait but did not go on to Baghdad to topple Saddam Hussein's government. Many border wars have this character: after occupying the land it wants, a state may stop short and defend its gains.

Raids are limited wars that consist of a single short action—a bombing run or a quick incursion by land. For example, in 1982 Israeli warplanes bombed an Iraqi nuclear research facility to stop Iraq from making progress toward the development of nuclear weapons. (Without this raid, Iraq might have had nuclear weapons by the time it invaded Kuwait in 1990.) The action had a narrow objective—the destruction of the facility—and was over within hours. Raids fall into the gray area between wars and nonwars because their destruction is limited and they are over quickly. Raiding that is repeated or fuels a cycle of retaliation usually becomes a limited war or what is sometimes called "low-intensity conflict."

Civil war refers to war between factions within a state trying to create, or prevent, a new government for the entire state or some territorial part of it. (The aim may be to change the entire system of government, to merely replace the people in it, or to split a region off as a new state.) The U.S. Civil War of the 1860s is a good example of a secessionist civil war; so is the war of Eritrea province in Ethiopia (now the internationally recognized state of Eritrea) in the 1980s. The war in El Salvador in the 1980s is an example of a civil war for control of the entire state (not secessionist). Civil wars seem to be often among the most brutal wars—sometimes brother fighting brother, often with no clearly defined front lines. One might think that people fighting their fellow citizens would act less cruelly than those fighting people from another state, but this is not so. The 50,000 or more deaths in the civil war in El Salvador included many at the hands of death squads—massacres, torture, and the like—killings that were not based on ethnic differences. (Of course, many of today's civil wars do contain ethnic conflicts as well.)

Guerrilla war, which includes certain kinds of civil wars, is warfare without front lines. Irregular forces operate in the midst of, and often hidden or protected by, civilian populations. The purpose of guerrilla war is not to engage an enemy army in direct confrontation but rather to harass and punish it so as to gradually limit its operation and effectively liberate territory from its control. U.S. military forces in South Vietnam fought against Viet Cong guerrillas for years in the 1960s, with rising frustration. The United

States could go almost anywhere by daylight and occupy a location, but by night the guerrillas would slip back and reclaim control. Efforts to combat such a guerrilla army—**counterinsurgency**—often include programs to "win the hearts and minds" of rural populations so that they stop sheltering the guerrillas.

In guerrilla war, without a fixed front line, there is much territory that neither side controls; both sides exert military leverage over the same places at the same time. This makes guerrilla wars extremely painful for civilians. The situation is doubly painful because conventional armies fighting against guerrillas often cannot distinguish them from civilians, and so punish both together. In one famous case in South Vietnam, a U.S. officer, who had ordered an entire village burned to deny its use as a sanctuary by the Viet Cong, commented, "We had to destroy the village to save it."

Warfare increasingly is irregular and guerrilla-style; it is less and less often an open conventional clash of large state armies.[31] But conventional wars like the Gulf War do still occur. On the whole, state and nonstate actors have a range of political goals that lead them to employ violent forms of leverage, and a range of options for employing force.

Terrorism

Terrorism is basically just another step along the spectrum of violent leverage, from total war to guerrilla war. Indeed terrorism and guerrilla war often occur together. Clausewitz might say that "terrorism is the continuation of war by other means." Yet terrorism differs from other kinds of wars. *Terrorism* refers to political violence that targets civilians deliberately and indiscriminately. Beyond this basic definition other criteria can be applied, but the definitions become politically motivated: one person's freedom fighter is another's terrorist. More than guerrilla warfare, terrorism is a shadowy world of faceless enemies and irregular tactics marked by extreme brutality.[32]

The purpose of terrorism is to demoralize a civilian population in order to use their discontent as leverage on national governments or other parties to a conflict. Related to this is the aim of creating drama in order to gain media attention for a cause. For instance, when the IRA planted bombs in London, it was hoping to make life miserable enough for Londoners that they insist their government settle the Northern Ireland issue; the bombing also sought to keep the issue of Northern Ireland in the news week after week. The

---

[31]Levite, Ariel E., Bruce W. Jentleson, and Larry Berman, eds. *Foreign Military Intervention: The Dynamics of Protracted Conflict.* New York: Columbia University Press, 1992. Klare, Michael, and Peter Kornbluh, eds. *Low-Intensity Warfare: Counterinsurgency, Proinsurgency, and Antiterrorism in the Eighties.* New York: Random/Pantheon, 1991. Azar, Edward E., and Chung-in Moon, eds. *National Security in the Third World: The Management of Internal and External Threats.* Aldershot, U.K.: Edward Elgar, 1988.

[32]Rapoport, David C., ed. *Inside Terrorist Organizations.* New York: Columbia University Press, 1988. Herman, Edward S., and Gerry O'Sullivan. *The "Terrorism" Industry: The Experts and Institutions That Shape Our View of Terror.* New York: Random/Pantheon, 1991. Reich, Walter, ed. *Origins of Terrorism: Psychologies, Ideologies, Theologies, States of Mind.* New York: Cambridge University Press, 1990. Falk, Richard. *Revolutionaries and Functionaries: The Dual Face of Terrorism.* New York: Dutton, 1988.

government would then be pressured to concede terms more favorable to the IRA than would otherwise be the case. Terrorism is seldom mindless; it is usually a calculated use of violence as leverage. However, motives and means of terrorism vary widely, having in common only that some actor is using violence to send a message to another actor.

The effect of terrorism is psychological. It actually harms very few victims. The number of U.S. citizens killed by terrorists each year is far less than the number killed in fires caused by faulty wiring, for instance. Yet terrorism, and not faulty wiring, is a national political issue. In part the effectiveness of terrorism in capturing attention is due to the dramatic nature of the incidents, especially as shown on television news. Terrorism also gains attention because of the randomness of its choice of victims. Although only a few dozen people may be injured by a bomb left in a market, millions of people realize that "it could have been me," because they, too, shop in markets. In attacks on airplanes this fear is heightened by many people's fears of flying. Terrorism thus amplifies a small amount of power through its psychological effect on large populations; this is why it is usually a tool of the powerless.

Terrorist attacks, such as the bomb that killed three people in the Frankfurt airport (June 1985), often reflect the weakness of the perpetrators and their lack of access to other means of leverage.

In the past, most terrorism has occurred in the Middle East, Europe, and South Asia. While U.S. interests and citizens abroad have been repeatedly targeted, little terrorism has taken place within the United States itself. The 1993 bombing of the World Trade Center in New York was an exception. But in an interdependent world, the United States may find increasingly that global problems like terrorism cannot be kept at a distance.

The classic cases of terrorism—including those that drew attention to the phenomenon in the 1970s—are those in which a *nonstate* actor uses attacks against *civilians* by secret *nonuniformed* forces, operating *across international borders*, as a leverage against *state* actors. Radical political factions or separatist groups may hijack or blow up airplanes, or plant bombs in cafes, clubs, or other crowded places. For example, a Palestinian faction seized and held hostage (then killed) Israeli athletes at the Olympic Games in Munich in 1972. Such tactics create spectacular incidents that draw attention to the terrorists' cause. Typically, the message is, "We won't go away; we will make you unhappy until you deal with us."

Often terrorism is used by radical factions of movements that have not been successful in getting attention or developing other effective means of leverage. It is often a tactic of desperation, and it almost always reflects weakness in the power position of the attacker. For instance, the Palestinian radicals in 1972 had seen Arab states defeated by Israel in war and could not see a way to gain even a hearing for their cause. By capturing media attention worldwide with dramatic incidents of violence—even at the cost of rallying world public opinion against their cause—the radicals hoped to make Palestinian aspirations an issue that Western governments could not ignore when deciding on policies toward the Middle East. Terrorists are more willing than states are to violate the norms of the international system because, unlike states, they do not have a stake in that system.

States themselves carry out acts designed to terrorize their own populations or those of other states, but scholars tend to avoid the term "terrorism" for acts taken by states (preferring to call it repression or war). Russia's indiscriminate attacks on civilian areas of Chechnya province in 1995 are an example. In fact, any violent act taken during a civil or international war—by or toward a warring party—cannot easily fit into the category of terrorism. Of course, because war itself is hard to define, so is terrorism; warring parties often call each other terrorists. In the Central American civil wars of the 1980s, both the states and the guerrillas employed tactics that, if taken in peacetime, would easily qualify as terrorism.

The narrowest definition of terrorism would exclude acts carried out either by or against *uniformed military forces* rather than civilians. For instance, this definition would exclude the killing of 243 U.S. Marines by a car bomb in Lebanon in 1983 because it was directed at a military target. It would also exclude the bombing of German cities in World War II even though the purpose was to terrorize civilians. But in today's world of undeclared war, guerrilla war, civil war, and ethnic violence, there is a large gray zone around clear cases of terrorism.

State-sponsored terrorism refers to the use of terrorist groups by states—usually under control of the state's intelligence agency—to achieve political aims.[33] For example, in

---

[33]Stohl, Michael, and George A. Lopez, eds. *Terrible Beyond Endurance? The Foreign Policy of State Terrorism.* Westport, CT: Greenwood, 1988.

1988 a bomb scattered pieces of Pan Am flight 103 over the Scottish countryside. Investigators converged on the scene and combed the fields for debris that could help identify the cause of the explosion. They found fragments of a tape recorder that had contained a sophisticated plastic-explosive bomb. A tiny strand of wire from the triggering device turned out to be a rare variety, through which the investigators traced the origins of the bomb after several years of intensive work. The U.S. and British governments identified two Libyan intelligence agents who had brought the tape recorder to Malta and smuggled it onto flight 103 in Frankfurt. In 1992, backed by the UN Security Council, they demanded that Libya turn over the two agents for trial. When Libya refused, the UN imposed sanctions including a ban on international flights to or from Libya (which was still in effect in 1995).

More often, state involvement in terrorism is very difficult to trace. Indeed, had the bomb on flight 103 exploded as scheduled over the Atlantic Ocean, instead of prematurely, the clues would not have been found. Western leaders in the Cold War suspected the hand of the Soviet intelligence service, the KGB, behind many terrorist incidents in the 1970s and 1980s. When the KGB files were opened after the collapse of the Soviet Union, some of these suspicions were confirmed, although many mysteries remained. When a political faction issues a communiqué claiming credit for a terrorist action, it never includes a statement like "the participants wish to thank the Iranian government for its generous support which made today's action possible."

Counterterrorism has become a sophisticated operation as well as a big business. International agencies, notably the *Interpol* police agency (and in Europe, Europol), coordinate the actions of states in tracking and apprehending suspected terrorists (as well as drug traffickers, and other criminals). National governments have investigative agencies, such as the FBI and CIA in the United States, to try to break through the wall of secrecy around terrorist operations. Lately, many private companies have expanded the business of providing security services, including antiterrorist equipment and forces, to companies and individuals doing business internationally.

Conflict Resolution

The development and implementation of peaceful strategies for settling conflicts—using alternatives to violent forms of leverage—is known by the general term **conflict resolution.** These methods are at work, competing with violent methods, in virtually all international conflicts. Recently the use of conflict resolution has been increasing, becoming more sophisticated, and succeeding more often.[34]

---

[34]Fisher, Roger, Elizabeth Kopelman, and Andrea Kupfer Schneider. *Beyond Machiavelli: Tools for Coping with Conflict.* Cambridge, MA: Harvard University Press, 1995. Zartman, William I., ed. *Elusive Peace: Negotiating an End to Civil Wars.* Washington, DC: The Brookings Institution, 1995. Sandole, Dennis J. D., and Hugo Van der Merwe, eds. *Conflict Resolution: Theory and Practice.* New York: St. Martin's Press, 1993. Miall, Hugh. *The Peacemakers: Peaceful Settlement of Disputes Since 1945.* New York: St. Martin's Press, 1992. Väyrynen, Raimo, ed. *New Directions in Conflict Theory: Conflict Resolution and Conflict Transformation.* Newbury Park, CA: Sage, 1991. Burton, John W. *Conflict Resolution and Prevention.* New York: St. Martin's Press, 1990. Kriesberg, Louis, Terrell A. Northrup, and Stuart J. Thorson, eds. *Intractable Conflicts and Their Transformation.* Syracuse: Syracuse University Press, 1989.

Most conflict resolution uses a third party whose role is **mediation** between two conflicting parties.[35] Most of today's international conflicts have one or more mediating parties working regularly to resolve the conflict short of violence. There is no hard and fast rule saying what kinds of third parties mediate what kinds of conflicts. Today the UN is the most important mediator on the world scene. Some regional conflicts are mediated through regional organizations such as the European Community and the Organization of American States, or by single states or even private individuals. Individuals can make a critical difference. For instance, the former president of Costa Rica, Oscar Arias, won the 1987 Nobel peace prize for mediating a multilateral agreement among Central American presidents to end several brutal wars in the region.[36]

In the mid-1990s, former president Jimmy Carter emerged as a virtual one-man band for international mediation. He closed agreements on nuclear proliferation in North Korea, democratic transition in Haiti, and ceasefires in Bosnia and the Sudan. Each agreement was criticized—the North Korean agreement let North Korea buy time for its nuclear program; the Haiti agreement worked only because of an imminent threat of military force (with U.S. planes already en route); the Bosnia ceasefire lasted only for one winter when snow prevented much fighting anyway. Still, it was clear by 1995 that Carter had become available as a specialized instrument that states could bring into play in international bargaining—in some cases as a genuine alternative to military options.

The involvement of the mediator can vary. Some mediation is strictly *technical*—a mediator may take an active but strictly neutral role in channeling communication between two states that lack other channels of communication.[37] For example, Pakistan secretly passed messages between China and the United States before the breakthrough in U.S.-Chinese relations in 1971. Such a role is sometimes referred to as offering the mediator's *good offices* to a negotiating process.

In facilitating communication, a mediator listens to each side's ideas and presents them in a way the other side can hear. The mediator works to change each side's view of difficult issues. In these roles the mediator operates in the mode of a translator between the two sides, or of a therapist helping them work out psychological problems in their relationship.

Mediators may also actively *propose solutions* based on an assessment of each side's demands and interests. Such solutions may be compromises, may recognize the greater validity of one side's position (or power), or may be creative ideas that meet the needs of both parties in ways they had not thought of. A 50-50 compromise is not always the best or fairest solution—it may simply reward the side with the more extreme starting position.

---

[35]Bercovitch, Jacob, and Jeffrey Z. Rubin, eds. *Mediation in International Relations: Multiple Approaches to Conflict Management*. New York: St. Martin's Press, 1992. Princen, Thomas. *Intermediaries in International Conflict*. Princeton: Princeton University Press, 1992.

[36]Child, Jack. *The Central American Peace Process, 1983–1991: Sheathing Swords, Building Confidence*. Boulder, CO: Lynne Rienner, 1992.

[37]Stein, Janice Gross, ed. *Getting to the Table: The Processes of International Prenegotiation*. Baltimore: Johns Hopkins University Press, 1989.

If both sides agree in advance to abide by a solution devised by a mediator, the process is called *arbitration*. In that case both sides present their arguments to the arbitrator, who decides on a "fair" solution. For example, the Israelis and Egyptians submitted their border dispute over the hotel at Taba (see p. 185) to arbitration when they could not come to an agreement on their own. Similarly, El Salvador and Honduras turned to the World Court to arbitrate their territorial disputes in 1992; and Chile and Argentina gave their border problems to a panel of Latin American judges in the 1980s and 1990s. In arbitration it is not uncommon to empower a panel of three people, one chosen by each side unilaterally and a third on whom both sides agree.

Why should a state settle nonviolently a conflict that might be settled by military means? It must see that doing so would be in its interest. To get national leaders to come to this conclusion one must create conditions to bring into play mutual interests that already exist or to create new mutual interests.

In many situations two conflicting parties could benefit from a solution other than war but lack the trust and communication channels to find such a solution. Neutral mediation with various degrees of involvement can bring about awareness of the two parties' common interests. For example, Egypt and Israel had a common interest in making peace in the late 1970s, but they also had a high level of mistrust. U.S. president Jimmy Carter invited the two heads of state to a private and relaxed setting—his Camp David retreat—where they could go through the issues in a productive manner over nearly two weeks of discussions. Without the restrictions of formal negotiations, it was easier for the two leaders to find their common interests.

Sometimes, when heads of state do not see their common interests, ordinary citizens try to raise awareness of such mutual interests on both sides. Travel and discussion by private individuals and groups toward this end has been called *citizen diplomacy*, and it occurs fairly regularly (though not very visibly) when conflicting states are stuck in a cycle of hostility.[38] Sometimes a private trip takes on historical significance, as when the U.S. table tennis team was invited to China in 1971 at the outset of the U.S.-China rapprochement.

Conflicting parties (and mediators) can also work to *restructure* the terms of bargaining—in effect extending the possible solutions for one or both sides so that their interests overlap. Often a mediator can come up with a *win-win* solution.[39] This may be as simple as providing means for one or both parties to *save face* when giving up some demand—which may lower the cost of giving up the point enough that the benefits of a deal outweigh the costs. In other cases, creative solutions may satisfy both parties. For instance, at the Camp David negotiations, Egypt insisted on regaining sovereignty over all its territory in the Sinai desert. Israel insisted on security against the threat of attack from the Sinai. The win-win solution was a return of the territory to Egyptian sovereignty but with most of it demilitarized (with a few U.S. observers present) so that Egypt could not use it to stage an attack. A win-win solution often trades off two disputed items on which the

[38]Warner, Gale, and Michael Shuman. *Citizen Diplomats: Pathfinders in Soviet-American Relations and How You Can Join Them*. New York: Continuum, 1987.

[39]Fisher, Roger, and William Ury, with Bruce Patton, ed. *Getting to Yes: Negotiating Agreement Without Giving In*. New York: Penguin, 1983.

Conflict resolution offers an alternative avenue for settling conflicts short of violence. Aung San Suu Kyi, a leading practitioner of nonviolent conflict resolution, sought reconciliation with the Burmese military government that had denied her election victory and placed her under house arrest for years (1989 photo).

states place different priorities. Each side can then prevail on the issue that it considers important while yielding on an issue it does not care about as much.

Another way to create mutual interests is to break a conflict into pieces (fractionation) and start with those pieces in which a common interest and workable solution can be found. These may be largely symbolic *confidence-building* measures at first but can gather momentum as the process proceeds. A gradual increase in trust reduces the risks of nonviolent settlements relative to their costs and creates an expectation that the issues at stake can be resolved nonviolently.

A mediator who is in a position to apply positive or negative leverage to the two parties can use that leverage to influence each side's calculation of interests (again opening up new mutual interests). For instance, the promise of future U.S. aid to both Israel and Egypt was an important sweetener in bringing them to a substantive agreement at Camp David. Likewise, the reluctance of states in the Middle East to incur U.S. displeasure (since the Gulf War) played a role in bringing parties in the Arab-Israeli conflict into peace talks in 1991.

Just as there are many possible outcomes of conflict, many types of war, and varied propensities for violence among different states, so too is there great diversity in the ways and means of using force if conflict resolution fails to offer a better alternative. States develop a wide array of military forces, which vary tremendously in their purposes and capabilities—having in common only that they are instruments used to apply violence in some form. It is to these military forces that we now turn.

❖ CHAPTER SUMMARY

◆ War and other forms of international violence are used as leverage to try to improve the terms of settlement of conflicts.

◆ Many theories have been offered as general explanations about when such forms of leverage come into play—the causes of war. Contradictory theories have been proposed at each level of analysis, and with two exceptions none have strong empirical support. Thus, political scientists cannot reliably predict the outbreak of war.

◆ The two exceptions are (a) that there are few if any societies in which war and intergroup violence as means of leverage are unknown, and (b) that democratic states almost never fight wars against other democracies.

◆ States come into conflict with each other and with nonstate actors for a variety of reasons. Conflicts will always exist among international actors.

◆ Territorial disputes are among the most serious international conflicts because states place great value on territorial integrity. With a few exceptions, however, almost all the world's borders are now firmly fixed and internationally recognized.

◆ Conflicts over the control of entire states (through control of governments) are also serious and are relatively likely to lead to the use of force.

◆ Economic conflicts lead to violence much less often, because positive gains from economic activities are more important inducements than negative threats of violence. Some particular kinds of economic conflict, however, have special implications for national security.

◆ Drug trafficking creates several kinds of conflict that draw in state and nonstate actors alike.

◆ Ethnic conflicts, especially when linked with territorial disputes, are very difficult to resolve because of the psychological biases they create. It is hard to explain why people's loyalties are sometimes to their ethnic group, sometimes to a multiethnic nation.

◆ Fundamentalist religious movements pose a broad challenge to the rules of the international system in general and state sovereignty in particular. Islamic fundamentalism is especially strong because it taps into anti-Western sentiment in the Middle East.

◆ Ideologies do not matter very much in international relations, with the possible exception of democracy as an ideology. State leaders can use ideologies to justify whatever actions are in their interests.

◆ When violent means are used as leverage in international conflicts, a variety of types of war result. These vary greatly in size and character, from guerrilla wars and raids to hegemonic war for leadership of the international system. Along this spectrum of uses of violence, the exact definition of war is uncertain.

◆ Like other violent means of leverage, terrorism is used to gain advantage in international bargaining situations. Terrorism is effective if it damages morale in a population and gains media exposure for the cause.

◆ Mediation and other forms of conflict resolution are alternative means of exerting leverage on participants in bargaining. Increasingly these means are succeeding in settling conflicts without (or with no further) use of violence.

❖ THINKING CRITICALLY

1. Suppose that you were the mediator in negotiations between two states each claiming the same piece of land. What principles could you follow in developing a mutually acceptable plan for ownership of the territory? What means could you use to convince the two states to accept your plan?

2. How many of the six types of international conflict discussed in this chapter can you connect with the phenomenon of nationalism discussed on pp. 31–33? What are the connections in each case?

3. European textbooks were revised after World War II to reduce ethnic and national stereotypes and give a fairer portrayal of Europe's various nations. What about the textbooks you used to learn your country's history? Did they give an accurate picture, or did they overstate the virtues of your own ethnic group or nation at the expense of others? How?

4. The rise of fundamentalism among the world's major religions challenges traditional notions of state sovereignty. Do you think that this trend will strengthen, or weaken, the United Nations and other attempts to create supranational authority (which also challenge state sovereignty)?

5. Given the definition of war provided on p. 210, name three current international situations that clearly fit the definition of war and three that are ambiguous "quasi wars" (almost but not quite fitting the definition). Which do you think are more serious, the wars or the quasi wars? Do they involve different types of actors? Different kinds of conflicts?

❖ KEY TERMS

conflict
settlement
irredentism
territorial waters
airspace
(theory of) lateral pressure
ethnic groups
ethnocentrism
dehumanization
secular (state)

Islam/Muslims
hegemonic war
total war
limited war
civil war
guerrilla war
counterinsurgency
state-sponsored terrorism
conflict resolution
mediation

*Russian soldier in
Chechnya, 1995.*

MILITARY FORCE

❖ THE USE OF FORCE

A state leader in a conflict bargaining situation can apply various kinds of leverage to reach a more favorable outcome (see Figure 6.1). One set of levers represent nonviolent means of influencing other states, such as foreign aid, economic sanctions, personal diplomacy, and so forth (less-tangible means include use of norms, morality, and other ideas). A second set of levers—the subject of this chapter—make violent actions occur. They set armies marching or missiles flying.

When state leaders resort to force in an international conflict, they do not push all the violence levers at once. Rather, they choose applications of force that suit their objectives in the situation and their strategies for achieving those objectives. Furthermore, leaders of different states have different levers available to them—different military capabilities that they earlier decided to create and maintain (see p. 227). In order to understand the decisions that leaders make about using military force, it is important to know how various military capabilities work, how much they cost, and what effects they have.

Violence as a means of leverage tends to be costly to both the attacker and the attacked. It is therefore not the most effective instrument in most situations: states can generally achieve their objectives in a more cost-effective way using means of leverage such as economic actions (Chapters 8 and 9), foreign aid (Chapter 13), communication (Chapter 10), or international organizations (Chapter 7). Military force tends to be a last resort. There is also evidence that the utility of military force relative to nonmilitary means is slowly declining over time.

Yet most states still devote vast resources to military capabilities compared to other means of influence. For example, the United States has about 20,000 diplomats but 2 million soldiers; it spends about $10 billion a year on foreign aid but $250 billion on military forces.

For many states, the reason for this dedication of resources is largely defensive. Military capabilities are maintained in an effort to ensure *security*—the ability to feel safe against the threat of military attack (or of other uses of force as leverage by other states). The overall utility of military force in IR may be declining, but for the narrow purpose of repelling a military attack there is often no substitute for military means. Because of the

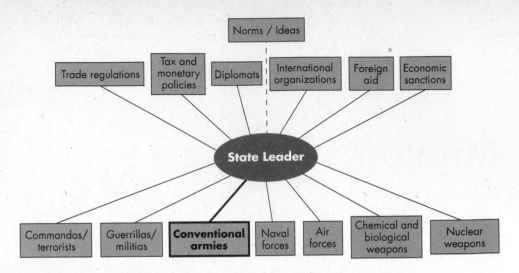

FIGURE 6.1 Military and Nonmilitary Means of Leverage
Conventional armed force is the most commonly used military form of leverage.

security dilemma, states feel they must devote large resources to military capabilities if even a few other states are doing so.

Military capabilities are generally divided into two types—conventional forces and weapons of mass destruction (nuclear, chemical, and biological weapons). Virtually all of the actual uses of military force to date have involved conventional forces. The weapons of mass destruction nonetheless come into play in international bargaining because even the implicit threat of their use is a means of leverage. Although the superpower nuclear arms race has ended, the proliferation of weapons of mass destruction to new states is an increasing concern.

This chapter discusses the various kinds of military forces used by state leaders. It first considers the major strategic concerns of state leaders in acquiring and maintaining military forces, especially in deciding how much to spend on military budgets. The chapter then considers the civil-military link that allows political leaders to control military forces to be used as leverage in international bargaining. Finally the chapter sketches the variety of types of military forces that states maintain, including efforts to obtain weapons of mass destruction.

❖ CONFIGURING FORCES

Given the range of military capabilities available to states (at various costs), how should state leaders choose which to acquire?

Military Economics

Choices about military forces depend on the connection between a state's military spending and its economic health. Not long ago, it was widely believed in the United

States that "war is good for the economy" (a lesson drawn from World War II, when military spending seemed to help end the Great Depression). If this were true, state leaders would not face difficult choices in setting military budgets. High military spending would give them both more military capabilities for use in international conflicts *and* more economic growth for domestic needs (buying popular and political support in various ways).

Unfortunately for state leaders, the economics of military spending are not so favorable. Over the long run, military spending tends to compete with other economic needs such as investment in civilian industry or government projects. Over time, economic resources used for military purposes deprive the rest of the economy and reduce its growth. High-technology military development (using engineers, scientists, technicians, etc.) tends to starve civilian sectors of talent and technology. Fewer jobs are created, per dollar of U.S. government funds, in the military than in education, housing, construction, and similar purposes (military spending is more capital-intensive and less labor-intensive). Conversely, reductions in military spending tend to free up economic resources for more productive purposes and strengthen the growth of the economy in the long term.

Thus, over the long term state leaders face a trade-off between increasing their available military leverage and increasing their overall economic health. This trade-off explains in part why, during the Cold War, the great power with the *highest* military spending—the Soviet Union, at perhaps 20 percent of GDP—had the *worst* economic performance, whereas the great power with the *lowest* military spending (Japan, with around one percent of GDP) had the *best* economic performance.[1]

As the Cold War ended, U.S. leaders cut military spending in hopes of reaping a *peace dividend* (more money for cities, education, the environment, and so forth).[2] U.S. citizens and politicians also began to demand that prosperous U.S. allies in Europe and Japan pay more of the costs for maintaining U.S. military forces there—a concept known as *burden sharing*. At the same time, Russia and the other former Soviet republics drastically curtailed military spending, which their tattered economies could no longer support.

Unfortunately, the short-term effects of military spending (or reductions in spending) tend to run counter to the long-term effects. The immediate effect of a sharp reduction in military spending (as at the end of a war) is often to throw people out of work and disrupt economic growth. Conversely, the effect of increased military spending in the short term can be to pick up the slack in a national economy operating below capacity (as the United States was in the 1930s, for example). As with any government spending, the immediate effect of pumping money into the economy is to stimulate growth (even while undermining longer-term growth by increasing inflation and debt).

---

[1]Mintz, Alex, and Steve Chan. *Defense, Welfare and Growth: Perspectives and Evidence.* New York: Routledge, 1992. Samuels, Richard J. *Rich Nation, Strong Army: National Security and the Technological Transformation of Japan.* Ithaca: Cornell University Press, 1994.

[2]Mintz, Alex, ed. *The Political Economy of Military Spending in the United States.* New York: Routledge, 1992. Ward, Michael D., and David R. Davis. Sizing Up the Peace Dividend: Economic Growth and Military Spending in the United States, 1948–1996. *American Political Science Review* 86 (3), 1992: 748–58. Kaufmann, William W. *Glasnost, Perestroika, and U.S. Defense Spending.* Washington, DC: The Brookings Institution, 1990.

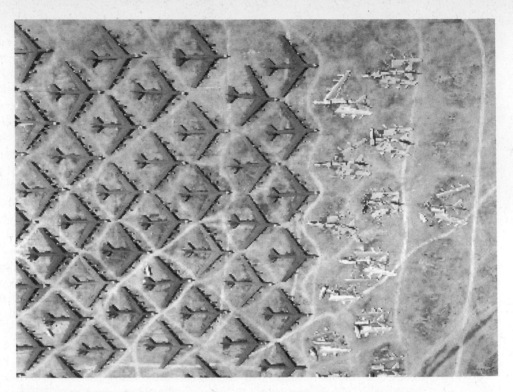

U.S. and Russian nuclear forces are being greatly reduced under the START treaties. Here U.S. B-52 bombers are being chopped up, under the eye of Russian satellites, to bring force levels down.

Because of these short-term effects, U.S. military spending cuts after the Cold War deepened a serious recession and did not produce a quick peace dividend. Russia's cuts in military spending likewise did little to stop its economic free fall. There and throughout the former Soviet Union—and somewhat less desperately in the United States and the West—political leaders scrambled to develop plans for **economic conversion**—the use of former military facilities and industries for new civilian production.[3]

Both the long- and short-term effects of military spending are magnified by actual *warfare.* War not only stimulates very high military spending, it destroys capital (people, cities, farms, and factories in battle areas) and causes inflation (by reducing the supply of various goods while increasing demand for them). Governments must pay for war goods

[3]Anthony, Ian. *The Future of the Defense Industries in Central and Eastern Europe.* New York: Oxford University Press, 1994. Klein, Lawrence R., Fu-chen Lo and Warwick J. McKibbin, eds. *Arms Reduction: Economic Implications in the Post Cold War Era.* New York: United Nations University Press, 1995. Dumas, Lloyd J., and Marek Thee, eds. *Making Peace Possible: The Promise of Economic Conversion.* New York: Pergamon Press, 1989. Melman, Seymour. Swords into Plowshares: Converting from Military to Civilian Production. *Technology Review* 89 (1), 1986: 62–71.

by borrowing money (increasing government debt), by printing more currency (fueling inflation), or by raising taxes (reducing spending and investment). U.S. revolutionary Thomas Paine warned in 1787 that "war. . . has but one thing certain, and that is to increase taxes."[4]

Nonetheless, war and high military spending can have certain economic benefits. The short-term stimulation resulting from a boost in military spending has been mentioned. Another potential benefit is the acquisition of territory (containing resources and capital). If Saddam Hussein had gotten away with his quick grab of Kuwait, for example, it would have been worth many times the cost of the military attack. And Serbian ultra-nationalists made fortunes off the plunder of Bosnians who were "ethnically cleansed." Another potential economic benefit of war is to stir up a population's patriotism so it will work harder for less pay. But overall, the benefits rarely equal the economic costs of war.

State leaders, then, face somewhat complex choices in setting overall levels of military spending. Over the long term, lower military spending is economically preferable, but in the short term higher military spending can stimulate the economy. Sudden changes in military spending, up or down, are usually disruptive to economic health and stability. But such sudden changes usually reflect the beginnings or ends of wars, which entail even more complex trade-offs of costs and benefits (both economic and political) for state leaders.

The Choice of Capabilities

Despite the complexity of these trade-offs, state leaders must adopt military budgets, choose particular military capabilities to obtain, and often structure other economic activities to support those choices (for instance, nurturing the military-industrial complex). Leaders try to assess the threats to their state from other states' military capabilities and then develop affordable strategies to reduce those threats.

The most basic choice facing state leaders is *how much* to spend on military capabilities. This varies widely, from Costa Rica (with virtually no military spending at all) to states such as North Korea, which devotes 20 percent or more of all economic activity to military purposes. If military budgets are too low, states may be unprepared to meet a security threat; in the worst case, they may even be overrun and conquered militarily. But if leaders set military budgets too high, they will overburden the national economy in the long run. (So far, Costa Rica has not been attacked despite recent wars in neighboring Nicaragua and Panama, whereas North Korea is virtually bankrupt.)

Since the end of the Cold War, U.S. leaders have had to rethink military capabilities. Politicians generally agreed that U.S. leadership in world affairs required having the world's most capable military forces. But given a tremendous U.S. lead over other great powers in this respect (after the Soviet Union collapsed), it was not clear how much was enough for such a purpose. Rationales for various policies (short and long term) were developed by the Pentagon, members of Congress, and private think tanks—matching up certain configurations of forces with certain scenarios in which the United States might

---

[4]Paine, Thomas. *The Writings of Thomas Paine*. Volume 2. New York: Knickerbocker Press, 1894.

want military options. One master of such analyses, former congressman Les Aspin, was secretary of defense in 1993–1994 and began a review of U.S. military force structures. But no definitive vision of the U.S. role in world politics, and the types of scenarios to expect, had emerged by the mid-1990s.[5]

The primary mission of U.S. armed forces during the Cold War—containing the Soviet Union, especially from attacking Western Europe—suddenly became irrelevant. However, the Gulf War suggested a new type of mission based on the ability to deploy a large armed force to a regional conflict area. Does the United States need enough military forces to put down one such regional crisis at a time? Or two at once in different parts of the world? Should the United States assume that it would have to fight such a war single-handed, or can it count on the participation of allies? These are the kinds of questions on which the level of future U.S. military spending depends.

Outside the United States, other states were making similar assessments—most dramatically in Russia and the other republics of the former Soviet Union. Although they tried to reduce military spending as quickly as possible, there were no jobs for laid-off soldiers and military-industrial workers and no housing for troops brought home from Eastern Europe. Until the economic transitions in the region are sorted out, the long-term outlook for the size of military forces there is impossible to assess.

The cutbacks are less dramatic in Western Europe, where NATO members spend several percent of GDP on military forces. And in Japan military spending was already only one percent of GDP, so dramatic cutbacks are not in the works. In China the question of military spending is not critical for economic growth because the army is largely self-supporting (running its own farms, factories, etc.). Chinese military forces were cut back substantially in the 1980s, but in the early 1990s a new buildup was underway.

Great powers continue to dominate the makeup of world military forces. Table 6.1 summarizes the most important forces of the great powers. Together, they account for a third of the world's soldiers, two-thirds of world military spending, 90 percent of arms exports, and 99 percent of nuclear weapons. The table also reflects the sizable military forces maintained by Germany and Japan despite their nontraditional roles in international security affairs since World War II.

In the global South, military spending varies greatly from one country to another, depending in part on the government in power (military or civilian).[6] Spending also depends heavily on the availability of hard currency, from exports of oil or other products to pay for arms purchases. In the 1980s, well over half of all arms imports by third-world countries were in the Middle East, where oil exports created a ready source of funding for military purchases on world arms markets. The remaining arms purchases were spread fairly evenly across Latin America, South Asia, East Asia, and Africa. More than half these arms came from the United States and the Soviet Union, with two-thirds of the re-

---

[5]Betts, Richard K. *Military Readiness: Concepts, Choices, Consequences.* Washington, DC: The Brookings Institution, 1995.

[6]Graham, Norman A., ed. *Seeking Security and Development: The Impact of Military Spending and Arms Transfers.* Boulder, CO: Lynne Rienner, 1994. Ball, Nicole. *Security and Economy in the Third World.* Princeton: Princeton University Press, 1988. Barnett, Michael N. *Confronting the Costs of War: Military Power, State, and Society in Egypt and Israel.* Princeton: Princeton University Press, 1992.

During the Cold War, the superpowers poured money into military budgets, at rates ranging from 5 to 10 percent of GDP for the United States and perhaps 20 percent for the Soviet Union. What theories can explain the superpowers' military spending levels, including the sharp decreases in military spending in the 1990s?

One approach is based on reciprocity (see pp. 63–66). Each superpower responds to the other's military spending by raising or lowering its own military budget in the next time period. From this perspective, the superpower arms race may fit the model of a repeated Prisoner's Dilemma, in which the two players use reciprocity to make sure that the other side's defections do not pay. As in laboratory experiments in which college students play PD repeatedly, both sides eventually learn to get out of the cycle of mutual defection (the spiraling arms race), and lock in to stable cooperation. This could explain the recent sharp decrease in military spending.

An alternative model has each superpower's military spending domestically driven. This would follow from such ideas as the organizational process model of foreign policy (see p. 141) and the power of the military-industrial complex (see pp. 156–158). The recent decreases in military spending would probably then be best explained by internal economic problems in both superpowers.

Hundreds of research studies have tried to test these models against the empirical evidence provided by forty years of military budgets. Typically they use a mathematical model of the arms race, and then use quantitative data on arms spending to test statistically whether the model explains the

THINKING THEORETICALLY
❖

data well. The statistical test shows how well, on average, a country's military spending correlates with the other country's previous spending.

So which theory is supported by these tests? The answer is that neither can be evaluated with much confidence because the quantitative data on military spending are unreliable. Not only did both superpowers conceal military spending (and even military activity from which spending levels might be inferred), but comparing the two was problematical. Costs of weapons and salaries were very different in the two countries; the soldiers and equipment were not of comparable quality; rubles were not convertible into dollars; and macroeconomic indicators like GDP were not compatible across communist and capitalist economies. As a result, no one could say for sure if Soviet military spending was going up or down in a given year, or whether Soviet spending was more or less than U.S. spending. Some research studies found ways around some of these problems, but overall the arms race models have been more useful as purely theoretical models than as testable propositions about the real Cold War arms race.

Thus, military spending can be explained by at least two good theories—good in the sense that they can explain the outcome in terms of a general model with implications for other cases—and neither model can be ruled out by empirical evidence. Note that both the reciprocity model and the domestically driven model have liberal underpinnings, though they operate at different levels of analysis (interstate and domestic). Do conservative or revolutionary world views suggest to you other models that explain military spending levels, beyond these two?

Table 6.1 Estimated Great-Power Military Capabilities, Circa 1994

	Military Expenditures (Billions of U.S. $)	Soldiers[a] (Millions)	Weapons[a]			Nuclear Warheads[b]	1993 Arms Exports[c] (Billions of U.S. $)
			Tanks	Carriers/ Warships/ Submarines	Combat Airplanes		
United States	280	1.6	15,000	11/126/104	6,300	8,300	11.6
Russia	80?	1.7	20,000	2/159/185	4,100	8,900	5.0
China	35	2.9	8,000	0/ 55/ 50	5,800	400	0.5
France	35	0.4	1,000	2/ 41/ 18	900	500	1.0
Britain	35	0.3	1,000	3/ 35/ 17	600	300	1.1
Germany	30	0.4	3,000	0/ 12/ 20	500	0	2.0
Japan	65	0.2	1,000	0/ 62/ 17	400	0	0
Approximate % of world total	70%	35%				99%	95%

In the early 1990s, military forces of all these states—Russia above all—were being profoundly restructured. Figures are estimates of levels in or around 1994. Numbers of weapons or soldiers do not indicate quality (levels of technology) or predict how armed forces would actually perform in combat; in particular, Chinese forces are lower-tech than the others. Russian forces are disorganized and in disrepair, with rampant desertion, nonoperational equipment, and drastic declines in military spending. Expenditure data are notoriously unreliable for Russia. Data on soldiers exclude reserves. Tanks are main battle tanks. Warships (major surface warships) include cruisers, destroyers, and frigates. Airplanes exclude reconnaissance, command, electronics, and trainer aircraft. Nuclear warheads exclude thousands of tactical warheads in storage; data as of December 1994.

Sources: Author's estimates based on the following: [a] *The Military Balance* (IISS); Chinese military expenditures from *SIPRI Yearbook 1994:* 443. [b] *Arms Control Today, December 1994:* 29. [c] Calculated from *SIPRI Yearbook 1994:* 484 (1993 data).

mainder coming from Western Europe.[7] In the 1990s, arms exports to the global South have been dominated by the United States.

From a global perspective, the amount of world military spending is decreasing substantially in the post–Cold War era. However, it is decreasing from high levels. World military spending has been about five percent of the total goods and services in the world economy—about the same proportion as in the United States. This is nearly a trillion dollars every year—the equivalent of about one million dollars every forty seconds. Most of it is spent by a few big states and over one-quarter of it by the United States alone. World military spending is a vast flow of money that could, if redirected to other pur-

[7]Forsberg, Randall, ed. *The Arms Production Dilemma: Contraction and Restraint in the World Combat Aircraft Industry.* Cambridge, MA: M.I.T. Press, 1994. O'Prey, Kevin P. *The Arms Export Challenge: Cooperative Approaches to Export Management and Defense Conversion.* Washington, DC: The Brookings Institution, 1995. Kolodziej, Edward A. *Making and Marketing Arms: The French Experience and Its Implications for the International System.* Princeton: Princeton University Press, 1987.

poses, change the world profoundly and improve major world problems.[8] Of course, "the world" does not spend this money or choose how to direct it; states do.

Beyond these considerations about the size of military forces, the *configuration* of a state's military forces also presents difficult choices. Should the United States emphasize its navy or its air force? Should the army have more soldiers or more tanks? Which bases should be closed in periods of military cutbacks? Should Japan build nuclear weapons? Should Syria buy medium-range missiles?

Different missions require different forces. During the Cold War, about half of all military spending in the U.S. budget—and of world military spending—was directed toward the East-West conflict in Europe. Now other missions—such as intervention in regional conflicts like Iraq-Kuwait or in civil conflicts like Somalia and Haiti—are more important. Some scholars think such interventions are less necessary now that Soviet influence in third-world regions is not a concern; others think that interventions are more important now because North-South issues are replacing East-West ones as major security threats.[9] Other new missions for military forces include humanitarian assistance, drug interdiction, and nation-assisting missions (using military forces to build roads and schools, and to offer similar assistance).

Decisions about a state's military role give direction to its entire economy. During the Cold War, U.S. scientific research and industrial innovation was concentrated in the military sector. By contrast, Japan's research and development in those years focused on commercial products, contributing to Japan's prosperity. In the 1990s, the reconfiguration of U.S. military forces will be undertaken with an eye to the economic spin-offs of military or commercial research and development.

Whatever configuration of military forces a state maintains, the leaders of the state then face ongoing decisions about when and how to use those forces.

❖ CONTROL OF MILITARY FORCES

The first issue of concern to a state leader in pulling a lever to exert influence is whether the lever is attached to anything. That is, how are the decisions of leaders translated into actual actions in distant locations that carry out the leaders' plans?

Command

The use of military force generally requires the coordination of the efforts of thousands, sometimes millions, of individuals performing many different functions in many locations. Such coordination is what is meant by *command*. One cannot take for granted the ability

---

[8]Forsberg, Randall, Robert Elias, and Matthew Goodman. Peace Issues and Strategies. In Institute for Defense and Disarmament Studies. *Peace Resource Book 1986.* Cambridge, MA: Ballinger, 1985.

[9]O'Hanlon, Michael. *Defense Planning for the Late 1990s: Beyond the Desert Storm Framework.* Washington, DC: The Brookings Institution, 1995. Haass, Richard N. *Intervention: The Use of American Military Force in the Post–Cold War World.* Washington, DC: The Brookings Institution, 1994. Murray J. Douglas and Paul R. Viotti, eds. *The Defense Policy of Nations: A Comparative Study.* 3rd ed. Baltimore: Johns Hopkins University Press, 1994.

of a state leader to make military forces take desired actions. At best military forces are large and complex institutions, operating in especially difficult conditions during wartime. At worst military forces have a mind of their own (see pp. 234–235). Sometimes, as in the Russian Army's occupation of Chechnya province in 1995, the state leader (President Yeltsin) appears to exert partial but not complete control over the military.

States control military forces through a **chain of command** running from the highest authority through a hierarchy spreading out to the lowest-level soldiers. The highest authority, or commander in chief, is usually the top political leader—the U.S. president, Russian president, and so forth. The military hierarchy consists of levels of *officers*.

The value of this military hierarchy is illustrated by a story from ancient China in which a king was thinking of hiring Sun Tzu (see pp. 52, 67) as an advisor. As a test, the king asked Sun Tzu if he could turn his harem of 200 concubines into troops. Sun Tzu divided them into two units, commanded by the king's two favorites. He explained the signals to face forward, backward, right, and left. But when he gave the signals, the women just laughed. Sun Tzu then had the two "officers" executed on the spot and put the next most senior concubines in their places. When he gave the signals again, the women obeyed flawlessly. Sun Tzu declared that "the troops are in good order and may be deployed as the King desires." Thus, military hierarchy and discipline make armed forces function as instruments of state power.

In actual conditions of battle, controlling armed forces is especially difficult, because of complex operations, rapid change, and the *fog of war* created by chaos on the battlefield. Participants are pumped up with adrenalin, deafened by noise, and confused by a mass of activity that—from the middle of it—may seem to make no sense. They are called on to perform actions that may run against basic instincts as well as moral norms—killing people and risking death. It is difficult to carry out overall plans of action, to coordinate forces effectively.

These factors reduce the effectiveness of military forces as instruments of state power. But military forces have developed several means for counteracting these problems. First is the principle of military *discipline*. Orders given from higher levels of the hierarchy must be obeyed by the lower levels—whether or not those at the lower level agree. Failure to do so is *insubordination*, or a *mutiny* if a whole group is involved. Leaving one's unit is called *deserting*. These are serious offenses punishable by prison or death.

But discipline depends not only on punishment but on patriotism and professionalism on the part of soldiers. Officers play to nationalist sentiments, reminding soldiers that they fight for their nation and family. No military force is better than the soldiers and officers that make it up. Combat, logistics, communication, and command all depend on individual performance; motivation matters.

Whatever the motivation of soldiers, they require *training* in order to function as instruments of state power. Military training includes both technical training and training in the habit of obeying commands—a central purpose of basic training in every military force. Soldiers are deliberately stripped of their individuality—hair styles, clothes, habits, and mannerisms—to become part of a group. This has both good and bad effects for the individuals (varying from person to person), but it works for the purposes of the military. Then in *exercises*, soldiers practice over and over until certain operations become second nature.

Through a hierarchical chain of command, states control the actions of millions of individual soldiers, creating effective leverage in the hands of state leaders. Here, Chinese women soldiers march in a military parade, Guangzhou, 1991.

To maintain control of forces in battle, military units also rely on soldiers' sense of group solidarity—emotional bonds among the group members.[10] Soldiers risk their lives because their "buddies" depend on them. Abstractions such as nationalism, patriotism, or religious fervor are important, but loyalty to the immediate group (along with a survival instinct) is a stronger motivator. Recent debates about the participation of women and homosexuals in the U.S. armed forces revolve around the question of whether their presence disrupts group solidarity. (Evidence, though sparse, suggests that it need not.)

Troops operating in the field also rely on *logistical support* in order to function effectively. For states to use military leverage, they cannot just push armies around on a map like chess pieces. Rather, they must support those armies with large quantities of supplies. Leaders in Prussia (Germany) over a century ago used well-oiled logistics based on railroads to defeat both Austria and France which were using rapid offensives.

A further difficulty that states must overcome in order to use military forces effectively is that top officers and political leaders need accurate information about what is going on in the field—*intelligence*—in order to make good decisions.[11] They also need extensive

[10]Kellett, Anthony. The Soldier in Battle: Motivational and Behavioral Aspects of the Combat Experience. In Betty Glad, ed. *Psychological Dimensions of War*. Newbury Park, CA: Sage, 1990, pp. 215–35. Dyer, Gwynne. *War*. New York: Crown, 1985.

[11]Laqueur, Walter. *A World of Secrets: The Uses and Limits of Intelligence*. New York: Basic Books, 1985. Hastedt, Glenn. Intelligence Studies After the Cold War. *International Studies Notes* 16 (3), 1991: 39–42.

communications networks, including the ability to use codes to ensure secrecy as information flows up and down the military hierarchy. Such functions are known as "command and control" or sometimes *C3I*—for command, control, communications, and intelligence. This information side of controlling military forces has become ever more important. For example, in the Gulf War, a top U.S. priority was to target Iraqi communications facilities so as to disable Iraq's command and control. Meanwhile, the U.S. side used computers, satellite reconnaissance, and other information technologies to amplify its effectiveness.

Finally, states rely on their military officers to develop and implement effective *strategies and tactics*. Strategies bring the state's military (and nonmilitary) capabilities to bear in an overall coordinated manner to achieve an end. Tactics do the same but in a more localized setting (a single battle) and in a more standardized way. Often when state leaders want to achieve certain political aims in international conflicts, they ask military officers to suggest strategies for employing force toward those ends. Strategy and tactics become especially important when a state employs military force in a conflict with another state whose military capabilities are larger or technically superior. For example, Israel defeated the larger Egyptian military forces in 1967 and 1973 partly by employing clever tactics.

States and Militaries

Overcoming chaos and complexity is only part of the task for state leaders seeking to control military forces. Sometimes they must overcome their own military officers as well. Although militaries are considered instruments of state power, in many states the military forces themselves control the government. These **military governments** are most common in third-world countries, where the military may be the only large modern institution in the country.

Military leaders are able to exercise political control because the same violent forms of leverage that work in international politics also work in domestic politics. In fact, domestically there may be little or no counterleverage to the use of military force (whereas internationally there are other states' armies to contend with). Military officers thus have an inherent power advantage over civilian political leaders. Ironically, the disciplined central command of military forces, which makes them effective as tools of state influence, also allows the state to lose control of them to military officers. Soldiers are trained to follow the orders of their commanding officers, not to think about politics.

A **coup d'état** (French for "blow against the state") is the seizure of political power by domestic military forces—a change of political power outside the state's constitutional order.[12] Coups are often mounted by ambitious junior officers against the top generals. Officers who thus break the chain of command can take along with them the sections of the military hierarchy below them. Coup leaders move quickly to seize centers of power before other units of the military can come into play (putting down the coup attempt or even creating a civil war). These power centers typically include official state buildings in the capital city, such as the presidential palace and parliament, as well as television sta-

---

[12]David, Steven R. *Third World Coups d'État and International Security*. Baltimore: Johns Hopkins University Press, 1987. Maniruzzaman, Talukder. Arms Transfers, Military Coups, and Military Rule in Developing States. *Journal of Conflict Resolution* 36 (4), 1992: 733–55. Foltz, William J., and Henry S. Bienen, eds. *Arms and the African: Military Influences on Africa's International Relations*. New Haven: Yale University Press, 1985. Jackman, Robert S., Rosemary H. T. O'Kane, Thomas H. Johnson, Pat McGowan, and Robert O. Slater. Explaining African Coups d'État. *American Political Science Review* 80 (1), 1986: 225–50.

tions and transmitters. Civilian politicians in power and uncooperative military officers are arrested or killed. The coup leaders try to create a sense of inevitability around the change in government and hope that fellow officers throughout the military defect to their side.

The outcome of a coup is hard to predict. If most or all of the military goes along with the coup, civilian leaders are generally helpless to stop it. But if most of the military officers follow the existing chain of command, the coup is doomed. For instance, in the Philippines in the late 1980s, the top general, Fidel Ramos, remained loyal to the civilian president, Corazón Aquino, in seven coup attempts by subordinate officers. In each case the bulk of the Philippine military forces stayed loyal to the popular Ramos, and the coups failed. In 1992 Ramos himself was elected president with the backing of a grateful Aquino.

Coups may also be put down by outside military force. A government threatened with a coup may call on foreign friends for military assistance. But because coups are considered largely an internal affair—and because they are over so quickly—direct foreign intervention in them is relatively rare.

Military governments often have difficulty in establishing popular legitimacy for their rule because their power is clearly based on force rather than a popular mandate (although the public may support the new government if the old one was particularly bad). In order to stay in power, both military and civilian governments require at least passive acceptance by their people.

A coup is a change of government carried out by domestic military forces operating outside the state's constitution. The number of military governments is declining but dozens remain. Soldiers are shown outside the Haitian legislature, which is being forced at gunpoint to name a new president after a coup against elected president Jean-Bertrand Aristide, October 1991. (Aristide returned as president in 1995.)

Even in nonmilitary governments, the interaction of civilian with military leaders—called *civil-military* relations—is an important factor in how states use force. Military leaders may undermine the authority of civilian leaders in carrying out foreign policies, or they may even threaten a coup if certain actions are taken in international conflicts.

The traditions of civil-military relations in a state do not necessarily reflect the extent of democracy there. States in which civilians traditionally have trouble controlling the military include as well some with long histories of democracy, notably in Latin America. And states with strong traditions of civilian control over military forces include some authoritarian states such as the former Soviet Union (where the Communist party controlled the military). This tradition helps to explain the failure of the attempted coup in August 1991 against the head of the Communist party (Gorbachev). Even with most of the second echelon of party leaders behind them, the coup leaders could not gain the legitimacy needed to take power and to get soldiers to follow their orders.[13]

The tradition of civilian (Communist party) control of the military in China is more ambiguous. Regional military leaders coordinate their activities through the Military Commission, under direction of the Communist party. But during the Cultural Revolution in the 1960s, and again in the Tiananmen protests in 1989, military forces essentially held power at times of internal splits in the party. Both Mao Zedong and Deng Xiaoping made it a point to control the Military Commission personally.

In a few states, certain military forces operate beyond the reach of the government's chain of command. Certainly this is true when rebel guerrilla armies control territories nominally under the jurisdiction of the central government. It is also true in the infrequent but dramatic cases when governmental authority breaks down—in Lebanon in the 1980s and Somalia in 1991–1992, for example. Private armies or militias then answer to local warlords rather than to any national government. In such situations one cannot speak of military force as an instrument of state leverage. But in most of the world, most of the time, military forces follow the commands of state leaders (or are themselves the state leaders).

No matter how firmly state leaders control the military forces at their disposition, those forces are effective only to the extent that they are equipped and trained for the purposes the state leaders have in mind. To understand decisions to use military force one must understand the various types of forces and weapons and the missions they are each adapted to perform.

❖ CONVENTIONAL FORCES

The bargaining power of states depends not only on the overall size of their military forces but on the particular capabilities of those forces in various scenarios. State leaders almost always turn to conventional military forces for actual missions, reserving weapons of mass destruction for making or deterring threats.

---

[13]Lepingwell, John W. R. Soviet Civil-Military Relations and the August Coup. *World Politics* 44 (4), 1992: 539–72.

If a leader decides that an international conflict could be more favorably settled by applying military force, it matters a great deal whether the application involves bombing another state's capital city, imposing a naval blockade, or seizing disputed territory. Armed forces can apply negative leverage at a distance, but various types of forces have evolved over time for different situations and contexts—on water, on land, or in the air.[14] They match up against each other in particular ways. A tank cannot destroy a submarine, and vice versa. A tank can generally prevail against foot soldiers with rifles, though foot soldiers with antitank missiles might prevail.

Types of Forces

Whatever their ultimate causes and objectives, most wars involve a struggle to *control territory*. Territory holds a central place in warfare because of its importance in the international system, and vice versa. Borders define where a state's own military forces and rival states' military forces are free to move. Military logistics make territoriality all the more important because of the need to control territories connecting military forces with each other. An army's supplies must flow from home territory along *supply lines* to the field. Thus the most fundamental purpose of conventional forces is to take, hold, or defend territory on land.

Armies *Armies* are adapted to this purpose. Infantry soldiers armed with automatic rifles can generally control a local piece of territory—using their guns as leverage to "bargain" with people in that zone. When an organized military unit has guns and the other people in the area do not, the latter will tend to obey the commands of the former. Military forces with such a presence are considered to *occupy* a territory militarily. Although inhabitants may make the soldiers' lives unhappy through violent or nonviolent resistance, generally only another organized, armed military force can displace occupiers.

Iraq's occupation of Kuwait illustrates the principle of occupying territory. Even after the U.S.-led forces had pummeled Iraqi forces for six weeks with massive bombing raids, Iraq remained in control of the territory of Kuwait. In the end, ground forces had to move in on land to take control of the territory of Kuwait. A U.S. officer said that to win the war you had to have your soldier standing there with a rifle in his hand and nobody shooting at him.

Foot soldiers are called the **infantry.** They use assault rifles and other light weapons (mines, machine guns, and the like), as well as heavy artillery of various types. *Artillery* is extremely destructive and not very discriminating: it usually causes the most damage and casualties in wars. *Armor* refers to tanks and armored vehicles. In *open terrain*, such as desert, mechanized ground forces typically combine armor, artillery, and infantry. In *close terrain*, such as jungles and cities, however, foot soldiers are most important.

---

[14]Keegan, John. *A History of Warfare.* New York: Random House, 1993. Van Creveld, Martin. *Technology and War: From 2000 B.C. to the Present.* New York: Free Press, 1989. O'Connell, Robert L. *Of Arms and Men: A History of War, Weapons and Aggression.* New York: Oxford University Press, 1989. Luttwak, Edward, and Stuart L. Koehl. *The Dictionary of Modern War.* New York: HarperCollins, 1991.

For this reason, the armies of industrialized states have a greater advantage over poor armies in open conventional warfare, such as in the Kuwaiti desert. In jungle, mountain, or urban warfare, however—such as in Bosnia or Cambodia, for example—such advantages are eroded, and a cheaper and more lightly armed force of motivated foot soldiers or guerrillas may survive and ultimately prevail over an expensive conventional army. These factors might help explain why U.S. military commanders were more willing to send U.S. forces into Kuwait than into Bosnia in 1991–1992. But then Somalia (open terrain) should have been an easy mission for the U.S.-led coalition in 1993–1994; instead it turned into a fiasco.

Navies *Navies* are adapted primarily to control passage through the seas and to attack land near coastlines.[15] Unlike armies, navies are not tied to territory because the oceans beyond coastal waters are not owned by any state. Controlling the seas in wartime allows states to move their own goods and military forces by sea while preventing enemies from doing so. In particular, navies protect *sealift* logistical support. Navies can also blockade enemy ports. As of 1995, Western navies were enforcing naval blockades against both Iraq and Yugoslavia.

Aircraft carriers—mobile platforms for attack aircraft—are instruments of **power projection** that can exert negative leverage against virtually any state in the world. Merely sending an aircraft carrier sailing to the vicinity of an international conflict implies a threat to use force—a modern version of what was known in the nineteenth century as "gunboat diplomacy" (the United States does so several times a year). However, aircraft carriers are extremely expensive and typically require 20 to 25 supporting ships for protection and supply. Few states can afford even one. The United States has 12, France two, Russia one, and several other states have a few smaller and less capable carriers. (In 1992 Russia announced it would sell its second aircraft carrier, still under construction, to raise hard currency.)

Most warships are *surface ships* of various sizes and designs, which rely increasingly on guided *missiles* and are in turn vulnerable to attack by missiles (fired from ships, planes, submarines, or land). Since the ranges of small missiles now reach from dozens to hundreds of miles, naval warfare emphasizes detection at great distances without being detected oneself—a cat-and-mouse game of radar surveillance and electronic countermeasures.

Missile-firing ships are much cheaper and faster than aircraft carriers. They are becoming potent instruments of power projection themselves. (Cruise missiles are discussed later.) Submarines are specialized to attack ships but can also fire missiles at land targets. (Those that fire nuclear missiles are discussed later.) Submarine and antisubmarine warfare places a great premium on detection and evading detection.

Marines (part of the navy in the United States, Britain, and Russia) move to battle in ships but fight on land—*amphibious warfare*. Marines are also useful for great-power *intervention* in distant conflicts where they can insert themselves quickly and establish local control. In the 1992–1993 intervention in Somalia, U.S. Marines were already waiting

---

[15]Keegan, John. *The Price of Admiralty: The Evolution of Naval Warfare*. New York: Viking, 1988.

Different types of military forces are adapted to different purposes. Aircraft carriers are used for power projection in distant regions. They are so expensive that only a few states have one and only the United States has a dozen. Here, the USS *Independence* enters the Persian Gulf, October 1990.

offshore while the UN Security Council was debating whether to authorize the use of force.

Air Forces *Air forces* are specialized for controlling airspace (attacking other aircraft), land and sea attack, reconnaissance, and airlift. As at sea, missiles—whether fired from air, land, or sea—are increasingly important. Air forces have developed various means to try to fool such missiles, but with mixed results. In the Afghanistan war, the U.S.-made portable Stinger missile used by guerrillas took a heavy toll on the Soviet air force.

Traditionally, and still to a large extent, aerial bombing resembles artillery shelling in that it causes great destruction with little discrimination. This has begun to change in a few cases as *smart bombs* improve accuracy. For instance, laser-guided bombs have maneuverable fins in the rear and a sensor in front; they follow a laser beam pointed at the target from the air. Television viewers during the Gulf War watched video images of bombs scoring direct hits (not all were as accurate as those shown on TV). But most of the bombing in that war was high-altitude *saturation bombing* using very large numbers of dumb bombs.

In other more typical wars, such as Russia's repression of Chechnya in 1995, bombing of cities causes high civilian casualties. In cases of low-intensity conflicts and guerrilla wars, especially where forces intermingle with civilians in closed terrain such as Vietnamese jungles or Somali cities, bombing is of limited utility.

Even more than ships, aircraft rely heavily on electronics, especially radar. The best-equipped air forces have specialized AWACS (Airborne Warning and Control System) airplanes to survey a large area with radar and coordinate the movements of dozens of aircraft. The increasing sophistication of electronic equipment and the high performance requirements of attack aircraft make air forces quite expensive—out of the reach of some states altogether. This gives rich states tremendous advantages over poor ones in air warfare. Despite the expense, air superiority is often the key to the success of ground operations in open terrain.

Logistics All military operations rely heavily on logistical support such as food, fuel, and ordnance (weapons and ammunition). Military logistics are a huge operation, and in most armed forces the majority of soldiers are not combat troops. Before the Gulf War, the United States moved an army of half a million people and a vast quantity of supplies to Saudi Arabia in a six-month effort that was the largest military logistical operation in such a time frame in history.

Global reach capabilities combine long-distance logistical support with various power projection forces.[16] These capabilities allow a great power to project military power to distant corners of the world and to maintain a military presence in most of the world's regions simultaneously. Only the United States today fully possesses such a capability—with worldwide military alliances, air and naval bases, troops stationed overseas, and aircraft carriers plying the world's oceans (see Figure 6.2). Britain and France are in a distant second place, able to mount occasional distant operations of modest size such as the Falkland Islands War. Russia is preoccupied with internal conflicts and its CIS neighbors, and China's military forces are oriented toward regional conflicts and are not global in scope.

Space forces are military forces designed to attack in or from outer space.[17] Ballistic missiles, which travel through space briefly, are not generally included in this category. Only the United States and Russia have substantial military capabilities in space. The development of space weapons has been constrained by the technical challenges and expenses of space operations, and by norms against militarizing space.

Satellites are used extensively for military purposes, but these purposes do not include attack. Satellites perform military surveillance and mapping, communications, weather assessment, and early warning of ballistic missile launches. Analysts pore over masses of satellite reconnaissance data every day in Washington, DC, and other capitals.

---

[16]Harkavy, Robert E. *Bases Abroad: The Global Foreign Military Presence*. New York: Oxford University Press, 1989.

[17]Jasani, Bhupendra, ed. *Space Weapons and International Security*. Oxford: Oxford University Press, 1987. Kirby, Stephen, and Gordon Robson, eds. *The Militarisation of Space*. Boulder, CO: Lynne Rienner, 1987. Colino, R. R. The U.S. Space Program: An International Viewpoint. *International Security* 11 (4), 1987: 157–64. Militarizing the Last Frontier: The Space Weapons Race. *The Defense Monitor* 12 (5), 1983. Dyson, Freeman. *Weapons and Hope*. New York: Harper & Row, 1984.

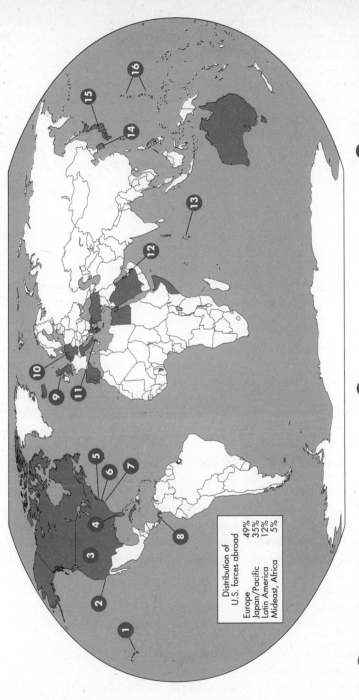

1. Hawaii: U.S. Army Pacific, Pacific Air Forces, U.S. Navy Pacific Fleet, Marine Forces Pacific
2. 1st Marine Force, 3rd Fleet
3. Strategic Command (nuclear); Space Command
4. Central Command (for Middle East); Special Operations Command
5. Military Sealift Command; Transportation Command
6. Atlantic Fleet, 2nd Fleet
7. 2nd Marine Force
8. Panama: Southern Command (Army, Navy)
9. Britain: U.S. Navy Europe
10. Germany: U.S. Army Europe, U.S. Air Force Europe
11. Italy: 6th Fleet
12. Bahrain: Middle East Force
13. Diego Garcia
14. South Korea: 8th U.S. Army
15. Japan: U.S. Army Japan, 7th Fleet, 3rd Marine Force
16. Guam, Marianas, and other Pacific islands

Distribution of
U.S. forces abroad

Europe	49%
Japan/Pacific	35%
Latin America	12%
Mideast, Africa	5%

FIGURE 6.2 Global U.S. Military Network, 1994
Shaded countries are those hosting U.S. military installations. Headquarters of major commands are also indicated.

Poorer states can buy satellite photos on the commercial market—now including high-resolution pictures that Russia has begun selling to earn hard currency.

Satellites now provide navigational information to military forces—army units, ships, planes, and even guided missiles in flight. Locations are calculated to within about fifty feet by small receivers that pick up beacons transmitted from a network of 18 satellites known as a *Global Positioning System (GPS)*; the United States and Russia each have a GPS. Hand-held receivers are available commercially, so the military forces of non-superpowers can ride free on these satellite navigation beacons. But in general outer space is an area in which great powers have great advantages over smaller or poorer states. For instance, U.S. forces in the Gulf War took extensive advantage of satellite reconnaissance, communications, and navigation in defeating Iraqi forces.

Evolving Technologies

Through the centuries, the lethal power of weapons has increased continuously—from swords to muskets, machine guns to missiles. Technological developments have changed the nature of military force in several ways. First, the resort to force in international conflicts now has more profound costs and consequences than it did at the outset of the international system several centuries ago. Great powers in particular can no longer use force to settle disputes among themselves without risking massive destruction and economic ruin.

A second long-term effect of technological change is that military engagements now occur across greater *standoff distances* between opposing forces. Missiles of all types are accelerating this trend. Its effect is to undermine the territorial basis of war and of the state itself. The state once had a hard shell of militarily protected borders, but today the protection offered by borders is diminishing.[18] It is harder for any state to unilaterally assure its own security within a defensive perimeter. For example, Israel's successful defensive of its borders could not stop Iraqi Scud missiles from hitting Israeli cities during the Gulf War. This change makes states more interdependent; in the case of Israel the realization of its vulnerability may have accelerated the search for a peace settlement with its Arab neighbors.

Technology is also changing the loss of *power gradient* that defines a state's loss of effective power over distance.[19] The gradient still exists; for instance, the United States can more readily apply military force in Haiti or Panama than in Iraq (partly because of the importance of logistics). But technological change is making the gradient less steep. Even smaller states can occasionally extend a long military reach, as Israel did when it once bombed the PLO headquarters in Algeria, 1800 miles away.

Historically, technological developments have often given an inherent advantage to either defense or offense, changing the offense-defense balance over time.[20] Currently,

---

[18]Herz, John H. The Rise and Demise of the Territorial State. *World Politics* 9 (4), 1957: 473–93.

[19]Boulding, Kenneth E. *Conflict and Defense*. New York: Harper & Row, 1962.

[20]Levy, Jack S. The Offensive/Defensive Balance of Military Technology: A Theoretical and Historical Analysis. *International Studies Quarterly* 28, 1984: 219–38. Hopf, Ted. Polarity, the Offense-Defense Balance, and War. *American Political Science Review* 85 (2), 1991: 475–94. Anderton, Charles H. Toward a Mathematical Theory of the Offensive/Defensive Balance. *International Studies Quarterly* 36 (1), 1992: 75–100.

The information revolution is making smaller weapons more potent. The U.S.-made Stinger antiaircraft missile helped turn the tide against the Soviet Union in the war in Afghanistan in the 1980s, with far-reaching consequences.

electronics seem to be making small defensive weapons more effective relative to large offensive ones.

The pace of technological change has also made national security more intertwined with economics. *Critical technologies* with potential military applications are developed by industrialized states and guarded from export. In the 1980s a major scandal erupted when it was discovered that the Japanese company Toshiba had sold the Soviet Union advanced machinery that would allow the Soviets to produce quieter submarine propellers (an important feature for evading detection). Throughout the Cold War, a committee of the Western allies called COCOM (for "coordinating committee") had to approve of any exports to the Soviet bloc with possible military applications. This put the individual economic interests of Western states (to stimulate exports) in conflict with their communal security interests (to keep advanced technology out of the wrong hands)—a classic collective security problem (see pp. 106–108).

In recent decades, the technological revolution in electronics has profoundly affected military forces, especially their command and control. **Electronic warfare** refers to the uses of the electromagnetic spectrum (radio waves, radar, infrared, etc.) in war—employing electromagnetic signals for one's own benefit while denying their use to an enemy.[21] Electromagnetic signals are used for *sensing* beyond the normal visual range, through radar, infrared, and *imaging* equipment to see in darkness, through fog, or at great distances. These and other technologies have illuminated the battlefield so that forces cannot be easily hidden.

Electronic countermeasures are technologies designed to counteract enemy electronic systems such as radar and radio communications. **Stealth** technology uses special radar-absorbent materials and unusual shapes in the design of aircraft, missiles, and ships to scatter enemy radar. However, stealth is extremely expensive (each B-2 stealth bomber costs about $500 million) and is prone to technical problems.

Electronics are changing the costs and relative capabilities of weapons across the board. Computer chips in guided missiles have made them a formidable weapon on land, sea, and air. The miniaturization of such weaponry is making smaller and cheaper military forces more powerful than ever. An infantry soldier now can use a shoulder-fired missile costing $10,000 to destroy a main battle tank costing $1 million. Similarly, a small boat firing an antiship missile costing $250,000 can destroy a major warship costing hundreds of millions of dollars. Technological developments are in some ways increasing the advantages of great powers over less-powerful states while in other ways they undermine those advantages.

Proposals have recently been put forward for restructuring great-power military forces to take advantage of these changes. The idea of *nonoffensive defense* is to radically reshape forces for purely defensive missions by taking advantage of electronic technologies that make defense cost-effective.[22] Weapons such as guided antitank missiles would be used to create border zones that could be reliably defended at modest cost. These forces would have little offensive capability, so they would not pose a threat to neighbors and would not create a security dilemma that could fuel an arms race. Such a configuration would put less money into jets and tanks, and more money into sophisticated defensive installations. The concept was developed for NATO (with reference to a potential Soviet invasion of West Germany) but might be applied more generally in other situations. It is noteworthy that when Yugoslavia broke up, the republic of Slovenia used antitank missiles effectively (in mountains) to repel federal Yugoslav armored forces, despite being outnumbered and outspent overall.

---

[21]Munro, Neil. *The Quick and the Dead: Electronic Combat and Modern Warfare*. New York: St. Martin's Press, 1991. Arnett, Eric H. Welcome to Hyperwar. *Bulletin of the Atomic Scientists* 48 (7), 1992: 14–21. Evangelista, Matthew. *Innovation and the Arms Race: How the United States and the Soviet Union Develop New Military Technologies*. Ithaca: Cornell University Press, 1988.

[22]Booth, Ken, ed. *New Thinking About Strategy and International Security*. Boston: Unwin Hyman, 1991. Møller, Bjørn. *The Dictionary of Alternative Defence*. Boulder, CO: Lynne Rienner, 1992. Møller, Bjørn. *Common Security and Nonoffensive Defense: A Neorealist Perspective*. Boulder, CO: Lynne Rienner, 1992. Forsberg, Randall. Keep Peace by Pooling Armies. *Bulletin of the Atomic Scientists* 48 (4), 1992: 41–42.

❖ NUCLEAR, CHEMICAL, AND BIOLOGICAL WEAPONS

Weapons of mass destruction include three general types—nuclear, chemical, and biological weapons. They are distinguished from conventional weapons by their enormous potential lethality, especially relative to their small size and modest costs, and by their relative lack of discrimination in whom they kill. Because of these differences, weapons of mass destruction offer state leaders types of leverage that differ from conventional military forces. When deployed on ballistic missiles, these weapons can potentially be fired from the home territory of one state and wreak great destruction on the home territory of another state.

Until now *this has never happened*. But the mere threat of such an action undermines the territorial integrity and security of states in the international system. Thus scholars pay special attention to such weapons and the missiles that can deliver them. Of central concern in the 1990s are the potentials for proliferation—the possession of weapons of mass destruction by more and more states.

Weapons of mass destruction serve different purposes from conventional weapons. With a few exceptions, their purpose is to deter attack (especially by other weapons of mass destruction) by giving state leaders the means to inflict great pain against a would-be conqueror or destroyer. For middle powers, these weapons also provide destructive power more in line with the great powers, serving as symbolic equalizers.

Nuclear Weapons

Nuclear weapons are, in sheer explosive power, the most destructive weapons available to states. A single weapon the size of a refrigerator can destroy a city. Defending against nuclear weapons is extremely difficult at best.

To understand the potentials for nuclear proliferation, one has to know something about how nuclear weapons work. There are two types. *Fission* weapons (atomic bombs or A-bombs) are simpler and less expensive than *fusion* weapons (also called *thermonuclear* bombs, *hydrogen* bombs or H-bombs). The term *bomb* refers to a *warhead* that can be delivered by missile, bomb, artillery shell, or other means.

When a fission weapon explodes, one type of atom (element) is split, or "fissioned," into new types with less total mass. The lost mass is transformed into energy according to Albert Einstein's famous formula, $E = mc^2$, which shows that a little bit of mass is equivalent to a great deal of energy. In fact, the fission bomb that destroyed Nagasaki, Japan, in 1945 converted to energy roughly the amount of mass in a single penny.

Two elements can be split in this way, and each has been used to make fission weapons. These elements—known as **fissionable material**—are *uranium-235* (or U-235) and *plutonium* (plutonium-239). In these elements, speeding neutrons can collide with atoms and split them apart, releasing energy (including speeding neutrons). A *chain reaction* occurs, with a release of energy, only if the fissionable atoms are packed together closely enough to make a *critical mass*. Nuclear reactors maintain a nonexplosive chain reaction by keeping the number of speeding neutrons constant. By contrast, nuclear weapons trigger an explosive chain reaction by maximizing the number of speeding neutrons.

Fission weapons work by taking *subcritical* masses of fissionable material—amounts not dense enough to start a chain reaction—and compressing them into a critical mass, which explodes. In the simplest design, one piece of uranium is propelled down a tube (by conventional explosives) into another piece of uranium. A more efficient but technically demanding design has high explosives arranged precisely around a hollow sphere of plutonium so as to implode the sphere and create a critical mass. Enhanced designs add an outer sphere of neutron-reflecting material to increase the number of speeding neutrons during the explosion.

Plutonium and uranium are fissionable materials, with which many countries could make nuclear weapons. Here, Greenpeace activists in France protest the first shipment of plutonium to Japan for use in commercial nuclear power reactors (November 1992). The shipment of 1.7 tons would be enough to make more than a hundred nuclear weapons.

Although these designs require sophisticated engineering, they are well within the capabilities of many states and some private groups.[23] The obstacle is obtaining fissionable material. Only ten pounds or less are required for each bomb, but even these small amounts are not easily obtained. U-235, which can be used in the simplest bomb designs, is especially difficult to obtain. Natural uranium (mined in various countries) has less than one percent U-235, mixed with nonfissionable uranium. Extracting the fissionable U-235 is referred to as *enriching* the uranium up to *weapons grade* (or high grade). It is slow, expensive, and technically complex—a major obstacle to proliferation.

Plutonium is more easily produced, from low-grade uranium in nuclear power reactors—although extracting the plutonium requires a *separation plant.* But a plutonium bomb is more difficult to build than a uranium one—another obstacle to proliferation. Plutonium is also used in commercial breeder reactors, which Japan in particular has built recently—another source of fissionable material. In 1992 Japan began a controversial program of shipping plutonium from separation plants in Europe by sea to Japan—creating a possible temptation for theft and a weapons-capable stockpile for Japan.

Fission weapons were invented fifty years ago by U.S. scientists in a secret World War II science project known as the *Manhattan Project.* In 1945 one uranium bomb and one plutonium bomb were used to destroy Hiroshima and Nagasaki, killing one hundred thousand civilians in each city and inducing Japan to surrender unconditionally. By today's standards those bombs were crude, low-yield weapons. But they are the kind of weapon that might be built by a relatively poor state or a nonstate actor.

Fusion weapons are extremely expensive and technically demanding; hence, they are available as leverage to only the richest, largest, most technologically capable states. In fusion weapons, two small atoms (variants of hydrogen) fuse together into a larger atom, releasing energy. This reaction occurs only at extremely high temperatures (the sun "burns" hydrogen through fusion). Weapons designers use *fission* weapons to create these high energies and trigger an explosive fusion reaction. The explosive power of most fission weapons is between 1 and 200 *kilotons*—each kiloton being the equivalent of a thousand tons of conventional explosive. The power of fusion weapons is typically 1 to 20 *megatons* (a megaton equaling a thousand kilotons). In the post–Cold War era fusion weapons have become less important.

The effects of nuclear weapons include not only the blast of the explosion, but also heat and radiation. The heat can potentially create a self-sustaining firestorm in a city. The radiation creates radiation sickness, which at high doses kills people in a few days and at low doses creates long-term health problems, especially cancers. Radiation is most intense in the local vicinity of (and downwind from) a nuclear explosion, but some is carried up into the atmosphere and falls in more distant locations as nuclear *fallout.* Nuclear weapons also create an *electromagnetic pulse (EMP)* that can disrupt and destroy electronic equipment (some weapons are designed to maximize this effect). In addition, using many nuclear weapons at once (as in a war) would have substantial effects on global climate, possibly including a *nuclear winter* in which years of colder and darker conditions would trigger an environmental catastrophe.

---

[23]McPhee, John. *The Curve of Binding Energy.* New York: Ballantine Books, 1973.

Ballistic Missiles and Other Delivery Systems

Nuclear weapons are of little use unless they can be detonated remotely—preferably very remotely! *Delivery systems* for getting nuclear weapons to their targets—much more than the weapons themselves—are the basis of states' nuclear arsenals and strategies (discussed shortly). Inasmuch as nuclear warheads can be made quite small—weighing a few hundred pounds or even less—they are adaptable to a wide variety of delivery systems.

During the Cold War, nuclear delivery systems were divided into two categories. *Strategic* weapons were those that could hit an enemy's homeland, usually at long range (for instance, Moscow from Nebraska). They were once carried on long-range bombers, now mainly on missiles. *Tactical* nuclear weapons were those designed for battlefield use in a theater of military engagement. In the Cold War years both superpowers integrated tactical nuclear weapons into their conventional air, sea, and land forces using a variety of delivery systems—gravity bombs, artillery shells, short-range missiles, land mines, depth charges, and so forth. As with all conventional forces, missiles assumed a greater role over time, and nuclear warheads were paired with short-range ground-to-ground missiles, ship-to-ship missiles, air-to-ground missiles, ground-to-air missiles, and so forth. Some conventional weapons systems were *dual use*, carrying either nuclear or conventional warheads.

In part, the integration of nuclear weapons into conventional forces was meant to deter a conventional East-West war (such as a Soviet invasion of Western Europe). In part, military planners simply found nuclear weapons cost-effective. From a strictly military perspective, if an enemy tank column was advancing, if an enemy airfield had to be neutralized, if an aircraft carrier had to be taken out of the picture, the results would be faster and more reliable using tactical nuclear weapons than conventional weapons.

However, the tens of thousands of nuclear warheads integrated into superpower conventional forces required special precautions and posed dangers such as theft or accident. Their actual use would have entailed grave risks of escalation to strategic nuclear war, putting home cities at risk. Because of these problems, the United States and Russia both phased out tactical nuclear weapons almost entirely when the Cold War ended. The tactical weapons deployed in the former Soviet republics were shipped back to Russia for storage and eventual disassembly.

The main *strategic* delivery vehicles are **ballistic missiles;** unlike airplanes, they are extremely difficult to defend against. Ballistic missiles carry a warhead up along a trajectory and let it drop on the target. These trajectories typically rise out of the atmosphere—at least 50 miles high—before descending. A powerful rocket is needed, and a guidance system adjusts the trajectory (early in its ascent) so that the warhead drops closer to the target. Various ballistic missiles differ in their *range* (the distance it can travel), *accuracy* (how close to the target the warhead lands), and *throw weight* (how heavy a warhead it can carry). In addition, some missiles fire from fixed sites, whereas others are *mobile* (making them hard to target).

The longest-range missiles are *intercontinental ballistic missiles*—ICBMs—with ranges over 5000 miles (the distance from Chicago to Moscow). Some carry up to ten warheads that can hit different targets. Most ICBMs are owned by the United States and Russia, a few by China. Intermediate- and medium-range missiles have ranges from somewhat under 1000 miles to a few thousand miles. They include most *submarine-launched ballistic*

TABLE 6.2 BALLISTIC MISSILE CAPABILITIES (1992)

Country	Range (miles)	Potential Targets
United States[a]	8,100	World
Russia[a]	8,100	World
China[a]	8,100	World
Britain[a]	2,900	Europe or ?; submarine-launched
France[a]	2,200	Europe or ?; land- and submarine-launched
Saudi Arabia	1,700	Iran, Iraq, Syria, Israel, Turkey, Kuwait, Yemen, Egypt, Libya, Sudan
Israel[a]	900	Syria, Iraq, Saudi Arabia, Egypt
Iran[b]	175	Iraq, Kuwait
Syria	175	Israel, Jordan, Iraq, Turkey
Egypt	175	Libya, Sudan, Israel
Libya	175	Egypt, Sudan, Israel
Yemen	175	Saudi Arabia, Djibouti
Afghanistan	175	Pakistan, Tajikistan
Pakistan[a]	175	India
India[a]	150	Pakistan, Bangladesh
North Korea[b]	375	South Korea, Russia, China
South Korea	150	North Korea
Poland	175	Germany, Russia
Czech Republic	300	Germany
Bulgaria	300	Turkey, Albania, Bosnia, Serbia, Greece
Romania	175	Serbia, Ukraine, Moldova
Cuba	45	—

Number of missile-capable states: 22

Note: Potential targets listed include both hostile and friendly states. Iraq's missile capability (range 500 miles) was (in theory) destroyed under UN supervision after the Gulf War.
[a]States believed to have nuclear weapons.
[b]States believed to be trying to build nuclear weapons.
Source: Range data are from *Bulletin of the Atomic Scientists,* March 1992: 31.

missiles (SLBMs)—which are valued for their protectability under attack—and most of the British, French, and Chinese missiles (and some U.S. and Russian ones).

Of special interest today are *short-range ballistic missiles (SRBMs)* with ranges of well under 1000 miles. The modified *Scud* missiles fired by Iraq at Saudi Arabia and Israel during the Gulf War were (conventionally armed) SRBMs. In regional conflicts, the long range of more powerful missiles may not be necessary; for example, the largest cities of Syria and Israel are only 133 miles from each other. The capital cities of Iraq and Iran are less than 500 miles apart, as are those of India and Pakistan. All these states own ballistic missiles. Short-range and some medium-range ballistic missiles are cheap enough to be obtained and even home-produced by small middle-income states. Table 6.2 lists the capabilities of the 22 states with ballistic missiles.

Many short-range ballistic missiles, including those used by Iraq during the Gulf War, are highly inaccurate but still very difficult to defend against.[24] With conventional warheads they have more psychological than military utility (demoralizing an enemy population by attacking cities indiscriminately). With nuclear, chemical, or biological warheads, however, these missiles could be deadlier. A number of states now possess short-range ballistic missiles armed with weapons of mass destruction, but none has ever been used.

The accuracy of delivery systems of all ranges improves as one moves to great powers, especially the United States. After traveling thousands of miles, the best U.S. missiles can land within 50 feet of a target half of the time. The trend in the U.S. nuclear arsenal has been toward less-powerful warheads but more accurate missiles, for flexibility.

The newest and most capable class of delivery system, owned only by the United States and Russia, is the **cruise missile** (which can also use conventional warheads). This is a small winged missile that can navigate across thousands of miles of previously mapped terrain to reach a particular target. A U.S. cruise missile can attack distant targets without risking U.S. lives. During the Gulf War, surprised reporters in Baghdad watched from a hotel window as a U.S. cruise missile flew up the river, turned right at an intersection, and hit a telecommunications building. Cruise missiles can be launched from ships, submarines, airplanes, or land. In 1993 President Clinton attacked the Iraqi intelligence headquarters with dozens of cruise missiles fired from hundreds of miles away—the first all-cruise-missile attack in history. U.S. leaders were embarrassed when one missile hit the Baghdad hotel where foreign journalists stayed, but the attack did destroy the target without risking American lives.

Conceivably, small states or substate groups that may acquire nuclear weapons in the future could deliver them through innovative means. Because nuclear weapons are small, one (or a few) could be smuggled into a target state by car, by speedboat, in diplomatic pouches, or by other such means, and then detonated like any terrorist bomb. One advantage of such methods would be the ease of concealing the identity of the perpetrator.

In all the world's nuclear arsenals, delivery systems include special provisions for command and control.[25] Because the weapons are so dangerous, control is highly centralized. In the United States and Russia, the president is accompanied everywhere by a military officer carrying a briefcase with the secret codes required to order such an attack. So far, at least, control procedures have succeeded in preventing any accidental or unauthorized use of nuclear weapons.

Chemical and Biological Weapons

Several times during the 1991 Gulf War, most of the population of Israel—millions of people—spent nights huddled in special sealed-off rooms in their houses, wearing gas masks and putting infants into little tents. This action was caused by fear of chemical weapons on Iraqi missiles (which turned out to have only conventional warheads).

A *chemical weapon* is a weapon that releases chemicals that kill and disable people.[26]

---

[24]Postol, Theodore A. Lessons of the Gulf War Experience with Patriot. *International Security* 16 (3), 1991/1992: 119–71.

[25]Sagan, Scott D. *The Limits of Safety: Organizations, Accidents, and Nuclear Weapons.* Princeton: Princeton University Press, 1993. Nolan, Janne E. *Guardians of the Arsenal: The Politics of Nuclear Strategy.* New York: Basic Books, 1989. Allard, C. Kenneth. *Command, Control, and the Common Defense.* New Haven: Yale University Press, 1990.

[26]Adams, Valerie. *Chemical Warfare, Chemical Disarmament.* Bloomington: Indiana University Press, 1990. Spiers, Edward M. *Chemical Weaponry: A Continuing Challenge.* New York: St. Martin's Press, 1989. Findlay, Trevor, ed. *Chemical Weapons and Missile Proliferation: With Implications for the Asia/Pacific Region.* Boulder, CO: Lynne Rienner, 1991.

A variety of types of chemicals can be used, from lethal ones such as nerve gas to merely irritating ones such as tear gas. Different chemicals interfere with the nervous system, blood, breathing, or other body functions. Some can be absorbed through the skin; others must be inhaled. Some persist in the target area long after their use; others disperse quickly.

It is possible to *defend* against most chemical weapons by dressing troops in protective clothing and gas masks and following elaborate procedures to decontaminate equipment. But protective suits are hot, and antichemical measures reduce the efficiency of armies. In general, civilians are much less likely to have protection against chemicals than are military forces (the well-prepared Israeli civilians were an exception). Chemical weapons are by nature indiscriminate about whom they kill. Several times, chemical weapons have been *deliberately* used against civilians (most recently against Iraqi Kurds). During World War II Germany also killed millions of Jews, homosexuals, and Gypsies in gas chambers using lethal chemicals. (Germany was embarrassed in 1991 when its companies turned out to have been major suppliers of chemical weapons materials to Iraq.)

Use of chemical weapons in war has been rare. Mustard gas, which produces skin blisters, was widely used (in artillery shells) in World War I. After the horrors of that war, the use of chemical weapons was banned in the 1925 *Geneva protocol*, a treaty that is still in effect. In World War II, both sides were armed with chemical weapons but neither used them, for fear of retaliation (the same was true in the Gulf War). Since then (with possibly a few unclear exceptions) only Iraq has violated the treaty—against Iran in the 1980s. Unfortunately, Iraq's actions not only breached a psychological barrier against using chemical weapons, but also showed such weapons to be cheap and effective against human waves of attacking soldiers without protective gear. This stimulated more third-world states to begin acquiring chemical weapons. Dozens now have them.

Chemical weapons have been called "the poor country's atom bomb"—although nuclear weapons are far more destructive—because chemical weapons are a cheap way for states to gain weapons of mass destruction as potential leverage in international conflicts. Production of chemical weapons can use similar processes and facilities as for pesticides, pharmaceuticals, and other civilian products. It is difficult to locate chemical weapons facilities in suspect countries, or to deny those states access to the needed chemicals and equipment. For instance, Western states accused Libya in the early 1990s of building a chemical weapons complex at a certain facility in the desert. Not so, said the Libyans, it is a pharmaceutical plant (probably untrue, but hard to prove false).

The 1925 treaty did not ban the production or possession of chemical weapons, and several dozen states currently have stockpiles of them. The United States and the Soviet Union maintained large arsenals of chemical weapons during the Cold War but have reduced them greatly in the past decade. In 1992 a new **Chemical Weapons Convention** to ban the production and possession of chemical weapons was concluded after years of negotiation; it was signed by over 120 states, including all the great powers. The new treaty includes strict verification provisions and the threat of sanctions against violators and (an important extension) against nonparticipants in the treaty.

Biological weapons resemble chemical ones, except that instead of chemicals they use microorganisms or biologically derived toxins. Some use viruses or bacteria that cause fatal diseases, such as smallpox, bubonic plague, and anthrax. Others cause nonfatal, but incapacitating, diseases or diseases that kill livestock. Theoretically, a single weapon could spark an epidemic in an entire population, but this is considered too dangerous and less-contagious diseases are preferred.

Civilians are more vulnerable to chemical weapons than soldiers are. A new treaty aims to ban chemical weapons worldwide. Here, Israeli kindergarteners prepare against chemical warfare threat from Iraqi Scud missiles during the Gulf War, 1991.

Biological weapons have *never been used* in war. Their potential strikes many political leaders as a Pandora's box that could let loose uncontrollable forces if opened. For this reason, the development, production, and possession of biological weapons are banned under the 1972 **Biological Weapons Convention,** signed by over 100 countries including the great powers. The superpowers destroyed their stocks of biological weapons and had to restrict their biological weapons complexes to defensive research rather than the development of weapons. However, because the treaty makes no provision for inspection and because biological weapons programs are (like chemical ones) relatively easy to hide, several states—including Iraq, Libya, and Syria—remain under suspicion of having biological weapons. Evidence surfaced after the collapse of the Soviet Union that a secret biological weapons program was under way there as well.

Today the United States and perhaps a dozen other countries maintain biological weapons *research* (not banned by the treaty). Research programs are trying to ascertain the military implications of advances in biotechnology. Most states doing such research claim that they are doing so only to deter another state from developing biological weapons. There is a security dilemma here (see p. 74) with the potential for a future arms race. But so far such a race has been avoided.

Proliferation

Proliferation is the spread of weapons of mass destruction—nuclear weapons, ballistic missiles, and chemical or biological weapons—into the hands of more actors. Poor states and middle powers want ballistic missiles capable of delivering nuclear weapons—or if that is infeasible, then chemical or biological weapons. This capability is desired because it provides states with a potentially powerful means of leverage in international conflicts—a threat to cause extreme damage that is impossible to defend against. Because the only practical counterleverage is a threat to retaliate in kind, states also want ballistic missiles with weapons of mass destruction in order to deter their use by others. This causes a security dilemma (as in the India-Pakistan example on pp. 70–71).

The implications of proliferation for international relations are difficult to predict but evidently profound. Ballistic missiles with weapons of mass destruction remove the territorial protection offered by state borders and make each state vulnerable to others. Some realists, who believe in the basic rationality of state actions, are not so upset by this prospect, and some even welcome it. They reason that in a world where the use of military force could lead to mutual annihilation, there would be fewer wars—just as during the superpower arms race of the Cold War.

Other IR scholars who put less faith in the rationality of state leaders are much more alarmed by proliferation. They fear that with more and more nuclear (or chemical/biological) actors, miscalculation or accident could lead to the use of weapons of mass destruction on a scale unseen since 1945.[27]

The leaders of great powers tend to side with the second group.[28] They would like to keep the existing oligopoly on weapons of mass destruction, in which five great powers have these capabilities but other states generally do not. Slowing down proliferation is a central foreign policy goal of the Clinton administration. Proliferation erodes the great powers' advantage relative to middle powers. Furthermore, there is a widespread fear that weapons of mass destruction may fall into the hands of terrorists or other nonstate actors, who would be immune from threats of retaliation (they have no territory or cities to defend) and who therefore might be much more willing to use such weapons.

However, states that sell technology with potentials for aiding proliferation can make money doing so. For example, Russia in 1995 was under U.S. pressure to cancel a nuclear deal with Iran (which the U.S. said was trying to build nuclear weapons), but doing so would cost Russia about a billion dollars. Industrialized states have competed to sell technology and have simultaneously worked to restrain such sales by other states. This is another international collective-goods problem, in which states pursuing their individual interests end up collectively worse off.

Nuclear proliferation could occur simply by a state or nonstate actor's buying (or stealing) one or more nuclear weapons or the components to build one. The means to prevent this range from covert intelligence to tight security measures to safeguards preventing a stolen weapon from being used. But there are rumors that one or more of the thousands of Soviet tactical nuclear weapons may have disappeared after that state split up.

A more serious form of nuclear proliferation is the development by states of *nuclear*

---

[27]Spector, Leonard S., with Jacqueline R. Smith. *Nuclear Ambitions: The Spread of Nuclear Weapons, 1989–90.* Boulder, CO: Westview, 1990.

[28]Clausen, Peter A. *Nonproliferation and the National Interest: America's Response to the Spread of Nuclear Weapons.* New York: HarperCollins, 1993.

complexes to produce their own nuclear weapons on an ongoing basis.[29] Here larger numbers of weapons are involved and there are strong potentials for arms races in regional conflicts and rivalries. The relevant regional conflicts are those between Israel and the Arab states, Iran and its neighbors, India and Pakistan,[30] the two Koreas, and possibly Taiwan and China. In addition, South Africa reported in 1993 that it had built several nuclear weapons but then dismantled them in the 1980s. North Korea was of greatest concern in the mid-1990s. A U.S.–North Korean agreement froze the North Korean program in exchange for economic assistance, but put off some crucial decisions into the late 1990s.

Israel has never test-exploded nuclear weapons nor admitted it has them. It claims simply that "Israel will not be the first country to introduce nuclear weapons into the region" (which might imply that weapons hidden away have not been "introduced"). In fact Israel is widely believed to have a hundred or more nuclear warheads on combat airplanes and medium-range missiles. Israel wants these capabilities to use as a last resort if Israel were overrun and about to be conquered by its neighbors—just as the Biblical figure Samson brought down the house upon himself and everyone else.[31] By implicitly threatening such action, Israeli leaders hope to convince Arab leaders that a military conquest of Israel is impossible. But by keeping its weapons secret, Israel tries to minimize the provocation to its neighbors to develop their own nuclear weapons. To prevent Iraq from doing so, Israel carried out a bombing raid on the main facility of the Iraqi nuclear complex in 1982.

Efforts to limit the development of nuclear complexes by these states hinge on stopping the flow of necessary materials and expertise—such as enriched uranium, enrichment equipment, electronic timers, and nuclear engineers. A particular fear in the 1990s is that the nuclear complex of the former Soviet Union could be a source of fissionable material, equipment, or nuclear expertise (low-paid technicians might sell out to third-world states). From 1992 to 1994, over one hundred attempts to smuggle uranium or plutonium from the former Soviet Union were reported. Shipments of weapons-grade fissionable material were intercepted on at least five occasions in 1994.

The **Non-Proliferation Treaty (NPT)** of 1968 created a framework for controlling the spread of nuclear materials and expertise.[32] The *International Atomic Energy Agency (IAEA)*, a UN agency based in Vienna, is charged with inspecting the nuclear power industry in member states to prevent secret military diversions of nuclear materials. However, a number of potential nuclear states (such as Israel) have not signed the NPT, and even those states that have signed may sneak around its provisions by keeping some facil-

---

[29]Lewis, John Wilson, and Xue Litai. *China Builds the Bomb*. Stanford: Stanford University Press, 1988.

[30]Albright, David, and Mark Hibbs. India's Silent Bomb. *Bulletin of the Atomic Scientists* 48 (7), 1992: 27–31. Albright, David, and Mark Hibbs. Pakistan's Bomb: Out of the Closet. *Bulletin of the Atomic Scientists* 48 (6), 1992: 38–43.

[31]Hersh, Seymour M. *The Samson Option: Israel's Nuclear Arsenal and American Foreign Policy*. New York: Random House, 1991.

[32]Bellany, Ian, Coit D. Blacker, and Joseph Gallacher, eds. *The Nuclear Non-Proliferation Treaty*. Totowa, NJ: F. Cass, 1985.

ities secret (as Iraq did). Under the terms of the Gulf War cease-fire, Iraq's nuclear program was uncovered and dismantled by the IAEA.[33]

North Korea withdrew from the IAEA in 1993, then bargained with Western leaders to obtain economic assistance, including safer reactors, in exchange for freezing its nuclear program. North Korea's leader died just months later, and the ultimate outcome of this compromise was unclear as of 1995. Either the United States and its allies had been suckered into letting the North Koreans stall for several years, or they had succeeding in reining in the most dangerous potential new nuclear power.

Nuclear proliferation has been less widespread than was feared a few decades ago. The five permanent members of the Security Council, who all had nuclear weapons by 1964, have continued to make up the nuclear club of states with openly acknowledged arsenals. Several other states are believed to have nuclear weapons, but in smaller quantities (only one was test-exploded, by India almost twenty years ago).

A number of middle powers and two great powers (Japan and Germany) have the potential to make nuclear weapons but have chosen not to do so. The reasons for deciding against "going nuclear" include norms against using nuclear weapons, fears of retaliation, and practical constraints including cost. Several republics of the former Soviet Union have recently been added to the non-nuclear-by-choice category. Ukraine dragged its feet on commitments to get rid of strategic nuclear missiles—hoping to use them as bargaining chips to obtain Western aid and security guarantees—but ultimately came around. Members of the Ukrainian parliament, according to one of their leaders, "don't care where these things are aimed. They know that they must get something for them."[34]

At present, *Israel* is widely believed to have a hundred or more nuclear weapons on missiles and airplanes, although it has never acknowledged their existence. *India* has the ability to produce nuclear weapons and has probably produced about twenty. *Pakistan* is believed to have developed a modest nuclear weapons production capability in recent years, and may possess about ten weapons. *South Africa* developed nuclear weapons but dismantled its program and weapons prior to black majority rule. *North Korea*'s active pursuit of a nuclear weapons program in the early 1990s was frozen, at least in theory, in 1995. North Korea may already have one or more nuclear weapons, making it possibly the ninth nuclear-armed State. *Iran* was singled out by the United States in the early to mid-1990s for trying to develop nuclear weapons (as it had begun to do under the shah in the 1970s), but was not expected to succeed before late in the decade at best. *Brazil* and *Argentina* seemed to be headed for a nuclear arms race in the 1980s but then called it off as civilians replaced military governments in both countries.[35]

In 1995 the NPT came up for a 25-year review. In that period the non-nuclear states were supposed to stay non-nuclear; they had largely done so, except for Israel, India, and Pakistan, which had never signed the treaty. The nuclear states were supposed to undertake serious nuclear disarmament (to reduce the power advantage against non-nuclear

[33]Albright, David, and Mark Hibbs. Iraq's Nuclear Hide-and-Seek. *Bulletin of the Atomic Scientists* 47 (7), 1991: 14–23.

[34]*The New York Times*, January 7, 1993, A1.

[35]Leventhal, Paul L., and Sharon Tanzer, eds. *Averting a Latin American Nuclear Arms Race: New Prospects and Challenges for Argentine-Brazil Nuclear Cooperation.* New York: St. Martin's Press, 1992.

Nuclear proliferation makes it more likely that nuclear weapons will be used in a future regional war in South Asia or the Middle East. Here U.S. soldiers watch a test explosion in 1951, near the start of the nuclear age, before the medical effects of nuclear radiation were fully understood. Since then, tens of thousands of nuclear weapons have been built; eight or nine countries possess at least a few.

states); they had largely failed to do so until the 1990s, and still possessed far more potent nuclear arsenals than 25 years earlier. Despite these complaints, the 172 signers of the treaty agreed in 1995 to extend it indefinitely.

The proliferation of ballistic missiles has been more difficult to control.[36] There is a **Ballistic Missile Control Regime** through which industrialized states try to limit the flow of missile-relevant technology to third-world states. One success was the interruption of an Egyptian-Argentinean-Iraqi partnership in the 1980s to develop a medium-range missile. West German companies were induced to stop selling technology secretly to the project. But in general the regime has been less successful. At present, short- and medium-range missiles (ranges up to about 2000 miles) apparently are being developed by Iraq,

[36]Fetter, Steve. Ballistic Missiles and Weapons of Mass Destruction: What Is the Threat? What Should Be Done? *International Security* 16 (1), 1991: 5–42. Nolan, Janne E. *Trappings of Power: Ballistic Missiles in the Third World*. Washington, DC: The Brookings Institution, 1991. Harvey, John R. Regional Ballistic Missiles and Advanced Strike Aircraft: Comparing Military Effectiveness. *International Security* 17 (2), 1992: 41–83.

Iran, Israel, Saudi Arabia, Pakistan, India, and possibly Argentina and Brazil. Soviet-made short-range ballistic missiles are owned by a number of third-world states. China has continued to sell its missiles and technology in the third world (bringing lower prices to buyers and hard currency to China)—a sore point in relations with the West.[37]

Nuclear Strategy

Certainly the decision to acquire or forgo nuclear weapons is the most fundamental aspect of a state's *nuclear strategy*. But the term generally is applied to states that have already decided to acquire nuclear weapons; it refers to their decisions about how many nuclear weapons to deploy, what delivery systems to put them on, and what policies to adopt regarding the circumstances in which they would be used.[38]

The reason for possessing nuclear weapons is almost always to deter another state from a nuclear or conventional attack by threatening ruinous retaliation. Deterrence should work if state leaders are rational actors wanting to avoid the huge costs of a nuclear attack. But it will work only if other states believe that one's threat to use nuclear weapons is *credible*. The search for a credible deterrent by two or more hostile states tends to lead to an ever growing arsenal of nuclear weapons, for reasons that have their own logic.

To follow this logic, begin with a decision by a state to deploy a single nuclear weapon (say, on a ballistic missile) as a deterrent to attack by a hostile neighbor. We may again use India and Pakistan as a hypothetical example. Suppose that Pakistan deployed a single nuclear missile aimed at India (not that Pakistan would really do this or be more likely to than India). Then India would not attack—that is, unless it could prevent Pakistan from using its missile. India could do this by building offensive forces capable of wiping out the Pakistani missile (probably using nuclear weapons, but that is not the key point here). Then the Pakistani missile, rather than deter India, would merely spur India to destroy the missile before any other attack. An attack intended to destroy—largely or entirely—a state's nuclear weapons before they can be used is called a *first strike*.

Pakistan could make its missile survivable (probably by making it mobile). It could also build more nuclear missiles so that even if some were destroyed in an Indian first strike, some would survive with which to retaliate. Weapons that can ride out a first strike and still strike back give a state *second-strike capabilities*. A state that deploys the fewest nuclear forces needed for an assured second-strike capability (which turns out to be between tens and hundreds) has a *minimum* deterrent. The possession of second-strike capabilities by both sides is called **mutually assured destruction (MAD)** because neither side can prevent the other from destroying it. The term implied that the strategy although reflecting "rationality" was actually insane (mad) because deviations from rationality could destroy both sides.

[37]Bitzinger, Richard A. Arms to Go: Chinese Arms Sales to the Third World. *International Security* 17 (2), 1992: 84–111.

[38]Glaser, Charles L. *Analyzing Strategic Nuclear Policy*. Princeton: Princeton University Press, 1990. Sagan, Scott D. *Moving Targets: Nuclear Strategy and National Security*. Princeton: Princeton University Press, 1989. Nye, Joseph S., Graham T. Allison, and Albert Carnesdale, eds. *Fateful Visions: Avoiding Nuclear Catastrophe*. Cambridge, MA: Ballinger, 1988. Rhodes, Edward. *Power and Madness: The Logic of Nuclear Coercion*. New York: Columbia University Press, 1989. Jervis, Robert. *The Meaning of the Nuclear Revolution: Statecraft and the Prospect of Armageddon*. Ithaca: Cornell University Press, 1989. Kull, Steven. *Minds at War*. New York: Basic Books, 1988. Talbott, Strobe. *The Master of the Game: Paul Nitze and the Nuclear Peace*. New York: Knopf, 1988.

If India could not assuredly destroy Pakistan's missile, it would undoubtedly deploy its own nuclear missile to deter Pakistan from using its missile. India, too, could achieve a second-strike capability. Now the question of credibility becomes quite important. In theory, India could launch a *non-nuclear* attack on Pakistan, knowing that rational Pakistani leaders would rather lose such a war than use their nuclear weapons and bring on an Indian *nuclear* response. The nuclear missiles in effect cancel each other out.

During the Cold War, this was the problem faced by U.S. war planners trying to deter a Soviet conventional attack on Western Europe. They could *threaten* to use nuclear weapons in response, but rational Soviet leaders would know that rational U.S. leaders would never act on such a threat and risk escalation to global nuclear war. Better to lose West Germany, according to this line of thinking, than lose both West Germany *and* New York.

During the Cold War, U.S. planners tried to convince the Soviets that such an attack would be too risky no matter how rational U.S. leaders were. They did this by integrating thousands of tactical nuclear weapons into conventional forces so that the escalation to nuclear war might happen more or less automatically in the event of conventional war. This was the equivalent of "throwing away the steering wheel" in a game of Chicken (see p. 71).

Another approach used in the Cold War was to build U.S. nuclear forces that could effectively strike Soviet missiles, not just destroy Soviet cities. Then the United States in case of war might fight a nuclear war without committing suicide. This is called a *nuclear warfighting,* or *counterforce,* capability (because it targets the other state's forces). Without such a capability, a state's only available lever is to blow up another state's cities—a *countervalue* capability (targeting something of value to the other side).

The trouble with nuclear warfighting forces, however, is that they must be very accurate, powerful, and massive in order to successfully knock out the other side's nuclear weapons. This makes them effective first-strike weapons—very threatening to the other state and likely to provoke a further buildup of the other state's weapons in response. First-strike weapons are considered inherently *unstable* in a crisis, because they are so threatening that the other side would be tempted to attack them quickly in a first strike of its own. Knowing that this could happen, the first state would itself be tempted to launch its weapons before such an attack—"use 'em or lose 'em."[39]

The problem is accentuated by the use of multiple warheads on a single missile (MIRVs). The more warheads on a missile, the more tempting a target it makes for the other side. (One successful strike can prevent multiple enemy strikes.) Thus, fixed land-based MIRVed missiles are considered destabilizing weapons: the United States and Russia agreed in the 1992 START II treaty to phase them out.

Defense plays little role in nuclear strategy because no effective defense against missile attack has been devised. However, the United States has spent several billion dollars a year for a decade, *trying* to develop defenses that could shoot down incoming ballistic missiles. The program was called the **Strategic Defense Initiative (SDI),** or *"star wars."* It originated in President Reagan's 1983 call for a comprehensive shield that would make nuclear missiles obsolete.[40] However, the mission soon shifted to a (slightly) more realis-

---

[39]Wagner, R. Harrison. Nuclear Deterrence, Counterforce Strategies, and the Incentive to Strike First. *American Political Science Review* 85 (3), 1991: 727–50.

[40]Chace, James, and Caleb Carr. *America Invulnerable: The Quest for Absolute Security from 1812 to Star Wars.* New York: Summit Books, 1988. Franklin, H. Bruce. *War Stars: The Superweapon and the American Imagination.* New York: Oxford University Press, 1988.

tic one of defending some U.S. missiles in a massive Soviet attack. After the Cold War the mission shifted again, to one of protecting U.S. territory from a very limited missile attack (at most a few missiles), such as might occur in an unauthorized launch, an accident, or an attack by a small state. Current plans call for deploying, within this decade, ground-based, non-nuclear missiles to try to intercept incoming warheads.

In addition to the technical challenges of stopping incoming ballistic missile warheads, a true strategic defense would also have to stop cruise missiles and airplanes, if not more innovative delivery systems. If a rogue state or terrorist group struck the United States with a nuclear weapon, it would probably not use an ICBM to do so. Nobody has an answer to this problem. For now, virtually the only defense against a nuclear weapon is a good offense—the threat to retaliate.

Nuclear Arsenals and Arms Control

During the Cold War, the superpowers' nuclear forces grew and technologies developed. These evolving force structures were codified (more than constrained) by a series of arms control agreements. *Arms control* is an effort by two or more states to regulate by formal

Cruise missiles helped convince superpower leaders in the late 1980s that a nuclear war could never be won and that a "star wars" shield would not work. A U.S. nuclear cruise missile can deliver a 200-kiloton warhead over 1500 miles, within about 50 feet of a target. Here a conventionally armed cruise missile is fired at Iraq by the USS *Missouri* during the Gulf War, January 1991.

agreement their acquisition of weapons.[41] Arms control is broader than just nuclear weapons—for instance, after World War I the great powers negotiated limits on sizes of navies—but in recent decades nuclear weapons have been the main focus of arms control. Arms control agreements typically require long formal negotiations with many technical discussions, culminating in a treaty. Some arms control treaties are multilateral, but during the Cold War most were bilateral (U.S.-Soviet). Some stay in effect indefinitely; others have a limited term.

At first, the United States had far superior nuclear forces and relied on a strategy of *massive retaliation* for any Soviet conventional attack. This threat became less credible as the Soviet Union developed a second-strike capability. When the superpowers realized in the 1960s that MAD could not be avoided, they turned to nuclear arms control to regulate their relations. The superpowers gained confidence from arms control agreements that they could do business with each other and that they would not let the arms race lead them into a nuclear war—fear of which had increased after the Cuban Missile Crisis of 1962. Nuclear arms control talks and agreements did not stop either superpower from developing any weapon it wanted, but they did *manage* the arms race and bring about a convergence of expectations about its structure.

For example, the first agreements, in the 1960s, banned activities that both sides could easily live without—testing nuclear weapons in the atmosphere (the *Limited Test Ban Treaty* of 1963), and placing nuclear weapons in space (the *Outer Space Treaty* of 1967). The Non-Proliferation Treaty (1968) built on the superpowers' common fears of China and other potential new nuclear states. Other confidence-building measures were directed at the management of potential crises. The *hot line* agreement connected the U.S. and Soviet heads of state by telephone in the early 1960s. A later agreement on *incidents at sea* provided for efforts to control escalation after a hostile encounter or accident on the high seas. Eventually, centers and systems for the exchange of information in a crisis were developed.

Several treaties in the 1970s locked in the superpowers' basic parity in nuclear capabilities under MAD. The 1972 *Antiballistic Missile (ABM)* treaty prevented either side from using a ballistic missile defense as a shield from which to launch a first strike. Some U.S. officials now want to renegotiate the ABM treaty to allow the deployment of U.S. defenses under SDI. The *Strategic Arms Limitation Treaties (SALT)* put formal ceilings on the growth of both sides' strategic weapons. *SALT I* was signed in 1972 and *SALT II* in 1979—but SALT II was never ratified by the U.S. Senate (due to the subsequent Soviet invasion of Afghanistan). The U.S. arsenal peaked in the 1960s at over 30,000 warheads; the Soviet arsenal peaked in the 1980s at over 40,000.

In the past decade, new arms control agreements have culminated in the substantial reduction of nuclear forces after the end of the Cold War.[42] The *Intermediate Nuclear Forces (INF)* treaty of 1988 banned an entire class of missiles that both sides had deployed in Europe—for the first time actually reducing nuclear forces instead of just limiting their growth. The 1991 **Strategic Arms Reduction Treaty (START I)**, which took a decade to

---

[41]Adler, Emanuel, ed. *The International Practice of Arms Control.* Baltimore: Johns Hopkins University Press, 1992.

[42]Romberg, Bennet, ed. *Arms Control Without Negotiation: From the Cold War to the New World Order.* Boulder, CO: Lynne Rienner, 1993. Flournoy, Michele A., ed. *Nuclear Weapons After the Cold War: Guidelines for U.S. Policy.* New York: HarperCollins, 1993. Glaser, Charles L. Nuclear Policy Without an Adversary: U.S. Planning for the Post-Soviet Era. *International Security* 16 (4), 1992: 34–78.

negotiate, called for reducing the superpowers' strategic arsenals by about 30 percent.[43] The 1992 **START II** treaty, negotiated in less than a year, proposes to cut the remaining weapons by more than half in the next decade (if ratified by Russia's parliament). The United States will end up with 3500 strategic warheads and Russia with 3000—down from over 11,000 each in 1990. (These reductions are in addition to the elimination of most tactical nuclear weapons.) The terms of the START treaties favored the United States, especially in reducing the most threatening Soviet land-based MIRVed ICBMs. The INF and START treaties provide for strict verification, including *on-site inspection* of facilities in the other side's nuclear complex. When coupled with satellite reconnaissance, these agreements create considerable transparency in nuclear matters.

A potential future arms control measure being considered in the mid-1990s was a *Comprehensive Test Ban Treaty (CTBT)* to halt all nuclear test-explosions. This would impede the development of new types of nuclear weapons. Russia, France, and the United States have all unilaterally imposed some form of temporary testing moratorium in recent years. China still tested occasionally, as of 1995, but the great powers seemed close to an agreement to end nuclear testing in 1996.

Overall, the United States has the most potent nuclear arsenal in the world by far, because it has not only the most weapons but the most accurate delivery systems. The reductions in U.S. and Russian arsenals still leave them much larger than those of China, France, and Britain, which each have several hundred weapons. These smaller arsenals are, however, enough for a credible second-strike capability. Britain tends to use U.S.-built nuclear weapons systems; China and France rely on their own efforts. Britain's arsenal includes about 100 warheads on long-range submarine-launched missiles and 200 more on tactical aircraft. France has 400 warheads on submarine-launched long-range missiles, 18 on long-range land missiles, and about 50 on tactical aircraft. China is thought to have about 50 warheads on long-range land missiles, 100 on intermediate-range missiles, 30 on submarines and 200 or more on long-range bombers.

Arms control efforts outside the area of nuclear arms have not been very successful. For decades the NATO and Warsaw Pact countries carried on the *Mutual and Balanced Force Reduction (MBFR)* talks aimed at limiting conventional military forces in Europe. These were hopelessly deadlocked until the last years of the Cold War, when the *Conventional Forces in Europe (CFE)* treaty was signed in 1990. That treaty provided for asymmetrical reductions in Soviet forces and limited the conventional forces of both sides. But by the time it was signed, the Warsaw Pact was breaking up; within two years it was virtually obsolete. The signatories have kept the treaty in effect as a guard against any future arms buildup in Europe, but relaxed limits on Russian forces deployed near southern Russia, a new conflict zone.

Efforts to control the conventional *arms trade* through arms control treaties have had no success. After the Gulf War, the five permanent Security Council members tried to negotiate limits on the supply of weapons to the Middle East. The five participants account for the overwhelming majority of weapons sold in the Middle East. But no participant wanted to give up its own lucrative arms sales in the region, which each naturally saw as justified.

All the weapons of mass destruction have in common that they are relatively difficult and expensive to build, yet they provide only specialized capabilities that are rarely if ever

---

[43]*Bulletin of the Atomic Scientists* 47 (9), 1991: 12–40. Special issue on START.

actually used. This is why a number of states have decided that such weapons are not worth acquiring, even though it would be technically possible to do so. That kind of cost-benefit thinking also applies more broadly to states' decisions about the acquisition of all kinds of military forces.

States face complex choices regarding the configuration of their military forces in the post–Cold War era. Not only have the immediate contingencies and threats changed drastically, but the nature of threats in the new era is unknown. Perhaps most important, world order itself is evolving even as military technologies do. The next chapter discusses the evolving structures and norms governing international political relations and how they are changing the nature of world order.

❖ CHAPTER SUMMARY

- ◆ Military forces provide states with means of leverage beyond the various nonmilitary means of influence widely used in international bargaining.
- ◆ Political leaders face difficult choices in configuring military forces and paying for them. Military spending tends to stimulate economic growth in the short term but reduce growth over the long term.
- ◆ In the 1990s, military forces of the great powers are being radically restructured and military spending reduced—most dramatically in Russia and Eastern Europe.
- ◆ Military forces include a wide variety of capabilities suited to different purposes. Conventional warfare requires different kinds of forces from those needed to threaten the use of nuclear, chemical, or biological weapons.
- ◆ Except in time of civil war, state leaders—whether civilian or military—control military forces through a single hierarchical chain of command.
- ◆ Military forces can threaten the domestic power of state leaders, who are vulnerable to being overthrown by coups d'état.
- ◆ Control of territory is fundamental to state sovereignty and is accomplished primarily with ground forces.
- ◆ Small missiles and electronic warfare are increasingly important, especially for naval and air forces. The role of satellites is expanding in communications, navigation, and reconnaissance.
- ◆ Weapons of mass destruction—nuclear, chemical, and biological—have been used only a handful of times in war.
- ◆ The production of nuclear weapons is technically within the means of many states and some nonstate actors, but the necessarily fissionable material (uranium-235 or plutonium) is very difficult to obtain.
- ◆ Most industrialized states, and many poor ones, have refrained voluntarily from acquiring nuclear weapons. These states include two great powers, Germany and Japan.
- ◆ More states are acquiring ballistic missiles capable of striking other states from hundreds of miles away (or further, depending on the missile's range). But no state has ever attacked another with weapons of mass destruction mounted on ballistic missiles.
- ◆ Chemical weapons are cheaper to build than nuclear weapons, they have similar threat value, and their production is harder to detect. More middle powers have chemical weapons than nuclear ones. A new treaty bans the possession and use of chemical weapons.

◆ Several states conduct research into biological warfare, but by treaty the possession of such weapons is banned.

◆ Slowing the proliferation of ballistic missiles and weapons of mass destruction in the third world is a central concern of the great powers.

◆ The United States and Russia have arsenals of thousands of nuclear weapons; China, Britain, and France have hundreds. Weapons deployments are guided by nuclear strategy based on the concept of deterrence.

◆ Arms control agreements formally define the contours of an arms race or mutual disarmament process. Arms control helped build confidence between the superpowers during the Cold War.

❖ THINKING CRITICALLY

1. If you were the leader of, say, Vietnam, what size and kinds of military forces would you want your country to have? To meet what kinds of threats would you choose each type of capability?

2. Suppose that Libya turned out to have obtained three tactical nuclear warheads from the former Soviet arsenal and was keeping them in unknown locations. What, if anything, should the great powers do about this? What consequences might follow from their actions?

3. Imagine a world in which most of the states, rather than just a few, had nuclear weapons and long-range ballistic missiles. Would it be more peaceful or more war-prone? Why?

4. Most of the great powers are reconfiguring their military forces in the post–Cold War era. What kinds of capabilities do you think your own country needs in this period? Why?

5. World military spending is close to $1 trillion every year. If you could redirect these funds, how would you use them? Would such uses be better or worse for the states involved? Do you think there is a realistic chance of redirecting military spending in the way you suggest?

❖ KEY TERMS

economic conversion
chain of command
military government
coup d'état
infantry
power projection
electronic warfare
stealth (technology)
weapons of mass destruction
fissionable material
ballistic missile

cruise missile
Chemical Weapons Convention
Biological Weapons Convention
proliferation
Non-Proliferation Treaty (NPT)
Ballistic Missile Control Regime
mutually assured destruction (MAD)
Strategic Defense Initiative (SDI)
Strategic Arms Reduction Treaties
    (START I & II)

*U.S. ambassador to the
UN Madeleine Albright votes
to authorize force in Haiti,
July 1994.*

CHAPTER 7

Joost
skype

INTERNATIONAL ORGANIZATION AND LAW

❖ WORLD ORDER

Most international conflicts are not settled by military force. Despite the anarchic nature of the international system based on state sovereignty, the security dilemma does not usually lead to a breakdown in basic cooperation among states. States generally refrain from taking maximum short-term advantage of each other (such as by invading and conquering). States work *with* other states for mutual gain and take advantage of each other only "at the margin." Unfortunately the day-to-day cooperative activities of states often are less newsworthy than states' uses of force.

States work together by following rules they develop to govern their interactions. States usually *do* follow the rules. Over time, the rules have become more firmly established and institutions have grown up around them. States then develop the habit of working through those institutions and within the rules. They do so because of self-interest; great gains can be realized by regulating international interactions through institutions and rules, thereby avoiding the costly outcomes associated with a breakdown of cooperation (see pp. 101–104).

International anarchy thus does not mean a lack of order, structure, and rules. In many ways, actors in international society now work together as cooperatively as actors in domestic society—more so than some domestic societies. Today, most wars are civil wars, not interstate wars per se; this reflects the general success of international norms, organizations, and laws—in addition to the balance of power—in maintaining peace among states.

International anarchy, then, means simply that states surrender sovereignty to no one. Domestic society has government with powers of enforcement; international society does not. When the rules are broken in IR, actors can rely only on the power of individual states (separately or in concert) to restore order.[1]

---

[1]Suganami, Hidemi. *The Domestic Analogy and World Order Proposals*. New York: Cambridge University Press, 1989.

The Evolution of World Order

Over the centuries, international institutions and rules have grown stronger, more complex, and more important. International order started out based largely on raw power, but it has evolved and become based more on legitimacy and habit (as well as power). *Domestic law*, too, at one time was enforced only by the most powerful on behalf of the most powerful. The first states and civilizations were largely military dictatorships. Law was what the top ruler decreed. International law and organization likewise started out as terms imposed by powerful winners on losers after wars.

The international institutions and rules that operate today took shape especially during periods of hegemony (see "Hegemony" on pp. 81–82), when one state predominated in international power following a hegemonic war among the great powers. The international organizations that today form the institutional framework for international interactions—such as the UN, the Organization of American States, and the World Bank—were created after World War II under U.S. leadership.

Rules of international behavior have become established over time as norms and are often codified as international law. This is a more incremental process than the creation of institutions; it goes on between and during periods of war and of hegemony. But still the most powerful states, especially hegemons, have great influence on the rules and values that have become embedded over time in a body of international law.

For example, the principle of free passage on the open seas is now formally established in international law.[2] But at one time warships from one state did not hesitate to seize the ships of other states and make off with their cargoes. This was profitable to the state that pulled off such raids, but of course their own shipping could be raided in return. More important, such behavior made long-distance trade itself more dangerous, less predictable, and less profitable. The trading states could benefit more by getting rid of the practice. So over time a norm developed around the concept of freedom of navigation on the high seas. It became one of the first areas of international law developed by the Dutch legal scholar *Hugo Grotius* around the time of the Thirty Years' War (1618–1648)—a time when the Dutch dominated world trade and could benefit most from free navigation.

Dutch power, then, provided the backbone for the international legal concept of freedom of the seas. Later, when Britain dominated world trade, the principle of free seas was enforced through the cannons of *British* warships. As the world's predominant trading state, Britain benefited from a worldwide norm of free shipping and free trade. And with the world's most powerful navy, Britain was in a position to define and enforce the rules for the world's oceans.

Likewise, twentieth-century world order has depended heavily on the power of the United States (and, for a few decades, on the division of power between the United States and the Soviet Union). The United States at times came close to adopting the explicit role of "world police force." But in truth the world is too large for any single state—even a hegemon—to police effectively. Rather, the world's states usually go along with the rules established by the most powerful state without constant policing. Meanwhile they try to influence the rules by working through international institutions (to which the hegemon cedes some of its power). In this way, although states do not yield their sov-

---

[2]Booth, Ken. *Law, Force and Diplomacy at Sea*. Winchester, MA: Allen & Unwin, 1985.

ereignty, they vest some power and authority in international institutions and laws and generally work within that framework.[3]

International Norms and Morality

The rules that govern most interactions in IR are rooted in moral norms.[4] **International norms** are the expectations held by national leaders about normal international relations. For example, the invasion of Kuwait by Iraq was not only illegal, it was widely viewed as immoral—beyond the acceptable range of behavior of states (that is, beyond the normal amount of cheating that states get away with). Political leaders in the United States and around the world drew on moral norms to generate support for a collective response to Iraq. Thus morality is an element of power (see "Elements of Power" on pp. 56–60).

These norms are widely held; they shape expectations about state behavior and set standards that make deviations stand out. International morality differs somewhat from morality within states, which is strongly influenced by the particular culture and traditions of the particular state. By contrast, international morality is a more universal set of moral standards and rules applicable to the interactions of states themselves.

The attempt to define universal norms follows a centuries-long philosophical tradition. Philosophers like Kant argued that it was natural for autonomous individuals (or states) to cooperate for mutual benefit because they could see that pursuing their individual interests too narrowly would end up hurting all. Thus, sovereign states could work together through structures and organizations (like Kant's proposed world federation) that would respect each member's autonomy and not create a world government over them. In the nineteenth century, such ideas were embodied in practical organizations in which states participated to manage specific issues such as international postal service and control of traffic on European rivers.

Agreed norms of behavior, institutionalized through such organizations, become *habitual* over time and gain *legitimacy*. State leaders become used to behaving in a normal way and stop calculating, for each action, whether violating norms would pay off. For instance, the U.S. president does not spend time calculating whether the costs of invading and plundering Canada would outweigh the benefits. The willingness to maintain normal behavior has psychological roots in "satisficing" and in aversion to risk (see "Individual Decision Makers" on pp. 142–146). Legitimacy and habit explain why international norms can be effective even when they are not codified and enforced.

International norms and standards of morality do not help, however, when different states or world regions hold different expectations of what is normal. To the United States it was a moral imperative to punish Iraqi aggression against Kuwait. But from the perspective of leaders in Jordan and Yemen, the U.S. response represented immoral imperialistic aggression. Likewise, during the Cold War the two superpowers did not share the same notions of normal relations; for example, they had different conceptions of détente in the 1970s, when the Soviets thought that their support of third-world liberation movements should not undermine superpower cooperation on other issues, whereas U.S. leaders

[3]Falk, Richard. *Explorations at the Edge of Time: The Prospects for World Order.* Philadelphia: Temple University Press, 1992. Kim, Samuel S. *The Quest for a Just World Order.* Boulder, CO: Westview, 1984.

[4]Kratochwil, Friedrich V. *Rules, Norms, and Decisions: On the Conditions of Practical and Legal Reasoning in International Relations and Domestic Affairs.* New York: Cambridge University Press, 1989.

International norms are evolving in the areas of humanitarian assistance and national sovereignty. A multinational intervention helped feed Somalis in 1992–1993, but after problems arose there the international community failed to respond when genocide took half a million lives in Rwanda in 1994. Here Rwandan children are buried in a mass grave.

thought Soviet cooperation should extend to such conflicts. In cases of diverging norms, morality can be a factor for misunderstanding and conflict rather than a force of stability.

The **"New World Order"** envisioned by U.S. president Bush during the Iraq-Kuwait crisis included four principles: peaceful settlement of disputes, solidarity against aggression, reduced and controlled arsenals, and just treatment of all peoples. Note that some of the principles are based more on practical considerations (reduced arsenals) and others on more explicitly moral standards (just treatment of all peoples). These principles, which President Clinton generally embraced as well, represent the interests of the United States and other great powers in a stable world order.

This new order found little solid ground to stand on in the post–Cold War era, however. One problem with rapid change is that nobody knows what to expect; norms break down because leaders do not have common expectations. Through a long process of coping with a sequence of cases, international leaders build up new understandings of the rules of the game. For example, President Bush's last secretary of state, who helped keep the United States aloof from the Bosnia crisis in 1992, said later that if the Cold War had still been going on he would have advised U.S. leaders to "jump in with both feet." Thus, the end of the Cold War put basic expectations, such as when U.S. military intervention is warranted, up for grabs. The new norms were still rather unsettled by the mid-1990s.

Roles of International Organizations

Especially in times of change, when shared norms and habits may not suffice to solve international dilemmas and achieve mutual cooperation, institutions play a key role. They are concrete, tangible structures with specific functions and missions to focus on. These institutions have proliferated rapidly in recent decades, and continue to play an increasing role in international affairs. **International organizations (IOs)** include *intergovernmental organizations* (IGOs) such as the UN, and *nongovernmental organizations* (NGOs) such as the International Committee of the Red Cross.

The number of IOs has grown roughly fivefold since 1945, reaching about five hundred IGOs and five thousand NGOs. On average, a new NGO is created somewhere in the world every few days. This weaving together of people across national boundaries through specialized groups reflects world interdependence (see "Interdependence" on pp. 324–327).[5]

Some IGOs are global in scope, others are regional or just bilateral (having only two states as members). Some are general in their purposes, others have specific functional purposes. Overall, the success of these IGOs has been mixed; the regional ones have had more success than the global ones, and those with specific functional or technical purposes have worked better than those with broad purposes (see pp. 390–392). IGOs hold together because they promote the national interests (or enhance the leverage) of their member states—not because of vague ideals.

Among *regional* IGOs, the European Union encompasses some of the most important (see Chapter 10), but is not the only example. Others include the Association of South East Asian Nations (ASEAN), the Latin American Integration Association, and locust control organizations in Africa (on regional security alliances, see pp. 86–90). The functional roles of IOs are important to their overall effect on international relations, but those roles are taken up in Chapter 10 on international integration. For now we may continue to rely on the more general theoretical discussion of international institutions begun in Chapter 3.

---

[5]Kratochwil, Friedrich V., and Edward D. Mansfield, eds. *International Organization: A Reader.* New York: HarperCollins, 1994.

The Catholic Church is prominent among the many IOs that influence international affairs. Here the Pope, speaking in Croatia, urges reconciliation in the former Yugoslavia.

Global IGOs (aside from the UN) usually have functional purposes involving coordinating actions of some set of states around the world. The IGO called Intelsat, for example, is a consortium of governments and private businesses that operates communications satellites. Members of the Organization of Petroleum Exporting Countries (OPEC) are major oil producers, which meet periodically in Vienna to set production quotas for members in an effort to keep world oil prices high and stable. Similar organizations exist for other commodities from copper to bananas.

NGOs tend to be more specialized in function than IGOs. For instance, someone who wants to meet political scientists from other countries can join the International Political Science Association. Many NGOs have economic or business-related functions. The International Air Transport Association, for example, coordinates the work of airline companies. Other NGOs have global political purposes—for example, Greenpeace (for the environment), Amnesty International (for human rights), or Planned Parenthood (for reproductive rights and family planning). Still other NGOs have cultural purposes—for example, the International Olympic Committee.

Religious groups are among the largest NGOs, whose memberships often span many countries. Both in today's world and historically, sects of Christianity, Islam, Buddhism, Judaism, Hinduism, and other world religions have organized themselves across state borders, often in the face of hostility from one or more national governments. Missionaries have deliberately built and nurtured these transnational links. The Catholic Church historically held a special position in the European international system, especially before the seventeenth century. NGOs with broad purposes and geographical scope often maintain observer status in the UN so that they can participate in UN meetings about issues of concern. For example, Greenpeace attends UN meetings about the global environment.

A web of international organizations of various sizes and types now connects people in all countries. The rapid growth of this network, and the increasingly intense communications and interactions that occur within it, are indicative of rising international interdependence. These organizations in turn provide the institutional mesh to hold together some kind of world order even when leaders and contexts come and go, and even when norms are undermined by sudden changes in power relations. At the center of that web of connection stands the most important international organization today, the UN.

❖ THE UNITED NATIONS

The UN and other international organizations have both strengths and weaknesses in the anarchic international system. State sovereignty creates a real need for such organizations on a practical level, because no central world government performs the function of coordinating the actions of states for mutual benefit. However, state sovereignty also severely limits the power of the UN and other IOs, because governments reserve power to themselves and are stingy in delegating it to the UN or anyone else. The UN has had a mixed record with these strengths and weaknesses—in some ways providing remarkable global-level management and in other ways appearing helpless against the sovereignty of even modest-sized states (much less of the great powers).

The UN System

The UN is a relatively new institution, only fifty years old. Even newer is the more prominent role that the UN has played in international security affairs since the Cold War ended. Despite this new prominence, the main purposes of the UN are the same now as when it was founded right after World War II.[6]

Purposes of the UN The UN is the closest thing to a world government that has ever existed, but it is not a world government. Its members are sovereign states who have not empowered the UN to enforce its will within states' territories except with the consent of those state's governments. Thus, although the UN strengthens world order, its design acknowledges the realities of international anarchy and the unwillingness of states to surrender their sovereignty. Within these limits, the basic purpose of the UN is to

---

[6]Luard, Evan, and Derek Heater. *The United Nations: How It Works and What It Does.* 2nd ed. New York: St. Martin's Press, 1994. Chadwick, F. Alger, Gene M. Lyons, and John E. Trent, eds. *The United Nations System: The Policies of Member States.* New York: United Nations University Press, 1995.

provide a global institutional structure through which states can sometimes settle conflicts with less reliance on use of force.

The **UN Charter** is based on the principles that states are *equal* under international law; that states have full *sovereignty* over their own affairs; that states should have full *independence* and *territorial integrity*; and that states should carry out their international *obligations*—such as respecting diplomatic privileges, refraining from committing aggression, and observing the terms of treaties they sign. The Charter also lays out the structure of the UN and the methods by which it operates.

The UN does not exist because it has power to force its will on the world's states; it exists because states have created it to serve their needs. A state's membership in the UN is essentially a form of indirect leverage. States gain leverage by using the UN to seek more beneficial outcomes in conflicts (especially on general multilateral issues where a global forum brings all parties together). The cost of this leverage is modest—UN dues and the expenses of diplomatic representatives, plus the agreement to behave in accordance with the Charter (most of the time).

States get several useful benefits from the UN. Foremost among these benefits is the international stability (especially in security affairs) that the UN tries to safeguard; this stability allows states to realize gains from trade and other forms of exchange (see Chapter 8). The UN is a *symbol* of international order and even of global identity. It is also a *forum* where states can promote their views and bring their disputes. And it is a mechanism for *conflict resolution* in international security affairs.

The UN also promotes and coordinates development assistance (see Chapter 13) and other programs of *economic and social development* in third-world countries. This reflects the belief that economic and social problems—above all, poverty—are an important source of international conflict and war. Finally, the UN is a coordinating system for *information* and planning by hundreds of internal and external agencies and programs, and for the collection and publication of international data.

Despite its heavy tasks, the UN is still a small and fragile institution—a fifty-year-old infant. Compare, for instance, what states spend on two types of leverage for settling conflicts—military forces and the UN. Every year the world spends almost a *thousand* billion dollars on the military and *less than five* billion on the UN operating and peacekeeping budgets. That proportion is about the same in the United States: each U.S. citizen pays (on average) about $1000 a year for U.S. military forces and less than $5 for UN dues, U.S. contributions to UN peacekeeping forces, and voluntary U.S. contributions to all UN programs.

Structure of the UN The UN's structure, shown in Figure 7.1, centers around a **General Assembly,** where representatives of all states sit together in a huge room, listen to speeches, and pass resolutions. The General Assembly coordinates a variety of third-world development programs and other autonomous agencies through the *Economic and Social Council (ECOSOC)*. Parallel to the General Assembly is the **Security Council,** in which five great powers and ten rotating member-states make decisions about international peace and security. The Security Council has responsibility for the dispatch of peacekeeping forces to trouble spots. The administration of the UN takes place through the **Secretariat** (executive branch), led by the secretary-general of the UN. The

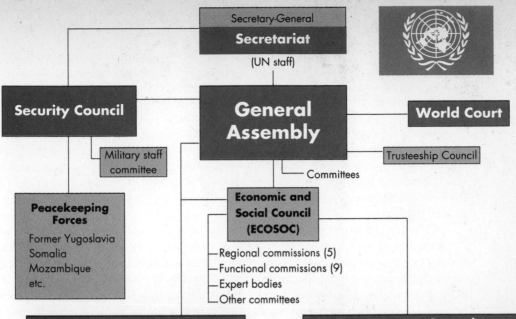

Secretary-General

Secretariat

(UN staff)

Security Council

General Assembly

World Court

Military staff committee

Trusteeship Council

Committees

Peacekeeping Forces

Former Yugoslavia
Somalia
Mozambique
etc.

Economic and Social Council (ECOSOC)

— Regional commissions (5)
— Functional commissions (9)
— Expert bodies
— Other committees

UN Programs

UNEP	(UN Environment Program)
UNICEF	(UN Children's Fund)
UNDRO	(Office of the UN Disaster Relief Coordinator)
UNHCR	(Office of the UN High Commissioner for Refugees)
UNRWA*	(UN Relief Works Agency [for Palestinian Refugees])
UNDP	(UN Development Program)
UNITAR*	(UN Institute for Training and Research)
UNIFEM	(UN Development Fund for Women)
INSTRAW	(UN International Research and Training Institute [for women])
UNCTAD	(UN Conference on Trade and Development)
WFP	(World Food Program)
WFC	(World Food Council)
UNCHS	Human Settlements (Habitat)
UNFPA	(UN Population Fund)
UNU	(UN University)
UNDCP	(Drug Control Program)
ITC	(International Trade Center)

* Does not report to ECOSOC.

Autonomous Agencies

IAEA*	(International Atomic Energy Agency, Vienna)
WHO	(World Health Organization, Geneva)
FAO	(Food and Agriculture Organization, Rome)
IFAD	(International Fund for Agricultural Development, Rome)
ILO	(International Labor Organization, Geneva)
UNESCO	(UN Educational, Scientific, and Cultural Organization, Paris)
UNIDO	(UN Industrial Development Organization, Vienna)
ITU	(International Telecommunications Union, Geneva)
UPU	(Universal Postal Union, Berne)
ICAO	(International Civil Aviation Organization, Montreal)
IMO	(International Maritime Organization, London)
WIPO	(World Intellectual Property Organization, Geneva)
WMO	(World Meteorological Association, Geneva)
MIGA	(Multilateral Investment Guarantee Agency)
IMF	(International Monetary Fund, Washington)
IBRD	(International Bank for Reconstruction and Development [World Bank], Washington)
IDA	(International Development Association, Washington)
IFC	(International Finance Corporation, Washington)
GATT*	(General Agreement on Tariffs and Trade, Geneva)

* Does not report to ECOSOC.

FIGURE 7.1 The United Nations

World Court (International Court of Justice), which is discussed later in the chapter, is a judicial arm of the UN. (A *Trusteeship Council* oversaw the transition of a handful of former colonial territories to full independence; with the last trust territory's independence in 1994, the Council became obsolete.)

National delegations to the UN, headed by ambassadors from each member state, work and meet together at UN headquarters. They have diplomatic status in the United States, which as host country also assumes certain other obligations to facilitate the UN's functioning. For example, the U.S. government has permitted people such as Fidel Castro—normally barred from entry to the United States—to visit New York long enough to address the UN.

A major strength of the UN structure is the *universality of its membership*. There were 185 members in 1995. Virtually every territory in the world is either a UN member or formally a province or colony of a UN member. Switzerland, which maintains a strict autonomy from the international system, is not a UN member but maintains an "observer" mission to participate in meetings. Formal agreement on the Charter (even if sometimes breached in practice) commits all states to a common set of basic rules governing their relations. (A major flaw in the old League of Nations was the absence of several important actors.)

One way the UN induced all the great powers to join was to reassure them that their participation in the UN would not harm their national interests. Recognizing the role of power in world order, the UN Charter gave five great powers each a veto over substantive decisions of the Security Council.

The UN Charter establishes a mechanism for *collective security*—the banding together of the world's states to stop an aggressor. Chapter 7 of the Charter explicitly authorizes the Security Council to use military force against aggression if the nonviolent means called for in Chapter 6 have failed. However, because of the great-power veto, the UN cannot effectively stop aggression by (or supported by) a great power. Thus Chapter 7 was used only once during the Cold War—in the Korean War when the Soviet delegation unwisely boycotted the proceedings (and when China's seat was held by the Nationalists on Taiwan). It was under Chapter 7 that the UN authorized the use of force to reverse Iraqi aggression against Kuwait in 1990.

History of the UN The UN was founded in 1945 in San Francisco by 51 states. It was the successor to the League of Nations, which had failed to effectively counter aggression in the 1930s—Japan simply quit when the League condemned Japanese aggression against China. Like the League, the UN was founded to increase international order and the rule of law to prevent another world war.

There has long been a certain tension between the UN and the United States as the world's most powerful state. (The United States had not joined the League, and it was partly to assure U.S. interest that the UN headquarters was placed in New York.) The UN in some ways constrains the United States by creating the one coalition that can rival U.S. power—that of all the states. A certain isolationist streak in U.S. foreign policy (see pp. 173–174) runs counter to the UN concept. However, the UN also *amplifies* U.S. power because the United States leads the global UN coalition. Furthermore, the United States in the 1990s is not rich or strong enough to keep order in the world single-handed.

And as a great trading nation the United States benefits from the stability and order that the UN helps to create.

In the 1950s and 1960s the UN's membership more than doubled as colonies in Asia and Africa won independence. This changed the character of the General Assembly, where each state has one vote regardless of size. The new members had different concerns from the Western industrialized countries and in many cases resented having been colonized by Westerners. Many third-world states, even more so then than today, felt that the United States enjoyed too much power in the UN—that the UN too often promoted U.S. interests. They noticed that the UN is usually effective in international security affairs only when the United States leads the effort (because U.S. interests are at stake in the matter).

The growth in membership thus affected voting patterns in the UN. During the UN's first two decades, the Assembly had regularly sided with the United States, and the Soviet Union was the main power to use its veto in the Security Council to counterbalance this tendency. But as newly independent third-world states began to predominate, the United States found itself in the minority on many issues and by the 1970s and 1980s had become the main user of the veto.[7]

Another change in UN membership took place in 1971. China's seat on the Security Council (and in the General Assembly) had been occupied by the Nationalist faction on Taiwan island, which had lost power in mainland China in 1949. The exclusion of Communist China was an exception to the principle of universal membership in the UN, and in 1971 the Chinese seat was taken from the Nationalists and given to the Communist government. However, now the government on Taiwan—which functions autonomously in many international matters despite its formal status as a Chinese province—is not represented in the UN.

Throughout the Cold War, the UN had few successes in international security because the U.S.-Soviet conflict prevented consensus. The UN appeared somewhat irrelevant in a world order structured by two opposing alliance blocs. There were a few notable exceptions, such as agreements to station peacekeeping forces in the Middle East on several occasions, but the UN did not play a central role in solving international conflicts. The General Assembly, with its predominantly third-world membership, concentrated on the economic and social problems of poor countries, and this became the main work of the UN.

Third-world states also used the UN as a forum to criticize rich countries in general and the United States in particular. By the 1980s, the U.S. government showed its displeasure with this trend by withholding hundreds of millions of dollars in U.S. dues owed to the UN and by withdrawing from membership in one UN agency, UNESCO. (The back dues were still over $1 billion by 1995, and the United States also unilaterally lowered its contributions to peacekeeping.)

After the Cold War, however, the bipolar world order gave way to one in which multilateral action was more important. The great powers could finally agree on effective measures regarding international security. Also, third-world states could not hope to play

[7]Gregg, Robert W. *About Face: The United States and the United Nations.* Boulder, CO: Lynne Rienner, 1993. Vincent, Jack E. *Support Patterns at the United Nations.* Lanham, MD: University Press of America, 1991.

off the superpowers against each other, so they cautiously avoided alienating the United States. In this context the UN moved to center stage in international security affairs.[8]

The UN had several major successes in the late 1980s in bringing to an end violent regional conflicts (in Central America and the Iran-Iraq War). Cease-fires were negotiated under UN auspices, and peacekeeping forces were dispatched to monitor the situation. In Namibia (Africa), a UN force oversaw independence from South Africa and the nation's first free elections. By the 1990s, the UN had emerged as the world's most important tool for settling international conflicts. Between 1987 and 1993, Security Council resolutions increased from 15 to 78, peacekeeping missions from 5 to 17, peacekeepers from 12,000 to 78,000, and countries sending troops from 26 to 76.

The new missions were not without problems, however. Inadequate funding undermined peacekeeping efforts to some extent. In Angola, the UN sent only a few peacekeepers, and when the government won internationally observed elections in 1992, the rebels took to arms and the civil war resumed. In Cambodia, the Khmer Rouge faction refused to disarm according to the UN-brokered peace plan it had signed.

Such problems came to a head in the former Yugoslavia, where the UN undertook its largest peacekeeping mission with nearly 40,000 foreign troops, costing over $1 billion annually. As we have seen, the mission was deeply flawed by the mismatch between the types of forces sent (lightly armed, equipped for humanitarian operations) and the situation into which they were sent (territorial aggression by heavily armed forces). After several years of hunkering down and becoming less and less relevant to the war in Bosnia, the *UN Protection Force (UNPROFOR)* had been renamed by Bosnians the "Self-Protection Force." It performed good work in delivering humanitarian aid (where allowed to do so by the Serbian military forces), but did nothing for collective security. It was replaced by a NATO peace implementation force in 1996.

After fifty years, the UN finally is beginning to work as it was originally intended to, through a concert of great powers and universal recognition of the Charter. However, as states turn increasingly to the UN, its modest size and resources are becoming seriously overburdened. At its fiftieth anniversary (1995), the UN is bigger and more important than ever, yet (ironically) in danger of failing. UN management practices have received increasing criticism, as has the UN's record on gender equality. The coming few years will see the UN continuing to grapple with the challenges of its new role and the limitations of its new budget, cut back 5 percent for 1996.

The Security Council

The Security Council is responsible for maintaining international peace and security, and for restoring peace when it breaks down. Its decisions are *binding* on all UN member-states. The Security Council has tremendous power to *define* the existence and nature of a security threat, to *structure* the response to such a threat, and to *enforce* its decisions through mandatory directives to UN members (such as to halt trade with an aggressor).

---

[8]Weiss, Thomas G., ed. *The United Nations and Civil Wars.* Boulder, CO: Lynne Rienner, 1995. Berridge, G. R., ed. *Return to the U.N.: U.N. Diplomacy in Regional Conflicts.* New York: St. Martin's Press, 1991. Baehr, Peter R., and Leon Gordenker. *The United Nations in the 1990s.* New York: St. Martin's Press, 1992. Taylor, Paul, and A. J. R. Groom, eds. *Global Issues in the United Nations Framework.* New York: St. Martin's Press, 1989.

Collective security rests with the UN Security Council, here voting in November 1990 to authorize the use of force if Iraq did not withdraw from Kuwait by January 15. Foreign ministers attended personally on this occasion, and the presidency, which rotates monthly, was held by U.S. secretary of state James Baker (top right). Soviet foreign minister Shevardnadze (top center) voted "yes." China (at right) abstained but did not use its veto, and the resolution passed 12-2 with only Cuba and Yemen opposed. UN staff sit in center, with UN secretary-general Perez de Cuellar next to Baker.

In fifty years the Council has passed fewer than a thousand resolutions. These resolutions represent the great powers' blueprints for resolving the world's various security disputes, especially in regional conflicts. (Because of the veto system the Council avoids conflicts between great powers themselves, such as on arms control.)

The five *permanent members* of the Council—the United States, Britain, France, Russia, and China—are the most important. The Council also has ten *nonpermanent members* who rotate onto the Council for two-year terms. The nonpermanent members are elected (five each year) by the General Assembly from a list of nominees prepared by informal regional caucuses. Usually there is a mix of regions and country sizes represented, though not by any strict formula. The Council's *chairperson* rotates among the Council members monthly. Occasionally this matters: in late 1990 the United States pushed for action against Iraq before the chair passed at the end of the month from the United States to Yemen (which opposed the U.S. position).

Substantive Security Council resolutions require *nine* votes from among the 15 members. A "no" vote by a permanent member defeats the resolution—the *veto* power. Many resolutions have been vetoed by the permanent members.

A permanent member wishing to register misgivings about a resolution without vetoing it may *abstain*. China abstains with some regularity, because it generally reserves its veto for matters directly affecting Chinese security. As a power with more regional than global interests, China avoids alienating other great powers by blocking their actions in distant parts of the world. (If the Security Council tried to condemn China, no such restraint would apply.) The United States has used the abstention tactic several times to register a middle position on resolutions critical of Israel.

The Security Council *meets irregularly* (in the New York UN headquarters) upon request of a UN member—often a state with a grievance regarding another state's actions. When Kuwait was invaded, when the United States accused Libya of harboring terrorists, when Bosnia was being shelled by Serbians, the victim called on the Security Council—a kind of 911 phone number for the world (but one without a standing police force). Because international security continues to be troublesome in many regions and because these troubles often drag on for months or years, meetings of the Council are frequent.

The Security Council's *power is limited* in two major ways, both of which reflect the strength of state sovereignty in the international system. First, the Council's decisions depend entirely on the interests of the Council's member states. The ambassadors who represent those states at the UN cannot change a Council resolution without authorization from their governments. Second, although Security Council resolutions in theory bind all UN members, member states in practice often try to evade or soften their effect. For instance, trade sanctions are difficult to enforce because it is tempting and relatively easy to cheat by trading with a sanctioned state. A Security Council resolution can be enforced in practice only if enough states with enough power care enough about it.

The Security Council has a formal mechanism for coordinating multilateral military action in response to aggression, called the *Military Staff Committee*. It is composed of military officers from the permanent Council members. But the United States opposes placing its forces under non-U.S. commanders, and the committee has never been used. Instead, military forces responding to aggression under the auspices of Security Council resolutions have remained under national command. For example, U.S. forces in the Gulf War had the mission of enforcing UN resolutions but did not display UN insignia or flags. The same was true of the 20,000 U.S. soldiers sent to Somalia in late 1992 to restore humanitarian relief efforts disrupted by civil war. In most peacekeeping operations, however, UN forces operate under UN command, wear UN insignia (including blue helmets or berets), travel in UN-marked vehicles, and so forth. In Haiti in 1994–1995, U.S. forces occupied the country at first, then turned over command to a UN force which included a smaller number of U.S. troops.

Even when the Security Council cannot agree on means of enforcement, its resolutions shape the way disputes are seen and ultimately how they are resolved. For instance, Security Council Resolution 242 after the Arab-Israeli war of 1967 laid out the principles for a just peace in that conflict—primarily the right of all states in the region to live within secure and well-defined borders and the return by Israel of territories captured in the 1967 war. (The parties are still arguing about whether territories to be returned by Israel means "all" territories.) These principles were reaffirmed in Resolution 338 after the

1973 war. Twenty years later, these resolutions formed the basis for peace negotiations between Israel and its Arab neighbors that began in 1991.

After the end of the Cold War, the prestige of the Security Council rose and it became more active than before. The first *summit meeting* of Council members in 1992 brought together for the first time ever the leaders of the "big five." The summit reaffirmed the universal commitments of states to the security principles embodied in the UN Charter and to the Council as a structure for implementing those principles.

Proposed Changes The structure of the Security Council is not without its problems, however. Japan and Germany are great powers that contribute substantial UN dues (based on economic size) and make large contributions to UN programs and peacekeeping operations. Yet they have exactly the same formal representation in the UN as tiny states with less than 1/100 of their population: one vote in the General Assembly and the chance to rotate onto the Security Council (in practice they rotate on more often than the tiny states). As global trading powers, Japan and Germany have huge stakes in the ground rules for international *security* affairs, because a stable security climate is good for doing business internationally. Japan and Germany see that the security rules are written in the Security Council. Naturally they would like seats at the table.

But including Japan and Germany as permanent Council members would not be simple. If Germany joined, three of the seven permanent members would be European, giving that region unfair weight (especially from the viewpoint of former European colonies in the third world). The three European seats could be combined into one (a rotating seat or one representing the European Union), but this would water down the power of Britain and France, which can veto any such change in the Charter. Also, if Japan or Germany were given a seat, then what about India, with 20 percent of the world's population? It, too, has only a lone vote in the General Assembly and so is badly underrepresented in the present scheme. But China (with a veto) would not welcome rival India onto the Council. Furthermore, what about the Islamic states—powerful states like Iran, rich ones like Saudi Arabia, and populous ones like Indonesia? How could they be excluded from the Security Council if states like India were included? But which Islamic state could represent such a diverse set of states? Finally, what about Latin America and Africa? One plan to overhaul the Security Council, proposed by Brazil in 1992, would give permanent seats, but without veto power, to Japan, Germany, India, Brazil, Nigeria, Egypt, and perhaps others—expanding the Council's size to around twenty-five. The future of this plan and others was still uncertain in 1995.

Any overhaul of the Security Council would require a change in the UN Charter, possibly opening other issues of Charter reform on which members states disagree. For all these reasons, changes in the structure of the Security Council may be difficult to achieve, barring a compelling reason to act.

Peacekeeping Forces

Peacekeeping forces are not mentioned in the UN Charter. Secretary-General Dag Hammarskjöld in the 1960s joked that they were allowed under "Chapter Six and a Half"— somewhere between the nonviolent dispute resolution called for in Chapter 6 of the Charter and the authorization of force provided for in Chapter 7.

The Charter requires member states to place military forces at the disposal of the UN, but such forces were envisioned as being used in response to aggression (under collective security). In practice, when the UN has authorized force to reverse aggression—as in the Gulf War in 1990—the forces involved have been *national* forces not under UN command.

The UN's *own* forces—borrowed from the armies of member states but under the flag and command of the UN—have been *peacekeeping* forces working to calm regional conflicts, playing a neutral role between warring forces.[9] These forces won the Nobel peace prize in 1988 in recognition of their growing importance and success. As was learned in Bosnia, however, such forces acting as neutrals do not succeed well in a situation where the Security Council has identified one side as the aggressor.

Peacekeeping Missions The secretary-general assembles a peacekeeping force for each mission, usually from a few states totally uninvolved in the conflict, and puts it under a single commander. The soldiers put on helmets or berets in the UN color, blue, with UN insignia—and are commonly called **blue helmets.** Their vehicles are white with a large black "UN" painted on them. Peacekeeping forces serve at the invitation of a host government and must leave if that government orders them out (as Egypt did in 1967 and Croatia briefly threatened to do in 1995).

Authority for peacekeeping forces is granted by the Security Council, usually for a period of three to six months that may be renewed—for decades on end in some cases. In one early case, the Suez crisis in 1956, the General Assembly authorized the forces under the "Uniting for Peace" resolution, allowing the Assembly to take up security matters when the Security Council was deadlocked. In the Congo in 1960 it was the secretary-general who took the initiative. But today the Security Council controls peacekeeping operations.

Funds must be voted by the General Assembly, and lack of funds is today the single greatest constraint on the use of peacekeeping forces. Special assessments against member states pay for peacekeeping operations. With the expansion of peacekeeping since 1988, the expenses of these forces exceed the rest of the UN budget by more than 2 to 1. Peacekeeping missions now cost over $3 billion annually. Member states owed over half a billion dollars in unpaid contributions in the mid-1990s (in addition to a like amount owed in back UN dues). The United States alone owed over $1 billion in assessments by 1995 and unilaterally reduced its share of peacekeeping contributions from 31 to 25 percent.

Current Missions As of 1995 the UN maintained 70,000 troops from over seventy countries in 17 separate peacekeeping or observing missions, spanning five world regions (Russia/Eastern Europe, South Asia, Africa, the Middle East, and Latin America). These are listed in Table 7.1. (Missions change from year to year.)

The largest peacekeeping missions (they were one mission until 1995) were in the former republics of *Yugoslavia*—Bosnia-Herzegovina, Croatia, and Macedonia. There, nearly forty thousand UN troops helped secure the supply of minimal humanitarian relief

---

[9]Durch, William J., ed. *The Evolution of UN Peacekeeping: Case Studies and Comparative Analysis.* New York: St. Martin's Press, 1993. Fetherston, A. B. *Towards a Theory of United Nations Peacekeeping.* New York: St. Martin's Press, 1994. James, Alan. *Peacekeeping in International Politics.* New York: St. Martin's Press, 1991. Liu, F. T. *United Nations Peacekeeping and the Non-Use of Force.* Boulder, CO: Lynne Rienner, 1992. Rikhye, Indar Jit, and Kjell Skjelsbaek, eds. *The United Nations and Peacekeeping: Results, Limitations and Prospects: The Lessons of 40 Years of Experience.* New York: St. Martin's Press, 1991.

TABLE 7.1 UN PEACEKEEPING MISSIONS AS OF JANUARY 1995

Location	Region	Size	Annual Cost (millions)	Role	Since
Former Yugoslavia	Russia/E. Europe	40,000	$1600	Peacekeeping, humanitarian relief	1992
Somalia	Africa	9,500	900	Peacekeeping, humanitarian relief	1992
Rwanda	Africa	5,500	200	Peacekeeping, humanitarian relief	1993
Lebanon	Middle East	5,000	150	Monitor cease-fire near border with Israel	1978
Mozambique	Africa	5,000	300	Oversee cease-fire, disarmament, elections	1992
Cyprus	Middle East	1,200	40	Monitor cease-fire	1964
Iraq-Kuwait	Middle East	1,100	60	Observe cease-fire along border	1991
Golan Heights	Middle East	1,000	30	Monitor cease-fire between Israel and Syria	1974
Western Sahara	Middle East	300	40	Organize referendum in Moroccan-held territory	1991
Israel	Middle East	200	30	Observe Arab-Israeli truce	1948
Georgia	Russia/E. Europe	100	10	Observe cease-fire in civil war	1993
Liberia	Africa	100	1	Observe cease-fire in civil war	1993
Haiti	Latin America	100	1	Observe elections, democratic transition	1993
Angola	Africa	100	30	Observe transition process ending civil war	1989
India-Pakistan	South Asia	40	7	Observe cease-fire	1949
El Salvador	Latin America	30	30	Observe transition process ending civil war	1989
Tajikistan	Russia/E. Europe	20	1	Observe cease-fire in civil war	1994
	Total	69,300	$3430		

Note: Size indicates total personnel (mostly troops but some civilian administrators). The "Protection Force" in former Yugoslavia was split into three parts, then replaced by NATO. Cost figures are for 1994.

to many civilians displaced by the war, especially in the besieged Bosnian capital of Sarajevo, which lived under siege for more than three years. The UN forces monitored numerous cease-fires, which were continually broken. In 1996 this force was replaced by a NATO-led implementation force (IFOR). Croatia relented on its threat to expel UN forces from its country (where, the Croatian leaders complained, the UN was merely solidifying Serbian conquests by protecting the status quo without any political progress), instead bypassing the UN to recapture territory militarily. As we have seen, the debacle in the former Yugoslavia became a major test for the credibility of the UN as an effective actor in international security affairs.

The UN's second-largest peacekeeping operation in the early 1990s was in *Cambodia*. There, 15,000 peacekeepers were coupled with a large force of UN administrators who took over substantial control of the Cambodian government under a fragile pact which ended a long civil war that had decimated the country in the 1970s and 1980s. Despite difficulty in obtaining the cooperation of the Khmer Rouge faction (which refused to disarm as it had agreed), the UN pressed forward to make this arrangement work, and held elections in 1993 that chose a Cambodian government. The operation did not solve all problems, but overall it was judged a reasonable success.[10]

The lessons learned in Cambodia helped the UN accomplish a similar mission more easily in *Mozambique*. A peace agreement ended a long and devastating civil war there, setting up mechanisms for disarmament, the integration of military forces, and the holding of internationally supervised elections for a new government. In 1992 the UN tried to accomplish a similar mission in *Angola* with only 500 personnel. The peace process was on track until the government won the elections; the rebels refused to accept the results and resumed an even more destructive civil war for three more years. Learning from this failure, the UN sent a force fifteen times larger to Mozambique. As of 1995 Mozambique was the most successful of the UN's five largest missions; those in the former Yugoslavia, Somalia, Rwanda, and Lebanon had all experienced major problems.

Observing and Peacekeeping What we call "peacekeepers" actually perform two different functions—observing and peacekeeping. *Observers* are unarmed military officers sent to a conflict area in small numbers simply to watch what happens and report back to the UN. This can be helpful because with the UN watching, the parties to a conflict are often less likely to break a cease-fire. Observers can *monitor* various aspects of a country's situation—cease-fires, elections, respect for human rights, and other areas. (Often this monitoring—such as that to certify whether an election is fair—is organized by IGOs and NGOs outside the UN as well.)

The function of *peacekeeping* itself is carried out by lightly armed soldiers (in armored vehicles with automatic rifles but without artillery, tanks, and other heavy weapons). Such forces play several roles. They can *interpose* themselves physically between warring parties to keep them apart (more accurately, to make them have to attack the UN forces in order to get to their enemy). UN peacekeepers often try to *negotiate* with military officers on both sides. This channel of communication can bring about tactical actions and understandings that support a cease-fire. But the UN forces in a war zone cannot easily move around and get from one side's positions to those of the other to conduct such negotiations.

Peacekeeping is much more difficult if one side sees the UN forces as being *biased* toward the other side. Israel feels this way about UN forces in southern Lebanon, for example. On occasion Israeli forces have broken through UN lines to attack enemies. In Cambodia and the former Yugoslavia in the early 1990s, one party deliberately attacked UN forces many times, causing a number of deaths. In general, when cease-fires break down, UN troops get caught in the middle. More than 800 have been killed over the years—most of them in the Congo (Zaire) in 1960–1964, in Cyprus since 1964, in southern Lebanon since 1978, and in the former Yugoslavia. In some conflicts, peacekeepers organized outside the UN framework have been used instead of UN-commanded forces; CIS troops have played this role occasionally in the former Soviet Union, and U.S. forces have acted as peacekeepers in Egypt's Sinai desert.

Peacemaking In the past, peacekeeping forces have generally been unable to make peace, only to keep it. As the UN commander in Bosnia once said in response to criticisms of inaction, "I'm not going to fight a war in white tanks." To go into a shooting

---

[10]Doyle, Michael W. *UN Peacekeeping in Cambodia: UNTAC's Civilian Mandate*. Boulder, CO: Lynne Rienner, 1995.

war and suppress hostilities requires military forces far beyond those of past UN peacekeeping missions. Thus, peacekeepers are usually not sent until a cease-fire has been arranged, has taken effect, and has held up for some time. Often dozens of cease-fires are broken before one sticks. The problem is that wars may simmer along for years, taking a terrible toll, before the UN gets its chance. At times it is as though the fire department arrives on the scene after the house has burned to the ground.

To address this problem, the secretary-general in 1992 proposed to create UN peace-making (or peace enforcement) units that would not only monitor a cease-fire but enforce it if it broke down. These forces would be more heavily armed than peacekeeping forces because they would weigh into the battle. Also, these forces would be able to respond to hot spots within a few days, rather than within several months as with past peacekeeping forces.[11] The secretary-general called for member states to make available, on a rapid deployment basis, one thousand soldiers each—specially trained volunteers—to create a standby UN army that could respond quickly to crises. Chapter 7 of the UN Charter allows the UN to draw on resources of member states in this way, but these provisions have not been used in the past. Control over the deployment and operation of these forces would be held by the Security Council.

Not only did the member states refuse the request for soldiers, they shot down the idea of peacemaking and did not provide peace enforcement forces for Bosnia where the need was most obvious. (In 1995, a more combat-ready "reaction force" was tried out in Bosnia.) Indeed, the great powers forced a slowdown in the expansion of peacekeeping operations generally, and in some cases turned down the secretary-general when he urgently requested a peacekeeping mission to head off an impending disaster. This was the case for example in Burundi in 1995, when the same Hutu-Tutsi conflict as in neighboring Rwanda threatened to erupt into another genocide.

The Secretariat

The secretary-general of the UN is the closest thing to a "president of the world" that exists. But the secretary-general represents member states—especially the five permanent Security Council members—and not the world's five billion people. The current secretary-general, Boutros Boutros-Ghali, is fond of calling himself just the "humble servant" of the member states. Judging from his inability to get the Security Council to follow his lead on peacekeeping, his humility would seem well justified. The secretary-general is *nominated* by the Security Council—requiring the consent of all five permanent members—and must be *approved* by the General Assembly. The term of office is five years and may be renewed.

The Secretariat of the UN is its executive branch, headed by the secretary-general. It is a bureaucracy for administering UN policy and programs, just as the State Department is a bureaucracy for U.S. foreign policy (the State Department is somewhat larger). In security matters the secretary-general personally works with the Security Council; third-world development programs are coordinated by a second-in-command—the Director-General for Development and International Economic Co-operation. The Secretariat is divided into functional areas, with undersecretaries-general and assistant secretaries-general.

---

[11]Boutros-Ghali, Boutros. *An Agenda for Peace: Preventive Diplomacy, Peacemaking and Peace-keeping*. New York: United Nations, 1992.

With limited powers and resources, Secretary-General Boutros Boutros-Ghali tried to expand the scope and size of UN peacekeeping missions but ran into severe constraints. Here is Boutros-Ghali in Sarajevo, Bosnia, December 1992.

The *UN staff* in these various areas includes administrative personnel as well as technical experts and economic advisors working on various programs and projects in the member countries. The staff numbers about five thousand people at the New York headquarters and about ten thousand more around the world. The largest concentration of the latter is in Geneva, Switzerland, where several UN programs and agencies are headquartered (even though Switzerland itself is not a UN member). Geneva is a frequent site for various kinds of negotiations and is almost a second UN headquarters city—one that is seen as more neutral than New York. A few third-world development programs are headquartered in third-world cities.

One purpose of the UN Secretariat is to begin to develop an *international civil service* of diplomats and bureaucrats whose loyalties are at the global level, not to their particular states of origins. The UN Charter sets the secretary-general and staff apart from the authority of national governments and calls on member states to respect the staff's "exclusively international character." The UN has been fairly successful in this regard; the secretary-general is most often seen as an independent diplomat thinking about the whole world's interests, not a pawn of any state.

But in the early 1990s the UN bureaucracy came under increasing criticism for both inefficiency and corruption. These criticisms, coming especially from the United States, which saw itself as bearing an unfair share of the costs, led to a reform program by the mid-1990s.

The secretary-general is more than a bureaucratic manager. He (it has not yet been a she) is a visible public figure whose personal attention to a regional conflict can move it toward resolution. The Charter allows the secretary-general to use the UN's "good offices" to serve as a neutral mediator in international conflicts—to bring hostile parties together in negotiations. For example, Boutros-Ghali was personally involved in trying to mediate conflicts in Somalia, the former Yugoslavia, and elsewhere, as his predecessor had done in Central America a few years earlier.

The secretary-general also works to bring together the great-power consensus on which Security Council action depends—a much harder job than mere bureaucratic management. The secretary-general has the power under the Charter to bring to the Security Council any matter that might threaten international peace and security, and so to play a major role in setting the UN's agenda in international security affairs.

Boutros Boutros-Ghali is the secretary-general from 1992 through 1996. He is a "diplomat's diplomat" from Egypt, with decades of experience in foreign service and the UN, who played a role in the Egyptian-Israeli peace treaty of 1978. Boutros-Ghali is trying to expand UN peacekeeping and peacemaking in local conflicts before they escalate and spread. His assertiveness in the Security Council has caused frictions with permanent members of the Council, including his scolding them for giving him big mandates without adequate resources to carry them out.

Just as the U.S. president has tensions with Congress over foreign policy, the secretary-general sometimes has tensions with the Security Council. But the secretary-general is chosen by the Security Council and has less autonomy than the U.S. president. When the secretary-general asks for authority for a peacekeeping mission for six months, the Security Council is likely to say, "Three months." If the secretary-general asks for ten million dollars he might get five. Thus the secretary-general remains, like the entire UN system, constrained by state sovereignty.

Past secretaries-general have come from various regions of the world but never from a great power. They are Trygve Lie (from Norway, 1946–1952), Dag Hammarskjöld (Sweden, 1953–1961), U Thant (Burma, 1961–1971), Kurt Waldheim (Austria, 1972–1982), and Javier Perez de Cuellar (Peru, 1982–1992).

The General Assembly

The General Assembly is made up of all 185 member states of the UN, each with one vote. It usually meets every fall, from late September through January, in *plenary session*. State leaders or foreign ministers generally come through one by one to address this assemblage. For instance, the U.S. president usually addresses the Assembly once during this fall gathering. The Assembly sessions, like most UN deliberations, are simultaneously translated into dozens of languages so that delegates from around the world can carry on a single conversation. This global town hall is a unique institution and provides a powerful medium for states to put forward their ideas and arguments. Presiding over it is a president elected by the Assembly—a post without much power.

The Assembly convenes for *special sessions* every few years on general topics such as economic cooperation. The UN special session on disarmament in June 1982 provided the occasion for the largest political rally in U.S. history—a peace demonstration of a million people in New York. The Assembly has met in *emergency session* in the past to deal with an immediate threat to international peace and security, but this has happened only nine times and has now become uncommon.

The General Assembly has the power to accredit national delegations as members of the UN (through its Credentials Committee). For instance, in 1971 the delegation of the People's Republic of China was given China's seat in the UN (including on the Security Council) in place of the Nationalists on Taiwan. For decades neither North nor South Korea became members of the UN (because both claimed the whole of Korea), but they finally took seats as separate delegations in 1991. Some political entities that fall short of state status send *permanent observer missions* to the UN, which participate without a vote in the General Assembly; these include, for instance, the Vatican (Holy See) and the Palestine Liberation Organization (PLO). This is also what the Koreas did before becoming members.

The General Assembly's main power lies in its *control of finances* for UN programs and operations, including peacekeeping. It also can *pass resolutions* on various matters, but these are not binding on the members. They are purely advisory and at times have served largely to vent frustrations of the third-world majority. The Assembly also *elects members* of certain UN agencies and programs. Finally, the Assembly coordinates UN programs and agencies through its own system of committees, commissions, councils, and so forth.

The Assembly coordinates UN programs and agencies through the Economic and Social Council (ECOSOC), which has 54 member states elected by the General Assembly for three-year terms. ECOSOC manages the overlapping work of a large number of programs and agencies. Its *regional commissions* look at how UN programs work together in a particular region; its *functional commissions* deal with global topics such as population growth, narcotics trafficking, human rights, and the status of women; and its *expert bodies* work on technical subjects that cut across various UN programs in areas such as crime prevention, public finances, and geographical names. Outside of ECOSOC, the General Assembly operates many *other specialized committees*. Standing committees facilitate the work of the Assembly in issue areas such as decolonization, legal matters, or disarmament.

Many of the activities associated with the UN do not take place under tight control of either the General Assembly or the Security Council. They occur in functional agencies and programs having various amounts of autonomy from UN control.

UN Programs

Through the Economic and Social Council, the General Assembly oversees more than a dozen major programs to advance economic development and social stability in poor states of the third world. Through its programs, the UN helps to manage global North-South relations: it organizes a flow of resources and skills from the richer parts of the world to support development in the poorer parts.

The programs are *funded* partly by General Assembly allocations and partly by contributions that the programs raise directly from member states, businesses, or private charitable contributors. In one case, UNICEF, the program has for decades organized U.S. children in an annual Halloween fund drive on behalf of their counterparts in poorer countries. The degree of General Assembly funding, and of operational autonomy from the Assembly, varies from one program to another. Each UN program has a staff, a headquarters, and various operations in the field, where it works with host governments in member states.

Several of these programs are of growing importance today. The *UN Environment Program* (UNEP) has become prominent in the 1990s as the economic development of the third world and the growing economies of the industrialized world take a toll on the world environment (see Chapter 11). UNEP grapples with global environmental strategies, guided by principles adopted at the Earth Summit (the UN Conference on Environment and Development) in Brazil in 1992. UNEP provides technical assistance to member states, monitors environmental conditions globally, develops standards, and recommends alternative energy sources.

UNICEF is the UN Children's Fund, which gives technical and financial assistance to third-world countries for programs benefiting children, including emergency relief. Unfortunately, the needs of children in many countries are still urgent, and UNICEF is kept busy. It is financed by voluntary contributions. The *Office of the UN High Commissioner for Refugees (UNHCR)* has also been kept quite busy in recent years. UNHCR coordinates efforts to protect, assist, and eventually repatriate the large numbers of refugees who flee across international borders each year to escape from war and political violence. (The longer-standing problem of Palestinian refugees is handled by a different program, the *UN Relief Works Agency*, or *UNRWA*.)

The *UN Development Program (UNDP)*, funded by voluntary contributions, coordinates all UN efforts related to third-world development. With about five thousand projects operating simultaneously around the world, UNDP is the world's largest international agency providing technical development assistance. The UN also operates several development-related agencies for training and for the promotion of women's role in development.

The office of the UN High Commissioner for Refugees (UNHCR)—one of dozens of UN programs—has assumed growing importance in caring for refugees displaced by war. Here UNHCR brings Pakistani peacekeepers to help feed refugees in Somalia.

Many third-world countries depend on export revenues to finance economic development, making those countries vulnerable to fluctuations in commodity prices and other problems involved in international trade. The **UN Conference on Trade and Development (UNCTAD)** seeks to negotiate international trade agreements to stabilize commodity prices and promote third-world development. Because third-world countries do not have much power in the international economy, however, UNCTAD has little leverage with which to promote third-world interests in trade (see p. 538).

Other UN programs manage problems such as disaster relief, food aid, housing, and population issues. Throughout the poorer countries, the UN maintains an active presence in economic and social affairs.

Autonomous Agencies

In addition to its own programs, the UN General Assembly maintains formal ties with about twenty autonomous international agencies not under its control. Most are specialized technical organizations through which states pool their efforts to address problems such as health care or labor conditions.

The only such agency in international security affairs is the International Atomic Energy Agency (IAEA), headquartered in Vienna, Austria. It was established under the UN but is formally autonomous. Although the IAEA has an economic role in helping to develop civilian nuclear power plants, it mainly works to prevent nuclear proliferation (see p. 254). With nuclear proliferation threats causing great international concern in the 1990s, the IAEA is a busy agency.

In the area of health care, the **World Health Organization (WHO)** based in Geneva provides technical assistance to improve conditions in the third world and conducts major immunization campaigns in poor countries. In the 1960s and 1970s, WHO led one of the great public health victories of all time—the worldwide eradication of smallpox. Today WHO is a leading player in the worldwide fight to control AIDS (see pp. 457–459).

In agriculture, the *Food and Agriculture Organization (FAO)* is the lead agency. In labor standards it is the *International Labor Organization (ILO)*. UNESCO—the *UN Educational, Scientific, and Cultural Organization*—facilitates international communication and scientific collaboration. The *UN Industrial Development Organization (UNIDO)* promotes industrialization in the third world.

The longest-established IOs, with some of the most successful records, are those easily taken for granted—specialized agencies dealing with technical aspects of international coordination in functional areas such as aviation or postal exchange. For instance, the *International Telecommunications Union (ITU)* allocates radio frequencies. The *Universal Postal Union (UPU)* sets standards for international mail. The *International Civil Aviation Organization (ICAO)* sets binding standards for international air traffic. The *International Maritime Organization (IMO)* facilitates international cooperation on shipping at sea. The *World Intellectual Property Organization (WIPO)* seeks world compliance with copyrights and patents, and promotes third-world development and technology transfer within a legal framework that protects such intellectual property (see pp. 333–335). Finally, the *World Meteorological Association (WMO)* operates a world weather watch and promotes the exchange of weather information.

The major coordinating agencies of the world economy (discussed in Chapters 8, 9, and 13) are also UN-affiliated agencies. The World Bank and the International Monetary

Fund (IMF) give loans, grants, and technical assistance for economic development (and the IMF manages international balance-of-payments accounting). The General Agreement on Tariffs and Trade (GATT) is a complex multilateral treaty and an ongoing negotiation, setting rules for international trade.

Overall, the density of connections across national borders, both in the UN system and through other IOs, is increasing year by year. In a less-tangible way, people are also becoming connected across international borders through the meshing of ideas, including norms and rules. And gradually the rules are becoming international laws.

❖ INTERNATIONAL LAW

IOs impinge on state sovereignty by creating new structures (both supranational and transnational) for regulating relations across borders. International law and international norms limit state sovereignty in another way. They create principles for governing international relations that compete with the core realist principles of sovereignty and anarchy.

International law, unlike national laws, applies to relations *between states*. It differs from national laws in deriving not from actions of a legislative branch or other central authority, but from tradition and agreements signed by states. It also differs in the difficulty of enforcement, which depends not on the power and authority of central government but on reciprocity, collective action, and international norms.[12]

Sources of International Law

Laws within states come from central authorities—legislatures or dictators. Because states are sovereign and recognize no central authority, international law rests on a different basis. The declarations of the UN General Assembly are not laws, and most do not bind the members. The Security Council can compel certain actions by states, but these are commands rather than laws: they are specific to a situation. No body of international law has been passed by a legislative body. Where, then, does international law come from? Four sources of international law are recognized: treaties, custom, general principles of law (such as equity), and legal scholarship (including past judicial decisions).

Treaties and other written conventions signed by states are the most important source.[13] International treaties now fill more than a thousand thick volumes, with tens of thousands of individual agreements. There is a principle in international law that treaties once signed and ratified must be observed (*pacta sunt servanda*). States violate the terms of treaties they have signed only if the matter is very important or the penalties for such a violation seem very small. In the United States, treaties duly ratified by the Senate are considered to be the highest law of the land, equal with acts passed by Congress.

---

[12]Ku, Charlotte, and John King Gamble. International Law: "State of the Discipline" 1992. *International Studies Notes* 16 (3), 1991: 47–52. Moynihan, Daniel Patrick. *On the Law of Nations*. Cambridge, MA: Harvard University Press, 1990. Falk, Richard, Friedrich Kratochwil, and Saul H. Mendlovitz, eds. *International Law: A Contemporary Perspective*. Boulder, CO: Westview, 1985. Franck, Thomas M. *Political Questions, Judicial Answers: Does the Rule of Law Apply to Foreign Affairs?* Princeton: Princeton University Press, 1992.

[13]Reuter, Paul. *Introduction to the Law of Treaties*. London: Pinter, 1992.

Treaties and other international obligations such as debts are *binding on successor governments* whether the new government takes power through an election, a coup, or a revolution. For example, after the revolutions in Eastern Europe around 1990, newly democratic governments were held responsible for debts incurred by their communist predecessors. Even when the Soviet Union broke up, Russia as the successor state had to guarantee that Soviet debts would be paid and Soviet treaties honored (some of the latter required complex agreements involving other former Soviet republics). Although revolution does not free a state from its obligations, some treaties have built-in escape clauses that let states legally withdraw from them, after giving due notice, without violating international law.

Because of the universal commitment it entails for all states to respect certain basic principles of international law, the UN Charter is one of the world's most important treaties. Its implications are broad and far-reaching, in contrast with more specific treaties such as a fishery management treaty. The specialized agreements are usually easier to interpret and more enforceable than broad treaties like the Charter.

Custom is the second major source of international law. If states behave toward each other in a certain way for long enough, their behavior becomes generally accepted practice with the status of law. Western international law (though not Islamic law) tends to be *positivist* in this regard—which means that it draws on actual customs, the practical realities of self-interest, and the need for consent rather than on a concept of divine or natural law derived from abstract principles.

General principles of law also serve as a source of international law. Actions such as theft and assault that are recognized in most national legal systems as crimes tend to have the same meaning in an international context. Consider an action such as Iraq's invasion of Kuwait. This act was illegal under treaties signed by Iraq (including the UN Charter and that of the Arab League) and under the custom Iraq and Kuwait had established of living in peace as sovereign states. Beyond treaty or custom, the invasion violated international law because the general principle is recognized that one state may not overrun its neighbor's territory and annex it by force. (Of course a state may still think it *can get away* with such a violation of international law.)

The fourth source of international law, recognized by the World Court as subsidiary to the others, is *legal scholarship*—the written arguments of judges and lawyers around the world on the issues in question. Only the writings of the most highly qualified and respected legal figures can be taken into account, and then only to resolve points not resolved by the first three sources of international law.

Often international law lags behind changes in norms; law is quite tradition-bound. Certain activities such as espionage are technically illegal but are so widely condoned that they cannot be said to violate international norms. Other activities are still legal but have come to be frowned upon and seen as abnormal. For example, China's shooting of student demonstrators in 1989 violated international norms but not international law.

Enforcement of International Law

Although these sources of international law distinguish it from national law, an even greater difference arises in regard to the *enforcement* of the two types of law. International law is much more difficult to enforce. There is no world police force, no prison cell in the

Even basic points of international law, such as prohibiting attacks on diplomats, can ultimately be enforced only by applying the power of other states (through such leverage as economic sanctions, freezing relations, or threatening military force). Here are U.S. diplomats on their first day as hostages in the U.S. embassy, Tehran, Iran, November 1979.

basement of the UN building to hold aggressors. Rather, enforcement of international law depends on the power of states themselves, either individually or collectively, to punish transgressors or force compliance.

Enforcement of international law depends heavily on practical reciprocity (see pp. 64–66). States follow international law most of the time because they want other states to do so. For instance, the reason neither side in World War II used chemical weapons on the battlefield was not that anyone could *enforce* the treaty banning use of such weapons. It was that the other side would probably respond by using chemical weapons too, and the costs would be high to both sides. International law recognizes the legitimacy of *reprisals*: actions that would have been illegal under international law may be legal if taken in response to the illegal actions of another state.

States also follow international law because they fear general or long-term costs that could come from a reputation for disregarding international law (rather than just fear of immediate retaliation). If a state fails to pay its debts, it will not be able to borrow money on world markets. If it cheats on the terms of treaties it signs, other states will not sign future treaties with it. The resulting isolation could be very destructive to the state's security interests.

A state that breaks international law may also face a collective response by a group of states, such as the imposition of *sanctions* on the violator. Sanctions are agreements among other states to stop trading with the violator, or to stop some particular commodity trade (most often military goods) as punishment for its violation of some international law. Over time, a sanctioned state can become a *pariah* in the community of nations, cut off from normal relations with others. This is very costly in today's world, when economic well-being everywhere depends on trade and economic exchange in world markets. Iraq and Serbia had been in the pariah category for years on end as of 1995.

International law enforcement through reciprocity and collective response has one great weakness—it depends entirely on national power. Reciprocity works only if the aggrieved state has the power to inflict costs on the violator. Collective response works only if the collectivity cares enough about an issue to respond. This makes it relatively easy to cheat on small issues (or to get away with major violations if one has enough power). For example, as we have seen, the international community repeatedly condemned Serbia's violations of international law in 1992 but was reluctant to bear the costs of punishing and reversing them.

If international law extends only as far as power reaches, what good is it? The answer lies in the uncertainties of power (see Chapter 2). Without common expectations regarding the rules of the game and adherence to those rules most of the time by most actors, power alone would create great instability in the anarchic international system. International law, even without perfect enforcement, creates expectations about what constitutes legal behavior by states. This makes violations or divergences from those expectations stand out, which makes it easier to identify and punish states that deviate from accepted rules. When states have agreed to the rules by signing treaties (such as the UN Charter), violations become more visible and clearly illegitimate. Thus, in most cases, although power continues to reside in states, international law establishes workable rules for those states to follow. The resulting stability is so beneficial that usually the costs of disrupting it by breaking the rules outweigh the short-term benefits that could be gained from such violations.

The World Court

As international law has developed, a general world legal framework in which states can pursue grievances against each other has begun to take shape. The rudiments of such a system now exist in the **World Court** (formally called the *International Court of Justice*), although its jurisdiction is limited and its caseload light.[14] The World Court is a branch of the UN.

Only states, not individuals or businesses, can sue or be sued in the World Court. When a state has a grievance against another, it can take the case to the World Court for an impartial hearing. The Security Council or General Assembly may also request advisory Court opinions on matters of international law.

The Court is a panel of 15 judges elected for nine-year terms (five judges every three years) by a majority of both the Security Council and General Assembly. The court meets

---

[14]Falk, Richard. *Reviving the World Court*. Charlottesville: University Press of Virginia, 1986.

The World Court hears international disputes but with little power to enforce judgments. Here, U.S. representatives (at right) in March 1992 press Libya to hand over two agents suspected of bombing Pan Am flight 103 in 1988. The Court rejected Libya's arguments, and UN sanctions banning commercial flights were imposed on Libya.

in The Hague, Netherlands. It is customary for permanent members of the Security Council to have one of their nationals as a judge at all times. Ad hoc judges may be added to the 15 if a party to a case does not already have one of its nationals as a judge.

The great *weakness* of the World Court is that states have not agreed in a comprehensive way to subject themselves to its jurisdiction or obey its decisions. Almost all states have signed the treaty creating the Court, but only about a third have signed the *optional clause* in the treaty agreeing to give the Court jurisdiction in certain cases—and even many of those signatories have added their own stipulations reserving their rights and limiting the degree to which the Court can infringe on national sovereignty.

The United States, for example, withdrew from the optional clause when it was sued by Nicaragua in 1986 (over the CIA's mining of Nicaraguan harbors): it refused to give the Court any power over U.S. policy in Central America.[15] A few years earlier, Iran refused to acknowledge the jurisdiction of the Court when sued by the United States in 1979 over its seizure of the U.S. embassy in Iran. In such cases the Court may hear the case without one side participating—and usually rules in favor of the participating side—but has no means to enforce the ruling.

---

[15]Forsythe, David P. *The Politics of International Law: U.S. Foreign Policy Reconsidered.* Boulder, CO: Lynne Rienner, 1990.

In one of its most notable successes, the World Court in 1992 settled a complex border dispute between El Salvador and Honduras. By mutual agreement, the two states had asked the Court in 1986 to settle territorial disputes along six stretches of border, three islands, and territorial waters. The disputes dated from 1861 and had led to a war in 1969. This was the most complex case ever handled by the Court, entailing 50 court sessions and years of deliberation over documents and precedents. The case was heard by a five-judge panel headed by a Brazilian and including judges from Britain and Japan in addition to Honduras and El Salvador. In its ruling, the World Court drew borders that gave about two-thirds of the total land to Honduras and split the territorial waters among both countries and Nicaragua. Despite some misgivings among residents of certain disputed territories, the national governments pledged to abide by the decision.

A main use of the World Court now is to arbitrate issues of secondary importance between countries with friendly relations overall. For instance, the United States has settled commercial disputes with Canada and with Italy through the Court. Because national security interests are not at stake, and because the overall friendly relations are more important than the particular issue in such cases, states have been willing to submit to the Court's jurisdiction.

There are other international forums for the arbitration of grievances (by mutual consent) as well. Some regional courts, notably in Europe, resemble the World Court in function. Various bodies are capable of conducting arbitration—as when Israel and Egypt submitted their dispute about the tiny territory of Taba to binding arbitration after failing to reach a settlement. Arbitration can remove domestic political pressures from national leaders by taking the decision out of their hands. But for major disputes involving issues of great importance to states, there is still little effective international legal apparatus.

Because of the difficulty of winning enforceable agreements on major conflicts through the World Court, states have used the Court infrequently over the years—a dozen or fewer cases per year. The number has been increasing, however.

International Cases in National Courts

Most legal cases concerning international matters—whether brought by governments or by private individuals or companies—remain entirely within the legal systems of one or more states. National courts hear cases brought under national laws and can enforce judgments by collecting damages (in civil suits) or imposing punishments (in criminal ones).

For a party with a grievance or dispute that crosses national boundaries, several advantages are gained by pursuing the matter through the national courts of one or more of the relevant states, rather than through international channels. First, judgments are *enforceable*. The party that wins a lawsuit in a national court can collect from the other party's assets within the state. Second, private *individuals and companies* can pursue legal complaints through national courts (as can subnational governmental bodies), whereas in most areas of international law states must themselves bring suits on behalf of their citizens rather than let the citizens pursue suits directly. (In truth, even national governments pursue most of their legal actions against each other through national courts.)

Third, there is often a *choice* of more than one state within which a case could legally be heard; one can pick the legal system most favorable to one's case. It is up to each state's court system to decide whether it has *jurisdiction* in a case (the right to hear it), and courts tend to extend their own authority with a broad interpretation. Traditionally, a national court may hear cases concerning any activity on its national *territory*, any actions of its own *citizens* anywhere in the world, and actions taken *toward* its citizens elsewhere in the world. Noncitizens can use the national courts to enforce damages against citizens, because the national court has authority to impose fines and if necessary seize bank accounts and property.

Consider a hypothetical example: a government in the third world nationalizes its oil industry, which includes installations of a U.S. oil company. The company considers the compensation offered to be inadequate, so the company has a grievance against that government. Where should the company take its case? It could get the U.S. government to act on its behalf through international channels such as the World Court. Or it could sue in the courts of the third-world country or in U.S. courts. The company would be most likely to win in U.S. courts, because U.S. judges and juries would be sympathetic. It could then collect damages from assets of the third-world government that are located in the United States. The company could seize U.S. bank accounts maintained by that government, or buildings it owned (except its embassy, which is not considered to be on U.S. territory). Or the company could wait for a state-owned airplane or ship to enter a U.S. port, and seize it. It would be hard for the third-world government to do business in the United States without paying the damages awarded to the oil company.

The United States is a favorite jurisdiction within which to bring cases for two reasons: First, U.S. juries have the reputation of awarding bigger settlements in lawsuits than juries elsewhere in the world (if only because the United States is a rich country). Second, because many people and governments do business in the United States, it is often possible to collect damages awarded by a U.S. court.

There are important limits to the use of national courts to resolve international disputes, however. Most important is that the authority of national courts stops at the state's borders, where sovereignty ends. A court in Zambia cannot compel a resident of Thailand to come and testify; it cannot authorize the seizure of a British bank account to pay damages; it cannot arrest a criminal suspect (Zambian or foreigner) except on Zambian soil.

To bring a person outside the state's territory to trial in a national court, the state's government must ask a second government to arrest the person on the second state's territory and hand him or her over for trial. This is called *extradition*, which is a matter of international law because it is a legal treaty arrangement *between* states. If there is no such treaty, the individual generally remains immune from a state's courts by staying off its territory.

There are gray areas in the jurisdiction of national courts over foreigners. If a government can lure a suspect onto the high seas, it can nab the person without violating another country's territoriality. Israel did this to recover one of its own citizens wanted for trial. He had taken refuge in Europe but was foolish enough to go for a yacht ride with a new girlfriend who turned out to be an Israeli secret agent.

More troublesome are cases in which a government obtains a foreign citizen from a foreign country for trial without going through extradition procedures. A famous case occurred in the 1980s when a Mexican doctor was wanted by U.S. authorities for allegedly participating in the torture and murder of a U.S. drug agent in Mexico. The U.S. government organized and paid a group of bounty hunters to kidnap the doctor in Mexico, carry him forcibly across the border, and deliver him to the custody of U.S. courts. The U.S. Supreme Court gave the U.S. courts jurisdiction in the case—showing the tendency to extend state sovereignty wherever possible—although international lawyers and Mexican officials sharply disagreed. The U.S. government had to reassure the Mexican government that the United States would not kidnap Mexican citizens for trial in the United States in the future. (After all of that, the doctor returned home after the case was thrown out for lack of evidence.)

The principle of territoriality also governs **immigration law.** When people cross a border into a new country, the decision about whether they can remain there, and under what conditions, is up to the new state on whose soil they stand. The state of origin cannot compel their return. National laws establish conditions for foreigners to travel and visit on a state's territory, to work there, and sometimes even to become citizens (*naturalization*). Many other legal issues are raised by people traveling or living outside their own country—passports and visas, babies born in foreign countries, marriages to foreign nationals, bank accounts, businesses, taxes, and so forth. Practices vary from country to country, but the general principle is that *national laws prevail on the territory of a state*.

Despite the continued importance of national court systems in international legal affairs and the lack of enforcement powers of the World Court, it would be wrong to conclude that state sovereignty is supreme and international law impotent. Rather, there is a balance of sovereignty and law in international interactions.

❖ LAW AND SOVEREIGNTY

The remainder of this chapter discusses particular areas of international law, beginning with the most firmly rooted and widely respected, and moving to newer and less-established areas. In each area, the influence of law and norms runs counter to the unimpeded exercise of state sovereignty. This struggle becomes more intense as one moves from long-standing traditions of diplomatic law to recent norms governing human rights.

Laws of Diplomacy

The bedrock of international law is respect for the rights of diplomats. The standards of behavior in this area are spelled out in detail, applied universally, and taken very seriously. The ability to conduct diplomacy is necessary for all other kinds of relations among states, except perhaps all-out war. Since the rise of the international system five centuries ago, it has been considered unjustifiable to harm an emissary sent from another state as a means of influencing the other state. Such a norm has not *always* existed; it is natural in some ways to kill the messenger who brings an unpleasant message, or to use another state's official as a hostage or bargaining chip. But today this kind of behavior is universally condemned, though it still happens from time to time.

The status of embassies and of an ambassador as an official state representative are explicitly defined in the process of **diplomatic recognition.** Diplomats are *accredited* to each other's governments (they present "credentials"), and thereafter the individuals so defined enjoy certain rights and protections as foreign diplomats in the host country.

Diplomats have the right to occupy an *embassy* in the host country as though it were their own state's territory. On the grounds of the U.S. embassy in Kuwait, for instance, the laws of the United States, and not those of Kuwait, apply. The U.S. armed forces (marines) occupy the territory, and those of Kuwait may not enter without permission. This principle of international law explains why, when Iraq invaded Kuwait, it did not set foot inside the U.S. embassy compound even though it could have overrun the facility easily. (Iraq claimed that since Kuwait no longer existed, the embassies there no longer enjoyed diplomatic status, but it was not willing to press the point.) Instead Iraq placed the compound under siege, eventually forcing the staff and ambassador to leave.

A flagrant violation of the sanctity of embassies occurred in Iran after Islamic revolutionaries took power in 1979. Iranian students seized and occupied the U.S. embassy compound, holding the U.S. diplomats hostage for over a year. The Iranian government did not directly commit this act but did condone it and did refuse to force the students out of the embassy. (Host countries are expected, if necessary, to use force against their own citizens to protect a foreign embassy.)

Diplomats enjoy **diplomatic immunity** even when they leave the embassy grounds and travel around. (The right to travel varies from one country to another; diplomats may be restricted to one city or free to roam about the countryside.) Alone among all foreign nationals, diplomats are beyond the jurisdiction of the host country's national courts. If they commit crimes, from jaywalking to murder, they may not be arrested and tried. All the host country can do is to take away a diplomat's accreditation and *expel* the person from the host country.

U.S. commitments as host country to the UN include extending diplomatic immunity to the diplomats accredited to the UN. The UN delegates thus cannot be prosecuted under U.S. law. Given this immunity, where do delegates park their cars in New York City? Wherever they want! Each year they simply tear up thousands of parking tickets. Occasionally UN representatives are accused of more serious crimes (murder, in one case in the 1980s), but they cannot be brought to trial in the United States for those crimes—much less for their parking offenses.

Because of diplomatic immunity, it is common to conduct espionage activities through the diplomatic corps, out of an embassy. Spies are often posted to low-level positions in embassies, such as cultural attaché, press liaison, or military attaché. If the host country catches them spying, it cannot prosecute them, so it merely expels them. Diplomatic norms (though not law) call for politeness when expelling spies; the standard reason given is "for activities not consistent with his/her diplomatic status." If a spy operates under cover of being a business person or tourist, then no immunity applies: the person can be arrested and prosecuted under the host country's laws.

A *diplomatic pouch* is a package sent between an embassy and its home country. As the name implies, it started out historically as a small and occasional shipment, but today there is a large and steady volume of such shipments all over the world. Diplomatic pouches, too, enjoy the status of home country territoriality: they cannot be opened, searched, or confiscated by a host country. Although we do not know how much mischief goes on in diplomatic pouches (because they are secret), it is safe to assume that illicit goods such as guns and drugs regularly find their way across borders in diplomatic pouches.

To *break diplomatic relations* means to withdraw one's diplomats from a state and expel its diplomats from one's own state. This tactic is used to show displeasure with another government; it is a refusal to keep doing business as usual. When a new revolutionary government comes into power, for instance, some countries may withdraw recognition. The U.S. has not had diplomatic relations with Cuba since the 1959 revolution, for example.

When two countries lack diplomatic relations, they often do business through a third country willing to represent a country's interests formally through its own embassy. This is called an *interests section* in the third country's embassy. In this way, the practical needs of diplomacy can overcome a formal, legal lack of relations between states. For instance, U.S. interests are represented by the Swiss embassy in Cuba, and Cuban interests are represented by the Swiss embassy in the United States. In practice, these interests sections are located in the former U.S. and Cuban embassy buildings and staffed with U.S. and Cuban diplomats.

States register lower levels of displeasure by *recalling their ambassadors* home for some period of time; diplomatic norms call for announcing a trip home "for consultations" even when everyone knows the purpose is to signal annoyance. Milder still is the expression of displeasure by a *formal complaint*. Usually the complaining government does so in its own capital city, to the other's ambassador. Complaints often relate to the treatment of a citizen or business from one state in another.

The law of diplomacy is repeatedly violated in one context—terrorism. Because states care so much about the sanctity of diplomats, the diplomats make a tempting target for terrorists, and because terrorist groups do not enjoy the benefits of diplomatic law (as states do), they are willing to break diplomatic norms and laws. An attack on diplomats or embassies is an attack on the territory of the state itself—yet can be carried out far from the state's home territory. Being a diplomat has become a dangerous occupation, and many have been killed in recent decades. Because terrorist actions are seldom traceable to governments, international law (enforced through reciprocity or collective response) is of limited use in stopping terrorist attacks on diplomats.

War Crimes

After the law of diplomacy, international law regarding war is one of the most developed areas of international law. Laws concerning war are divided into two areas—laws in war (*jus in bello*) and laws of war (*jus ad bellum*).[16] Consider these in turn, beginning with laws in wartime, violations of which are considered **war crimes.**[17]

The Roman politician Cicero said: "Laws are silent in time of war."[18] This is no longer true. In wartime, international law is especially difficult to enforce, but there are extensive norms of legal conduct in war that are widely followed. After a war, losers can be punished for violations of the laws of war (war crimes). In the 1990s, for the first time since World War II, the UN Security Council authorized an international war crimes tribunal, directed against war crimes in the former Yugoslavia. A similar tribunal was later established for genocide in Rwanda. Both tribunals were established in The Hague, Netherlands. The tribunal on the former Yugoslavia issued indictments against the top Bosnian Serb leaders and other Serbian and Croatian officers, but was severely hampered

---

[16]Walzer, Michael. *Just and Unjust Wars: A Moral Argument with Historical Illustrations.* 2nd ed. New York: Basic Books, 1992.

[17]Howard, Michael, George J. Andreopoulos, and Mark R. Shulman, eds. *The Laws of War: Constraints on Warfare in the Western World.* New Haven: Yale University Press, 1994. De Lupis, Ingrid Detter. *The Law of War.* New York: Cambridge University Press, 1987.

[18]Cicero. Pro Milone. In *The Speeches of Cicero.* Edited and translated by N. H. Watts. Cambridge, MA: Harvard University Press, 1931.

both by lack of funding and by its lack of power to physically arrest suspects who enjoyed the sanctity of Serbia and Croatia. Only one person (accused as a concentration camp guard) could be brought to trial by 1996, since the others were not in custody. Unlike at Nuremberg, the aggressor had not been conquered and its leaders arrested. So, as with most international law, the enforcement of laws of war occurs mostly through practical reciprocity and group response, reinforced by habit and legitimacy. A state that violates laws of war can find itself isolated without allies and subject to reprisals.

The most important principle in the laws of war is the effort to limit warfare to the *combatants* and to protect *civilians* when possible. It is illegal to target civilians in a war unless there is a compelling military utility in doing so. Even then the amount of force used must be *proportional* to the military gain, and only the *necessary* amount of force can be used.

To help separate combatants from civilians, soldiers must wear *uniforms and insignia;* for example, U.S. armed forces typically have a shoulder patch with a U.S. flag. This provision is frequently violated in guerrilla warfare, making that form of warfare particularly brutal and destructive of civilian life. If one cannot tell the difference between a bystander and a combatant, one is likely to kill both when in doubt (and in the "fog of war" soldiers are in doubt a lot). By contrast, in a large-scale conventional war such as the Gulf War, it is much easier to distinguish civilians from soldiers, although the effort is never completely successful.[19]

Soldiers have the right under the laws of war to *surrender,* which is to abandon their status as combatants and become **prisoners of war (POWs).** They give up their weapons and their right to fight, and earn instead the right (like civilians) not to be targeted. POWs may not be killed, mistreated, or forced to disclose information beyond their name, rank, and serial number. During the Gulf War, the United States took many thousands of Iraqi prisoners and respected their right to drop out of the fight. Iraq's treatment of a handful of U.S. POWs—including physical mistreatment—was among Iraq's many violations of international law in that war. The law of POWs is enforced through practical reciprocity. Once, late in World War II, German forces executed 80 POWs from the French partisan forces (whom Germany did not recognize as legitimate belligerents). The partisans responded by executing 80 German POWs.

The laws of war reserve a special role for the **International Committee of the Red Cross (ICRC).** The ICRC provides practical support—such as medical care, food, and letters from home—to civilians caught in wars and to POWs. Exchanges of POWs are usually negotiated through the ICRC. Armed forces must respect the neutrality of the Red Cross, and most of the time they do so (again, guerrilla war is more problematic).

The laws of warfare impose moral responsibility on *individuals* in wartime, as well as on states. The Nuremberg Tribunal after World War II established that participants can be held accountable for war crimes they commit. German officers defended their actions as "just following orders," but this was rejected; the officers were punished, some executed, for their war crimes.

Not all Nuremberg defendants were found guilty, however. For example, laws of war

---

[19]Fotion, Nicholas G. The Gulf War: Cleanly Fought. *Bulletin of the Atomic Scientists* 47 (7), 1991: 24–29. Lopez, George A. The Gulf War: Not So Clean. *Bulletin of the Atomic Scientists* 47 (7), 1991: 30–35.

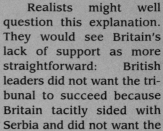

The UN Security Council has established a war crimes tribunal for the former Yugoslavia. Its effectiveness was limited by inadequacy of funding necessary to hire investigators and translators, rent offices and phone lines, and so forth. The contributions of the great powers varied, with the United States providing the most support (though still not adequate to the need) and Great Britain providing virtually nothing. What theories could help explain why one great power would make a large contribution and its closest ally a negligible one?

Liberal theorists would quickly recognize a collective goods problem in paying for the tribunal. The world community benefits from the work of the tribunal (inasmuch as it deters future aggression and genocide), but each individual state gains this benefit—however beneficial it ends up being—regardless of its own contribution. By this logic Britain is being rational to "free ride" because the United States and others are willing to pick up enough of the tab to make the tribunal at least minimally effective. The United States for its part exhibits a lingering hegemonic impulse by paying the largest relative share for the tribunal; as the world's most powerful state and leading international trader, the United States has the greatest interest in maintaining world order.

Realists might well question this explanation. They would see Britain's lack of support as more straightforward: British leaders did not want the tribunal to succeed because Britain tacitly sided with Serbia and did not want the tribunal to upset the gradual return of Serbia to the world community despite its crimes. By this line of thinking, a strong power is needed in the Balkans to maintain order in a relatively unimportant corner of Europe, and Serbia is the logical power to do so. The same geopolitical factors that led Britain in the past to side with Serbia (and Russia and France) against Croatia (and Germany, Austria, and Turkey) still operate today. War crimes come and go, by this reasoning, but great-power interests remain fairly constant.

Both theories seem to have merit. Can you think of any ways to tease out whether Britain was "free riding" by hoping that others would pay for the tribunal, or whether Britain actually was trying to impede the success of the tribunal by withholding support?

limit the use of force against civilians to that which is necessary and proportional to military objectives. That can be a high limit in a total war. In World War II, the German army besieged the Russian city of Leningrad (St. Petersburg) for two years, and civilians in the city were starving. Sieges of this kind are permitted under international law if an army cannot easily capture a city. Once, a large group of Russian civilians left the city and began walking toward the German lines, looking for food and water. The German commander ordered artillery to fire on the civilians, driving them back into the city. At Nuremberg after the war, the German commander defended his actions as militarily necessary since forcing the civilians to remain in the city would deplete its provisions and force a quicker surrender (while accepting them behind German lines would only drain German provisions). The judges agreed that the commander's actions were necessary and proportional to the ends they served; he was acquitted.[20]

---

[20]Walzer, Michael. See footnote 16 in this chapter.

Changing Context The laws of warfare have been undermined by the changing nature of war. Conventional wars by defined armed forces on defined battlegrounds are giving way to irregular and "low-intensity" wars fought by guerrillas and death squads in cities or jungles. The lines between civilians and soldiers blur in these situations, and war crimes become more commonplace. In the Vietnam War, one of the largest problems faced by the United States was an enemy that seemed to be everywhere and nowhere. This led frustrated U.S. forces into attacking civilian villages seen as supporting the guerrillas. In one infamous case a U.S. officer was court-martialed for ordering his soldiers to massacre hundreds of unarmed civilians in the village of My Lai in 1968 (he was convicted but given a light sentence). In today's irregular warfare, frequently inflamed by ethnic conflicts, the laws of war are increasingly difficult to uphold.

Another factor undermining laws of war is that states now rarely issue a *declaration of war* setting out whom they are warring against and the cause of their action. This practice, common until about fifty years ago, helped distinguish belligerents from bystanders, protecting neutral countries and invoking the rights and responsibilities of the warring states. Today, such declarations are seldom used because they bring little benefit to the state declaring war and incur obligations under international law. States just fight wars without declaring them. In many cases, such as revolutionary and counterrevolutionary civil wars in the third world, a declaration would not even be appropriate, because wars are declared only against states, not internal groups. In undeclared wars the distinctions between participants and nonparticipants are undermined (along with the protection of the latter).

Just War Doctrine

In addition to the laws about how wars are fought (war crimes), international law distinguishes **just wars** (which are legal) from wars of aggression (which are illegal). This area of law grows out of centuries-old religious writings about just wars (which once could be enforced by threats to excommunicate individuals from the church). Today, the legality of war is defined by the UN Charter, which outlaws aggression. Above and beyond the legal standing of just war doctrine, it has become a strong international norm, not one that all states follow but an important part of the modern intellectual tradition governing matters of war and peace which evolved in Europe.

The idea of *aggression,* around which the doctrine of just war evolved, is based on a violation of the sovereignty and territorial integrity of states. It assumes recognized borders that are legally inviolable. Aggression refers to a state's use of force, or an imminent threat to do so, against another state's territory or sovereignty—unless the use of force is in *response* to aggression. Tanks swarming across the border constitute aggression, but so do tanks massing at the border if their state has threatened to invade. The lines are somewhat fuzzy between aggression and response to aggression: tanks swarming across the border in *response* to tanks massing on the other side *might* not be considered aggression, depending on the context. For a threat to constitute aggression (and justify the use of force in response) it must be a clear threat of using force, not just a hostile policy or general rivalry.

In Iraq's invasion of Kuwait, for instance, Iraq's complaint that Kuwait had unfairly taken joint oil resources could not justify Iraq's invasion. Instead, Iraq justified its invasion on the grounds that Kuwait's territorial integrity had never really existed, because it was historically a province of Iraq. The flaw in this argument was that Iraq and Kuwait had both signed the UN Charter binding them to respect each other's territorial integrity! The international community had little trouble in determining that Iraq's invasion was aggression.

States have the right to *respond to aggression* in the only manner thought to be reliable—military force. Just war doctrine is not based on nonviolence. Responses can include both the *repelling* of the attack itself and the *punishment* of the aggressor. Responses can be taken by the victim of aggression or by other states not directly affected—as a way of maintaining the norm of nonaggression in the international system. The collective actions of UN members against Iraq after its invasion of Kuwait are a classic case of such response.

Response to aggression is the *only allowable use* of military force according to just war doctrine. The just war approach thus explicitly rules out war as an instrument to change another state's government or policies, or in ethnic and religious conflicts. In fact, the UN Charter makes no provision for "war" but rather for "international police actions" against aggressors. The analogy is with law and order in a national society, enforced by police when necessary. Because only aggression justifies military force, if all states obeyed the law against aggression there would be no international war. Another way to say this is that both sides in a war cannot both be just (though both can be unjust). There is always at least one party to *blame* for a war, and just war doctrine is based on being able to identify an aggressor.

Just war doctrine has been undermined, even more seriously than laws of war crimes, by the changing nature of warfare, which is less often fought across defined borders by sovereign states.[21] In civil wars and low-intensity conflicts, the belligerents range from poorly organized militias to national armies, and the battleground is often a patchwork of enclaves and positions with no clear front lines (much less borders). It is harder to identify an aggressor in such situations, and harder to balance the relative merits of peace and justice.

Another change in the nature of warfare that has undermined just war doctrine is the development of nuclear weapons. It is generally recognized that nuclear war could not be an adequate response to aggression. Thus, the use of nuclear weapons could never be just in the view of most scholars of the subject. More difficult to answer is whether it can be just to possess weapons that could not be justly used in war.

For a war to be *morally* just, it must be more than merely a response to aggression; it must be waged for the *purpose* of responding to aggression. The *intent* must be just. A state may not take advantage of another's aggression to wage a war that is essentially aggressive—waged to grab territory or wealth, for instance. Although the U.S.-led war effort to oust Iraq from Kuwait was certainly a response to aggression, critics found the justness of the war to be compromised by the U.S. interest in obtaining cheap oil from the Middle East—not an allowable reason for waging war.

---

[21]Johnson, James Turner. *Can Modern War Be Just?* New Haven: Yale University Press, 1984.

Human Rights

One of the newest and least developed areas of international law concerns human rights—the universal rights of human beings against certain abuses of their *own* governments.[22] The very idea of human rights flies in the face of the sovereignty and territorial integrity of states. Efforts to promote human rights are routinely criticized by governments with poor human rights records (like China) as "interference in our internal affairs"—a violation of the norms of international relations. This charge puts human rights law on shaky ground.

Yet norms and even laws concerning human rights continue to develop, if only because what happens within one state can so easily spill over national borders these days. A prime example occurred after the Gulf War, when Iraq cracked down brutally on a Kurdish uprising in northern Iraq. The norm of noninterference in Iraq's internal affairs would dictate that however many Kurds were slaughtered was Iraq's business alone. But when the Kurds fled in huge numbers to the Turkish border, they threatened to overwhelm the resources of Turkey and perhaps inflame a Kurdish uprising in Turkey itself. The anti-Iraqi alliance therefore declared the matter an international concern and imposed their own armed forces within northern Iraq to provide security and coax the Kurds back home. Eventually the Kurdish groups gained virtual autonomy under foreign military cover, compromising Iraq's sovereignty. Because of Iraq's lack of military reach into the area, Turkey was able to invade in 1995 to try to cut off the roots of the Kurdish guerrillas operating in Turkey.

Even in cases that do not so directly spill over national borders, the world is now more interconnected and interdependent than ever. A government's abuses of its own citizens can inflame ethnic conflicts, undermine moral norms of decency, and in other ways threaten the peace and stability of the international community. At least this is the rationale for treating human rights as a question of international law and norms. Human rights are also considered by some state leaders as a legitimate international concern because the presence or absence of democracy (including respect for rights) is thought to strongly influence states' foreign policies and propensities for violence (see "Democracy" on pp. 160–163).

Law concerning human rights dates back to the Nuremberg trials after World War II. Beyond the war crimes committed by German officers were their acts of *genocide* (attempts to exterminate a whole people) in which about ten million civilians had been killed in death camps. Clearly this ranked among the most wicked crimes ever committed, yet it did not actually violate either international law or German law. The solution was to create a new category of legal offenses—**crimes against humanity**—under which those responsible were punished. The category was not used again in practice until 1994–1995, when the tribunal for the former Yugoslavia handed down indictments for genocide.

---

[22]Robertson, A. H., and J. G. Merrills. *Human Rights in the World: An Introduction to the Study of the International Protection of Human Rights.* 3rd ed. Manchester, U.K.: Manchester University Press, 1992. Donnelly, Jack. *Universal Human Rights in Theory and Practice.* Ithaca: Cornell University Press, 1989. Newsom, David D., ed. *The Diplomacy of Human Rights.* Lanham, MD: University Press of America, 1986. Novak, Michael. *Human Rights and the New Realism: Strategic Thinking in a New Age.* Lanham, MD: University Press of America, 1986.

Soon after the experience of World War II, in 1948, the UN General Assembly adopted the *Universal Declaration of Human Rights*. It does not have the force of international law, but it sets forth (hoped-for) international norms regarding behavior by governments toward their own citizens and foreigners alike. The declaration roots itself in the principle that violations of human rights upset international order (causing outrage, sparking rebellion, etc.) and in the fact that the UN Charter commits states to respect fundamental freedoms. The declaration proclaims that "all human beings are born free and equal" without regard to race, sex, language, religion, political affiliation, or the status of the territory on which they were born. It goes on to promote norms in a wide variety of areas, from banning torture to guaranteeing religious and political freedom to the right of economic well-being.

Clearly this is a broad conception of human rights, and one far from today's realities. No state has a perfect record on human rights, and states differ in terms of which areas they respect or violate. When the United States criticizes China for prohibiting free speech, for example, China responds that the United States does not provide jobs for all citizens. Overall, despite the poor record of the world's states on some points, progress has been made on others. For example, slavery has been abandoned worldwide in the past one hundred and fifty years.

The *Helsinki agreements* in the 1970s, reached during a period of détente in U.S.-Soviet relations, made human rights a legitimate subject in an East-West treaty for the first time in the Cold War. The Soviet Union and Eastern European states agreed to guarantee certain basic rights of political dissent in their countries. These agreements were often breached but still provided important norms by which governments' behavior was judged (including, ultimately, by their own people who overthrew those governments more than a decade later).

Today, human rights efforts center on winning basic political rights in authoritarian countries—beginning with a halt to torture, execution, and imprisonment of those expressing political or religious beliefs. The leading organization pressing this struggle is **Amnesty International,** an NGO that operates globally to monitor and try to rectify glaring abuses of human rights.[23] Amnesty International has a reputation for impartiality and has criticized abuses in many countries, including the United States. A variety of other groups, such as Human Rights Watch (and its affiliated Asia Watch, Middle East Watch, etc.), work in a similar way but often with a more regional or national focus. The UN also operates a Commission on Human Rights with a global focus.[24] In 1993 the General Assembly after forty years of debate created the position of high commissioner for human rights (whose powers do not, of course, include making states do anything, but do include publicizing their abuses).

Enforcement of norms of human rights is very difficult, because it involves interference in a state's internal affairs. Cutting off trade or contact with a government that violates human rights sends a signal but tends to hurt the citizens whose rights are being violated (by further isolating them). The most effective method yet discovered is a combination of *publicity* and *pressure*. Publicity entails digging up information about human rights abuses, as groups like Amnesty International do. Then the pressure of other

---

[23]Amnesty International. *Amnesty International Report*. London: author, annual. Amnesty International. *Torture in the Eighties: An Amnesty International Report*. London: author, 1984.

[24]Tolley, Howard, Jr. *The UN Commission on Human Rights*. Boulder, CO: Westview, 1987.

International norms concerning human rights conflict with state sovereignty, causing friction in relations such as China's with the United States. Here, teenagers accused of prostitution are sentenced at a show trial in Shanxi province, 1988. A student-led movement for democracy was crushed the next year. China considers these internal affairs.

governments, as well as private individuals and businesses, consists of threats to punish the offender in some way through nonviolent means. For instance, one faction in the U.S. Congress repeatedly sought in the early 1990s to link the terms of U.S.-Chinese trade to China's human rights record. But inasmuch as most governments seek to maintain normal relations with each other most of the time, this kind of intrusive punishment by one government of another's human rights violations is rare—and its effect is not reliably successful. In 1994 the U.S. government unlinked China's trade status from its human rights record.

The U.S. State Department has actively pursued human rights since the late 1970s, when President Carter made human rights a major goal of U.S. foreign policy. An annual U.S. government report assesses human rights in states around the world. In cases where abuses are particularly severe or becoming worse, U.S. foreign aid has been withheld from these states or their armed forces. (But in other cases, CIA funding supported the abusers.)

Four **conventions on human rights** have been drawn up as legally binding (though still not easily enforceable) treaties. These deal with genocide, racial discrimination, political rights, and economic and social rights, respectively. The treaties have been ratified by about half the world's states. The United States has ratified only the genocide convention (and even that one only recently). In addition to specific concerns about the terms of the other three treaties, the United States (along with many other states) has general concerns about the loss of sovereignty implicit in such treaties.

Yet despite all these limitations, concern about human rights *is* a force to be reckoned with in international relations. There are now widely held norms about how governments *should* behave, and someday government may actually adhere to those norms—as they have already begun to do in select areas like the abolition of slavery. With the downfall of authoritarian and military governments in the former Soviet Union, Eastern Europe, Latin America, Africa, and elsewhere, a growing emphasis on human rights in the 1990s seems likely.

The concern of states for the human rights of individuals living in other states is a far cry from the realist concerns that have dominated the theory and practice of IR in the past. Indeed, the entire area of international law and organization runs counter to the fundamental assertions about international anarchy made by realists. The remaining chapters of this book move away from realism in two other ways—its emphasis on military force above other forms of leverage, and its pessimism about the potentials for international cooperation as an outcome of bargaining. If Part One of this book began with realism and subsequently challenged it on theoretical and practical grounds, Part Two begins with liberalism, and then finds realism (power politics) shadowing even the least security-oriented issue areas.

❖ CHAPTER SUMMARY

- International anarchy is balanced by world order—rules and institutions through which states cooperate for mutual benefit.
- World order has always been grounded in power, but order mediates raw power by establishing norms and habits that govern interactions among states.
- States follow the rules—both moral norms and formal international laws—much more often than not.
- The "New World Order" is a set of norms, proposed by President Bush, for international behavior in the post–Cold War era.
- International rules operate through institutions (IOs), with the UN at the center of the institutional network.
- The UN embodies a tension between state sovereignty and supranational authority. In its Charter and history, the UN has made sovereignty the more important principle. This has limited the UN's power.
- The UN particularly defers to the sovereignty of great powers, five of whom as permanent Security Council members can each block any security-related resolution binding on UN member states.
- In part because of its deference to state sovereignty, the UN has attracted virtually universal membership of the world's states, including all the great powers.
- Each of the 185 UN member states has one vote in the General Assembly, which serves mainly as a world forum and an umbrella organization for third-world social and economic development efforts.
- The Security Council has ten rotating member states and five permanent members—the United States, Russia, China, Britain, and France.
- The UN is administered by five thousand international civil servants in the Secretariat, headed by the secretary-general.
- The regular UN budget plus all peacekeeping missions together amount to less than one percent of what the world spends on military forces.

◆ Voting patterns and coalitions in the UN have changed over the years with the expanding membership and changing conditions. Currently the U.S. role is strong, and the Security Council is relatively united in purpose.

◆ UN peacekeeping forces are deployed in regional conflicts in five world regions. Their main role is to monitor compliance with agreements such as cease-fires, disarmament plans, and fair election rules.

◆ UN peacekeepers operate under UN command and flag. Sometimes national troops operate under their own flag and command to carry out UN resolutions (as in the U.S.-led multinational coalition in the Gulf War).

◆ The secretary-general has proposed to strengthen UN forces to create more heavily armed peace enforcement units that could respond more quickly to conflict flare-ups. But this proposal hit serious obstacles.

◆ IOs include UN programs (mostly on economic and social issues), autonomous UN agencies, and organizations with no formal tie to the UN. This institutional network helps to strengthen and stabilize the rules of IR.

◆ International law, the formal body of rules for state relations, derives from treaties (most importantly), custom, general principles, and legal scholarship—not from legislation passed by any government.

◆ International law is difficult to enforce and is enforced in practice by national power, international coalitions, and the practice of reciprocity.

◆ The World Court hears grievances of one state against another but cannot infringe on state sovereignty in most cases. It is an increasingly useful avenue for arbitrating relatively minor conflicts.

◆ Most cases involving international relations are tried in national courts, where a state can enforce judgments within its own territory.

◆ In international law, the rights of diplomats have long had special status. Embassies are considered to be the territory of their home country.

◆ Laws of war are also long-standing and well-established. They distinguish combatants from civilians, giving each certain rights and responsibilities. Guerrilla wars and ethnic conflicts have blurred these distinctions.

◆ Wars of aggression violate norms of just war—one waged only to repel or punish aggression. It is sometimes (but not always) difficult to identify the aggressor in a violent international conflict.

◆ International norms concerning human rights are becoming stronger and more widely accepted. However, human rights law is problematical because it entails interference by one state in another's internal affairs.

❖ THINKING CRITICALLY

1. Suppose you were asked to recommend changes in the structure of the UN Security Council (especially in permanent membership and the veto). What changes would you recommend, if any? Based on what logic?

2. The UN secretary-general proposed to create a standby army of peacemaking forces loaned by member states. This would reduce state sovereignty a bit and increase supranational authority. Discuss this plan's merits and drawbacks.

3. Collective security against aggression depends on states' willingness to bear the costs of fighting wars to repel and punish aggressors. Sometimes great powers have been

willing to bear such costs; at other times they have not. What considerations do you think should guide such decisions? Give examples of situations (actual or potential) that would and would not merit the intervention of great powers to reverse aggression.

4. Given the difficulty of enforcing international law, how might the role of the World Court be strengthened in future years? What obstacles might such plans encounter? How would they change the Court's role if they succeeded?

5. Although international norms concerning human rights are becoming stronger, some states continue to consider human rights an internal affair over which the state has sovereignty within its territory. Do you think human rights are a legitimate subject for one state to raise with another? If so, how do you reconcile the tensions between state autonomy and universal rights? What practical steps could be taken to get sovereign states to acknowledge universal human rights?

❖ KEY TERMS

international norms
"New World Order"
international organizations (IOs)
UN Charter
General Assembly
Security Council
Secretariat
blue helmets (peacekeeping forces)
UN Conference on Trade and
   Development (UNCTAD)
World Health Organization
   (WHO)

World Court
immigration law
diplomatic recognition
diplomatic immunity
war crimes
prisoners of war (POWs)
International Committee of the
   Red Cross (ICRC)
just wars
crimes against humanity
Amnesty International
conventions on human rights

PART TWO

INTERNATIONAL POLITICAL ECONOMY

Hong Kong

FROM SECURITY TO POLITICAL ECONOMY

Liberalism and
  Mercantilism

MARKETS

Global Patterns of Trade
Comparative Advantage
Prices and Markets
Centrally Planned
  Economies
Politics of Markets
Balance of Trade
Interdependence

TRADE STRATEGIES

Autarky
Protectionism
Industries and Interest
  Groups
Cooperation in Trade

TRADE REGIMES

The GATT (World Trade
  Organization)
Bilateral and Regional
  Agreements
Cartels

*Cars being loaded for export,
South Korea, 1986.*

TRADE

❖ FROM SECURITY TO POLITICAL ECONOMY

We move now from security to political economy. Scholars of **international political economy (IPE)** study the politics of international economic activities.[1] The most frequently studied such activities are trade, monetary relations, and multinational corporations (see this chapter and Chapter 9). Two topics of special interest in recent years are the economic integration of Europe and other regions (Chapter 10) and the international politics of the global environment (Chapter 11). Most scholars of IPE focus on the industrialized regions of the world, where most of the world's economic activity occurs. However, the global South has received growing attention, especially because economic relations and conditions there may be a more frequent source of international conflict and war in the post–Cold War era. The international aspects of these third-world issues include the gap between the global North and South (Chapter 12), and the North's role in the South's economic development (Chapter 13). Although all of these issues overlap (to varying degrees) with international security matters, they all deal primarily with political bargaining over economic issues and thus fit within IPE broadly defined.

The conceptual framework used to study international security affairs applies to IPE as well. The core concepts of power and bargaining developed from Chapter 2 on will continue to inform the IPE chapters, as will the emphasis on states as the most important actors (though not the only important actors) and the idea that states tend to act in their own interests.

---

[1]Caporaso, James A., and David P. Levine. *Theories of Political Economy*. New York: Cambridge University Press, 1993. Frieden, Jeffry A., and David A. Lake. *International Political Economy: Perspectives on Global Power and Wealth*. 3rd ed. New York: St. Martin's Press, 1995. Chase-Dunn, Christopher, ed. *The Historical Evolution of the International Political Economy*. Brookfield, VT: Edward Elgar, 1995. Gayle, Dennis J., Robert A. Denemark, and Kendall W. Stiles. International Political Economy: Evolution and Prospects. *International Studies Notes* 16 (3), 1991: 64–68. Murphy, Craig N., and Roger Tooze, eds. *The New International Political Economy*. Boulder, CO: Lynne Rienner, 1991. Stiles, Kendall W., and Tsuneo Akaha, eds. *International Political Economy: A Reader*. New York: HarperCollins, 1991.

However, the major approaches to IPE diverge from realism by downplaying the importance of military leverage in international bargaining. Most conflicts studied in IPE—conflicts over economic transactions—occur in situations where military force would not be a very effective means of influence. The main reason for this ineffectiveness is that using military force would disrupt a range of mutually profitable economic exchanges. Another (related) divergence from realism is in the conception of self-interest; in IPE the realist concept of narrow short-term self-interest competes poorly with the liberal idea that mutually beneficial long-term cooperation can often better achieve a state's self-interest (see Chapter 3). The collective goods problem presented in Chapter 3 is important throughout IPE.

Liberalism and Mercantilism

On another key assumption of realism—international anarchy—two major approaches within IPE differ.[2] One approach, called **mercantilism,** generally shares with realism the belief that each state must protect its own interests at the expense of others—not relying on international organizations to create a framework for mutual gains. Mercantilists therefore emphasize relative power (as do realists): what matters is not so much a state's absolute amount of well-being but its position relative to rival states.[3]

Liberalism, an alternative approach, generally shares the assumption of anarchy (lack of world government) but does not see this condition as precluding extensive cooperation to realize common gains.[4] It holds that with some attention to building international organizations, institutions, and norms, states can mutually benefit from economic exchanges. It matters little to liberals whether one state gains more or less than another—just whether the state's wealth is increasing in *absolute* terms (see Chapter 3). This concept parallels the idea that IOs allow states to relax their narrow, short-term pursuit of self-interest in order to realize longer-term mutual interests (see Chapter 3 and "The Evolution of World Order" on pp. 266–267).

Liberalism and mercantilism are *theories* of economics and also *ideologies* that shape state policies. Liberalism is the dominant approach in Western economics, though more so in *microeconomics* (the study of firms and households in markets) than in *macroeconomics* (the study of national economies). Marxism is often treated as a third theoretical/ideological approach to IPE, along with mercantilism and liberalism. Marxist approaches are attuned to economic exploitation as a force shaping political relations. We will explore these theories in depth in Chapter 12 since they find their greatest explanatory power in North-South relations.

---

[2]Crane, George T., and Abla M. Amawi, eds. *The Theoretical Evolution of International Political Economy: A Reader.* New York: Oxford University Press, 1991.

[3]Gilpin, Robert. *The Political Economy of International Relations.* Princeton: Princeton University Press, 1987. Nowell, Gregory P. *Mercantile States and the World Oil Cartel, 1900–1939.* Ithaca: Cornell University Press, 1994. Conybeare, John A. *Trade Wars: The Theory and Practice of International Commercial Rivalry.* New York: Columbia University Press, 1987. Pollins, Brian M. Does Trade Still Follow the Flag? *American Political Science Review* 83 (2), 1989: 465–80.

[4]Neff, Stephen C. *Friends but No Allies: Economic Liberalism and the Law of Nations.* New York: Columbia University Press, 1990. Ward, Benjamin. *The Ideal Worlds of Economics: Liberal, Radical and Conservative Economic World Views.* New York: Basic Books, 1979.

In IPE, contrary to international security, liberalism is the dominant tradition of scholarship and mercantilism is secondary. Thus, IR has a split personality. In matters of military force and security, scholars focus on anarchy and inherently conflicting interests. In matters of international political economy, however, they focus on international regimes and institutions that allow states to achieve mutual interests.

In truth, most international economic exchanges (as well as security relationships) contain some element of mutual interests—joint gains that can be realized through cooperation—and some element of conflicting interests. Game theorists call this a "mixed interest" game. For example, in the game of Chicken (see p. 71), the two drivers share an interest in avoiding a head-on collision; yet their interests diverge in that one can be a hero only if the other is a chicken. In international trade, even when two states both benefit from a trade (a shared interest), one or the other will benefit more depending on the price of the transaction (a conflicting interest).

Liberalism places most emphasis on the shared interests in economic exchanges, whereas mercantilism emphasizes the conflicting interests. Liberals see the most important goal of economic policy as the maximum creation of total wealth through achieving optimal *efficiency* (maximizing output, minimizing waste). Mercantilists see the most important goal as the creation of the most favorable possible *distribution* of wealth.

The main reason for the dominance of liberalism in IPE is that in practice great gains have been realized from free trade. In any economic exchange that is not coerced by negative leverage, both parties gain. Both can gain because they place different values on the items being exchanged. Each party places less value on the item it starts with than the other party does. For instance, when a supermarket sells a head of cabbage, the consumer values the cabbage more than the cash paid for it, and the supermarket values the cash more than the cabbage. This simple principle is the basis for economic exchange.

However, even though both parties gain in an exchange, they may not gain equally: the distribution of benefits from trade may not be divided equally among participating states. One party may benefit greatly from an exchange, whereas the other party benefits only slightly. Liberal economists are most interested in maximizing the overall (joint) benefits from exchange—a condition they call *Pareto-optimal* (after an economist named Pareto). They have little to say about how the total benefits are distributed among the parties (see Figure 8.1).

Rather, the distribution of benefits is a matter for implicit or explicit *bargaining,* and hence a matter for politics and the use of leverage to influence the outcomes.[5] States as participants in the international economy try to realize the greatest overall gains for *all* states while simultaneously bargaining to maximize *their own* share of those gains. Power does matter in such bargaining, but the most relevant forms of leverage are positive (the prospect of gains by striking a deal) rather than negative. Because the exchange process creates much wealth, there is much room for bargaining over the distribution of that wealth.

Liberalism sees individual households and firms as the key actors in the economy and views government's most useful role as one of noninterference in economics except to

[5] Grieco, Joseph M. *Cooperation Among Nations: Europe, America, and Non-Tariff Barriers to Trade.* Ithaca: Cornell University Press, 1990. Gowa, Joanne. *Allies, Adversaries, and International Trade.* Princeton: Princeton University Press, 1993. Sideri, S. *Trade and Power.* Rotterdam: Rotterdam University Press, 1970. Hirschmann, Albert O. *National Power and the Structure of Foreign Trade.* Berkeley: University of California Press, 1945.

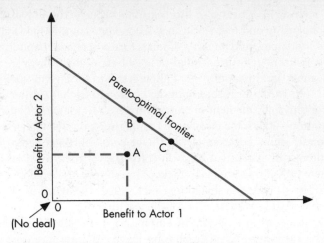

FIGURE 8.1 Joint and Individual Benefits
Any deal struck, such as at point A, yields certain benefits to each actor (dotted lines). Joint benefits are maximized at the Pareto-optimal frontier, but the distribution of those benefits, as between points B and C (both of which are better than A for both actors), is a matter for bargaining. Liberalism is more concerned with joint benefits, mercantilism more with the relative distribution.

regulate markets in order to help them function efficiently (and to create infrastructure such as roads that also help the economy function efficiently). Politics in this view should serve the interests of economic efficiency. With the hand of government removed from markets, the invisible hand of supply and demand can work out the most efficient patterns of production, exchange, and consumption (through the mechanism of prices). Because of the benefits of free trade, liberals disdain realists' obsession with international borders, because borders constrain the maximum efficiency of exchange.

For mercantilists, by contrast, economics should serve politics: the creation of wealth underlies state power. Because power is relative, trade is desirable only when the distribution of benefits favors one's own state over rivals. The terms of exchange shape the relative rates at which states accumulate power and thus shape the way power distributions in the international system change over time. As Japan and Germany, for instance, have achieved great prosperity, mercantilists saw them potentially threatening to overtake the United States. Liberals, by contrast, thought Japanese and German wealth boosted the entire world economy and ultimately benefited the United States.

Mercantilism achieved prominence several hundred years ago, and Britain used trade to rise in relative power in the international system around the eighteenth century. At that time mercantilism meant specifically the creation of a trade surplus (see "Balance of Trade" later in this chapter) in order to stockpile money in the form of precious metal (gold and silver), which could then be used to buy military capabilities (mercenary armies and weapons) in time of war.

Mercantilism declined in the nineteenth century as Britain decided it had more to gain from free trade than from protectionism. It returned as a major approach in the period between World Wars I and II, when liberal global trading relations broke down.

Again in recent years, with the weakening of the liberal international economic order created after World War II, mercantilism has begun to become more prominent.[6]

The distinction between liberalism and mercantilism is reflected in the difference between hegemony and empire. Under hegemony (see pp. 81–82), a dominant state creates an international order that facilitates free trade, but does not try to control economic transactions by itself. An empire, by contrast, controls economic transactions in its area centrally. Historically, empires have a poor record of economic performance whereas hegemony has been much more successful in achieving economic growth and prosperity.[7] Of course, under hegemony, rival states also share (with the hegemon) in the overall growth and prosperity, which can ultimately erode the hegemon's relative power and end its hegemony.

❖ MARKETS

International exchanges of goods and services now occur in *global markets*. Liberalism supports the use of market processes, relatively unhindered by political elements; mercantilism favors greater political control over markets and exchanges. The stakes in this debate are high because of the growing volume and importance of international trade for most national economies.

Global Patterns of Trade

International trade amounts to nearly 20 percent of the total production of goods and services in the world. Around $4 trillion worth of trade crosses international borders each year.[8] This is a very large number, more than four times larger than the world's military spending, for example. The great volume of international trade reflects the fact that trade is profitable.

The role of trade in the economy varies somewhat from one region to another, but it is at least as important overall in the third-world regions as in the industrialized regions of the world. Nonetheless, in the world economy as a whole, the global South accounts for only a small part of all trade, because the third world's economic activity itself is only one-third of the world total (see pp. 22–23). This creates an asymmetrical dependence in North-South trade (see Chapters 12 and 13).

Overall, most political activity related to trade is concentrated in the industrialized West (North America, Western Europe, and Japan/Pacific), which accounts for 75 percent of all international trade. Trade between these areas and the global South, although less important in volume, is also a topic of interest to IPE scholars (see Chapter 13).[9] Of special interest in the 1990s are trade issues in the former communist transition

---

[6]Sylvan, David J. The Newest Mercantilism [review article]. *International Organization* 35 (2), 1981: 375–81.

[7]Rosecrance, R. *The Rise of the Trading State: Commerce and Conquest in the Modern World.* New York, Basic Books, 1986.

[8]Data in this chapter calculated from: United Nations. *World Economic and Social Survey 1994: Current Trends and Policies in the World Economy.* New York: United Nations, 1994. Totals not adjusted for purchasing-power parity.

[9]McKeown, Timothy J. A Liberal Trade Order? The Long-Run Pattern of Imports to the Advanced Capitalist States. *International Studies Quarterly* 35 (2), 1991: 151–72.

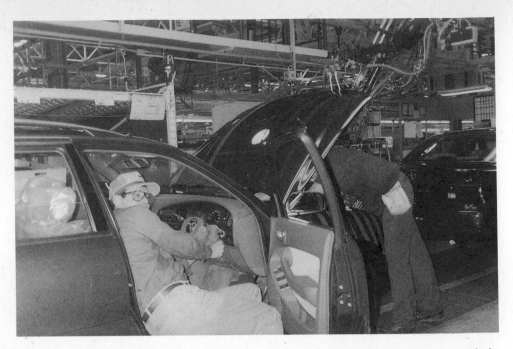

At a Toyota factory in Kentucky, U.S. workers assemble a Japanese car for export to Britain and Japan (car has right-hand drive). As the world economy becomes more integrated, markets and production are becoming global in scope.

economies of Russia and Eastern Europe, which face formidable challenges in the 1990s as they try to join the capitalist world economy.

Two contradictory trends are at work in global trading patterns today. One trend is toward the integration of the industrialized regions with each other in a truly global market. The GATT (discussed later in this chapter) is especially important to this global integration process. The second trend is the emerging potential division of the industrialized West into three competing trading blocs, each internally integrated but not very open to the other two blocs. Regional free-trade areas in Europe and North America, and perhaps in Asia in the future, raise the possibility of trading zones practicing liberalism inwardly and mercantilism outwardly.

Comparative Advantage

The overall success of liberal economics is due to the substantial gains that can be realized through trade.[10] These gains result from the **comparative advantage** that different states enjoy in producing different goods (a concept pioneered by economists Adam Smith and David Ricardo two hundred years ago). States differ in their abilities to produce certain goods because of differences in natural resources, labor force characteristics, and other

---

[10]Lake, David A., ed. *The International Political Economy of Trade*. Brookfield, VT: Edward Elgar, 1993. Odell, John S. Understanding International Trade Policies: An Emerging Synthesis [review article]. *World Politics* 43 (1), 1990: 139–66. Cohen, Benjamin J. The Political Economy of International Trade [review article]. *International Organization* 44 (2), 1990: 261–78.

such factors. In order to maximize the overall creation of wealth, each state should specialize in producing the goods for which it has a comparative advantage and then trade for goods that another state is better at producing. Of course, the costs of transportation and of processing the information in the trade (called *transaction costs*) must be included in the costs of producing an item. But both of these are low (and declining) relative to the differences in the cost of producing items in different locations.

Consider the example of Denmark, a small industrialized European country with 5 million people and a GDP of $20,000 per capita. Denmark has few domestic energy sources, almost no mineral resources, and modest amounts of land for agriculture. It has to import most of the raw material and many of the manufactured products on which its economy depends. To pay for these imports, Denmark specializes in two export products for which it has a comparative advantage on European and world markets. One is butter, which does not require large amounts of land, energy, or raw materials but does require a specialized and skilled dairy industry. The other is Lego™—the children's toy bricks. Manufacturing Lego is not easy: the bricks must fit together precisely even after years of harsh treatment. By creating a superior product Denmark gained predominance in the world market for children's plastic building bricks. By specializing in export products where it has a comparative advantage—butter and Lego—Denmark balances its trade and pays for its various imports.

Two commodities of much greater importance in the world economy are oil and cars. It is *much* cheaper to produce oil (or an equivalent energy source) in Saudi Arabia than in Japan, and much cheaper to produce cars in Japan than in Saudi Arabia. Japan needs oil to run its industry (including its car industry), and Saudi Arabia needs cars to get around its vast territory (including reaching its remote oil wells). Even after accounting for the shipping and transaction costs, it saves a huge amount of money to ship Japanese cars to Saudi Arabia and Saudi oil to Japan, compared to the costs if each were self-sufficient.

A state need not have an absolute advantage over others in producing one kind of good in order to make specialization pay. It need only specialize in producing goods that are lower in cost than other goods *relative* to world market prices. To illustrate this, imagine hypothetically that Japan discovered a way to produce synthetic oil using roughly the same mix of labor and capital that it now uses to produce cars, and that this synthetic oil could be produced a bit more cheaply than what it cost Saudi Arabia to produce oil, but that Japan could still produce cars *much* more cheaply than could Saudi Arabia. From a strictly economic point of view, Japan should keep producing cars (where it had the greatest comparative advantage) and not divert capital and labor to make synthetic oil (where it had only a slight advantage). In essence, the extra profits Japan would make from exporting more cars would more than compensate for the slightly higher price it would pay to import oil.

Thus, international trade generally expands the Pareto-optimal frontier by increasing the overall efficiency of production. Free trade allocates global resources to states that have the greatest comparative advantage in producing each kind of commodity. As a result, prices are both lower overall and more consistent worldwide. Increasingly, production is oriented to the world market.

Trade is not without drawbacks, however, when seen from a political rather than purely economic vantage point. One drawback is familiar from the preceding discussions of international security—long-term benefits may incur short-term costs. When a state begins to import goods that it had been producing domestically, there may be disruptions to its economy: workers may need to retrain and find new jobs, and capital (such as factories) may not be easy to convert to new uses. Another problem with trade is that its benefits and costs tend not to be evenly distributed *within* a state. Some industries or communities may benefit at the expense of others. For example, if a U.S. manufacturing company moves its factory to Mexico to take advantage of cheaper labor there, and exports its goods back to the United States, the workers at the old U.S. factory lose their jobs, but U.S. consumers enjoy cheaper goods. The costs of such a move fall heavily on a few workers, but the benefits are spread thinly across many consumers. This kind of unequal distribution of costs and benefits often creates political problems even when the *overall* economic benefits outweigh the costs.

Between states (as well as within each state) the distribution of benefits from trade can also be unequal. The new wealth created by international trade can be divided in any manner between the participants. For instance, it would be worthwhile for Saudi Arabia to import cars even at a price much higher than what it cost Japan to produce them, as long as the price was less than what it would cost Saudi Arabia to produce cars itself (or to buy them elsewhere). Similarly, Saudi Arabia would profit from selling oil even at a price just a bit above what the oil costs to produce (or what it can sell the oil for elsewhere). In such a case, with very expensive cars and cheap oil, most of the benefits of trade would go to Japan, but Saudi Arabia would still make an absolute (though not relative) gain in wealth. Alternatively, Saudi Arabia could buy the cars very inexpensively and sell the oil very expensively so that most of the benefits of trade would go to the Saudis and less to the Japanese. With so much added value from the exchange process, there is a great deal of room for bargaining over the distribution of benefits.

If there were only two states in the world, the bargaining over prices (that is, over the distribution of benefits from trade) would essentially be a political process entailing the use of leverage, possibly including military force. But in a world of many states (and even more substate economic actors such as companies and households), this is less true. Prices are set instead by market competition. If Japan's cars are too expensive, Saudi Arabia can buy German cars; if Saudi oil is too expensive, Japan can buy Alaskan oil.

Prices and Markets

The *terms* of an exchange are defined by the price at which goods are traded. Often the *bargaining space*—defined by the difference between the lowest price a seller would accept and the highest price a buyer would pay—is quite large. For example, Saudi Arabia would be willing to sell a barrel of oil (if it had no better option) for as little as, say, ten dollars a barrel, and industrialized countries are willing to pay as much as fifty dollars a barrel for the oil. (In practice, oil prices have fluctuated in this broad range in recent decades.) How are prices determined within this range? That is, how do the participants decide on the distribution of benefits from the exchange?

When there are multiple buyers and sellers of a good (or equivalent goods that can be substituted for it), prices are determined by market competition. In terms of the bargaining framework we have been using, sellers bargain for a high price, using as leverage the threat to sell to a different buyer. Meanwhile buyers bargain for a low price, with the leverage being a threat to buy from a different seller. In practice, free markets are supposed to (and sometimes do) produce stable patterns of buying and selling at a fairly uniform price, which is the *market price*. At this price, sellers know that an effort to raise the price would drive the buyer to seek a different seller, and buyers know that an effort to lower the price would drive the seller to seek a different buyer. Because of this stability, the process of bargaining is greatly simplified and most economic exchanges take place in a fairly routine manner.

Buyers vary in the value they place on an item (like a barrel of oil); if the price rises, fewer people are willing to buy it, and if the price drops, more people are willing to buy it. This is called the *demand curve* for the item. Sellers also vary in the value they place on the item. If the price rises, more sellers are willing to supply the item to buyers; if the price drops, fewer sellers are willing to supply the item. This is called the *supply curve*.

In a free market, the price at which the supply and demand curves cross is the *equilibrium* price. At this price sellers are willing to supply the same number of units that buyers are willing to purchase. (In practice, prices reflect *expectations* about supply and demand in the near future.) In a trade of Saudi oil for Japanese cars, for example, the prices would be determined by the world demand for, and supply of, oil and cars.

This means that in liberal economics, *bilateral* relations between states are less important than they are in security affairs. The existence of world markets reduces the leverage that one state can exert over another in economic affairs (because the second state can simply find other partners). Imagine Japan trying to exert power by refusing to sell cars to Saudi Arabia. It would only hurt itself; Saudi Arabia would just buy cars elsewhere. In IPE, then, power is more diffuse and involves more actors at once than in international security.

The *currency* in which world prices are expressed is somewhat arbitrary. Prices were once pegged to the value of gold or silver. Now prices are expressed in national currencies, most prominently the U.S. dollar, Japanese yen, and German mark. In practice, the conversions of money among national currencies is complex (see Chapter 9), but for the sake of simplicity we may proceed as if there were a common currency.

Centrally Planned Economies

One major alternative to a market economy is a **centrally planned** (or *command*) **economy,** in which political authorities set prices and decide on quotas for production and consumption of each commodity according to a long-term plan. This type of economy was for decades the standard in the communist states of the former Soviet Union, Eastern Europe, China, and several smaller countries (it is still in place in Cuba and North Korea). Within the Soviet economic bloc (which included Eastern Europe and Mongolia), international trade also took place at government-controlled prices.

The proponents of central planning claimed it would make economies both more rational and more just. By controlling the economy, governments could guarantee the basic needs of citizens (as in China's "iron rice bowl" policy under Chairman Mao) and could mobilize the state fully for war if necessary (as the Soviet Union did in World War II under Stalin). Proponents of central planning also hoped that government's long-term view of resources and needs would smooth out the business cycles and avoid the recessions that periodically afflict capitalist economies.

Instead, communist economics has in recent years been discredited as hopelessly inefficient and discarded in whole or in part by virtually all of its former followers. The economies of Russia and Eastern Europe stagnated over the Cold War decades while environmental damage and military spending both took an increasing economic toll. Now the

East German Trabant—discarded as Germany unified—in East Berlin, 1990. The unreliable, polluting Trabant reflected the inefficiency of production in the centrally planned economies of the communist countries during the Cold War. All those countries are now making transitions—by various routes and with various degrees of success—toward market-based economies.

former Soviet republics and Eastern Europe are almost all trying to make a *transition* to a market-based economy connected to the world capitalist economy.[11] This transition has proven very difficult. In the first half of the 1990s, the total GDP of the region *shrank* by about *35 percent*—a great depression worse than the one the United States experienced in the early 1930s (see p. 373). Living standards dropped dramatically for most citizens. A program of *shock therapy*—a radical, sudden shift over to market principles—seemed to work in Poland despite short-term dislocation. But a similar program in Russia stalled (or was effectively blocked by old-time Communist officials).

China, whose government continues to follow a Marxist *political* line (central control by the Communist party), has shifted substantially toward a market *economy*.[12] This transition dramatically increased China's economic growth in the 1980s, reaching an annual rate of 8 percent in 1991 and 13 percent in 1992 and 1993 (see "The Chinese Experi-

[11]Aslund, Anders. *How Russia Became a Market Economy*. Washington, DC: The Brookings Institution, 1995. Hewett, Ed A., with Clifford G. Gaddy. *Open for Business: Russia's Return to the Global Economy*. Washington, DC: The Brookings Institution, 1992. Haus, Leah A. *Globalizing the GATT: The Soviet Union's Successor States, Eastern Europe, and the International Trading System*. Washington, DC: The Brookings Institution, 1992.

[12]Jacobson, Harold K., and Michel Oksenberg. *China's Participation in the IMF, the World Bank, and GATT: Toward a Global Economic Order*. Ann Arbor: University of Michigan Press, 1990.

ence" on pp. 514–516). Perhaps because China is not yet industrialized (and hence more flexible about how it invests capital profitably), the introduction of market principles in China's economy has been less painful than in the (mal)developed economies of Russia and Eastern Europe.

Today, the world's economic activity follows the principles of free markets more than central planning but often falls somewhere between the extremes. Many governments control domestic prices on some goods (for instance, subsidizing certain goods to win political support). Many states *own* (all or part of) industries thought to be vital for the national economy—**state-owned industries** such as oil production companies or national airlines. There are also types of goods, such as electricity service, where it would be inefficient for competing suppliers to provide the good (each with its own transmission lines running along the street); in such cases governments often regulate prices or supply the service themselves. Furthermore the government sector of the economy (military spending, road building, Social Security, and so on) make up a substantial fraction of the industrialized countries' economies. Because they contain both some government control and some private ownership, the economies of the industrialized West are called **mixed economies.**

Politics of Markets

A free and efficient market requires a fairly large number of buyers looking for the same item and a large number of sellers supplying it. It also requires that participants have fairly complete information about the other participants and transactions in the market. Also, the willingness of participants to deal with each other should not be distorted by personal (or political) preferences but should be governed only by price and quality considerations. Failures to meet these various conditions are called *market imperfections;* they reduce efficiency (to the dismay of liberal economists). Most political intrusions into economic transactions are market imperfections.

International trade occurs more often at world market prices than does *domestic* economic exchange. There is no world government to own industries, provide subsidies, or regulate prices. Nonetheless, world markets are often affected by politics. For one thing, when states are the principal actors in international economic affairs, the number of participants is often small (especially for certain goods). When there is just one supplier of an item—a *monopoly*—the supplier can set the price quite high. An *oligopoly* is a monopoly shared by just a few large sellers—often allowing for tacit or explicit coordination to force the price up. To the extent that companies band together along national lines, monopolies and oligopolies are more likely.

Governments can use antitrust policies to break up monopolies and keep markets competitive. But home governments often *benefit* from the ability of their companies to distort international markets and bring in more revenue (whether those companies are state-owned or just taxed by the state). *Foreign* governments have little power to break up such monopolies.

Another common market imperfection in international trade is *corruption;* individuals may receive payoffs to trade at nonmarket prices. The government or company involved may lose some of the benefits being distributed, but the individual government official or company negotiator gets increased benefits (see pp. 525–527).

Politics provides the *legal framework* for markets—assuring that participants keep their commitments (contracts are binding), that buyers pay for goods they have purchased, that counterfeit money is not used, and so forth. In the international economy, lacking a central government authority, rules are less easily enforced. As in security affairs, such rules can be codified in international treaties, but enforcement depends on practical reciprocity (see pp. 290–292).

Taxation is another political influence on markets. Taxes are used both to generate revenue for the government and as a means of regulating economic activity through incentives. For instance, a government may keep taxes low on foreign companies in hopes of attracting them to locate and invest in the country. Taxes applied to international trade itself are called tariffs, and are a frequent source of international conflict (see "Protectionism" later in this chapter).

Political interference in free markets is most explicit when governments apply *sanctions* against economic interactions of certain kinds or between certain actors. Political power then prohibits an economic exchange that would otherwise have been mutually beneficial. Enforcing sanctions is always a difficult task, because there is an incentive (money to be made) to break the sanctions through black markets or other means.[13] For instance, despite UN sanctions against trading with Serbia in the early 1990s, many people and companies took risks to smuggle goods across Serbia's borders, because doing so was profitable. Without broad multilateral support for international sanctions, they generally fail. For example, when the United States tried to punish the Soviet Union in the 1970s by applying trade sanctions against a Soviet oil pipeline to Western Europe, it did not stop the pipeline. It just took profitable business away from a U.S. company (Caterpillar) and allowed European companies to profit instead (because European states did not join in the sanctions).

The difficulty of applying sanctions reflects a more general point made earlier—that power in IPE is more diffused among states than it is in security affairs. If one state tries to use economic means of leverage (like sanctions) to influence another, other states can profitably take over. Refusing to participate in mutually profitable economic trade often harms oneself more than the target of one's actions, unless nearly all other states follow suit.

Balance of Trade

Mercantilists, as was mentioned, favor political control of trade so that trade relations serve a state's political interests—even at the cost of some lost wealth that free markets might have created. Their preferred means of accomplishing this end is to create a favorable balance of trade. The **balance of trade** refers to the value of a state's imports relative to its exports.

A state that exports more than it imports has a *positive balance of trade*, or *trade surplus*. Japan has run a trade surplus in recent years: it gets more money for the cars and

---

[13]Martin, Lisa L. *Coercive Cooperation: Explaining Multilateral Economic Sanctions.* Princeton: Princeton University Press, 1992. Miyagawa, Makio. *Do Economic Sanctions Work?* New York: St. Martin's Press, 1992. Doxey, Margaret P. *International Sanctions in Contemporary Perspective.* New York: St. Martin's Press, 1987. Baldwin, David A. *Economic Statecraft.* Princeton: Princeton University Press, 1985.

Economic sanctions, such as the UN embargo on trade with Yugoslavia, are among the most obvious ways that politics interferes in markets. But sanctions are hard to enforce because smuggling is profitable. Here is one shipment of fuel going from Albania to Yugoslavia (across the lake) by barge, to support Serbian military operations and the Yugoslavian economy. The flow of fuel was estimated to have reached a million gallons a day at times.

other goods it exports than it pays for oil and other imported goods. By contrast, if a state imports more than it exports, it has a *negative balance of trade (trade deficit)*. (This is different from a budget deficit in government spending, sometimes called simply "the deficit," though the United States runs both trade and budget deficits.) In the early 1990s, the U.S. trade deficit was around $75 billion per year, of which roughly 80 percent was accounted for by trade with Japan, China, and Taiwan.

The balance of trade must ultimately be reconciled, one way or another. It is tracked financially through the system of national accounts (see pp. 365–366). In the short term, a state can trade for a few years at a deficit and then a few years at a surplus. The imbalances are carried on the national accounts as a kind of loan. But a trade deficit that persists for years becomes a problem for the state. For instance, Japan in recent years has run a trade surplus overall (and in U.S.-Japanese bilateral trade) while the United States has run a deficit. To balance trade, the United States then "exports" currency (dollars) to Japan, which can use the dollars to buy such things as shares of U.S. companies, promissory notes from the U.S. government (treasury bills), or U.S. real estate. In essence (oversimplifying a bit), a state with a chronic trade deficit must export part of its standing wealth (real estate, companies, bank accounts, etc.) by giving ownership of such wealth to foreigners.

This is one reason mercantilists favor national economic policies designed to create a trade *surplus.* Then the state can "own" parts of other states, which gives it power over them. Rather than being indebted to others, the state holds IOUs from others. Rather than being unable to find the money it might need someday to cope with a crisis or fight a war, the state sits on a pile of money that represents potential power. Historically, mercantilism literally meant stockpiling gold (gained as a result of running a trade surplus) as a fungible form of power (see Figure 8.2). Such a strategy is attuned to realism's emphasis on relative power. For one state to have a trade surplus, another must have a deficit.

There is a price for mercantilist-derived power. Often a trade surplus lowers the short-term standard of living. For instance, if the Japanese people cashed in their trade surplus each year for imported goods, they could enjoy those goods now instead of piling up money for the future. Mercantilists are willing to pay such short-term costs because they are more concerned with power than with standards of living.

Interdependence

When the well-being of a state depends on the cooperation of a second state, the first state is *dependent* on the second. When two or more states are simultaneously dependent on each other, they are **interdependent.** Interdependence is a political and not just economic phenomenon. When states trade, they become mutually dependent on each other's *political* cooperation in order to realize economic gains through trade.

In IPE, interdependence refers less often to a *bilateral* mutual dependence than to a *multilateral* dependence in which each state depends on the political cooperation of most or all of the others to keep world markets operating efficiently. Most states depend on the world market, not on specific trading partners (though for large industrialized states each bilateral trade relationship is important as well).

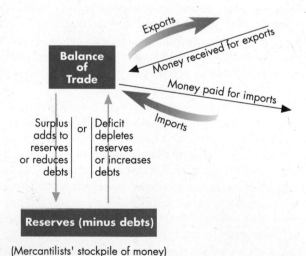

FIGURE 8.2 Balance of Trade

The mutual dependence of two or more states does not mean that their degree of dependence is equal or symmetrical. Often one is more dependent than another. This is especially true because world markets vary in their openness and efficiency from one commodity and region to another. Saudi Arabia, for instance, has more power over the price of oil than Japan has over the price of cars.

The degree of a state's *short-term* dependence on another may differ from its *long-term* dependence. The short-term dislocation that would be caused by disrupting exchange with another country has been called the *sensitivity* of supply. For example, when oil prices rose sharply in the early 1970s, Japan and other industrialized states did not have policies in place to cope with the increases: they were *sensitive* to the disruption, and long lines formed at gas stations as a result. Over the longer term, states may be able to change their policies to take advantage of alternatives that could substitute for disrupted trade. For instance, Japan expanded nuclear power in response to oil price increases—a long-term strategy. A state that *cannot* adjust its policies to cope with disrupted trade, even over the long run, suffers from *vulnerability* of supply.[14]

Over time, as the world economy develops and technology advances, states are becoming *increasingly interdependent*. Some IR scholars point out that this is not entirely new. The great powers were very interdependent before World War I; for instance, international trade was about the same percentage of GDP then as now. But several other dimensions of interdependence show dramatic change. One is the extent to which individual *firms*, which used to be nationally based, now are international in their holdings and interests (becoming MNCs), which makes them dependent on the well-being of other states in addition to their home state and makes them tend to favor free trade.[15]

Another key aspect of interdependence is the tight integration of world markets through the ever-expanding flow of *information* and communication worldwide (see pp. 405–414). This facilitates the free competition of goods and services in global markets as well as the expanding volume of money (capital) that moves around the world every day. Yet another dimension of change is the expansion of *scope* in the global economy, from one based in Europe to a more diffuse network encompassing the world. The rise of China and Southeast Asia, and the integration of Russia and Eastern Europe into the world market economy in the 1990s, are accelerating this trend.

Whether based on a specific bilateral trading relationship, an integrated global (or regional) market, or the international nature of corporate holdings, interdependence arises from comparative advantage—that is, from the greater absolute wealth that two or more states can produce by collaborating. This wealth depends on international political cooperation, which is therefore in the interests of all participants. Furthermore, violence is usually not an effective leverage in bringing about such cooperation. Thus, many IR scholars argue that *interdependence inherently promotes peace*.[16] It alters the cost-benefit calculations of national leaders so as to make military leverage less attractive. (Some IR

---

[14]Keohane, Robert O., and Joseph S. Nye. *Power and Interdependence*. 2nd ed. New York: HarperCollins, 1989.

[15]Milner, Helen V. *Resisting Protectionism: Global Industries and the Politics of International Trade*. Princeton: Princeton University Press, 1988.

[16]Mansfield, Edward D. *Power, Trade, and War*. Princeton: Princeton University Press, 1994.

Trade is increasing interdependence among states. Interdependence may promote peace, by making the severing of a relationship too expensive to be rational. For example, some scholars expect U.S.-Chinese relations to be more cooperative as a result of those states' increasing trade. Here U.S. trade negotiator and Chinese trade minister announce agreement that averted a trade war, 1995.

scholars saw similar trends in international interdependence just before World War I, but war occurred anyway.)

Despite the added wealth that states enjoy as a result of trade and the power that such wealth creates, interdependence does have drawbacks. The more a state gains from trade cooperation, the more its own well-being depends on other states, which therefore have power over it. In situations of asymmetrical interdependence, in particular, the economic benefits of cooperation may come with inherent vulnerabilities. For example, it is cheaper for Japan to import energy than to produce it domestically, but dependence on energy imports has historically put Japan at a disadvantage in terms of international power. In the 1930s, the United States cut off its oil exports to Japan to protest Japanese foreign policy. Similarly, in the two world wars, Britain and Germany blockaded each other's food imports in an effort to turn dependence on imports into a power element. Exports as well as imports can create dependence; UN sanctions against Iraq's oil exports deprived it of revenue after its 1990 invasion of Kuwait.

Interdependence thus ties the well-being of a state's population and society to policies and conditions in other states, outside its control. The price of trade-generated wealth (and the power it brings) is a loss of state autonomy and sovereignty. These problems are intensifying as world markets become more closely interwoven, especially in regional integration such as in Europe (see Chapter 10).

As states become more interdependent, power is becoming more, not less, important in IR. The intensification of linkages among states multiplies the number of issues affecting the relations of states and the avenues of influence by which outcomes are shaped. It is true that because power operates on multiple complex dimensions in a highly interdependent world, the importance of one dimension—military power—is gradually diminishing relative to other means of influence (diplomatic, economic, cultural, etc.). But the overall importance of international power on all dimensions combined is increasing as the world becomes more interdependent.

❖ TRADE STRATEGIES

To manage these trade-offs of gains and losses in power and wealth, states develop economic strategies—trade strategies in particular—that seek to maximize their own wealth while minimizing their vulnerability and dependence on others. Some strategies can be implemented by single states; most involve participation in some broader framework.

Autarky

One obvious way to avoid becoming dependent on other states, especially for weak states whose trading partners would tend to be more powerful, is to avoid trading altogether and instead try to produce everything one needs by oneself. Such a strategy is called *self-reliance* or **autarky**. As the theory of comparative advantage would suggest, such a policy has proven ineffective. A self-reliant state pays a very high cost to produce goods for which it does not have a comparative advantage. Meanwhile, other states can cooperate among themselves to maximize their joint creation of wealth—so an autarkic state tends to be left further and further behind. Over time its relative power in the international system falls.

In practice, when states have relied on a policy of autarky they have indeed lagged behind others. A classic case in recent decades was the small state of Albania, next to Yugoslavia and near Italy. When the communist giants China and the Soviet Union split in the 1960s, Albania's communist government alone sided with China, putting Albania at odds with both its Western and Eastern European neighbors. Albania did not participate in world markets but relied on a centrally planned economy designed for self-sufficiency. Then, in the 1970s, Albania split from China as well, becoming totally isolated. Few foreigners were allowed to visit, little trade took place, and Albania pursued autarky to prevent outsiders from gaining power over it. Around 1991, when this curtain of isolation finally fell, Albania looked about the same as it had decades earlier. Little additional wealth had been generated; little economic development had taken place. It was among the weakest of the European countries, East or West.

China's experience also illustrates the problems with autarky. China's economic isolation in the 1950s and 1960s, resulting from an economic embargo imposed by the United States and its allies, was deepened during its own Cultural Revolution in the late 1960s when it broke ties with the Soviet Union as well. In that period, all things foreign were rejected. For instance, Chinese computer programmers were not allowed to use foreign software such as Assembler language and Fortran—standards in the rest of the world. Instead they had to create all software from scratch; China would not depend on foreigners for goods, services, or technology. As a result, the computer industry lagged far behind, "reinventing the wheel," as the world's computer industry sped ahead.

When China opened up to the world economy in 1980s, the pattern was reversed. The rapid expansion of trade, along with some market-oriented reforms in its domestic economy, resulted in rapid economic growth, which continued into the mid-1990s.

Protectionism

Although few states pursue strategies of autarky, many states try to manipulate international trade in such a manner as to strengthen one or more domestic industries and shelter them from world markets. Such policies are broadly known as **protectionism**—protection of domestic industries against international competition. Although this term encompasses a variety of trade policies arising from various motivations, all are contrary to liberalism in that they seek to distort free markets to gain some advantage for the state (or substate actors within it), generally by discouraging imports of competing goods or services.[17]

Government policies that discourage imports can help domestic industries or communities avoid the costs that would come with full participation in world markets. As was mentioned earlier, those costs often fall disproportionately on a small part of the population, which often leads that group to pressure the government for protection. The benefits of greater global efficiency, by contrast, are spread more broadly across the population and do not create similar pressures in domestic politics.

A state's *motivation* to protect domestic industry can arise from several sources. Often governments simply cater to the political demands of important domestic industries and interests, regardless of the overall national interest. An industry may lobby or give campaign contributions in order to win special tax breaks, subsidies, or restrictions on competing imports (see "Industries and Interest Groups" later in this chapter).

States often attempt to protect an *infant industry* as it starts up in the state for the first time, until it can compete on world markets. For instance, when South Korea first developed an automobile industry, it was not yet competitive with imports from Japan, the United States, and Europe. Under protectionism, South Korean consumers were in effect given incentives to buy more Korean-built Hyundais and fewer Toyotas and Fords. From this sales base, Hyundai developed in size and experience until eventually it was able to compete with foreign producers and even to export Hyundais profitably to the United States and other countries. In a number of poor states, the *textile* trade has been a favored infant industry (adding value without heavy capital requirements) that governments have protected.[18] Protection of infant industry is considered a relatively legitimate reason for (temporary) protectionism.

---

[17]Goldstein, Judith. The Political Economy of Trade: Institutions of Protection. *American Political Science Review* 80 (1), 1986: 161–84.

[18]Aggarwal, Vinod K. *Liberal Protectionism: The International Politics of Organized Textile Trade.* Berkeley: University of California Press, 1985.

Another motivation for protection is to give a domestic industry breathing room when market conditions shift or new competitors arrive on the scene. Sometimes domestic industry requires time to adapt and can emerge a few years later in a healthy condition. For instance, when gas prices jumped in the 1970s, U.S. auto producers were slow to adapt by shifting toward smaller cars, and smaller Japanese cars gained a great advantage in the U.S. market. The U.S. government used a variety of measures, including import quotas and loan guarantees, to help the U.S. industry through this transition.

Another motivation is the protection of industry considered vital to national security. For example, in the 1980s U.S. officials sought to protect the U.S. electronics and computer industries against being driven out of business by Japanese competitors, because those industries were considered crucial to military production. A government-sponsored consortium of U.S. computer-chip companies called Sematech was formed to promote the U.S. capability to produce chips cheaply (ordinarily the government would discourage such a consortium as an antitrust violation). Likewise, in the machine-tool industry (equipment for cutting metal) the U.S. government extended protection in the 1980s for fear of losing a militarily important asset. Autarky may not pay in most economic activities, but for military goods states are often willing to sacrifice some economic efficiency for the sake of self-sufficiency. Then in the event of war the state will be less vulnerable.

Finally, protection may be motivated by a defensive effort to ward off predatory practices by foreign companies or states. Predatory generally refers to efforts to unfairly capture a large share of world markets, or even a near-monopoly, so that eventually the predator can raise prices without fearing competition. Most often this entails **dumping** products in foreign markets at prices below the minimum level necessary to make a profit. For instance, Japan was accused in 1992 of dumping minivans on the U.S. market. How can a company make money selling its products below cost, and why would the importing state complain about getting such a good deal? It is indeed a good deal for U.S. consumers in the short term, but it weakens the competing U.S. automobile industry over the longer term. The reason a state would want its companies to dump products in foreign markets is that money lost in the short term could lead to dominance of a market, which eventually lets the state raise prices enough to recoup its losses and to profit more.

Within a domestic economy, the government can use antitrust laws to break up an impending monopoly, but in IR no such mechanism exists, so governments try to restrict imports in such situations to protect their state's industries. Such restrictions are recognized as legitimate, but there are great disagreements about whether a given price level is predatory or merely competitive.

Just as there are several motivations for protectionism, so too governments use several methods to restrict imports. The simplest is a **tariff** (or **duty**) on certain types of imported goods. This is a tax imposed on goods (usually as a percentage of their value) as they enter the country. Tariffs not only restrict imports but can be an important source of state revenues as well. If a state is going to engage in protectionism, international norms favor tariffs as the preferred method of protection because they are straightforward and not hidden (see "The GATT (World Trade Organization)" later in this chapter). Most states maintain a long and complex schedule of tariffs, based on thousands of categories and subcategories of goods organized by industry.

Other means to discourage imports are called **nontariff barriers** to trade. Imports can be limited by a *quota*. Quotas are ceilings on how many goods of a certain kind can be im-

Protectionism uses various means to keep foreign imports from competing fairly with domestic products. Japan prevented the import of U.S. rice for over twenty-five years, until partly lifting the ban in 1993. Here the first U.S. rice arrives in 1993.

ported; they are imposed to restrict the growth of such imports. The extreme version is a flat prohibition against importing a certain type of good (or goods from a certain country). The U.S. government used quotas to restrict the number of Japanese-made cars that could enter the United States in the 1980s, when the U.S. automobile industry was losing ground rapidly to Japanese imports. Most of those quotas were *voluntary* in that Japan and the United States negotiated a level that both could live with. A disadvantage of this type of numerical quota (based on number, not value, of cars) is that Japan could raise the price on its cars (demand remained while supply was restricted) and shift its exports toward more expensive cars (such as the Lexus rather than the Tercel). This increased the profits of Japanese automakers relative to their U.S. counterparts. Partly using these profits, Japanese companies then set up their own factories within the United States. These competed effectively with the U.S. automobile companies. U.S. jobs, but not U.S. companies, were protected.

A third way to protect domestic industry—in addition to tariffs and quotas—is through *subsidies* to a domestic industry, which allow it to lower its prices without losing money. Such subsidies are very extensive in, but not limited to, state-owned industries. Subsidies can be funneled to industries in a variety of ways. A state can give *tax breaks* to an industry struggling to get established or facing strong foreign competition. Or it can make *loans* (or government guarantees of private loans) on favorable terms to companies in a threatened industry. Sometimes governments buy goods from domestic producers at high *guaranteed prices* and resell them on world markets at lower prices; the European Community does this with agricultural products, to the dismay of U.S. farmers.

Fourth, imports can be restricted by various *restrictions and regulations* that make it hard to distribute and market a product even though it can be imported. For instance, in marketing U.S. products in Japan, U.S. manufacturers often complain of complex bureaucratic regulations and the tight system of corporate alliances funneling the supply of parts from Japanese suppliers to Japanese manufacturers. Imports can also be discouraged by restricting a foreign manufacturer's ability to advertise in local markets. Finally, of course, when a state nationalizes an entire industry, such as oil production or banking, foreign competition is shut out.

Sometimes a country's culture, rather than state action, discourages foreign imports. The citizens may (with or without government encouragement) follow a philosophy of *economic nationalism*—the use of economics to influence international power and relative standing in the international system (a form of mercantilism). For example, many U.S. citizens ignore the advice of liberal economists to buy the best car they can find at the best price, regardless of where it is produced—to participate freely in an international marketplace. Many U.S. citizens prefer instead to "Buy American" even if it means paying a bit more for an equivalent product. Although such a bias reduces the overall efficiency of world production, it does result in more of the benefits being distributed to U.S. workers. In Japan, consumers have shown a preference for Japanese-made products even when their government has urged them to buy more imported goods (to reduce Japanese trade frictions with the United States).

Protectionism has both positive and negative effects on an economy, most often helping producers but hurting consumers. For instance, although U.S. automobile manufacturers were aided somewhat by the restrictions imposed on Japanese imports in the 1980s, U.S. automobile consumers paid more for cars as a result (several hundred dollars more per car by some estimates). The costs to consumers may outweigh the benefits to producers (as liberal economists stress), but those costs are spread among millions of households, whereas the benefits are concentrated on a few firms, which are more motivated and politically more powerful.

Another problem with protectionism is that domestic industry may use protection to avoid needed improvements and may therefore remain inefficient and uncompetitive—especially if protection continues over many years. When the U.S. steel industry was protected against cheap imports in the late 1970s, it had little incentive to improve quality and efficiency. Only the 1982 recession, which caused a painful crisis in the steel industry, triggered improvements that made the industry more competitive.

Although it violates liberal principles, temporary protectionism can have a stabilizing effect under certain conditions. For example, when U.S. motorcycle manufacturer Harley-Davidson lost half its U.S. market share in just four years, the U.S. government imposed tariffs on imported Japanese motorcycles such as Hondas. The tariffs started at 45 percent in 1983; they were to decline each year for five years and then be eliminated. With the clock running and the tariffs decreasing each year, Harley scrambled to improve efficiency and raise quality. As a result, Harley regained its market share and the tariffs were lifted a year early. In the late 1980s a reinvigorated Harley raised its market share even more and began exporting Harleys to Japan. Protectionism worked in this case because it was short-term and straightforward. Most protectionist policies are longer-term, more complex, and more likely to backfire.

Industries and Interest Groups

As has been mentioned, industries and other domestic political actors often seek to influence a state's foreign economic policies (see "Interest Groups" on pp. 153–156).[19] These pressures do not always favor protectionism. Industries that are advanced and competitive in world markets often try to influence their governments to adopt free-trade policies. This strategy promotes a global free-trade system in which such industries can prosper. By contrast, industries that lag behind their global competitors tend to seek government restrictions on imports or other forms of protection.

Means to influence foreign economic policy include lobbying, forming PACs, paying bribes, even encouraging coups. Actors include industry-sponsored groups, companies, labor unions, and individuals (from corporate executives to factory workers). Within an industry, such efforts usually work in a common direction because, despite the competition among companies and between management and labor, all share common interests regarding the trade policies that affect the industry. However, a different industry may be pushing in a different direction. For instance, some U.S. industries supported the North American Free Trade Agreement (NAFTA); others opposed it.

A good example of how competing domestic interests can pull in opposite directions on state trade policy is U.S. tobacco exports. U.S. companies have a comparative advantage globally in producing cigarettes. As the U.S. market for cigarettes shrank in the 1980s (due to education about the dangers of smoking), manufacturers became more aggressive in marketing U.S. cigarettes overseas. They challenged regulations in foreign countries restricting cigarette advertising, claiming that these regulations were protectionist measures aimed at excluding a U.S. product from lucrative markets. Often the foreign government had a state-owned tobacco industry, which the U.S. companies saw as being unfairly favored. In the late 1980s, the U.S. government sided with the U.S. tobacco companies and pressed foreign states to open their markets to U.S. cigarettes, threatening retaliatory trade measures if they refused. Health groups like the American Cancer Society opposed such U.S. policies, which they saw as unethical since they contributed to creating a future health nightmare in third-world countries whose smoking rates went up as incomes rose. Thus, the conflicting interests of domestic interest groups came to bear on policy regarding this issue.

In many countries, government not only *responds* to industry influence, but works actively *with* industries to promote their growth and tailor trade policy to their needs.[20]

[19]Simmons, Beth A. *Who Adjusts? Domestic Sources of Foreign Economic Policy During the Interwar Years*. Princeton: Princeton University Press, 1994. Ikenberry, G. John, David A. Lake, and Michael Mastanduno, eds. The State and American Foreign Economic Policy [special issue]. *International Organization* 42 (1), 1988. Destler, I. M. *American Trade Politics*. 2nd ed. Washington, DC: Institute for International Economics, 1992. Katzenstein, Peter J., ed. *Between Power and Plenty: Foreign Economic Policies of Advanced Industrial States*. Madison: University of Wisconsin Press, 1978. Verdier, Daniel. *Democracy and International Trade: Britain, France, and the United States, 1860–1990*. Princeton: Princeton University Press, 1994.

[20]Strange, Susan. *States and Markets: An Introduction to International Political Economy*. 2nd ed. New York: St. Martin's Press, 1994.

Such **industrial policy** is especially common in states where one or two industries are crucial to the entire economy (and of course where states own industries directly). But it is becoming a major issue in economic relations among great powers as well.[21] In Japan (where industries are mostly not state-owned), the government coordinates industrial policy through the powerful *Ministry of International Trade and Industry (MITI)*. MITI tries to plan an overall strategy to take best advantage of Japan's strengths and to direct capital and technology into promising areas. It has had both successes and failures in recent decades. In the Clinton administration, the United States is moving toward a more active industrial policy.

Interest groups not organized along industry lines also have particular interests in state trade policies. U.S. environmentalists, for example, do not want U.S. companies to use the free-trade agreement to avoid pollution controls by relocating to Mexico (where environmental laws are less strict). U.S. labor unions do not want companies to use the free-trade agreement to avoid paying high wages. However, Mexican-American citizens' groups in the United States tend to support the free-trade agreement because it strengthens ties to relatives in Mexico.

Several industries are particularly important in trade negotiations in the 1990s. First is *agriculture,* which has traditionally been protected from foreign competition on grounds that self-sufficiency in food reduces national vulnerability (especially in time of war). Although such security concerns have now faded somewhat, farmers are well-organized and powerful domestic political actors in Japan, Europe, the United States, and other countries. For instance, farmers are a key constituency in the Liberal Democratic Party (LDP), which governed Japan for decades. The farmers exercise greater political influence than their numbers would suggest, and they naturally tend to think that the soul of Japan would be wounded if rice (an important part of the culture) were freely imported. In France, farmers enjoy wide political support and have a huge stake in the trade policies of the European Community; subsidies to farmers in France (and elsewhere in Europe) protect them against competition from U.S. farmers.

Intellectual property rights are a second contentious area of trade negotiations in the 1990s. Intellectual property rights are the rights of creators of books, films, computer software, and similar products to receive royalties when their products are sold. The United States has a major conflict with some third-world states over *piracy* of computer software, music, films, and other creative works—products in which the United States has a strong comparative advantage globally. It is technically easy and cheap to copy such works and sell them in violation of the copyright, patent, or trademark. Because U.S. laws cannot be enforced in foreign countries, the U.S. government wants foreign governments to prevent and punish such violations. In 1991, the United States threatened China with punitive tariffs unless China enforced a new copyright law. An agreement was reached in

[21]Tyson, Laura D'Andrea. *Who's Bashing Whom?: Trade Conflict in High Technology Industries*. Washington, DC: Institute for International Economics, 1992. Thurow, Lester. *Head to Head: The Coming Economic Battle Among Japan, Europe, and America*. New York: Morrow, 1992. Hart, Jeffrey A. *Rival Capitalists: International Competitiveness in the United States, Japan, and Western Europe*. Ithaca: Cornell University Press, 1993. Rapkin, David P., and William P. Avery, eds. National Competitiveness in a Global Economy. Boulder, CO: Lynne Rienner, 1994. Bergsten, C. Fred, and Marcus Noland. *Reconcilable Differences? United States–Japan Economic Conflict*. Washington, DC: Institute for International Economics, 1993. Katzenstein, Peter J. *Small States in World Markets: Industrial Policy in Europe*. Ithaca: Cornell University Press, 1985.

1992, but lack of progress led to (not over) the brink of a trade war in 1995. In addition to China, countries that reportedly pirate large amounts of computer software and music and entertainment products include Taiwan, India, Thailand, and the former Soviet Union. Infringement of intellectual property rights is widespread in many third-world countries, on products ranging from videotaped movies to prescription drugs.

Companies trying to protect intellectual property in an international context cannot rely on enforcement of rules the way they can in domestic contexts. They need to bring their own state's government to bear, as well as using their own resources. For example, Microsoft Corporation's MS-DOS is one of the world's most profitable software products. In 1991 Microsoft added a hologram (three-dimensional image) to the package and manual to thwart software pirates, who were making an estimated $1 billion per year in unauthorized copies of Microsoft products. But within weeks a Taiwan-based counterfeiting ring commissioned a firm in China to produce fake holograms, and in a few months the pirates had assembled hundreds of thousands of fake MS-DOS packages in five languages and sold them in countries from Germany to Singapore to the United States—costing Microsoft up to $150 million. Not trusting foreign governments to act vigorously, Mi-

Intellectual property rights have been an important focus of recent trade negotiations. Here the U.S. film *Platoon* is being shown in Japan, and it is likely the owners of rights to the film are being paid royalties. The same film sold on videotape in Russia or the third world would frequently be a pirated version, without royalties being paid.

crosoft hired private investigators in four countries to track down the ring, and received partial cooperation from the governments in Taiwan and China in halting the operation. But Taiwan would not prosecute the alleged ringleader, and China balked at giving Microsoft the valuable fake hologram molds seized in a raid. Representatives of the U.S. Commerce Department accompanied Microsoft's lawyer in negotiating with the Chinese government for the return of the molds. Because of state sovereignty in legal matters, private international economic conflicts easily become government-to-government issues.[22]

Another key trade issue is the openness of countries to trade in the **service sector** of the economy. This sector includes many services, especially those concerning information, but the key focus in international trade negotiations is on *banking, insurance,* and related *financial services*. U.S. companies enjoy a comparative advantage in these areas because of their information-processing technologies and experience in financial management. The North American Free Trade Agreement will, for the first time in decades, allow U.S. banks and insurance companies to operate in Mexico. In general, as telecommunications become cheaper and more pervasive, services offered by companies in one country can be efficiently used by consumers in other countries.

Another especially important industry in international trade is the *arms trade*, which operates largely outside of the framework of normal commercial transactions because of its national security implications.[23] Governments in industrialized countries want to protect their domestic arms industries rather than rely on imports to meet their weapons needs. And those domestic arms industries become stronger and more economically viable by exporting their products (as well as supplying their own governments). Governments usually participate actively in the military-industrial sector of the economy, even in countries such as the United States that lack industrial policy in other economic sectors (see "The Military-Industrial Complex" on pp. 156–158). Even when arms-exporting countries agree in principle to try to limit arms exports to a region—as the great powers did for the Middle East in 1991—they have found it extremely difficult to give up the power and profits that such arms exports bring.

Major weapons like fighter jets are another class of products for which the United States enjoys a global comparative advantage. Indeed, the United States dominates the sale of arms to the global South, with over 70 percent of such sales in 1993 ($15 billion worth, of which $12 billion was to Saudi Arabia and Kuwait). Britain and Russia were far behind, with about 10 percent each. But generally the third-world arms market (two-thirds of the world arms trade) declined from $60 billion in 1988 to $20 billion in 1993, with Soviet/Russian sales dropping from over $25 billion to just $1 billion. The Middle East has been and still is the leading arms-importing region.

Illicit Trade A somewhat different kind of problem is presented by the "industry" of illicit trade, or *smuggling*. No matter what restrictions governments put on trading certain goods, someone is usually willing to risk punishment to make a profit in such trade. Smuggling exists because it is profitable to sell fake Taiwanese copies of MS-DOS in Germany, or Colombian cocaine in the United States, even though these products are

---

[22]King, Harriet. Microsoft Nails Some Pirates. *The New York Times*, May 10, 1992: F7.

[23]Richardson, J. David. The Political Economy of Strategic Trade Policy [review essay]. *International Organization* 44 (1), 1990: 107–34.

illegal in those countries. Even with legal goods, profits can be increased by evading tariffs (by moving goods secretly, mislabeling them, or bribing customs officials).

Illegal goods, and legal goods imported illegally, often are sold in *black markets*, which are unofficial (sometimes secret) markets. Black markets are widespread, and flourish particularly in economies heavily regulated by government, such as centrally planned economies. In many third-world countries, black markets make up a substantial fraction of the total economic activity (though it is hard to measure), and deprive the government of significant revenue. Black markets also exist for foreign currency exchange (see Chapter 9).

The extent of illicit trade varies from one country and industry to another, depending on profitability and enforcement. Drugs and weapons are most profitable, and worldwide illegal trade networks exist for both. International black markets for weapons trade, beyond government controls, are notorious. A state with enough money can buy—although at premium prices—most kinds of weapons.

In illicit trade, different states have different interests in enforcing political control over the trade. For instance, in illegal arms exports, the exporting state may gain economically from the trade and the importing state gains access to the weapons; the losers are the other exporters that neither got the export revenue nor kept the weapons out of the hands of the importer. Thus, illicit trade often creates conflicts of interest among states and leads to complex political bargaining among governments, each looking after its own interests.

Cooperation in Trade

Successful trade strategies are those that achieve mutual gains from cooperation with other states, without being taken advantage of by those states. A global system of free trade is a collective good. In the absence of a world government, the benefits of trade depend on international cooperation—to enforce contracts, prevent monopolies, and discourage protectionism. A single state can profitably subsidize its own state-owned industries, create its own monopolies, or erect barriers to competitive imports as long as not too many other states do the same thing. If other states break the rules of free trade as well, the benefits of free exchange slip away from all parties involved.

As with international law generally, economic agreements between states depend strongly on reciprocity for enforcement (see pp. 64–66, 291). If one state protects its industries, or puts tariffs on the goods of other states, or violates the copyright on works produced in other countries, the main resort that other states have is to apply similar measures against the offending state. The use of reciprocity to enforce equal terms of exchange is especially important in international trade, where states often negotiate complex agreements—commodity by commodity, industry by industry—based on reciprocity.[24]

Enforcement of fair trade is complicated by differing interpretations of what is fair. States generally decide what practices of other states they consider unfair (often prodded

---

[24]Bayard, Thomas O., Kimberly Ann Elliott, Amelia Porges, and Charles Iceland. *Reciprocity and Retaliation in U.S. Trade Policy.* Washington, DC: Institute for International Economics, 1994. Rhodes, Carolyn. Reciprocity in Trade: The Utility of a Bargaining Strategy. *International Organization* 43 (2), 1989: 273–300.

Trade cooperation depends on reciprocity for "enforcement." For example, when U.S. producers complain of being excluded from Japanese markets, they pressure the U.S. government to exclude Japanese products from U.S. markets in return. Through multiple threats and deals, U.S. trade negotiators have won openings in Japan's food market, but less so in auto parts. Opening Japan's construction industry is a current goal of U.S. negotiators.

by affected domestic industries) and then take (or threaten) retaliatory actions to punish those practices. For instance, a U.S. law, the Super 301 provision, mandates retaliation against states that restrict access of U.S. goods to their markets. However, if the other state does not agree that its practices were unfair, the retaliatory actions may themselves seem unfair and call for counterretaliation. One disadvantage of reciprocity is that it can lead to a downward spiral of noncooperation, popularly called a trade war (the economic equivalent of the arms races discussed on pp. 65–66). To prevent this, states often negotiate agreements regarding what practices they consider unfair. In some cases, third-party arbitration can also be used to resolve trade disputes.

Retaliation for unfair trade practices usually is based on an attempt to match the violation in type and extent. For instance, European barriers to U.S. food exports have caused the United States to raise barriers to food imports from Europe. In the early 1990s, U.S. soybean growers complained to the U.S. government that their cattle-feed products were suffering in European markets due to the European Community's subsidies to farmers. An arbitration panel set up under GATT (discussed shortly) ruled in early 1992 against the European subsidies, permitting U.S. retaliation if Europe did not lower the barriers. The U.S. government then threatened to impose tariffs of up to 100 percent on $1 billion of imported European "fine foods" such as wine and cheese.

The list of targeted European products drawn up by the U.S. trade representative included $2 billion of *possible* target imports—focused especially on French products because French farmers were considered the main political force behind the European agricultural subsidies. The process of imposing the tariffs was extended over several months to allow negotiations to proceed. In late 1992, at the last minute, the U.S. and European Community negotiators reached agreement on the phased reduction of European subsidies and a trade war was averted.

In cases of dumping, retaliation is aimed at offsetting the advantage enjoyed by goods imported at prices below the world market. Retaliatory tariffs raise the price back to market levels. For example, U.S. automakers complained to the U.S. government in 1991 that Japanese carmakers were dumping minivans on the U.S. market at below-production cost, in an aggressive effort to take away market share from U.S. producers in one of their few remaining areas of strength. (U.S. producers held 88 percent of the U.S. minivan market, but Japanese producers had gone from 3 to 12 percent in three years.) In 1992 the Commerce Department ruled that Mazda had sold minivans in the United States at 12.7 percent below fair market value and Toyota had sold minivans at 6.75 percent below fair market value. It proposed the use of tariffs to raise prices by these amounts, back to market levels.

Before such tariffs are imposed, another U.S. government agency, the *International Trade Commission (ITC)*, determines whether the low-priced imports have actually hurt the U.S. industry.[25] In the meantime, importers must put down deposits with the government equal to the difference from market prices—about $1000 to $2000 per van in this case. The ITC ruled that U.S. automakers had indeed been hurt, even though the minivans were still profitable at prices pulled down by Japanese imports. The deposits were kept, and tariffs were imposed on the imported minivans. As a result, U.S. consumers paid substantially more for both domestic and imported minivans.

In this case, there was no third-party ruling as in the European farm subsidy case. The United States unilaterally decided that the minivans were being dumped, and retaliated in its own way. The Japanese companies never agreed with the charges and pointed out that their pricing of minivans *within* Japan was comparable. In fact, the Japanese companies saw the entire incident as election-year pandering by the U.S. government.[26] Was it fair retaliation for unfair trade or an unfair tariff imposed on fair trade? The two sides disagreed.

In practice, states keep close track of the exact terms on which they trade. Large bureaucracies monitor international economic transactions—prices relative to world market levels, tariffs, taxes, etc.—and develop detailed policies to reciprocate any other state's deviations from cooperation.

Trade cooperation is easier to achieve under hegemony (see the discussions of hegemonic stability on pp. 82, 103–104). The efficient operation of markets depends on a sta-

[25]Hansen, Wendy L. The International Trade Commission and the Politics of Protectionism. *American Political Science Review* 84 (1), 1990: 21–46.

[26]Greenhouse, Steven. Unfair Pricing Is Found on Japanese Mini-Vans. *The New York Times*, May 20, 1992: D1.

In two U.S.-European trade disputes in the early 1990s, a trade war loomed as the United States prepared target lists for retaliatory tariffs. Both trade wars were averted at the last minute, as was the U.S.-Chinese trade war that loomed until (at the last minute) China agreed to stronger enforcement of intellectual property rights on U.S. products in 1995. Similarly, agreement on the Uruguay round of the GATT came at the last moment before a deadline. Why do these economic agreements so often come at the last moment?

Game theorists might look to the game of Chicken as an explanatory model. In most trade disputes, each state would rather get to a deal, even on terms that somewhat favor the other state if need be. But each would like even more to get a deal on their own terms. Similarly, in a game of Chicken each player would rather avoid the head-on collision, and being a hero or a chicken is a secondary con-

THINKING THEORETICALLY

❖

sideration. In trade negotiations, both states hold out for their own terms (not swerving) for as long as possible, then come to agreement only when faced with an imminent collision—the expiration of a deadline past which there will be no deal at all.

A different theoretical explanation would be that decision makers in trading states hold out for their best terms, but always avert a trade war in the end because their ideas and belief systems have been shaped by historical experiences. The failure of the Smoot-Hawley tariffs and the trade wars that followed, in the 1930s, led to the acceptance by foreign policy elites (in the United States and elsewhere) of the idea that trade wars are disastrous and must be avoided. The power of that idea, rather than rational calculations of national interest per se by the decision makers of the moment, would explain why trade wars keep being averted at the last minute.

ble political framework such as hegemony can provide. Political power can protect economic exchange from the distorting influences of violent leverage, of unfair or fraudulent trade practices, and of uncertainties of international currency rates. A hegemon can provide a world currency in which value can be universally calculated. It can punish the use of violence and can enforce norms of fair trade. Because its economy is so large and dominating, the hegemon has a potent leverage in the threat to break off trade ties, even without resort to military force. For example, to be denied access to U.S. markets today would be a serious punishment for export industries in many states. (Being denied access to markets in, say, India, would not hurt nearly as much.)

U.S. hegemony helped create the major norms and institutions of international trade in the post-1945 era. Now that U.S. hegemony seems to be giving way to a more multipolar world—especially in economic affairs among the great powers—institutions are even more important for the success of the world trading system. The role and operation of the major trade regimes and institutions occupies the remainder of this chapter.

❖ TRADE REGIMES

Trade regimes are the common expectations governments have about the rules for international trade. A variety of partially overlapping regimes concerned with international trade have developed, mostly since World War II. The most central of these is the GATT, which became the World Trade Organization in 1995.

The GATT (World Trade Organization)

The **General Agreement on Tariffs and Trade (GATT)** is a world organization working for freer trade on a multilateral basis. Established in 1947, the GATT has been more of a negotiating framework than an administrative institution. It has not actually regulated trade: before GATT, proposals for a stronger institutional agency were rejected (due to U.S. fears that overregulation would stifle free trade). GATT was more a regime than an institution until the mid-1990s, though it did have a small secretariat with headquarters in Geneva, Switzerland. The GATT also helped to *arbitrate* trade disputes (as in the European agricultural subsidy case), helping clarify the rules and helping states observe them. Over time the membership of the GATT grew, most recently with the addition of states from the former Soviet bloc and China. Today almost all the world's major trading states are among the 120 members.

In 1995 GATT members began to operate at a higher level of institutionalization, becoming the **World Trade Organization (WTO).** They also expanded the GATT's traditional focus on manufactured goods to include services and intellectual property. The WTO will have some powers of enforcement and an international bureaucracy to keep track of the politics of international trade. It is unclear how much power the WTO will be able to wield over states in practice.

The GATT framework is based on the principles of reciprocity—that one state's lowering of trade barriers to another should be matched in return—and of nondiscrimination. The latter principle is embodied in the **most-favored nation (MFN) concept,** which says that trade restrictions imposed by a GATT member must be applied equally to all GATT members. That is, every member is entitled to the same treatment that a state gives its most-favored trading partner. If Australia applies a 20 percent tariff on auto parts imported from France, it is not supposed to apply a 40 percent tariff on auto parts imported from the United States. In this way, GATT does not get rid of barriers to trade altogether but equalizes them in a global framework in order to create a level playing field for all member states. States are not prevented from protecting their own industries by a variety of means but cannot play favorites among their trading partners.

An exception to the MFN system is the **Generalized System of Preferences (GSP)** through which industrialized states began in the 1970s to give trade concessions to third-world states to help the latter's economic development. These preferences amount to a promise by rich states to allow imports from poor ones under even lower tariffs than those imposed under MFN.[27]

The GATT is a *negotiating forum* for multilateral trade agreements that lower trade barriers on a fair and reciprocal basis. These are detailed and complex agreements that specify the commitments of various states and regions to lower certain trade barriers by certain amounts on fixed schedules. Almost every such commitment entails domestic political costs, because domestic industries lose protection against foreign competition.

---

[27]Hirata, Akira, and Ippei Yamazawa, eds. Trade Policies Towards Developing Countries. New York: St. Martin's Press, 1993. Glover, David J., and Diana Tussie, eds. *The Developing Countries in World Trade: Policies and Bargaining Strategies.* Boulder, CO: Lynne Rienner, 1993. Finlayson, Jock A., and Mark W. Zacher. *Managing International Markets: Developing Countries and the Commodity Trade Regime.* New York: Columbia University Press, 1988.

Even when other states agree to make similar commitments in other areas, the lowering of trade barriers is often a hard commitment for national governments to make.

As a result, GATT negotiations on these multilateral agreements are long and difficult. Typically they stretch on for several years or more. This is called a *round* of negotiations, and after it is completed the GATT members begin on a new round. There have been five rounds of GATT negotiations since 1947. Among these, the *Kennedy round* in the 1960s—so called because it started during the Kennedy administration—paid special attention to the growing role of the (increasingly integrated) European Economic Community (EEC), which the United States found somewhat threatening. The *Tokyo round* (begun in Tokyo) in the 1970s had to adjust trading rules to new conditions of interdependence in the world economy as, for instance, OPEC raised oil prices and Japan began to dominate the automobile export business.

The **Uruguay round** started in 1986 (in Uruguay). Although the rough outlines of a new GATT agreement emerged after a few years, efforts to wrap up the Uruguay round failed at five successive G7 summit meetings in 1990–1994. As the round dragged on year after year, participants renamed GATT the "general agreement to talk and talk." It was estimated that a successful conclusion to the round would add hundreds of billions of dollars to the world economy over the remainder of the decade. But that money was a collective good, which would be enjoyed both by states that made concessions in the final negotiations to reach agreement and those that did not.

Agreement was finally reached in late 1994. In this round the United States had pressured Europe to reduce agricultural subsidies, and third-world states to protect intellectual property rights. In the end the United States got some, but not all, of what it wanted. France held out adamantly and won the right to protect its film industry against U.S. films.

Since 1947 the GATT has tried to encourage states to use import tariffs rather than other means of protecting industries and to lower those tariffs over time. The GATT has concentrated on manufactured goods and has succeeded in reducing the average tariffs on these goods substantially since 1947. At present, average tariff rates on manufactured goods in the industrialized West are around 10 to 15 percent of the goods' value. Tariff rates in the regions of the global South are around 30 percent (reflecting the greater protection that industry in the third world is seen as needing).

Agricultural trade is politically more sensitive than trade in manufactured goods (as noted earlier) and was seriously addressed only in the recent Uruguay round.[28] Trade in services, such as banking and insurance, will likely become the next major issue area tackled in GATT/WTO negotiations, as such trade approaches one-quarter of the total value of world trade in the 1990s.

In general, states continue to participate in GATT and the WTO, because the benefits, in terms of global wealth creation, outweigh the costs, in terms of harm to domestic industries or painful adjustments in national economies. States try to change the rules in their favor during the rounds of negotiations (never with complete success), and between

---

[28]Avery, William P., ed. *World Agriculture and the GATT*. Boulder, CO: Lynne Rienner, 1992. Marlin-Bennett, Renée Elizabeth. *Food Fights: International Regimes and the Politics of Agricultural Trade Disputes*. New York: Gordon and Breach, 1993.

rounds they try to evade the rules in minor ways. But the overall benefits are too great to jeopardize by nonparticipation or by allowing frequent trade wars to occur.

Bilateral and Regional Agreements

Although the GATT/WTO provides an overall framework for multilateral trade in a worldwide market, most international trade is governed by more specific international political agreements. These are of two general types—bilateral trade agreements and regional free-trade areas.

Bilateral Agreements Bilateral treaties covering trade are reciprocal arrangements to lower barriers to trade between two states. Usually they are fairly specific. For instance, one country may reduce its prohibition on imports on product X (which the second country exports at competitive prices) while the second country lowers its tariff on product Y (which the first country exports).

Part of the idea behind GATT is to strip away the maze of bilateral agreements on trade and simplify the system of tariffs and preferences. This has only partially succeeded. Bilateral trade agreements continue to play an important role.[29] They have the advantages of reducing the collective goods problem inherent in multilateral negotiations and facilitating reciprocity as a means to achieve cooperation. As the Uruguay round of GATT negotiations bogged down, some state leaders began to favor bilateral agreements as more achievable than the global GATT agreements. Inasmuch as most states have only a few most-important trading partners, a few bilateral agreements can go a long way in structuring a state's trade relations.

Free-Trade Areas Regional free-trade areas are also very important in the structure of world trade. In such areas, groups of neighboring states agree to clear away the entire structure of trade barriers (or most of it) within their area. With outside countries, trade continues to be governed by bilateral treaties and the GATT framework. A free-trade area may be called a "common market" or "customs union" (see p. 395). The creation of a regional free-trade area allows a group of states to cooperate in increasing their own wealth without waiting for the rest of the world. In fact, from an economic nationalist perspective a free-trade area can enhance a region's power at the expense of other areas of the world.

The most important free-trade area is in Europe; it is connected with the European Union but with a somewhat larger membership. Europe contains a number of small industrialized states living close together, so the creation of a single integrated market allows these states to gain the economic advantages that come inherently to a large state such as the United States. The European free-trade experiment has been a great success overall, contributing to Europe's accumulation of wealth since World War II (see Chapter 10).

---

[29]Yarbrough, Beth V., and Robert M. Yarbrough. *Cooperation and Governance in International Trade: The Strategic Organizational Approach.* Princeton: Princeton University Press, 1992. Oye, Kenneth A. *Economic Discrimination and Political Exchange: World Political Economy in the 1930s and 1980s.* Princeton: Princeton University Press, 1992.

Workers at RCA factory in Juarez, Mexico. U.S. companies are expanding production in Mexico, where labor is cheap, under the North American Free Trade Agreement (NAFTA). Under NAFTA, goods produced in Mexico have freer access to U.S. and Canadian markets, and vice versa.

The United States and Canada signed the **North American Free Trade Agreement (NAFTA)** in 1988 and expanded it to include Mexico as of 1994.[30] As of the early 1990s, Canada and Mexico were the largest and third-largest U.S. trading partners, respectively (Japan was second). U.S. policy makers plan to add South American states such as Chile in the future, working toward the eventual creation of a single free-trade area in the Western hemisphere. In its first year, U.S.-Mexican free trade under NAFTA expanded, but was made more complex and difficult when Mexico's currency dropped drastically relative to the dollar in 1994–1995.

Efforts to create a free-trade area, or perhaps just a semi-free-trade area, in Asia began in the late 1980s but moved fairly slowly. Malaysia was the leading country promoting such an arrangement, which it hoped would boost Malaysian economic development (though economists expected Japan would benefit most). In contrast to the European and North American arrangements, an Asian bloc would include very different kinds of states—rich ones like Japan, poor ones like the Philippines; democracies, dictatorships,

---

[30]Baer, Delal M., and Sidney Weintraub, eds. *The NAFTA Debate: Grappling with Unconventional Trade Issues*. Boulder, CO: Lynne Rienner, 1994. Lustig, Nora, Barry P. Bosworth, and Robert Z. Lawrence, eds. *North American Free Trade: Assessing the Impact*. Washington, DC: The Brookings Institution, 1992.

and communist states. It is unclear how well such a diverse collection could coordinate their common interests, especially because their existing trade patterns are not focused on each other but are spread out among other states including the United States (again in contrast to trade patterns existing before the creation of the EFTA and NAFTA).

During the Cold War, the Soviet bloc maintained its own trading bloc, the *Council for Mutual Economic Assistance (CMEA)*, also known as COMECON. After the Soviet Union collapsed, the members scrambled to join up with the world economy, from which they had been largely cut off. The *Commonwealth of Independent States (CIS)*, formed by 12 former Soviet republics, may become an economic coordinating body and quite possibly a free-trade area. The existing patterns of trade favor a CIS free-trade area because it was previously a free-trade zone by virtue of being part of a single state. Transportation, communication, and other infrastructural links run across borders frequently.

Other efforts to create free-trade areas have had mixed results. A *Caribbean common market (CARICOM)* was created in 1973, but the area is neither large nor rich enough to make regional free trade a very important accelerator of economic growth. Eleven countries created a Latin American Free Trade Association (LAFTA) in 1960 (changed in 1980 to the *Latin American Integration Association*), but the effort was held back by the different levels of poverty and wealth among the members and their existing patterns of trade (as in the Asian efforts just mentioned). Venezuela, Colombia, Ecuador, Peru, and Bolivia created the *Andean Common Market* in 1969; it had modest successes but not dramatic results, because trade within the bloc was not important enough (compared with, say, Venezuelan oil exports to the United States). The *Southern Common Market (Mercosul)* tripled trade among its members—Brazil, Argentina, Uruguay, and Paraguay—in its first four years, in the early 1900s. By 1995 Chile and Bolivia were expected to join and Mercosul planned a free-trade agreement with the Andean countries. Politicians in North and South America spoke of creating a single free-trade zone from Canada to Argentina.

If regional free-trade areas such as EFTA and NAFTA gain strength and new ones arise, it is possible that the GATT framework and WTO will be weakened. The more states are able to meet the political requirements of economic growth through bilateral and regional agreements, the less they may depend on the worldwide agreements developed through the GATT and WTO.

Cartels

A **cartel** is an association of producers or consumers, or both, of a certain product—formed for the purpose of manipulating its price on the world market. It is an unusual but interesting form of trade regime. Most often it is producers and not consumers that form cartels. This is because there are usually fewer producers than consumers, and it seems possible for them to coordinate their actions so as to keep prices high. Cartels can use a variety of means to affect prices; the most effective is to coordinate limits on production by each member so as to lower the supply, relative to demand, of the good.

The most prominent cartel in the international economy is the *Organization of Petroleum Exporting Countries (OPEC)*. Its member states together control about $125 billion in oil exports annually (as of 1993)—about half the world total and enough to significantly affect the price. (A cartel need not hold a monopoly on production of a good to be effective in limiting supply and raising prices.) One to two decades ago—at OPEC's peak of strength—the proportion was even higher. OPEC maintains a headquarters in Vienna, Austria (not a member), and holds negotiations several times a year to set quotas for each country's production of oil in order to keep world oil prices in a target range. Members and their export levels (before and after the Gulf War) are shown in Table 8.1. Note how Saudi Arabia increased its exports to compensate for the loss of Iraqi and Kuwaiti production, keeping prices relatively stable on world markets before and after the Gulf War.

OPEC illustrates the potential that a cartel creates for serious collective goods problems. Individual members of OPEC can (and do) cheat a bit by exceeding their production quotas while still enjoying the collective good of high oil prices. The collective good breaks down when too many members exceed their quotas, as has happened repeatedly to OPEC. Then world oil prices drop. (Iraq's accusations that fellow OPEC member Kuwait was exceeding production quotas and driving oil prices down was one factor in Iraq's invasion of Kuwait in 1990.)

OPEC may have worked as well as it has only because a single member, Saudi Arabia, has enough oil to unilaterally manipulate supply sufficiently to drive prices up or down. This is a form of "hegemonic stability" within the cartel. Saudi Arabia can take up the slack from some cheating in OPEC (cutting back its own production) and keep prices up. Or if too many OPEC members are cheating on their quotas, Saudi Arabia can punish them by flooding the market with oil and driving prices down until the other OPEC members collectively come to their senses. Even with Saudi predominance, the high oil prices of the 1970s led non-OPEC states to increase production and importing states to

TABLE 8.1 OPEC MEMBERS AND VALUE OF OIL EXPORTS

Member State	Exports (Billion $)		
	1989	1991	1993
Saudi Arabia	24	44	41
Iraq	15	0	0
Iran	11	15	15
United Arab Emirates	11	15	13
Venezuela	10	12	11
Kuwait	9	1	11
Libya	8	10	8
Nigeria	7	12	11
Algeria	7	10	6
Indonesia	6	6	4
Qatar	2	2	3
Gabon	1	2	2
Total	111	129	125

Note: Major oil exporters *not* in OPEC include Russia and Kazakhstan (the Soviet Union was the world's largest exporter in the late 1980s, although exports have since dropped sharply), Mexico, China, Britain, and Norway. Ecuador, a minor exporter, left OPEC in 1992. The United States, until several decades ago a major oil exporter, is now a major importer.

Source: Data adapted from United Nations. *World Economic Survey 1994.* New York: United Nations, 1994, p. 306.

improve energy conservation, so that by the 1980s even OPEC could not prevent a severe decline in world oil prices.

Consumers usually do not form cartels. However, in response to OPEC the major *oil-importing* states formed their own organization, the *International Energy Agency (IEA)*, which has some of the functions of a cartel. The IEA coordinates the energy policies of major industrialized states—such as the maintenance of oil stockpiles in case of a shortage on world markets—in order to keep world oil prices low and stable. The largest importers of oil in descending order of volume are the United States, Japan, Germany, Italy, and France—five members of the G7.

For a few commodities that are subject to large price fluctuations on world markets—detrimental to both producers and consumers—joint producer-consumer cartels have been formed. In order to keep prices stable, producing and consuming states use the cartel to coordinate the overall supply and demand globally. Such cartels exist for coffee, several minerals, and some other products. In the coffee cartel, Colombia argued in the late 1980s for a higher target price for coffee, so that Colombian peasants would have an incentive to switch from growing coca (for cocaine production) to coffee. But the United States as the major coffee-consuming state would not agree to the proposal for higher prices.

In general, the idea of cartels runs counter to liberal economics because cartels are deliberate efforts to distort free markets. However, in occasional cases where free markets create large fluctuations in price, the creation of a cartel can bring some order to chaos and result in greater efficiency. Cartels usually are not as powerful as market forces in determining overall world price levels: too many producers and suppliers exist, and too many substitute goods can replace ones that become too expensive, for a cartel to corner the market. The exceptions, such as OPEC in the 1970s, are rare.

Whether through cartels, free-trade areas, GATT, or bilateral agreements, states have found it worthwhile to create regimes and institutions to structure their trading relations. Overall, despite a loss of state sovereignty as a result of growing interdependence, these efforts have benefited participating states. Stable political rules governing trade allow states to realize the great economic gains that can result from international exchange. Such political stability is equally important in international monetary and business relations, which are the subject of Chapter 9.

❖ CHAPTER SUMMARY

- ◆ Mercantilism emphasizes the use of economic policy to increase state power relative to other states. It is related to realism.
- ◆ Liberalism emphasizes international cooperation—especially through worldwide free trade—to increase the total creation of wealth (regardless of its distribution among states). Liberalism is conceptually related to idealism.
- ◆ Most international exchanges entail some conflicting interests and some mutual interests on the part of the states involved. Deals can be made because both sides benefit, but conflict over specific outcomes necessitates bargaining.
- ◆ The volume of world trade is very large—nearly 20 percent of global economic activity—and is concentrated heavily in the states of the industrialized West (Western Europe, North America, and Japan/Pacific).

◆ Trade creates wealth by allowing states to specialize in producing goods and services for which they have a comparative advantage (and importing other needed goods).

◆ The distribution of benefits from an exchange is determined by the price of the goods exchanged. With many buyers and sellers, prices are generally determined by market equilibrium (supply and demand).

◆ Communist states during the Cold War operated centrally planned economies in which national governments set prices and allocated resources. Almost all these states are now in transition toward market-based economies, which seem to be more efficient in generating wealth. The transition has been very painful in Russia and Eastern Europe, less so in China.

◆ Politics intrudes into international markets in many ways, including the use of economic sanctions as political leverage on a target state. However, sanctions are difficult to enforce unless all major economic actors agree to abide by them.

◆ Mercantilists favor trade policies that produce a trade surplus for their own state. Such a positive trade balance generates money that can be used to enhance state power.

◆ States are becoming more and more interdependent, in that the well-being of states depends on each other's cooperation. Some scholars have long argued that rising interdependence makes military force a less useful form of leverage in international bargaining.

◆ States that have reduced their dependence on others, by pursuing self-sufficient autarky, have failed to generate new wealth to increase their well-being. Self-reliance, like central planning, has been largely discredited as a viable economic strategy.

◆ Through protectionist policies, many states try to protect certain domestic industries from international competition. Such policies tend to slow down the global creation of wealth but do help the particular industry in question.

◆ Protectionism can be pursued through various means, including import tariffs (the favored method), quotas, subsidies, and other nontariff barriers.

◆ Industries often lobby their own governments for protection. Governments in many states develop industrial policies to guide their efforts to strengthen domestic industries in the context of global markets.

◆ Certain products—especially food, intellectual property, services, and military goods—tend to deviate more than others from market principles. Political conflicts among states concerning trade in these products are frequent.

◆ A world market based on free trade is a collective good (available to all members regardless of their individual contribution) inasmuch as states benefit from access to foreign markets whether or not they have opened their own markets to foreign products.

◆ Because there is no world government to enforce rules of trade, such enforcement depends on reciprocity and state power. In particular, states reciprocate each other's cooperation in opening markets (or punish each other's refusal to let in foreign products). Although it leads to trade wars on occasion, reciprocity has achieved substantial cooperation in trade.

◆ Over time the rules embodied in trade regimes (and other issue areas in IR) become the basis for permanent institutions, whose administrative functions provide yet further stability and efficiency in global trade.

◆ The World Trade Organization, formerly the GATT, is the most important multilateral global trade agreement. In successive rounds of GATT negotiations over nearly fifty years, states have lowered overall tariff rates (especially on manufactured goods).

◆ The Uruguay round of the GATT, completed in 1994, is expected to add hundreds of billions of dollars to the global creation of wealth over the remainder of the decade.

◆ The GATT was institutionalized in 1995 with the creation of the World Trade Organization (WTO).

◆ Although the WTO provides a global framework, states continue to operate under thousands of bilateral trade agreements specifying the rules for trade in specific products between specific countries.

◆ Regional free-trade areas (with few if any tariffs or nontariff barriers) have been created in Europe, North America, and several other less important instances. The North American area includes Canada, Mexico, and the United States; it is just now coming into effect.

◆ International cartels are occasionally used by leading producers (sometimes in conjunction with leading consumers) to control and stabilize prices for a commodity on world markets. The most visible example in recent decades has been the oil producers' cartel, OPEC, whose members control over half the world's exports of a vital commodity, oil.

❖ THINKING CRITICALLY

1. Suppose your state had a chance to reach a major trade agreement by making substantial concessions. The agreement would produce $5 billion in new wealth for your state, as well as $10 billion for each of the other states involved (which are political allies but economic rivals). What advice would a mercantilist give your state's leader about making such a deal? What arguments would support the advice? How would liberal advice and arguments differ?

2. China seems to be making a successful transition to market economics and is growing rapidly. Some projections indicate it could become the world's second-largest economy early next century or sooner. Do you think this is a good thing or a bad thing for your state? Does your reasoning reflect mercantilist or liberal assumptions?

3. Given the theory of hegemonic stability, what effects might a resurgence of U.S. power in the post–Cold War era have on the world trading system? How might those effects show up in concrete ways?

4. Before reading this chapter, to what extent did you have a preference for buying products made in your own country? Has reading this chapter changed your views on that subject? How?

5. NAFTA, the new free-trade agreement between Mexico and the United States, recently came into effect. Given that wages in Mexico are lower and technology is less developed than in the United States, which U.S. industries do you imagine supported the free-trade agreement? Specifically, do you think labor-intensive industries or high-technology industries were more supportive of the deal? Why?

❖ KEY TERMS

international political economy (IPE)
mercantilism vs. liberalism
comparative advantage
centrally planned economy
state-owned industries
mixed economies
balance of trade
interdependence
autarky
protectionism
dumping
tariff (duty)
nontariff barriers

industrial policy
intellectual property rights
service sector
General Agreement on Tariffs and Trade (GATT)
World Trade Organization (WTO)
most-favored nation (MFN) concept
Generalized System of Preferences (GSP)
Uruguay round
North American Free Trade Agreement (NAFTA)
cartel

*Traders at Hong Kong gold
and silver market.*

MONEY AND BUSINESS

❖ ABOUT MONEY

This chapter summarizes the politics of the world monetary system and then discusses the role of private companies as nonstate actors in the world economy. The monetary system is just one aspect of the political environment governments create, an environment that shapes the rules for international business and the context for the actions of multinational corporations (MNCs).

Imagine a world *without* money. In order to conduct an economic exchange, the goods being exchanged would have to be brought together in one place and traded in quantities reflecting the relative values the parties placed on them. This kind of trade, involving no money, is called *barter*. It still occurs sometimes when monetary systems do not operate well. For example, during the Chinese-Soviet hostility of the 1960s and 1970s, some barter trade along their border continued. Soviet money was worthless in China, and Chinese money was worthless in the Soviet Union. So traders brought goods to the border, agreed on their value (expressed nominally in Swiss francs), and traded the appropriate quantities.

The unit of currency used in an economy is arbitrary, but it must have roughly the same value for different people. In war-torn Angola in the 1980s, the money printed by the government became inflated until it was practically worthless. Over time, a new standard of value evolved in much of the country based on a commodity—cans of beer—for which there was stable demand and a consensus on value. Beer became the currency used by many Angolans in daily economic transactions at the local level. The use of such a currency is, of course, much less efficient than using printed money.

With money, goods can move directly from sellers to buyers without having to meet in a central place. In a world economy, goods can flow freely among many states, with just the exchange of money keeping track of who owes whom for what. Money exists to facilitate exchange by providing a single medium against which all goods can be valued. Different buyers and sellers place different values on goods, but all buyers and sellers place roughly the same value on money, so it serves as a standard against which other values can be measured.

Money itself has little or no inherent value. What gives it value is the widespread belief that it has value—that it can be exchanged for goods. Money is just an IOU. Because it depends on the willingness of people to honor and use it, money's value rests on trust. Governments have the job of creating money and of maintaining public confidence in its value. For money to have stable value, the political environment must be stable. Political instability such as war or revolution erodes public confidence that money today will be exchangeable for needed goods tomorrow. The result is inflation, bringing a devaluation of the nation's currency on world markets (discussed later in this chapter).

The international economy is based on national currencies, not a world currency, because of the nature of state sovereignty. One of the main powers of a national government is to create its own currency as the sole legal currency in the territory it controls. The national currencies are of no inherent value in another country, but can be exchanged one for another.[1] How can the value of goods or currencies be judged in a world lacking a central government and a world unit of money?

Traditionally, for centuries, the European state system used *precious metals* as a global currency, valued in all countries. *Gold* was most important, and *silver* second most important. These metals had inherent value because they looked pretty and were easily molded into jewelry or similar objects. They were relatively rare, and the mining of new gold and silver was relatively slow. These metals lasted a long time, and they were difficult to water down or counterfeit.

Over time, gold and silver became valuable *because* they were a world currency—that is, because other people around the world trusted that the metals could be exchanged for future goods—and this overshadowed any inherent functional value of gold or silver. Bars of gold and silver were held by states as a kind of bank account denominated in an international currency. Recall (from Chapters 2 and 8) that these piles of gold (literal and figurative) were the object of mercantilist trade policies in past centuries. Gold has long been a key power resource with which states could buy armies or other means of leverage.

In recent years the world has not used such a **gold standard** but has developed an international monetary system divorced from any tangible medium such as precious metal (or beer). Until very recently, and still to some extent, private investors have bought stocks of gold or silver at times of political instability, as a haven that would reliably have future value. But gold and silver have now become basically like other commodities, with unpredictable fluctuations in price, and their role even as private havens is diminishing. The change in the world economy away from bars of gold to purely abstract money makes international economics more efficient (no need to move bars of gold around); the only drawback is that without tangible backing in gold, currencies may seem less worthy of people's confidence.

---

[1]Cohen, Benjamin J., ed. *The International Political Economy of Monetary Relations.* Brookfield, VT: Edward Elgar, 1993. Eichengreen, Barry. *Elusive Stability: Essays in the History of International Finance, 1919–1939.* New York: Cambridge University Press, 1989. Eichengreen, Barry. *International Monetary Arrangements for the 21st Century.* Washington, DC: The Brookings Institution, 1995.

Money has value only because people trust its worth. Inflation erodes a currency's value if governments print too much money or if political instability erodes public confidence in the government. Counterfeiting is also a growing problem in this era of color copiers. Here a new device to test the authenticity of money is demonstrated in Tokyo (1993).

❖ THE CURRENCY SYSTEM

Today, national currencies are valued against each other, not against gold or silver. Each state's currency can be exchanged for a different state's currency according to an **exchange rate**—defining, for instance, how many Canadian dollars are equivalent to one U.S. dollar. These exchange rates are very important because they affect almost every international economic transaction—trade, investment, tourism, and so forth.[2] Consider first the mechanics by which exchange rates are set and adjusted, then the factors influencing the longer-term movements of exchange rates, and finally the banking institutions that manage these issues.

International Currency Exchange

In practice, most exchange rates are expressed in terms of the world's most important currencies—the U.S. dollar, Japanese yen, and German mark. That is, the rate for exchang-

---

[2] Aliber, Robert Z. *The International Money Game*. 5th ed. New York: Basic Books, 1987.

ing, say, Danish kroner for Brazilian cruzeiros depends on the value of each relative to these leading world currencies. The exchange rates that most affect the world economy are those *within* the G7 states—dollars, marks, yen, British pounds, French francs, Canadian dollars, and Italian lire.

The relative values of currencies at a given point in time are arbitrary; only the *changes* in values over time are meaningful. For instance, the German mark happens to be fairly close to the U.S. dollar in value, whereas the Japanese yen is denominated in units closer to the U.S. penny. In itself this says nothing about the desirability of these currencies or the financial positions of their states. However, when the value of yen rises (or falls) *relative* to dollars, because yen are considered more (or less) valuable than before, the yen is said to be strong (or weak).

Some states' currencies are not **convertible.** This means that the holder of such money has no guarantee of being able to trade it for another currency. Such is the case in states cut off from the world capitalist economy, like the former Soviet Union. Few such states remain, but a lingering challenge is to make the Russian ruble a fully convertible currency (see "The Position of Russia and Eastern Europe" later in this chapter). In practice, even nonconvertible currency can often be sold, in black markets or by dealing directly with the government issuing the currency, but the price may be extremely low.

Some currencies are practically nonconvertible because they are inflating so rapidly that holding them for even a short period means losing money (this is now the biggest problem with the ruble). For instance, if Angolans prefer to use beer as currency, the banknotes issued by the Angolan government obviously are not worth much to foreign governments, banks, or businesses. Nor were the 10-billion-dinar notes printed by Serbia in 1993, worth only pennies after hyperinflation passed 100 trillion percent per year. (In early 1994 a new currency tied directly to the German mark was issued, cutting inflation to nearly zero for a year.)

Nobody wants to hold currency that is rapidly inflating—losing value relative to goods and services. So inflation reduces a currency's value relative to more stable (more slowly inflating) currencies.

The industrialized West has kept inflation relatively low—mostly below 5 percent annually—since 1980 (see Table 9.1). (The 1970s saw inflation of over 10 percent per year in many industrialized economies, including the United States.) The global South

TABLE 9.1 INFLATION RATES BY REGION, 1993

Region	Inflation Rate
Industrialized West	3% per year
China	13%
Middle East	15%
Latin America	900%
South Asia	6%
Africa	200%
Former Soviet republics	1,500%

Note: Regions are not identical to those used elsewhere in this book. Data are estimates based on partial data from 1993.

Source: Adapted from United Nations. *World Economic and Social Survey 1994.* New York: United Nations, pp. 30, 263, 269.

has had much less success in taming inflation. China, South Asia, and the Middle East had inflation rates in the early 1990s of about 10 or 15 percent annually; but Africa (over 100 percent) and Latin America (around 1,000 percent) have not. Russia and some other transitional economies now have inflation rates comparable to those in Latin America. Extremely high, uncontrolled inflation—over 50 percent per month, or 13,000 percent per year—is called **hyperinflation.** Even at less extreme levels, such as Latin America's overall 1,700 percent rate in 1990, currencies can lose 95 percent of their value in a year. In such conditions, money loses 5 percent of its value every week, and it becomes hard to conduct business domestically (to plan, save, or invest), let alone internationally.

By contrast with nonconvertible currency, **hard currency** is money that can be readily converted to leading world currencies (which now have relatively low inflation). For example, a Russian oil producer can export oil and receive payment in German marks or another hard currency, which can then be used to pay for imported goods from outside Russia. But a Russian sausage producer selling products within Russia would be paid in rubles, which could not be used outside the country.

States maintain **reserves** of hard currency. This is the equivalent of the stockpiles of gold in centuries past. National currencies are now backed by hard-currency reserves, not gold. Some states continue to maintain gold reserves as well. The industrialized countries have financial reserves roughly in proportion to the size of their economies.

One form of currency exchange uses **fixed exchange rates.** Here governments decide, individually or jointly, to establish official rates of exchange for their currencies. For example, the Canadian and U.S. dollars were for many years equal in value; a fixed rate of 1-to-1 was maintained (this is no longer true). States have various means for trying to maintain, or modify, such fixed rates in the face of changing economic conditions (see "Why Currencies Rise or Fall" later in this chapter).

Floating exchange rates are now more common and are used for the world's major currencies. Rates are determined by global currency markets in which private investors and governments alike buy and sell currencies. There is a supply and demand for each state's currency, with prices constantly adjusting in response to market conditions. Just as investors might buy shares of General Motors stock if they expected its value to rise, so they would buy a pile of Japanese yen if they expected that currency's value to rise in the future. Through short-term speculative trading in international currencies, exchange rates adjust to changes in the longer-term supply and demand for currencies.

There are major international currency markets in a handful of cities—the most important being New York, London, Zurich (Switzerland), Tokyo, and Hong Kong—linked together by instantaneous computerized communications. These markets are driven in the short term by one question: What will a state's currency be worth in the future relative to what it is worth today? These international currency markets involve huge amounts of money—a trillion dollars every day—moving around the world (actually only the computerized information moves). They are private markets, not as strongly regulated by governments as are stock markets.[3]

National governments periodically *intervene* in financial markets, buying and selling currencies in order to manipulate their value. (These interventions may also involve

---

[3]Aronson, Jonathan David. *Money and Power: Banks and the World Monetary System*. Newbury Park, CA: Sage, 1977.

changing interest rates paid by the government; see pp. 360–362). Such government in-tervention to manage the otherwise free-floating currency rates is called a **managed float** system. The leading industrialized states often, but not always, work together in such in-terventions. If the price of the U.S. dollar, for instance, goes down too much relative to other important currencies (a political judgment), governments will step into the cur-rency markets, side by side with private investors, and buy dollars. With this higher de-mand for dollars, the price may then stabilize and perhaps rise again. (If the price got too high, governments would step in to sell dollars, increasing supply and driving the price down.) Such interventions usually happen quickly, in one day, but may be repeated sev-eral times within a few weeks in order to have the desired effect.[4]

In their interventions in international currency markets, governments are at a disad-vantage because even acting together they control only a small fraction of the money moving on such markets; most of it is privately owned. Governments do have one advan-tage in that they can work together to have enough impact on the market to make at least modest changes in price. A second advantage is that governments can operate in secret, keeping private investors in the dark regarding how much currency governments may eventually buy or sell, and at what price. Only *after* a coordinated multinational interven-tion into markets does the public find out about it. (If speculators knew in advance they could make money at the government's expense.)

A successful intervention can make money for the governments at the expense of private speculators. If, for example, the G7 governments step in to raise the price of dol-lars by buying them around the world (selling other hard currencies), and if this succeeds in raising the price of dollars, the governments can then sell again (most likely in small chunks, secretly, over time) and pocket a profit. However, if the intervention fails and the price of dollars keeps falling, the governments will *lose* money and may have to keep buy-ing and buying in order to stop the slide. In fact, the governments might run out of money before then and have to absorb a huge loss. So governments have to be realistic about the limited effects they can have on currency prices.

These limits were well illustrated in the *European currency crisis* of September 1992. The European Union (EU) tries to maintain the equivalent of a fixed exchange rate among the various European currencies while letting the European currencies as a whole float freely relative to the rest of the world (see "The Single European Act" on pp. 398–400). For 1992 the British pound was pegged at 2.95 German marks, and if it slipped from that rate, European governments were supposed to take various actions to bring it back into line. This is called the **Exchange Rate Mechanism (ERM),** and it is intended as a step toward an eventual single currency for Europe (see "The Maastricht Treaty" on pp. 400–402).

In September 1992, certain long-term forces were pushing apart the values of the German mark and British pound. In essence, Germans feared inflation due to the costs of reunifying their country and wanted to restrict money supply to prevent this. Britons, however, were worried about recession and unemployment, which a tight money supply

---

[4]Dominguez, Kathryn M., and Jeffrey A. Frankel. *Does Foreign Exchange Intervention Work?* Washington, DC: In-stitute for International Economics, 1993. Henning, C. Randall. *Currencies and Politics in the United States, Ger-many, and Japan.* Washington, DC: Institute for International Economics, 1994.

Private investors, not central banks, control most of the money traded internationally every day. Currency trader works from his California home, 1992.

would only worsen. As a result, currency speculators began to gamble that Britain would not be able to maintain the value of the British pound relative to the German mark.

As the pound began to fall, the British government intervened to buy pounds and drive the price back up. But speculators, who controlled far more money than the European governments, kept selling pounds. The speculators were convinced that the British government would be unable to prop up the pound's value, and they proved correct. With no way to stop the decline, Britain pulled out of the ERM and allowed the pound to float freely; it quickly fell in value. All the pounds that the British government had bought during its intervention were then worth less—a loss of billions of dollars. The government's loss was the private speculators' gain.

In this instance, a single speculator—a Hungarian-American financial fund manager named George Soros—sold off $10 billion worth of pounds in just a few weeks (borrowing money in pounds and selling those pounds for marks, dollars, or yen). He was convinced that the underlying weakness in the British economy relative to the German economy would thwart Britain's efforts to maintain a fixed exchange rate against the German mark. When Britain caved in and devalued the pound, Mr. Soros sold back his marks, dollars, and yen for (cheaper) pounds, and paid back the money he borrowed—walking away with a $1 billion profit at the expense of the British government. Although such large profits are rare, the story illustrates the problem governments have in controlling exchange rates when most money is privately owned. Soros went on to become a philanthropist, giving away millions of dollars to support democratic transitions in Russia and Eastern Europe. He proved to be mortal, however, losing over half a billion dollars in one day in 1994 when U.S.-Japanese trade talks collapsed.

Why Currencies Rise or Fall

In the short term, exchange rates depend on speculation about the future value of currencies. But over the long term, the value of a state's currency tends to rise or fall relative to others because of changes in the long-term supply and demand for the currency. Supply is determined by the amount of money that a government prints. Printing money is a quick way to generate revenue for the government, but the more money printed, the lower the price it will fetch on international currency markets. Domestically, printing too much money creates inflation because the amount of goods in the economy is unchanged but more money is circulating to buy them with. *Demand* for a currency depends on the state's economic health and political stability. People do not want to own the currency of an unstable country because political instability leads to the breakdown of economic efficiency and of trust in the currency issued by that government (as happened, for instance, during Angola's civil war).

A *strong* currency is one that increases its value relative to other currencies—not just in day-to-day fluctuations on currency markets, but in a somewhat longer-term perspective. A *weak* currency is the opposite. The strength of a state's currency tends to reflect that state's monetary policy and economic growth rate. Investors want to hold a currency that will not be watered down by inflation and that can be profitably invested in a growing economy.

To some extent, states have *common* interests—opposed to those of private investors—in maintaining stable currency exchange rates. But currency exchange also creates *conflicts* between states, as it did between Britain and Germany in the 1992 European currency crisis. States often prefer a *low* value for their own currency relative to others, because a low value promotes exports and helps turn trade deficits into surpluses—as mercantilists especially favor (see "Balance of Trade" on pp. 322–324).

For example, a U.S. dollar was worth 100 Japanese yen in January 1995. The United States runs a trade deficit with Japan (importing more goods from Japan than it exports to Japan). When the exchange rate suddenly dropped to 80 Japanese yen in early 1995, Japan could buy more U.S. goods for 80 yen (a dollar's worth instead of 80 cents as before), effectively lowering the price of U.S. goods in Japan. Japanese goods imported into the United States at the same time became more expensive (what had cost 80 cents now cost a dollar). So U.S. firms and households imported less from Japan and exported more to Japan. The U.S. trade balance improved.

But why should Japan agree to make Japanese exports to the United States more expensive? If Japanese politicians are economic liberals (which they are up to a point), they might want to enjoy cheaper goods imported from the United States. But if they are economic nationalists, they would want to maintain a trade surplus and would agree to intervene only at the point at which the stability of the world economic system was endangered (the collective good of stable exchange rates might not be provided). Decisions

U.S. made Apple computers for sale in Japan, 1992. Changes in the dollar-yen exchange rate—reflecting underlying trends in the two national economies as well as the two governments' monetary policies—directly affect the prices of imported goods like these computers.

about the target rates of currency exchange—those the great powers will cooperate to enforce through market interventions—are thus a major arena of international political bargaining. To keep currency speculators from profiting at the expense of all governments, most such bargaining occurs in secret.

To some extent, exchange rates and trade surpluses or deficits tend to adjust automatically toward equilibrium (the preferred outcome for liberals). An *overvalued* currency is one whose exchange rate is too high, resulting in a chronic trade deficit. The deficit can be covered by printing more money, which in turn waters down the currency's value and brings down the exchange rate (assuming it is allowed to float freely).

Because they see adjustments as harmless, liberals are not bothered by exchange rate changes such as the fall of the dollar relative to the yen, and of the Mexican peso relative to the dollar, in early 1995. These are mechanisms for allowing the world economy to work out inefficiencies and maximize overall growth.

A unilateral move to reduce the value of one's own currency by changing a fixed or official exchange rate is called a **devaluation.** Generally, devaluation is a quick fix for financial problems in the short term, but it can create new problems. It causes losses to foreigners who hold one's currency (which is suddenly worth less). This reduces the trust people place in the currency—that it will be worth as much in the future as today. As a result, demand for the currency drops, even at the new lower rate. Investors become wary of future devaluations, and indeed such devaluations often follow one after another in unstable economies. A currency may be devalued by allowing it to to float freely, often bringing a single sharp drop in values. This is what Britain did in the European currency crisis just discussed.

The weakening of a currency, while encouraging exports, carries dangers. For example, the Mexican peso dropped 20 percent in one day (50 percent over several months) when allowed to float freely at the end of 1994. With imported goods shooting up in price, inflation jumped to a 45 percent annualized rate and standards of living fell. And with dollar-denominated loans suddenly becoming more expensive to service, corporate profits dropped. The Bank of Mexico had to offer 50 percent interest rates to attract capital. The resulting economic dislocations were a big setback to Mexico's economic growth and development. Similarly, when the currency used by 14 African countries (based on the French franc) was devalued by half in early 1994, financial experts praised the long-term benefits the move would bring to those economies. But in the short term, the urban poor had to tighten their belts as prices jumped. Thus, depending on what goods an economy imports and exports, a weaker currency that raises the price of imported goods may disrupt economic growth. In general, any sharp or artificial change in exchange rates tends to disrupt smooth international trade and hence interfere with the creation of wealth.

Central Banks

As has been mentioned, governments control the printing of money. In some states, the politicians or generals who control the government directly control the amounts of money printed. It is not surprising that inflation tends to be high in those states, because political problems can often be solved by printing more money to use for various purposes. But in most industrialized countries, politicians know they cannot trust themselves with day-to-day decisions about printing money. To enforce self-discipline and enhance public trust in the value of money, these decisions are turned over to a **central bank.**

The economists and technical experts who run the central bank basically have the job of maintaining the value of the state's currency by limiting the amount of money printed and not allowing high inflation. Politicians appoint the people who run the bank, but generally for long terms that do not coincide with those of the politicians. Thus, central bank managers try to run the bank in the national interest, a step removed from partisan politics. For example, if a state leader orders a military intervention the generals obey; but if the leader orders an intervention in currency markets the central bank does not have to comply.

In the United States, the central bank is the *Federal Reserve*, or the Fed. The "reserve" is the government's stockpile of hard currency. The Fed can affect the economy by releasing or hoarding its money. Internationally, it does this by intervening in currency markets as described earlier. Multilateral interventions are usually coordinated by the heads of central banks and treasury (finance) ministries in the leading countries. The long-term, relatively nonpartisan perspective of central bankers makes it easier for states to achieve the collective good of a stable world monetary system.

Domestically, the Fed exercises its power mainly by setting the **discount rate**—the interest rate the government charges when it loans money to private banks. (Central

This and the next two "Thinking Theoretically" boxes will take up the "collective goods problem" (see pp. 100–101) in several areas of international political economy. Relatively stable exchange rates for international currency can be seen as a collective good, in that all members of the international economy benefit from a stable framework for making investments and sales, yet an individual country can benefit from devaluing its own currency. (Whether such benefits are actually economic, or merely political benefits tied to perceptions of national interest, does not matter here, as long as state leaders perceive that defection from existing exchange rates can benefit their countries.)

According to the theory of collective goods, international exchange rate stability should be more readily achieved under two circumstances—under hegemony and under a small-group arrangement. Hegemonic stability, in this theory, includes providing backing for world currency stability, using the hegemon's own economic clout and its influence over other great powers. Lacking a hegemon, collective goods are thought to be easiest to assure if controlled by a small group rather than one with many members. In the small-group setting, defectors stand out and mutual cooperation is more readily enforced.

Followers of hegemonic stability theory

THINKING THEORETICALLY

❖

would explain the currency turmoil of the mid-1990s—some major currencies shooting up and others collapsing—as a natural outcome of declining U.S. hegemony. If one believed that the effect works in the short term as well as the long term, one could hypothesize that international currency exchange should be more stable at times of temporary resurgence of U.S. power (as in the 1991 Gulf War), and should fluctuate more at times of U.S. retreat from hegemony (as in 1992–1994). Unfortunately there are not enough such cases of U.S. rise and decline to support a meaningful statistical test of the hypothesis.

Followers of the small-group theory (which is not incompatible with the hegemonic approach) would be interested in proposals around 1995 to expand the G7 to a G8 by including Russia. This might set a precedent for further expansion later. Furthermore, signs appeared in 1995 that control of international monetary coordination was shifting away from the G7 and toward the IMF's governing committee, which has 24 state members—a much larger group.

Collective goods theory would predict that such expansions would weaken exchange rate stability. Eventually, a new group with fewer members (for example, a U.S.-Japanese-German committee or meeting) might have to be formed to restore stability.

banks have only private banks, not individuals and corporations, as their customers.) In effect this rate controls how fast money is injected into the economy. If the Fed sets too low a discount rate, too much money will come into circulation and inflation will result. If the rate is set too high, too little money will circulate and consumers and businesses will find it hard to borrow as much or as cheaply from private banks; economic growth will be depressed. Again, a state leader cannot order the central bank to lower the discount rate and inject more money into the economy to stimulate economic growth (in an election year, for instance) but can only ask very nicely and very discreetly for such action. The central bankers will inject the money only if they are convinced that it will not be too inflationary.

Central bank decisions about the discount rate have important international consequences. If interest rates are higher in one state than another, foreign capital will tend to be attracted to the state with the higher rate. And if economic growth is high in a foreign country, more goods can be exported to it. So states care about other states' monetary policies. This often creates international conflicts that can be resolved only politically (such as at G7 summit meetings) and not technically—because each central bank, although removed from domestic politics, still looks out for its own state's interests in the international arena.

For example, in the recession of the early 1990s, the U.S. Fed worried more about slow economic growth than about inflation, so it lowered interest rates sharply. The central bank of Germany was more worried about inflation, resulting from the costs of German reunification, than about slow growth. (Germans still remember that in the 1920s hyperinflation devastated their economy.) To reduce inflation, the German central bank raised its lending rate. U.S. officials pleaded with German officials (mostly in vain) to lower the German interest rate in order to stimulate German economic growth and hence increase U.S. exports to Germany.

Low U.S. interest rates—like an infusion of money in the economy—helped pull the United States out of the recession of the early 1990s. But then the low U.S. interest rates (among other factors) led the dollar to fall dramatically relative to the mark in the mid-1990s. The Fed could stem this weakening of the dollar by raising interest rates (in effect choking off money and raising its value), but this would slow economic growth and possibly trigger a new recession.

Although central banks control sizable reserves of currency, they are constrained by the limited share of world money that they own. Most wealth is controlled by private banks and corporations. As economic actors, states do not drive the direction of the world economy; in many ways they follow it, at least over the long run. However, states still have key advantages as actors in the international economy. Most important, states control the monopoly on the legal use of force—violent leverage—against which even a large amount of wealth usually cannot stand. To put it another way, state leaders can jail corporate executives who do not follow the state's rules. Ultimately, then, political power is the state's trump card as an economic actor.

The World Bank and the IMF

Because of the importance of international cooperation for a stable world monetary system and because of the need to overcome collective goods problems, international regimes and institutions have developed around norms of behavior in monetary relations. Just as the UN institutionally supports regimes based on norms of behavior in international security affairs (see Chapter 7), the same is true in the world monetary regime.

As in security affairs, the main international economic institutions were created near the end of World War II. The **Bretton Woods** system was adopted at a conference of the winning states in 1944 (at Bretton Woods, New Hampshire). It established the *International Bank for Reconstruction and Development (IBRD)*, more commonly called the **World Bank,** as a source of loans to reconstruct the European economies after the war and to help states through future financial difficulties. (Later, the main borrowers were third-world countries and, in the 1990s, Eastern European ones.) Closely linked with the World Bank was the **International Monetary Fund (IMF).** The IMF coordinates international currency exchange, the balance of international payments, and national accounts (discussed shortly). The World Bank and the IMF continue to be the pillars of the international financial system. (The roles of the World Bank and the IMF in third-world development are taken up in Chapter 13.)

Bretton Woods established a regime of stable monetary exchange, based on the U.S. dollar and backed by gold, that lasted from 1944 to 1971.[5] During this period, the dollar was given a fixed value equal to 1/35 of an ounce of gold, and the U.S. government guaranteed to buy dollars for gold at this rate (from a stockpile at Fort Knox, Kentucky). Other states' currencies were exchanged at fixed rates relative to the dollar. These fixed exchange rates were set by the IMF based on the long-term equilibrium level that could be sustained for each currency (rather than short-term political considerations). The international currency markets operated within a very narrow range around the fixed rate. If a country's currency fell more than 1 percent from the fixed rate, the country was obligated to use its hard-currency reserves to buy its own currency back and thus shore up the price. (Or, if the price rose more than 1 percent, it was obligated to sell its currency to drive the price down.)

The gold standard was abandoned in 1971—an event sometimes called the "collapse of Bretton Woods." The term is not quite appropriate: the institutions survived, and even the monetary regime underwent more an adjustment than a collapse. The U.S. economy no longer held the overwhelming dominance it had in 1944—mostly because of European and Japanese recovery from World War II, but also because of U.S. overspending on the Vietnam War and other programs. Throughout the 1950s and 1960s, the U.S. had spent dollars abroad to stimulate world economic growth and fight the Cold War, but these had begun to far exceed the diminishing stocks of gold held by the Federal Reserve. So successful were the efforts to reinvigorate the economies of Japan and Europe that the United States suffered a relative decline in its trade position.

As a result, the dollar had become seriously overvalued. By 1971 the dollar was no longer worth 1/35 of an ounce of gold, and the United States had to abandon its fixed exchange rate—much as Britain did in the 1992 crisis discussed earlier. President Nixon unilaterally dumped the dollar-gold system (in two stages, in 1971 and 1973), and the dollar was allowed to float freely; before long it had fallen to a fraction of its former value (gold was worth several hundred dollars an ounce, not $35).

The abandonment of Bretton Woods was good for the United States and bad for Japan and Europe, where leaders expressed shock at the unilateral U.S. actions. (For Japan the shock was doubled when Nixon unilaterally opened relations with China without consulting Japan.) The interdependence of the world capitalist economy, which had produced record economic growth for all the Western countries after World War II, had also created the conditions for new international conflicts.

To replace gold as a world standard, the IMF created a new world currency, the **Special Drawing Right (SDR).** The SDR has been called "paper gold" because it is created in limited amounts by the IMF, is held as a hard-currency reserve by states' central banks, and can be exchanged for various international currencies. The SDR is today the closest thing to a world currency that exists, but it cannot buy goods—only currencies. And it is owned only by states (central banks), not by individuals or companies.

---

[5]Moffitt, Michael. *The World's Money: International Banking from Bretton Woods to the Brink of Insolvency.* New York: Simon & Schuster, 1983.

Bars of gold from U.S. reserves, San Francisco, 1974 (nearly $10 million worth at today's prices). Gold historically served as a world currency, but has now been largely replaced by the World Bank's SDRs ("paper gold").

The value of the U.S. dollar was pegged to the SDR rather than to gold, at a fixed exchange rate (but one that the IMF periodically adjusted to reflect the dollar's strength or weakness). SDRs are linked in value to a basket of several key international currencies. So when one currency rises a bit and another falls, the SDR does not change value much; but if all currencies rise (worldwide inflation), the SDR rises with them.

Since the early 1970s, the major national currencies have been governed by the managed float system. The transition from the dollar-gold regime to the managed float regime was difficult. The United States was no longer dominant enough to single-handedly provide stability to the world monetary system. Instead states had to bargain politically over the targets for currency exchange rates in the meetings we now know as G7 summits.

The technical mechanisms of the IMF are based on each member state's depositing financial reserves with the IMF. Upon joining the IMF, a state is assigned a *quota* for such deposits, partly of hard currency and partly of the state's own currency (this quota is not related to the concept of trade quotas, which are import restrictions). The quota is based on the size and strength of a state's economy. A state can then borrow against its quota (even exceeding it somewhat) to stabilize its economy in difficult times, and repay the

IMF in subsequent years. (This system works well for temporary imbalances in monetary relations but not for chronic ones.)

Unlike either the UN General Assembly or the Security Council, the IMF and the World Bank use a *weighted voting* system—each state has a vote equal to its quota. Basically this means that the G7 states control the IMF, although nearly all the world's states are members. The United States has the single largest vote, and its capital city is headquarters for both the IMF and the World Bank.

Since 1944 the IMF and the World Bank have tried to accomplish three major missions in turn. First they sought to provide stability and access to capital for states ravaged by World War II, especially for Japan and the states of Western Europe. This mission was a great success, leading to growth and prosperity in those states. Then, especially in the 1970s and 1980s, the Bank and the IMF tried to promote economic development in newly independent third-world countries. As we shall see in Chapter 13, that mission was far less successful—as evidenced by the lingering (and even deepening) poverty in much of the global South. The third mission, undertaken in the 1990s, is the integration of Eastern Europe and Russia into the world capitalist economy. By the mid-1990s, the outcome of this ambitious effort was far from certain.

❖ STATE FINANCIAL POSITIONS

As currency rates change and state economies grow, the overall positions of states relative to each other shift.

National Accounts

The IMF maintains a system of *national accounts* statistics to keep track of the overall monetary position of each state. A state's **balance of payments** is like the financial statement of a company: it summarizes all the flows of money in and out of the country. The system itself is technical and not political in nature. Essentially, three types of international transactions go into the balance of payments: the current account, flows of capital, and changes in reserves (see Table 9.2).

The *current account* is basically the balance of trade discussed in Chapter 8. Money flows out of a state to pay for imports and flows into the state in payment for exports. The goods imported or exported include both merchandise and services of various kinds. For instance, the money spent by a British tourist visiting Florida is equivalent to the money spent by a British consumer buying Florida oranges in a London supermarket; both are money flowing into the U.S. current account.

The current account includes two other items. *Government transactions* are military and foreign aid grants, as well as salaries and pensions paid to government employees abroad. *Remittances* are funds sent home by companies or individuals outside a country. For example, a Ford Motor Company subsidiary in Britain may send profits back to Ford in Detroit. Conversely, a British citizen working in New York may send money to her parents in London.

The second category in the accounts is *capital flows*, which are foreign investments in, and by, a country.[6] Capital flows are measured in *net* terms—the total investments and

---

[6]Kindleberger, Charles P. *International Capital Movements*. New York: Cambridge University Press, 1987.

TABLE 9.2 BALANCE OF PAYMENTS ACCOUNTS

In Billions of U.S. Dollars

	United States (1993)	Germany (1992)	Japan (1993)
Current Account			
Exports (goods & services)	755	563	555
– Imports (goods & services)	–827	–557	–417
= Trade balance	–72	6	138
+ Government transactions and remittances	–32	–32	–6
= Current account balance	–104	–26	132
Capital Flows (net money received)			
+ Direct foreign investment received	–37	–9	–14
+ Loans and other capital inflow	72	78	–90
Changes in Reserves			
= Changes in reserves	–69	+43	+28

Source: Data adapted from World Bank. *World Tables.* Washington, DC: The World Bank, 1995.

loans foreigners make *in* a country minus the investments and loans that country's companies, citizens, and government invest in *other* countries. Most of such investment is private, although some is by (or in) government agencies and state-owned industries. Capital flows are divided into **direct foreign investment** (or foreign direct investment)—such as building a factory in a foreign country or buying real estate there—and indirect *portfolio investment*, such as buying stocks and bonds or making loans to a foreign company. (Economists also distinguish *short-term* from *long-term* portfolio investments.) These various kinds of capital flows have somewhat different political consequences (see "International Debt" and "Direct Foreign Investment" later in this chapter), but they are basically equivalent in the overall national accounts picture.

The third category, *changes in foreign exchange reserves*, makes the payments balance in the national accounts. Any difference between the inflows and outflows of money (in the current account and capital flows combined) is made up by an equal but opposite change in reserves. These changes in reserves consist of the state's purchases and sales of SDRs, gold, and hard currencies other than its own, and changes in its deposits with the IMF. If a state has more money flowing out than in, it gets that money from its reserves. If it has more money flowing in than out, it puts the money in its reserves.

Thus, national accounts always balance in the end. At least, they almost balance; there is a residual category—errors and omissions—because even the most efficient and honest government (many governments are neither) cannot keep track of every bit of money crossing its borders. But basically the payments balance.

International Debt

In one sense, an economy is constantly in motion, with money moving around through the processes of production, trade, and consumption. But economies also contain *standing wealth*. The hard-currency reserves owned by governments are one form of standing wealth, but not the most important. Most standing wealth is in the form of homes and cars, farms and factories, ports and railroads. The various kinds of standing wealth are called *capital*. Nothing lasts forever, but standing wealth lasts for enough years to be treated differently than goods that are quickly consumed.

The main difference is that capital (standing wealth) can be used to create more wealth: factories produce goods, railroads support commerce, and so forth. Standing wealth creates new wealth, so the economy tends to grow over time. As it grows, more standing wealth is created. In a capitalist economy, money makes more money.

Interest rates reflect this inherent growth dynamic. *Real* interest rates are the rates for borrowing money above and beyond the rate of inflation (for instance, if money is loaned at an annual interest rate of 8 percent but inflation is 3 percent, the real interest rate is 5 percent). Businesses and households borrow money because they think they can use it to create new wealth faster than the rate of interest on the loan.

Borrowing and lending is like any other economic exchange; both parties must see it as beneficial. The borrower values the money now more than the promise of more money in the future (because the borrower can use the money profitably in the meanwhile), whereas the lender values the promise of more money in the future more than the money now. The distribution of benefits from the exchange is, as usual, subject to bargaining. Imagine that a profitable business can use a loan to generate 10 percent annual profit (above the inflation rate). At one extreme the business could pay 1 percent real interest and keep 9 percent for itself; at the other it could pay 9 percent interest and keep 1 percent.

The actual split, reflected in prevailing interest rates, is determined by a market process—the market for money. Lenders seek out businesses profitable enough to pay high interest, and businesses seek out lenders with enough idle cash to lend it out at low interest rates. In an imperfect but workable way, the supply and demand for money determine interest rates.

Imagine now that the business borrowing the money is an entire state—the government, companies, and households. If the state's economy is healthy, it can borrow money from foreign governments, banks, or companies and create enough new wealth to repay the debts a few years later. But states, like businesses, sometimes operate at a loss; then their debts mount up. In a vicious circle, more and more of the income they generate goes to paying interest, and more money must be borrowed to keep the state in operation. If its fortunes reverse, a state or business can create wealth again and over time pay back the principal on its debts to climb out of the hole. If not, it will have to begin selling off part of its standing wealth (buildings, airplanes, factories, and the like). The *net worth* of the state or business (all its assets minus all its liabilities) will decrease.

When a state's debts accumulate, the standing wealth of the state is diminished as assets are sold off to pay the debts. In some third-world countries, debts accumulated in the 1970s and 1980s to the point of virtual national bankruptcy, or zero net worth. The debts became unpayable, and the lenders (banks and governments) had to write them off the books or settle them at a fraction of their official value.[7]

The industrialized states, by contrast, have enough standing wealth that even in their most indebted times they still have substantial net worth. Still, rising debts are encumbrances against the future creation of wealth, and foreign lenders come to own a greater

---

[7]Stallings, Barbara. *Banker to the Third World: U.S. Portfolio Investment in Latin America, 1900–1986.* Berkeley: University of California Press, 1987.

share of the state's total standing wealth. Naturally, such a situation horrifies mercantilists. National debt to them represents a loss of power. It is the opposite of the pile of reserves that mercantilists would like to be sitting on.[8]

Why do states go into debt? One major reason is a trade deficit. In the balance of payments, a trade deficit must be made up somehow. It is common to borrow money to pay for a trade deficit. A second reason for international debt is the pattern of income and consumption among households and businesses. If people and firms spend more than they take in (live beyond their means), they must borrow to pay their bills. The credit card they use may be from a local bank, but that bank may be getting the money it lends to them from foreign lenders.

A third reason for national debt is government spending relative to taxation. Under the principles of **Keynesian economics** (named for economist John Maynard Keynes), governments sometimes spend more than they take in—*deficit spending*—in order to stimulate economic growth. If such a strategy works, the increased economic growth eventually generates higher tax revenues to make up the deficit. In effect the government lends money to the nation and recovers it later from a healthier economy. Where does the government get this money? It could print more money, but as we have seen, this would be inflationary and central banks try to prevent it. So the government often borrows the money, from both domestic and foreign sources.

Government decisions about spending and taxation are called **fiscal policy;** decisions about printing and circulating money are called **monetary policy.**[9] These are the two main tools available for government to manage an economy. There is no free lunch: high taxation chokes off economic growth, printing excess money causes inflation, and borrowing to cover a deficit places a mortgage on the state's standing wealth. This is why, for all the complexities of governmental economic policies and international economic transactions, a state's wealth and power ultimately depend more than anything on the underlying health of its economy—the education and training of its labor force, the amount and modernity of its capital goods, the morale of its population, and the skill of its managers. In the long run, international debt reflects these underlying realities.

The U.S. Position

The United States is an extraordinarily wealthy and powerful state. Its most *unique* strengths may be in the area of international security—as the world's only superpower—but its economic strengths are also striking. It is not only the world's largest economy but the most technologically advanced one in such growth sectors as computers, telecommunications, aviation and aerospace, and biotechnology. The U.S. position in scientific research and higher education is unparalleled in the world.

The U.S. position in the international economy, however, has shifted considerably since World War II. U.S. hegemony has declined, U.S. strengths have eroded, and com-

---

[8]Kapstein, Ethan B. *Governing the Global Economy: International Finance and the State.* Cambridge, MA: Harvard University Press, 1994. Helleiner, Eric. *States and the Reemergence of Global Finance: From Bretton Woods to the 1990s.* Ithaca: Cornell University Press, 1994. Cline, William R. *International Debt Reexamined.* Washington, DC: Institute for International Economics, 1994.

[9]Frieden, Jeffry A. Invested Interests: The Politics of National Economic Policies in a World of Global Finance. *International Organization* 45 (4), 1991: 425–52.

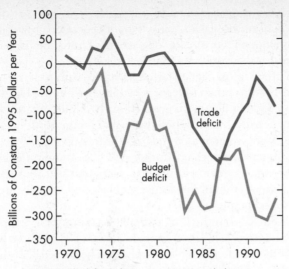

Note: Trade deficit refers to current account balance before official transactions

FIGURE 9.1 U.S. Financial Position, 1970–1992
Source: Data from World Bank, *World Tables on Diskette,* Fall 1994 edition. Washington, DC: The World Bank.

petitors have gained relative ground (especially in Western Europe and Asia). In the early 1950s, the U.S. economy (GDP) was about twice the size of the next six advanced industrial states *combined.* By the 1980s its relative share of world GDP had dropped almost by half. In 1950 the United States held half of the world's financial reserves; by 1980 it held less than 10 percent. As we have seen, the slide in U.S. financial strength was one reason for the abandonment of Bretton Woods in 1971. This long-term decline after the extraordinary post-1945 U.S. hegemony was a natural and probably unavoidable one.

In the 1980s, however, the U.S. financial position worsened much more rapidly, causing great alarm.[10] The U.S. national debt increased dramatically as the government used deficit spending—in part to finance a military buildup, in part to reduce taxes—but the economy was not stimulated into faster growth. In fact growth became even more sluggish and the country slipped into *recession* (a shrinking GDP) in the early 1990s. The U.S. government continued to slide further into debt by hundreds of billions of dollars each year. The United States is now losing net worth and having to sell off its standing wealth to pay the bills. Where once the U.S. was sitting on a pile of gold, now it sits under a pile of debt.

The deterioration of the U.S. position in the 1980s is illustrated in Figure 9.1. The budget deficit grew to $300 billion per year while the trade deficit (exports minus imports) grew from near zero to around $200 billion in just a few years, before recovering to a level under $100 billion (data are inflation-adjusted, in 1995 dollars).

As a result, the U.S. government's **national debt** grew from about one trillion dollars at the beginning of the 1980s to three trillion by the end of that decade. By the mid-

---

[10]Volcker, Paul A., and Toyoo Gyohten. *Changing Fortunes: The World's Money and the Threat to American Leadership.* New York: Random House, 1992.

1990s it was approaching the equivalent of one year's GDP. The interest payments were equivalent to what would otherwise be a healthy rate of economic growth (several percent of GDP in inflation-adjusted terms). Not long ago, the United States was the world's leading lender state; now it is the world's leading debtor state.

In the private sector, the United States started the 1980s with well over $100 billion more invested in foreign countries than foreigners had invested in the United States. By 1988, foreigners had over $500 billion more invested in the United States than U.S. investors had in foreign countries. Most of these were short-term portfolio investments, with nearly half being U.S. government securities such as treasury bills.[11]

These shifts in investment mean that ownership of U.S. standing wealth began to shift into the hands of foreigners. Mercantilists may decry that fact. But the foreign investment issue is just a manifestation of the deeper problems of U.S. debt and the underlying weakness of the U.S. economy.

The U.S. position is reflected in the U.S. national accounts for 1993, shown earlier in Table 9.2 (p. 366). The circled "−72" shows a trade deficit of $72 billion, whereas Germany and Japan had $6 billion and $138 billion surpluses. The circled "72" shows $72 billion more of investments and loans coming into the country than Americans were investing and loaning out outside the country (Japan was investing and loaning out $90 billion more than it was receiving from other states). And the circled "−69" indicates that in 1993 the United States depleted its reserves by $69 billion to make ends meet. All these numbers reflect the fall in U.S. economic standing in recent years.

The underlying causes—and even the extent—of U.S. economic decline are matters of dispute.[12] Some scholars tie U.S. economic problems to the costs of the Cold War—from the Vietnam War through the arms race of the 1980s. Some historians see a parallel to previous great powers which overstretched themselves with military and political commitments that their economies could not support, leading to economic and political decline. In this view, Japan (and to some extent Western Europe) benefited from lower military spending rates. Although this theory might help explain the Soviet collapse as well (because Soviet military spending was exceptionally high), it is controversial and does not fit some other cases such as the success of South Korea (which also had high military spending).

Other explanations of U.S. decline include U.S. politicians' aversion to setting tax rates high enough to cover spending, the high consumption and low savings rate of U.S. citizens, and possibly the failings of U.S. management style relative to that of other cultures (especially Japan). Some scholars attribute the decline to U.S. willingness to shoulder an unfair burden in providing collective goods like free trade and monetary stability, allowing Western Europe and Japan to become free riders. All these theories are controversial.

Whatever their cause, these U.S. financial trends have profound implications for the entire world political economy. They undermine the leading U.S. role since World War II in stabilizing international trade and monetary relations, in assuring the provision of col-

---

[11]Graham, Edward M., and Paul R. Krugman. *Foreign Direct Investment in the United States.* 3rd ed. Washington, DC: Institute for International Economics, 1994.

[12]Nau, Henry R. *The Myth of America's Decline: Leading the World Economy into the 1990s.* New York: Oxford University Press, 1990. Kennedy. *The Rise and Fall of the Great Powers.* See footnote 48 in Chapter 2.

lective goods, and in providing capital for the economic development of other world regions. In a more decentralized world economy with a weakened U.S. role, collective goods problems may be harder to solve and free trade may be harder to achieve. Some troubling signs of economic instability appeared in the early 1990s, in the turbulent, recession-plagued years that followed the end of the Cold War.

The U.S. financial decline creates problems in international security as well. U.S. global commitments and foreign aid may be scaled back. Again, collective goods may become more difficult to provide. Some scholars (and policy makers) worry that a power vacuum in world politics could invite aggression in the future.

The Position of Russia and Eastern Europe

Immediate victims of U.S. financial weakness are Russia and Eastern Europe, in the sense that the United States cannot provide the capital (investments, loans, and grants) to help get this region on its feet again after the Cold War. Were the United States stronger economically, it might repeat in Russia and Eastern Europe the successful aid program that stimulated new growth in Western Europe and Japan after World War II.

Instead, states in this region face daunting challenges as they try to convert from centrally planned to capitalist economies and to join the world capitalist economy. These challenges include integration into the world trading system (membership in GATT, bilateral trade agreements, and so forth) and attracting foreign investment. Among the most difficult tasks were the attempts of states in this region to join the international monetary system. This was perhaps the most important challenge, because having a stable and convertible currency is a key element in attracting foreign business and expanding international trade.

Most of the states of the former Soviet bloc became members of the IMF and were assigned quotas. But the IMF and the World Bank would not make loans available freely to these states until their governments took strong action to curb inflation, balance government budgets, and assure economic stability. Such stability would have been easier to achieve with the foreign loans, however, creating a chicken-and-egg problem.

All the economies of the region experienced a deep depression (shrinking GDP) in 1989–1991. By 1992, only Poland had resumed economic growth—a 1 to 4 percent annual growth of GDP following a 20 percent shrinkage in 1990–1991. The rest of Eastern Europe (except Bulgaria and Slovakia) stopped shrinking by 1994. But the states of the former Soviet Union continued downward, until by the mid-1990s the total economic activity of those states had been cut by more than a third over five years (see Table 9.3). In general the Eastern European countries appeared to have better prospects of stabilizing their economies than did the states of the former Soviet Union. Among the latter, Russia was better off than some others; it had inherited much of the Soviet Union's economic infrastructure and natural resources and was large enough to gain the attention of the West. But internal power struggles created political instability in Russia, discouraging foreign investment. And inflation reached 1,500 percent in 1992 and nearly 1,000 percent in 1993. The costs of the war in Chechnya in 1995 made matters worse, and as of 1995 there was no end in sight to Russia's ordeal, although inflation had abated somewhat.

Ukraine had even more severe economic woes (as did some other former Soviet republics). By 1992, Ukraine had inflation of 2,700 percent, with the government printing ever-larger quantities of coupons (denominated in Russian rubles) that served as money.

Russian pensioner reacts to 400 percent increase in milk prices, February 1992. Inflation in Russia has since become much worse, lowering standards of living for most of the population by about half on average, and creating political turmoil.

The coupons themselves had become devalued (against the Russian ruble, which itself was inflating rapidly) by more than half their value in less than a year. As a result, almost two-thirds of all economic transactions in Ukraine were on a barter basis. Meanwhile, the government had enacted almost no market-oriented economic reforms (former Communists were in power) and continued to funnel huge subsidies to state-owned industries (in the form of freshly printed coupons). Inflation was near 9,000 percent in 1993, according to one estimate.

By 1994, with Ukraine's GDP at half its 1990 level and inflation at around 5,000 percent, Ukrainian voters elected a reformer as president. He pushed through "shock therapy" economic reforms but faced a backlash from antireform political forces. The fate of Ukraine, along with the rest of the former Soviet Union, was still uncertain in 1995.

The various states of the region had varying experiences, ranging from Poland's relative speed in making the transition away from communism to Ukraine's relative slowness. Russia was somewhere in between—itself a mix of successes and failures. During the transition, the gold reserves of the former Soviet Union—previously among the world's largest—were sold off to make ends meet.

The region's financial problems were similar to those facing third-world countries trying to stabilize their economies (see Chapter 13), but they were compounded by special problems resulting from the breakup of the Soviet Union itself. First, some states

TABLE 9.3 MARCHING BACKWARD

Economic Collapse in Russia and Eastern Europe

Cumulative (4-Year) Change in GDP, 1990–1993	
Former Soviet Republics[a]	–39%
Poland	–15%
Czech Rep. and Slovakia	–25%
Hungary	–14%
Romania	–27%
Bulgaria	–42%
East Germany (1990 only)[b]	–25%

[a]Includes Russia, Ukraine, and 13 other states.
[b]Absorbed by West Germany in late 1990.
Source: United Nations, *World Economic and Social Survey 1994.* New York: United Nations, p. 261.

printed their own currency while others kept using the Russian ruble (through the framework of the CIS). In the case of a state like Ukraine that planned to print its own currency, the rubles already in circulation there (and even the temporary ruble-denominated coupons) threatened to flood back into Russia in trade for Russian goods—in effect expanding the ruble supply and fueling inflation in Russia.

The soaring inflation and general economic collapse throughout the region made it much harder to resolve all these problems and arrive at a stable political and economic environment in which IMF and World Bank assistance would be useful and not just wasted. In any case the amounts of money available for such assistance were limited because of the economic recession of the early 1990s in the world's leading economies. By 1994 almost all the former Soviet republics had joined the IMF (after negotiating reform plans).

Several billion dollars were collected from the major economic powers in the early 1990s to create a "ruble-convertibility fund" that could be used to intervene in currency markets to shore up the value of the Russian ruble if necessary. This fund, combined with other forms of economic assistance (mostly loans rather than grants), made about twenty billion dollars available for the task of helping the region through its transition. Experts doubted whether such a sum was anywhere near adequate for such a massive, historic, and unprecedented transition of an entire economic system. By way of comparison, twenty billion dollars would reduce the U.S. budget deficit by about 10 percent for one year— and the U.S. financial problems were much less severe than those of Russia.

To get access to these assistance funds, Russia had to take steps to control inflation and government spending, sell off state-owned industry, and institute a market system throughout its economy. The attempt to implement such measures turned out to be even more painful than expected. Russian president Yeltsin found himself challenged by a coalition of former Communists and industry leaders, who demanded continuing state subsidies of major industries. To stop those subsidies risked alienating these political forces, deepening the shrinkage of GDP, and throwing more people out of work. But continuing the subsidies risked widening the budget deficit and triggering hyperinflation.

These issues were unresolved several years after the Soviet Union broke up. The momentum of economic reform slowed down in Russia and throughout the region. In Russia, the prime minister who had pushed for shock therapy was replaced in late 1992 with an advocate of a slower pace of reform. In Lithuania, which had led the way among republics breaking away from the Soviet Union, severe economic problems led voters in late 1992, in that state's first free elections after independence, to return the former Communists to power. Then a number of other states in the region followed suit, leading to a resurgence of former Communist parties.

The economic and financial problems of the region were compounded by security problems—ethnic and national conflicts along the southern rim of the former union—which disrupted trade and monetary relations. For example, rail traffic from Russia was disrupted by separatists in Georgia, and Azerbaijan cut off energy supplies to Armenia. It appears that for the next few years at least, Russia and Eastern Europe will struggle to find the economic and political stability that will allow them to integrate into the world capitalist economy. Until then, most of these states remain largely cut off from the potential benefits that could result from stable convertible currencies, expanded trade, and increased foreign investment.

As Russia and Eastern Europe tried to make the transition from command economies to market-based ones, the role of private businesses expanded relative to that of the state. In the rest of the world, private business already plays a role in the economy that exceeds that of the state—as noted earlier in the case of currency interventions. The remainder of this chapter considers the international political issues related to the operation of private businesses across state borders.

❖ MULTINATIONAL BUSINESS

Although states are the main rule makers for currency exchange and other international economic transactions, those transactions are carried out mainly by private firms and individuals, not governments. Most important among these private actors are MNCs.

Multinational Corporations

Multinational Corporations (MNCs) are companies based in one state with affiliated branches or subsidiaries operating in other states. There is no exact definition, but the clearest case of an MNC is a large corporation that operates on a worldwide basis in many countries simultaneously, with fixed facilities and employees in each. With no exact definition, there is also no exact count of the number of MNCs worldwide, but a reasonable estimate is around ten thousand.

Most important are *industrial corporations*, which make goods in factories in various countries and sell them to businesses and consumers in various countries. For example, the Ford Motor Company has over three hundred thousand employees in thirty countries and in 1994 merged its European and North American operations into one administrative unit, producing a "world car." Many of the largest industrial MNCs are based in the United States, though the relative U.S. share has declined in recent decades while the shares of Japan and Germany have increased. The automobile, oil, and electronics industries have the largest MNCs. Of the largest 20 MNCs in terms of sales in 1992 (excluding trading companies), all were based in G7 states—eight in the United States, four in

Japan, three in Germany, and five in Britain (two of which were jointly based in the Netherlands). The top three were General Motors (GM), Exxon, and Ford.[13]

Beyond industrial corporations, *financial corporations* (the most important being banks) also operate multinationally—though often with more restrictions than industrial MNCs. Among the largest commercial banks worldwide, the United States does not hold a leading position—reflecting the traditional U.S. antitrust policy that limits banks' geographic expansion and restricts them from certain financial services (such as stock brokerage and insurance). Japanese banks, with fewer such restrictions, make up 23 of the 50 largest banks in the world. Twenty-two more are based in Europe, three in the United States, one in Canada, and one in Hong Kong (1993 data). The growing international integration of financial markets was spectacularly illustrated in 1995 when a single 28-year-old trader in Singapore lost $1 billion speculating on Japanese stock and bond markets and bankrupted his employer, a 200-year-old British investment bank.

Beyond industrial corporations and banks, some MNCs sell *services*.[14] The McDonald's fast-food chain and American Telephone and Telegraph (AT&T) are good examples. So are the international airlines, which sell tickets in dozens of states (and currencies) for travel all over the world. More down-to-earth service businesses such as retail grocery stores can also become MNCs. During the Gulf War, U.S. personnel could shop at Safeway supermarkets in Saudi Arabia. The United States predominates in service MNCs as it does in industrial ones (though service companies are generally somewhat smaller and less internationalized than the giant industrial corporations and banks).

The role of MNCs in international political relations is somewhat complicated and in some dispute.[15] Some scholars see MNCs as virtually being agents of their home national governments. This view resonates with mercantilism, in which economic activity ultimately serves political authorities. In this view, MNCs have clear national identities and act as members of their national society under authority of the state. A variant of this theme (from a more revolutionary world view) sees national governments as virtually being agents of their MNCs; state interventions (economic and military) serve private, monied interests.

An opposite, liberal view of MNCs sees them as virtual citizens of the world beholden to no government. The head of Dow Chemical once said he dreamed of buying an island beyond any state's territory and putting Dow's world headquarters there. In such a view, MNCs act globally in the interests of their (international) stockholders and owe loyalty to no state. In any case MNCs are motivated by the need to maximize profits, and managers who fail to do so are likely to be fired. Only in the case of state-owned MNCs—an important exception but a small minority of the total companies worldwide—do MNC actions reflect state interests. Even then, managers of state-owned MNCs have won greater autonomy to pursue profit in recent years (as part of the economic reforms instituted in many countries).

---

[13]United Nations. *World Investment Report 1994: Transnational Corporations, Employment and the Workplace.* New York: United Nations, 1994.

[14]Aronson, Jonathan D. The Service Industries: Growth, Trade, and Development Prospects. In John W. Sewell and Stuart K. Tucker, eds. *Growth, Exports and Jobs in a Changing World Economy: Agenda 1988.* New Brunswick, NJ: Transaction Books 1988.

[15]Gilpin, Robert. *U.S. Power and the Multinational Corporation.* New York: Basic Books, 1975.

As independent actors in the international arena, MNCs are increasingly powerful. Dozens of industrial MNCs have annual sales of tens of billions of dollars each ($100 billion for GM, Ford, and Exxon). Only about twenty-five states have more economic activity per year (GDP) than does the largest MNC, General Motors. And even MNCs one-tenth the size of GM, of which there are dozens, have more economic activity than the GDPs of the majority of the world's states. A more apt comparison might be between MNCs and IOs as nonstate actors operating in the international arena. MNCs more than match most such organizations in size and financial resources. For example, the largest IGO (the UN) has less than $10 billion a year in revenue, compared to about $100 billion for the largest MNC (GM). However, the largest *government* (the United States) has revenues of $1 trillion—ten times larger than GM. Thus the power of MNCs does not rival that of the largest states but exceeds that of many poorer states and many IOs; this affects MNC operations in the global South (see pp. 527–530).

Giant MNCs contribute to global interdependence. They are so deeply entwined in so many states that they have a profound interest in the stable operation of the international system—in security affairs as well as trade and monetary relations. MNCs prosper in a stable international atmosphere that permits freedom of trade, of movement, and of capital flows (investments)—all governed by market forces with minimal government interference. Thus MNCs are, overall, a strong force for liberalism in the world economy, despite the fact that particular MNCs in particular industries do push for certain mercantilist policies to protect their own interests.

Corporations that do business internationally and the states that host them have created a global *infrastructure* of facilities, services, communication links, and the like, that facilitate the conduct of business. The business infrastructure is a key aspect of *transnational relations*—linkages among people and groups across national borders.

Most MNCs have a world management system based on *subsidiaries* in each state in which they operate. The operations within a given state are subject to the legal authority of that state's government. But the foreign subsidiaries are owned (in whole or in substantial part) by the parent MNC in the home country. The parent MNC hires and fires the top managers of its foreign subsidiaries.

In addition to the direct connections among members of a single MNC, the operations of MNCs have supported the emergence of a global business infrastructure connecting a transnational community of businesspeople. A U.S. manager arriving in Spain or South Korea, for instance, does not find a bewildering scene of unfamiliar languages, locations, and customs. Rather, she or he moves through a familiar sequence of airport lounges, telephone calls and faxes, international hotels, business conference rooms, CNN broadcasts, and so forth—most likely hearing English spoken in all.

Direct Foreign Investment

MNCs do not just *operate* in foreign countries, they own capital (standing wealth) there—buildings, factories, cars, and so forth. For instance, U.S. and German MNCs own some of the capital located in Japan, and Japanese MNCs own capital located in the United States and Germany. *Investment* means exchanging money for ownership of capital (for the purpose of producing a stream of income that will, over time, more than compensate for the money invested). Investments in foreign countries are among the most important, and politically sensitive, activities of MNCs.

As was mentioned earlier, *portfolio* investment refers to paper securities like stocks, bonds, and T-bills, whereas *direct* foreign investment involves tangible goods like factories and office buildings. Paper can be traded on a global market relatively freely, but direct investments cannot be freely moved from one state to another as conditions change. For instance, it is expensive to move a factory if the state in which it is located suddenly raises tax rates on factories. Direct investment is long term, and it is more visible than portfolio investment. Investments in the *manufacturing* sector usually entail the greatest investment in fixed facilities, which are difficult to move, and in training workers and managers. Investments in the *extraction* of minerals or fuels are less expensive, but even less movable. Investments in the *service* sector tend to be less expensive and easier to walk away from if conditions change.

Mercantilists tend to view foreign investments in their own country suspiciously. In third-world countries, direct foreign investment often evokes concerns about a loss of sovereignty, because governments may be less powerful than the MNCs that invest in their country. These fears also reflect the historical fact that most foreign investment in the third world used to come from colonizers.[16]

But many poor and transitional states also desperately need capital from any source to stimulate economic growth, so direct foreign investment is generally welcomed and encouraged despite these fears of economic nationalists (North-South investment is discussed further in Chapter 13, pp. 535–538).[17] Most direct foreign investment is not in the third world, however, but in industrialized countries. (The same is true of portfolio investment: of the more than $400 billion raised on international credit markets through bonds and loans, 87 percent of the money was borrowed by the industrialized West.)

Economic nationalists in *industrialized* countries also worry about losing power and sovereignty due to foreign investment. In Canada, for instance, mercantilists are alarmed that U.S. firms own more than half of Canada's manufacturing industry and over two-thirds of Canada's oil and gas industry. Canada is much smaller than the United States, yet it depends heavily on U.S. trade. In this asymmetrical situation, some Canadians worry that they are being turned into an annex of the U.S.—economically, culturally, and ultimately politically—losing their own national culture and control of their economy. They do not welcome further investment by U.S.-based MNCs.

Meanwhile, U.S. economic nationalists have similar concerns over direct foreign investment in the United States. Partly this reflects alarm over the accumulation of U.S. debts. Mercantilists see a loss of power when foreign investors buy up companies and real estate in a debtor country. Such concerns seem to be stronger when a foreign MNC buys an *existing* company or building than when it builds a *new* factory or other facility. For example, when Japanese investors bought Columbia movie studios in Los Angeles and (temporarily) Rockefeller Center in New York, many Americans saw these properties as somehow representative of the American spirit, and their sale was seen as a U.S. loss. But when Honda builds a new car factory in Ohio, adding jobs and facilities to the U.S. economy, no such loss is perceived.

---

[16]Gomes-Casseres, Ben, and David B. Yoffie, eds. *The International Political Economy of Direct Foreign Investment.* Brookfield, VT: Edward Elgar, 1993.

[17]Biersteker, Thomas J. *Distortion or Development? Contending Perspectives on the Multinational Corporation.* Cambridge, MA: MIT Press, 1978. Pearson, Margaret M. *Joint Ventures in the People's Republic of China: The Control of Foreign Direct Investment Under Socialism.* Princeton: Princeton University Press, 1992.

Liberalism does not condone such arguments. Liberal economists emphasize that global efficiency and the increased generation of wealth result from the ability of MNCs to invest freely across international borders. Investment decisions should be made solely on economic grounds (profitability, efficiency), not nationalistic ones. Liberals also pointed out a glaring inconsistency in the U.S. public's preoccupation with Japanese investment in the United States in the late 1980s: over half of all foreign investment in the United States is from Western Europe (especially Britain and the Netherlands), and only a third as much is from Japan. Yet there is little outcry about a loss of U.S. sovereignty to Europe. Presumably this reflects either racism or a lingering shadow of World War II in the U.S. public's perceptions of foreign investment.

In the view of liberal economists, foreign investments in the United States help, rather than hurt, the U.S. economy. Many of the benefits of a profitable Japanese factory in the United States, for example, accrue to the U.S. workers at the plant and U.S. consumers of its products, even if some of the profits go back to Japan (and even those profits may be reinvested in the United States). Furthermore, U.S. MNCs still have over a trillion dollars of direct foreign investment outside the United States, so the picture is by no means one-sided.

Host and Home Government Relations

A state in which a foreign MNC operates is called the **host country** for such operations. The state where the MNC has its headquarters is called its **home country.** MNC operations create a variety of problems and opportunities for both the host and home countries' governments. Conflicts between the host government and the MNC may spill over to become an interstate conflict between the host government and home government. For example, if a host government takes an MNC's property without compensation or arrests its executives, the home government may step in to help the MNC.[18]

Because host governments can regulate activities on their own territories, in general an MNC cannot operate in a state against the wishes of its government. Conversely, because MNCs have many states to choose from, a host government cannot generally force an MNC to do business in the country against the MNC's wishes. Therefore, at least in theory, MNCs operate in host countries only when it is in the *interests of both* the MNC and the host government. Common interests result from the creation of wealth in the host country by the MNC. Both the MNC and the host government benefit from this wealth—the MNC as profits, the government directly by taxation and indirectly through economic growth (generating future taxes and political support).

However, there are also conflicts in the relationship. One obvious conflict concerns the distribution of new wealth between the MNC and host government. This distribution depends on the rate at which MNC activities or profits are taxed, as well as on the ground rules for MNC operations. Before an MNC invests or opens a subsidiary in a host country, it sits down with the government to negotiate these issues. Threats of violent leverage are largely irrelevant. Rather, the government's main leverage is to promise a favorable climate for doing business and making money; the MNC's main leverage is to threaten to take its capital elsewhere.

Governments can offer a variety of incentives to MNCs to invest. Special terms of

---

[18]Rodman, Kenneth A. *Sanctity Versus Sovereignty: U.S. Policy Toward the Nationalization of Natural Resource Investments in the Third World.* New York: Columbia University Press, 1988.

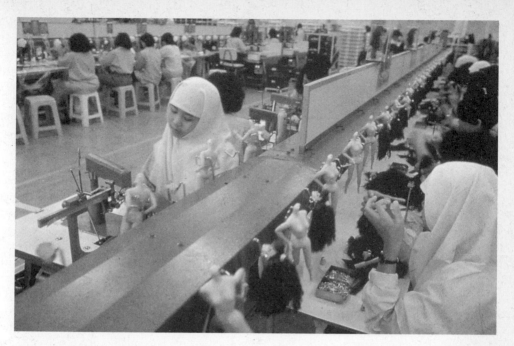

Direct foreign investment is often sought by host governments because it stimulates employment and economic growth, though at wages that home countries would not tolerate. Here Indonesian women assemble Barbies at a Mattel factory. Note that along with investment, a host country imports certain cultural trappings of the MNC's activity—such as Mattel's rendition of femininity in its doll. (This is a literal case of what postmodern feminists call the social construction of gender roles.)

taxation and of *regulation* are common. In cases of resource extraction, negotiations may revolve around the rates the government will charge to *lease* land and mineral rights to the MNC. National and local governments may offer to provide business *infrastructure*—such as roads, airports, or phone lines—at the government's expense. (However, an MNC could also offer to build such infrastructure if allowed to operate on favorable terms in the country.) Over time, certain locations may develop a strong business infrastructure and gain a comparative advantage in luring MNCs to locate there.

These kinds of issues basically all concern the distribution of the new wealth that will be created by MNC operations. MNCs seek host governments that will let the MNC keep more of that wealth; governments seek MNCs that will let governments keep more. With many MNCs and quite a few governments involved in such negotiations, there is a sort of market process at work in the worldwide investment decisions of MNCs.

In addition to these relatively straightforward questions of distribution, MNC relations with host governments contain several other sources of potential conflict. One is the potential for governments to *break their agreements* with MNCs and change the terms of taxes, regulations, or other conditions. The extreme case is *nationalization,* in which a host government takes ownership of MNC facilities and assets in the host country (with or without compensation). Once an MNC has invested in fixed facilities, it loses much of its leverage over the government because it cannot move to another country without incurring huge expenses. However, governments hesitate to break their word with MNCs because then other MNCs may not invest in the future. Nationalization of foreign assets is rare now.

Another source of conflict is *trade policies* of the host government. Government restrictions on trade seldom help foreign MNCs; more often they help the host country's own industries—which often directly compete with foreign MNCs. Ironically, although they favor global free trade, MNCs may funnel direct investment to states that restrict imports, because MNCs can avoid the import restrictions by producing goods in the host country (rather than exporting from the home country). Trade restrictions are thus another form of leverage that states have in luring direct foreign investment.

Trade regulations often seek to create as many jobs and as much taxable income as possible within the host country. For example, if Toyota assembles cars at a factory in the United States (perhaps to avoid U.S. import restrictions), the U.S. government tends to pressure Toyota to use more U.S. parts in building the cars (such "domestic content" rules were part of the 1992 North American Free Trade Agreement). MNCs generally want the freedom to assemble goods anywhere from parts made anywhere; governments by contrast want to maximize the amount of wealth created on their own territories. With parts and supplies now routinely converging from many countries to go into a product completed in one country, it is very difficult to say exactly where the product was made. The question is a complex one that entails long negotiations between MNCs and host governments.

Monetary policy also leads to conflicts between MNCs and host governments. When a state's currency is devalued, imports suddenly become more expensive. A foreign MNC selling an imported product (or a product assembled from imported parts) in the host country can be devastated by such a change. For example, if the dollar falls relative to the yen, Toyota-U.S.A. may have to charge more U.S. dollars for its cars in order to pay for the parts it brings in from Japan. Therefore, an MNC making a long-term investment in a host country wants the country's currency to be reasonably stable.

Finally, MNCs may conflict with host governments on issues of *international security* as well as domestic political stability. When an MNC invests in a country, it counts on its facilities there operating profitably over a number of years. If a war or revolution takes away the MNC's facility, the company loses not just income but capital—the standing wealth embodied in that facility. Governments that allow wars or allow revolutions to develop on their territories are generally bad hosts for MNCs.

In negotiating over these various sources of conflict, MNCs use a variety of means to influence host governments. These generally follow the same patterns as those used by domestic corporations (see "Interest Groups" on pp. 153–156 and "Industries and Interest Groups" on pp. 332–335). MNCs hire lobbyists, use advertisements to influence public opinion, and offer incentives to host-country politicians (such as locating new facilities in their districts). Such activities are politically sensitive because host-country citizens and politicians may resent foreigners' trying to influence them. For example, if Toyota-U.S.A. ran television ads supporting a U.S. presidential candidate who supported free trade, U.S. voters might react negatively to this foreign intrusion into U.S. politics.

Corruption is another means of influence over host governments that cannot be overlooked. Nobody knows the full extent to which MNCs use payoffs, kickbacks, gifts, and similar methods to win the approval of individual government officials for policies favorable to the MNC. Certainly this happens quite a bit with host governments in the third world (where government officials may be more desperate for income), but corruption also occurs regularly in rich industrialized countries. For example, in the 1970s U.S.-based Lockheed bribed top government officials in Japan to buy Lockheed jets for the Japanese military. In another infamous case in the early 1990s, the Bank of Commerce and Credit International (BCCI) was found to have operated a vast illegal worldwide network of money laundering, fraud, and corruption.[19]

MNCs have a range of conflicts with their *home* governments (where their headquarters are located), just as they do with their host states.[20] Because MNCs are not foreigners but citizens in their home states, they have somewhat more freedom of action in influencing their home governments than they do in influencing host governments. For instance, U.S. MNCs routinely contribute to U.S. politicians' campaigns in hopes that those politicians will support policies favorable to the MNCs' global operations.

Some MNC conflicts with home governments are the same as with host governments. *Taxation* is an important one. *Trade policies* are another. One recurrent complaint of MNCs against home governments is that policies adopted to punish political adversaries—economic sanctions and less extreme restrictions—end up harming the home-country MNCs more than the intended target. Usually, a competing MNC from another country is able to step into the gap when a government restricts its own MNCs (as in the Soviet gas pipeline mentioned on p. 322). Unless ordered to do so, MNCs tend to go on doing business wherever it is profitable, with little regard for the political preferences of their governments. True to the wealth-maximizing principles of liberalism, MNCs generally prefer to keep politics from interfering with business.

A prime example of this tendency was the decision by the U.S.-based Conoco oil company to undertake a billion-dollar oil development project in Iran, just when the U.S. government was trying to contain Iran as a rogue state. But under pressure from the U.S. government, Conoco quickly decided to back out of the deal. This saved both the U.S. government and Conoco embarrassment, though costing Conoco a lucrative contract that went instead to a European company.

In 1975, when a Soviet-backed Marxist party took control of Angola, several U.S. multinational oil companies operating there were responsible for much of the hard-currency revenue of that oil producing African country. Conservative U.S. politicians called for the U.S. companies to pull out of Angola, and the largest, Gulf Oil, decided to do so (though probably based on risk analysis more than on any political ideal). But Gulf's operations in Angola were bought by another U.S.-based company, Chevron Oil, which continues to operate them profitably today. It's not that Chevron executives were soft on communism; they just thought that the Cold War was irrelevant—as it was in Chevron's negotiations for drilling rights in the Soviet Union and its successor states. In the 1980s the U.S. government funded and trained a rebel army to destabilize the Angolan government—including a few attacks on U.S. companies like Chevron! The (Marxist) host government was called on to provide security for (capitalist) Chevron against such attacks.

The location of an MNC's headquarters determines its home nationality. The shareholders and top executives of an MNC are mostly from its home country. But as the world

---

[19]Adams, James Ring, and Douglas Frantz. *A Full Service Bank: How BCCI Stole Billions Around the World*. New York: Pocket Books, 1992.

[20]Cohen, Benjamin J. *In Whose Interest? International Banking and American Foreign Policy*. New Haven: Yale University Press, 1986.

economy becomes more integrated, this is becoming less true. Just as MNCs are increasingly doing business all over the world and assembling products from parts made in many countries, so are shareholders and managers becoming more international in composition.

Business Environments

All business activity takes place within an environment shaped by politics.[21] In some places, states allow private businesses to compete freely with little interference from government; elsewhere states own and operate their own businesses and forbid competition altogether. In some places goods flow freely from producers to consumers; elsewhere the same goods may be taxed, harassed, or even stolen on their way to the consumer. In some places markets are dominated by oligopolies; elsewhere large companies are forcibly broken up into smaller ones.

MNCs operating across international borders do business in a variety of business environments at once. MNCs do their best to influence the political environments in which they work, but for the most part the MNCs have to live with conditions created by governments and can at best avoid certain states and favor others. MNCs have definite preferences about political conditions. Beyond the obvious preference to keep more of the wealth they generate, MNCs have general preferences about the political business environments in which they live. As MNCs become more important actors in IR, it is likely that they will work to make our world resemble their ideal environment.

The international business environment most conducive to the creation of wealth by MNCs is one of *stable international security*. It is difficult and risky to make money in a situation of international conflict, especially one that threatens to degenerate into violence and war. War destroys wealth, reduces the supply of labor, and distorts markets in many ways. Certainly there are some businesses that profit from international instability and the threat of war—such as arms merchants and smugglers—but these are the exceptions.

In part, the MNCs' great interest in stability derives from the nature of investment, which pays back a stream of income over time. Money invested today may not be recovered for many years into the future. Any disruption of the economic framework in which MNCs expect to do business may mean the loss of investments. Large corporations, and especially banks, put much effort into political **risk assessment** before making international investments. They want to determine the probability that political conditions in future years (during which the investments will be paid back) will change so radically that the flow of income is disrupted. These future political conditions include not only wars but international exchange rates, taxation policies, and trade policies. But international security risks are among the most threatening to business.

In favoring stable international security, MNCs illustrate the fundamental connection between peace and prosperity in the liberal view of IPE. The world in which realists and mercantilists think we are doomed to live is, from a liberal perspective, an impover-

---

[21]Preston, Lee E., and Duane Windsor. *The Rules of the Game in the Global Economy: Policy Regimes for International Business*. Hingham, MA: Kluwer Academic, 1992.

International business prospers in stable political environments. Foreign investors tend to be wary of putting money into a business environment like Russia's, where inflation constantly erodes the value of currency, and rampant crime and corruption take a huge economic toll. Here a woman in Moscow trades rubles for dollars in October 1994, bailing out after a one-day drop of over 25 percent in the ruble's value.

ished world. According to liberalism, the growing interdependence and growing prosperity of our world go hand in hand and create the conditions for stable peace. MNCs are merely the leading edge of a strong trend in IR: actors would rather make money than make war, and making war is not an effective way to make money.

Beyond these international security concerns, MNCs favor political stability in the broader rules of the game governing international business. When an MNC decides to do business in a new country, it hopes to know at the outset what to expect in terms of trade regulations, monetary policies, tax rates, and even public sentiments toward foreign companies. In a way the actual policies of states regarding tax rates, exchange rates, tariffs, and so forth matter less than the stability of those policies. Businesses can easily adapt to a variety of conditions, but they adapt to rapid changes in those conditions less easily.

In monetary policy, international business benefits from the stability of rates that the managed float system tries to achieve. In trade policy, business benefits from the stability of tariff levels in the slowly shifting GATT framework. In norms of international law, business benefits from the traditions holding governments responsible for the predecessors' debts and requiring compensation for foreign assets nationalized.

MNCs also depend on national governments to provide security domestically for business operations. If Toyota builds a factory in Italy, it wants the Italian government to apprehend criminals who kidnap Toyota executives or steal Toyota payrolls, not to mention terrorists who might plant bombs to protest Toyota's presence. Foreigners make an inviting target for political and nonpolitical crimes alike. Many corporations have their own security personnel, and independent companies provide security services to businesses. But such capabilities do not compare with those of the armed forces maintained by states, so MNCs ultimately rely on host and home governments to provide a secure environment for business.

Occasionally, MNCs can get their home governments to provide security when host governments fail to do so. During the colonial era, home governments directly ran foreign colonies in which businesses could operate under the security guarantees of the home government. Many of these businesses continued to operate profitably after those colonies gained independence. In the postcolonial era, military interventions by industrialized countries in the third world continue to occur, and some IR scholars see those interventions as efforts to impose on smaller states the political arrangements for profitable MNC operations. This is an area of controversy, however. IR scholars continue to study the relationships between the international economic activities of MNCs and the international security activities of their home governments.[22]

MNCs themselves influence the evolving international security environment. Just as states form alliances to augment their capabilities, so do companies ally with other companies to enhance their pursuit of wealth. Corporate alliances involving MNCs often have international implications. When business alliances in an industry that has international markets occur *within* a single state, the alliances may in effect promote economic nationalism. Increasingly, however, corporate alliances are forming *across* national borders. Such alliances tend to promote liberalism rather than economic nationalism. For example, inter-MNC alliances have made the auto industry more international than ever. Chrysler cars have Mitsubishi engines, and so forth. A car can rarely be classified anymore as being made in *any* one country.

These international business alliances undermine both economic nationalism and the concept of a world splitting into rival trading blocs based in Europe, North America, and East Asia. In fact, international business alliances create interdependence among their home states. National interests become more intertwined and interstate conflicts tend to be reduced. By operating in multiple countries at once, all MNCs have these effects to some degree. But because they are based in one home country, MNCs are foreigners in other countries. International alliances of MNCs, however, are at home in several countries at once.

We do not yet live in a world without national borders—by a long shot—but the international activities of MNCs are moving us in that direction. Chapter 10 explores some of the ways in which people, companies, and ideas are becoming globally integrated across states.

---

[22]Krasner, Stephen D. *Defending the National Interest: Raw Materials Investments and U.S. Foreign Policy.* Princeton: Princeton University Press, 1978. Gibbs, David N. *The Political Economy of Third World Intervention: Mines, Money, and U.S. Policy in the Congo Crisis.* Chicago: University of Chicago Press, 1991. Lipson, Charles. *Standing Guard: Protecting Foreign Capital in the Nineteenth and Twentieth Centuries.* Berkeley: University of California Press, 1985.

❖ CHAPTER SUMMARY

- Each state uses its own currency. These currencies have no inherent value but depend on people's belief that they can be traded for future goods and services.

- Gold and silver were once used as world currencies that had value in different countries. Today's system is more abstract: national currencies are valued against each other through exchange rates.

- The most important currencies—against which most other states' currencies are compared—are the U.S. dollar, German mark, and Japanese yen.

- Inflation, most often resulting from the printing of currency faster than the creation of new goods and services, causes the value of a currency to fall relative to other currencies. Inflation rates vary widely but are generally much higher in the third world and former Soviet bloc than in the industrialized West.

- States maintain reserves of hard currency and gold. These reserves back a national currency and cover short-term imbalances in international financial flows.

- Fixed exchange rates can be used to set the relative value of currencies, but more often states use floating exchange rates driven by supply and demand on world currency markets.

- Governments cooperate to manage the fluctuations of (floating) exchange rates but are limited in this effort by the fact that most money traded on world markets is privately owned.

- Over the long term, the relative values of national currencies are determined by the underlying health of the national economies and by the monetary policies of governments (how much money they print).

- Governments often prefer a low (weak) value for their own currency, as this promotes exports, discourages imports, and hence improves the state's balance of trade. However, a sudden unilateral devaluation of the currency is a risky strategy because it undermines confidence in the currency.

- To ensure discipline in printing money—and avoid inflation—industrialized states turn monetary policy over to semiautonomous central banks like the U.S. Federal Reserve. By adjusting interest rates on government money loaned to private banks, a central bank can control the supply of money in a national economy.

- The World Bank and the International Monetary Fund (IMF) work with states' central banks to maintain stable international monetary relations. From 1945 to 1971 this was done by pegging state currencies to the U.S. dollar and the dollar in turn to gold (backed by gold reserves held by the U.S. government). Since then the system has used Special Drawing Rights—a kind of world currency controlled by the IMF—in place of gold.

- The IMF operates a system of national accounts to keep track of the flow of money into and out of states. The balance of trade (exports minus imports) must be balanced by capital flows (investments and loans) and changes in reserves.

- International debt results from a protracted imbalance in capital flows—a state borrowing more than it lends—in order to cover a chronic trade deficit or government budget deficit. The result is that the net worth of the debtor state is reduced and wealth generated is diverted to pay interest (with the creditor state's wealth increasing accordingly).

◆ The U.S. financial position declined naturally from an extraordinary predominance immediately after World War II. The fall of the dollar-gold standard in 1971 reflects this decline.

◆ In the 1980s (and continuing today), the U.S. position has worsened dramatically. A chronic budget deficit and trade deficit contribute to an ever-increasing debt burden.

◆ The positions of Russia and the other states of the former Soviet bloc have declined drastically in the past five years as they try to make the difficult transition from communism to capitalism. Economic growth rates are negative and large; inflation is almost out of control. Recession-bound Western states have not offered massive economic assistance to Russia and Eastern Europe.

◆ Multinational corporations (MNCs) do business in more than one state simultaneously. The largest are based in the leading industrialized states, and most are privately owned. MNCs are increasingly powerful in international economic affairs.

◆ MNCs contribute to international interdependence in various ways. States depend on MNCs to create new wealth, and MNCs depend on states to maintain international stability conducive to doing business globally.

◆ Direct foreign investment by MNCs takes years to pay back a stream of income; meanwhile, the MNC cannot easily move its operations from a state where it has invested. Governments seek such foreign investments on their territories so as to benefit from the future stream of income. MNCs try to negotiate favorable terms and look for states with stable currencies and political environments in which to make direct investments.

◆ MNCs try to influence the international political policies of both their headquarters state and the other states in which they operate. Generally MNCs promote policies favorable to business—low taxes, light regulation, stable currencies, and free trade. They also support stable international security relations, because war generally disrupts business.

◆ Increasingly, MNCs headquartered in different states are forming international alliances with each other. These alliances, even more than other MNC operations across national borders, are creating international interdependence and promoting liberal international cooperation.

◆ MNCs sometimes promote economic nationalism over liberalism, however, especially in the case of state-owned MNCs or alliances of MNCs based in a single country.

❖ THINKING CRITICALLY

1. Find a recent newspaper article about a change in currency exchange rates (usually in the business section). Analyze the various influences that may have been at work in the change of currency values—monetary policies, the underlying state of national economies, the actions of central banks (separately or in coordination), and the factors such as political uncertainty that affect investors' confidence in a currency.

2. Is the deteriorating U.S. economic position in the past decade a good thing or a bad thing for Japan? What arguments would you make on either side of this question? What steps could Japan take either to stop the U.S. slide or to accelerate it?

3. Many scholars and politicians alike think that private international investment is the best hope for the economies of Russia and Eastern Europe. Given the current economic and political disarray in that region, what kinds of investors from the industrialized West might be willing to invest there? What actions could the governments of Western states take to encourage such investment? What pitfalls would the governments and investors have to watch out for?

4. If you were representing an MNC like Toyota in negotiations over building an automobile factory in a foreign country, what kinds of concessions would you ask the host government for? What would you offer as incentives? In your report to Toyota's top management regarding the deal, what points would you emphasize as most important? What if you were representing the host state in the negotiations and reporting to top state leaders? Then what would be your negotiating goals and the focus of your report?

5. Suppose that the head of Dow Chemical had his way and established Dow's world headquarters on an island outside all state territory. How do you think this would change Dow's strategies or business operations? What problems might it create for Dow?

❖ KEY TERMS

gold standard
exchange rate
convertibility (of currency)
hyperinflation
hard currency
reserves
fixed vs. floating exchange rates
managed float
Exchange Rate Mechanism (ERM)
devaluation
central bank
Bretton Woods

World Bank
International Monetary Fund (IMF)
Special Drawing Right (SDR)
balance of payments
direct foreign investment
Keynesian economics
fiscal policy
monetary policy
national debt
multinational corporation (MNC)
host vs. home country
risk assessment

*Opening in the Berlin
Wall, 1989.*

INTEGRATION

❖ SUPRANATIONALISM

This chapter and the next continue to develop a theme from the discussion of MNCs—that of nonstate actors in interaction with state actors. Although MNCs are *substate* actors in the formation of state foreign policy (see pp. 151–160), they are also *transnational* actors bridging national borders and creating new avenues of interdependence among states.[1] This chapter discusses transnational and international nonstate actors whose roles and influences are *supranational*—they subsume a number of states within a larger whole.

The UN, as we have seen, has some supranational aspects, though they are limited by the UN Charter, which is based on state sovereignty. On a regional level, the *European Union (EU)* is a somewhat more supranational entity than the UN; other regional organizations have tried to follow Europe's path as well, with mixed success. These cases all contain a struggle between the contradictory forces of **nationalism** and **supranationalism**—between state sovereignty and the higher authority (in level but not yet in power or legitimacy) of supranational structures.

Formal IGOs like the UN or EU are not the only way that supranationalism is developing. Even more far-reaching in many ways are the effects of information technologies that operate globally and regionally across state boundaries without formal political structures. Here, too, supranational influences compete for influence with the sovereign state. This chapter considers these various supranational influences on international politics, from the formal structures of the EU to the globalizing effects of information.

❖ INTEGRATION THEORY

The theory of international integration can help to explain these new phenomena, which challenge once again the foundations of realism (state sovereignty and territorial in-

---

[1]Nye, Joseph S., Jr., and Robert O. Keohane, eds. *Transnational Relations and World Politics*. Cambridge, MA: Harvard University Press, 1981.

tegrity). **International integration** refers to the process by which supranational institutions come to replace national ones—the gradual shifting upward of sovereignty from the state to regional or global structures. The ultimate expression of integration would be the merger of several (or many) states into a single state—or ultimately into a single world government. Such a shift in sovereignty to the supranational level would probably entail some version of federalism, in which states (or other political units) would recognize the sovereignty of a central government while retaining certain powers for themselves. This is the form of government adopted (after some debate) in the U.S. Constitution.

Today one hears occasional calls for a "United States of Europe"—or even of the world—but in practice the process of integration has never gone beyond a partial and uneasy sharing of power between the state and supranational levels. States have been unwilling to give up their exclusive claim to sovereignty and have severely limited the power and authority of supranational institutions. The UN, certainly, falls far short of a federal model (see Chapter 7). It represents a step in the direction of international integration—but only a step.

Other modest examples of the integration process have been encountered in previous chapters. One is the creation of regional free-trade areas such as NAFTA. But these arrangements hardly challenge states' territorial integrity, much less their political sovereignty. Nor do states give up much sovereignty in either monetary regimes or dealings with MNCs, although all these aspects of IPE do have supranational elements.

The most successful example of the process of integration by far—though even that success is only partial—is the European Union. Although we can observe aspects of international integration at work elsewhere in the world, these processes have gone much further in Europe than anywhere else. The regional coordination now occurring in Western Europe is a new historical phenomenon achieved only since World War II.[2]

Until fifty years ago the European continent was the embodiment of national sovereignty, state rivalry, and war. The international system was invented in Europe. For five hundred years until 1945 the states of Europe were locked in chronic intermittent warfare, and in the twentieth century alone two world wars left the continent in ruins. The European states have historical and present-day religious, ethnic, and cultural differences. The 15 members of today's EU speak 13 different official languages. If ever there were a candidate for the failure of integration, Europe would appear to be it. Even more surprising, European integration began with the cooperation of Europe's two bitterest enemies over the previous hundred years, enemies in three major wars since 1870—France and Germany (references to "Germany" refer to West Germany from 1944 to 1990, and unified Germany since).

When Western European states began forming supranational institutions and creating an economic community to promote free trade and coordinate economic policies, it caught the attention of IR scholars. They used the term *integration* to describe what they observed happening in Europe. Seemingly, integration challenged the assumption of realism that states were strictly autonomous and would never yield power or sovereignty.

These scholars proposed that European moves toward integration could be explained by *functionalism*—the growth of specialized technical organizations that cross national

---

[2]Keohane, Robert O., and Stanley Hoffmann, eds. *The New European Community: Decisionmaking and Institutional Change.* Boulder, CO: Westview, 1991. Kahler, Miles. *International Institutions and the Political Economy of Integration.* Washington, DC: The Brookings Institution, 1995.

Integration processes in Europe and elsewhere are making state borders more permeable to people, goods, and ideas—increasing interdependence. Here Japanese tourists exchange currency at a 24-hour teller machine in Paris (1987).

borders.[3] According to functionalists, technological and economic development lead to more and more supranational structures as states seek practical means to fulfill necessary *functions* such as delivering mail or phone calls from one country to another or coordinating the use of rivers that cross borders. Some IR scholars tried to measure the extent of functional connections in Europe, for instance, by counting flows of mail and other communications among countries.[4] As these connections became denser and the flows faster, functionalism predicted that states would be drawn together into stronger international economic structures.

The European experience, however, went beyond the creation of specialized agencies to include the development of more general, more political supranational bodies, such as the European Parliament. **Neofunctionalism** is a modification of functional theory by IR scholars to explain these developments. Neofunctionalists argue that economic integration (functionalism) generates a *political* dynamic that drives integration further. Closer economic ties require more political coordination in order to operate effectively and eventually lead to political integration as well—a process called *spillover*.

[3]Mitrany, David. *The Functional Theory of Politics*. London: The London School of Economics/M. Robertson, 1975. Haas, Ernst B. *Beyond the Nation-State: Functionalism and International Organization*. Stanford: Stanford University Press, 1964. Haas, Ernst B. *When Knowledge Is Power: Three Models of Change in International Organizations*. Berkeley: University of California Press, 1989. Skolnikoff, Eugene B. *The Elusive Transformation: Science, Technology, and the Evolution of International Politics*. Princeton: Princeton University Press, 1994.
[4]Cioffi-Revilla, Claudio, Richard L. Merritt, and Dina A. Zinnes, eds. *Communication and Interaction in Global Politics*. Newbury Park, CA: Sage, 1987.

Some scholars focused on the less-tangible *sense of community* ("we" feeling) that began to develop among Europeans, running contrary to nationalist feelings that still existed as well. The low expectation of violence among the states of Western Europe created a **security community** in which such feelings could grow.[5] The emergence of a European identity was also assisted by such efforts as the textbook revision project mentioned on p. 202.

Elsewhere in the world, economies were becoming more interdependent at both the regional and global levels. The Andean Common Market, begun in 1969, promoted a limited degree of regional integration in the member states of Venezuela, Colombia, Ecuador, Peru, and Bolivia. In Asia, the Association of South East Asian Nations (ASEAN) chalked up some successes in promoting regional economic coordination over several decades.[6]

Interest in integration theory among IR scholars has waxed and waned with the uneven pace of European integration. In the 1960s and 1970s European integration seemed to slow down, and regional integration efforts elsewhere in the world also failed to develop as hoped. For most of the Cold War decades, integration took a secondary position among IR scholars (and policy makers) to the concerns of East-West conflict, nuclear weapons, and related security issues. Then in the 1980s, Europe accelerated its progress toward integration again, the Cold War ended, and the North American Free Trade Agreement took form; the scholarly interest in integration expanded again.

Costs of Integration Ironically, the new wave of integration in Europe and elsewhere is encountering limits and setbacks just as scholars are reinvigorating the theory of integration. Integration reduces states' ability to shield themselves and their citizens from the world's many problems and conflicts. For example, in the early 1990s Venezuela found that its open border with Colombia brought in large trans-shipments of cocaine bound for the United States. China found that its new openness to foreign trade also exposed it to the AIDS epidemic spreading in Asia. Germany and Western Europe found that accepting foreign refugees meant living with more domestic ethnic conflict.

Integration can mean greater centralization at a time when individuals, local groups, and national populations are demanding more say over their own affairs. The centralization of political authority, information, and culture as a result of integration can threaten both individual and group freedom. Ethnic groups want to safeguard their own cultures, languages, and institutions against the bland homogeneity that a global or regional melting pot would create. As a result of these costs of integration, many states and citizens, in Europe and elsewhere, have responded to the new wave of integration with resurgent nationalism in the 1990s.

Indeed these forces have set in motion a wave of *disintegration* of states running counter to (though simultaneous with) the integrating tendencies in today's world. The wave of disintegration in some ways began with the decolonization of former European empires in Africa, Asia, and the Middle East after World War II. Currently disintegration

---

[5]Deutsch, Karl W. *Political Community and the North Atlantic Area: International Organization in the Light of Historical Experience*. Princeton: Princeton University Press, 1957. Ullman, Richard H. *Securing Europe*. Princeton: Princeton University Press, 1991.

[6]Wallace, William. *Regional Integration*. Washington, DC: The Brookings Institution, 1995.

is most evident in Russia and Eastern Europe—especially in the former Soviet Union and former Yugoslavia. But states in other regions—Somalia, Iraq, Afghanistan, and Cambodia—appear in danger of breaking into pieces, in practice if not formally. The result of the Soviet breakup *might* end up resembling that of Western Europe under the most optimistic scenario for the future of the CIS. But the result of that experiment is not yet known, and few scholars are very optimistic. A challenge to integration theorists in the coming years will be to account for these various new trends running counter to integration in the 1990s.

Throughout the successful and unsuccessful efforts at integration runs a common thread—the tension between nationalism and supranational loyalties (regionalism or globalism). In the less-successful integration attempts, nationalism stands virtually unchallenged, and even in the most successful cases nationalism remains a potent force locked in continual struggle with supranationalism. This struggle is a central theme even in the most successful case of integration—the European Union.

❖ THE EUROPEAN UNION

Like the UN, the **European Union (EU)** was created after World War II and has developed since. But whereas the UN structure has changed little since the Charter was adopted, the EU has gone through several waves of expansion in its scope, membership, and mission over the past forty years.[7]

The Vision of a United Europe

Europe in 1945 was decimated by war. Most of the next decade was spent getting back on its feet with help from the United States through the Marshall Plan. But already two French leaders, Jean Monnet and Robert Schuman, were developing a plan to implement the idea of functionalism in Europe. Their vision was that Europe could be saved from future wars by creating crosscutting economic linkages that would eventually bind states together politically.

In 1950 Schuman as French foreign minister proposed a first modest step—the merger of the French and German steel (iron) and coal industries into a single framework that could most efficiently use the two states' coal resources and steel mills. Coal and steel were key to European recovery and growth. The Schuman plan gave birth in 1952 to the *European Coal and Steel Community (ECSC)*, in which France and Germany were joined by Italy (the third large industrial country of continental Europe) and by three smaller countries—Belgium, Netherlands, and Luxembourg (together called the Benelux countries). These six states worked through the ECSC to reduce trade barriers in coal and steel and to coordinate their coal and steel policies. For a French factory, it no longer mattered

---

[7]Nelsen, Brent F., and Alexander C. Stubb, eds. *The European Union: Readings on the Theory and Practice of European Integration.* Boulder, CO: Lynne Rienner, 1994. Dinan, Desmond. *Ever Closer Union? An Introduction to the European Community.* Boulder, CO: Lynne Rienner, 1994. Weigall, David, and Peter Stirk, eds. *The Origins and Development of the European Community: A Student Reader and Companion.* London: Pinter, 1992. Cafruny, Alan W., and Glenda G. Rosenthal, eds. *The State of the European Community: The Maastricht Debates and Beyond.* Boulder, CO: Lynne Rienner, 1993. Nelson, Brian, David Roberts, and Walter Veit, eds. *The European Community in the 1990s: Economics, Politics, Defence.* New York: Berg, 1992.

whether the coal it burned came from France, Germany, or Italy. The ECSC also established a High Authority that to some extent could bypass governments and deal directly with companies, labor unions, and individuals. Britain did not join, however.

If coal and steel sound like fairly boring topics, that was exactly the idea of functionalists. The issues involved were matters for engineers and technical experts, and did not threaten politicians. Since 1952, technical experts have served as the leaders of the integration process in other aspects of European life and outside Europe. As mentioned in Chapter 7, technical IOs like the Universal Postal Union came before political ones like the UN.

International scientific communities deserve special mention in this regard. If German and French steel experts had more in common than German and French politicians, this is even more true of scientists who understand each other's language, interests, and perspectives. Today the European scientific community is one of the most internationally integrated areas of society. For example, the CERN high-energy physics facility located in Switzerland—the most advanced of its kind in the world—is hardly a Swiss project but a thoroughly European one (though not an EU project). The EU operates the European Space Agency, the European Molecular Biology Laboratory, and the European Southern Observatory, among other facilities. This illustrates the importance of technical communities in functionalist integration.

Although technical cooperation succeeded in 1952, political and military cooperation proved much more difficult. In line with the vision of a united Europe, the six ECSC states signed a second treaty in 1952 to create a European Defense Community to work toward integrating Europe's military forces under one budget and command. But the French Parliament failed to ratify the treaty, and Britain refused to join such a force. The ECSC states also discussed formation of a European Political Community in 1953, but could not agree on its terms. Thus, in economic cooperation the supranational institutions succeeded but in political and military affairs state sovereignty prevailed.

The Treaty of Rome

In the **Treaty of Rome** in 1957, the same six states (France, Germany, Italy, Belgium, Netherlands, Luxembourg) created two new organizations. One extended the coal-and-steel idea into a new realm, atomic energy. **Euratom,** the European Atomic Energy Community, was formed to coordinate nuclear power development by pooling research, investment, and management in that issue area. It continues in operation today (with an expanded membership). The second organization was the *European Economic Community (EEC)*, later renamed the *European Community (EC)*.

After its founding in 1957 the EEC was often called simply the *Common Market*. Actually a common market was not immediately created but was established as a goal (which has since been largely realized). The treaty called for a sequence of steps to more closely coordinate the six states' economies over time.

In Chapter 8, the terms *free-trade area, customs union,* and *common market* were not distinguished; we may now define them more precisely. Creating a **free-trade area** meant that tariffs and restrictions on the movement of goods across borders (within the EEC) were lifted. This was done within a few years after 1957. Today the *European Free Trade Association (EFTA)* is an extended free-trade area associated with the EU; its members are

Norway, Iceland, Liechtenstein, and Switzerland. (All but Switzerland became, with the EU, the European Economic Area, participating in the "Europe 1992" single market described shortly.)

A **customs union** means that the participating states adopt a unified set of tariffs with regard to goods coming in from outside the free-trade area. Without this, the free-trade area could result in each type of good being imported into the state with the lowest tariff and then reexported (tariff-free) to the other states in the free-trade area; this would be inefficient. The Treaty of Rome committed the six states to creating a customs union by 1969. A customs union creates free and open trade within its member states, bringing great economic benefits. Because of these benefits the customs union remains the heart of the EU and the one aspect widely copied elsewhere in the world.

A **common market** means that in addition to the customs union, member states allow labor and capital (as well as goods) to flow freely across borders. For instance, a French doctor could work in Italy on the same terms as an Italian one, or a Belgian financier could invest in Germany on the same terms as a German investor. Although the Treaty of Rome adopted the goal of a common market, even today it has been only partially achieved.

One key aspect of a common market was achieved, at least in theory, in the 1960s when the EU (then the EC) adopted a **Common Agricultural Policy (CAP).** In practice, the CAP has led to recurrent conflicts among member states and tensions between nationalism and regionalism. Recall that agriculture has been one of the most difficult sectors of the world economy in which to achieve free trade (see p. 333). To promote national self-sufficiency in food, many governments give subsidies to farmers. The CAP was based on the principle that a subsidy extended to farmers in any EC country should be extended to farmers in all EC countries. That way no EC government was forced to alienate politically powerful farmers by removing subsidies, yet the overall policy would be equalized throughout the community in line with the common market principle. As a result, subsidies to farmers today absorb about two-thirds of the total EU budget and are the single greatest source of trade friction between Europe and the United States (including the 1992 trade dispute described on pp. 337–338).

The fourth step anticipated in the plan for European integration (after free trade, customs union, and a common market) was an *economic union* in which the overall economic policies of the member states would be coordinated for greatest efficiency and stability. In this step a *monetary union* would also be established, with a single currency instead of the separate national currencies now in use. These plans are still alive but will not be achieved until the end of the 1990s at best. A future fifth step in economic integration would be the supranational coordination of economic policies.

To reduce state leaders' fears of losing sovereignty, the Treaty of Rome provides that changes in its provisions must be approved by all member states. For example, France vetoed Britain's application for membership in the EEC in 1963 and 1967. However, in 1973 Britain did finally join, along with Ireland and Denmark. This expanded the EC's membership to nine, including the largest and richest countries in the region.

In 1981 Greece was admitted, and in 1986 Portugal and Spain joined. These were poorer countries with less industry and lower standards of living, and their inclusion created difficulties in effectively integrating Europe's economies. These difficulties persist today, and the richer European states are giving substantial aid to the poorer ones in hopes

Under the free-trade area first created by the 1957 Treaty of Rome, goods can move freely across European borders to reach consumers in any member country. In agriculture, creating an integrated free market in Europe has not been easy; the EC adopted a Common Agricultural Policy in the 1960s to address the problem. Prices in this French marketplace in 1991 reflect subsidies to French farmers.

of strengthening the weak links of Europe. Greece, Portugal, Spain, and Ireland are called the "poor four" within the EU.

Structure of the European Union

The structure of the EU reflects its roots in technical and economic cooperation. The coal and steel experts have been joined by experts on trade, agriculture, and finance at the heart of the community. The EU headquarters and staff have the reputation of colorless bureaucrats—sometimes called *"Eurocrats"*—who care more about technical problem solving than about politics. These supranational bureaucrats are balanced in the EU structure by provisions that uphold the power of states and state leaders.

Although the rule of Eurocrats follows the functionalist plan, it has created certain problems as the EU has progressed. Politicians in member states have certain qualms about losing power to the Eurocrats. Equally important, citizens in those states have become more uncomfortable in recent years with the growing power of faceless Eurocrats over their lives. Citizens can throw their own political leaders out of office in national elections, but the Eurocrats seem out of reach and less accountable.

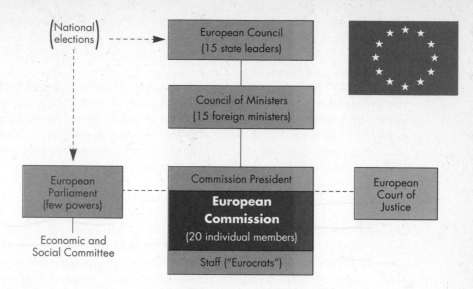

FIGURE 10.1 Structure of the European Union (EU)

The EU's structure is illustrated in Figure 10.1. The Eurocrats consist of a staff of about five thousand, organized under the **European Commission** at EU headquarters in Brussels, Belgium. The Commission has 20 individual members—one or two from each member state—who are chosen for four-year renewable terms. Their role is to identify problems and propose solutions to the Council of Ministers. They select one of their members as the commission president. These individuals are supposed to represent the interests of Europe as a whole (supranational interests) and not their own states, but this goal has been only imperfectly met. For instance, in the 1992 agricultural trade dispute with the United States, critics of Commission president Jacques Delors said he had impeded a settlement in order to appease French farmers because he planned a future political career in his native France. (But he opted not to run for president of France after his EU term.)

The Commission lacks formal autonomous power except in working out day-to-day EU operations. Formally the Commission reports to, and implements the policies of, the **Council of Ministers.** The Council is a meeting of the relevant ministers (foreign, economic, agriculture, finance, etc.) of each member state—politicians exercising control over the bureaucrats (or trying to). This formal structure reflects states' resistance to yielding sovereignty. This arrangement also means that the individuals making up the Council of Ministers vary from one meeting to the next, and that technical issues receive priority over political ones. The arrangement thus gives some advantage back to the Commission staff. Recall the similar tension between politicians and career bureaucrats in national foreign policy making (see "Bureaucracies" on p. 151–153).

The Council of Ministers in theory has a weighted voting system based on each state's population, but in practice it operates by consensus on major policy issues (all 15 members must agree). On other issues, decisions can be made by qualified majorities, overriding national sovereignty. The Council has a rotating presidency (with limited power). The Council of Ministers must approve the policies of the European Commission and give it general directions.[8]

In the 1970s, state leaders (prime ministers or presidents) created a special place for themselves in the EC, to oversee the direction of the community; this structure again shows the resistance of state leaders to being governed by any supranational body. The *European Council* consists of the 15 state leaders, who meet with the Commission president on a regular basis twice a year. They are the ones with the power to get things done in their respective national governments (which still control most of the money and power in Europe).

There is a **European Parliament,** which might someday operate as a true legislature passing laws for all of Europe.[9] At present it operates more as a watchdog over the Commission, with little power to legislate. The Parliament must approve the Commission's budget but cannot control it item by item. The Parliament serves mainly as a debating forum and a symbol of European unity. Since 1979, voters throughout Europe have directly elected their representatives to the European Parliament. Seats are allocated according to population. Political parties are organized across national lines, with all the Christian Democrats from all 15 countries, for instance, sitting together. However, many of the most heated debates are between national delegations *within* a party—reflecting the continuing influence of nationalism.

An *Economic and Social Committee* discusses continentwide issues that affect particular industries or constituencies. This committee is purely advisory; it lobbies the Commission on matters it deems important. It is designed as a forum in which companies, labor unions, and interest groups can bargain transnationally.

The EU also runs a **European Court of Justice** in Luxembourg. Its adjudicates disputes on matters covered by the Treaty of Rome—which covers many issues. Unlike the World Court (see pp. 292–294), the European Court has actively established its jurisdiction and not merely served as a mechanism of international mediation. The Court has established its right to overrule national law when in conflict with EU law—giving it unique powers among international courts. It hears cases brought by individuals, not just governments. In hundreds of cases, the Court has ruled on matters ranging from discrimination in the workplace to the pensions of Commission staff members.

The Single European Act

European integration has proceeded in a step-by-step process that produces tangible successes, reduces politicians' fears of losing sovereignty, and creates pressures to continue the process. In 1985 the EC passed the **Single European Act,** which set a target date of

[8]Kirchner, Emil Joseph. *Decision Making in the European Community: The Council Presidency and European Integration.* Manchester, U.K.: Manchester University Press, 1992.

[9]Smith, Julie. *Voice of the People: The European Parliament in the 1990s.* Washington, DC: The Brookings Institution, 1995.

the end of 1992 for the creation of a true common market in Europe.[10] This comprehensive set of changes was nicknamed *Europe 1992*.

The 1992 process was guided by about three hundred directives from the European Commission. Most of these were aimed at eliminating nontariff barriers to free trade in goods, services, labor, and capital within the EC. The issues tended to be complex and technical. For instance, professionals licensed in one state should be free to practice in another; but Spain's licensing requirements for, say, physical therapists, may have differed from those of Britain or the other EC countries. The Commission bureaucrats worked to smooth out such inconsistencies and create a uniform set of standards. Each national government had to pass laws to implement these measures.

For example, the German government had long set standards for the quality of beer sold in Germany—reflecting that nation's long history of beer making and beer drinking. These regulations in practice excluded most foreign beer from the German market. In a true common market, the same quality standards for beer have to apply in Germany as in France, Britain, and elsewhere. So, on orders of the European Commission, the German government rescinded the beer regulations, and foreign beers poured into Germany.

The Single European Act also called for the creation of a European Central Bank (which will be in Frankfurt, Germany) and a single currency and monetary system—not right away but in stages over time. Since 1979 the EC had linked its national currencies into a *European Monetary System* aimed at reducing exchange-rate fluctuations among nine European currencies (the most important being the mark, pound, and franc). The *Exchange Rate Mechanism (ERM)*, mentioned earlier on page 356, restricts currencies to a narrow band of fluctuation relative to each other while it lets them together fluctuate freely relative to world markets. It is called the "snake" because a graph of the values of the currencies moving together over time looks like a snake.

This close linkage of currencies may have been too ambitious. As we have seen, in the 1992 currency crisis, Britain, Italy, and Spain had to break from the ERM rates. As long as the economies of the EU members are tied to separate states (with separate central banks), efforts to maintain fixed exchange rates may prove difficult. British politicians are reluctant to deepen a recession (in an effort to maintain an overvalued pound) in order to save German politicians from inflation.

Such exchange rate problems could eventually be overcome by introduction of a European currency. That currency, the **ECU** (for "European Currency Unit"), will be called the **euro**. Today it is an abstract unit like the World Bank's SDR (see p. 363). It is used mostly by national governments to buy and sell other currencies. But EU leaders hope that within a decade the euro may replace all the national currencies of Europe. Because citizens use money every day, a European currency could deepen citizens' sense of identification with Europe—a victory for supranationalism over nationalism. However, precisely for this reason some state leaders and citizens resist the idea of giving up the symbolic value of their national currencies. After arguing about whose picture to put on the euro, the EU was moving in the mid-1990s toward letting each country print its own design.

---

[10]Moravcsik, Andrew. Negotiating the Single European Act: National Interests and Conventional Statecraft in the European Community. *International Organization* 45 (1), 1991: 19–56.

The 1992 process as a whole continued step-by-step economic integration. However, it continued to put aside for the future the difficult problems of political and military integration. The 1992 process also triggered certain fears, in the United States and elsewhere, of a "Fortress Europe" that would be more self-sufficient and less open to world trade. Non-Europeans worried that the supranationalism of the EU could emerge as a regional version of economic nationalism. Such fears may help to explain why, as "Europe 1992" was coming into effect, U.S.-European trade tensions intensified and GATT trade talks stalled.

The Maastricht Treaty

The **Maastricht Treaty,** signed in the Dutch city of Maastricht in December 1991, renamed the EC the EU and committed it to further progress in two main areas. The first was monetary union. Under the treaty, the existing European currencies would be abolished in 1997 or 1999 and replaced by the euro. A European Central Bank would be created to take over the functions of states' central banks.[11]

It is not surprising that the monetary union has met resistance from several quarters. Money is more politicized than steel tariffs or beer-brewing regulations. A monetary union infringes on a core prerogative of states—the right to print currency. German leaders, furthermore, worried that the euro would prove a poor substitute for the mark. There were also major technical problems connected with monetary union owing to the disparity between the richer and poorer EU states. Maastricht makes monetary union contingent on a certain financial stability being achieved in each member state: its budget deficit must be less than 3 percent of GDP and its inflation rate no more than 1.5 percentage points above the average of the three lowest-inflation EU members. (Divergent inflation rates would make a single currency unworkable; see "International Currency Exchange" on pp. 353–358.) By 1992, only France and Luxembourg met these conditions; some other states were within reach, but the "poor four" were far from meeting them.

To solve these problems, the Maastricht Treaty called for increasing the EU budget by $25 billion annually by 1997 to provide economic assistance to the poorer members. But the richer countries resent this subsidy to the poorer ones—in effect carrying the poor countries as free riders on the collective good of EU integration. Nor is it clear that the proposed sum would be enough to do the job.

The second main goal of Maastricht was even more controversial—political and military integration. The treaty commits European states to work toward a common foreign policy with a goal of eventually establishing a joint military force. Again this infringes a core area of state sovereignty. Although long a goal of integrationists, it has always taken a back seat to the functional and technical areas of economic integration. In addition, some leaders worried about the effect of EU security coordination on NATO and on U.S. participation in European military affairs. Britain was particularly wary of pushing aside NATO and the United States. France had fewer such qualms. In fact France and Ger-

---

[11]Nolling, Wilhelm. *Monetary Policy in Europe After Maastricht.* New York: St. Martin's Press, 1993.

many created a small joint military force in the early 1990s (see pp. 87–88), which they hoped to expand in the future.

The Maastricht Treaty encountered problems soon after its signing. One problem was the fractious response of EU members to the war in the former Yugoslavia—next door on the European continent. Efforts by the EU to mediate the conflict failed repeatedly, and the EU seemed powerless as the war spread and a humanitarian and refugee crisis deepened. In June 1992, French president Mitterand secretly flew straight from an EU summit meeting to the embattled Bosnian capital, Sarajevo; this unilateral initiative reflected the EU's inability to act in unison in the crisis. But overall, the EU's problem in the former Yugoslavia was not that its different members were acting at cross purposes, but rather that the unified policy of the EU didn't work.

Closer to home, the citizens of Europe began to react seriously against the loss of national identity and sovereignty implicit in Maastricht.[12] Through the years of European integration, public opinion has been largely supportive. In recent years polls have shown a strong majority of European citizens in favor of greater political and military integration, and in favor of expanding the powers of the European Parliament—although support for political union is weaker in Denmark and Britain than elsewhere. Perhaps the Eurocrats took public support too much for granted, for a substantial and growing minority was having second thoughts.

As an amendment to the Treaty of Rome, Maastricht had to be ratified by all (then 12) members. The ratification process suddenly stirred up strong public feelings against closer European union in several countries. British politicians had already gotten assurances in the treaty that allowed Britain to stay outside of a monetary union and of a unified European social policy, if it so chose. In other EU states, however, the political leaders and citizens had seemingly not given much thought to the public reactions to Maastricht before signing it. The treaty had been negotiated as though it were just another technical measure—a matter for experts, not politicians and citizens. Suddenly, citizens and leaders seemed to wake up and realize that the faceless Eurocrats in Brussels were actually stripping away their national sovereignty!

In a 1992 referendum, Danish voters narrowly rejected the treaty despite the support of the major political parties, industries, and labor unions (in a second vote Danes approved the treaty, with provisions like Britain's, in 1993). A referendum in Ireland passed easily, but one in France just barely passed after a hard-fought campaign. As a result, EU leaders had to admit that public opinion across the continent reflected deep reservations about a closer European union. The future of Maastricht is now uncertain. Economic and technical integration (possibly including a monetary union) seems likely to move forward, though more slowly than anticipated. But the future of political and military integration appears much shakier. In the struggle between nationalism and supranationalism, the balance seems once again to have shifted back to nationalism when it comes to sovereignty, money, and control of foreign and military policy. Even after thirty years of preparation, spillover is proving elusive.

---

[12]Lankowski, Carl, ed. *Europe's Emerging Identity: Opposition Movements vs. Regional Integration in the European Community.* Boulder, CO: Lynne Rienner, 1993.

The Maastricht Treaty encountered unexpected public resistance in several European countries. After a heated campaign, France barely approved the treaty in a 1992 referendum (here, "No to Maastricht; Rethink Europe"). Norwegians and Swiss voted against joining the EU.

Expanding the Union

Despite the problems emerging in the Maastricht process, the EU has been successful enough to attract neighboring states that want to join. In fact, the larger and more integrated the EU becomes, the less attractive is the prospect of remaining outside of it for any state in the vicinity of Europe. The EU is beginning to come to terms with the possibility of going from fifteen members to twenty or thirty, with potentially far-reaching changes in how the community operates.

Spain and Portugal, admitted in 1986 as the eleventh and twelfth members, filled out the western side of Europe. In 1995, Austria, Sweden, and Finland joined the EU. They are located on the immediate fringe of the present EU area, and as relatively rich countries they will not disrupt the EU economy (for instance, their currencies would not drag down the euro in a monetary union). Norway applied to join and was accepted, but its citizens voted down the idea in a referendum in 1994, leaving the EU with 15 members in 1995—all but two of the main states of Western Europe. (Switzerland's plans to join were, like Norway's, halted by a popular referendum in the early 1990s; citizens preferred to maintain their traditional strict neutrality even at a possible cost to the Swiss economy.)

To the south, three others have applied to join but face less hopeful prospects for acceptance—Turkey, Cyprus, and Malta. These are poorer states that could add to the problems the EU already has in absorbing the "poor four." Turkey has also drawn criticism for its human rights record (especially regarding the Kurds), and Cyprus is divided along cease-fire lines in an ethnic conflict. These countries are also located at the southern fringe of Europe, far from the EU's center of gravity.

In the southern tier of Eastern Europe (Albania, Romania, Bulgaria, and the former Yugoslavia), no states have good prospects for acceptance into the EU, with the possible exception of Slovenia, the richest of the former Yugoslav republics. Conceivably Croatia (and perhaps Bosnia) could someday follow; at least the possibility was being used in the mid-1990s to entice Croatian leaders to follow Western-backed policies.

Expansion eastward, now that Austria has joined, would take the EU into the territory of the former Soviet bloc, with no obvious stopping point short of Moscow. Next door to Austria is Hungary, which has asked to join the EU. If Hungary joined, then what about Ukraine, and then Russia? Several of the newly independent, newly capitalist countries of Russia and Eastern Europe are interested in joining the EU; Poland and Hungary were first to apply. These are, with the Czech Republic, the Eastern European states with the most developed capitalist economies, but by Western European standards they are still relatively poor. Existing EU members are wary of being dragged down by these economies, which are still embroiled in the painful transition from socialism to capitalism and lack stable currencies. It is hard to imagine their joining a European monetary union anytime in the 1990s.

Among the former Soviet republics, the most Western and independent-minded are the Baltic republics—Estonia, Latvia, and Lithuania. They are trying to reorient their economies away from Moscow and toward Finland, Sweden, Poland, and Germany; they are not members of the CIS. In 1995 they gained free-trade status with the EU (as Sweden joined the EU). They too will likely seek EU membership, but they are smaller, further from the center of Europe, and more closely tied to the former Soviet economy than states like Hungary (none of which helps their case for membership).

The implications of expanding the EU's membership are considerable. Even the simple expansion to 15 members in 1995 (with the addition of Austria, Finland, and Sweden) changed the dynamics of the EU in several ways. The Commission, previously a cumbersome committee with 17 members, became even more cumbersome with 20 members. The Parliament began to approach one thousand members. The ability of the EU to reach decisions by consensus could become more elusive. The working time required to make decisions in the Council of Ministers expanded with the larger number of potential cleavages and alliances on a particular issue among 15 rather than 12 members.

In addition to being cumbersome, and worsening collective goods problems (see box, p. 404), an expanded community could make the achievement of unified policies more difficult. The more states are represented in the EU, each with its particular national interests, the harder it may be to identify any coherent supranational interest of the group as a whole (one that also serves the interests of the individual members). The tensions between nationalism and supranationalism would presumably intensify, with more states pulling in more directions at once.

Beyond these problems of larger groups, the addition of new members in the south or east could accentuate the problems of disparity in wealth already being experienced with the "poor four." If at least $25 billion annually is needed to stabilize the currencies of the "poor four" and bring them into a monetary union this decade, much more would be required to bring in a few Eastern European states. The costs appear to be more than today's EU members would be willing to pay.

These realities seem to present a choice for the EU—*deepening* the community

Let us return to the proposition that the maintenance of collective goods is easier in a small group than a large one (see pp. 100–101). Over the years, the membership of the European Union has expanded, from six members to fifteen. Further expansion is being debated. According to collective goods theory, the expanding membership should make it easier to free ride on the community's larger, richer members without being so visible and disrupting the overall provision of collective goods by the community. One might expect a smaller core group, even a German-French duopoly or German hegemony, to emerge in the EU to dictate policy and enforce cooperation.

This approach could help to explain the difficulties faced by the EU in the early 1990s—popular resistance, disunity over foreign affairs like Bosnia, major obstacles to currency union, squabbles over future directions, and so forth. However, other theories could explain these outcomes as well. A realist could simply point to differences in national interests as creating a natural barrier to integration beyond a certain point. In this view it was the gradual infringement of national sovereignty (which could not be allowed to go beyond a certain point) rather than the expansion of membership, which explains the various problems of EU integration in the early 1990s.

THINKING THEORETICALLY ❖

Can you think of a similar case in which either integration gradually deepened or membership gradually expanded, but not both at once? For example, the extension of NAFTA to Mexico in the late 1990s is characterized by deeper economic integration but still a small number of members in the free-trade area (three). Such cases could help to begin testing the competing theories regarding the obstacles to European integration. If large numbers of members are the problem in Europe, NAFTA should not face similar problems; if the stubbornness of national sovereignty is the problem, then NAFTA *should* face such problems. (Of course, just a few cases usually are not sufficient to draw broad generalizations.)

through a monetary union and other measures envisioned by Maastricht, or *broadening* it by adding members. States that favor deepening the EU—France especially—argue that an enlarged membership would prove unwieldy and would endanger the gains the EU has made. Those that favor broadening (such as Britain) argue that the ideal of a united Europe requires the EU to take in those who wish to join, even though progress toward economic integration will be slowed down. Britain is less eager to deepen the European union and favors expansion partly because it will slow down such deepening.

By 1995 Europe had begun dividing more tangibly into an "inner" and "outer" group of countries. Seven countries abolished border controls and the need for passports from Portugal to Germany but tightened border controls between themselves and the eight other EU members that did not join the free-movement zone. For example, Germans who cross into Denmark (a nonparticipant) on Sunday mornings to buy bread because German bakeries are closed on Sunday now need identification at the border; formerly they had just waved their bags of bread at the guards as they crossed the border.

Beyond the EU itself, Europe is a patchwork of overlapping structures with varying memberships (see Figure 10.2). Despite the Single European Act, there are still many Eu-

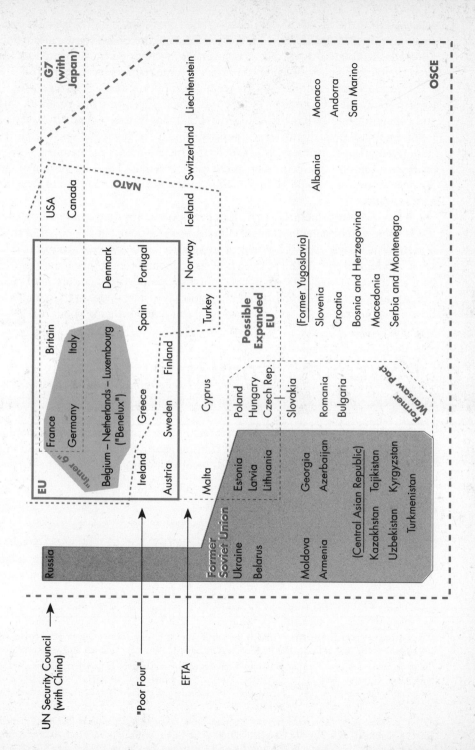

FIGURE 10.2 Overlapping Memberships of European States

ropes. Within the EU are the "inner six," the "poor four," and the possible new joiners, each with their own concerns. Around its edges are the EFTA states participating in the European Economic Area. NATO membership overlaps partly with the EU. Russia and even the United States are European actors in some respects but not others.[13]

One truly universal intergovernmental organization exists in Europe—the *Organization for Security and Cooperation in Europe (OSCE)*. Operating by consensus, with a large and expanding universal membership, the OSCE has little actual power except to act as a forum for multilateral discussions of security issues. (The name was upgraded in 1994 from "Conference" to "Organization"—CSCE to OSCE—when the members failed to agree on more substantive concerns such as the war in Bosnia.) Thus, international integration is not a matter of a single group or organization but more a mosaic of structures tying states together.

These various structures of the European political system, centered on the EU, are IGOs composed of states as members. But as was mentioned at the outset of this chapter, a more diffuse, less-tangible aspect of integration also deserves attention. That is the sense of identity that develops over time as economic (and other functional) ties bring people closer together across borders. Supranational identity, culture, and communication are also aspects of international integration. The remainder of this chapter considers how information technologies are bypassing states and bringing about this kind of integration globally.

❖ THE POWER OF INFORMATION

Global telecommunications are profoundly changing how information and culture function in international relations.[14] Information is now a vital tool of national governments in their interactions with each other. Yet technology is at the same time undermining and disempowering those governments and shifting power to substate actors and individuals. Those newly empowered individuals and groups have begun to create new transnational networks worldwide, bypassing states.

Wiring the World

The new international political possibilities are based on technological developments.[15] Just a hundred years ago, the idea of instant global communication was incomprehensible. It would have seemed unthinkable that anyone could push a dozen buttons on a

[13]Treverton, Gregory F. *America, Germany, and the Future of Europe*. Princeton: Princeton University Press, 1992. Treverton, Gregory F., ed. *The Shape of the New Europe*. New York: Council on Foreign Relations, 1992.

[14]Comor, Edward A., ed. *The Global Political Economy of Communication: Hegemony, Telecommunication and the Information Economy*. New York: St. Martin's Press, 1994. Hamelink, Cees J. *The Politics of World Communication*. Thousand Oaks, CA: SAGE Publications, 1994. Frederick, Howard H. *Global Communication and International Relations*. Belmont, CA: Wadsworth, 1993.

[15]Pool, Ithiel de Sola. *Technologies Without Boundaries: On Telecommunications in a Global Age*. Edited by Eli M. Noam. Cambridge, MA: Harvard University Press, 1990. Drake, William J., ed. *The New Information Infrastructure: Strategies for U.S. Policy*. Washington, DC: The Brookings Institution, 1995.

handheld instrument and be able to talk with any of billions of people anywhere in the economically developed areas of the world (and many of the poorer areas). Equally ridiculous was the idea that you could look at a box no bigger than a suitcase and see in it moving pictures of things happening at that moment in distant lands. For most of the history of the international system, until about one hundred and fifty years ago, the fastest way to send information was to write it down and bring it to the recipient by horse or sailing ship.

The *media* over which information travels—telephones, television, films, magazines, and so forth—shape the way ideas take form and spread from one place to another. The media with the strongest political impact are *radio* and (especially) *television*. There are about 800 million TV sets and over 2 billion radio receivers in the world (roughly one-third are in North America, one-third in Western and Eastern Europe and Russia, and the rest in the third world and Japan/Pacific).[16] The power of these media is to take a single source of information (a moving picture or a voice) and reproduce it in many copies in many locations.

Radio, and increasingly TV, reaches the poorest rural areas of the third world. Peasants who cannot read can understand radio. *Shortwave* radio—typically stations like Voice of America (VOA), the British Broadcasting Corporation (BBC), or Radio Moscow—is very popular in remote locations.

TV is especially powerful. The combination of pictures and sounds affects viewers emotionally and intellectually. Viewers can experience distant events more fully. Traditionally this participation has been passive. Everyone gets the same experience, spoon-fed from a TV studio. But as technology has developed in recent decades, the passive nature of TV is changing. There are more and more channels of information on TV, giving viewers more power over what they watch—from the local city council meeting, to simultaneous translation of the Russian evening news (in the United States), to MTV music videos (in Russia). Less and less are millions of TV viewers all forced to march to the beat of the same drummer; rather, the global TV audience is being fragmented into many small pieces, often *not* along national lines.

Ordinary over-the-air TV and radio signals are radio waves carried on specific frequencies. A limited number of frequencies are available in the radio-wave spectrum, so frequencies are a limited resource in high demand, which governments regulate and allocate to users. Because radio waves do not respect national borders, the allocation of frequencies is a subject of interstate bargaining. International regimes have grown up around the regulation of international communications technologies.[17]

Now the limitations of radio waves are yielding to new technologies. *Cable TV* does not use the airwaves of the radio spectrum and can carry dozens of signals at once (hun-

[16]UNESCO. *UNESCO Yearbook*. New York: United Nations (annual).

[17]Krasner, Stephen D. Global Communications and National Power: Life on the Pareto Frontier. *World Politics* 43 (3), 1991: 336–66. Cowhey, Peter F. The International Telecommunications Regime: The Political Roots of Regimes for High Technology. *International Organization* 44 (2), 1990: 169–200. Crandall, Robert W., and Kenneth Flamm, eds. *Changing the Rules: Technological Change, International Competition, and Regulation in Communications*. Washington, DC: The Brookings Institution, 1989.

Global communications, a very new capability on the time scale of the international system, are changing the rules of IR and empowering nonstate transnational actors. Here a villager in Iran brings home a color TV, 1995.

dreds, in the future). Cable also has the potential to carry signals in the opposite direction (from the viewer). *Satellite* transmissions also bypass the normal over-the-air radio spectrum and transmit signals over a huge area to dish-shaped antennas.

Images and sounds are also being recorded, reproduced, and viewed in new ways through *audiotapes* and *videotapes*. Video cassette recorders (VCRs) have proliferated in many countries in recent years. Information on audio- and videotapes can be played back repeatedly and passed from person to person, again giving the viewer more control than in ordinary TV programming. Furthermore, *video cameras* are empowering ordinary citizens to create their own visual records, such as videos of political demonstrations in one country that end up on the TV news in another country.

Even more empowering of ordinary citizens is the *telephone*. Unlike TV and radio, phones are two-way media through which users interact without any centralized information source. Increasingly, phones are becoming more powerful, thanks to fiber-optic cables, communication satellites, cellular phones, satellite phones, fax machines, and modems. New satellite networks will soon allow a portable phone to use a single phone number worldwide. These forms of communication do not slow down for even a millisecond when they cross an international border. The increased flows of information from state to state reflect the growing functional interdependence of states in today's world.

Information technologies have security implications. Capabilities such as fiber-optic cables or satellite communications serve governments in conducting their foreign and military policies (see "Evolving Technologies" on pp. 242–244). Because fiber-optic cables facilitate military command and control, the United States tried to prevent the sale of such cables to Russia even after the Cold War ended.

In a subtle but pervasive way, communication technologies may be diffusing power away from governments and toward ordinary people and other nonstate actors.[18] Recall that new "smart weapons" technologies are empowering the foot soldier relative to large-weapons systems (see p. 244). New communications technologies may be doing the same for ordinary citizens relative to governments and political parties.

Information as a Tool of Governments

Not all aspects of the information revolution work against governments, however. With so much more information traveling around the world than ever before, information has become an important instrument of governments' power (in both domestic and interstate dealings).[19] Above all, governments want *access to information*. In 1992, U.S. secretary of state Baker made his first visit to the newly independent Asian republics of the former Soviet Union (the poorest and most remote CIS members). At each stop, one of the first questions Baker was asked by the state leader was, "How do I get CNN?"[20] They were eager to find a source of news other than from Moscow. CNN, they hoped, would tie them directly to the Western world and symbolize their independence from Russia. Access to CNN was also considered something of a status symbol.

Governments spend large amounts of money and effort trying to gain information about what is happening both inside and outside their territories. They keep files on their citizens ranging from social security records to secret police files. They compile economic statistics to chart their own economic health and make estimates of the economic health of other states. Most operate intelligence-gathering agencies.

---

[18]Rosenau, James N. *Turbulence in World Politics: A Theory of Change and Continuity*. Princeton: Princeton University Press, 1990.

[19]Deutsch, Karl W. *The Nerves of Government: Models of Political Communication and Control*. New York: Free Press, 1969.

[20]*The New York Times*, February 2, 1992: A10.

Control of television news and other mass media has become an important instrument of political power, one that states often seek to control. Independent journalists are often directly or indirectly targeted in this effort. Here, 28-year-old American photographer Cynthia Elbaum works to show the world the effects of Russia's war in Chechnya (December 1994). She was killed an hour later in a Russian air raid on the site.

With today's information technologies, it is easier for governments to gather, organize, and store huge amounts of information. In this respect, the information revolution empowers governments more than ever. For example, in the past a wanted criminal, druglord, or terrorist could slip over the border and take refuge in a foreign country. Today, it is more likely that a computer at the border checkpoint would alert the border guard or that a routine traffic ticket in the foreign country could trigger an instant directive to arrest the person. Information technologies give repressive governments more power to keep tabs on citizens, spy on dissidents, and manipulate public opinion.

Just as domestic citizens find it harder to hide from their governments, so are state governments finding it harder to hide information from each other. The military importance of satellite reconnaissance has been mentioned (see p. 242). A powerful state like the United States can increase its power through information technologies. It can and does monitor (from a boat or satellite) the phone calls, faxes, data transmissions, and radio conversations in foreign countries.

Smaller and less-powerful governments, however, seem to gain even more power from information technology. As the cost of information decreases, it comes into reach of more states. The great powers have always been able to maintain a worldwide presence and gather information globally. Now small states can gain some of the same capabilities electronically—if only by monitoring world affairs on CNN. Even sophisticated information is becoming more available and cheaper; for instance, high-resolution satellite photos are now available commercially within the price range of most states. These images can be used for both military purposes and for natural-resource management—knowing what states (including one's own) have such resources as minerals, forests, and farmland, and the rate at which they are being used. The small but rich oil-producing state of Bahrain, for example, was seeking in 1993 to buy a satellite that would help it keep track of the production and movement of oil worldwide.

The very nature of interstate interactions is affected by changes in information technology. The risks of surprise in IR are reduced by the information revolution. The security dilemma is less severe as a result (states do not need to arm against unknown potential threats since they know what the real threats are). Similarly, the ability to monitor performance of agreements makes collective goods problems easier to resolve. (Recall that collective goods are more easily maintained when cheaters and free riders can be identified; see pp. 100–101).

The ability of governments to bargain effectively with each other and to reach mutually beneficial outcomes is enhanced by the availability of instant communications channels. During the Iraq-Kuwait crisis, the telephone was one of President Bush's most potent instruments of power in assembling the international coalition against Iraq.

In addition to gaining access to information, governments use information as a power capability by *disseminating* it internationally and domestically. In today's information-intensive world, TV transmitters may be more powerful than tanks. Even in war itself, propaganda plays a key role. For instance, in the Gulf War pamphlets and loudspeakers appealed to Iraqi soldiers, ultimately contributing to their mass surrenders.

The information disseminated by a government often crosses international borders, intentionally and otherwise. The government of Jordan, for example, is well aware that its Arabic programs are received by Arab citizens of Israel and that its English programs are watched by Israeli Jews. When Jordanian TV broadcasts, say, a U.S. documentary about the U.S. civil rights movement (with Arabic subtitles), the message influences Israeli-Palestinian relations across the border.

Most governments create explicit channels of information dissemination to influence domestic and international audiences. Stations like Radio Moscow broadcast radio programs in dozens of languages aimed at all the world's regions. The U.S. Information Agency (USIA) operates the U.S. government's VOA shortwave radio network, which is picked up in many third-world regions where it may be one of the few outside information sources. In the Cold War, ideological broadcasts were beamed into communist countries on networks like Radio Free Europe, Radio Liberty, and TV Marti. A similar effort aimed at China was started by the United States in the early 1990s.

Governments spread false as well as true information as a means of international influence. This is called *disinformation*. In the 1930s, the Nazis discovered that the "big lie," if repeated enough times, would be accepted as truth by most people. It is harder to fool international audiences these days, but domestic ones can still respond to propagandistic misinformation, as the Serbian regime in the early 1990s showed. Anyone who follows international events should remember that even stories reported in the Western news as fact are occasionally disinformation.

Most governments (but not the U.S. government) own and operate at least one main

TV station, and many hold a monopoly on TV stations. This suggests that TV signals often rank with military equipment and currency as capabilities so important to a government that it must control them itself. Indeed, in a military coup d'état, usually one of the first and most important targets seized is the television broadcasting facility. When power is up for grabs in a state, it is now as likely that fighting will occur in the government TV studios or at the transmitting antenna as at the legislature or presidential offices. As the Soviet Union broke up in the early 1990s, TV towers were the scene of confrontations in several republics. In Lithuania a crowd of Lithuanian nationalists surrounded the TV tower, and Soviet troops killed a dozen people shooting their way in.

During the attempted 1991 Soviet coup, the coup plotters failed to jam U.S. radio broadcasts into the country. Public opinion polls previously conducted by the USIA in the Soviet Union convinced U.S. officials that Boris Yeltsin and other opponents of the coup would receive wide support in the major Russian cities if people could find out about the opposition movement. The USIA gathered information on resistance to the coup and broadcast it back into the Soviet Union on the VOA, adding in foreign commentary like President Bush's statement that coups do not always succeed. The coup plotters' inability to control information channels ranging from the VOA to the international phone lines was a major reason for their failure.

Information as a Tool Against Governments

Information can be used against governments as well, by foreign governments or by domestic political opponents. Governments, especially repressive ones, fear the free flow of information, for good reason. When they are allowed to circulate among a population, ideas become a powerful force that can sweep aside governments, as when the idea of democracy swept away the white-rule system of apartheid in South Africa in the early 1990s. This has happened repeatedly in the past decade or so, nowhere more stunningly than in Russia and Eastern Europe. New information technologies have become powerful tools of domestic opposition movements and their allies in foreign governments. Television coverage fed popular discontent regarding the U.S. war in Vietnam in the late 1960s and the Russian war in Chechnya in 1995.

In Iran, the government was brought down in part by audiotapes. The tapes contained speeches and sermons by Ayatollah Khomeini, who spoke against the inequalities and harsh repression of the pro-Western government of the Shah of Iran. Khomeini advocated a revolution to create an Islamic state. The power of his sermons could never have been captured in newspapers and pamphlets. In addition, the shah's secret police could spot a subversive pamphlet with one glance, but the content of audiotapes cannot be determined instantly. Khomeini made the tapes while in exile in France and had them smuggled into Iran, where they were reproduced and passed around. When the Islamic revolution drove the shah from power in 1979, Khomeini arrived from France as a well-known and popular leader of a large movement.

Videotapes helped bring down the Marcos dictatorship in the Philippines. The leader of the opposition, Benigno Aquino, had been assassinated at the Manila airport as he returned from exile in 1983 (on Marcos's orders, it was widely believed). Videotapes of the assassination circulated secretly in the country afterward; they brought the repression of the government home in a graphic and emotional way that no printed words could.

Students on the barricades in pro-democracy movement, Bangkok, Thailand, 1992. The students survived brutal repression from the military regime and stayed organized by using cellular phones and other information technologies. Information, which easily crosses state borders, has become a major factor in both international and domestic politics.

Aquino's widow, Corazón Aquino, ran for president against Marcos and won; when Marcos tried to declare himself the victor, hundreds of thousands of residents of Manila converged on the army base and surrounded it, preventing Marcos from using military force to keep power. This "people power" revolution won over the army commanders, Marcos was swept from office, and Aquino became president.

In Thailand, military leaders lost power in what some Thais call "the cellular phone revolution."[21] Students protesting against the military government were joined by newly affluent Thais with access to cellular phones and fax machines. When the government shot the demonstrators in the streets, arrested them, and cut off their phone lines, the protesters stayed organized by using mobile phones and fax machines. Meanwhile, in next-door Burma a harsh military government faces the power of shortwave radio broadcasts by the opposition movement, made using a transmitter owned by the government of Norway.[22]

To counteract such uses of information, governments throughout the world try to limit the flow of unfavorable information—especially information from foreign sources.

---

[21]Shenon, Philip. Mobile Phones Primed, Affluent Thais Join Fray. *The New York Times,* May 20, 1992: A10.

[22]Crossette, Barbara. Burmese Opposition Gets Oslo Radio Service. *The New York Times,* July 19, 1992: 11.

During and after the 1989 Tiananmen protests, the Chinese government tried desperately to suppress the flow of information into and out of China. It stationed police at every fax machine in the country to screen incoming faxes after foreigners in Hong Kong, North America, and Europe began faxing in reports of the shooting of hundreds of protesters in Beijing.

During the Cold War, the Soviet Union prohibited all but a few photocopy machines because they allowed the uncontrolled replication of information. Thus, when dissidents wrote books or plays critical of the government, these works were passed from hand to hand with each person recopying the work on a typewriter. Similarly, the Soviet Union as late as 1987 had only 16 international long-distance circuits in and out of the country, all routed through Moscow. Of the nearly 300 million Soviet citizens, only 16 people could talk with the outside world at a time. This helped the government to reduce the influence of foreign ideas as well as to closely monitor contact with foreigners. At the time of the Soviet Union's breakup in 1991 there were still only 91 circuits.[23]

Efforts by one government to project power through media broadcasts often bring counterefforts by other governments to block such broadcasts. For instance, the VOA, the BBC, and other foreign media were routinely jammed by the Soviet Union and other closed societies during the Cold War. However, Soviet efforts to control information did not prevent the collapse of that society. To the contrary, the effort to run a modern economy without photocopy machines, international phone lines, computers, and other information technologies clearly *contributed* to the economic stagnation of the country.

All in all, the tide of technology seems to be running against governments (though not all scholars would agree with this assessment). Information gets through, and no political power seems capable of holding it back for long. As more and more communication channels carry more information to more places, governments become just another player in a crowded field—not unlike central banks trying to manage the rates of currencies on world markets where most money is privately owned.

As the information revolution continues to unfold, it will further increase international interdependence, making actions in one state reverberate in other states more strongly than in the past. Information is thus slowly undermining the assumptions of state sovereignty and territorial integrity held dear by realists. At the same time, by empowering substate transnational actors, information technology is undermining the centrality of states themselves in world affairs.

❖ INTERNATIONAL CULTURE

As the information revolution increases the power and importance of transnational actors, it puts into motion two contradictory forces. One we have just discussed—the empowering of substate actors. This force is a factor in the disintegration of states like the Soviet Union and Yugoslavia, and the proliferation of civil wars since the end of the Cold War. As substate groups gain power, they demand their own national rights of sovereignty and autonomy. Nationalism reasserts itself in smaller but more numerous units.

The second force, however, is the forging of transnational communities and supranational identities—a process alluded to earlier with reference to the EU. Here regionalism

---

[23]Ramirez, Anthony. Dial Direct to Moscow and Beyond. *The New York Times*, May 20, 1992: D1.

States do not control the global flow of information, which has become a potent force in world politics. State leaders are becoming just another set of players in a worldwide competition to reach audiences and markets and to "spin" stories a certain way. For example, President Clinton's Bosnia policy came under sharp questioning from such journalists as CNN's Christiane Amanpour (here in a satellite press conference with Clinton in 1994) and ABC's Peter Jennings.

or globalism asserts itself as an internationalized culture resting on communication links among people in different states. This second force, perhaps more than the first, challenges the realist emphasis on national borders and territorial integrity.

Telecommunications and Global Culture

Not only can people in one part of the world communicate with those elsewhere, they can also now find common interests to talk about. Riding the telecommunications revolution, a **global culture** is just beginning to develop, notwithstanding the great divisions remaining in culture and perspective (especially between the rich and poor regions of the world). In the global village, distance and borders matter less and less. Across dozens of countries, people are tuned in to the same news, the same music, the same sports events. Along with international politics, these activities now take place on a world stage with a world audience. The process might be seen as a form of cultural integration, similar to economic and technical integration.

Cultures, languages, and locations interact more quickly as the unfinished process of cultural integration proceeds. For example, in a rural town in Massachusetts, the local cable TV channel on weekends carries live news broadcasts from around the world (without translation), downloaded from a satellite consortium. One weekend, the Brazilian TV news on this broadcast included an ad for a U.S. film set in the Brazilian rain forest, dubbed in Portuguese. Information is bouncing around the world—Brazilian rain forest to Hollywood movie production to Brazilian movie theaters to Massachusetts cable TV. Such trends clearly undermine assumptions of state autonomy.

Ultimately, transnational cultural integration might lead to the emergence of supranational identities, including a global identity. If citizens in EU states can begin to think as Europeans, will citizens in UN member states someday begin to think as human beings and residents of Planet Earth? This is unclear. As we have seen, group identity is an important source of conflict between in-groups and out-groups (see "Ethnic Conflict" on pp. 198–204). Nationalism has tapped into the psychological dynamics of group identity in a powerful way that has legitimized the state as the ultimate embodiment of its people's aspirations and identity. Now the information revolution may aid the development of supranational identity. So far, nationalism continues to hold the upper hand. Global identity has not yet come to rival national identity in any state.

Cultural Imperialism Like international integration generally, global culture has its down side. The emerging global culture is primarily the culture of white Europeans and their descendants in rich areas of the world (mixed slightly with cultural elements of Japan and local third-world elites). For many people, especially in the global South, the information revolution carrying global culture into their midst is, despite its empowering potential, an invasive force in practice.

Above all, the emerging global culture is dominated by the world's superpower, the United States; this dominance has been referred to as **cultural imperialism.**[24] U.S. cultural influence is at least as strong as U.S. military influence. If there is a world language, it is English. If there is a "president of the world," it is more likely the U.S. president than the UN secretary-general.

U.S. films and TV shows dominate world markets. For instance, over 80 percent of the theaters in Jakarta, Indonesia, recently were showing *foreign* films, mostly U.S. ones. Indonesian filmmakers are being squeezed out by the U.S. film industry with its global comparative advantage.[25] Culture may be just another economic product, to be produced in the place of greatest comparative advantage, but culture also is central to national identity and politics. France held up the GATT agreement in 1994 until it could protect its film industry from U.S. competition. The prospect of cultural imperialism thus opens another front in the conflict of liberalism and mercantilism.

Industrialized countries have responded in various ways to U.S. cultural dominance. Canada has allowed U.S. cultural influence to become fairly pervasive, with some resentments but few severe frictions. France (especially) and other European states have been much more wary of U.S. influence; commissions periodically go through the French language trying to weed out expressions like "le cash-and-carry" (not an easy task). On the other hand, Japan seemingly incorporated whole segments of U.S. culture after World War II, from baseball to hamburgers, yet remained Japanese.

Global culture and cultural imperialism shape *the news* as reported on TV, radio, and print media. In the United States alone, 50 million viewers watch network news nightly.[26] To an increasing extent, everyone in the world follows the same story line of

---

[24]Tomlinson, John. *Cultural Imperialism: A Critical Introduction*. Baltimore: Johns Hopkins University Press, 1991.

[25]Shenon, Philip. Indonesian Films Squeezed Out by U.S. Giant. *The New York Times*, October 29, 1992: A17.

[26]Jordan, Donald L., and Benjamin I. Page. Shaping Foreign Policy Opinions: The Role of TV News. *Journal of Conflict Resolution* 36 (2), 1992: 227–41.

world news from day to day. (This "world news" story has become just one piece of the local news.) To some extent there is now a single drama unfolding at the global level, and the day's top international story on CNN very likely will also be reported by the other U.S. TV networks, the national TV news in France, Japan, Russia, and most other states, and the world's radio and print media. The fact that everyone is following the same story reflects the globalizing influence of world communications. Cultural imperialism is reflected in the fact that the story often revolves around U.S. actions, reflects U.S. values, or is reported by U.S. reporters and news organizations.

The attack on Iraq in 1991 illustrates in the extreme how the whole world watches one story—a story shaped by U.S. perspectives. When the bombing of Baghdad began, Saddam Hussein reportedly sat in his bunker watching the war unfold on CNN. The CNN signal he received originated from a nearby hotel room in Baghdad, traveled through an overland phone connection to Jordan, then went to CNN headquarters in Atlanta, where it was broadcast via satellite back to Baghdad. So Saddam Hussein got information about Baghdad—by way of Atlanta—at the same time it reached millions of viewers around the world, including U.S. leaders.

Some call it "global community," others "cultural imperialism." The power of information, opening up a wave of globalization in international business, is bringing together cultures in sometimes-incongruous ways. Chinese leaders seemed unsure whether McDonald's brought Western-style prosperity or spiritual pollution—maybe a bit of each.

Transnational Communities

Although a global culture is still only nascent and the most powerful identity is still at the national level, people have begun to participate in specific communities that bridge national boundaries. International journalists, for example, are members of such a community. They work with colleagues from various countries and travel from state to state with each other. Though a journalist's identity *as* a journalist rarely takes precedence over his or her national identity, the existence of the transnational community of journalists creates a new form of international interdependence.

Like journalists, scientists and church members work in communities spanning national borders. The effect once again is to undermine the state's role as the primary actor in international affairs. More important, the links forged in such transnational communities may create a new functionalism that could encourage international integration on a global scale.

International *sports* competition is one of the broadest-based transnational communities, especially strong at the regional level. Millions of fans watch their teams compete with teams from other countries. Of course, international sports competition can stir up animosities between neighbors, as when British soccer hooligans rampage through another European country after their team loses a game. But sports also create a sense of participation in a supranational community. This is especially true of world-level sports events in which a global athletic community participates. The *Olympic Games* (sponsored by the International Olympic Committee, an NGO) are a global event broadcast to a worldwide audience.[27] Sponsors broadcast universalistic commercial messages like Coca Cola's theme, "Shared Around the World."

Some people see sports as a force for peace. Sports events bring people from different countries together in shared activities. Citizens of different states share their admiration of sports stars, who become international celebrities. In Israel, one of the most successful programs for bridging the gap between Jewish and Arab children is a soccer camp in which Jewish and Arab star players (each admired in both communities) participate together as coaches. The U.S.-Chinese rapprochement of 1971 was so delicate that political cooperation was impossible until the way had first been paved by sports—the U.S. table tennis team that made the first official U.S. visit to China.

World sports competitions contribute to a supranational world culture and international integration. For example, Vanuatu is a Pacific island microstate with 120,000 people. Before 1992, Vanuatu had no televisions (just two radio stations and one newspaper). Then the country sent six athletes to the Olympics in Spain—and Vanuatuans just had to watch them on TV. So Vanuatu got its first TV station, along with 500 TV sets. A reporter from Radio Vanuatu described the people as "very, very happy"—although church leaders were concerned that people might start watching TV instead of going to church and might "learn bad things from other countries." For better or worse, sports deepened Vanuatu's interdependence with the world's other states.[28]

Most communication over the world's broadcasting networks is neither news nor sports, but *drama*—soap operas, films, situation comedies, documentaries, and so forth.

---

[27]Hill, Christopher R. *Olympic Politics*. Manchester, U.K.: Manchester University Press, 1992. Allison, Lincoln. *The Changing Politics of Sport*. New York: St. Martin's Press, 1993.

[28]National Public Radio, *Weekend Edition*, August 1, 1992.

Here U.S. cultural imperialism is strong, because so many films and TV shows watched around the world originate in Hollywood (home of the U.S. movie industry). The entertainment industry is a strong export sector of the U.S. economy. Large third-world countries like Brazil and India have concentrated their TV production efforts in an area where local contexts can gain viewers' interest and where production costs are modest—soap operas. They are immensely popular in these and other third-world countries.

The popularity of Brazilian soap operas notwithstanding, many international viewers see less of their own experiences than of dramas set in the United States. These dramas, of course, give a distorted view of U.S. life, such as the impression that all Americans are rich. Recall that "deconstruction" of such TV shows, according to postmodernists, reveals hidden political subtexts (see pp. 121–123).

The power of such messages was demonstrated in 1991, when Albania's communist government was crumbling along with its economy. Desperately poor Albanians flocked to ports and rode overloaded ferries to nearby Italy (where authorities eventually sent them back home). As it turned out, Albanians had an exaggerated view of Italian prosperity (though Italy was indeed more prosperous than Albania). Albanians had been receiving TV shows from nearby Italy and had seen commercials in which cats were fed their dinners on silver platters. Having been cut off from contact with the West for decades, many Albanians took such commercials literally and were amazed that even the cats in Italy were so rich!

Beyond TV and films, both live performances and recordings of *music* have become increasingly internationalized. In the world of classical music, a great conductor or violinist can roam the world in search of great orchestras and appreciative audiences, with almost complete disregard for national borders. International tours are a central element in rock music and jazz as well. Some genres of music, like Afro pop, are essentially more international than national, spanning several continents and explicitly global in outlook. Even highly specialized national music forms—such as Bulgarian chants or Mongolian throat singing—are gaining worldwide audiences. It is significant that people who speak different languages and cannot understand each other's words can understand each other's music.

Advertising is crucial to the emerging international culture. Advertising links the transnational products and services of MNCs with the transnational performances and works of actors, athletes, and artists. Most global broadcasts and performances—from the Olympic Games to reruns of *Dallas*—are paid for by advertising. As with the Italian cat food commercials just mentioned, advertising often carries subtle (or not so subtle) messages about culture, race, gender roles, and other themes. In Europe and Japan, international advertising may contain a subtext of U.S. superiority. In Eastern Europe and Russia, the advertising of products from Europe, Japan, and the United States may imply the superiority of the West over the East, whereas in the third world advertising may promote the values of the industrialized world over local and native cultures. For example, ads for cosmetics may portray stereotypical images of white Euro-American women as the ideal of beauty, even on billboards or TV shows in Asia or Latin America. Despite the cultural frictions that advertising can cause, it seems evident that without advertising the emerging global culture would lack the money needed to broadcast the Olympic Games or launch new communication satellites.

Finally, *tourism* also builds transnational communities. International tourists cross borders 500 million times a year. Tourism ranks among the top export industries worldwide. People who travel to another country often develop both a deeper understanding and a deeper appreciation for it. Person-to-person contacts and friendships maintained across borders make it harder for nationalism to succeed in promoting either war or protectionism. For example, a U.S. citizen who has visited Japan may be more likely to favor expanded U.S.-Japanese trade; a Greek who has visited Turkey and made friends there may be more likely to oppose a Greek-Turkish military confrontation.

Added to these contacts are exchange students and those who attend college in a foreign country. These students learn about their host countries, teach friends there about their home countries, and meet other foreign students from other countries. These kinds of person-to-person international contacts are amplified by electronic media. In the 1990s the Internet allows transnational dialogues to take place at a global level.

The transnational connections forged through these various communities—sports, music, tourism, and so forth—deepen the international interdependence that links the well-being of one state to that of other states. This may promote peace, because a person who knows more about a foreign country and has developed empathy for its culture is likely to act as a brake on political conflict with that country and an accelerator of positive cooperation with it. But sometimes cultural contact increases awareness of differences, creating distrust.

These supranational cultural influences are still in their infancy. Over the coming years and decades their shape will become clearer, and scholars will be able to determine more accurately how they are influencing world politics and state sovereignty. We need not wait as long to see the effects of a different kind of supranational influence, however. Environmental problems, which rarely recognize national borders, have forced states into ever-closer cooperation as political leaders find that the only effective responses are at a supranational level. These issues occupy Chapter 11.

❖ CHAPTER SUMMARY

- Supranational processes bring states together in larger structures and identities. These processes generally lead to an ongoing struggle between nationalism and supranationalism.
- International integration—the partial shifting of sovereignty from the state toward supranational institutions—is considered an outgrowth of international cooperation in functional (technical and economic) issue areas.
- Integration theorists thought that functional cooperation would spill over into political integration in foreign policy and military issue areas. This has not occurred. Indeed, powerful forces of disintegration are tearing apart previously existing states in some regions (especially in the former Soviet Union and Yugoslavia).
- The European Union (EU) is the most advanced case of integration. Its 15 member states have given considerable power to the EU in economic decision making. However, national power still outweighs supranational power even in the EU.
- Since the founding of the European Coal and Steel Community in 1952, the mission and membership of what is now the EU have expanded continually.
- The most important and most successful element in the EU is its customs union (and the associated free-trade area). Goods can cross borders of member states freely, and the members adopt unified tariffs with regard to goods entering from outside the EU.

◆ Under the EU's Common Agricultural Policy, subsidies to farmers are made uniform within the community. Carrying out this policy consumes two-thirds of the EU's budget. EU agricultural subsidies are a major source of trade conflict with the United States.

◆ The EU has long worked toward a monetary union with a single European currency (the ECU or "euro"). Such a union will require roughly comparable inflation rates and financial stability in all the member states. EU leaders hope to achieve a monetary union within the next decade.

◆ In structure, the EU revolves around the permanent staff of "Eurocrats" under the European Commission. The Commission's president, individual members, and staff all serve Europe as a whole—a supranational role. However, the Council of Ministers representing member states (in national roles) has power over the Commission.

◆ The European Parliament has members directly elected by citizens in EU states, but it has few powers and cannot legislate the rules for the community. The European Court also has limited powers, but has extended its jurisdiction more successfully than any other international court.

◆ The Single European Act, or "Europe 1992," created a common market throughout the EU, with uniform standards, open borders, and freedom of goods, services, labor, and capital within the EU.

◆ With its Exchange Rate Mechanism, the European Monetary System maintains relatively fixed rates of exchange within the EU while allowing EU currencies together to fluctuate in value relative to other world currencies. However, the system could not adapt to underlying differences in national financial conditions and was set back in 1992, as Britain, Italy, and Spain dropped out when they could not maintain the required value of their own currencies.

◆ The 1991 Maastricht Treaty on closer European integration (monetary union and political-military coordination) provoked a public backlash in several countries. Citizens began to resent the power of EU bureaucrats over national culture and daily life. Ratification of the treaty was narrowly rejected once by Danish voters and barely approved by French voters.

◆ The EU took in three new members recently—Austria, Finland, and Sweden—but Norwegians voted not to join. The EU faces challenges in deciding how far to expand its membership (especially regarding Eastern European states). To some extent the broadening of membership conflicts with the deepening of ties among the existing members.

◆ In addition to the EU and the associated European Free Trade Association, there are a variety of overlapping groupings, formal and informal, that reflect the process of integration in Europe.

◆ A different type of international integration can be seen in the growing role of communication and information operating across national borders. Supranational relationships and identities are being fostered by new information technologies, though such a process is still in an early stage.

◆ Greater access to information increases government power both domestically and internationally. Governments also use the dissemination of information across borders as a means of influencing other states. Thus information technologies can serve national and not just supranational purposes.

◆ Government access to information increases the stability of international relationships. The security dilemma and other collective goods problems are made less difficult in a transparent world where governments have information about each others' actions.

◆ The greater and freer flow of information around the world can undermine the authority and power of governments as well. It is now extremely difficult for authoritarian governments to limit the flow of information in and out of their states. Information technologies can empower ordinary citizens and contribute to transnational and supranational structures that bypass the state.

◆ Telecommunications are contributing to the development of global cultural integration. This process may hold the potential for the development of a single world culture. However, some politicians and citizens worry about cultural imperialism—that such a culture would be too strongly dominated by the United States.

◆ Transnational communities are developing in such areas as sports, music, and tourism. Such communities may foster supranational identities that could compete with the state for the loyalty of citizens someday.

❖ THINKING CRITICALLY

1. Functional economic ties among European states have contributed to the emergence of a supranational political structure, the EU, which has considerable though not unlimited power. Do you think the same thing could happen in North America? Could the U.S.-Canadian-Mexican NAFTA develop into a future North American Union like the EU? What problems would it be likely to face, given the experience of the EU?

2. Suppose you happened to be chatting with the president of the European Commission, who was complaining about the public reaction in European states against the growing power of the Commission's Eurocrats. What advice would you give? What steps could the Commission take to calm such fears without reversing the process of integration? How would your suggestions address the resentments that European citizens or governments have against Brussels?

3. Suppose the government of Turkey hired you as a consultant to help it develop a presentation to the EU about why Turkey should be admitted as a member. What arguments would you propose using? What kinds of rebuttals might you expect from the present EU members? How would you recommend responding?

4. Information technologies are strengthening transnational and supranational communications and identity. However, they are also providing states with new instruments of power and control. Which aspect do you find predominant now? Are these new capabilities helpful or harmful to state governments? Why? Do you expect your answer will change in the future, as technology continues to develop?

5. What are the good and bad effects, in your opinion, of the emergence of global communications and culture? Should we be cheering or lamenting the possibility of one world culture? Does the answer depend on where one lives in the world? Give concrete examples of the effects you discuss.

❖ KEY TERMS

nationalism vs. supranationalism
international integration
neofunctionalism
security community
European Union (EU)
Treaty of Rome
Euratom
free-trade area
customs union
common market
Common Agricultural Policy
  (CAP)

European Commission
Council of Ministers
European Parliament
European Court of Justice
Single European Act
ECU (euro)
Maastricht Treaty
global culture
cultural imperialism

*Protest at World Bank build-
ing, July 1994.*

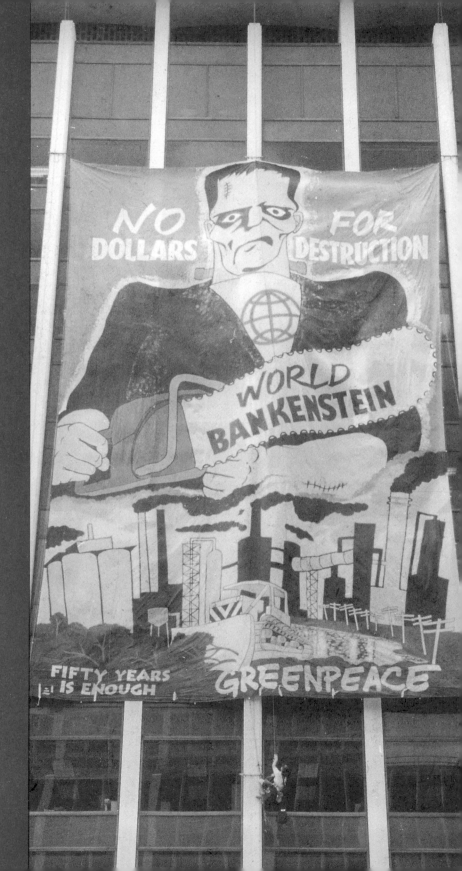

THE ENVIRONMENT

❖ INTERDEPENDENCE AND THE ENVIRONMENT

As we have seen, world industrialization and technological development have increased international interdependence through functional economic integration and transnational communication. Industrialization has also intensified international interdependence in another, less direct way, through its impact on the world's natural environment. Actions taken by one state now routinely affect other states' access to natural resources and to the benefits of a healthy environment.[1] The global threats to the natural environment are thus a major new source of interdependence.

Because environmental effects tend to be diffuse and long term, and because such effects easily spread from one location to another, international environmental politics creates difficult collective goods problems (see pp. 100–101). Essentially, a sustainable natural environment is a collective good, and states bargain over how to distribute the costs of providing that good. The technical, scientific, and ethical aspects of managing the environment are complex, but the basic nature of states' interests is not. The collective goods problem manifests itself in each issue area concerning the environment, natural resources, and population.

For example, the world's major fisheries in international waters are not owned by any state; they are a collective good. The various fishing states must cooperate (partly by regulating nonstate actors such as MNCs) to keep from depleting the stocks of fish. If too many states fail to cooperate, taking more than their share, the fish populations are wiped out and everyone's catch ends up much reduced. In fact, this has already happened in many of the world's largest fisheries in recent decades. As a result fish catches worldwide dropped sharply beginning around 1990. This has happened because each additional fishing boat—and the MNC that owns it as well as its state of origin—gains by catching an additional fish. The benefits of that fish go entirely to the one catching it, whereas the eventual costs of depleted stocks will be shared by all who fish there.

---

[1]Käkönen, Jyrki, ed. *Perspectives on Environmental Conflict and International Politics.* London: Pinter, 1992.

But what is a state's fair quota of fish? There is no world government to decide such a question, so states must enter into multilateral negotiations, agreements, and regimes. Such efforts create new avenues for functionalism and international integration, but also new potentials for conflict and "prisoner's dilemmas."

This type of collective goods dilemma has been called the **tragedy of the commons**.[2] The commons was originally shared grazing land in Britain, centuries ago. As with the fisheries, if too many people kept too many sheep there, the commons would be overgrazed. Yet adding one more sheep was profitable to that sheep's owner. Ultimately Britain solved this problem by the **enclosure** of the commons—splitting it into privately owned pieces on each of which a single owner would have an incentive to manage resources responsibly. The world's states are gradually taking a similar approach to fisheries by extending territorial waters to put more fish under the control of single states (see "Minerals, Land, Water" later in this chapter).

As in other areas of IPE, the solution of collective goods problems concerning the natural environment is based on achieving shared benefits that depend on overcoming conflicting interests.[3] *Regimes* are an important part of such a solution, providing some rules to govern the bargaining over who gets the benefits and bears the costs of environmental protection. So are functional IOs that specialize in technical and management aspects of the environment.[4]

Increasingly these IOs overlap with broader communities of experts from various states who structure the way states manage environmental issues; these have been called **epistemic communities** (knowledge-based communities). For example, the transnational community of experts and policy makers concerned with pollution in the Mediterranean is an epistemic community.[5]

In global environmental politics, it is hard to manage collective goods problems because of the large number of actors involved. Recall that collective goods are easier to provide in small groups, where individual actions have more impact on the total picture and where cheating is more noticeable. The opposite is true with the environment. The actions of nearly two hundred states (albeit some more than others) aggregate to cause indirect but serious consequences throughout the world. This large number of actors was reflected in the 1992 *UN Conference on Environment and Development* (nicknamed the *"Earth Summit"*) in Rio de Janeiro, Brazil; it was the largest summit meeting of state leaders ever, over a hundred in all.

---

[2]Ostrom, Elinor. *Governing the Commons: The Evolution of Institutions for Collective Action*. New York: Cambridge University Press, 1991. Hardin, Garrett. The Tragedy of the Commons. *Science* 162, December 16, 1968: 1243–48.

[3]Kingsbury, B., and A. Hurrell, eds. *The International Politics of the Environment*. Oxford: Oxford University Press, 1992. Mathews, Jessica Tuchman, ed. *Preserving the Global Environment: The Challenge of Shared Leadership*. New York: W. W. Norton, 1991.

[4]Keohane, Robert O., Marc A. Levy, and Peter M. Haas. Institutions for the Earth: Promoting International Environmental Protection. *Environment* 34 (4), 1992: 12–17, 29–36. Young, Oran R. *International Cooperation: Building Regimes for Natural Resources and the Environment*. Ithaca: Cornell University Press, 1989.

[5]Haas, Peter M. Introduction: Epistemic Communities and International Policy Coordination [special issue]. *International Organization* 46 (1), 1992: 1–36. Haas, Peter M. *Saving the Mediterranean: The Politics of International Environmental Cooperation*. New York: Columbia University Press, 1990.

Management of environmental issues is complicated by the large numbers of actors involved, which make collective goods problems hard to resolve (individuals may be more tempted to free ride). The largest gathering of heads of state in history took place in 1992 at the "Earth Summit" (UN Conference on Environment and Development) in Rio de Janeiro, Brazil.

With a few exceptions, only in the last two decades has the global environment become a major subject of international negotiation and of IR scholarship.[6] Interest in the environment has grown rapidly since the first "Earth Day" was held by environmental activists in 1970. The energy crises of the 1970s seemed to underline the issue in industrialized regions whose domestic fuel resources were dwindling. Oil spills, urban air pollution, pesticide residues, and difficulties at nuclear power plants—among other problems—elevated the environment on the international agenda.

The first UN conference on the international environment took place in Stockholm, Sweden, in 1972. It adopted general principles—that one state's actions should not cause environmental damage to another, for instance—and raised awareness about international aspects of environmental damage. A second conference was held, with less publicity, in 1982 in Nairobi, Kenya (headquarters of the UN Environment Program). The 1992 Earth Summit was the third conference; it was larger and more ambitious than its predecessors.

---

[6]Jancar, Barbara. Environmental Studies: State of the Discipline. *International Studies Notes* 16 (3), 1991: 25–31. Sprout, Harold, and Margaret Sprout. *The Ecological Perspective on Human Affairs, with Special Reference to International Politics.* Princeton: Princeton University Press, 1965.

Sustainable Economic Development

At the 1992 Earth Summit, the major theme was "sustainable" economic development. This refers to economic growth that does not deplete resources and destroy ecosystems so quickly that the basis of that economic growth is itself undermined. The concept applies to both the industrialized regions and the global South.[7]

In the past, the growth of population, industry, energy use, and the extraction of natural resources on the planet has been exponential—growing faster and faster over time. Such exponential growth cannot continue unchanged indefinitely into the future, almost by definition. Several possibilities emerge. First, new technologies may allow *unabated economic growth* to continue, but shift the basis of that growth away from the ever-increasing use of energy and other resources. This is what optimists with faith in technology expect. Goods and services would continue to multiply, raising the global standard of living, but would do so more and more efficiently to reduce strains on the environment.

A second possibility is a *collapse* of population and living standards in the world, as excessive growth leads to ecological disaster. Pessimists worry that the present course will overshoot the **carrying capacity** of the planetary ecosystem and cause ecosystems to break down because of long-term environmental problems such as species depletion and global warming. By the time such problems produced severe short-term effects, it would be too late to correct them. In effect, what happened to the world's largest fisheries off the coast of Peru would happen on a global scale—overuse and collapse.

Over the past twenty years scholars have produced computer models of the world—population, economic activity, pollution, and other key variables—which show that a finite earth cannot sustain infinite growth and that we are already reaching the "limits to growth."[8] These models are controversial, however. A variety of computer simulations have been developed to try to analyze the carrying capacity of the planet, given available resources and the demands of industrialization and population growth.[9] Some of these models explicitly consider international politics as a factor.[10]

A third possibility is that the past curve of exponential growth will flatten out to form an *S-curve*. The curve rises from a fairly flat slope to an exponential growth curve and then levels off back to a flat slope (at a higher level). This is the curve traced by the population of bacteria confined to a laboratory dish of limited size. It could also be the curve of human population and energy use on a planet of limited size. Instead of over-

[7]Harrison, Paul. *The Third World Revolution: Population, Environment, and a Sustainable World.* New York: Penguin USA, 1994. Brown, Lester R., et al. *State of the World 1995.* New York: W. W. Norton, 1995. Cooper, Richard N. *Environment and Resource Policies for the World Economy.* Washington, DC: The Brookings Institution, 1995.

[8]Meadows, Donella H., et al. *The Limits to Growth: A Report for the Club of Rome's Project on the Predicament of Mankind.* New York: Universe Books, 1972. Meadows, Donella, John Richardson, and Gerhart Bruckmann. *Groping in the Dark: The First Decade of Global Modelling.* Chichester, NY: Wiley, 1982.

[9]Herrera, Amilcar O., et al. *Catastrophe or New Society? A Latin American World Model.* Bariloche, Arg.: International Development Research Centre, 1976.

[10]Bremer, Stuart A., and Barry B. Hughes. *Disarmament and Development: A Design for the Future?* Englewood Cliffs, NJ: Prentice Hall, 1990. Bremer, Stuart A., ed. *The GLOBUS Model: Computer Simulation of Worldwide Political and Economic Developments.* Boulder, CO: Westview, 1987. Ward, Michael Don, ed. *Theories, Models, and Simulations in International Relations: Essays in Honor of Harold Guetzkow.* Boulder, CO: Westview, 1985.

shooting the planet's limits (triggering collapse), human beings would adapt to those limits in time to achieve a *steady-state* economy in which population, food production, energy use, and other key processes were stable from year to year. It has been argued that our generation is the "hinge of history," just past the middle point of the S-curve. If so, we are experiencing the most rapid change of any generation in the past *or* the future.[11] In this scenario the key task of our generation would be to adapt our economics and our politics, including IR, to level out into a sustainable long-term relationship with the environment.

The Earth Summit produced an overall plan, called Agenda 21, whereby large third-world states promise to industrialize along cleaner lines (at a certain cost to economic growth) and industrialized states promise to funnel aid and technology to them to assist in that process.[12]

The Earth Summit established the **Sustainable Development Commission;** it monitors states' compliance with the promises they made at the Earth Summit and hears evidence from environmental NGOs like Greenpeace. However, it lacks powers of enforcement over national governments—again reflecting the preeminence of state sovereignty over supranational authority (see pp. 272, 390). Of the 53 Commission members, 19 are from the industrialized regions, 12 from Africa, 12 from Asia, and 10 from Latin America. It was hoped that the Commission's ability to monitor and publicize state actions will discourage states from cheating on the deal reached at the Earth Summit.[13] But the Commission's first meeting, two years after the Earth Summit, found the states of the global North providing only half of the level of financial support pledged for sustainable development in the South.

Rethinking Interdependence

We have thus far treated international environmental issues as problems of interstate bargaining, an approach that reflects a neoliberal theoretical orientation. This approach has been challenged in recent years by an emerging theoretical framework that is more revolutionary in orientation, seeking more fundamental change in the nature of the international community's approach to environmental problems. This approach is well reflected in the grass-roots activism of Greenpeace and other environment-related NGOs. As discussed later (p. 435), environmentalists object to free-trade provisions that weaken environmental standards by empowering international bureaucrats who care more about wealth generation than eco-preservation. Similarly, environmental groups have objected to the international institutions managing economic development in the global South, in particular the World Bank whose development projects have been criticized as environmentally destructive.

In effect, the more revolutionary theoretical perspective rejects the liberal goal of maximizing wealth (see pp. 312–315). Although liberal concepts of rationality are longer-term than conservative ones (see p. 97), environmentalists take an even broader and longer-term view of rationality. From this perspective, the collective goods problem among states is not the problem; it is the growth of industrial civilization out of balance

---

[11]Platt, John R. The Step to Man. *Science* 149, August 6, 1965: 607–13.

[12]Miller, Marian A. L. *The Third World in Global Environmental Politics.* Boulder, CO: Lynne Rienner, 1995.

[13]Lewis, Paul. UN Implementing the Earth Summit. *The New York Times,* December 1, 1992: A16.

Pollution from Soviet industrialization caused great environmental damage, contributing to the stagnation and collapse of the Soviet economy—an unsustainable path. This steel plant in Novokuznetsk, Siberia, Russia, exemplifies the problem (1992). Today's third-world countries will have to industrialize along cleaner lines to realize sustainable development.

with the planetary ecosystem that must ultimately support it. True rationality, for environmentalists, must include very long-term calculations about how the self-interest of humanity itself is undermined by a greedy drive to exploit nature. To put it another way, interdependence and the collective goods problem are broadened to include humanity versus nature, not just state versus state.

The remainder of this chapter will remain focused primarily on interstate bargaining processes concerning the environment, but will include the broader forces of concern to environmentalists. If nothing else, these forces shape the contexts for interstate bargaining, and so must be of concern even to liberals and conservatives.

❖ MANAGING THE ENVIRONMENT

In discussing the issue areas in which states are bargaining over environmental problems, we may begin with the most global problems—those that are collective goods for all states and people in the world. Later sections consider more localized conflicts over pollution and natural resources.

The Atmosphere

Preserving the health of the earth's atmosphere is a benefit that affects people throughout the world without regard for their own state's contribution to the problem or its solution. Two problems of the atmosphere have become major international issues—global warming and depletion of the ozone layer.

Global Warming Global climate change, or **global warming,** is a slow, long-term rise in the average world temperature. Scientists are not certain that such a rise is occurring, or how fast if so, but there is growing evidence that global warming is a real problem, that it is caused by the emission of carbon dioxide and other gases, and that it will get worse in future decades. Many scientists believe that it would be prudent to address the problem soon, because once the symptoms become obvious it would be too late to intervene in time to prevent disaster.

It is not easy to guess who will be harmed and how soon. But over the next fifty years, according to most scientific estimates, global temperatures may rise by between two and nine degrees Fahrenheit if nothing is done. The high end of this temperature range corresponds with the difference between today's climate and that of the last ice age; it is a major climate change. At some point—possibly within a few decades—the polar ice caps would begin to melt a bit and cause the sea level to rise by as much as a few feet. Such a rise could flood many coastal cities and wipe out some island states altogether.

Global warming could also change weather patterns in many regions, causing droughts, floods, and widespread disruption of natural ecosystems. It is also possible that climate changes (at least mild ones) could *benefit* some regions and make agriculture more productive. Nobody knows for sure, but sudden environmental changes are usually much more harmful than helpful.

It is not easy to reduce the emissions of gases responsible for global warming. These gases result from the broad spectrum of activities that drive an industrial economy. They are a by-product of burning **fossil fuels**—oil, coal, and natural gas—to run factories, cars, tractors, furnaces, electrical generating plants, and so forth. These activities create **greenhouse gases**—so named because when concentrated in the atmosphere these gases act like the glass in a greenhouse: they let energy in as short-wavelength solar radiation but reflect it back when it tries to exit again as longer-wavelength heat waves. The greenhouse gases are *carbon dioxide* (responsible for two-thirds of the effect), *methane* gas, *chloroflourocarbons* (CFCs), and *nitrous oxide*. Over time, the concentration of these gases in the global atmosphere is slowly increasing, though the rates and processes involved are complicated (carbon is exchanged among the atmosphere, oceans, and trees).

Thus, the costs of reducing the greenhouse effect are high, because the solutions entail curbing economic growth or shifting it onto new technological paths.[14] For individual states, those costs are almost unrelated to the benefits of a solution. If one state reduces its industrial production or makes expensive investments in new technologies, this will have little effect on the long-term outcome unless other states do likewise. And if most states took such steps, a free rider that did not go along would save money and still benefit from the solution of the global warming problem. Furthermore, the costs (however distributed)

---

[14]Rubin, Edward S., et al. Realistic Mitigation Options for Global Warming. *Science* 257, July 10, 1992: 148.

begin taking their toll in the short term, but the benefits are decades in the future and hard to quantify.

Greenhouse gases are produced by each state roughly in proportion to its industrial activity. Eighty percent of greenhouse gases now come from the industrialized countries— 25 percent from the United States alone. Yet the most severe impacts of global warming are likely to be felt in the global South. Naturally, serious international conflicts are arising over who should pay the bills to avert greenhouse warming.[15]

All of these elements make for a difficult multilateral bargaining situation, one that has not yet been resolved. The *treaty on global warming* adopted at the 1992 Earth Summit did not commit the signatory states to meet target levels of greenhouse emissions by a particular date (due to U.S. objections to such a commitment). Meanwhile the **UN Environment Program (UNEP),** whose main function is to monitor environmental conditions, is working with the World Meteorological Organization to measure changes in global climate from year to year. Since 1989 the UN-sponsored *Intergovernmental Panel on Climate Change* has served as a negotiating forum for this issue.

Western Europe and Japan are more willing to regulate greenhouse emissions than is the United States (which burns more fossil fuel per person, partly because of its sprawling geography and reliance on automobiles). Europe and Japan have proposed that all states stabilize their emissions at 1990 levels by the year 2000. The United States has resisted a firm commitment to this target, although it may actually meet the standards unilaterally.

Technology may help to make the bargaining a bit easier in the future. Many technical experts now argue that dramatic gains can be made through energy efficiency measures and other solutions that do not reduce the amount of economic activity but only make it cleaner and more efficient. Although such investments might be costly, they would ultimately pay for themselves through greater economic efficiency. If this approach succeeds, international conflicts over global warming will be reduced.

Japanese leaders think their country can profit by developing a comparative advantage in environmental technologies. The government- and industry-funded *Research Institute of Innovative Technology for the Earth (RITE)*, among other projects, is developing methods to filter carbon dioxide out of industrial exhausts.[16] RITE is part of a MITI campaign (called *New Earth 21*) to coordinate a movement of Japanese industry into environmental technologies.

Ozone Depletion A second major atmospheric problem being negotiated by the world's governments is the depletion of the world's **ozone layer.**[17] Ozone high in the atmosphere screens out harmful ultraviolet rays from the sun. Certain chemicals used in industrial economies get into the air, float up to the top of the atmosphere, and interact with ozone in a way that breaks it down. The chief culprits are CFCs, which have been widely used in refrigeration and in aerosol sprays. (Unfortunately, ozone produced by

[15]Sebenius, James K. Designing Negotiations Toward a New Regime: The Case of Global Warming. *International Security* 15 (4), 1991: 110–48.

[16]Japan Bids for Global Leadership in Clean Industry. *Science* 256, May 22, 1992: 1144.

[17]Benedick, Richard Elliot. *Ozone Diplomacy*. Cambridge, MA: Harvard University Press, 1991. Liftin, Karen. *Ozone Discourse: Science and Politics in Global Environmental Cooperation*. New York: Columbia University Press, 1993.

International treaties have been much more successful in addressing ozone depletion (by phasing out the chemicals responsible) than global warming. A U.S.-European space shuttle mission in November 1994 studied the Antarctic ozone hole, which is the size of North America. Burning of fossil fuels—in the shuttle's rocket engines and throughout industrial societies—contributes to global warming.

burning fossil fuels does not replace the high-level ozone but only pollutes the lower atmosphere.)

As the ozone layer thins, more ultraviolet radiation is reaching the earth's surface. Over Antarctica, where the ozone is thinnest, there is a hole in the ozone for months each year, and it appears to be growing larger and lasting longer year by year. Depleted ozone levels over North America were detected in the early 1990s, and people have been warned to limit their exposure to the sun to lower the risk of skin cancer. Eventually, ozone depletion could have severe environmental consequences. The increased radiation could begin to kill off vegetation, reduce agricultural yields, and disrupt ecosystems.

Clearly, this is another collective goods problem in that one state benefits from allowing the use of CFCs in its economy, provided that most other states prohibit their use. But the costs of replacing CFCs are much lower than the costs of addressing global warming: CFCs can be replaced with other chemicals at relatively modest costs. Furthermore, the consequences of ozone depletion are both better understood and more immediate than those of global warming.

Therefore, states have had more success in negotiating agreements and developing regimes to manage the ozone problem. In the 1987 **Montreal Protocol,** 22 states agreed to reduce CFCs by 50 percent by 1998. In 1990 the timetable was accelerated and the signatories expanded: 81 states agreed to eliminate all CFCs by the year 2000. In 1992, as evidence of ozone depletion mounted, the schedule was again accelerated, with major industrial states phasing out CFCs by 1995. The signatories also agreed in principle to establish a fund (of unspecified size and source) to help third-world states pay for alternative refrigeration technologies not based on CFCs. Without such an effort, the third-world states would be tempted to free ride on the global CFC reduction efforts and could ultimately undermine the effort.

The Montreal Protocol on CFCs is the most important success yet achieved in international negotiations to preserve the global environment. It showed that states can agree to take action on urgent environmental threats, can agree on targets and measures to counter such threats, and can allocate the costs of such measures in a mutually acceptable way. Recent measurements of CFCs in the atmosphere show that the yearly rate of increase has slowed down—a promising start.[18] But the international cooperation on the ozone problem has not been widely repeated on other environmental issues.

Biodiversity

Biodiversity refers to the tremendous diversity of plant and animal species making up the earth's (global, regional, and local) ecosystems. Biologists believe that the 1.4 million species they have identified and named are only a small fraction of the total number of species in existence (most of which are microorganisms). Some species, such as humans, are distributed broadly around the world, whereas others live in just one locale.

Due to humans' destruction of ecosystems, large numbers of species are becoming *extinct* or are in danger of doing so. Extinct species can never be re-created. The causes of their extinction include overhunting, overfishing, and introducing nonnative species that crowd out previous inhabitants. But the most important cause of extinctions is *loss of habitat*—the destruction of rain forests, pollution of lakes and streams, and loss of agricultural lands to urban sprawl. Because ecosystems are based on complex interrelationships among species, often fragile and finely tuned, the extinction of a few species can cause deeper changes in the environment. For example, the loss of native microorganisms can lead to soil erosion, to chronic pollution of rivers, or to the transformation of arable land into deserts.

But because ecosystems are so complex, it is usually impossible to predict the consequences of a species' extinction or of the loss of a habitat or ecosystem. Generally the activities that lead to habitat loss are economically profitable, so there are real costs associated with limiting such activities. For example, logging in the U.S. Northwest has been restricted to save the northern spotted owl from extinction. Nobody can be sure what effect the owl's extinction would have, but the costs to loggers are clear and immediate.

Species preservation is thus a collective good resembling global warming; the costs are immediate and substantial but the benefits are long term and ill defined. In the case of biodiversity the effects of policies tend to be felt more locally than those of global warm-

---

[18]*Science* 256, May 22, 1992: 1109.

ing, so the problem to some degree can be enclosed within the purview of states. But to a surprising extent the biodiversity in one state's territory affects the quality of the environment in other states. Topsoil blown away in Africa is deposited in South America; monarch butterflies that failed to breed in Mexico in 1991 did not appear in New England in 1992.

It has been difficult to reach international agreement on sharing the costs of preserving biodiversity. At the 1992 Earth Summit, a treaty on biodiversity was adopted that committed signatories to preserving habitats and got rich states to pay poor ones for the rights to use commercially profitable biological products extracted from rare species in protected habitats (such as medicines from rain forest trees). However, because of fears that it could limit U.S. patent rights in biotechnology, the United States did not sign the treaty. Later it agreed to sign, with stipulations, but by mid-1995 was the only industrialized country that had not ratified the treaty. India began an effort to limit U.S. access to medicinal substances from the global South until the United States ratified the treaty.

Many environmentalists have a special concern for whales and dolphins, which like humans are large-brained mammals. In the past twenty years, environmental activists have gotten states to agree to international regimes to protect whales and dolphins. The **International Whaling Commission** (an IGO) sets quotas for hunting certain whale species; participation is voluntary, and Norway dropped out in 1992 when it decided unilaterally that it could increase its catch without endangering the species. The *Inter-American Tropical Tuna Commission* (another IGO) regulates methods used to fish for tuna, aiming to minimize dolphin losses.

The United States, which consumes half the world's tuna catch, has gone further and unilaterally requires—in the Marine Mammal Protection Act—that "dolphin-safe" methods be used for tuna sold in U.S. territory. Under this law the United States in 1990 banned imports of tuna from Mexico and Venezuela. These countries could not comply with the U.S. law as easily as the U.S. tuna industry could, and they called the law an unfair restriction on free trade. They took their case to the GATT (see pp. 340–342) and won. But the United States did not comply with the GATT ruling, despite appeals from the European Community and dozens of other states. Venezuela's tuna fleet was reduced to less than a third of its former size.[19]

Such conflicts portend future battles between environmentalists and free-trade advocates.[20] Free-traders argue that states must not use domestic legislation to seek global environmental goals. Environmentalists insist on doing just that, in the absence of meaningful international treaties accomplishing the same ends. In the 1990s a coalition of U.S. environmental groups campaigned against the "faceless bureaucrats" at GATT who override national laws like the tuna act; these bureaucrats are portrayed as agents of the MNCs, out to increase profits with no regard for the environment. Conflicts are developing over U.S. laws restricting imports of foods with pesticide residues, and over European laws on imports of tropical hardwoods from rain forests. Environmentalists feared that the successful Montreal Protocol on ozone protection, which relies on trade sanctions for enforcement, could be threatened by the new GATT/WTO agreements.

---

[19]Brooke, James. America—Environmental Dictator? *The New York Times*, May 3, 1992: F7.

[20]Esty, Daniel C. *Greening the GATT: Trade, Environment and the Future.* Washington, DC: Institute for International Economics, 1994. Leonard, H. Jeffrey. *Pollution and the Struggle for the World Product: Multinational Corporations, Environment, and International Comparative Advantage.* New York: Cambridge University Press, 1988.

Thus, unilateral approaches to biodiversity issues are problematical because they disrupt free trade; multilateral approaches are problematical because of the collective goods problem. It is not surprising that the international response to species extinction has been fairly ineffective to date.

Forests and Oceans

Two types of habitat—tropical rain forests and oceans—are especially important to both biodiversity and the atmosphere. Both are also reservoirs of commercially profitable resources like fish and wood. The difference is that forests are located almost entirely within state territory, but oceans are largely beyond any state territory, in the global commons.

Rain Forests As many as half the world's total species live in *rain forests;* they replenish oxygen and reduce carbon dioxide in the atmosphere—slowing down global warming. Rain forests thus benefit all the world's states; they are collective goods.

International bargaining on the preservation of rain forests has made considerable progress, probably because most rain forests belong to a few states. These few states have the power to speed up or slow down the destruction of forests—and international bargaining amounts to agreements to shift costs from those few states onto the broader group of states benefiting from the rain forests. This collective goods problem is simpler and has fewer actors than the global warming problem.

Although some rich states (including the United States) have large forests, most of the largest rain forests are in poor states such as Brazil (Latin America), Indonesia and Malaysia (Southeast Asia), and Madagascar (Africa). Such states can benefit economically from exploiting the forests freely—cutting lumber, clearing land for agriculture, and mining.[21] Until recently (and still to an extent), leaders of rich states have been most interested in encouraging maximum economic growth in poor states so that foreign debts could be paid—with little regard for environmental damage. The World Bank, for example, has been criticized by environmentalists for providing technical assistance and investment to build large dams in environmentally sensitive third-world areas.

Now that rich states have taken an interest in protecting rain forests, they are using money and development assistance as leverage to induce poorer states to protect their forests rather than exploiting them maximally. Several means have been used to do so. Under international agreements negotiated in the early 1990s, rich countries are contributing hundreds of millions of dollars in foreign aid for this purpose. In some third-world countries burdened by large foreign debts, environmentalists and bankers from rich countries have worked out "debt-for-nature swaps" in which a debt is canceled in exchange for the state's agreement to preserve tracts of forest.

Brazil in particular has responded to these agreements with significant steps. There, a major government-sponsored drive to settle and exploit the Amazon basin had begun in the 1960s. In the early 1990s, Brazil's government adopted sweeping new environmental policies to balance the economic exploitation of the Amazon basin with the needs of en-

---

[21]Guimãraes, Roberto P. *The Ecopolitics of Development in the Third World: Politics and Environment in Brazil.* Boulder, CO: Lynne Rienner, 1991.

vironmental preservation and the rights of indigenous peoples. Although the rain forest problem has not been solved, there is now widespread awareness of the problem and creative efforts are being made to solve it.

For example, Cultural Survival, a U.S.-based activist group, has developed creative ways to preserve native cultures and their environments. One idea is to make the rain forest economically profitable in its native state so that people do not need to cut down the trees to make money. One way to do this is to create new export markets for forest products, like Brazil nuts. Cultural Survival has helped Brazil nut gatherers form cooperatives and build a shelling factory. The nuts are shipped to Vermont and made into a brittle candy that goes into Ben and Jerry's "Rain Forest Crunch" ice cream. Such products satisfy the interests of U.S. consumers, Brazilian forest inhabitants, and the global environment.

Oceans The *oceans*, covering 70 percent of the earth's surface, are (like the rain forest) a key to regulating climate and preserving biodiversity. Oceans, like forests, are attractive targets for short-term economic uses that cause long-term environmental damage. Such uses include overfishing, dumping toxic and nuclear waste (and other garbage), and long-distance oil shipments with their recurrent spills.

Unlike rain forests, oceans belong to no state but are a global commons.[22] This makes the collective goods problem more difficult because no authority exists to enforce regulations. Preserving the oceans depends on the cooperation of the (over a hundred) states and (thousands of) nonstate actors involved in using them.

Free riders have great opportunities to profit. For example, *drift nets* are huge fishing nets, miles long, that scoop up everything in their path. They are very profitable but destructive of a sustainable ocean environment. Most states have now banned their use (under pressure from the environmental movement), but a few—notably Taiwan—have not. No state has the authority to go out into the oceans and stop Taiwanese fishing boats from using these nets.

One solution that states have pursued involves "enclosing" more of the ocean. Territorial waters have expanded to hundreds of miles off the coast (and around islands), so that state sovereignty encloses substantial resources (fisheries and offshore oil and mineral deposits). This solution has been pursued in the context of larger multilateral negotiations on ocean management.

Those negotiations centered on the **UN Conference on the Law of the Sea (UNCLOS)** from 1973 to 1982. Building on two earlier rounds (from 1958 to 1960), this conference created a world treaty governing uses of the oceans. The UNCLOS treaty established rules on territorial waters—12 miles for shipping and 200 miles for economic activities, such as fishing and mining. The 200-mile limit placed a substantial share of the economically profitable ocean resources in the control of about a dozen states (see Figure 11.1).

A conflict developed over a small piece of the continental shelf off Newfoundland that was just beyond the 200-mile range controlled by Canada. The Canadian Navy seized Spanish fishing ships there, which they claimed were overfishing and using too fine

[22]Pontecorvo, Giulio, ed. *The New Order of the Oceans*. New York: Columbia University Press, 1986. Osherenko, Gail, and Oran R. Young. *The Age of the Arctic: Hot Conflicts and Cold Realities*. New York: Cambridge University Press, 1989.

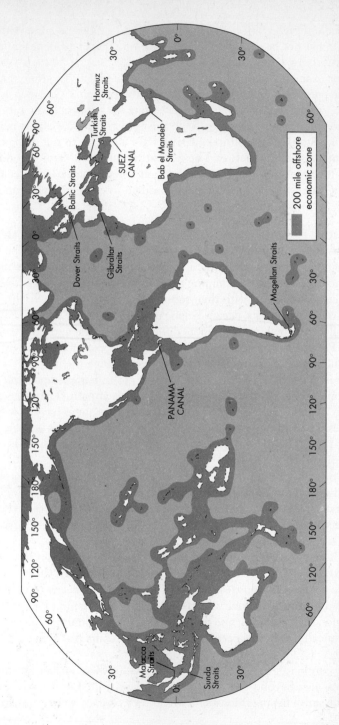

FIGURE 11.1 Overfishing, and similar problems of managing the "commons" of world oceans, have been addressed by enclosing the most important ocean areas as territorial waters of states. Shaded areas are within the 200-mile economic zones controlled by states under terms of the Law of the Sea treaty.

Source: Adapted from Andrew Boyd. *An Atlas of World Affairs.* 9th ed. New York: Routledge, 1992.

Ⅰn 1995, Canada began unilaterally enforcing fishing rules just outside its 200-mile territorial waters (economic zone), using military force several times to seize, disable, or drive away Spanish fishing ships. The actions seemed to set the stage for a nasty confrontation between allies (Canada and the European Union). Instead an agreement was reached, which limited fishing methods and catches in the area, as Canada had wanted. How might we explain this episode in theoretical terms?

Realism would note the effectiveness of Canada's resort to military leverage, which drove the cost of European resistance way up and made it worthwhile for the EU to come to terms with Canadian demands. Since treaties like UNCLOS are viewed with some skepticism by realists, they would attribute Canada's success to its proximity—the greater ease with which its navy could deploy to the disputed area—and its stronger will to prevail (reflecting the fact that the issue affected Canada's national interests much more than those of the EU).

Liberals could note, however, that the EU is far more powerful than Canada overall, so sheer power politics does not provide a very good starting point for explaining the outcome. Rather, liberals might emphasize

THINKING THEORETICALLY

the collective goods problem involved in overfishing, and note that Canada's willingness to unilaterally take on the enforcement costs effectively resolved the dilemma. It remained only to negotiate the terms of what was being enforced (the specific rules for fishing), and there the conflicts of interest were small compared to the overall range of mutual benefits produced by the close economic cooperation of Canada and the EU. The idea that unilateral enforcement could resolve collective goods dilemmas is supported by the comments of the chairman of a UN conference working on an international fishing treaty. He noted that the Canadian-EU agreement "will help our discussions here because it establishes the principle that there can be boarding and monitoring on the high seas."

In what other cases might we find unilateral enforcement of norms for using the global commons? How would you begin to test the theory that unilateral enforcement can be good for multilateral cooperation? Would there have to be one logical enforcer (like Canada in this case), or could any state step into the role? What effect would you expect the strength or weakness of hegemony in the international system to have in these cases?

a netting—endangering fish populations that were mostly within the 200-mile limit. Although the European Union accused Canada of "piracy" on the high seas, the two sides in 1995 reached an agreement on fishing levels and practices. The agreement in turn stimulated progress in UN talks that had been trying to develop global rules and norms for ocean fishing. (It is not clear in 1995 how successful the UN effort would be.) Earlier in 1994 Russian warships drove away dozens of foreign fishing ships in the Sea of Okhotsk. Similar conflicts were developing near Norway, West Africa, the South Pacific and the Indian Ocean.

UNCLOS also developed the general principle that the oceans are a common heritage of humankind. A mechanism was created, through an International Sea-Bed Authority, for sharing some of the wealth that rich states might gain from extracting minerals on the ocean floor (beyond 200 miles).

The UNCLOS treaty faced uncertain prospects when the United States at the last minute decided not to sign the treaty. U.S. leaders felt that their country bore too great a share of the costs in the plan. The United States is the dominant naval power with de facto military control in much of the world's ocean space. It is also the state most likely to benefit from unilateral deep-sea mining. The United States was not willing to underwrite the costs of providing the collective good of ocean management. After more than a decade's delay, and after renegotiating some aspects of the deep-sea mining provisions, the United States signed UNCLOS in 1994.

Private environmental groups have been active players on oceans, as in rain forests—pressuring governments and MNCs to change policies and activities. Tactics include direct action (such as Greenpeace ships shadowing whaling ships or garbage barges), lobbying, lawsuits, and public education. These tactics have effectively used global communications (see Chapter 10, pp. 412–414). A dramatic event isolated in a remote location on the high seas can be videotaped and reproduced on millions of TV sets.

Antarctica Like the oceans, *Antarctica* belongs to no state.[23] But the continent's strategic and commercial value are both limited, and not many states care about it. Thus, states have been successful in reaching agreements on Antarctica because the costs were low and the players few. The **Antarctic Treaty of 1959**—one of the first multilateral treaties concerning the environment—forbids military activity in Antarctica as well as the presence of nuclear weapons or the dumping of nuclear waste there. It sets aside territorial claims on the continent for future resolution and establishes a regime under which various states conduct scientific research in Antarctica. The treaty was signed by all states with interests or activities in the area, including both superpowers. In the 1980s, Greenpeace set up a permanent base in Antarctica to monitor conditions and by 1991 had convinced the treaty signatories to turn the continent into a "world park." Antartica is largely a success story in international environmental politics.

Pollution

Pollution generally creates a collective goods problem, but one that is not often global in scale. Pollution is more often a regional or bilateral issue. With some exceptions—such as dumping at sea—the effects of pollution are limited to the state where it occurs and its close neighbors. For example, U.S. industrial smokestack emissions affect acid rain in Canada but do not directly affect distant states. Even when pollution crosses state borders, it often has its strongest effects closest to the source. This makes it a somewhat less intractable collective goods problem, because a polluting state can seldom get an entirely free ride, and there are a limited number of actors. In addition, the effects of pollution tend to be visible in the short term and are not distant abstractions like global warming.

In several regions—notably Western and Eastern Europe and the Middle East—states are closely packed in the same air, river, or sea basins. In these cases, pollution controls must often be negotiated multilaterally. In Europe during the Cold War, the international

---

[23]Peterson, M. J. *Managing the Frozen South: The Creation and Evolution of the Antarctic Treaty System*. Berkeley: University of California Press, 1988.

pollution problem was exacerbated by the inability of Western European states to impose any limits on Eastern ones, whose pollution was notorious under the communist policy of massive industrialization. These problems are only now beginning to be addressed.

Several regional agreements seek to limit **acid rain,** which is caused by air pollution. Acid rain damages trees and often crosses borders. European states—whose forests have been heavily damaged—have agreed to limit air pollution and acid rain for their mutual benefit. In 1988, twenty-four European states signed a treaty to limit nitrogen oxide emissions to 1988 levels by 1995. After long negotiations, the United States and Canada have signed bilateral agreements to limit such pollution as well.

Water pollution often crosses borders as well, especially because industrial pollution, human sewage, and agricultural fertilizers and pesticides all tend to run into rivers and seas. Long-standing international regional agencies that regulate shipping on heavily used European rivers like the Rhine now also deal with pollution. The Mediterranean basin is severely polluted, and difficult to manage because so many states border it.[24] In North America, the Great Lakes on the U.S.-Canadian border had become heavily polluted by the 1970s. But because the issue affected only two countries, it was easier to address, and the situation has improved in recent years.

Toxic and nuclear wastes are a special problem because of their long-term dangers. States occasionally try to ship such wastes out of the country. International agreements now ban the dumping of toxic and nuclear wastes at sea (an obvious collective goods problem). But such wastes have been sent to third-world countries for disposal, for a fee. For instance, toxic ash from Pennsylvania became material for bricks in Guinea, and Italian nuclear waste was shipped to Nigeria.

Norms have developed in recent years against exporting toxic wastes—a practice seen as exploitive of the receiving country. In 1989 a hundred states signed a treaty under UN auspices to regulate shipments of toxic and nuclear wastes and prevent their secret movements under corrupt deals. Forty more countries, in Africa, did not sign the treaty but called for a complete halt to toxic waste shipments to Africa.

In one famous case, 14,000 tons of toxic waste—ash from Philadelphia's trash incinerator—was loaded on a ship in 1985 to be exported. The would-be recipients of the waste refused to accept it, and the ship spent nearly three years traveling from continent to continent in search of a state that would take its cargo. Finally, with the ash mislabeled as "fertilizer," the ship was allowed into Haiti; it dumped 4,000 tons of ash on a beach where it remained years later (despite a Haitian order to remove it). The other 10,000 tons apparently were illegally dumped in the Indian Ocean. In 1993 the ship's owners were convicted of perjury for denying the dumping.

In the 1950s, atmospheric nuclear tests created radioactive fallout that traveled thousands of miles before falling back to the ground. After milk drunk by U.S. schoolchildren was found to contain radioactive iodine, alarm over fallout led to the 1963 limited test ban, which stopped nuclear tests above ground. In 1986 a meltdown at the Soviet nuclear power plant at **Chernobyl,** in Ukraine, created airborne radioactivity that

---

[24]Haas, Peter M. *Saving the Mediterranean*. See footnote 5 in this chapter.

spread over much of Europe, from Italy to Sweden. The accident exemplified the new reality—that economic and technical decisions taken in one state can have grave environmental consequences for other countries. Soviet leaders made matters worse by failing to notify neighbors promptly of the accident.

On the various issues of water and air pollution, both unilateral state actions and international agreements have often been feasible and effective. In the past two decades, river water quality has improved in most industrialized regions. Market economies have begun to deal with pollution as just another cost of production that should be charged to the polluter instead of to society at large. Some governments have begun to allocate "pollution rights" that companies can buy and sell on a free market.

In the former Soviet bloc, decades of centrally planned industrialization has created more severe environmental problems, which may prove more intractable.[25] The environmental damage and human health risks in that region are staggering. The economically strapped former Soviet republics now must bargain over limiting pollution and repairing the damage. For example, the severely polluted Aral Sea formerly contained within one state, the Soviet Union, is now shared by two (Kazakhstan and Uzbekistan). Once the world's fourth largest inland sea, it has shrunk in half, its huge fisheries destroyed, after a Soviet-era mega-irrigation project (to grow cotton in the desert) diverted the Aral Sea's inlet rivers. In 1994 environmentalists gave up efforts to save the Aral Sea, after local and international political leaders failed to implement plans to address the problem. Local populations suffered from widespread health effects of the disaster. Decisions by the former Soviet republics to keep operating old and unsafe nuclear power reactors, as well as the problems associated with dismantling nuclear weapons, also add to the region's long environmental agenda.

❖ NATURAL RESOURCES

The natural environment is not only a delicate ecosystem requiring protection, it is also a repository of natural resources. The extraction of such resources brings states wealth (and hence power), so these resources regularly become a source of international conflicts.[26] Because these resources are mostly located within individual states' territories, they do not present a collective goods problem. Rather, states bargain (with leverage) over trade in these vital resources.

Three aspects of natural resources shape their role in international conflict. First, they are required for the operation of an industrial economy (even an agrarian one in the

---

[25]Feshbach, Murray. *Ecological Disaster: Cleaning Up the Hidden Legacy of the Soviet Regime*. Washington, DC: The Brookings Institution, 1995. Schleicher, Klaus, ed. *Pollution Knows No Frontiers: A Reader*. New York: Paragon, 1992. DeBardeleben, Joan, ed. *To Breathe Free: Eastern Europe's Environmental Crisis*. Baltimore: Johns Hopkins University Press, 1991. Singleton, Fred, ed. *Environmental Problems in the Soviet Union and Eastern Europe*. Boulder, CO: Lynne Reinner, 1987.

[26]Zacher, Mark W., ed. *The International Political Economy of Natural Resources*. Brookfield, VT: Edward Elgar, 1993. Ghee, Lim Teck, and Mark J. Valencia, eds. *Conflict over Natural Resources in South-East Asia and the Pacific*. New York: Oxford University Press, 1991. Lipschutz, Ronnie D. *When Nations Clash: Raw Materials, Ideology, and Foreign Policy*. New York: Ballinger, 1989. Pirages, Dennis. *Global Technopolitics: The International Politics of Technology and Resources*. Pacific Grove, CA: Brooks/Cole, 1989.

Pollution easily crosses national borders, as exemplified by the nuclear reactor accident at Chernobyl, Ukraine (USSR), in May 1986, which spread a radioactive cloud across Europe. Pollution's effects are mainly regional rather than global in scope, however, reducing the collective goods problem somewhat.

case of some resources). Second, their sources—mineral deposits, rivers, and so forth—are associated with particular territories over which states may fight for control. Third, natural resources tend to be unevenly distributed over the earth's surface, with plentiful supplies in some states and an absence in others. These aspects mean that trade in natural resources is extremely profitable; much additional wealth is created by such trade. They also mean that trade in resources is fairly politicized—creating market imperfections like monopoly, oligopoly, price manipulation, and so on (see "Politics of Markets" on pp. 321–322).

World Energy

Of the various natural resources required by states, energy resources (fuels) are central. The commercial fuels that power the world's industrial economies are *oil* (39 percent of world energy consumption), *coal* (32 percent), *natural gas* (24 percent), and *hydroelectric and nuclear power* (5 percent). The fossil fuels (coal, oil, gas) thus account for 95 percent of world energy consumption. (Some energy consumed as electricity comes from hydroelectric dams or nuclear power plants, but much of it comes from burning fossil fuels in electric-generating plants.)

Imagine a pile of coal weighing 22,000 pounds—ten metric tons. (That's about the weight of ten automobiles.) The energy released by burning that much coal is equivalent to the amount of energy North Americans use per person each year. Wealthier people, of course, consume more energy per person than do poorer people, but ten tons is the average.

Table 11.1 shows the energy consumption per person in the nine world regions. The four industrialized regions of the North use much more energy per person than those of the South. North America uses thirty times as much energy per person as do Asia or Africa. This is because Asia and Africa have little industry. Among industrialized countries there are differences in the *efficiency* of energy use—GDP produced per unit of energy consumed. The least-efficient region is Russia and Eastern Europe (even before that region's current economic depression); North America is also rather inefficient; and Europe and Japan are the most energy efficient of the industrialized regions.

International trade in energy plays a vital role in the world economy. As Table 11.1 shows, the regions of the industrialized West are all net importers of energy. Together they import from the rest of the world, each year, energy equivalent to 1.5 *billion* tons of coal. The other six world regions are net exporters of energy.

Although all forms of energy are traded internationally, the most important by far is oil, which is cheapest to transport over long distances (in pipelines and tanker ships). Russia and Eastern Europe receive vital hard currency earnings from exporting oil. Venezuela and Mexico (in Latin America) and Nigeria and Angola (in Africa) are major oil exporters. But by far the largest source of oil exports is the Middle East—especially the countries around the Persian Gulf (Saudi Arabia, Kuwait, Iraq, Iran, and the small sheikdoms of United Arab Emirates, Qatar, Bahrain, and Oman). Saudi Arabia is the largest oil exporter and sits atop the largest oil reserves (see Table 8.1 on page 345). The politics of world energy revolve around Middle East oil shipped to Western Europe, Japan/Pacific, and North America.

TABLE 11.1 PER CAPITA ENERGY CONSUMPTION AND NET ENERGY TRADE

1992, in Coal Equivalent

	Per Capita Consumption (Metric Tons)	Total Net Energy Exports (Million Metric Tons)
North America	10.8	−330
Western Europe	5.0	−680
Japan/Pacific	4.5	−510
Russia/Eastern Europe	5.1	275
China	0.8	50
Middle East	1.7	1,300
Latin America	1.2	240
South Asia	0.4	65
Africa	0.3	190
World as a whole	2.0	

Note: "Net exports" refers to production minus consumption. Net exports worldwide do not equal net imports for technical reasons.
Source: Calculated from United Nations. *Energy Statistics Yearbook.* New York: United Nations (annual).

The importance of oil in the industrialized economies helps to explain the political importance of the Middle East in world politics.[27] Iraq's 1990 invasion of Kuwait (and the mere possibility that Iraq's army could roll on into Saudi Arabia) threatened the West's access to stable and inexpensive supplies of oil. World oil prices immediately more than doubled in response. But Saudi Arabia was able to increase its own rate of oil exports massively enough to compensate for both Kuwaiti and Iraqi exports cut off in the wake of the invasion and the UN sanctions against Iraq. When it became clear that Saudi exports would not be disrupted, the price of oil dropped again on world markets. Thus, not only is energy a crucial economic sector (on which all industrial activity depends), it is also one of the most politically sensitive (because of the dependence of the West on energy imported from the Middle East and other third-world regions).

To secure a supply of oil in the Middle East, Britain and other European countries colonized the area early this century, carving up the territory into protectorates in which European power kept local monarchs on their thrones. (Iraq, for instance, argues that Kuwait is part of Iraq, that it was cut off and made into a separate state by the British.) The United States did not claim colonies or protectorates in the Middle East, but U.S. MNCs were heavily involved in the development of oil resources in the area from the 1920s through the 1960s—often wielding tremendous power. Local rulers depended on the technical expertise and capital investment of U.S. and European oil companies. The "seven sisters"—a cartel of Western oil companies—kept the price paid to local states low and their own profits high.

After World War II the British gave up colonial claims in the Middle East, but the Western oil companies kept producing cheap oil there for Western consumption. Then in 1973, during an Arab-Israeli war, the oil-producing Arab states of the region decided to punish the United States for supporting Israel. They cut off their oil exports to the United States and curtailed their overall exports. This sent world oil prices skyrocketing. OPEC realized its potential power and the high price the world was willing to pay for oil. After the war ended, OPEC agreed to limit production to keep oil prices high.

This 1973 **oil shock** had a profound effect on the world economy and on world politics. Huge amounts of hard currency accumulated in the treasuries of the Middle East oil-exporting countries, which in turn invested them around the world (these were called *petrodollars*). High inflation plagued the United States and Europe for years afterward. The economic instability and sense of U.S. helplessness—coming on top of the Vietnam debacle—seemed to mark a decline in American power and perhaps the rise of the third world.

In 1979, the revolution in Iran led to another major increase in oil prices. This **second oil shock** further weakened the industrialized economies. But these economies were already adjusting to the new realities of world energy. Higher oil prices led to the *expansion of oil production* in new locations outside of OPEC—in the North Sea (Britain and Norway), Alaska, Angola, Russia, and elsewhere. By the mid-1980s, the Middle East was

---

[27]Kapstein, Ethan B. *The Insecure Alliance: Energy Crises and Western Politics Since 1944.* New York: Oxford University Press, 1990. Yergin, Daniel. *The Prize: The Epic Quest for Oil, Money, and Power.* New York: Simon & Schuster, 1991. Ikenberry, G. John. *Reasons of State: Oil Politics and the Capacities of American Government.* Ithaca: Cornell University Press, 1988. Kupchan, Charles A. *The Persian Gulf and the West: The Dilemmas of Security.* Boston: Allen & Unwin, 1987.

rapidly losing its market share of world trade in oil. At the same time, industrialized economies learned to be more *energy efficient*. With slackening demand (due also to economic stagnation) and growing supply, world oil prices dropped from over $50 (in today's dollars) per barrel in 1980 to around $20 per barrel in 1986.

Due to these market adjustments, the industrialized West is now somewhat less dependent on Middle East oil and the power of OPEC has been greatly reduced. Low oil prices and competition within OPEC contributed to Iraq's economic problems in 1990 and its invasion of Kuwait—but world oil prices ended up lower after the Gulf War. Still, energy continues to be a crucial issue in which the Middle East plays a key role.

Low oil prices help the industrialized economies, but they have two major drawbacks. First, burning oil contributes to global warming, and low prices make it profitable to burn more oil and be less energy efficient. Second, low oil prices reduce the export earnings of oil producing countries. Those like Saudi Arabia, with huge financial reserves and plenty of oil, feel only modest pain. But countries like Venezuela and Mexico had counted on oil revenues in their economic development plans and had borrowed foreign money to be repaid from future oil earnings. Some of these countries face major debt problems as a result.

Minerals, Land, Water

To build the infrastructure and other manufactured goods that create wealth in a national economy, states need other raw materials in addition to energy. These include metals, other minerals, and related materials extracted through mining.

A combination of energy sources, other raw materials, and capital (machines, etc.) that all work together in an economy has been called a *technological style*. For instance, the combination of hay, farms, horse carts, and roads (etc.) makes up one technological style, and the combination of oil, steel, automobiles, and freeways (etc.) makes up a different style. The raw materials and fuels that a state requires depend on both its overall level of economic development (industrialization) and its technological style.

The political economy of minerals—iron, copper, platinum, and so forth—differs from that of world energy. The value of international trade in oil is many times greater than that of any mineral. Furthermore, mineral production is distributed more evenly than is oil production, with the result that supply is not so concentrated in one region of the world. Industrialized countries have further reduced their vulnerability by stockpiling strategic minerals (which is easier to do with minerals than with energy because the quantities and values are much smaller).

Nonetheless, industrialized countries do have certain vulnerabilities with regard to mineral supply, and these do affect international politics. Among the industrialized regions, Japan and Europe are most dependent on mineral imports; the United States is more self-sufficient. The former Soviet Union was a leading exporter of key minerals—a role that Russia may continue in the future. Despite its economic problems, one great strength of the Russian economy is being self-sufficient in both energy and mineral resources. During the Cold War, Western states feared becoming dependent on the Soviet Union to supply strategic minerals (especially those needed for military production, such as metal alloys for military aircraft).

Another major exporter of key minerals is South Africa. For a few strategic minerals, notably manganese and chromium, South Africa controls three-quarters or more of the world's reserves. Western leaders worry that political instability in South Africa (where the black majority has struggled for years under white minority rule) could disrupt the supply of these minerals. This is one reason why for years the industrialized countries were reluctant to impose trade sanctions on South Africa over human rights issues. South Africa's leading position in supplying diamonds, gold, and platinum to world markets gave South Africa a valuable source of income, but in the end the West did apply economic sanctions that hurt the South African economy.

Most important to industrialized economies are the minerals that go into making industrial equipment, from automobiles to computers. Traditionally most important is iron, from which steel is made. The leading producers of steel are the former Soviet Union, Japan, the United States, China, and Germany, followed by Brazil, Italy, South Korea, France, and Britain. Thus, major industrialized countries produce their own steel (Germany and Japan are the leading exporters worldwide). To preserve self-sufficiency in steel production, the United States and others have used trade policies to protect domestic steel industries.

Some industrialized countries, notably Japan, depend heavily on importing iron ore to feed their steel industry. But unlike oil, iron ore is not concentrated in a "Persian Gulf" but is exported from both third-world and industrialized countries around the world. There is an *Association of Iron Ore Exporting Countries (AIOEC)*, but it is limited to consultation, and the United States, Canada, and the former Soviet Union are exporters not among the twelve members.

For other important industrial minerals such as copper, nickel, and zinc, the pattern of supply and trade is much more diffuse than for oil, and the industrialized countries are largely self-sufficient—not dependent on third-world suppliers (see Table 11.2). Even when third-world states are the main suppliers, as they are for tin and bauxite, they have not gained the power that OPEC members have in oil. There is a producer cartel in some cases (copper), a producer-consumer cartel in some (tin), and separate producer and consumer cartels in others (bauxite).

Certain agricultural products have spawned producer cartels such as the Union of Banana Exporting Countries (UBEC) or the African Groundnut Council. Like minerals, some export crops come mainly from just a few countries. These include sugar (Cuba), cocoa (Ivory Coast, Ghana, Nigeria), tea (India, Sri Lanka, China), and coffee (Brazil, Colombia). Despite these regional concentrations, producer cartels have not been very successful in boosting prices of these agricultural products, which are less essential than energy.

Water Disputes In addition to energy and minerals, states need *water*. Requirements for water increase as a society industrializes, as it undertakes intensive agriculture, and as its population grows. World water use is thirty-five times higher than just a few centuries ago. Yet water supplies are relatively unchanging, and are becoming depleted in many places. Furthermore, those supplies—rivers and water tables—often cross international boundaries, so access to water is increasingly a source of international conflict. Sometimes—as when several states share access to a single water table or lake—these conflicts are collective goods problems.

Water problems are especially important in the Middle East, where water is not widely abundant and where supplies often cross borders. For instance, the Euphrates

TABLE 11.2 WORLD MINERALS

Major Producers and Exporters, 1988

Mineral (Main Uses)	Major Producers	Major Exporters
Iron (steel)	Soviet Union, China, Brazil, Australia, India, United States, Canada	Brazil, Australia, Soviet Union, India, Canada
Copper (electrical)	United States, Soviet Union, Chile, Japan, Canada	Chile, Zambia, Canada, Zaire, Peru
Nickel (stainless steel)	Soviet Union, Canada, Japan, Norway, Australia	Soviet Union, Norway, Dominican Republic, Britain, Finland
Zinc (galvanized steel)	Soviet Union, Canada, Japan, China, Germany, United States	Canada, Australia, Netherlands, Belgium, Spain
Lead (batteries)	United States, Soviet Union, Britain, Germany, Japan	Canada, Australia, Mexico, Germany
Tin (solder, plating)	Malaysia, Brazil, Indonesia, China, Soviet Union	Malaysia, Brazil, Singapore, Indonesia, Britain
Bauxite (aluminum)	Guinea, Australia, Jamaica, Brazil	Guinea, Australia, Jamaica, Brazil

Source: 1988 data from The Economist. *Book of Vital World Statistics.* New York: Random House, 1990.

River runs from Turkey through Syria to Iraq before reaching the Persian Gulf. Iraq objects to Syrian diversion of water from the river, and both Iraq and Syria object to Turkey's diversion.

The Jordan river originates in Syria and Lebanon and runs through Israel to Jordan. Soon after its independence in 1948 (never recognized by Syria, Lebanon, and Jordan), Israel began building a canal to take water from the Jordan river to "make the desert bloom." Jordan and its Arab neighbors complained to the UN Security Council, which tried (with the U.S. government) to mediate the dispute from 1953 to 1955. Israel's representative called the Jordan's water "the bloodstream and the life artery of our country" and "the very essence of national economic independence." The UN mediation efforts failed, and each state went ahead with its own water plans (although Israel and Jordan each agreed to stay within allocations suggested in a UN plan). In 1964, Israel's Arab neighbors decided to construct their own storage dams and diversion systems on three rivers in Syria and Lebanon to divert water before it reached Israel. This would have made Israel's water system, almost completely constructed, worthless. Turning to military leverage in this international bargaining situation, Israel launched air and artillery attacks on the Syrian construction site in 1964, forcing Syria to abandon its diversion project. Israel's capture of the Golan Heights in 1967 prevented Syria from renewing efforts to divert water from the Jordan river.[28]

[28]Lowi, Miriam L. *Water and Power: The Politics of a Scarce Resource in the Jordan River Basin.* New York: Cambridge University Press, 1993. Saliba, Samir N. *The Jordan River Dispute.* The Hague: Martinus Nijhoff, 1968, p. 28.

Water also contains other resources such as fish and offshore oil deposits. As was mentioned, the UNCLOS treaty enclosed more of these resources within states' territory. However, this enclosure creates new problems. Norms regarding territorial waters are not firmly entrenched yet; some states disagree on who owns what. Furthermore, control of small islands now implies rights to the surrounding oceans with their fish, offshore oil, and minerals. A potentially serious international dispute is brewing in the South China Sea, where China has laid claim to some tiny islands also claimed by Vietnam and other nearby countries. With the islands come nearby oil drilling rights and fisheries. China has invited a U.S. company to explore for oil there, promising protection by the Chinese Navy. This conflict could lead to military clashes. For similar reasons, Iran and the United Arab Emirates are disputing control of several small islands in the Persian Gulf.

A common theme runs through the conflicts over fuels, minerals, agricultural products, and territorial waters. They are produced in fixed locations but traded to distant places. Control of the territory containing resources gives a state both self-sufficiency (valued by mercantilists) and market commodities that generate wealth (valued by liberals).

International Security and the Environment

In recent years, IR scholars have expanded their studies of environmental politics to systematically study the relationship of military and security affairs with the environment.[29] One side of this relationship is the role of the environment as a *source* of international conflict. We have seen how environmental degradation can lead to collective goods problems among large numbers of states, and how competition for territory and resources can create conflicts among smaller groups of states.

The other side of the environment security relationship concerns the effect of activities in the international security realm on the environment. Military activities—especially warfare—are important contributors to environmental degradation, above and beyond the degradation caused by economic activities like mining and manufacturing.

These damaging effects were spotlighted during the Gulf War. Iraqi forces spilled large amounts of Kuwaiti oil into the Persian Gulf—either to try to stop an amphibious invasion, or simply to punish Saudi Arabia (in whose direction the currents pushed the oil). Then, before retreating from Kuwait, the Iraqis blew up hundreds of Kuwaiti oil wells, leaving them burning uncontrollably and covering the country with thick black smoke. This might have been intended to make air strikes more difficult, but seems to have been more an act of pure revenge. Air pollution and weather effects lasted over a year and were felt in other countries around the Gulf (such as Iran). Large lakes of oil formed in the Kuwaiti desert. Iraq's environment also suffered tremendous damage from the massive bombing campaign. (Since the war, Iraq has built a giant canal to drain marshes used for refuge by rebels, another potential environmental disaster.)

The deliberate environmental destruction seen in the Gulf War is not without precedent. Armies sometimes adopt a "scorched earth policy" to deny sustenance to their adversaries. Fields are burned and villages leveled. In China's civil war in the 1930s, the Nationalists used such a policy while closing in on the Communist base. In World War II,

---

[29]Homer-Dixon, Thomas F. On the Threshold: Environmental Changes as Causes of Acute Conflict. *International Security* 16 (2), 1991: 76–116.

Wars often bring environmental destruction—sometimes deliberately and sometimes as a by-product. Military operations in peacetime also contribute to environmental problems. Hundreds of Kuwaiti oil wells, set on fire by retreating Iraqi troops in 1991, burned for months.

the Soviets left a scorched earth behind as they retreated before the Nazi invasion. Other wars have seen less drastic forms of environmental warfare. During World War II, Japan used incendiary devices carried in high-altitude balloons to start forest fires in the U.S. Northwest. The Dutch flooded fields to keep out the French army in the seventeenth century. The United States sprayed defoliants massively in Vietnam to destroy jungles in an attempt to expose guerrilla forces. The Vietnamese countryside still shows effects from these herbicides, as do U.S. veterans who suffer lingering health effects due to contact with chemicals like *Agent Orange*.

Military activity short of war also tends to damage the environment. Military exercises tear up the countryside. Military industries pollute. Military forces use energy less efficiently than civilians do. Military aircraft and missiles contribute to ozone depletion. Military bases contain many toxic-waste dump sites.

The greatest *potential* environmental disaster imaginable would be a large nuclear war. Ecosystems would be severely damaged throughout the world by secondary effects of nuclear weapons—radioactive fallout and the breakdown of social order and technology. Some scientists also think that global climate changes, leading to famine and environmental collapse, could result—the "nuclear winter" mentioned on page 247.

❖ POPULATION

The international system is having to cope with increasing conflict and complexity in managing the global environment. The problem is increasing over time because human demands on the environment keep growing but the environment tends to remain static. The growing demands have two causes—economic growth (higher GDP per person) and a growing number of people.

We have so far focused on the first cause—world industrialization as a source of demands. This cause is the more important one in the industrialized regions. But in the global South, with less industry and more people, population pressures are more important. The rest of this chapter, which focuses on population issues, thus also serves to lead into the following chapters on North-South relations.

World Population Trends

Global population reached a record high today, as it does every day. In the 1990s, world population is growing by nearly 100 million each year—over a quarter of a million more people every day. It will grow from 5.8 billion in 1995 to 6.3 billion in 2000.

Forecasting future population is easy in some respects. Barring a nuclear war or an environmental catastrophe, today's children will grow up and have children of their own. For the coming twenty to thirty years, world population growth will be driven, rather mechanistically, by the large number of children in today's third-world populations. The projected world population in thirty years will be around 8 to 9 billion people, and there is very little anyone can do to change that projection. Of the increase in population in that period, 97 percent will be in the global South, with one-third in Africa alone.[30]

Forecasting beyond thirty years is more difficult. When today's children grow up, the number of children they bear will be affected by their incomes (due to the "demographic transition" discussed shortly). To the extent that third-world countries accumulate wealth—a subject taken up in Chapter 13—their populations will grow more slowly. A second factor affecting the rate of population growth will be government policies regarding women's rights and birth control.

Because of these two uncertainties, projections beyond a few decades have a range of uncertainty (see Figure 11.2). In the year 2050, world population will most likely be around 10 billion, and the rate of increase will probably be leveling out. But there is great uncertainty about how fast the leveling out may occur. Around 2050 to 2150, world population itself is expected to level out, but when it will reach a steady state, and at what level, is hard to predict. UN experts in 1980 predicted that it would level out after the year 2100 at 10.6 billion. By 1990 their estimates were revised to the year 2150 and 11.6 billion—roughly double today's population.

This revision was necessary because in the 1980s the decline in birthrates stalled in a number of countries[31] and economic growth in the third world fell below expectations.

---

[30]UNFPA data. See Lewis, Paul. Curb on Population Growth Needed Urgently, U.N. Says. *The New York Times*, April 30, 1992.

[31]Horiuchi, Shiro. Stagnation in the Decline of the World Population Growth Rate During the 1980s. *Science* 257, August 7, 1992: 761–65.

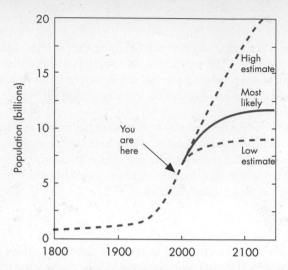

FIGURE 11.2 World Population Trends and Projections
Source: Based on data from the UN Population Office.

Under a high alternative forecast, the UN projects the population in 2150 at above 20 billion. A low forecast puts it below 10 billion. The actions of states and IOs *now* will determine which estimate will materialize in one hundred and fifty years.

Two hundred years ago, British writer *Thomas Malthus* warned that population tends to increase faster than food supply and predicted that population growth would limit itself through famine and disease. Today, experts and officials who warn against world overpopulation are sometimes called *Malthusian*. Critics point out that technology has kept pace with population in the past, allowing more food and other resources to be extracted from the environment even as population keeps growing.

However, leaders of most third-world states now recognize that unrestrained population growth drags down per capita income. The trouble is that, as with issues of environmental damage, actions taken to slow population growth tend to have short-term costs and long-term benefits. Doing nothing is the cheapest and often most politically acceptable course in the short run—and the most expensive in the long run.

The Demographic Transition

Population growth results from a difference between rates of birth (per thousand people) and rates of death. In agrarian (preindustrial) societies, both birthrates and death rates are high. Population growth is thus slow—even negative at times when death rates exceed birthrates (during a famine or plague, for instance).

The process of economic development—of industrialization and the accumulation of wealth on a per capita basis—brings about a change in birth and death rates that follows a fairly universal pattern called the **demographic transition** (see Figure 11.3). First death rates fall as food supplies increase and access to health care expands. Later birthrates fall as people become educated, more secure, and more urbanized, and as the status of women in society rises. At the end of the transition, as at the beginning, birthrates and death

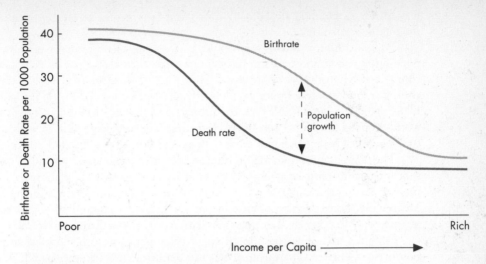

FIGURE 11.3 The Demographic Transition
As income rises, first death rates and then birthrates fall. The gap between the two is the population growth rate. Early in the transition, the population contains a large proportion of children; later it contains a large proportion of elderly people.

rates are fairly close to each other, and population growth is limited. But during the transition, when death rates have fallen more than birthrates, population grows rapidly.

One reason poor people tend to have many children is that under harsh poverty a child's survival cannot be taken for granted. Disease, malnutrition, or violence may claim the lives of many children (unpredictably), potentially leaving parents with no one to look after them in their old age. Having many children helps ensure that some survive. (The collective goods problem appears again, because each family wants more children but when all pursue this strategy the economic development of the whole community or state is held back.)

As a state moves through the demographic transition, the structure of its population in terms of age groups changes dramatically. Toward the beginning and middle of the process, most of the population is quite young. Families have many children, and adults do not have a very long life expectancy. Because children are not very productive economically, the large number of children in poor countries tends to slow down the accumulation of wealth. But by the end of the demographic transition, adults live longer and families have fewer children, so the average age of the population is much older. Eventually a substantial section of the population is elderly—a different nonproductive population that the economy must support.

The industrialized countries have been through the demographic transition and now have slow population growth—even negative growth in a few states.[32] Most third-world countries are in the middle of the transition and have rapid population growth.

The catch-22 of the demographic transition is this: Rapid population growth and a child-heavy population are powerful forces dragging down per capita income. Yet the best

---

[32]Cipolla, Carlo M. *The Economic History of World Population*. Harmondsworth, U.K.: Penguin, 1979.

way to slow population growth is to raise per capita income in order to complete the demographic transition.

Population growth thus contributes to a vicious cycle in many poor states. Where population rises at the same rate as overall wealth, the average person is no better off over time. Even when the economy grows faster than population, so that the *average* income rises, the total *number* of poor people may increase. From 1970 to 1985, according to the UN Population Fund (UNFPA), the proportion of people living in poverty in the third world dropped from 52 to 44 percent. But these are percentages of a growing total: the actual *number* of people living in poverty increased from about 950 million to 1.1 billion.[33]

The demographic transition tends to widen international disparities of wealth. States that manage to raise incomes a bit enter an upward spiral—population growth slows, so income levels per capita rise more, which further slows population growth, and so forth. Meanwhile, states that do not raise incomes have unabated population growth; per capita incomes stay low, which fuels more population growth—a downward spiral.

Globally, this disparity contributes to the gap in wealth between the North and South (see Chapter 12). Within the South disparities are also sharpened, as a few countries manage to slow population growth and raise incomes while others fail to do so. And even within a single country, the demographic transition sharpens disparities. Cities, richer classes, richer ethnic groups, and richer provinces tend to have low birthrates compared to the countryside and the poorer classes, ethnic groups, and provinces. In countries such as France, Israel, and the United States, wealthier ethnic groups (often white) have much slower population growth than poorer ethnic groups (often nonwhite).

Recent trends suggest that the third world is splitting into two groups of states. Around 1970, nearly fifty states including China and India entered the phase of the demographic transition marked by falling birthrates. But in nearly seventy other poor states, death rates were still falling faster than birthrates, leading to accelerating population growth. In the 1980s few new states moved from the second category to the first. Thus, while some third-world states move through the demographic transition, others remain stuck.

Although the demographic transition is universal in its outlines, particular changes in birthrates and death rates vary depending on local conditions and government policies.

Population Policies

The policies that governments adopt—and not just economic and demographic conditions—influence the birthrate. Among the most important policies are those regarding birth control (contraception). State policies vary widely.

At one extreme, China uses its strong government control of society to try to enforce a limit of one child per couple. Penalties for having a second child include being charged for services that were free for the first child and being stigmatized at work. Beyond two children, the penalties escalate. Contraceptives are free (as are abortions), and citizens are educated about them. China's policy has lowered population growth rates considerably in the cities but less so in the countryside, where 80 percent of the people live. Still, overall, in a single decade (the 1970s) China's fertility rate fell from 6 children per woman to about 2.5, a dramatic change.

But the Chinese policy has drawbacks as well. It limits individual freedom in favor of

---

[33]See footnote 30 in this chapter.

government control. Forced or coerced abortions have been reported. In traditional Chinese society (as in some other countries), sons are valued more than daughters. Couples who have a daughter first may keep trying until they have a son. In some cases Chinese peasants have reportedly had abortions if the baby would be female or have even killed newborn daughters so they could try for a son and still conform to the one-child policy.

India's policies are less extreme but have also been slower to reduce the birthrate, which fell from just under 6 per woman to about 4.7 in the 1970s. India's government has been strongly committed to birth control and has tried to make information and means widely available, but India does not have China's extreme government control over society (India is a democracy). India's birthrate leveled out from about 1977 to 1984 but resumed a gradual decline in the late 1980s.

At the other extreme from China are governments that encourage or force childbearing, and outlaw or limit access to contraception. Such a policy is called **pronatalist** (pro-birth). Traditionally many governments have adopted such policies because population was seen as an element of national power. More babies today meant more soldiers later. For example, recall (from p. 55) that the major difference in potential power between Iraq and Iran was population—Iran's being three times larger. On the battlefield, this power played out as "human wave" assaults of Iranian men and boys (who were slaughtered by the tens of thousands), which ultimately wore the Iraqis down.

Communist countries, including the Soviet Union, often adopted pronatalist policies. They gave special awards for mothers who produced large numbers of children for the socialist fatherland—a kind of extension of the factory quota system of centrally planned production.

Today, only a few third-world governments have strongly pronatalist policies, but many do not make birth control or sex education available to poor women. In some such states population is not considered a problem (and may even be seen as an asset); in other states the government simply cannot afford effective measures to lower birthrates. (Again, birth control has short-term costs and long-term benefits.) According to the UNFPA, 300 million women today do not have access to effective contraception.

Industrialized states have provided financial assistance for family planning programs in poor countries. One reason the drop in birthrates slowed down in the 1980s is that international financial assistance slowed down. After growing by 460 percent from the 1960s to the 1970s, such assistance grew by only 16 percent from the 1970s to the 1980s. U.S. assistance declined by 10 percent in that period. The U.S. government had provided over a quarter of the voluntary contributions that finance the UNFPA's annual budget of $225 million. These contributions were terminated in 1976 after U.S. antiabortion activists protested that some UNFPA funds were financing abortions. Some U.S. funding of the UNFPA was restored in the early 1990s.

Women's Status   Perhaps most important, birthrates are influenced by sexism and the status of women in society. In cultures that traditionally see women as valuable only in producing babies, there are great pressures against women who stop doing so. Many women do not use birth control because their husbands will not allow them to. These husbands may think that having many children is proof of their manliness, without which other men will look down on them. As women's status improves and they are allowed to work in various occupations, to own property, and to vote, women gain the power (as well as the education and money) necessary to limit the size of their families.

Few governments still promote high birthrates (pronatalism), but states vary widely in their family planning policies. The two most populous countries, China and India, have different approaches to birth control, each with strengths and weaknesses. This poster promotes China's one-child policy, advising "practice birth control to benefit the next generation" (1983).

According to the UNFPA, improving the status of women is one of the most important means of controlling world population growth. Government policies regarding women's status vary from one state to another. International programs and agencies, such as the UN ECOSOC commission on the status of women, are working to address the issue on a global scale. International economic aid programs have been criticized for paying insufficient attention to the status of women, focusing on economic development in isolation from population growth (see "Women in Development" on pp. 493–494).

Mortality and AIDS

Population growth is determined by the death rate as well as the birthrate. In a way the death rate is more complicated than the birthrate: births have only one source (sex involving women of childbearing age), whereas people die from many different causes at different ages. In poor countries people tend to die younger, often from infectious diseases (especially when children are weakened by malnutrition); in richer countries people live longer and die from cancer and heart disease more often. The proportion of babies who die within their first year is the **infant mortality** rate. It reflects a population's access to nutrition, water, shelter, and health care. In rich countries, infant mortality is 1 percent or below. In the poorest countries it is as high as 20 percent, and it is even higher in local pockets of extreme poverty.

Although death rates vary greatly from one state or region to another, the overall trends are quite stable from decade to decade. Wars, droughts, epidemics, and disasters have an effect locally but hardly matter globally. In the poorest countries, which are just beginning the demographic transition (with barely declining birthrates), the death rate has declined on a straight line from nearly 30 deaths per thousand population in 1950 to below 15 in 1990. In the *industrialized countries*, the death rate bottomed out around 10 per thousand by 1960. And in the *midtransition* countries in between (including China and India), the death rate fell from 25 in 1950 to 10 in 1980 and has been slightly lower than in the rich countries since then (because more of the population is younger in these poorer countries). In this middle group of developing countries, infant mortality is generally much lower than in the poorest countries.

These stable trends in mortality mean that the death rate is not a means by which governments or international agencies can affect population growth. For instance, worsening poverty may cause famine and a rising death rate, but this is not a realistic way to control population growth. It would mean moving backward through the demographic transition, which would wreck any chance of lowering birthrates. Nor can wars kill enough people to reduce population growth (short of global nuclear war). Even a major famine or war, one killing a million people, hardly alters world population trends because every year about 75 million people die—200,000 every day. In short, most of the world is already at or near the end of the transition in *death* rates; the key question is how long birthrates take to complete the transition.

Two mortality factors, however—smoking and AIDS—deserve special attention because they have begun to exact very high costs even if they do not alter overall population trends. In both cases, actions taken in the short term have long-term consequences, and once again there are short-term costs and long-term benefits. In the case of smoking, states that fail to curb the spread of nicotine addiction face high future costs in health care—costs that are just beginning to come due in many third-world countries. Although the tobacco trade makes smoking an international issue, the costs are largely limited to the state itself; its own citizens and economy pay the price.

AIDS   By contrast, AIDS is a worldwide epidemic in which the failure of one state to control the spread of HIV (human immunodeficiency virus) makes it more likely that people in other states will eventually become infected as well. There is a delay of five to ten years after infection by the virus before symptoms appear, and during this period an infected individual can infect others (through sex or blood). AIDS spreads internationally, through travel, reflecting the interdependence of states.

By 1995 an estimated 20 million people had been infected with HIV worldwide. Of these about 13 million were in Africa, 3 million in South Asia, 2 million in Latin America, over a million in North America, half a million in Europe, and under 100,000 each in East Asia, the Middle East, and Russia/Eastern Europe. Of these 20 million, only about 5 million had yet developed AIDS, so most of the costs (human, economic, and political) are yet to come as infected individuals become ill. Of the infected population, 55 percent were men, 35 percent (and growing) were women, and 10 percent were children. Because of systematic underreporting none of the totals are firm, and each new estimate seems to revise them upward.

No region has stopped the spread of the epidemic, although North America has slowed it down. The worldwide spread of HIV is explosive, especially in Southeast Asia.

By the year 2000, the World Health Organization (WHO) estimates, up to 40 million people may be infected worldwide. An independent estimate by a group of leading experts is higher still—40 million to 110 million. According to this estimate, by the year 2000 Asia will account for about 40 percent of infections worldwide, Africa for 30 percent, Latin America for 15 percent, and the industrialized regions for 15 percent.[34]

There are policies that states can adopt to slow the spread of AIDS. It is primarily a sexually transmitted disease, and its transmission can be prevented by using condoms. Drug users and medical personnel can use only new or disinfected needles; hospitals can screen blood. Although there is a massive scientific effort underway to develop a vaccine, for now the most effective measures boil down to public education and the distribution of condoms—neither of which can necessarily make individuals act responsibly.

States have only two means to protect themselves from infection from outside the country (a particular concern in countries with current low infection rates, such as China). First is to seal themselves off from contact with foreigners or to monitor foreigners on their territory. Considering the benefits of economic exchange (and the realities of interdependence) discussed in Chapter 8, this is not a very practical approach.

The second and more practical approach is to cooperate with other states worldwide to try to bring the epidemic under control. These international efforts are coordinated primarily by WHO and funded mainly by the industrialized countries. But WHO depends on national governments to provide information and carry out policies, and governments have been slow to respond. Governments falsify statistics to underreport the number of cases (lest tourists be driven away), and many governments are reluctant to condone or sponsor sex education and distribution of condoms because of religious or cultural taboos. A 1992 survey of 38 countries found that one-third of the leaders had never spoken about AIDS and another third had spoken only occasionally on the topic.

Asia is expected to be hardest hit by AIDS in the 1990s. Thailand is especially vulnerable because of its huge prostitution industry and acceptance of male promiscuity. Thailand's AIDS epidemic—300,000 or more people are thought to be infected—has special international significance because of Thailand's large tourism industry. Tourism and prostitution overlap in "sex tours" that attract thousands of foreign men each year to visit Thai brothels. The Thai government has developed an effective anti-AIDS program focusing on public education. The head of the program, Mechai Viravaidya, is known to Thais as "Mr. Condom." He handed out condoms at the annual meeting of the World Bank, held in Thailand in 1991, and started a restaurant called "Cabbages and Condoms." Thanks to these education efforts, Thailand may contain its AIDS epidemic sooner than other Asian countries, which largely continue to ignore the problem.[35]

Of worldwide spending on AIDS, only 6 percent was in third-world countries (where 80 percent of infected people live). For instance, in 1991, AIDS-prevention spending was $2.70 per person in the United States, but only 7 cents in Africa. Financial assistance from the industrialized countries for AIDS prevention and care in the third world was less

[34]Mann, Jonathan, Daniel J. M. Tarantola, and Thomas W. Netter, eds. *AIDS in the World 1992*. Cambridge, MA: Harvard University Press, 1992. Altman, Lawrence K. Researchers Report Much Grimmer AIDS Outlook. *The New York Times*, June 4, 1992: A1. Eckholm, Erik. AIDS, Fatally Steady in the U.S., Accelerates Worldwide. *The New York Times*, June 28, 1992: E5. 1995 data are from WHO.

[35]Shenon, Philip. Brash and Unabashed, Mr. Condom Takes on Sex Death in Thailand. *The New York Times*, December 20, 1992.

AIDS is spreading rapidly in Southeast Asia and Africa. The worldwide effort to slow AIDS, coordinated by the World Health Organization (WHO), illustrates how global-level problems like AIDS are making IOs like WHO more important. Here, AIDS poster in Hanoi, Vietnam, December 1992.

than $800 million and was increasingly being directed to favored governments rather than channeled through the WHO where it could be more efficiently used.

The international response to the AIDS epidemic will be crucial in determining its ultimate course. AIDS illustrates the transnational linkages that make international borders less meaningful than in the past. Effective international cooperation and commitment to halting the epidemic could save millions of lives and significantly enhance the prospects for economic development in the poorest countries in the coming decades. However, there is once again a collective goods problem regarding the allocation of costs and benefits from such efforts.

Population and International Conflict

Population issues are sometimes portrayed as simply too many people using up too little food and natural resources. This is too simplified a picture. In particular, the idea that overpopulation is the cause of hunger in today's world is not really accurate. Poverty and politics—more than population—are the causes of malnutrition and hunger today (see "World Hunger" on pp. 490–492). There is enough food in the world to feed all the world's people. There is also enough water, enough petroleum, enough land, and so forth—but these are unequally distributed.

Nonetheless, growing populations do put more strain on resources, regionally and globally. Even though resources do not usually run out, it costs more to extract them as the quantity needed increases (there is a supply curve as with any commodity). New food production techniques increase yields but cost money to implement; new agricultural land is less productive than existing plots; new oil or water supplies must come from greater depths; and so on. For example, food production grew more slowly than population in two-thirds of the developing countries in the 1980s.[36] In the 1960s and 1970s the "green revolution" increased yields enough to stay ahead of population growth (see "Technology Transfer" on pp. 530–532). But local environmental damage—such as soil erosion and water table depletion—has begun to reduce agricultural productivity in some areas. The faster populations grow, the more pressing will be world food problems.

Growing populations exacerbate all the international conflicts over natural resources discussed earlier. Conflicts over water, which are very serious in several regions, become worse as populations grow. So do a range of issues such as overfishing, deforestation, and the loss of agricultural land to urban sprawl. Although it does not cause these problems, population growth affects how severe they become and how quickly they develop.

There is not a simple linear relationship between the number of people in a state and its need for resources. Rather, as an economy develops, population growth slows but the demand for resources continues to rise. The resources are then needed for raising incomes (industrialization) rather than just feeding more mouths. The type of resources needed also changes—less food and more petroleum in the mix—as the state's technological style evolves. But overall, more states moving through the demographic transition more quickly—while it will slow population growth—will not decrease the quantity of resources they use or the environmental damage they cause. More likely the opposite is true.

However, if population growth can be limited at lower income levels—shifting the demographic curve by using government policies to encourage lower birthrates—then strains on the environment will be less. A country would then not only increase its per capita income sooner and faster but would do so at lower total population levels. This would reduce the load on the environment and resources as compared with industrializing at a higher level of population. Presumably, the international conflicts discussed earlier would be reduced accordingly.

Some IR scholars have argued that population growth leads states to expand outward in search of needed resources (the theory of lateral pressure mentioned on pp. 194–195). During the rise of Germany from the mid-nineteenth century through World War II, for instance, a consistent theme of German expansionists was the need for "living space" for the growing German population. This need was as much psychological as physical, but it was used to justify German territorial expansion, imperialism, and aggression.

Another source of international conflict connected with demographics is migration from poor states with high population growth to rich states with low population growth. For example, illegal immigration from Mexico to the United States is an irritant in U.S.-Mexican relations. Refugees are a recurrent source of interstate conflict as well. Palestinians living in refugee camps for several generations have become a chronic focal point of Arab-Israeli conflict. Population growth steadily increases the number of people living

---

[36]See footnote 30 in this chapter.

(in poverty) in the camps. Migration and refugees are population issues, but discussion of them is reserved for Chapter 12 (pp. 494–498) in the context of North-South relations.

Demographics can exacerbate ethnic conflicts (which in turn often fuel international conflicts due to ethnic ties with foreign states). Often one ethnic group is richer than another, and usually the poorer group has a higher rate of population growth (because of the demographic transition). For instance, in Lebanon, Muslims have a higher birthrate than Christians. At the time of Lebanese independence in 1944, a power-sharing arrangement was devised between Christian and Muslim political groups in Lebanon. By the 1970s the size of the two populations had changed but the political structure had remained frozen in place. This was a factor in the Lebanese civil war of the late 1970s and 1980s. That civil war, in turn, pulled in outside states including Syria, Israel, and the United States. The seizure of (Christian) U.S. hostages by (Muslim) militants in Lebanon set the stage for the arms-for-hostages scandal in Ronald Reagan's presidency.

Thus, population pressures are not a simple explanation for the world's problems but contribute in various ways to international conflicts. Demographic and environmental factors are playing a larger role and receiving more attention from IR scholars.

As we have seen, the implications of population issues differ greatly in the world's North and South. Strains on the environment and on natural resources are global in scope, yet in the North they arise from industrialization (growing GDP per capita), whereas in the South they are more affected by growing populations.

These differences in environmental impacts are by no means the only such North-South difference. In many ways the world seems to be splitting in two, with different realities in the rich and poor regions—a trend running contrary to the integration theme of the last few chapters. The next two chapters turn to that global North-South divide.

❖ CHAPTER SUMMARY

- ◆ Environmental problems are an example of international interdependence and often create collective goods problems for the states involved. The large numbers of actors involved in global environmental problems make them more difficult to solve.
- ◆ To resolve such collective goods problems, states have used international regimes and IOs, and have in some cases extended state sovereignty (notably over territorial waters) to make management a national rather than international matter.
- ◆ International efforts to solve environmental problems aim to bring about sustainable economic development. This was the theme of the 1992 UN Earth Summit.
- ◆ Global warming results from burning fossil fuels—the basis of industrial economies today. The industrialized states are much more responsible for the problem than are third-world states. Solutions are difficult to reach because costs are substantial and dangers are somewhat distant and uncertain.
- ◆ Damage to the earth's ozone layer results from the use of specific chemicals, which are now being phased out under international agreements. Unlike global warming, the costs of solutions are much lower and the problem is better understood.
- ◆ Many species are threatened with extinction due to loss of habitats such as rain forests. An international treaty on biodiversity and an agreement on forests aim to reduce the destruction of local ecosystems, with costs spread among states.

- The UN Conference on the Law of the Sea (UNCLOS) established an ocean regime that put most commercial fisheries and offshore oil under control of states as territorial waters. The United States signed the treaty after a decade's delay.
- Pollution—including acid rain, water and air pollution, and toxic and nuclear waste—tends to be more localized than global and has been addressed mainly through unilateral, bilateral, and regional measures rather than global ones.
- The economies of the industrialized West depend on fossil fuels. Overall, these economies import energy resources, mostly oil, whereas the other world regions export them. Oil prices rose dramatically in the 1970s but declined in the 1980s as the world economy adjusted by increasing supply and reducing demand.
- The most important source of oil traded worldwide is the Persian Gulf area of the Middle East. Consequently, this area has long been a focal point of international political conflict, including the 1991 Gulf War.
- States need other raw materials such as minerals, but no such materials have assumed the importance or political status of oil. Water resources are a growing source of local international conflicts, however.
- War and other military activities cause considerable environmental damage—sometimes deliberately inflicted as part of a war strategy.
- World population—approaching 6 billion—will reach 8 or 9 billion in thirty years. Thereafter it is expected to level out over one hundred and fifty years, ultimately reaching a stable level somewhere between about 10 and 20 billion.
- Future world population growth will be largely driven by the demographic transition. Death rates have fallen throughout the world, but birthrates will fall proportionally only as per capita incomes go up. The faster the economies of poor states develop, the sooner their populations will level out.
- The demographic transition sharpens disparities of wealth globally and locally. High per capita incomes and low population growth make rich states or groups richer, whereas low incomes and high population growth reinforce each other to keep poor states and groups poor.
- Within the overall shape of the demographic transition, government policies can reduce birthrates somewhat at a given level of per capita income. Effective policies are those that improve access to birth control and raise the status of women in society. Actual policies vary, from China's very strict rules on childbearing to pronatalist governments that encourage maximum birthrates and outlaw birth control.
- Death rates are stable and little affected in the large picture by wars, famines, and other disasters. Raising the death rate is not a feasible way to limit population growth.
- Although the global AIDS epidemic may not greatly slow world population growth, it will impose huge costs on many poor states in the coming years. Despite international efforts led by the World Health Organization, the epidemic has not been controlled. By the end of the 1990s, as many as 40 million to 100 million people are expected to be infected, nearly three-quarters of them in Asia and Africa.
- AIDS demonstrates that growing international interdependence—the shrinking world—has costs and not just benefits. Because states cannot wall themselves off from the outside world, international cooperation in addition to unilateral state actions will be necessary to contain AIDS.

◆   Population pressures do not cause, but do contribute to, a variety of international conflicts including ethnic conflicts, economic competition, and territorial disputes.

❖ THINKING CRITICALLY

1. Given the collective goods problem in managing environmental issues—heightened by the participation of large numbers of actors—what new international organizations or agreements could be created in the coming years to help solve this problem? Are there ways to reduce the number of actors participating in the management of global problems like ozone depletion? What problems might your proposals run into regarding issues like state sovereignty?

2. Few effective international agreements have been reached to solve the problem of global warming. Given the several difficulties associated with managing this problem, what creative international solutions can you think of? What would be the strengths and weaknesses of your solutions in the short term and in the long term?

3. Does the record of the international community on environmental management reflect the views of mercantilists, of liberals, or of both? In what ways?

4. Some politicians call for the Western industrialized countries, including the United States, to be more self-sufficient in energy resources in order to reduce dependence on oil imports from the Middle East. In light of the overall world energy picture and the economics of international trade, what are the pros and cons of such a proposal?

5. Dozens of poor states appear to be stuck midway through the demographic transition; death rates have fallen, birthrates remain high, and per capita incomes are not increasing. How do you think these states, with or without foreign assistance, can best get unstuck and complete the demographic transition?

❖ KEY TERMS

tragedy of the commons	biodiversity
enclosure	International Whaling Commission
epistemic communities	UN Conference on the Law of the Sea (UNCLOS)
carrying capacity	
Sustainable Development Commission	Antarctic Treaty of 1959
global warming	acid rain
fossil fuels	Chernobyl
greenhouse gases	oil shocks (1973, 1979)
UN Environment Program (UNEP)	demographic transition
ozone layer	pronatalist
Montreal Protocol	infant mortality

POVERTY

THEORIES OF ACCUMULATION

Economic Accumulation
Capitalism
Socialism
Economic Classes

IMPERIALISM

**The Globalization of
  Class**
The World-System
European Colonialism
Anti-Imperialism
Postcolonial Dependency

THE STATE OF
THE SOUTH

Basic Human Needs
World Hunger
**Rural and Urban
  Populations**
Women in Development
Migration and Refugees

REVOLUTION

Revolutionary Movements
Islamic Revolutions
**Postrevolutionary
  Governments**

*Rwandan refugee camp,
Zaire, August 1994.*

THE NORTH-SOUTH GAP

❖ POVERTY

The next two chapters concern the world's poor regions—the global South—where most people live. States in these regions are called by various names, used interchangeably—third-world countries, **less-developed countries** (LDCs), *underdeveloped countries (UDCs)*, or **developing countries**.[1] This chapter discusses the gap in wealth between the industrialized regions (the North) and the third world (the South). Chapter 13 discusses international aspects of economic development in the South.

Third-world poverty may be viewed from several theoretical perspectives. IR scholars do not all agree on the causes or implications of such poverty, or on solutions (if any) to the problem. Thus, they also disagree about the nature of relations between rich and poor states (North-South relations).[2] Everyone agrees, however, that much of the global South is extremely poor.[3]

Such poverty is difficult for North Americans to grasp. It is abject poverty—not the poverty of U.S. ghettos, but much worse. The extreme on the scale is starvation. As conveyed in pictures from places like Somalia or Sudan, starvation is dramatic and horrible.

[1]Swatuk, Larry A., and Timothy M. Shaw, eds. *The South at the End of the Twentieth Century: Rethinking the Political Economy of Foreign Policy in Africa, Asia, the Caribbean and Latin America.* New York: St. Martin's Press, 1994. Dorraj, Manochehr, ed. *The Changing Political Economy of the Third World.* Boulder, CO: Lynne Rienner, 1995.

[2]Haggard, Stephan, ed. *The International Political Economy and the Developing Countries.* Brookfield, VT: Edward Elgar, 1994. Davidian, Zaven N. *Economic Disparities Among Nations: A Threat to Survival in a Globalized World.* New York: Oxford University Press, 1994. Seligson, Mitchell A., and John T. Passe-Smith, eds. *Development and Underdevelopment: The Political Economy of Inequality.* Boulder, CO: Lynne Rienner, 1993. Slater, Robert O., Barry M. Schutz, and Steven R. Dorr, eds. *Global Transformation and the Third World.* Boulder, CO: Lynne Rienner, 1993. Stewart, Frances. *North-South and South-South: Essays on International Economics.* New York: St. Martin's Press, 1991. Zartman, I. William, ed. *Positive Sum: Improving North-South Relations.* New Brunswick: Transaction Books, 1987.

[3]World Bank. *World Development Report 1995.* New York: Oxford University Press, 1995. Morris, Morris David. *Measuring the Condition of the World's Poor: The Physical Quality of Life Index.* New York: Pergamon Press, 1979.

But it is not the most important aspect of poverty, because it affects relatively few of the world's poor people. Starvation is generally caused by war or extreme drought, or both. In most places, people who die from poverty do not starve but succumb to diseases after being weakened by *malnutrition* (lack of adequate quality of nutrition). Malnutrition kills many more people than outright starvation does—but less dramatically because people die in many locations day in and day out rather than all at once in one place. Hunger and malnutrition are sometimes caused by war but more often by other factors that displace people from farmable land to cities where many are unable to find other income (see "World Hunger" later in this chapter).

People who die from malnutrition do not die because of a lack of food in the world, or usually even a lack of food in their own state, but because they cannot *afford* to buy food. Likewise, people lack water, shelter, health care, and other necessities because they cannot afford them. The widespread, grinding poverty of people who cannot afford necessities is more important than the dramatic examples of starvation triggered by war or drought, because chronic poverty affects many more people.

Of all the world's people, about half are without adequate supplies of safe drinking water. About half live in substandard housing or are homeless altogether. About a third are malnourished, and one in seven is chronically undernourished (unable to maintain body weight). Nearly half are illiterate, and 99 percent do not have a college education. Multiplied by over five billion people, these percentages add up to a staggering number of extremely poor people.

Nearly a billion people in the global South live in abject poverty; the majority lack such basic needs as safe water, housing, food, and the ability to read. Here, open sewer runs through slum in Port-au-Prince, Haiti, 1986.

In all, about one billion people live in utter, abject poverty, without access to basic nutrition or health care. Two-thirds of them live in the densely populated states of Bangladesh, India, Indonesia, and Pakistan.[4] As noted earlier (p. 22), the average income per person in South Asia—home to one and a half billion people—is only about $1000 per year (or about $500 if not corrected for the lower costs of living in these regions compared to richer ones). Hundreds of millions have incomes far *below* that average. In Africa, another 600 million people live at similar income levels.[5]

If these statistics are difficult to digest, consider the bottom line. Every three seconds, somewhere in the world, a child dies as a result of malnutrition. That's over 1,000 every hour, 30,000 every day, 10 million every year. The world produces enough food to nourish these children and enough income to afford to nourish them, but their own families or states do not have enough income. They die, ultimately, from poverty. Consider that in the same three seconds in which another child dies this way, the world spends over $50,000 on military forces. A thousandth of that amount would save the child's life. This reality shadows the moral and political debates about North-South relations.

❖ THEORIES OF ACCUMULATION

How do we explain the enormous gap between income levels in the world's industrialized regions and those in the third world? And what are the implications of that gap for international politics? There are several very different approaches to these questions; we will concentrate on two contrasting theories of wealth accumulation, presented in simplified form. These approaches are based on more-liberal and more-revolutionary world views.

Economic Accumulation

A view of the problem from the perspective of capitalism is based on liberal economics—stressing overall efficiency in maximizing *economic growth*. This view sees the third world as merely lagging behind the industrialized North. More wealth creation in the North is seen as a good thing, as is wealth creation in the South, and the two are not in conflict.

A more revolutionary view of things, from the perspective of socialism, is concerned with the distribution of wealth as much as the absolute creation of wealth. It sees the North-South divide as more of a zero-sum game in which the creation of wealth in the North most often comes at the expense of the South. It also gives politics (the state) more of a role in redistributing wealth and managing the economy than does capitalism. Socialism thus parallels mercantilism in some ways. But socialists see economic classes rather than states as the main actors in the political bargaining over the distribution of the world's wealth. And mercantilism promotes the idea of concentrating wealth (as a power element), whereas socialism promotes the broader distribution of wealth.

For socialists, international exchange is shaped by capitalists' exploitation of cheap labor and cheap resources—using states to help create the political conditions for this exploitation. (Some socialists focus on workers in poor third-world countries, some on workers in richer industrialized countries, and some on both.) Thus, whereas mercantilists

---

[4]Brandt, Willy, et al. *North-South: A Programme for Survival*. Cambridge, MA: MIT Press, 1980.

[5]Callaghy, Thomas M., and John Ravenhill, eds. *Hemmed In: Responses to Africa's Economic Decline*. New York: Columbia University Press, 1993. Bender, Gerald J., ed. International Affairs in Africa [special issue]. *Annals of the American Academy of Political and Social Science* 489, 1987.

see political interests (of the state) as driving economic policies, socialists see economic interests (of capitalists and of workers) as driving political policies.

Capitalist and socialist approaches are rather incompatible in their language and assumptions about the problem of third-world poverty and its international implications. This chapter somewhat favors socialist approaches, focusing on the past history of imperialism as a central cause of the North-South divide and on revolutionary strategies and massive redistribution of wealth as solutions to it. Chapter 13 in turn leans toward capitalist approaches in discussing the prospects for economic development in the global South.

Economic development is based on **capital accumulation**—the creation of standing wealth (capital) such as buildings, roads, factories, and so forth. In order for human populations and their capital to grow, they must produce an **economic surplus** by using capital to produce more capital. This is done by investing money in productive capital rather than using it for consumption (there is a short-term trade-off between investing and consuming). The more surplus an economy produces, the more resources are available for investment above the minimum level of consumption needed to sustain human life.

Early human societies had a very simple stock of capital—mostly clothes and hand tools—and produced little surplus. Then came the discovery of agriculture about ten thousand years ago. A group of people could reliably produce a surplus—more grain than they could eat—decade after decade. The extra grain could feed specialists who made tools from metals, built houses, and constructed irrigation works. Ever since, the human species has been on an uninterrupted growth cycle based on the creation of economic surplus. More and more wealth has accumulated, and the human population has also grown larger and larger.

The Industrial Revolution, which began several centuries ago, greatly accelerated this process of world accumulation, drawing on large amounts of energy from fossil fuels. However, industrialization has occurred very unevenly across the world regions. The North has accumulated vast capital. The South produces spurts of wealth and has pockets of accumulation, but in most areas it remains in a basically preindustrial economy. This is why the North consumes about ten times as much commercial energy per person as the South does (see Table 11.1, p. 444).

The size of GDP alone does not indicate whether a national economy is making a profit or losing money, any more than the size of a company indicates whether it is profitable. Accumulation, or profit, in a national economy corresponds with the *economic growth rate*. States that operate profitably grow from year to year; those that operate at a loss shrink. (GDP and related concepts refer here to real values after adjusting for inflation.)

A state's economic growth rate does not indicate how much wealth it has accumulated in the past. For instance, in recent years the United States has grown only slowly—even shrinking a bit at times of recession (see "The U.S. Position" on pp. 368–371). But it starts from a large amount of standing wealth accumulated over the previous two hundred years. By contrast, a country like Mexico may have stronger economic growth (rate of accumulation), but because it starts from a much poorer position, it still lags far behind in total wealth. On a global scale, the South will continue to lag the North in GDP (income), even if its economic growth rate continues to be higher than the North's, as it has been in the last few years. The concentration of surplus in the world economy (in the

North) tends to be self-reinforcing for two reasons. First, concentrating wealth allows it to be invested more efficiently, which generates more wealth. Second, the more wealth is concentrated, the more power its owners gain. They can shape the rules of the world economy for their own benefit. With over 80 percent of the world's wealth, the North dominates world politics. Because socialists see a conflict of interest between the rich and poor, they see the North's political power as oppressive to the South.

Ultimately, the distribution of the benefits of world accumulation is an issue for international bargaining, just as the distribution of benefits from trade is (see Chapter 8, pp. 313–314). In the bargaining between rich and poor regions over the process of world accumulation, the two sides have very unequal power.[6]

Capitalism

Earlier chapters referred to capital in a general way as standing wealth. More precisely, *capital* is the set of goods that are used in producing other goods. Thus, a warehouse full of refined tin is capital, as is a tin can or a canning factory—all these goods go into producing further goods. But a stamp collection, a set of Lego™ toys, a freezer full of ice cream, or a pleasure boat are not capital in this sense, even though they have value; they are **consumption** goods. Their consumption does not contribute directly to the production of other goods and services.

A cycle of accumulation depends on capital goods more than consumption goods. Mines, factories, oil refineries, railroads, and similar goods contribute directly to the cycle of surplus production by which more factories and oil refineries are produced.

Investment competes with consumption. Forgoing consumption for investment is another case where short-term costs produce long-term benefits (as we have seen in aspects of trade, environmental, and population policies where collective goods problems are successfully overcome).

Capitalism is a system of *private ownership of capital* that relies on market forces to govern the distribution of goods. Under capitalism, the cycle of accumulation is largely under the control of private individuals and companies. When a surplus is produced, it is profit for the owners of the capital that produced the surplus (after the government takes out taxes). Private ownership encourages reinvestment of surplus because private individuals and companies seek to maximize their own wealth. The concentration of capital ownership in few hands also allows investment to be shifted easily from less-productive sectors and technologies to more productive ones (again maximizing growth and accumulation). Capitalism concentrates wealth, promoting efficient and rapid accumulation; it does not seek an equitable distribution of benefits.

In reality, no state is purely capitalistic. Almost all have some form of mixed economy that includes both private and state ownership.[7] Furthermore, in most capitalist countries the government balances the inhuman side of capitalism by redistributing some wealth downward (and by regulating capitalists). A "welfare state" provides education, certain health benefits, welfare for the poor, and similar services. Over the past century,

---

[6]Lake, David A. Power and the Third World: Toward a Realist Political Economy of North-South Relations [review essay]. *International Studies Quarterly* 31 (2), 1987: 217–34.

[7]Freeman, John R. *Democracy and Markets: The Politics of Mixed Economies.* Ithaca: Cornell University Press, 1989.

Production in the global South uses relatively little capital and much labor (at low wages), reflecting an early stage of industrialization. To develop economically, poor countries must generate self-sustaining capital accumulation. Banana production, as here in Ecuador (1995), is a classic cash crop export from the global South, capital-poor and labor-intensive.

capitalism has evolved and become more responsive to the need to balance efficiency with equity.

The principles of capitalism underlie the global economy with its great disparities of wealth. The concentration of capital in the global North furthers the development of global trade, of technology, and of reinvestment for maximum profit (overall growth). The private ownership of companies and of currency makes international markets operate more efficiently. Capital can be moved around from less productive to more productive countries and economic sectors. If wealth were distributed equally across world regions, these efficiencies might be lost and world economic growth might be slower.

Socialism

Socialism—the idea that workers should have political power—favors the *redistribution of wealth* toward the workers who produce that wealth. Because such redistribution does not happen naturally under capitalism, socialism generally endorses the use of the state for this purpose. It favors *governmental planning* to manage a national economy rather than leaving such management to market forces. Often, socialists advocate *state ownership* of capital, rather than private ownership, so that the accumulation of wealth is controlled by the state, which can distribute it equitably.

Socialism encompasses many political movements, parties, and ideologies, both historical and present-day. No socialist party has been very influential in U.S. politics since the 1930s, but in Europe and Japan, socialist parties are often either the governing party (as in France under Mitterand), part of a governing coalition (as in Japan after 1994), or the main opposition party (as in Britain). In the third world, where great poverty and disparities of wealth make the idea of redistributing wealth popular, most revolutionaries and many reformers consider themselves socialists of one variety or another.

Communist governments, including those in China and the former Soviet Union, base their political philosophy on socialism as well. In practice, however, they tend to extract wealth toward the center and have thus been called a form of state capitalism. For example, in the Soviet Union under Stalin in the 1930s there was a tremendous concentration of capital, which allowed rapid industrialization but starved millions of people. This took place under dictatorial political control rather than workers' control.

Marxism is a branch of socialism that includes both communism and other approaches. (Not all socialists are Marxist.) In the mid-nineteenth-century, *Karl Marx* emphasized labor as the source of economic surplus. At that time, the Industrial Revolution was accompanied by particular hardship among industrial workers (including child laborers) in Europe. Marxists today still believe that the surplus created by labor should be recaptured by workers through political struggle. Today, Marxism is most influential in third-world countries where capital is still scarce and labor conditions are wretched.

Like capitalism, socialism does not exist anywhere in a pure form. There is an element of socialism in mixed economies. China now calls its economic system "market socialism"—a combination of continuing state ownership of many large industries, capitalism at the local level, and openness to international investment and trade.

Some socialist theories argue that state ownership of industry increases efficiency by avoiding the problems that arise from the fragmentation of decision making under capitalism. In theory, central planners can use resources in a rational way that maximizes overall efficiency. But after decades of experimentation, it is clear that whatever its benefits in equity, state ownership is not very efficient. State planners who set quotas for production at each factory cannot adjust to economic conditions as efficiently as market-based prices can. State ownership is still promoted in many countries in order to redistribute wealth, to coordinate the development of certain key industries, or to maintain self-sufficiency in military production—but not because it is more efficient in general.

Russia and Eastern European states are now trying to make a transition to market economies because of the failure of centrally planned economies. Many third-world countries are also moving to sell off large state-owned industries—*privatization*—in hopes of increasing growth. Phone companies, oil companies, railroads—all are going on the auction block. France joined the auctioneers in 1993.

This privatization is proceeding quickly in several Eastern European and former Soviet republics, where the state owned virtually the whole economy during decades of communism. In Czechoslovakia (before it split in two), citizens received coupons representing a small bit of stock in state-owned companies. They could then sell the coupons for cash or invest them in any of several new mutual funds established by entrepreneurs. The mutual fund managers pooled the coupons they collected and bought up state-owned companies they thought would be profitable. Lured by promises of large profits, most

Czechoslovak citizens invested as new capitalists in this way. But when a similar scheme was tried in Russia, citizens weary from economic depression did not generally put much value in the coupons. Many Russians invested in a leading mutual fund that promised high profits but then went bankrupt.

Thus, in the region of Russia and Eastern Europe, communism had collapsed under the weight of inefficiency, but then the beginning stages of capitalism were even more inefficient, leading to a general economic collapse (a reduction of economic activity by roughly half over several years). Some countries, including Russia, slowed the pace of reforms in response, while reformists argued that what was needed was a speedup to get through the transition. Some countries democratically threw out the reformers and brought back the old Communist leaders to power. Over the remainder of the 1990s, it is likely that the various experiments being tried by the different countries of Eastern Europe and the former Soviet Union will sort themselves out, making clearer the best routes of transition for former communist economies.

In any event, the collapse of Soviet communism, along with the new emphasis on markets rather than central planning throughout the world, has closed the books on a historic experiment in one type of socialism that failed. Old-style communism as articulated and practiced by **Stalin**—*Stalinism,* which was marked by totalitarian state control under the Communist party—has been abandoned. But the failures of state-owned enterprises do not mean that socialism is dead. Rather, other types of socialism are now more salient. And new mixes of socialism and capitalism are being created.

Economic Classes

Socialists argue that IR and domestic politics alike are structured by unequal relationships between **economic classes.** (This emphasis on classes denies the realist dichotomy between domestic and international politics.) The more-powerful classes oppress and exploit the less-powerful by denying them their fair share of the surplus they create. The oppressed classes try to gain power, to rebel, to organize, in order to seize more of the wealth for themselves. This process is called **class struggle.** It is one way of looking at the political relationships between richer and poorer people, and between richer and poorer world regions.

Marx used a particular language to describe the different classes in an industrial economy; Marxists still use these terms. The **bourgeoisie** is the class of owners of capital—people who make money from their investments rather than from their labor. Under capitalism they are also the ruling class (sometimes in concert with politicians, military officers, or other powerful allies). The *petty bourgeoisie* are small-time owners of capital, like shopkeepers and other small businesspeople. They tend to think like owners and to identify with the bourgeoisie.

Intellectuals (including college professors and students) are treated ambiguously in most Marxist analyses; they often slip into a "petty bourgeois mentality" and see the world from the perspective of the rich, yet they sometimes are radicalized and side with the oppressed.

The **proletariat**—industrial factory workers—are considered potentially the most powerful class because their labor is necessary for the production of surplus. They are supposed to lead the revolution against the bourgeoisie. But factories have changed since the time of Marx: they are more capital-intensive, and workers in them are much better paid.

Various Marxist theories have tried to come to terms with this, none very successfully. Marxists also do not agree how to categorize increasingly important classes such as technical workers and managers. The class of economically unproductive people at the bottom of society is the *lumpenproletariat*—prisoners, criminals, drug addicts, and so forth. They are so down-and-out that they seldom become effective political revolutionaries.

One very important class in revolutions during this century (contrary to Marxist expectations) has been *peasants*.[8] Marxists traditionally consider peasants backward, ignorant, individualistic, and politically passive as compared to the well-educated and class-conscious proletariat. But in practice the successful third-world revolutions have been peasant rebellions (often led by Marxists talking about the proletariat). The largest was the Chinese revolution in the 1930s and 1940s.

According to Marxism, capitalism is just one stage of social evolution, preceded by feudalism and followed by socialism (when workers seize the state and use it to redistribute wealth) and eventually by communism (when everyone would be equal and the state would wither away as unnecessary). Each stage has its own forms of politics and culture, which make up the **superstructure** of the society. This superstructure is shaped by the **economic base** of society—its mode of production, such as slavery, feudalism, or capitalism.

In their particulars, Marxist analyses have been more often wrong than right in their predictions about the stages of social development, about class alliances, and about the results of revolutions. But Marxist revolutions have occurred in many third-world states, and Marxism (along with other forms of socialism) remains a force in third-world development and North-South relations.

❖ IMPERIALISM

Marx's theories of class struggle were oriented toward *domestic* society in the industrializing countries of his time, not toward poor countries or international relations. Traditional Marxists have looked to the advanced industrialized countries for revolution and socialism, which would grow out of capitalism. In their view, the third world would have to develop through its own stages of accumulation from feudalism to capitalism before taking the revolutionary step to socialism.

What actually happened was the opposite. Proletarian workers in industrialized countries enjoyed rising standards of living and did not make revolutions. Meanwhile, in the backward third-world countries, oppressed workers and peasants have staged a series of revolutions, successful and failed, over the past seventy years.

The Globalization of Class

Why did this happen? The answer largely shapes how one sees North-South relations today.[9] Marxists have predominantly (though not exclusively) followed a line of argument developed by V. I. **Lenin,** founder of the Soviet Union, before the Russian Revolution of

---

[8]Scott, James C. *Weapons of the Weak: Everyday Forms of Peasant Resistance.* New Haven: Yale University Press, 1986.

[9]Brewer, Anthony. *Marxist Theories of Imperialism: A Critical Survey.* Boston: Routledge and Kegan Paul, 1980. Kubalkova, Vendulka, and Albert Cruickshank. *Marxism and International Relations.* Oxford: Clarendon, 1985.

Squatter huts next to luxury houses in Manila, Philippines (1986). Such disparity of wealth is a microcosm of global North-South relations. Marxists see international relations and domestic politics alike as being shaped by class struggle between the rich and the poor.

1917.[10] At that time, Russia was a relatively backward state, like the third world today, and most Marxists considered a revolution there unlikely (looking instead to Germany).

Lenin's theory of **imperialism** basically argued that European capitalists were investing in colonies where they could earn big profits, and then using part of those profits to *buy off* the working class back home. The only limit that Lenin saw to this process was that after the scramble for colonies in the 1890s, few areas of the world were left to be colonized. After that, imperialist expansion could occur only at the expense of other imperialist states, leading to interimperialist competition and wars like World War I (which Lenin vehemently opposed). Seizing on Russia's weakness during that war, Lenin led the first successful communist revolution there in 1917.

Lenin's general idea still shapes one major approach to North-South relations. That is the idea that industrialized states exploit poor countries (through both formal and informal colonization) and buy off their own working classes with the profits. Through this *globalization of class relations*, world accumulation concentrates surplus toward the rich parts of the world and away from the poor ones. Revolutions, then, would be expected in poor regions.

---

[10]Lenin, V. I. Imperialism, the Highest Stage of Capitalism [1916]. In *Essential Works of Lenin*. New York: Bantam Books, 1966: 177 270.

Many third-world revolutionaries have sought to break loose from exploitation by the European colonizers. After European colonization ended, the United States as the world's richest country (with large investments in the third world and a global military presence) became the target of revolutionaries agitating against exploitation in poor countries. In a number of countries, imperialists were thrown out (often violently, sometimes not) and revolutionary nationalists took power.

One of the most important such revolutions was in China, where Mao Zedong's communists took power in 1949 on a Leninist platform adapted to the largely peasant-based movement they led. Mao declared that "China has stood up"—on its own feet, throwing off foreign domination and foreign exploitation. In India at the same time, the movement led by Gandhi used a different means (nonviolence) to achieve similar ends—national independence from colonialism. Indonesia threw out the Dutch. Lebanon threw out the French. Cuba threw out the Americans. This pattern was repeated, with variations, in dozens of countries.

According to the revolutionaries in these countries, exploitation of third-world countries by rich countries takes away the economic surplus of the third world and concentrates the accumulation of wealth toward the rich parts of the world. By breaking free of such exploitation, third-world states can then retain their own surplus and begin to accumulate their own wealth. Eventually they can generate their own self-sustaining cycles of accumulation and lift themselves out of poverty.[11]

In reality such an approach has not worked well. A policy of autarky does not foster growth (see pp. 327–328). And within a single poor country, trade-offs arise between concentrating or distributing wealth. For former colonies, the realities of economic development after independence have been complex.

Not all Marxist approaches favor a policy of self-reliance after revolution. For instance, Leon **Trotsky** was a Russian revolutionary who felt that after the 1917 revolution Russia would never be able to build socialism alone and so should make its top priority the spreading of revolution to other countries to build a worldwide socialist alliance. Trotsky's archrival Stalin wanted to build "*socialism in one country*," and he prevailed (and had Trotsky killed).[12] Mao also followed Stalin's path, and most third-world revolutions since then have had a strongly nationalist flavor.

The World-System

The global system of regional class divisions has been characterized by some IR scholars as a **world-system** or a *capitalist world-economy*.[13] This way of looking at IR is Marxist in orientation (focusing on economic classes) and relies on a global level of analysis.

---

[11]Tickner, J. Ann. *Self-Reliance Versus Power Politics*. New York: Columbia University Press, 1987.

[12]Mandel, Ernest. *From Stalinism to Eurocommunism: The Bitter Fruits of "Socialism in One Country."* Translated by Jon Rothschild. London: N.L.B., 1978.

[13]Wallerstein, Immanuel. *The Modern World-System*. 2 volumes. New York: Academic Press, 1974, 1980. Amin, Samir, Giovanni Arrighi, André Gunder Frank, and Immanuel Wallerstein. *Dynamics of Global Crisis*. New York: Monthly Review Press, 1982. Frank, André Gunder. *World Accumulation, 1492–1789*. New York: Monthly Review Press, 1978.

In the world-system, class divisions are regionalized. Third-world regions mostly extract raw materials (including agriculture)—work that uses much labor and little capital, and pays low wages. Industrialized regions mostly manufacture goods—work that uses more capital, requires more skilled labor, and pays workers higher wages. The manufacturing regions are called the **core** (or *center*) of the world-system; the extraction regions are called the **periphery.**

The most important class struggle today, in this view, is between the core and periphery of the world-system.[14] The core uses its power (derived from its wealth) to concentrate surplus from the periphery, as it has been doing for about five hundred years. Conflicts among great powers, including the two world wars and the Cold War, basically result from competition among core states over the right to exploit the periphery.

The core and periphery are not sharply delineated. Within the periphery, there are also centers and peripheries (for instance, the city of Rio de Janeiro compared to the Amazon rain forest) as there are within the core (such as New York City compared to the Mississippi Delta). The whole global structure is one of overlapping hierarchies. The concentration of capital and the scale of wages each form a continuum rather than a sharp division into two categories.[15]

In world-system theory, the **semiperiphery** is an area in which some manufacturing occurs and some capital concentrates, but not to the extent of the most advanced areas in the core. Eastern Europe and Russia are commonly considered to be semiperipheral, as are some of the newly industrializing countries (see pp. 511–514) such as Taiwan or Singapore. The semiperiphery acts as a kind of political buffer between the core and periphery because poor states can aspire to join the semiperiphery instead of aspiring to rebel against domination by the core.

Over time, membership in the core, the semiperiphery, and the periphery change somewhat, but the overall global system of class relations remains.[16] Areas that once were beyond the reach of Europeans, such as the interior of Latin America, become incorporated as periphery. Areas of the periphery can become semiperiphery and even join the core, as North America did. And core states can slip into the semiperiphery if they fall behind in accumulation, as Spain did in the late sixteenth to early seventeenth centuries. Because world-system theory provides only general concepts but not firm definitions of what constitutes the core, semiperiphery, and periphery, it is hard to say exactly which states belong to each category.[17]

The actual patterns of world trade support world-system theory to some extent. Table 12.1 shows the net exports (exports minus imports) of each world region for several types

---

[14]Boswell, Terry, ed. *Revolution in the World-System.* New York: Greenwood, 1989.

[15]Chase-Dunn, Christopher. *Global Formation: Structures of the World-Economy.* Cambridge, MA: Basil Blackwell, 1989.

[16]Friedman, Edward, ed. *Ascent and Decline in the World-System.* Beverly Hills: Sage, 1982. Goldgeier, James M., and Michael McFaul. A Tale of Two Worlds: Core and Periphery in the Post–Cold War Era. *International Organization* 46 (2), 1992: 467–92.

[17]Thompson, William R., ed. *Contending Approaches to World System Analysis.* Beverly Hills: Sage, 1983. Hopkins, Terence K., and Immanuel Wallerstein. *World-Systems Analysis: Theory and Methodology.* Beverly Hills: Sage, 1982. Bergesen, Albert, ed. *Studies of the Modern World-System.* New York: Academic Press, 1980.

TABLE 12.1 COMMODITY STRUCTURE OF WORLD TRADE BY REGION

Net Exports (Exports Minus Imports) in Billions of 1995 Dollars (1991 Data)

Region[a]	Manufactured Goods		Raw Materials	
	Machinery/ Chemicals[b]	Textiles and Other Light	Agriculture and Minerals	Energy
North America/Western Europe/Japan	(275)	−63	−23	−139
Russia and Eastern Europe	−23	−9	−10	13
China[c]	−15	(22)	5	3
Middle East[d]	−58	−14	−10	(76)
Latin America	−62	−14	(38)	27
Asia[c]	−60	(92)	−1	−5
Africa[d]	−44	−8	2	(38)

[a]Regions do not exactly match those used elsewhere in this book. A small residual is not included in any region.
[b]Machinery, metal manufactures, and chemicals.
[c]Taiwan, Hong Kong, and South Korea are here included in Asia.
[d]North African oil exporting states here are included in Africa, not the Middle East as elsewhere in this book.
Source: Calculated from UNCTAD data reported in United Nations. *World Economic and Social Survey* 1994. New York: United Nations, pp. 272–273.

of goods. As the circled numbers indicate, different regions specialize in exporting different kinds of goods. The core (industrialized West) exports $275 billion more than it imports in machinery, chemicals, and similar heavy manufactured goods. All the other regions import more than they export in such goods.

South and East Asia—here including Taiwan, Hong Kong, and South Korea—have a niche in light manufacturing including textile production; they export $92 billion more of these goods than they import. Such a pattern fits the semiperiphery category. China's $22 billion in net exports of light manufactures suggests that China is rising into the global semiperiphery.

The Middle East and Africa (here including North Africa) specialize in exporting oil ($76 billion and $38 billion respectively). This is an extraction role typical of the periphery. And Latin America has net exports of $38 billion in food, agricultural products, and minerals—also typical of the periphery. These regions' patterns of specialization must be kept in perspective, however: all regions both import and export all these types of goods, and the net exports listed in the table amount to only a small part of the world's $4 trillion in trade.

European Colonialism

For most third-world states, the history of having been colonized by Europeans is central to their national identity, foreign policy, and place in the world. For these states—and especially for those within them who favor socialist perspectives—international relations revolves around their asymmetrical power relationships with industrialized states. The

North plays a central role in creating, maintaining, and perhaps someday solving poverty in the South. (Capitalists tend to pay less attention to history and to focus on present-day problems in the South such as unbalanced economies, unskilled workforces, and corrupt governments.)

Today's global disparities did not exist until a few centuries ago. Eight hundred years ago there were a variety of relatively autonomous, independent civilizations in the world, none of which held power over each other—the Sung dynasty in China, the Arab empire in the Middle East, the Aztecs and Incas in Central America, the African kingdoms near present-day Nigeria, the shoguns in Japan, Genghis Khan's society in Siberia, and the feudal society of Europe (see pp. 25–26).

Europe between the twelfth and fifteenth centuries saw the rise of capitalism, a merchant class, science, and stronger states. Technological improvements in agriculture, industry, and the military gave Europe an edge over other world civilizations for the first time. European states conquered and colonized different world regions at different times (see "Imperialism" on pp. 29–31). Decolonization in some regions (such as the United States in 1776) overlapped with new colonizing in other regions.[18] But most of the world's territory was colonized by Europe at one time or another (see Figure 12.1).

Decolonization occurred only twenty to fifty years ago in most of Asia, Africa, and the Middle East. In Asia, the most important British colony was India (which included today's Pakistan and Bangladesh). Hong Kong was (and remains until 1997) a British colony serving as the gateway to China. British possessions also included Malaysia, Singapore, New Guinea, Australia, New Zealand, and others. Almost all the Asian colonies became independent around the time of World War II and the two decades afterward.

In Africa, European colonizers included Portugal, the Netherlands, Britain, France, Belgium, Germany, and Italy. In the late nineteenth century, European states rushed to grab colonies there (France and Britain ending up with most the territory). As a result, Africa was divided into a patchwork collection of colonies without coherent ethnic or geographic foundations.

The Middle East came under European influence as the Ottoman Empire disintegrated in the late nineteenth and early twentieth centuries—and as oil became a key fuel. Britain and France were most prominent there as well. Present-day Israel and Jordan were British-run until 1948. Syria and Lebanon were French. Iraq's claims on Kuwait stem from Britain's creation of Kuwait as an independent territory. The Arab-Israeli conflict also is strongly influenced by the history of British rule.

European conquerors treated their colonies as possessions that could be traded, seized as booty in wars, or given as mandates to new rulers. For instance, the island of Guam in the Pacific was once Spanish territory, then German, then Japanese, and then American.

Being colonized has a devastating effect on a people and culture. Foreigners overrun one's territory with force and take it over. They install their own government, staffed by their own nationals. The inhabitants are forced to speak the language of the colonizers, to adopt their cultural practices, and to be educated at schools run under their guidance. The inhabitants are told that they are inherently, racially inferior to the foreigners.

---

[18]Strang, David. Global Patterns of Decolonization, 1500–1987. *International Studies Quarterly* 35 (4), 1991: 429–54.

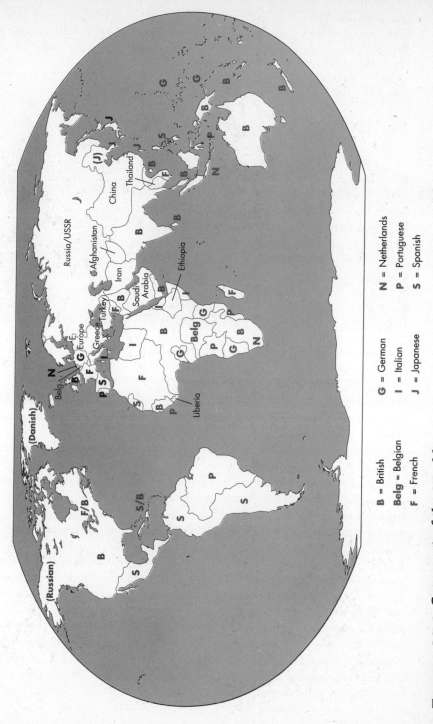

FIGURE 12.1 Conquest of the World
Former colonial territories of European states.

European colonialism worldwide promoted values and norms implying that the colonizer's culture is superior to the indigenous culture. Lingering effects remain in postcolonial societies. Here, mixed-race girls play with European-featured doll, Lima, Peru, 1992.

White Europeans in third-world colonies in Africa and Asia were greatly outnumbered by native inhabitants but maintained power by a combination of force and (more important) psychological conditioning. After generations under colonialism, most native inhabitants either saw white domination as normal or felt that nothing could be done about it. The whites often lived in a bubble world separated from the lives of the local inhabitants. They went to white clubs, bought products shipped in from Europe, made friends with other whites, and so forth.

Colonialism also had certain negative *economic* implications. The most easily accessible minerals were dug up and shipped away. The best farmland was planted in export crops rather than subsistence crops, and was sometimes overworked and eroded. The infrastructure that was built served the purposes of imperialism rather than the local population—for instance, railroads going straight from mining areas to ports. The education and skills needed to run the economy were largely limited to whites. As a result, when colonies attained independence and many of the whites departed, what remained was an undereducated population with a distorted economic structure and many of the valuable natural resources gone.

The economic effects were not all negative, however. Colonialism often fostered local economic accumulation (although controlled by whites). Cities grew up. Mines were dug and farms established. It was in the colonial administration's interest to develop the economy, to foster local cycles of capital accumulation. Much of the infrastructure that exists today in many third-world countries was created by colonizers. In some cases colonization brought together disparate communities into a cohesive political unit with a common religion, language, and culture, thus creating more opportunities for economic accumulation. Furthermore, in some cases the local political cultures replaced by colonialism were themselves oppressive to the majority of the people.

Anti-Imperialism

Wherever there were colonizers, there were anticolonial movements. Independence movements throughout Africa and Asia gained momentum during and after World War II, when the European powers were weakened. Through the 1960s, a wave of successful independence movements swept from one country to the next, as people stopped accepting imperialism as normal or inevitable (see Figure 12.2 on African decolonization).

Although many third-world countries gained independence around the same time, the methods by which they did so varied. In India, the most important colony of the largest empire (Britain), Gandhi led a movement based on nonviolent resistance to British rule (see "Nonviolence" on pp. 132–134). However, nonviolence broke down in the subsequent Hindu-Muslim civil war, which split India into two states—India mostly with Hindus, and Pakistan (including what is now Bangladesh) mostly with Muslims.

Some colonies won independence through warfare to oust their European masters; others won it peacefully by negotiating a transfer of power with weary Europeans. In Algeria, France abandoned its colonial claims in 1962 only after fighting a bitter guerrilla war. Some colonial liberation movements fought guerrilla wars based on communist ideology. The Viet Minh, for instance, defeated the French occupiers in 1954 and established communist rule in all of Vietnam by 1975. The Soviet Union supported such movements, and the United States opposed them. But in most cases the appeal of liberation movements was the general theme of anticolonialism rather than any ideology.

Across the various methods and ideologies of liberation movements in the third world, one common feature was reliance on nationalism as a strong source of popular support. Nationalism was only one of the ideas that these movements took from Europe and used to undermine European control; others included democracy, freedom, progress, and

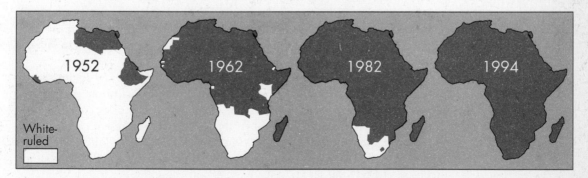

FIGURE 12.2 Areas of White Minority Rule in Africa, 1952–1994
Colonialism as a factor in international relations has been swept away over the past forty years. However, postcolonial dependency lingers on in many former colonies.
Source: Adapted from Andrew Boyd. *An Atlas of World Affairs.* 9th ed. London & New York: Routledge, 1992, p. 91.

Marxism. The leaders of liberation movements often had gone to European universities. Furthermore, under European control many states developed infrastructures, educational and religious institutions, health care, and military forces—all on the European model. Europe's conquest of the third world thus gave the third world tools to undo that conquest.[19]

Postcolonial Dependency

If imperialism concentrated the accumulation of wealth in the core and drained economic surplus from the periphery, then one might expect that accumulation in the third world would take off once colonialism was overthrown. Generally this had not been the case. A few states, such as Singapore, have accumulated capital successfully since becoming independent. But others, including many African states, seem to be going backward— the colonial cities slowly decaying and little new capital accumulating to replace the old colonial infrastructure. Most former colonies are making only slow progress in accumulation. Political independence has not been a cure-all for poor countries.

One reason for these difficulties is that under colonialism the training and experience needed to manage the economy were often limited to white Europeans. A few native inhabitants went to Europe for university training, but most factory managers, doctors, bankers, and so forth were whites. In many cases the white Europeans fled the country at the time of independence, leaving a tremendous gap in technical and administrative skills.

Another economic problem faced by newly independent states was that as colonies their economies had been developed in a narrow way to serve the needs of the European home country. Many of these economies rested on the export of one or two products. For Zambia, it was copper ore; for Ethiopia and El Salvador, coffee; for Botswana, diamonds; for Ghana, cocoa; and so forth.

Such a narrow export economy would seem well suited to use the state's comparative advantage to specialize in one niche of the world economy. But it leaves the state vulnerable to price fluctuations on world markets (which are out of its control). Given the North-South disparity in power, the raw materials exported by third-world countries do not tend to receive high prices (oil, from the mid-1970s to the mid-1980s, was an exception). The liberal free-trade regime based around GATT corrected only partially (through the General System of Preferences) for the North's superior bargaining position in North-South trade. And GATT has allowed agriculture (exported by the periphery) to remain protected in core states (see p. 337).

It is not easy to restructure an economy away from the export of a few commodities. Nor do state leaders generally want to do so, because the leaders benefit from the imports that can be bought with hard currency (including weapons). In any case, coffee plantations and copper mines take time and capital to create, and they represent capital accumulation—they cannot just be abandoned. In addition, local inhabitants' skills and training are likely to be concentrated in the existing industries. Furthermore, infrastructure such as railroads most likely was set up to serve the export economy. For instance, in Angola and Namibia the major railroads lead from mining or plantation districts to ports

---

[19]Barraclough, Geoffrey. *An Introduction to Contemporary History.* New York: Penguin Books, 1964.

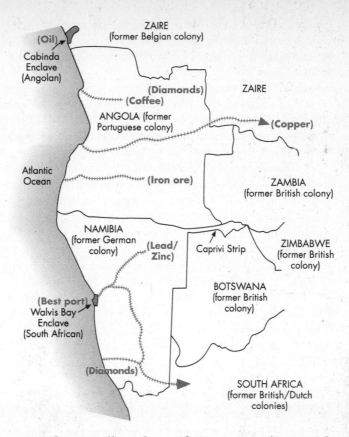

FIGURE 12.3 Borders, Railroads, and Resources in Angola and Namibia
Despite the independence of Angola and Namibia, colonial times shaped the borders and infrastructure in the region.

(see Figure 12.3). Political borders also may follow lines dictated by colonial economies. For example, an enclave (surrounded by Zaire) contains Angola's most profitable oil wells. A South African enclave, surrounded by Namibia, controls the best port in the area.

The newly independent states inherited borders that were drawn in European capitals by foreign officers looking at maps. As a result, especially in Africa, the internal rivalries of ethnic groups and regions made it very difficult for the new states to implement coherent economic plans. In a number of cases, ethnic conflicts within third-world states contributed to civil wars, which halted or reversed capital accumulation.

In quite a few cases the newly independent countries of Africa were little more than puppet governments serving their former colonizers. For example, according to a recently published memoir by a French official, France in the 1960s punished and even helped assassinate African leaders who opposed French policies. Those who supported France had direct phone lines to the French ambassadors' bedrooms, and gave France open-ended permission for military intervention. French officials auditioned a potential president of Gabon before allowing him to take office, and the self-declared emperor of the Central African Republic (later accused of cannibalism) used to call President de Gaulle of France "Papa."[20]

Finally, governments of many postcolonial states did not function very effectively, creating another obstacle to accumulation. In some cases corruption became much worse after independence (see "Corruption" on pp. 525–527). In other cases, governments tried to impose central control and planning on their national economy, based on nationalism, mercantilism, or socialism.

In sum, liberation from colonial control did not change underlying economic realities. The main trading partners of newly independent countries were usually their former colonial masters. The main products were usually those developed under colonialism. The administrative units and territorial borders were those created by Europeans. The state continued to occupy the same peripheral position in the world-system after independence as it had before. And in some cases it continued to rely on its former colonizer for security—protection against internal rebels or neighbors. For instance, France sent troops to Chad in the 1980s to help put down a Libyan-backed insurgency.

For these reasons, the period after independence is sometimes called **neo-colonialism**—the continuation of colonial exploitation without formal political control. This concept also covers the relationship of the third world with the United States, which (with a few exceptions) was not a formal colonizer in the first place. And it covers the North-South international relations of Latin American states that have been independent for almost two centuries.

Dependency Marxist IR scholars have developed **dependency** theory to explain the lack of accumulation in the third world.[21] They noticed that after World War II, Latin American states seemed on the verge of self-sustaining growth, in which a country's own capital would produce goods for its own markets. But this had not happened. These scholars define dependency as a situation where the accumulation of capital cannot sustain itself internally. A dependent country essentially has to borrow capital in order to produce goods, and then the debt payments reduce the accumulation of surplus. (Dependency is a form of international interdependence—the rich regions need to loan out their money just as the poor ones need to borrow it—but it is an interdependence marked by an extreme power imbalance.)

Dependency theorists focus not on the overall structure of the world-system (center and periphery) but on how a peripheral state's own internal class relationships play out. The development (or lack of development) of a third-world state depends on its local

---

[20]French, Howard W. French Held the Strings in Africa. *The New York Times*, February 28, 1995: A14.

[21]Cardoso, Fernando Henrique, and Enzo Faletto. *Dependency and Development in Latin America*. Translated by Marjory Mattingly Urquidi. Berkeley: University of California Press, 1979. Packenham, Robert A. *The Dependency Movement: Scholarship and Politics in Dependency Studies*. Cambridge, MA: Harvard University Press, 1992. Tetreault, Mary Ann, and Charles Frederick Abel, eds. *Dependency Theory and the Return of High Politics*. New York: Greenwood, 1986. Painter, James. *Bolivia and Coca: A Study in Dependency*. Boulder, CO: Lynne Rienner, 1994. Evans, Peter. *Dependent Development: The Alliance of Multinational, State, and Local Capital in Brazil*. Princeton: Princeton University Press, 1979.

conditions and history, even though it is affected by the same global conditions as other countries located in the periphery. Recall that within the third world there are local centers and local peripheries. There are capitalists and a national government within the state in addition to the external forces such as MNCs and governments of industrialized countries. These various forces can take on different configurations.

One historically important configuration of dependency is the **enclave economy,** in which foreign capital is invested in a third-world country to extract a particular raw material in a particular place—usually a mine, oil well, or plantation. Here the cycle of capital accumulation is primed by foreign capital, is fueled by local resources, and completes itself with the sale of products on foreign markets. Such an arrangement leaves the country's economy largely untouched except to give employment to a few local workers in the enclave and to provide taxes to the state (or line the pockets of some state officials). Over time, it leaves the state's natural resources depleted.

A different historical pattern is that of *nationally controlled production,* in which a local capitalist class controls a cycle of accumulation based on producing export products. The cycle still depends on foreign markets, but the profits now accrue to the local capitalists, building up a powerful class of rich owners *within* the country. This class—the local bourgeoisie—will tend to behave in a manner consistent with the interests of rich industrialized countries (on whose markets the class depends). They are not unpatriotic, but their interests tend to converge with those of foreign capitalists. For instance, they want to keep local wages as low as possible, to produce cheap goods for consumers in the rich countries. The local capitalists, in alliance with political authorities, enforce a system of domination that ultimately serves the foreign capitalists. This is another form of dependency.

After World War II a third form of dependency became more common—the penetration of national economies by MNCs. Here the capital is provided externally (as with the enclaves), but production is for local markets. For instance, a GM factory in Brazil would produce cars mostly for sale within Brazil. In order to create local markets for such manufactured goods, income must be concentrated enough to create a middle class that can afford such goods. This sharpens disparities of income within the country (most people remain poor). The cycle of accumulation depends on local labor and local markets, but because MNCs provide the foreign capital they take out much of the surplus as profit.

According to dependency theory, the particular constellation of forces within a country determines what coalitions form among the state, the military, big landowners, local capitalists, foreign capitalists (MNCs), foreign governments, and middle classes (such as professionals and skilled industrial workers). On the other side, peasants, workers, and sometimes students and the church, form alliances to work for more equal distribution of income, human and political rights, and local control of the economy. These class alliances and the resulting social relationships are not determined by any general rule but by concrete conditions and historical developments in each country. Like other Marxist theories, dependency theory pays special attention to class struggle as a source of social change.

Some people think that under conditions of dependency, economic development is almost impossible. Others think that development is possible under dependency, though it presents certain difficulties. We will return to these possibilities in Chapter 13.

Let us return to the example of genocide in Rwanda in 1994. We have discussed the theory that ethnic groups develop in-group biases that can lead to dehumanization of a rival group. Conservative realists might even say that violence of this type between ethnic groups is inevitable and natural, if deplorable. Since these conflicts are driven by "ancient ethnic hatreds," there is little the international community can do about them. Similar arguments were used, as we saw earlier, to justify the international community's feeble response in Bosnia as well.

Socialist approaches provide some different perspectives on the violence in Rwanda, pointing us to different kinds of explanations and evidence. For starters, the position of a peripheral country like Rwanda in the world-system can help explain violence and social upheaval there. Rwanda is one of the world's poorest countries, with a dense, fast-growing, and extremely poor population, over 90 percent rural. Typically for a peripheral state, Rwanda's main exports are coffee and tin; it imports machinery, fuel, and other manufactured goods. But income from its exports pays less than half the costs of its imports. Before its recent troubles the GDP was only $1,000 per person, and the land is depleted. Naturally such poverty drives a desperate struggle to survive, in which human life is cheapened.

Furthermore, dependency theories point to specific colonial histories as sources of explanation for the current problems of former colonies. Rwanda was colonized by Germany in the scramble for colonies by European powers at the end of the nineteenth century, and then grabbed by Belgium as Germany lost World War I. Although the minority Tutsi group (about 10 percent of the population) had ruled the majority Hutu group for several centuries before colonialism, it was under Belgian rule that large-scale Hutu violence against Tutsis first erupted.

It might be hypothesized that Belgium's interest would be to undermine the strongest political powers in a colony and support rival political forces that would be dependent on Belgium. Ultimately, among other things, keeping Rwanda down in this way could keep coffee prices low for Belgian consumers (who would then, according to Lenin's theory, live more comfortable lives and not make trouble for their bosses and politicians). In 1959, the Tutsi king and hundreds of thousands of Tutsis were driven into exile (from where they fought back for thirty-five years). Rwanda under Hutu rule was then granted independence from Belgium in 1962. In the following decade, the government repeatedly used massacres of Tutsis to respond to efforts of the Tutsi rebels in exile to return to power. As late as 1990, when Tutsi rebels advanced back into Rwanda, it was the Belgian army that showed up to save the Rwandan government—demonstrating the lasting nature of colonial ties. Ultimately the government of Hutu extremists that perpetrated genocide against the Tutsi in 1994 must be understood in the context of Rwanda's colonial history. (This telling is of course highly simplified, but the point is that the colonial element, while not necessarily determinative of outcomes, must be a part of any useful explanation.)

THINKING THEORETICALLY

❖

❖ THE STATE OF THE SOUTH

In the postcolonial era, some third-world states have made progress toward accumulation; some have not. The picture is a mixed one. Some (though not all) are caught in a cycle of abject poverty. Until incomes rise, the population will not move through the demographic transition (see pp. 452–454); population growth will remain high and incomes low.

Basic Human Needs

In order to put accumulation on a firm foundation, and to move through the demographic transition, the **basic human needs** of most of the population must be met.[22] They need food, shelter, and other necessities of daily life in order to feel secure. Furthermore, as long as people in the third world blame imperialism for a lack of basic needs, extreme poverty fuels revolution, terrorism, and anti-Western sentiments.

Children are central to meeting a population's basic needs. In particular, *education* opens up the possibility for a new generation to meet other basic needs and move through the demographic transition.[23] *Literacy*—which UNESCO defines as the ability to read and write a simple sentence—is the key component of education. A person who learns how to read and write can find out a wealth of information about small-scale agriculture, health care, birth control, and so forth. Some third-world countries have raised literacy rates substantially; others lag behind. In industrialized states, over 95 percent of the population is literate. In most middle-income third-world countries, the majority of the population is literate—over 90 percent in a few states. But in poorer countries the rate varies from over 50 percent down to just 10 percent of the population.

There is also great variation in schooling. Primary school attendance is fairly high in most poor states, which bodes well for future literacy. Secondary education—middle and high school—is another matter. In the North, about 90 percent are enrolled, but in most of the third world, less than half are enrolled. The rest are already working full-time and are unable to continue their schooling. College is available to only a small fraction of the population. Relative to population size, the United States has over thirty times more college students than Africa.

Effective *health care* in poor countries is not expensive—just four dollars per person per year for primary care. For instance, UNICEF has promoted four inexpensive methods that together are credited with saving the lives of millions of children each year. One method is *growth monitoring*—keeping regular records of a child's growth so that failure to gain weight will be noticed and action can be taken in time. It is estimated that regular weighing and advice could prevent half of all cases of malnutrition. A second method is *oral rehydration therapy (ORT)*, which consists of mixing two tablespoons of sugar and a half teaspoon of salt in a quart of clean water to stop diarrhea in children before they die from dehydration. A facility that produced 300 packets of the sugar-salt mixture daily at a cost of 1.5 cents each was built in Guatemala for just $550. Child deaths from diarrhea

---

[22]Streeten, Paul, et al. *First Things First: Meeting Basic Human Needs in the Developing Countries*. New York: Oxford University Press, 1981. Goldstein, Joshua S. Basic Human Needs: The Plateau Curve. *World Development* 13, 1985: 595–609.

[23]Noor, Abdun. *Education and Basic Human Needs*. Washington, DC: World Bank, 1981.

were cut in half in one year. The third method is *immunization* against six common deadly diseases—measles, polio, tuberculosis, tetanus, whooping cough, and diphtheria. In the past two decades, the number of children immunized in third-world countries has risen from 5 percent to over 50 percent.

The fourth method is the promotion of *breast feeding* as opposed to the use of infant formula. Many poor mothers consider baby formula more modern and better for a baby—a view promoted at times by unethical MNCs from industrialized states eager to market infant formula to large third-world countries. In the worst cases, salespeople dressed like nurses gave out free samples to new mothers. But once mothers started using formula, their own milk dried up and they were forced to continue with the costly formula, which is inferior to breast milk and can be dangerous when water supplies are unsafe and means of sterilization and refrigeration are lacking. After a consumer boycott of a well-known MNC gained attention, formula producers agreed in the 1980s to abide by WHO guidelines for selling formula in poor countries.

Globally, the disparities in access to health care are striking. The 75 percent of the world's people living in the South have about 30 percent of the world's doctors and nurses. In medical research under 5 percent of world expenditures are directed at problems in developing countries, according to WHO. The biggest killers are acute respiratory infections (7 million deaths per year), diarrhea (4 million), tuberculosis (3 million), and malaria and hepatitis (1 to 2 million each). About 600 million people are infected with tropical diseases—almost 300 million with malaria alone. Yet, because the people with

Children are a main focus of efforts to provide basic human needs in the global South. In Sudan (1993), famine and war forced this starving girl to set out for a feeding center, stalked by a vulture. She survived the incident, but the photographer committed suicide the next year.

such diseases are poor, there is often not a large enough market for drug companies (MNCs) in the industrialized world to invest in medicines for them.

In one case the U.S. Army created a lotion that can protect against infection by snail-borne worms that carry schistosomiasis, which WHO considers the second-worst public health problem in the world. Soldiers who serve in tropical areas can now be protected, but the drug company that produces the lotion has no plans to make it available to ordinary people because the market cannot afford the product.[24] In another case, a drug used against "river blindness" disease was profitably marketed by a drug company as a veterinary medicine in the United States, but was not profitable as a human medicine in the third world (some was donated by the manufacturer).

Safe water is another essential element of meeting basic human needs. In shantytowns there are usually no sanitary facilities, and in many rural locations people must walk for miles every day to fetch water. Access to water does not mean running water in every house, but a clean well or faucet for a village. Unfortunately, many third-world people lack such access—half or more of the population in India, Bangladesh, and Pakistan; two-thirds in Nigeria and Indonesia; one-quarter even in relatively well-off Brazil and Mexico.

For *shelter,* like water, the needs are minimal—safe structures that keep weather out and do not collapse on the inhabitants. It is taken for granted that large families live in a single room. But even so, in shantytowns at the edge of third-world cities shelter is inadequate and unsafe—especially in potential areas of earthquakes or monsoons (hurricanes). Refugees from war also lack shelter unless they are lucky enough to reach a well-equipped refugee camp.

In theory, providing for basic needs should give poor people hope of progress and should ensure political stability. However, it does not always work out. In Sri Lanka, a progressive-minded government implemented one of the world's most successful basic needs strategies, addressing nutrition, health care, and literacy. The policy showed that even a very poor country could meet basic needs at low levels of per capita income. Then an ethnic civil war broke out, with the ethnic group living in one province demanding autonomy. The civil war became more and more brutal—with death squads and indiscriminate reprisals on civilians—until it consumed the progress Sri Lanka had made. Today Sri Lanka is one of the world's most dangerous places, with basic needs in great jeopardy.

War in the third world—both international and civil war—is a leading obstacle to the provision of basic needs and political stability.[25] War causes much greater damage to society than merely the direct deaths and injuries it inflicts. In war zones, economic infrastructure such as transportation is disrupted, as are government services such as health care and education. Civil wars now kill more children than soldiers, according to a 1994 UNICEF report. Wars also drastically reduce the confidence in economic and political stability on which investment and trade depend.

In this context, it is noteworthy that almost all the wars of the past forty years have taken place in the third world (see p. 211). The shadow of war stretches from Central America through much of Africa, the Middle East, and South Asia. These wars may be

---

[24]*Science* 246, December 8, 1989: 1242.

[25]Dixon, William J., and Bruce E. Moon. Domestic Political Conflict and Basic Needs Outcomes: An Empirical Assessment. *Comparative Political Studies* 22 (2), 1989: 178–98.

the single greatest obstacle to economic development in the third world. To some extent these wars are caused by the poverty and instability of the third world; to some extent the wars are themselves a cause of poverty and instability. War is often part of a vicious circle for states unable to rise out of poverty.

There is a trade-off for third-world governments between spending funds on the military or on poor people. Many third-world governments import expensive weapons— whether because of real security conflicts with their neighbors, to put down internal challenges (secessionist movements or revolutions), or just as status symbols. These military forces are so expensive that even if they are never used they may deplete a state's ability to pursue basic needs and economic development. From a global perspective, the nearly $1 trillion spent annually on military forces (mostly in the North) could easily provide for the basic needs of all the world's poor people, giving states in the South a head start on accumulation. Instead, industrialized states compete to sell their advanced weapons to third-world governments as a source of export earnings. Disarmament alone would not solve all the problems of poor states, but continual militarization certainly makes those problems worse.[26]

World Hunger

Of all the basic needs of people in the third world, the most central is *food*. As was mentioned earlier, about 15 million children die each year from causes related to **malnutrition** (malnourishment)—the lack of needed foods including protein and vitamins. The term hunger refers broadly to malnourishment or outright **undernourishment**—a lack of calories. Hunger does not usually kill people through outright starvation, but it weakens them and leaves them susceptible to infectious diseases that would not ordinarily be fatal.[27]

Nearly 800 million people—about one in seven worldwide—are chronically undernourished (see Table 12.2). Their potential contribution to economic accumulation is wasted because they cannot do even light work. They cannot forgo short-term consumption for long-term investment. And they are a potential source of political instability— including international instability—as long as they stay hungry.

The world has the potential to produce enough food to feed all the world's people. The problem is not so much that there is an absolute shortage of food (though that condition does exist in some places) but that poor people do not have money to buy food.

Traditionally, rural communities have grown their own food—**subsistence farming.** Colonialism disrupted those traditional patterns, and the disruption has continued in postcolonial times. Third-world states have shifted land from subsistence to commercial

[26]Thomas, Caroline, and Paikiasothy Saravanamuttu, eds. *Conflict and Consensus in South/North Security*. New York: Cambridge University Press, 1989. Ayoob, Mohammed. *The Third World Security Predicament: State Making, Regional Conflict, and the International System*. Boulder, CO: Lynne Rienner, 1995. Rice, Edward E. *Wars of the Third Kind: Conflict in Underdeveloped Countries*. Berkeley: University of California Press, 1988. Slater, Robert O., Barry M. Schutz, and Steven R. Dorr, eds. *Global Transformation and the Third World*. Boulder, CO: Lynne Rienner, 1992.

[27]Dréze, Jean, and Amartya Sen, eds. *The Political Economy of Hunger*. 3 volumes. New York: Oxford University Press, 1991. Foster, Phillips. *The World Food Problem: Tackling the Causes of Undernutrition in the Third World*. Boulder, CO: Lynne Rienner, 1992. Tullis, F. LaMond, and W. Ladd Hollist, eds. *Food, the State, and International Political Economy: Dilemmas of Developing Countries*. Lincoln: University of Nebraska Press, 1986. Hollist, W. Ladd, and F. LaMond Tullis, eds. *Pursuing Food Security: Strategies and Obstacles in Africa, Asia, Latin America, and the Middle East*. Boulder, CO: Lynne Rienner, 1987.

TABLE 12.2 WHO'S HUNGRY?

Chronically Undernourished People by Region, Late 1980s

Region	Number (Millions)	Percentage of Population	20 Years Earlier
South Asia & China	528	19%	40%
Africa	168	33%	35%
Latin America	59	13%	19%
Middle East	31	12%	22%
Total "South"	786	20%	36%

Notes: Data are from 1988–1990 and 1969–1971. Regions do not exactly match those used elsewhere in this book. Chronic undernourishment means failing to consume enough food on average over a year to maintain body weight and support light activity.
Source: Based on 1992 FAO report as reported in *Science* 257, August 14, 1992: 876.

agriculture. Small plots have been consolidated into big plantations, often under the control of wealthy landlords. By concentrating capital and orienting the economy toward a niche in world trade, this process is consistent with liberal economics. But it displaces subsistence farmers from the land. Wars, of course, displace farmers even more quickly, with similar results.

Commercial agriculture relies on machinery, commercial fuels, and artificial fertilizers and pesticides. These goods must be purchased with cash and often must be imported. To earn the money to pay for these supplies, big farms grow **cash crops**—agricultural goods produced as commodities for export to world markets.[28] Such crops typically provide little nutrition to local peasants; examples include coffee, tea, cocoa, and sugar cane. When a plantation is built or expanded, subsistence farmers end up working in the plantation at very low wages or migrating to the cities in search of jobs. Often they end up hungry.

Even crops that could provide excellent nutrition to local populations become cash crops and slip out of the reach of hungry people nearby. For example, soybeans are produced on large commercial farms in Brazil using mechanized techniques (thereby displacing traditional labor-intensive agriculture). But instead of feeding hungry people in Brazil, the soybeans feed livestock to produce meat for the middle class and for export.

Many third-world governments support commercial agriculture with loans, subsidies, irrigation projects, or technical help. This government support reflects both the political power of the big landowners and the government's ability to obtain hard-currency revenues from export crops, but not from subsistence crops.

International food aid itself can sometimes contribute to these problems.[29] Agricultural assistance may favor mechanized commercial agriculture. And if an international agency floods an area with food, prices on local markets drop, which may force even more local farmers out of business and increase dependence on handouts from the government or international community. Also, people in a drought or famine often have to travel to

---

[28]Barkin, David, Rosemary L. Batt, and Billie R. DeWatt. *Food Crops vs. Feed Crops: Global Substitution of Grains in Production.* Boulder, CO: Lynne Rienner, 1990.

[29]Uvin, Peter. Regime, Surplus, and Self-Interest: The International Politics of Food Aid. *International Studies Quarterly* 36 (3), 1992: 293–312.

Subsistence farmers displaced from their land—such as by civil war in Somalia—risk chronic hunger and sometimes starvation. Here, mother and daughter in Baidoa, Somalia, December 1992.

feeding centers to receive the food, halting their work on their own land. For example, after drought hit the Sahel area of Africa in the 1970s, international agencies gave $8 billion in aid over a decade, but only about a sixth of this money supported the cultivation of nonirrigated crops for local consumption.

Rural and Urban Populations

The displacement of peasants from subsistence farming contributes to a massive population shift that typically accompanies the demographic transition. More and more people move to the cities from the countryside—**urbanization.** This is hard to measure exactly; there is no standard definition of when a town is considered a city. But industrialized states report that about 70 to 90 percent of their populations live in cities. By contrast, China is only 20 percent urbanized—a level typical of Asia and Africa. Most Middle Eastern states are a bit more urban (40 to 50 percent), and South American ones are 70 to 85 percent urban.

Urbanization is not caused by higher population growth in cities than in the countryside. In fact, the opposite is true. In cities the people are generally better educated, with higher incomes. They are further along in the demographic transition, and have lower growth rates than people in the countryside. Rather, the growth of urban population is caused by people moving to the cities from the countryside. They do so because of the higher income levels in the cities—economic opportunity—and the hope of more chances for an exciting life. They also move because population growth in the countryside stretches available food, water, arable land, and other resources—or because they have been displaced from subsistence farming as land is turned to commercial cultivation (or have been displaced by war).

Capital accumulation is concentrated in cities. To some extent this makes urban dwellers more politically supportive of the status quo, especially if a sizable middle class has developed in the city. Governments extend their influence more readily to cities than to the countryside. For instance, Chinese government policies adopted in Beijing often have little bearing on actual village life. But urban dwellers can also turn against a government: they are better educated and have rising expectations for their futures. Often rebellions arise from frustrated expectations rather than absolute levels of poverty. By contrast, the conservatism of peasants can make them a base of governmental support, as happened in China after the 1989 protests in Beijing.

In many cities the influx of people cannot be accommodated with jobs, housing, and services. In third-world slums and shantytowns, basic human needs often go unmet.

Many states have considered policies to break up large land holdings and redistribute land to poor peasants for use in subsistence farming—**land reform.**[30] Socialists almost always favor land reform, and many capitalists also favor it in moderation. The standards of moderation change over time; for instance, the El Salvadoran land reform favored by the United States in the 1980s was more sweeping than one that U.S. officials took as a sign of communism in Guatemala when the United States intervened there militarily in 1954.

The main opponents of land reform are large landowners, who often wield great political power because of their wealth and their international connections to markets, MNCs, and other sources of hard currency. Landowners have great leverage in bargaining with peasants—from using the legal system to maintaining virtual private armies.

Women in Development

Economic accumulation in poor countries is closely tied to the status of women in those societies.[31] This is a recent revelation; most attention in the past has focused on men as supposedly the main generators of capital. Governments and international agencies con-

---

[30]Dorner, Peter. *Latin American Land Reform in Theory and Practice.* Madison: University of Wisconsin Press, 1992. Montgomery, John D., ed. *International Dimensions of Land Reform.* Boulder, CO: Westview, 1984.

[31]Scott, Catherine V. *Gender and Development: Rethinking Modernization and Dependency Theory.* Boulder, CO: Lynne Rienner, 1994. Massiah, Joycelin, ed. *Women in Developing Economies: Making Visible the Invisible.* New York: Berg, 1992. Kardam, Nüket. *Bringing Women In: Women's Issues in International Development Programs.* Boulder, CO: Lynne Rienner, 1990. Nelson, Barbara J. The Role of Sex and Gender in Comparative Political Analysis: Individuals, Institutions, and Regimes [book review essay]. *American Political Science Review* 86 (2), 1992: 491–502.

centrated on work performed by male wage earners, which appears in financial statistics like the GDP. Women's work, by contrast, often is not paid for in money and does not show up in financial statistics. But women in much of the world work harder than men and contribute more to the economic well-being of their families and communities. Women hold together rural households when men move to cities. Women are also key to efforts to improve the lot of children and reduce birthrates. In nutrition, education, health care, and shelter, women are central to providing the basic needs of people in poor countries.

Yet women hold inferior social status to men in the countries of the South (at least as much as in the North). For instance, when food is in short supply, men and boys often eat first, with women and girls getting what's left. Because of this, of the world's malnourished children *80 percent are female*, according to Oxfam America.

Discrimination against girls is widespread in education and literacy. For example, in Pakistan 50 percent of boys but less than 30 percent of girls receive primary education. Throughout Asia, Africa, and the Middle East (though not in Latin America), more boys receive education, especially at the secondary level. At university level, only 30 percent of students are women in China and the Middle East, a bit over 20 percent in South Asia and Africa (but 45 percent in Latin America). Literacy rates among adults tell a similar story. In China, 80 percent of men, but only 50 percent of women, are literate. In India the rates are 55 percent for men and 25 percent for women. Only in Latin America do women's literacy rates approach those of men.

To meet basic human needs and achieve economic accumulation with equity, states and international agencies have begun to pay attention to ending discrimination in schooling, assuring women's access to health care and birth control, educating mothers about prenatal and child health, and generally raising women's status in society (allowing them a greater voice in decisions). These issues occupied the 1995 UN women's conference in Beijing, China, attended by tens of thousands of state and NGO representatives.

For example, international agencies help women organize small businesses, farms, and other income-producing activities. UNICEF has helped women get bank loans on favorable terms to start up small businesses in Egypt and Pakistan, and cooperative farms in Indonesia. Women have organized cooperatives throughout the third world, often in rural areas, to produce income through weaving and other textile and clothing production, retail stores, agriculture, and so forth.[32] In the slums of Addis Ababa, Ethiopia, for example, women heads of household with no land for subsistence farming had been forced into begging and prostitution. Women in three neighborhoods organized the Integrated Holistic Approach Urban Development Project to improve their lot. The project organized income-producing businesses from food processing to cloth weaving and garment production. These profitable businesses earned income for the women and helped subsidize health and sanitation services in the slums.

Migration and Refugees

The processes just outlined—basic-needs deprivation, displacement from land, urbanization—culminate in one of the biggest political issues affecting North-South relations—

---

[32]Bystydzienski, Jill, ed. *Women Transforming Politics: Worldwide Strategies for Empowerment.* Bloomington: Indiana University Press, 1992. Basu, Amrita. *Two Faces of Protest: Contrasting Modes of Women's Activism in India.* Berkeley: University of California Press, 1992.

The status of women in countries of the global South affects their prospects for economic development. Women are central to rural economies, to population strategies, and to the provision of basic human needs including education. This Asian 12-year-old, a prostitute's daughter, wears a wedding dress to invite a marriage proposal.

migration from poorer to richer states.[33] Millions of people from the global South have crossed international borders, often illegally, to reach the North.

Someone who moves to a new country in search of better economic opportunities, a better professional environment, or better access to their family, culture, or religion is engaging in migration (*emigration* from the old state and *immigration* to the new state). Such migration is considered voluntary. The home state is not under any obligation to let such people leave, and, more important, no state is obligated to receive migrants. As with any trade issue, migration creates complex patterns of winners and losers. Immigrants often provide cheap labor, benefiting the host economy overall, but also compete for jobs with (poor) citizens of the host country.

Most industrialized states try to limit immigration from the third world. Despite border guards and fences, many people migrate anyway, illegally. In the United States, such immigrants come from all over the world, but mostly from nearby Mexico, Central America, and the Caribbean. In Western Europe they come largely from North Africa, Turkey,

---

[33]Weiner, Myron. *The Global Migration Crisis: Challenge to States and to Human Rights*. New York: HarperCollins, 1995. Kritz, Mary M., Lin Lean Lim, and Hania Zlotnik, eds. *International Migration Systems: A Global Approach*. New York: Oxford University Press, 1992.

and (increasingly) Eastern Europe.[34] Some Western European leaders worry that the loosening of border controls under the process of integration (see pp. 400–401) will make it harder to keep out illegal immigrants. Indeed, fear of immigration is one reason why Swiss voters rejected membership in the EU.

International law and custom distinguish **refugees** from migrants. Refugees are people fleeing to find refuge from war, natural disaster, or political persecution.[35] (Fleeing from chronic discrimination may or may not be considered grounds for refugee status.) International norms obligate countries to accept refugees who arrive at their borders. Refugees from wars or natural disasters are generally housed in refugee camps temporarily until they can return home (this can drag on for years). Refugees from political persecution may be granted *asylum*, which allows them to stay in the new state. Acceptance of refugees—and the question of which states must bear the costs—is a collective goods problem.

The number of international refugees in the world grew from 3 million in 1976 to 23 million by 1995. In addition, 26 million more people are displaced within their own countries. In 1995, 40 million people were at risk of becoming dependent on international humanitarian aid. Most were displaced by wars (see Table 12.3).

The political impact of refugees have been demonstrated repeatedly in recent years. After the Gulf War, Iraq's persecution of rebellious Iraqi Kurds sent large numbers of Kurdish refugees streaming to the Turkish border, where they threatened to become an economic burden to Turkey. Turkey closed its borders, and the Iraqi Kurds were left stranded in the mountains without sustenance. The United States and its allies then sent in military forces to protect the Kurds and return them to their homes in Iraq (violating Iraq's territorial integrity but upholding the Kurds' human rights). When the Kurdish-controlled area of Iraq became a base for Kurdish guerrillas in Turkey, the Turkish Army in 1995 invaded the area (another violation of Iraqi sovereignty, which was not operative there anyway). The close connection of economics and international security is illustrated by this episode—a security-related incident (the war) caused an economic condition (starving Kurds) that in turn led to other security ramifications (U.S. military protection of Kurdish areas of Iraq; Turkish invasion of the area).

The connection of economics and security appears in other refugee questions as well. For example, the Palestinian refugees displaced in the 1948 and 1967 Arab-Israeli wars (and their children and grandchildren) live in "camps" that have become long-term neighborhoods, mainly in Jordan and Lebanon. Economic development is impeded in these camps because the host states and Palestinians insist that the arrangement is only temporary. The poverty of the refugees in turn fuels radical political movements among the camp inhabitants.

It is not always easy to distinguish a refugee fleeing war or political persecution from a migrant seeking economic opportunity. Illegal immigrants may claim to be refugees in

---

[34]Brubaker, William Rogers, ed. *Immigration and the Politics of Citizenship in Europe and North America.* Lanham, MD: University Press of America, 1989. Miller, Mark J., ed. Strategies for Immigration Control: An International Comparison. *The Annals of the American Academy of Political and Social Science* 534, July 1994. Larrabee, F. Stephen. Down and Out in Warsaw and Budapest: Eastern Europe and East-West Migration. *International Security* 16 (4), 1992: 5–33.

[35]Zolberg, Aristide, Astri Suhrke, and Sergio Aguayo. *Escape from Violence: Conflict and the Refugee Crisis in the Developing World.* New York: Oxford University Press, 1989. Gordenker, Leon. *Refugees in International Politics.* New York: Columbia University Press, 1987.

TABLE 12.3 POPULATIONS NEEDING EMERGENCY INTERNATIONAL AID

Country	Cause	Number at Risk[a] (millions)
Sudan	war	4
Ethiopia	postwar	4
Rwanda, Burundi (incl. Tanzania, Zaire)	war/genocide	4
Angola	war	4
Afghanistan (incl. Iran, Pakistan)	war	4
Bosnia	war	3
Liberia	war	2
Sierra Leone	war	2
Haiti	coup/sanctions	2
Eritrea	postwar	2
Iraq	war	2
Azerbaijan	war	1
Tajikistan	war	1
Georgia	war	1
Other		4

[a]Estimated number of people who will depend on emergency international assistance for food or survival needs, 1995.

order to be allowed to stay, when really they are seeking better economic opportunities. In the past decade this has become a major political issue throughout the North.

In Germany, France, Austria, and elsewhere, resentment of foreign immigrants has fueled upsurges of right-wing nationalism in domestic politics. Germany, with lax regulations for asylum seekers (they could live for years at state expense while applications for refugee status were processed), became a favored destination for growing numbers of immigrants—most of whom were not political refugees. At a time of economic difficulty following German reunification, around 1992, neo-Nazi youths staged violent attacks on foreigners and forced the government to tighten restrictions on immigration. (Hundreds of thousands of Germans then demonstrated against the neo-Nazis.)

In the United States, people arriving from war-torn El Salvador and Guatemala in the 1980s were often sent home after the U.S. government denied that they had reason to fear persecution from their (U.S.-supported) home governments. (A "sanctuary" movement in U.S. churches broke the law by sheltering such Central Americans.) And after a 1991 coup in Haiti deposed the elected (socialist) president, tens of thousands of poor people set off for U.S. shores in small boats. Were they fleeing from persecution by the Haitian military or just looking for better economic opportunities (especially plausible in light of the U.S.-led economic sanctions that had damaged Haiti's economy)? The U.S. government screened the Haitians, granted asylum to a few, and shipped most back to Haiti. As the numbers grew, the United States began intercepting boats on the high seas and returning them directly to Haiti—a practical response that nonetheless violated international law (boats on the high seas are not within U.S. jurisdiction). President Clinton promised to change the U.S. policy if elected, but he reversed himself when thousands of Haitians built boats and prepared to set sail on Clinton's inauguration day.

North-South economic disparities, as between Haiti and the United States, affect international security affairs. After a 1991 coup in Haiti, tens of thousands of Haitian refugees were turned back by the U.S. military. Ultimately U.S. military intervention was called in. Here, the U.S. Coast Guard intercepts Haitian refugees in July 1988.

Evidently the only solution to the Haitian problem was to seek a political solution within Haiti itself (and then drop the U.S. sanctions). Thus, the United States ultimately intervened militarily to restore Haiti's president to power. Similarly, the problem of illegal immigration from Mexico seems to lack any real solution except to improve economic conditions in Mexico (as it was hoped the NAFTA treaty would help accomplish).

In general, South-North migration creates problems for the industrialized states that, it seems, can only be solved by addressing the problems of the South itself. To the extent that the North does not help address those problems, people in the South seem likely to turn to their own solutions, which often include revolutionary strategies.

❖ REVOLUTION

Poverty and lack of access to basic human needs are prime causes of revolutions, especially when relatively poor people see others living much better.[36] Most revolutionary

[36]Skocpol, Theda. *Social Revolutions in the Modern World.* New York: Cambridge University Press, 1994. Skocpol, Theda. *States and Social Revolutions: A Comparative Analysis of France, Russia, and China.* New York: Cambridge University Press, 1979. Schutz, Barry M., and Robert O. Slater, eds. *Revolution and Political Change in the Third World.* Boulder, CO: Lynne Rienner, 1990. Gurr, Ted Robert. *Why Men Rebel.* Princeton: Princeton University Press, 1970. Lichbach, Mark Irving. An Evaluation of "Does Economic Inequality Breed Political Conflict?" Studies. *World Politics* 41 (4), 1989: 431–70.

movements espouse egalitarian ideals—a more equal distribution of wealth and power. Most third-world countries have had active revolutionary movements at one time or another since their independence.

Revolutionary Movements

During the Cold War years, the classic third-world revolutionary movement was a communist insurgency based in the countryside. Such a revolution typically was organized by disenchanted students, professionals, and educated workers—usually committed to some variant of Marxist ideology—who won support from laborers and peasants. Its targets were the state, the military forces backing up the state, and the upper classes whose interests the state served. Usually "U.S. imperialism" or another such foreign presence was viewed as a friend of the state and enemy of the revolution.[37]

Sometimes the U.S. government gave direct military aid to governments facing such revolutionary movements; in a number of countries, U.S. military advisors and even combat troops were sent to help put down the revolution and keep communists from taking power. The United States often tried (but rarely with success) to find a third force, between repressive dictators and communist revolutionaries, that would be democratic, capitalist, and committed to peaceful reform. For its part, the Soviet Union often armed and helped train the revolutionaries. If a revolution won power, then it was the Soviet Union that armed the new government and sent military advisors, and the United States that supported antigovernment rebels.

In this way, the domestic politics of third-world countries became intertwined with great-power politics in the context of the North-South gap. But in reality, many of these governments and revolutions had little to do with global communism, capitalism, or imperialism. They were local power struggles—sometimes between the haves and the have-nots, sometimes between rival ethnic groups—into which great powers were drawn.

Some third-world revolutions succeeded in taking power: they gained strength, captured some cities, and (often following the defection of part of the government army) marched on the capital city and took control. New foreign policies quickly followed (see "Postrevolutionary Governments" later in this chapter).

Elsewhere, and more frequently, revolutions failed: ever-smaller numbers of guerrillas were forced ever further into the countryside with dwindling popular support. A third outcome became more common in recent years—a stalemated revolution in which it becomes clear after ten or twenty years of guerrilla warfare that neither the revolutionaries nor the government can defeat the other. In these cases, the international community may step in to negotiate a cease-fire and the reincorporation of the revolutionaries, under some set of reforms in government practices, into peaceful political participation. This happened successfully in El Salvador (Central America), and elsewhere in the late 1980s with varying degrees of success.

The Chinese revolution of the 1930s and 1940s was the model of a successful communist revolution for decades thereafter. In Southeast Asia, communist guerrillas ultimately took power in South Vietnam, Cambodia, and Laos but withered away in Thailand, Burma, and Malaysia. In Latin America, Fidel Castro's forces took power in Cuba in

---

[37]Parenti, Michael. *The Sword and the Dollar: Imperialism, Revolution, and the Arms Race.* New York: St. Martin's Press, 1988.

1959 after years of guerrilla war. But when Castro's comrade-in-arms, Che Guevara, tried to replicate the feat in Bolivia, he failed and was killed.[38]

By the early 1990s, these communist third-world revolutions seemed to have played themselves out—winning in some places, losing in others, and coming to a stalemate in a few countries. The end of the Cold War removed superpower support from both sides, and the collapse of the Soviet Union and the adoption of capitalist-oriented economic reforms in China undercut the ideological appeal of communist revolutions.

One revolutionary movement that lingered after the Cold War was the Shining Path (*Sendero Luminoso*) in Peru.[39] Based on communist ideology, the Shining Path advocated the violent overthrow of the Peruvian government, the distribution of wealth, smashing U.S. imperialism, and giving power to indigenous peoples instead of descendants of Spanish colonizers. In practice, Shining Path seized power in villages and neighborhoods by killing anyone who refused to join and by destroying any alternative political forces (such as labor unions and political leaders) working for the poor or promoting socialism.

These tactics aimed to force a choice between Shining Path and a corrupt government whose army disrespected human rights. However, given that choice, most Peruvians sided with the government! A reformist president, Alberto Fujimori, received popular support in 1992 when he seized emergency powers, cracked down on the Shining Path, and managed to arrest its top leader (around whom the group had built a cult of personality). He easily won reelection in 1995.

Islamic Revolutions

Although third-world revolutions almost always advocate for the poor versus the rich and for nationalism versus imperialism, the particular character of these movements varies across regions and time periods. For instance, in Africa, where colonialism left state boundaries at odds with ethnic divisions, many revolutionary movements have a strong tribal and provincial base; this may fuel secessionism by a province (such as Eritrea from Ethiopia). Asian revolutionary movements tapped into general anticolonial sentiments, as when Vietnamese communists fought to oust the French colonizers and then saw the war against the United States as a continuation of the same struggle. In Latin America, where national independence was won long ago, revolutions tended to be couched in terms of class struggle against rich elites and their foreign allies (states and MNCs).

In the post–Cold War era, the most potent revolutionary movements are Islamic ones in the Middle East, not communist ones in Asia or Latin America. Islam is now a key focal point of global North-South conflict. Islamic revolutionaries in most Middle East countries are not just concerned with religious practice, although that is certainly one area of conflict (see "Religious Conflict" on pp. 204–207). Like revolutionaries elsewhere, they derive their main base of strength from championing the cause of the poor masses against rich elites. Like other revolutionaries throughout the third world, Islamic movements draw their base of support from poor slums, where the revolutionaries sometimes operate basic services unmet by the government.

---

[38]Dominguez, Jorge. *To Make a World Safe for Revolution: Cuba's Foreign Policy.* Cambridge, MA: Harvard University Press, 1989. Wickham-Crowley, Timothy P. *Guerrillas and Revolution in Latin America: A Comparative Study of Insurgents and Regimes Since 1956.* Princeton: Princeton University Press, 1991.

[39]Palmer, David Scott, ed. *The Shining Path of Peru.* New York: St. Martin's Press, 1992. Radu, Michael. Can Fujimori Save Peru? *Bulletin of the Atomic Scientists* 48 (6), 1992: 16–21.

Islamic revolutionary movements are rooted in reaction against the colonial experience. They criticize imperialism in the postcolonial period as reflected in the Westernized ways of the ruling elites in Middle Eastern countries. For example, in Iran the shah had been armed by the United States as a bulwark against Soviet expansion into the Middle East. The Islamic revolutionaries who overthrew him in 1979 (led by Khomeini) declared the United States, as the leading political and cultural force in the industrialized West, to be the world's "great Satan."

Islamic revolutionaries reject the entire European-based cultural framework on which the modern international system rests. This rejection was dramatically illustrated when, after its revolution, Iran refused to protect the safety of U.S. diplomats and the territorial integrity of the U.S. embassy in Iran (see "Laws of Diplomacy" on pp. 296–298). Islamic revolutionaries likewise reject Western norms concerning the rights of individuals; this was exemplified by Khomeini's 1989 offer of a large reward to anyone who killed a British author, Salman Rushdie, whose book Khomeini considered blasphemous. Western values regarding human rights and women's roles are similarly rejected.

Recall that in most third-world revolutions in the past, the guiding ideas such as nationalism or Marxism were imported from the North (through, for instance, attendance at European universities by future revolutionaries from Africa and Asia). The Islamic revolutions are different in this regard. They seek to overthrow ideas imported from the North and to substitute home-grown ideas rooted in their own region for many centuries. This is part of the appeal of Islam as an anti-imperialist ideology.

Whereas Iran's revolution was directed against a U.S.-backed leader, an Islamic guerrilla war in Afghanistan showed that similar ideas could prevail against a Soviet-backed leader. Here it was communism and Soviet domination, rather than capitalism and Western domination, that Islamic revolutionaries overthrew. After a decade of destructive civil war (in which U.S. aid helped the revolutionaries), the Islamic forces took power in 1992. However, the Islamic factions then began fighting among themselves—based partly on ethnic and regional splits and partly on the different foreign allies of different factions.

In Algeria, Islamic revolutionaries organized against the ruling party that itself had kicked out the French colonizers in 1962 but was now seen as corrupt, inept, and not revolutionary enough. The Islamic parties won preliminary parliamentary elections in 1991 and were assured of coming to power in the final elections. Instead, the military took over, canceled the elections, and arrested thousands of Islamic activists. Nonetheless, the revolutionaries continued to agitate and staged a growing number of violent attacks on government targets. Several years of escalating violence ensued, with tens of thousands of people killed. Increasingly as the conflict wore on, the revolutionaries targeted intellectuals, prominent women, journalists, and other independent-minded symbols of secular Algerian society.

Elsewhere in the Middle East, Islamic movements are particularly active in Tunisia, Jordan, and Tajikistan. In Jordan, Islamic parties control the largest bloc of seats in the parliament. In the former Soviet republic of Tajikistan they are a major faction in civil strife (since the Soviet Union's demise). Middle Eastern Islamic revolutionaries also took a keen interest in the fate of Muslims targeted for genocide in Bosnia from 1992 on. They saw this conflict as part of a broad regional (almost global) struggle of Western, Christian imperialism against Islam—a struggle dating back to the Crusades almost a thousand years ago. By 1995 Muslims were being bloodied by Christians in wars in Bosnia, Azerbaijan, and Chechnya.

In many Muslim-populated countries, Islam serves as a rallying point against the West and its colonial past. The Algerian government canceled democracy after Islamic parties won parliamentary elections in 1991. Here, supporters of the Islamic Salvation Front in Algiers protest martial law in June 1991; tens of thousands of people died in the following years of civil strife.

Postrevolutionary Governments

When revolutionaries succeed in taking power, their state's domestic and international politics alike are affected. This occurred in China in 1949; Cuba in 1959; Algeria in 1962; South Vietnam, Cambodia, Angola, and Mozambique in 1975; Nicaragua and Iran in 1979; and Afghanistan in 1992.

Even though revolutionaries advocate the broad distribution of wealth, they tend to find after taking power that centralizing accumulation is more practical: it gives the state more control of wealth and power (with which to meet the needs of the masses, or line the pockets of the new leaders, as the case may be). Over time, the new elite may come to resemble the old one, although individuals change places. Similarly, revolutionaries often advocate improving women's status, but after taking power male revolutionaries have tended to push aside their female comrades, and traditional sex roles have reappeared.[40]

---

[40]Urdang, Stephanie. *And Still They Dance: Women, War and the Struggle for Change in Mozambique.* New York: Monthly Review Press, 1989.

More relevant to international relations are the problems that beset successful revolutionaries due to violence—usually backed directly or indirectly by foreign states. After many revolutions, the meeting of basic human needs has been severely impeded by continuing political violence and even civil war. For example, the socialist government that took power in Angola in 1975 wanted to improve the lot of poor people, but instead civil war ravaged the country for more than fifteen years and the poor ended up much hungrier than ever. Likewise, the Nicaraguan Sandinistas after taking power fell into a protracted civil war with U.S.-backed counterrevolutionaries—a war that wiped out gains in basic needs in much of the country. In Vietnam, the war that brought the communists to power was so fierce that it left the country devastated.

Such problems reached an extreme under the communist Khmer Rouge faction that took power in Cambodia in 1975. They sought to radically alter the society by destroying economic classes, destroying concentrations of capital, destroying ideas that ran contrary to the revolution, abolishing money, and rebuilding the entire nation in the image of their own ideology. To implement this plan the Khmer Rouge executed almost everyone associated with government, business, or universities, or who had independent ideas. They then evacuated the populations of cities into the countryside, where hundreds of thousands starved to death. After losing power in 1979 (when Vietnam invaded and installed a new government), the Khmer Rouge continued to wage guerrilla war for more than a decade afterwards. A UN-administered peace plan was implemented in the 1990s (though against continuing Khmer Rouge resistance), but the country had been decimated. The Khmer Rouge disaster showed that merely destroying concentrations of capital does not help meet poor people's basic needs.

Violence and war—both international and civil war—are tremendous obstacles to economic accumulation and the provision of basic human needs. It is a great contradiction of violent revolutions that they rely on the methods of war to gain power, supposedly to redistribute wealth and meet people's basic needs. Yet rich and poor alike are often caught in a downward spiral of indiscriminate violence and destruction that leaves poor people worse off than before. And after taking power, violent revolutionaries often face continuing civil or international war in the struggle to keep power. Successful revolutions often induce neighboring states either to contain the revolution or to take advantage of the new government's instability. For example, within a year of the 1979 revolution in Iran, Iraq had attacked in hopes of conquering Iran while it was weak. (European states did much the same to France after the French Revolution of 1789.)

In foreign policy, revolutionary governments often start out planning radically different relationships with neighbors and great powers (as Trotsky planned to do after the 1917 Soviet revolution). And indeed, the pattern of international alliances often shifts, as when a Cold War client of one superpower shifted to the other after a change of government.

But over time the new government usually discovers that, now that it holds power, it has the same interest as other states in promoting national sovereignty and territorial integrity. The rules of the international system work for the revolutionaries instead of against them, once they control a state. Their state also has the same geographical location as before, the same historical conflicts with its neighbors, and the same ethnic ties. So it is not unusual over time to find similar foreign policies emanating from a revolutionary government as from its predecessor.

South Africa's president, Nelson Mandela (here shown at a march of the African National Congress in Boipatong, 1992), has had unusual success in making the difficult transition from revolutionary to state leader. He has the advantage of coming to power nonviolently (relatively speaking), enjoying tremendous world respect, and leading a country that is relatively prosperous (though with huge inequalities) in a very poor continent.

In general, after revolutionaries have been in power for a decade or two, they tend to become less revolutionary. Power does tend to corrupt or co-opt even the best-intentioned socialists, and officials find some of the same opportunities for corruption as those in the previous government did. For example, corruption is rampant in the Chinese government, four decades after the revolution. Even for the most honest leaders, the need to develop the economy often creates pressures to build up new concentrations of capital. Perhaps these are now owned by the state, rather than by private banks or landowners. But hierarchies tend to reappear. Furthermore, violent revolutions most often lead to authoritarian rule (for fear that counterrevolutionaries will retake power), not to multiparty democracy. This means that the revolutionary party has a monopoly on power, year after year, which leads to a certain conservatism.

These tendencies are illustrated in the experiences of Algeria and China. The young revolutionaries of the National Liberation Front drove the French colonialists out of Algeria in 1962. Twenty years later, these revolutionaries were moderate enough to play the role of intermediaries between revolutionary Iran and the United States in the hostage crisis of 1980. And ten years later the old revolutionaries were the entrenched rulers against whom young Islamic revolutionaries rose up. Similarly, in China the revolutionaries who took power in 1949 were able to make common cause with the U.S. imperialists by 1971, and by 1989 they were the conservative rulers shooting down student protesters in the streets of Beijing.

Thus, although revolutions create short-term shifts in foreign policy, over the longer term the rules of international relations have tended to triumph over revolutionary challenges. Likewise, though revolutions promise great economic change, the overall state of economic conditions and relations—especially between North and South—has been resistant to change.

Overall, North-South relations show how difficult it has become to separate political economy from international security. The original political relations contained in European imperialism led to economic conditions in the South—from high population growth to urbanization and concentrations of wealth—that in turn led to political movements for independence, and later to revolutions. The various aspects of the North-South gap considered in this chapter—from hunger and refugees to the structure of commodity exports—all contain both economic and political-military aspects.

Marxists emphasize that the economic realities of accumulation, or the lack of accumulation, lie beneath all the political struggles related to global North-South relations. But Marxists' strategies—from armed revolutions to self-reliance to state ownership—have not been very successful at changing those realities. Chapter 13 therefore turns in depth to the question of how economies in the South can develop the accumulation process and what role the North can play in that process.

❖ CHAPTER SUMMARY

- Most of the world's people live in poverty in the third world. About one billion live in extreme poverty, without access to adequate food, water, and other necessities.

- Moving from poverty to well-being requires the accumulation of capital. Capitalism and socialism take different views on this process. Capitalism emphasizes overall growth with considerable concentration of wealth, whereas socialism emphasizes a fair distribution of wealth.

- Most states have a mixed economy with some degree of private ownership of capital and some degree of state ownership. However, state ownership has not been very successful in accumulating wealth. Consequently, many states are selling off state-owned enterprises (privatization), especially in Russia and Eastern Europe.

- Marxists view international relations, including global North-South relations, in terms of a struggle between economic classes (especially workers and owners) that have different roles in society and different access to power.

- Since Lenin's time, many Marxists have attributed poverty in the South to the concentration of wealth in the North. In this theory capitalists in the North exploit the South economically and use the wealth thus generated to buy off workers in the North. Revolutions thus occur in the South and are ultimately directed against the North.

- IR scholars in the world-system school argue that the North is a core region specializing in producing manufactured goods and the South is a periphery specializing in extracting raw materials through agriculture and mining. Between these are semiperiphery states with light manufacturing.

- Today's North-South gap traces its roots to the colonization of the third-world regions by Europe over the past several centuries. This colonization occurred at different times in different parts of the world, as did decolonization.

◆ Because of the negative impact of colonialism on local populations, anticolonial movements arose throughout the third world at various times and using various methods. These culminated in a wave of successful independence movements after World War II in Asia and Africa. (Latin American states gained independence much earlier.)

◆ Following independence, third-world states were left with legacies of colonialism, including their basic economic infrastructures, that made wealth accumulation difficult in certain ways. These problems still remain in many countries.

◆ Wealth accumulation (including the demographic transition discussed in Chapter 11) depends on the meeting of basic human needs such as access to food, water, education, shelter, and health care. Third-world states have had mixed success in meeting their populations' basic needs.

◆ War has been a major impediment to meeting basic needs, and to wealth accumulation generally, in poor countries. Almost all the wars of the past fifty years have been fought in the third world.

◆ Hunger and malnutrition are rampant in the third world. The most important causes are the displacement of subsistence farmers from their land—because of war, population pressures, and the conversion of agricultural land into plantations growing export crops to earn hard currency.

◆ Urbanization is increasing throughout the third world as more people move from the countryside to cities. Huge slums have grown in the cities as poor people arrive and cannot find jobs.

◆ Women's central role in the process of accumulation has begun to be recognized. International agencies based in the North have started taking women's contributions into account in analyzing economic development in the South.

◆ Poverty in the South has led huge numbers of migrants to seek a better life in the North; this has created international political frictions. War and repression in the South have generated millions of refugees seeking safe haven. Under international law and norms, states are generally supposed to accept refugees but do not have to accept migrants.

◆ Many people throughout the third world have turned to political revolution as a strategy for changing economic inequality and poverty. Often, especially during the Cold War, states in the North were drawn into supporting one side or the other during such revolutions.

◆ Today the most potent third-world revolutions are the Islamic revolutions in the Middle East. Even more than the communist revolutions of the past, Islamic revolutions are directed against the North and reject the Western values on which the international system is based. Like communist ones, Islamic revolutions draw support and legitimacy from the plight of poor people.

◆ When revolutionaries succeed in taking power, they usually change their state's foreign policy. Over time, however, old national interests and strategies tend to reappear. After several decades in power, revolutionaries usually become conservative and in particular come to support the norms and rules of the international system (which are favorable to them as state leaders).

◆   North-South relations, although rooted in a basic economic reality—the huge gap in accumulated wealth—reflect the close connections of economics with international security.

❖ THINKING CRITICALLY

1. In what ways does the North American Free Trade Agreement (NAFTA) discussed in Chapter 8 reflect the overall state of North-South relations as described in this chapter? How would capitalism and socialism as general approaches to the theory of wealth accumulation differ in their views of the agreement?

2. The zones of the world economy as described by world-system theorists treat the North as a core and the South as largely a periphery. Can you think of exceptions to this formula? How seriously do such exceptions challenge the overall concept as applied to North-South relations generally? Be specific about why the exceptions do not fit the theory.

3. In North and South America, independence from colonialism was won by descendants of the colonists themselves. In Asia and Africa it was won mainly by local populations with a long history of their own. How do you think this has affected the postcolonial history of one or more specific countries from each group?

4. Suppose you lived in an extremely poor slum in the third world and had no money or job—but retained all the knowledge you now have. What strategy would you adopt for your own survival and well-being? What strategies would you reject as unfeasible? Would you adopt or reject the idea of revolution? Why?

5. Suppose that Islamic revolutions succeeded in taking power throughout most of the Middle East. How, if at all, might this change the relations of states in that region with states in the North? What historical precedents or other evidence supports your view?

❖ KEY TERMS

less-developed countries
developing countries
capital accumulation
economic surplus (growth)
consumption vs. investment
capitalism vs. socialism
Marxism
Stalin, Lenin, Trotsky
economic class/class struggle
bourgeoisie vs. proletariat
superstructure and economic base
imperialism
world-system

core, periphery, semiperiphery
neocolonialism
dependency
enclave economy
basic human needs
malnutrition and undernourishment
subsistence farming
cash crop
urbanization
land reform
migration
refugees

*Hong Kong business
district, 1987.*

CHAPTER 13

INTERNATIONAL DEVELOPMENT

❖ WHAT IS DEVELOPMENT?

Economic development refers to the combined processes of capital accumulation, rising per capita incomes (with consequent falling birthrates), the increasing of skills in the population, the adoption of new technological styles, and other related social and economic changes.[1] The most central aspect is the accumulation of capital (with its ongoing wealth-generating potential). The concept of development has a subjective side that cannot be measured statistically—the judgment of whether a particular pattern of wealth creation and distribution is good for a state and its people. But one simple measure of economic development is the per capita GDP—the amount of economic activity per person.

By this measure, most of the third world made progress on economic development in the 1970s, with real per capita GDP growth of almost 3 percent annually. This rate was a bit higher than in the global North (despite the higher population growth in the South, which pulls down per capita GDP). However, in the 1980s this economic development came to a halt except in Asia. Per capita GDP *decreased* from 1981 to 1991 in Latin America, Africa, and the Middle East. Only in South and East Asia did 3.6 percent annual growth continue in that decade, and in China the rate was 7.5 percent annually (compared to 2 percent in the industrialized countries).[2]

By 1992–1993, real economic growth had returned across the South—about 5 percent annual growth for the South as a whole, but varying from about 1 percent growth in

---

[1]Weiner, Myron, and Samuel B. Huntington, eds. *Understanding Political Development: An Analytic Study.* Boston: Little Brown, 1987. Lewis, John P., and Valeriana Kallab, eds. *Development Strategies Reconsidered.* New Brunswick: Transaction Books, 1986. Newman, Barbara A., and Randall J. Thomson. Economic Growth and Social Development: A Longitudinal Analysis of Causal Priority. *World Development* 17 (4), 1989: 461–71.

[2]South and East Asia here includes South Korea, Taiwan, and Hong Kong. United Nations. *World Economic Survey 1992*, p. 185.

Africa and 2 to 5 percent in Latin America, the Middle East and Asia, to 13 percent annual growth in China. But still, on a per capita basis, GDP was the same or lower as ten years earlier, in all regions except China and East Asia. And inflation also picked up in the early 1990s, reaching more than 200 percent annually for the entire global South as a whole in 1993. Inflation was 900 percent in Latin America, around 60 percent in Africa and the Middle East, and about 10 percent in Asia and China. Thus by the mid-1990s China stood out among the regions as making rapid progress toward economic development. All the other regions of the global South showed much slower progress if any, and faced serious problems moving development forward.[3]

The average amount of income per capita does not indicate how income is distributed or to what purposes it is put. Here the perspectives and prescriptions of capitalism and socialism again diverge (see pp. 469–472). Capitalists tend to favor the concentration of capital as a way to spur investment rather than consumption (and to realize economies of scale and specialization). In line with liberalism, capitalists favor development paths that tie third-world states closely to the world economy and international trade.[4] They argue that although they defer equity, such development strategies maximize efficiency. Once a third-world state has a self-sustaining cycle of accumulation underway, it can better redress poverty in the broad population. To do so too early would choke off economic growth, in this view.

The same concept applies broadly to the world's development as a whole. From a capitalist perspective, the North-South gap is a stage of world development in which capital accumulation is concentrated in the North. This unequal concentration creates faster economic growth, which ultimately will bring more wealth to the South as well (a "trickle down" approach). There is no practical way, in this view, to shift wealth from the North to the South without undermining the free-market economics responsible for global economic growth.

Socialists disagree with these views. They argue that meaningful third-world development should improve the position of the whole population and of the poor—sooner rather than later. Thus, socialists tend to advocate a more equitable distribution of wealth, and they dispute the idea that greater equity will impede efficiency or slow down economic growth. On the contrary, by raising incomes among the poorer people, a strategy based on equity will speed up the demographic transition and thus lead more quickly to sustained accumulation. Such a strategy seeks to develop a state's economy from the bottom up instead of the top down.

On a global level, socialists do not see the North-South disparities as justified by global growth benefits. They favor political actions to shift income from North to South in order to foster economic growth in the South. Such a redistribution, in this view, would create faster, not slower, global economic growth—has well as more-balanced and stable growth.

In reality, most states in the global South use a mix of the two strategies in their economic policies, as do the industrialized states in shaping their roles in third-world development. Welfare capitalism, such as most industrialized states practice, distributes enough

[3]Kennedy, Paul. *Preparing for the Twenty-First Century*. New York: Random House, 1993.

[4]Colclough, Christopher, and James Manor, eds. *States or Markets? Neo-Liberalism and the Development Policy Debate*. New York: Oxford University Press, 1991.

wealth to meet the basic needs of almost everyone while letting most wealth move freely in capitalist markets. Such a mix is harder to achieve in a third-world state where the smaller total amount of wealth may force a choice between welfare and capitalism. Fortunately, the amount of income that a state needs to satisfy most of its population's basic needs is not very large—around $2000 per capita per year even if that income is distributed unequally as it typically is. Unfortunately, many states are still below this level of per capita income.

The capitalist theory that unequal income distributions are associated with higher economic growth is only weakly supported by empirical evidence. Many states with fairly equitable income distributions have achieved high growth rates (including South Korea, Taiwan, Singapore, and Hong Kong), and many with unequal distributions have grown only slowly if at all (e.g., Zambia, Argentina, and Ghana). But there are also cases of relatively equitable countries that grow slowly (e.g., India) and inequitable ones that grow rapidly (e.g., Malaysia).

❖ EXPERIENCES

Although much of the third world went backward in the 1980s, some Asian states continued to develop and China in particular increased its GDP rapidly (see Figure 13.1). This indicates that a single, simplified model of the South does not apply to all third-world countries. One must consider the various experiences of different countries as they try different approaches to development.[5]

The Newly Industrializing Countries

Given the extent of third-world poverty, is it even possible for a third-world country to get economic development rolling and lift itself out of poverty? The answer is "yes," at least for some countries. A handful of poor states have achieved self-sustaining capital accumulation, with impressive economic growth. They are called the **newly industrializing countries (NICs).**[6] These states posted strong economic growth in the 1980s. They are semiperiphery states that export light manufactured goods (see "The World-System" on pp. 475–477).

The most successful NICs are the **"four tigers"** or **"four dragons"** of East Asia—South Korea, Taiwan, Hong Kong, and Singapore. Each has succeeded in developing particular sectors and industries that are competitive on world markets.[7] These sectors and industries can create enough capital accumulation within the country to raise income levels not just among the small elite but across the population more broadly.

---

[5]Arnold, Guy. *The End of the Third World.* New York: St. Martin's Press, 1993.

[6]Haggard, Stephan. *Pathways from the Periphery: The Politics of Growth in the Newly Industrializing Countries.* Ithaca: Cornell University Press, 1990. Haggard, Stephan. *Developing Nations and the Politics of Global Integration.* Washington, DC: The Brookings Institution, 1995.

[7]Hughes, Helen, ed. *Achieving Industrialization in East Asia.* New York: Cambridge University Press, 1988. Wade, Robert. East Asia's Economic Success: Conflicting Perspectives, Partial Insights, Shaky Evidence [review article]. *World Politics* 44 (2), 1992: 270–318. Wade, Robert. *Governing the Market: Economic Theory and the Role of Government in East Asian Industrialization.* Princeton: Princeton University Press, 1992.

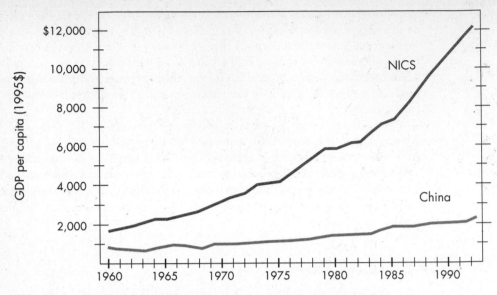

Note: NICs include South Korea, Taiwan, Hong Kong, and Singapore

FIGURE 13.1 Economic Growth of NICs and China

Many third-world countries are trying to apply the model of the NICs, but so far few have succeeded. Most poor states remained mired in poverty, with as many failures as successes. Scholars do not know whether the NICs are just the lucky few that have moved from the periphery to the semiperiphery of the world-system (see p. 476), or whether their success can eventually be replicated throughout the world to allow the whole third world to accumulate capital.

South Korea, which has iron and coal resources, developed competitive steel and automobile industries that export globally, creating a trade surplus (see "Balance of Trade" on pp. 322–324). For example, Hyundai cars and trucks, sold in the United States and other world markets, are produced by the giant South Korean MNC, Hyundai. The state is strongly involved in industrial policy, trying to promote and protect such industries. *Taiwan* too has a strong state industrial policy. It specializes in the electronics industry, where Taiwanese products are very successful worldwide, and in other light manufacturing.

Hong Kong also has world-competitive electronics and other light industries, but its greatest strengths are in banking and trade—especially trade between southern China and the rest of the world. Hong Kong is a small territory with great internal disparities of wealth. Its rich neighborhoods are jammed with high-rise office buildings and expensive apartments; nearby are huge refugee camps providing cheap labor. Hong Kong is a financial center for much of Asia. *Singapore* is a trading city located at the tip of the Malaysian peninsula—convenient to the South China Sea, the Indian Ocean, and Australia. Singapore has developed some niches in light manufacturing.

For different reasons, each of these states holds a somewhat unusual political status in the international system. South Korea and Taiwan—both former colonies of Japan—both have unusual status in the international system. South Korea and North Korea are sepa-

Singapore (1991) is one of the "four tigers" (with Hong Kong, Taiwan, and South Korea). Other third-world countries are trying to emulate the success of these NICs. But no single, simple lesson applicable to other states emerges from the NICs.

rate states in practice, but people on both sides consider Korea one nation. Taiwan is an island province of China, which neither its own government nor that in Beijing considers independent (but in practice operates independently). Both South Korea and Taiwan were scenes of fighting in the 1950s (the Korean War in 1950–1953 and the less severe Taiwan Straits crises of 1955 and 1958), and both came under the U.S. security umbrella during the Cold War. Both were militarized, authoritarian states intolerant of dissent during those decades.

U.S. spending in East Asia during the Cold War benefited South Korea and Taiwan. In these cases military conflict did not impede development—as military spending and war usually do—because the conflicts served to transfer some wealth from the United States to these states.

Hong Kong and Singapore have a different political profile. They were both British colonies (Hong Kong still is until 1997). They are more city-states than nation-states, and their cities are trading ports and financial centers. Although not as repressive nor as militarized as South Korea and Taiwan during the Cold War era, Hong Kong and Singapore were not democracies either. Hong Kong is ruled by a British governor, Singapore by a dominant individual (who once banned sales of the *Asian Wall Street Journal*, hardly a radical newspaper, after it criticized him).

A few other states have had some success in industrializing, but are not considered to be models as widely applicable as the "four tigers." *Israel*, for instance, has developed economically in an unusual manner. It received sustained infusions of outside capital from several sources—German reparations, U.S. foreign aid (economic and military), and contributions from Zionists in foreign countries. This outside assistance was particular to the history of German genocide against Jews during World War II and the efforts of Jews worldwide to help build a Jewish state afterward. Few if any third-world countries could hope to receive such outside assistance (relative to Israel's small size). In common with the other NICs, however, Israel had a strong state involvement in key industries, and it carved out a few niches for itself in world markets (notably in cut diamonds and military technology).

Thailand has been suggested as a potential fifth tiger. It received enormous foreign investment in the 1980s (mostly from Japan) and created a sizable middle class (recall the "cellular phone revolution" mentioned on p. 413). But it is not yet clear whether it will succeed in following the other NICs. *Malaysia* is also trying to follow closely in the footsteps of the tigers. Again, it is too soon to say whether this will succeed. *Indonesia* set itself a goal in 1969 to become a NIC by 1994. It fell short of that goal, but has made some progress in attracting foreign investment. With nearly 200 million people, Indonesia's major assets are cheap labor (an average wage of about 25 cents per hour) and exportable natural resources, including oil.

Thus, it is unclear whether there are general lessons applicable to other third-world countries to be learned from the success of the "four tigers." Two NICs (Hong Kong and Singapore) are small trading cities located at the intersection of industrialized and third-world regions (Japan/Pacific, South Asia, and China). There are no equivalents elsewhere in the third world. The other two came of age while enmeshed in security relationships with the United States that no longer apply to most third-world countries, if they ever did.

The Chinese Experience

Very few of the third world's people live in NICs. The largest, South Korea, has fewer than 50 million. China is more than twenty times its size. This alone makes China's efforts to generate self-sustaining accumulation worthy of study. But China has also had one of the fastest-growing third-world economies in recent years.

Between the communist victory of 1949 and the Cultural Revolution of 1966–1976, Chinese economic policy emphasized national self-sufficiency and communist ideology. The state controlled all economic activity through central planning and state ownership. An "iron rice bowl" policy guaranteed basic food needs to all Chinese citizens (at least in theory).

After Mao died in 1976, China under Deng Xiaoping instituted waves of economic reforms and transformed its southern coastal provinces (near Hong Kong and Taiwan) into **free economic zones** open to foreign investment and run on capitalist principles. Peasants work their own fields, instead of collective farms, and "get rich" (by Chinese standards) if they do well. Entrepreneurs start companies, hire workers, and generate profits. Foreign investment has flooded into southern China, taking advantage of its location, cheap labor, and relative political stability. Other areas of China have gradually opened up to capitalist principles as well, under China's market socialism. The state now requires more industries to turn a profit and gives more initiative to managers to run their own companies and spend the profits as they see fit.

Economic growth has been rapid since these policies were instituted. Standards of living are rising substantially. However, China is also re-creating some of the features of capitalism that Mao's revolutionaries had overturned. New class disparities are emerging, with rich entrepreneurs driving fancy imported cars while poor workers find themselves unemployed (earlier, socialism guaranteed everyone employment even though this reduced efficiency). Social problems like prostitution have returned, as have economic problems like inflation. Most frustrating for ordinary Chinese is the widespread official corruption that has accompanied the get-rich atmosphere.

Popular resentment over these problems (mainly inflation and corruption) led industrial workers and even government officials to join students in antigovernment protests at Beijing's Tiananmen Square in 1989. Authorities used the military to violently suppress the protests, signaling its determination to maintain tight political control while economic reform proceeded. This policy, combining economic reform with political orthodoxy, was reaffirmed at the next Party Congress in 1992. Economic growth roared ahead at 12 percent per year in 1992–1994, but inflation returned, reaching 22 percent in 1994 as a result of what the government called "mistakes." (As of 1995, it remained to be seen what course China would take after the death of Deng Xiaoping.)

China's rapid economic growth has put appliances like refrigerators and washing machines in reach of a growing middle class. Chinese economic successes followed China's opening to the world economy and adoption of market-oriented reforms. Here, consumers in Beijing, 1989.

China's get-rich-quick climate was illustrated by an unusual riot which took place in 1992 in the southern city of Shenzhen after a million Chinese citizens flooded into the city to buy applications to purchase stock during an expansion of the tiny stock market. (Only one in ten applicants would actually get to buy stock.) There were few other investment outlets for these citizens' rising incomes, and they shared a perception that stocks could only go up in value. When applications ran out and rumors spread that corrupt officials had made off with the applications themselves, the remaining would-be investors rioted in the streets. This incident illustrates the intensity of get-rich fever in China as well as the popular discontent over corruption.[8]

It is unclear what lessons China's economic success over the past decade holds for the rest of the third world. The shift away from central planning and toward private ownership was clearly a key factor in success, yet the state continued to play a central role in overseeing the economy (even more than in the NICs). Perhaps the earlier socialist policies, such as the "iron rice bowl," had met basic needs adequately enough to allow capitalism into the mix without impoverishing most of the population. Then again, China's socialist policies may merely have delayed its accumulation of wealth. Perhaps authoritarian political control facilitated the difficult transition to a more capitalist, growth-oriented economy. Then again, such control may only have closed off economic opportunities. These topics are being debated vigorously as China looks to the future (post-Deng), and other poor states look to China.

Other Experiments

Other sizable third-world states have pursued various development strategies, with mixed successes and failures. *India*, like China, deserves special attention because of its size. Its economy was until recently based loosely on socialism and state control of large industries but private capitalism in agriculture and consumer goods. The state subsidizes basic goods (setting affordable prices) and gives special treatment to farmers (who pay no income tax and receive free electricity and cheap fertilizer). Unlike China, India has a relatively democratic government—and a fractious one, with various autonomy movements and ethnic conflicts. India's government is ridden with corruption from top to bottom; this has held back accumulation.

Indian state-owned industries, like those elsewhere, are largely unprofitable. To take an extreme example, twelve years after a fertilizer plant was built, it employed 3000 workers but had not produced any fertilizer. India's socialist philosophy and widespread poverty also limit the growth of a middle class to support capital accumulation and state revenue: less than 1 percent of the population pays any income tax. Furthermore, bureaucracy in India has discouraged foreign investment. For instance, in the first quarter of 1992 India received only $300 million in foreign investment (35 cents per person), whereas China received over twenty times that amount.[9]

The 1991 collapse of the Soviet Union—India's main ally and trading partner—threw India into a severe economic crisis that nearly caused it to default on its international debts. India sought help from the IMF and the World Bank, and committed itself

---

[8]Kristoff, Nicholas D. After Riots, Will Beijing Sell Reform Short? *The New York Times*, August 16, 1992: E1. Lieberthal, Kenneth. *Governing China*. New York: W.W. Norton, 1995.

[9]Gargan Edward A. India's Rush to a Free Market Economy Stumbles. *The New York Times*, August 15, 1992: 2.

China's economic growth in the 1980s and 1990s stands out (along with a few other East Asian countries) from the pattern of sluggish development (if any) elsewhere in the global South. Several different explanations can be offered for China's success. One explanation rooted in a conservative world view is that China's traditional Confucian culture (shared to some extent by its East Asian neighbors) provides the discipline and social cohesion that allows rapid economic development and relative political stability. (China's path, then, would not apply to other areas of the global South.) The trouble with this explanation is that China's cultural traditions are fairly fixed from decade to decade, yet China's politics have careened from civil war to totalitarian stability to Cultural Revolution to reformism, and its economic development has varied from the disaster of the Great Leap Forward in the 1950s to the success of market socialism since the 1980s. A theoretical explanation in which the outcome varies so much while the hypothesized cause remains fixed is not very appealing.

A more liberal approach—and the dominant one now for explaining China's success—emphasizes the effect of market-oriented reforms in opening the way for rapid growth and rising incomes. Since liberals tend to favor open economies and free trade, they make much of the fact that as China moved its economic system in these directions, growth picked up rapidly. This explanation is appealing in that it can be applied widely to other countries of the South. However, the evidence that it actually works well across the board is not very strong. After all, economic reforms similar to China's have

THINKING THEORETICALLY

❖

been implemented in many other countries, yet China's performance far exceeds most of those other cases. This line of thinking then suggests avenues for further refinement of this theoretical approach. For example, one could tease apart the various elements of China's economic reforms—ranging from agricultural reforms to privatization to allowing foreign investment and so forth—and see which ones coincide with other successful cases in the global South.

A different explanation can be found in world-system theory (a more revolutionary approach). China can be seen as moving from the periphery zone of the world-economy to the semiperiphery (along with some East Asian neighbors). As we have seen, China's exports of light-industrial products supports this characterization. In this theory, however, such a movement between zones does not change the overall structure of the world-system. Some regions like China move up a zone; others like Russia and Eastern Europe move down a zone (from core to semiperiphery). But the periphery itself must remain, and only a small part of the world can ever belong to the core. Thus, China's economic rise does not provide lessons or a viable path for states elsewhere in the global South. This theoretical approach, as compared to the liberal one, is a bit vague on its predictions ("some move up, some move down") and thus hard to test. But its main conclusion—that the success of one region does not indicate any overall convergence of the South with the North—is borne out by the data we first reviewed in Chapter 1. China is, so far, the exception to a persistent (even growing) North-South gap.

to far-reaching economic reforms such as reducing bureaucracy, freeing markets, and selling money-losing state-owned industries (see "IMF Conditionality" later in this chapter). It was unclear several years later how far these reforms would go and what effect they would have on India's economic growth.

Among other sizable Asian countries, *Indonesia* and *Thailand* are trying, with some limited success, to follow a Pacific Rim NIC strategy, following in the path of South Korea and Taiwan. Thailand's military government followed China's example in 1992 by shooting student demonstrators (in the "cellular phone revolution" mentioned on p. 419), but this did not work. In the aftermath, some military commanders were forced off lucrative positions on the boards of directors of state-owned enterprises.

Other large Asian states—*Bangladesh, Pakistan, Vietnam,* and the *Philippines*—are more deeply mired in poverty and have dimmer prospects for capital accumulation in the coming years. All have problems with state bureaucracies and corruption. Vietnam is a communist state trying to follow a reform model parallel to China's. The Philippines is trying to overcome a rebellion in the countryside and a history of political instability that discourages foreign investment. It never fully recovered from the looting of its economy and treasury under the Marcos dictatorship in the 1970s and early 1980s. Pakistan also faces political instability and a chronic danger of war with India. Bangladesh is just extremely poor, with no apparent foothold to get accumulation started.

Brazil and *Mexico* are the largest third-world states in the Western hemisphere. Brazil built up a sizable internal market by concentrating income in a growing middle and upper class, especially after a military coup in 1964. However, its cities are still ringed with huge slums filled with desperately poor people. In the 1980s Brazil returned to democratic civilian rule and began economic reforms such as selling off unprofitable state-owned enterprises, promoting free markets, and encouraging foreign investment. The first sale of a state-owned company, in 1991, caused street riots; but a dozen more in the following year proceeded more smoothly.

Nonetheless, by the early 1990s, despite three major debt renegotiations in a decade, Brazil remained well over $100 billion in debt (the largest foreign debt in the third world). It had annual inflation of 200 percent and more, causing the currency's value to fall drastically. The president, who had been elected on promises to clean up corruption, was impeached in a corruption scandal. The positive side of this embarrassing episode for Brazil was a constitutional, civilian transfer of power. With faster economic growth and foreign investment, a bigger grain harvest, and a substantial trade surplus, Brazil's main problem by 1993 was inflation. Dependency theorist Fernando Cardoso (see footnote 21 in Chapter 12) became finance minister, in charge of controlling inflation. His anti-inflation plan was so successful that he was elected president in 1995, and other countries tried to copy his methods.

In Mexico, similar economic reforms were undertaken in the 1980s. Like Brazil, Mexico had pockets of deep poverty and a sizable foreign debt. Unlike Brazil, Mexico had oil to export (a good source of hard currency, despite low world prices). Mexico has also enjoyed relative political stability, though corruption is a problem. Mexico in the early 1990s tied its economic future to the NAFTA free-trade area with the United States and Canada. Leaders hoped this agreement would accelerate foreign investment, creating jobs and export opportunities. Mexico also sold off over $20 billion of state-owned companies (sparing the strategic oil industry) to help lower its debt and bring down inflation by the early 1990s. But assassinations and other political upheaval, including an armed rebellion in the South that broke out in response to the NAFTA accord, complicated Mexico's development problems. In 1994–1995 Mexico's currency collapsed and standards of living for many consumers took a sharp drop. With help from the United States, Mexico undertook new economic reforms to try to rebuild the economy and restore international and domestic confidence in its political system.

In Africa, *Nigeria* is the largest country and, with oil to export, one of the less impoverished. In 1980, when oil prices were high, Nigeria began building a huge, Soviet-style steel plant, two hundred and fifty miles inland, which leaders hoped would serve as the cornerstone of Nigerian economic development. Twelve years and $5 billion later, the plant was ready to start producing steel. It is the biggest industrial project in sub-Saharan Africa. But its products will not be competitive in the world steel industry, so government subsidies may be required indefinitely. Meanwhile, as world oil prices fell drastically in the 1980s, state revenues dropped and the country went in debt by $35 billion. Corruption consumed a sizable sum of money in the course of building the steel plant. This pattern of centralized industrialization under Nigeria's military government faces uncertain prospects at best, although oil exports provide continuing income.[10] Nigeria canceled a planned experiment in democracy in the early 1990s, and a military dictatorship continued in power by mid-decade. African-Americans began an unusual campaign to press for democracy in Nigeria, in order to move Africa's largest country forward in both human rights and overall development.

In the Middle East, the small countries with large oil exports—like *Saudi Arabia, Kuwait,* and *Bahrain*—have done well economically. But they are in a special class; their experience is not one that third-world states without oil can follow. *Iran* and *Iraq* are somewhat larger countries that have also benefited from oil exports. After the Iran-Iraq War ended in 1988, Iran began to grow robustly and to attract foreign investment. However, its Islamic radicalism creates frictions with Western powers and makes some investors wary. Meanwhile, Iraq squandered oil revenues on military adventures in Iran and Kuwait; its economic development was set back enormously by the bombing of its infrastructure during the Gulf War.

Turkey has been fairly successful in developing its economy without oil revenues, a rare case. Like South Korea and Taiwan, Turkey was an authoritarian state for many years but has allowed political liberalization in recent years; it has developed under a U.S. security umbrella (NATO) and has received considerable U.S. foreign aid. Like Mexico, Turkey is trying to join its richer neighbors—the European Union. Turkey also hopes to develop strong ties with the five former Soviet Asian republics. In contrast to Iran, Turkey espouses a secular politics, with Islam relegated to the religious and cultural sphere. (In the 1990s a small but growing Islamic movement began challenging the secular basis of Turkish society).

Egypt is mired in poverty despite substantial U.S. aid since the late 1970s. The state owns 70 percent of industry, operates the economy centrally, imposes high import tariffs, and provides patronage jobs and subsidized prices in order to maintain political power. A major portion of Egypt's foreign debt was forgiven after it helped the anti-Iraq coalition in

---

[10]Noble, Kenneth B. Nigeria's Monumental Steel Plant: Nationalist Mission or Colossal Mistake? *The New York Times,* July 11, 1992: 3.

the Gulf War, but Egypt remains about $30 billion in debt. It runs a trade deficit of billions of dollars each year, and 20 percent of the workforce is unemployed. Corruption is widespread at all levels of the bureaucracy. Islamic militants have gained increasing strength as Egypt's economy weakens, despite state repression against them.

These examples from all the third-world regions illustrate the variety of approaches toward economic development that third-world states have tried and the mixed success they have met. Such experiences have been generalized into "lessons" for economic development.

❖ LESSONS

Clearly, the largest third-world states are following somewhat different strategies with somewhat different results; no single model applies to all of them. But several common themes recur. These themes concern trade, the concentration of capital, authoritarianism, and corruption.

Import Substitution and Export-Led Growth

Throughout the third world, states are trying to use international trade as the basis of accumulation. For the reasons discussed in Chapter 8, a policy of self-reliance or autarky is at best an extremely slow way to build up wealth. But through the creation of a trade surplus, a state can accumulate hard currency and build industry and infrastructure.

One way to try to create a trade surplus—used frequently a few decades ago—is **import substitution.** This refers to the development of local industries to produce items that a country had been importing. These industries may receive state subsidies or tariff protection. On the surface, this would seem to be a good policy for reducing dependency—especially on the former colonial master—while shrinking a trade deficit or building a trade surplus. But it is against the principle of comparative advantage and has not proven effective in most cases. Some scholars think that import substitution is a useful policy but only at a very early phase of economic development, after which it becomes counterproductive. Others think it is never useful.

In recent years more and more states have shifted to a strategy of **export-led growth,** which is the strategy used by the NICs. This strategy seeks to develop industries that can compete in specific niches in the world economy. The chosen industries may receive special treatment such as subsidies, tax breaks, and protected access to local markets. Exports from these industries generate hard currency and create a favorable trade balance. The state can then spend part of its money on imports of commodities produced more cheaply elsewhere.

As we have seen, such a strategy has risks, especially when a state specializes in the export of a few raw materials (see "Postcolonial Dependency" on pp. 482–484). Such a specialty leaves poor countries vulnerable to sudden price fluctuations for their export products. For example, when world copper prices fell from $3000 to $1300 per ton in just eight months in 1974, income fell accordingly in Zambia, which got 94 percent of export earnings from copper. It had to cut back imports of needed goods drastically and suffered a 15 percent decline in its (already low) GDP.[11]

---

[11]Brandt, Willy, et al. *North-South: A Programme for Survival.* Cambridge, MA: MIT Press, 1980, p. 145.

Successful economic development in South Korea meant investing in moderately capital-intensive factories to manufacture such goods as TVs and cars competitively. Foreign investment, international debt, and domestic incquality all can help concentrate the necessary capital for manufacturing. Here, TV factory assembly line, South Korea.

The overall relationship between the prices of exported and imported goods—called the *terms of trade*—affects an export strategy based on raw materials. There is some evidence that in the 1950s and 1960s, and again in the 1980s, the terms of trade eroded the value of raw materials. A third-world state trying to create trade benefits by exporting such goods would have to export more and more over time in order to import the same manufactured goods—a major obstacle to accumulation.

Because of both terms of trade and price fluctuations, states have looked to exporting manufactured goods, rather than raw materials, as the key to export-led growth. However, in seeking a niche for manufactured goods, a third-world state must compete against industrialized countries with better technology, more educated workforces, and much more capital. For example, Nigeria's steel exports are unlikely to provide the desired trade surplus (although South Korean steel did so). Thus, third-world countries need to be careful and selective in developing export-oriented industrial strategies. It is not enough just to subsidize and protect an industry until it grows in size; someday it has to be able to stand its own ground in a competitive world or it will not bring in a trade surplus.

Concentrating Capital for Manufacturing

Manufacturing emerges as a key factor in both export-led growth and self-sustaining industrialization (home production for home markets). It is not surprising that third-world states want to increase their own manufacturing base and change the global division of labor based on manufacturing in the core and resource extraction in the periphery. In 1975 the UN Industrial Development Organization (UNIDO) set a goal of having 25 percent of world manufacturing occur in the South by the year 2000, compared to less than 10 percent at that time. This goal will be nowhere near met, however.

One great difficulty in getting manufacturing started is that capital is required to build factories. Competitive factories in technologically advanced industries can require large amounts of capital—such as the $5 billion for Nigeria's steel plant. Nigeria obtained much of the money from oil exports, but most third-world states lack such a source of funds.

To invest in manufacturing, these countries must *concentrate* what surplus their economies produce. They face the familiar trade-off between short-term consumption and long-term investment. Money spent building factories cannot be spent subsidizing food prices, providing make-work jobs for unemployed people, or building better schools. Thus the concentration of capital for manufacturing often sharpens disparities in income. A political price must often be paid in the short term for reducing public consumption, even in industrialized states. And in third-world states there is little margin for reducing consumption without causing extreme hardship. So the result may be crowds rioting in the streets or guerrillas taking control of the countryside.

The problem is compounded by the need to create domestic markets for manufactured goods. Because it is unlikely that a manufacturing industry in a poor country will become immediately competitive on world markets, one common strategy is to build up the industry with sales to the home market (protected by tariffs and perhaps subsidies) before pursuing world markets. But home markets for manufactured goods do not come from poor peasants in the countryside or from the unemployed youth in city slums. Rather, wealth must be concentrated in a *middle class* that has rising income to buy manufactured goods like cars or TVs.

The growing disparity of income in such a situation often triggers intense frustration on the part of poorer people, even those whose own income is slowly rising. (Again, political rebellion is fueled by relative deprivation as much as by absolute poverty.) A common way states respond to such problems is to crack down hard with force to stamp out the protests of the poor and of other political opponents of the government (see "Authoritarianism and Democracy," discussed next).

Such problems might be minimized by reducing the amount of capital that needs to be squeezed from a third-world state's domestic economy. Capital for manufacturing can come from foreign investment or foreign loans, for instance. This strategy reduces short-term pain, but it also reduces the amount of surplus (profit) available to the state in the long term. Another way to minimize the capital needs of manufacturing industry is to start out in low-capital industries. These industries can begin generating capital, which can in turn be used to move into somewhat more technologically demanding and capital-intensive kinds of manufacturing. A favorite starter industry is *textiles*. The industry is fairly labor-intensive, giving an advantage to countries with cheap labor, and does not require huge investments of capital to get started. Many third-world states have built their own textile industries as a step toward industrialization. For this reason, many states impose high tariffs on textiles, which are among the least freely traded commodities.

There are some inherent problems with concentrating capital for manufacturing. One is that it creates conditions ripe for corruption (discussed shortly). The problem is especially severe when authoritarian political control (a military government or communist state) is used to enforce compliance with the hardships that may accompany the concentration of wealth. In many cases—Brazil, Nigeria, India, China, and others—too much of the money ends up in the hands of corrupt bureaucrats (who do not invest it for future national economic growth).

A new approach that has received international attention is based on a Peruvian entrepreneur's analysis of the **informal sector** in Lima's economy—black markets, street vendors, and other private arrangements.[12] These modes of business are often beyond state control and may not even show up in state-compiled economic statistics. Markets operate rather freely, and some scholars have begun to see such markets, rather than large manufacturing industries, as the core of a new development strategy.

Authoritarianism and Democracy

Several decades ago, many scholars expected that third-world states would follow the European and North American states in economic and political development. The gradual accumulation of capital would be accompanied by the gradual extension of literacy and education, the reduction of class and gender disparities, and the strengthening of democracy and political participation. The United States could be a model for third-world development in this view. It had gone from poor colony to industrializing state to rich superpower. Political rights (including the vote) had been steadily extended to more segments of the population.[13]

In reality, however, democracy has not accompanied economic development in a systematic or general way. In fact, as was noted earlier, the fastest-growing states have generally been authoritarian states, not democracies. This has led to the theory that economic development is incompatible with democracy. According to this line of thought, political repression and the concentration of political control are necessary to maintain order during the process of concentrating capital and getting accumulation started. Demands by poor people for greater short-term consumption must be refused. Class disparities must be sharpened. Labor discipline must be enforced at extremely low wage levels. Foreign investors must be assured of political stability—above all, that radicals will not take power and that foreign assets will not be nationalized in a revolution. A democracy may be inherently incapable of accomplishing these difficult and painful tasks, according to this way of thinking.

---

[12]De Soto, Hernando. *The Other Path: The Invisible Revolution in the Third World.* New York: HarperCollins, 1989.

[13]Huntington, Samuel P. *The Third Wave: Democratization in the Late Twentieth Century.* Norman: University of Oklahoma Press, 1991. Diamond, Larry, ed. *Political Culture and Democracy in Developing Countries.* Boulder, CO: Lynne Rienner, 1993.

The NICs did not achieve their success through free and open democratic politics, but through firm state rule permitting little dissent. Chinese leaders contrast their recent economic successes, achieved under tight political control, with the failed Soviet efforts under Gorbachev to promote economic reform by first loosening political control. And when Brazil had a military coup in 1964, foreign investment increased, presumably because a military government was seen as better able to enforce stable conditions favorable to MNCs (if not to local workers, and certainly not to socialist organizers).

It has been suggested that a strong state facilitates capital accumulation.[14] Only a strong state in this view has the power to enforce and coordinate the allocations of wealth required to start accumulation going. But scholars do not agree on the definition of a strong state; some refer to the size of the state bureaucracy or its ability to extract taxes, others to its legitimacy or its ability to enforce its will on the population. The idea of a strong state is often connected with economic nationalism (see pp. 314–331), and sometimes with socialism (using the state for downward rather than upward wealth distribution, see pp. 470–472).

In reality, the theory that authoritarianism leads to economic development does not hold up, just as the theory that democracy automatically accompanies economic development does not hold up. Many authoritarian states have achieved neither political stability nor economic development. Others have realized political stability but have failed at economic accumulation. The many military dictatorships in Africa are among the least successful models in the third world. In Latin America, the poorest country, Haiti, had the most authoritarian government for decades. As was shown by the Philippines under Marcos, an absolute dictatorship invites absolute corruption, with the potential to drain away the state's surplus for personal gain. By contrast, in relatively democratic Brazil in 1992, the president could be removed before stealing nearly as much as Marcos did. In both Brazil and Argentina, democratization in the 1980s was eventually followed by financial progress in increased growth in the mid-1990s.

Furthermore, authoritarian states can lead to greater political instability, not less. The harder the state cracks down, the more resentment the population feels. Instead of peaceful protests, violent insurgencies often grow out of such resentments. In Guatemala (Central America), for example, a military government has harshly repressed rural revolutionaries and their peasant sympathizers for decades. Since the 1960s, in this country of 9 million, repression and war have killed 100,000 people, and another 45,000 have "disappeared" (suspected dissidents are taken away by the military or by "death squads" and never heard from again; most are killed and buried in mass graves).[15] Guatemala's government has at times received substantial U.S. aid (based on "anticommunism") and at other times been banned from receiving such aid (based on violations of "human rights"). But after several decades its authoritarian rule has not stopped dissent, brought political stability, attracted much foreign investment, or created much economic accumulation.

[14]Evans, Peter B., Dietrich Rueschemeyer, and Theda Skocpol, eds. *Bringing the State Back In*. New York: Cambridge University Press, 1985. Krasner, Stephen D. *Structural Conflict: The Third World Against Global Liberalism*. Berkeley: University of California Press, 1985.

[15]Human Rights Watch World Report 1990. Cited in *Science* 257, July 24, 1992: 479.

Meanwhile, elsewhere in Latin America a wave of civilian governments replaced military ones in the late 1980s.[16] Economic conditions there have improved, not worsened, as a result. In states like South Korea and Taiwan, which began industrializing under authoritarianism but have since shifted toward democracy, economic progress was not harmed. Relatively free elections and tolerance of dissent signaled greater stability and maturity, and did not discourage investment or slow economic growth (although the 1992 world recession did).

It has been suggested that authoritarian rule and the concentration of income in few hands represent a phase in the development process. First, capital must be concentrated to get accumulation started, and tight political control must be maintained during this painful phase. Later, more wealth is generated, income spreads to more people, the middle class expands, and political controls can be relaxed. Peru in the early 1990s provides an example of this authoritarian-phase model compressed in time. President Alberto Fujimori was elected in 1990, ten years into an increasingly bloody war with Maoist guerrillas (feeding partly on Peru's income inequality) that had choked off foreign investment and tourism. Meanwhile, government mismanagement, corruption, and military abuses (and the war) had driven inflation to over 7000 percent in 1990. Fujimori suspended Peru's democracy and its Congress, seizing authoritarian powers to prosecute the war against the guerrillas and stem government corruption and inflation. The guerrilla leader was captured in 1992 and the rebellion largely suppressed; meanwhile inflation dropped sharply in 1991 and came down to 15 percent by 1994. Fujimori restored democratic institutions, liberalized rules for foreign investment, and reduced state-owned industry from 35 percent to 5 percent of the economy in 1992–1994. As a result, in 1994 foreign investment nearly doubled in one year and Peru's economy grew at a world-record 12 percent rate. Fujimori easily won reelection in 1995.

But again, the empirical reality does not support such a theory as a general rule. There is no guarantee that, even in the early phases of accumulation, authoritarian control leads to economic development. If anything, flagrant human rights abuses seem to cause political instability at any stage of economic development. Some successful accumulators, such as China and Saudi Arabia, have maintained tight political control throughout the process. Others, such as South Korea and Turkey, have started with authoritarian rule and evolved into democracies. Still others, such as Costa Rica and Malaysia, have achieved good economic results while maintaining relative democracy and little repression. Similarly, among the countries that have done poorly in economic accumulation one finds both authoritarian regimes and democratic ones. Therefore, a state's form of political governance does not determine its success in economic development.

Corruption

Corruption is an important negative factor in economic development in many states; corruption also plays a role in some of the theories just discussed about various strategies for using trade, industry, and government to promote economic development.

---

[16]O'Donnell, Guillermo, Philippe C. Schmitter, and Lawrence Whitehead, eds. *Transitions from Authoritarian Rule: Prospects for Democracy* [series]. Baltimore: Johns Hopkins University Press, 1986. Reilly, Charles A., ed. *New Paths to Democratic Development in Latin America: The Rise of NGO-Municipal Collaboration.* Boulder, CO: Lynne Rienner, 1995. Przeworski, Adam. *Democracy and the Market: Political and Economic Reforms in Eastern Europe and Latin America.* New York: Cambridge University Press, 1991.

Corruption centers on the government as the central actor in economic development, especially in its international aspects. Through foreign policy, the government mediates the national economy's relationship to the world economy. The government regulates the conditions under which MNCs operate in the country. It enforces worker discipline—calling out the army if necessary to break strikes or suppress revolutions. It sets tax rates and wields other macroeconomic levers of control over the economy. And in most third-world states it owns a sizable stake in major industries—a monopoly in some cases.

Government officials, ranging from the state leader to the petty bureaucrat or police officer in a remote province, have power to shape the process of accumulation. Their approval or disapproval can determine whether an MNC can drill a new oil well, whether a trader (or smuggler) can import foreign goods, or which local capitalist gets a contract to build a bridge. With such power comes a great temptation for corruption.

Corruption is a kind of privatization of politics in that it concerns the distribution of benefits from economic transactions (exchange and capital accumulation). For example, when a foreign MNC comes into a country to drill for oil, the surplus produced will be shared among the MNC (through profits), the state (through taxation and fees), the local capitalists who make money supplying the operation, the local workers who earn wages, and the foreign consumers who use the oil (which, due to the added supply, will be slightly cheaper on world markets).

Corruption is a major impediment to third-world development. Brazil's President Collor promised to clean up government corruption but resigned from office (here, 1992) after being implicated in a corruption scandal involving payoffs funneled through his wife (in photo).

State officials will decide whether to let the MNC into the country, which MNC to give the drilling rights to, and what terms to insist on (leasing fees, percentages of sales, etc.). These are complex deals struck after long negotiations. Corruption merely adds another player, the corrupt official, to share the benefits. For instance, a foreign oil company can pay off an official to award a favorable contract, and both can profit.

Corruption is by no means limited to the third world. But for several reasons corruption has a deeper effect in poor countries. First, there is simply less surplus around to keep economic growth going; accumulation is fragile. (In rich countries, accumulation is more robust and can withstand some corruption without grinding to a halt.) Another difference is that in those third-world countries dependent on exporting a few products, the revenue arrives in a very concentrated form—large payments in hard currency. This presents a greater opportunity for corruption than in a more diversified economy with more (smaller) deals. Furthermore, in third-world countries incomes are often so low that corrupt officials are more tempted to accept payments. In industrialized countries officials tend to live reasonably well, and only the greedier among them will risk being caught at corruption.

Occasionally, government officials serve not their own private interests but those of a foreign state. Such a government is called a *puppet government*. The officials of such a government (sometimes just a single dictator) are bought off to serve the interests of a more powerful state (which may have installed the government through military conquest). For example, the government installed in Afghanistan after the Soviet invasion was considered a puppet of the Soviet Union. Certain Latin American dictators were once considered to be in the pocket of the United States. During the Cold War, both superpowers justified installing friendly governments by reference to global power politics. Critics, however, believed the puppet governments served business interests of the controlling state, not security interests. This and other issues concern the role of international business in third-world accumulation.

❖ NORTH-SOUTH BUSINESS

Given the importance of international trade and investment to third-world economic development, not only governments but private banks and MNCs from the North are major participants in the economies of the South. (Several large third-world states have also managed to create their own MNCs, though these play a fairly minor role compared to MNCs from the North.)

Foreign Investment

Poor countries have little money available to invest in new factories, farms, mines, or oil wells. Foreign investment—investment in such capital goods by foreigners (most often MNCs)—is one way to get accumulation started (see "Direct Foreign Investment" on pp. 376–378). Foreigners then own the facilities; the investor by virtue of its ownership can control decisions about how many people to employ, whether to expand or shut down, what products to make, and how to market them. Also, the foreign investor can usually take the profits from the operation out of the country (repatriation of profits). However, the host government can share in the wealth by charging fees and taxes, or by leasing land or drilling rights (see "Host and Home Government Relations" on pp. 378–382).

Because of past colonial experiences, many third-world governments have feared the loss of control that comes with foreign investments by MNCs.[17] Sometimes the presence of MNCs was associated with the painful process of concentrating capital and the sharpening of class disparities in the host state. Although such fears remain, they are counterbalanced in most third-world states by the ability of foreign investors to infuse capital and generate more surplus. By the 1980s and 1990s, as models based on autarky or state ownership were discredited and the NICs gained success, many poor states rushed to embrace foreign investment.

One way in which states have sought to soften the loss of control implicit in foreign investment is through *joint ventures*. These are companies owned partly by a foreign MNC and partly by a local firm or the host government itself. Sometimes foreign ownership in joint ventures is limited to some percentage (often 49 percent), to ensure that ultimate control rests with the host country even though a large share of the profits go to the MNC. The percentage of ownership is usually proportional to the amount of capital invested, so if a host government wants more control it must put up more of the money. Joint ventures work well for MNCs because they help ensure the host government's cooperation in reducing bureaucratic hassles and ensuring success (by giving the host government a direct stake in the outcome).

MNCs invest in a country because of some advantage of doing business there. In some cases it is the presence of minerals or other natural resources. Sometimes it is cheap labor. Sometimes geographical location is a factor. Some states have better *absorptive capacity* than others—the ability to put investments to productive use—because of more highly developed infrastructure and a higher level of skills among workers or managers. These are most often middle-income states, so the funneling of investments to states with high absorptive capacity tends to sharpen disparities *within* the third world.

MNCs also look for a favorable *regulatory environment* in which a host state will facilitate, rather than impede, the MNC's business. For example, Motorola had decided to invest well over $1 billion in new facilities in India in the 1990s, but changed its mind after encountering India's bureaucracy and shifted its investments toward China instead.[18]

MNC decisions about foreign investment also depend on prospects for *financial stability*, especially for low inflation and stable currency exchange rates. If a currency is not convertible into hard currency, an MNC will not be able to take profits back to its home state or reinvest them elsewhere.

Beyond these financial considerations, a foreign investor producing for local markets wants to know that the host country's *economic growth* will sustain demand for the goods being produced. Similarly, whether producing for local consumption or export, the MNC wants the local *labor* supply—whether it is semiskilled labor or just cheap labor—to be stable. Foreign investors often look to international financial institutions, such as the World Bank and the IMF, and to private analyses, to judge a state's economic stability before investing in it.

Of equal importance in attracting investment is *political stability* (see pp. 382–384). Banks and MNCs conduct *political risk analyses* to assess the risks of political disturbances in third-world states in which they might invest.

---

[17]Biersteker, Thomas. *Multinationals, the State and Control of the Nigerian Economy.* Princeton: Princeton University Press, 1987.

[18]See footnote 9 in this chapter.

Foreign investment is an important source of capital for economic development in the global South. But the relationship of foreign investors and host countries transcends economics and draws in culture, politics, and identity. This man in Shanghai, the historical (and perhaps future) center of foreign economic penetration in China, ponders the choice of Pepsi or 7-Up.

Host countries for their part seek to assure potential foreign investors that they are stable political environments in which investments will not be at risk. For example, foreign states occasionally take out pages of advertising in U.S. newspapers to promote their country as a site for investment. Sometimes these appeals coincide with a summit meeting, as when Pakistan's Benazir Bhutto visited the United States in 1995. Or they may follow events in the host country. For example, in 1992 the military government of Thailand, a would-be NIC in Asia, suppressed student protests in Bangkok, shooting hundreds dead. Within months, the revamped Thai government took out an expensive double-page ad in the *New York Times* titled "Thailand: Still on Track." The ad played up the king and queen, who had mediated between the military and students and who represented national stability. It quoted top officials of Monsanto (an MNC) and Citicorp (an international bank) expressing confidence in Thailand. It declared that the recent "events" (or "tragedy") had resolved the inevitable political tension that comes with economic growth and had now been put behind. The ad stated that "Thailand is inherently politically stable." The prime minister reassured readers that, despite 16 coups in the past forty years, "Thailand was not much affected" by them. Although "politicians and military figures came and went, . . . they were not material to what was a rather stable process" of economic growth, internationalization, and market-oriented reform. Such ads reflect the importance of political stability for foreign investments.

Beyond their usual role in providing foreign investment, technology transfer, and loans (in the case of banks)—all in the normal course of business and all with the expectation of future repayment or profit—MNCs also sometimes participate in more broadly conceived development projects in a host state. This is a way of investing in political goodwill as well as helping provide political stability by improving the condition of the population. It is good business practice to build positive, cooperative relationships with third-world states in which the MNC does business. The attitude of the government and the goodwill of the population affect the overall business prospects of the MNC. In the long run, blatant exploitation is not the most profitable way to do business.

For example, consider the operations of Conoco, a U.S.-based oil company, in the poor oil-exporting African state of Angola. Areas of potential offshore oil production are leased by the Angolan government to foreign oil companies, which then explore for oil and tap any commercially viable finds. The MNCs typically pay for the right to explore and then share the revenues of the oil extracted (if any) with the government. Negotiations over the terms of such leases tend to be complex, and there is strong competition among MNCs from around the world, some of which are state-owned oil companies (from France, Brazil, and elsewhere) that can get their governments to offer favors such as military aid to Angola.

In this environment, Conoco in the late 1980s realized it was at a disadvantage compared to its global competitors, particularly because Conoco's home government was supporting armed rebels against the Angolan government. (To make matters worse, Conoco's parent company, the Du Pont chemical company, has been targeted by Greenpeace because it produces ozone-destroying CFCs.) Another disadvantage was Conoco's unwillingness to bribe Angolan officials to secure contracts (a philosophy that its competitors did not always share).

What leverage could Conoco employ to gain an edge in this bargaining situation? Conoco decided to use development assistance to local communities as a kind of legal bribe in lease negotiations. Give us the lease, said Conoco, and we will fund specific development projects such as schools. A politician would not gain personal income from such a scheme but would win political capital in local communities.

The Angolan government accepted several such proposals, and Conoco won several offshore leases. As it turned out, a few years later under the agreement to end the Angolan civil war, the government politicians found themselves standing for election for the first time. Popular goodwill turned out to be a good investment for the ruling party, which won the elections. (The happy outcome of this case did not, unfortunately, lead to a happy end to the story overall. The civil war resumed when rebels rejected the election results, and as often happens in the risky business of oil exploration, Conoco's leases did not lead to commercially viable oil discoveries.)

Technology Transfer

The productive investment of capital depends on the knowledge and skills—business management, technical training, higher education, as well as basic literacy and education—of workers and managers. Of special importance are the management and technical skills related to the key industries in a state's economy. Recall that in many former colonies, whites with such skills left after independence (see "Postcolonial Dependency" on pp. 482–484). In other states the skills needed to develop new industries have never existed. A few states in the Persian Gulf with very large incomes and small populations have imported a whole workforce from foreign countries. But this is rare.

Most third-world states seek to build up their own educated elite with knowledge and skills to run the national economy. One way to do so is to send students to industrialized states for higher education. This entails some risks, however. Students may enjoy life in the North and fail to return home. In most third-world countries, every student talented enough to study abroad represents a national resource and usually a long investment (in primary and secondary education), which is lost if the student emigrates and does not return. The same applies to professionals (for example, doctors or architects) who emigrate later in their careers. The problem of losing skilled workers to richer countries is called the **brain drain.** It has impeded economic development in such states as India, Pakistan, Sri Lanka, the Philippines, and China.

Technology transfer refers to a third-world state's acquisition of technology (knowledge, skills, methods, designs, specialized equipment, and so on) from foreign sources, usually in conjunction with direct foreign investment or similar business operations. For example, a third-world state may allow an MNC to produce certain goods in the country under favorable conditions, provided the MNC shares knowledge of the technology and design behind the product. The state may try to get its own citizens into the management and professional workforce of factories or facilities created by foreign investment. In this way not only does physical capital accumulate in the country, so does the related technological base for further development. However, MNCs are sometimes reluctant to share proprietary technology.

Technology transfer sometimes encounters difficulty when the technological style of the source country does not fit the needs of the recipient country. A good fit has been called *appropriate technology*.[19] In particular, the Soviet Union was fond of creating the "world's largest" factory of some type, and it tended to apply the same overly centralized approach to its investments and development projects in the third world (such as the huge Nigerian steel plant mentioned earlier). Furthermore, technology that seemed useful to bureaucrats in Moscow might not be appropriate to a recipient country; in 1960 the Soviets sent snowplows to the tropical country of Guinea.[20]

The **green revolution**—a massive transfer of agricultural technology coordinated through international agencies—deserves special mention.[21] This effort, which began in the 1960s, transplanted a range of agricultural technologies from rich countries to poor ones—new seed strains, fertilizers, tractors to replace oxen, and so forth. The green revolution increased crop yields in a number of states, especially in Asia, and helped food supplies keep up with growing populations.

---

[19]Betz, Matthew J., Pat McGowan, and Rolf T. Wigand, eds. *Appropriate Technology: Choice and Development*. Durham: Duke University Press, 1984. Jequier, Nicolas, ed. *Appropriate Technology: Problems and Promises*. Paris: OECD, 1976.

[20]Legvold, Robert. *Soviet Policy in West Africa*. Cambridge, MA: Harvard University Press, 1970, p. 124.

[21]Alauddin, Mohammed, and Clement Tisdell. *The "Green Revolution" and Economic Development: The Process and Its Development in Bangladesh*. New York: St. Martin's Press, 1991.

However, it did have drawbacks. Critics said the green revolution made recipients dependent on imported technologies like tractors and oil, that it damaged the environment with commercial pesticides and fertilizers, and that it disrupted traditional agriculture (driving more people off the land and into cities). Environmental reactions to the green revolution—including the emergence of pesticide resistance in insect populations—have led to recent declines in crop yields, forcing changes in the green revolution.[22]

For example, in Indonesia pesticides introduced in the green revolution created resistant strains of a rice parasite and killed off the parasite's natural predators. The pesticides also polluted water supplies. Recognizing the need to adapt imported technologies to local needs, the Indonesian government banned most pesticides in 1986 and adopted organic methods instead. In recent years the Food and Agriculture Organization (FAO) has spread information about organic pest control through traditional village theater plays. Pesticide usage has declined sharply while rice production has increased.

Meanwhile, on the Indonesian island of Bali, "water priests" traditionally controlled the allocation of scarce water resources to agriculture. In the green revolution, such practices were often dismissed as superstitious nonsense and replaced with modern water-allocation schemes. But the water priests actually had more experience with local conditions over many years, and more legitimacy with the local farmers, than did the foreign experts. A U.S. anthropologist recently developed graphical software for Macintosh computers that the water priests could use to gain access to technical information about water supplies without sacrificing their own experience and authority.

In the 1990s, states in the North are focusing on technology transfer that promotes *environmentally sustainable development* (see pp. 428–429). Japan's MITI-funded International Center for Environmental Technology Transfer hopes to train 10,000 people from third-world countries, over ten years, in energy conservation, pollution control, and other environmental technologies. Japan also hosts the International Environmental Technology Center, a project of the UN Environment Program (UNEP). Among other motives, Japan hopes these projects will encourage developing countries to choose Japanese technology and products.[23]

Third-World Debt

Borrowing money is an alternative to foreign investment as a way of obtaining funds to prime a cycle of economic accumulation. If accumulation succeeds, it produces enough surplus to repay the loan and still make a profit. Borrowing has several advantages. It keeps control in the hands of the state (or other local borrower) and does not impose painful sacrifices on local citizens, at least in the short term.

Debt has its disadvantages too. The borrower must service the debt—making regular payments of interest and repaying the principal according to the terms of the loan. **Debt service** is a constant drain on whatever surplus is generated by the investment of the money. With direct foreign investment, a money-losing venture is the problem of the for-

---

[22]*Science* 256, May 22, 1992: 1140. *Science* 256, May 29, 1992: 1272.
[23]*Science* 256, May 22, 1992: 1145.

Under pressure of debt, IMF conditionality, and other constraints on state finances, many third-world governments are privatizing state-owned enterprises, including large development projects. This privatized toll road runs from Cuernavaca to Acapulco, Mexico (1994).

eign MNC; with debt, such a failure is the problem of the borrowing state (which must find the money elsewhere). Not infrequently, a debtor must borrow new funds to service old loans, slipping ever further into debt.

The failure to make scheduled payments is called a **default** and is considered a drastic action because it destroys lenders' confidence and results in future loans being cut off. Rather than defaulting, borrowers try to **renegotiate** their debts with lenders, coming up with a mutually acceptable payment scheme to keep at least some money flowing to the lender. If interest rates have fallen since a loan was first taken out, the borrower can refinance (just as home buyers do with their mortgages). Borrowers and lenders can also negotiate to restructure a debt by changing the length of the loan (usually to a longer payback period) or the other terms. Occasionally state-to-state loans are written off altogether—forgiven—for political reasons, as happened with U.S. loans to Egypt after the Gulf War.

Third-world debt encompasses several types of lending relationships, all of which are influenced by international politics. The borrower may be a private firm or bank in a third-world country, or it may be the government itself. Loans to the government are somewhat more common because lenders consider the government less likely to default than a private borrower. The *lender* may be a private bank or company, or a state (both are important). Usually banks are more insistent on receiving timely payments and firmer in renegotiating debts than are states. Some state-to-state loans are made on artificially favorable *concessionary* terms, in effect subsidizing economic development in the borrowing state. For instance, a rich state may lend money to a poor ally at little or no interest, with a long repayment period.

In the 1970s and 1980s, many third-world states borrowed heavily from banks and states in the North, which encouraged the borrowing. The anticipated growth often did not materialize. In oil-exporting states like Venezuela and Mexico, for instance, price declines reduced export earnings with which states planned to repay the loans. Other exporting states found that protectionist measures in the North, combined with a global economic slowdown, limited their ability to export. Sometimes borrowed funds were simply not spent wisely and produced too little surplus to service the debt.

As a result, by the 1980s a *third-world debt crisis* had developed, particularly in Latin America.[24] Many third-world states could not generate enough export earnings to service their debts, much less to repay them—not to speak of retaining some surplus to generate sustained local accumulation. Major states of the global South like Brazil, Mexico, and India found foreign debt a tremendous weight on economic development (see Table 13.1).

Many private banks in industrialized countries had overextended themselves with loans that third-world states could not repay, and some economists worried that the banking system in the North could collapse. But the banking system rode out this crisis, writing off a portion of the uncollectible debts each year. Banks sold off the debts at a discount, which means that a buyer might pay, for example, $5 million to buy an IOU from Brazil for $10 million. The buyer would then try to settle the debt with Brazil for somewhat more than $5 million (forgiving the rest) or renegotiate a plan to service the debt at lower interest or better terms than the original debt. There is now a *secondary market* in third-world debts, and the financial pages of newspapers show the prevailing rates that people will pay to buy each state's debts. From 1986 to 1989 the average price for the bank debts of 15 heavily indebted countries in this secondary market dropped from 65 percent of face value to 30 percent. In the worst cases, holders of debts of some poor states could not unload them for more than 1 cent on the dollar. (By 1991 the average was back to 45 percent of face value.)[25]

Debt renegotiation has become a perennial occupation of third-world states. Brazil had to do so three times in a decade, in the 1980s and early 1990s. Such renegotiations are complex international bargaining situations, like international trade or arms control negotiations but with more parties. The various lenders—private banks and states—try to extract as much as they can, and the borrower tries to hold out for more favorable terms.

---

[24]Jorge, Antonio, and Jorge Salazar-Carrillo, eds. *The Latin American Debt*. New York: St. Martin's Press, 1992. Frieden, Jeffry A. *Debt, Development, and Democracy: Modern Political Economy and Latin America, 1965–1985*. Princeton: Princeton University Press, 1992. Kahler, Miles, ed. *The Politics of International Debt*. Ithaca: Cornell University Press, 1986. Bradshaw, York W., and Ana-Maria Wahl. Foreign Debt Expansion, the International Monetary Fund, and Regional Variation in Third World Poverty. *International Studies Quarterly* 35 (3), 1991: 251–72. Wood, Robert E. *From Marshall Plan to Debt Crisis: Foreign Aid and Development Choices in the World Economy*. Berkeley: University of California Press, 1986.

[25]United Nations. *World Economic Survey 1992*. New York: United Nations, p. 80.

TABLE 13.1 THIRD-WORLD DEBT, 1991

	Foreign Debt		Annual Debt Service	
Region	*Billion $*	*% of GDP*	*Billion $*	*% of Exports*
Latin America	445	37%	48	29%
Asia	440	26%	58	9%
Africa	275	100%	27	26%
Other	100	—	15	—
Total "South"	1260	36%	148	16%

Notes: Regions do not exactly match those used elsewhere in this book. Africa here includes North Africa. Asia includes China.
Source: Based on IMF, OECD, and World Bank data compiled by UN and listed in United Nations. *World Economic Survey 1992.* New York: United Nations, pp. 224–27.

If a borrowing government accepts terms that are too burdensome, it may lose popularity at home; the local population and opposition politicians may accuse it of selling out to foreigners, neocolonialists, and so on. But if the borrowing state does not give enough to gain the agreement of the lenders, it might have to default and lose out on future loans and investments, which could greatly impede economic growth.

For the lenders, debt renegotiations involve a collective goods problem: all of them have to agree on the conditions of the renegotiation but each really cares only about getting its own money back. To solve this problem, state creditors meet together periodically as the **Paris Club,** and private creditors as the **London Club,** to work out their terms.

Through such renegotiations, and the corresponding write-offs of debts by banks, third-world states have largely avoided defaulting on their debts. Some large states have threatened (overtly or subtly) to default—or even to lead a coalition of third-world states all defaulting at once—but ultimately have backed off from such threats. Default is a risky course because of the integrated nature of the world economy, the need for foreign investment and foreign trade in order to accumulate wealth, and the risks of provoking international confrontations with more powerful states. Lenders too have always proven willing to absorb losses in the end rather than push a borrower over the edge and risk financial instability. Through various efforts, including the *Baker Plan* and *Brady Plan* in the 1980s (named after the U.S. treasury secretaries who proposed them), and the work of multilateral institutions like the World Bank and the IMF, the third-world debt situation had stabilized somewhat by the early 1990s.

Despite this recent improvement, third-world states have not yet solved the debt problem. As shown in Table 13.1, the South in 1991 owed over $1.2 trillion in foreign debt, and paid about $150 billion a year to service that debt. The debt service (in hard currency) absorbed more than one-quarter of the entire hard-currency export earnings in Latin America and Africa—the regions most affected. Africa's debt was equal to the annual GDP of the region. Asia had less-serious debt problems, especially relative to the region's exports, but particular states were hard hit there as well.

IMF Conditionality

The International Monetary Fund (IMF) and the World Bank have a large supply of capital from their member states (see "The World Bank and the IMF" on pp. 362–365). This capital plays an important role in funding the early stages of accumulation in third-world states and in helping developing countries get through short periods of great difficulty (such as a drought, bad harvest, or recession). Furthermore, as a political entity rather than a bank, the IMF can make funds available on favorable terms.

The IMF does not give away money indiscriminately. Quite the opposite, it scrutinizes third-world states' economic plans and policies, withholding loans until it is satisfied that the right policies are in place. Then it makes loans to help states through the transitional process of implementing the IMF-approved policies. The IMF also sends important signals to private lenders and investors: The IMF's approval of a state's economic plans is a "seal of approval" that bankers and MNCs use to help assess the wisdom of investing in that state. For all these reasons the IMF wields great power to influence the economic policies of third-world states.

An agreement to loan IMF funds on the condition that certain government policies are adopted is called an **IMF conditionality** agreement.[26] Dozens of third-world states have entered into such agreements with the IMF in the past two decades. The terms insisted on by the IMF are usually painful for the citizens (and hence for national politicians). The IMF demands that inflation be brought under control, which requires reducing state spending and closing budget deficits. This often spurs unemployment and requires that subsidies of food and basic goods be reduced or eliminated. Short-term consumption is curtailed in favor of longer-term investment. Surplus must be concentrated to service debt and invest in new capital accumulation. The IMF wants to ensure that money lent to a country is not frittered away on politically popular but economically unwise purposes. It wants to ensure that inflation does not eat away all progress and that the economy is stable enough to attract investment. In addition, the IMF demands steps to curtail corruption.

Because of the pain inflicted by a conditionality agreement—and to some extent by any debt renegotiation agreement—such agreements are often politically unpopular in the third world.[27] On quite a few occasions, a conditionality agreement has brought rioters into the streets demanding the restoration of subsidies for food, gasoline, and other essential goods. Sometimes governments have backed out of the agreement or have broken their promises (partly or totally) under such pressure. Occasionally, governments have been toppled. As a Peruvian economist noted in 1992, "You can reduce the debt, but is it worth it? [Terms are] too harsh, and it results in mass unemployment and the abandonment of any kind of social program."[28] In a country like Peru, facing a violent leftist guerrilla war that fed on mass poverty, such a choice was especially difficult.

---

[26]Williamson, John, ed. *IMF Conditionality*. Washington, DC: Institute for International Economics, 1983. Biersteker, Thomas J. Reducing the Role of the State in the Economy: A Conceptual Exploration of IMF and World Bank Prescriptions. *International Studies Quarterly* 34 (4), 1990: 477–92.

[27]Haggard, Stephan, and Robert R. Kaufman, eds. *The Politics of Economic Adjustment: International Constraints, Distributive Conflicts, and the State*. Princeton: Princeton University Press, 1992. Sidell, Scott R. *The IMF and Third-World Political Instability: Is There a Connection?* New York: St. Martin's Press, 1988.

[28]Nash, Nathaniel C. Latin Debt Load Keeps Climbing Despite Accords. *The New York Times*, August 1, 1992: 40.

The IMF formula for stability and success is remarkably universal from one country to the next. When the IMF negotiated terms for economic assistance to Russia and the former Soviet republics in the early 1990s, the conditions were similar to those for any third-world state: cut inflation, cut government spending, cut subsidies, crack down on corruption. Critics of the IMF argue that it does not adapt its program adequately to account for differences in the local cultural and economic conditions in different states. (It is interesting to note that the United States since the 1980s would not qualify for IMF assistance because it has not found the political will to cut the government deficit.)

The South in International Economic Regimes

Because of the need for capital and the wealth created by international trade, most third-world states now see their future economic development as resting on a close interconnection with the world economy, not on national autarky or third-world regional economic communities. This means that third-world states must play by the rules embedded in international economic regimes, as discussed in Chapters 8 and 9.

The GATT trading regime tends to work against third-world states relative to industrialized ones. A free-trade regime makes it harder for poor states to protect infant industries in order to build self-sufficient capital accumulation. It forces competition with more technologically advanced states. A poor state can be competitive only in low-wage, low-capital niches—especially those using natural resources that are scarce in the North, like tropical agriculture, extractive (mining and drilling) industries, and textiles.

Yet just these economic sectors in which third-world states have comparative advantages on world markets—agriculture and textiles in particular—are largely excluded from the free-trade rules of the GATT (see pp. 340–342). The GATT instead has concentrated on free trade in manufactured goods, in which states in the North have comparative advantages. As a result, some third-world states find that they are expected to open their home markets to foreign products, against which home industries are not competitive, yet their own export products are shut out of foreign markets.

To compensate for this inequity and help third-world states use trade to boost their economic growth, the GATT created the Generalized System of Preferences (p. 340). These and other measures—such as the Lomé conventions in which EU states relaxed tariffs on third-world goods—are exceptions to the overall rules of trade, intended to ensure that participation in world trade advances rather than impedes third-world development.[29] Nonetheless, critics claim that third-world states are the losers in the overall world trading regime.

The World Bank came under criticism on its fiftieth anniversary in 1994. A coalition of activist groups including Greenpeace and Oxfam America accused the Bank of supporting authoritarian regimes and underwriting huge infrastructure projects (like dams) that displaced poor people. Critics alleged that the Bank's portfolio of loans in the global South, totaling well over $100 billion, was more a hindrance than a help to true develop-

---

[29]Tussie, Diana, and David J. Glover, eds. *The Developing Countries in World Trade: Policies and Bargaining Strategies.* Boulder, CO: Lynne Rienner, 1993. Ravenhill, John. *Collective Clientelism: The Lomé Conventions and North-South Relations.* New York: Columbia University Press, 1985.

ment. Bank officials responded that despite a few mistakes and some management inefficiency, the Bank and its mission were sound.

The tenuous position of the third world in international economic regimes reflects
the role of power in IR. The global North, with two-thirds of the world's wealth, clearly
has more power—more effective leverage—than the South. The global disparity of power
is accentuated by the fact that the South is split up into over a hundred actors whereas
the North's power is concentrated in seven large states (the G7 members). Thus, when
the rules of the world economy were created after World War II, and as they have been
rewritten and adjusted over the years, the main actors shaping the outcome have been a
handful of large industrialized states.

Third-world states have responded in several ways to these problems with world economic regimes. In the 1970s, OPEC shifted the terms of trade for oil—bringing huge
amounts of capital into the oil exporting countries. Some third-world states hoped such
successes could be repeated for other commodities, resulting in broad gains for the third
world, but this did not occur (see "Cartels" on pp. 344–346 and "Minerals, Land, Water"
on pp. 446–449).

Also in the 1970s, many third-world states tried to form a broad political coalition to
push for restructuring the world economy so as to make North-South economic transactions more favorable to the South. A summit meeting of the nonaligned movement (see
p. 91) in 1973 first called for a **New International Economic Order (NIEO).**[30] Central
to the NIEO was a shift in the terms of trade to favor primary commodities relative to
manufactured goods. The NIEO proposal also called for the promotion of industrialization in the third world, and for increased development assistance from the North.

The NIEO never became much more than a rallying cry for the global South, however—partly because of the South's lack of power in world politics, and partly because disparities within the South created divergent interests among states there. In the 1980s, in
fact, the terms of trade further deteriorated for raw material exporters, and (as we have
seen) economic development slowed down in much of the third world. But in China and
some other Asian countries, development accelerated.

Third-world states have continued to pursue proposals to restructure world trade to
benefit the South. These efforts now take place mainly through the **UN Conference on
Trade and Development (UNCTAD),** which meets periodically but lacks power to implement major changes in North-South economic relations.[31] Recurrent attempts to promote South-South trade (reducing dependence on the North) have proven largely impractical. Efforts continue, however, to boost third-world cooperation and solidarity
through a variety of groups like the nonaligned movement and the UN.[32] Nonetheless,
such efforts have done little to change the South's reliance on assistance from the North.

[30]Murphy, Craig N. *The Emergence of the NIEO Ideology.* Boulder, CO: Westview, 1984. Galtung, Johan. *The
North/South Debate: Technology, Basic Human Needs, and the New International Economic Order.* New York: Institute for World Order, 1980.

[31]Williams, Marc. *Third World Cooperation: The Group of 77 in UNCTAD.* New York: St. Martin's Press, 1991.
Weiss, Thomas G. *Multilateral Development Diplomacy in UNCTAD.* New York: St. Martin's Press, 1986.

[32]Folke, Steen, Niels Fold, and Thyge Enevoldsen. *South-South Trade and Development: Manufacturers in the New
International Division of Labour.* New York: St. Martin's Press, 1993. Bobiash, Donald. *South-South Aid: How Developing Countries Help Each Other.* New York: St. Martin's Press, 1992. Erisman, H. Michael. *Pursuing Postdepen-
dency Politics: South-South Relations in the Caribbean.* Boulder, CO: Lynne Rienner, 1992.

❖ FOREIGN ASSISTANCE

Foreign assistance (or *overseas development assistance*) is money or other aid made available to third-world states in order to help them speed up economic development or simply meet basic humanitarian needs.[33] Along with the commercial economic activities just discussed (investments and loans), foreign assistance is a second major source of money for third-world development. It covers a variety of programs—from individual volunteers lending a hand to massive government packages—in which money or some other form of value flows from North to South. (A special case not involving the North is development funding distributed by Middle East oil-producing states, for instance through the Arab Development Bank.)

Different kinds of development assistance have different purposes. Some are humanitarian in nature, some are political, and others are intended to create future economic advantages for the giver (these purposes often overlap). The state or organization that gives assistance is called a *donor,* and the state or organization receiving the aid is the *recipient.* Foreign assistance creates, or extends, a relationship between donor and recipient that is simultaneously political and cultural as well as economic.[34] Foreign assistance can be a form of power in which the donor seeks to influence the recipient, or it can be a form of interdependence in which the donor and recipient create a mutually beneficial exchange.

Patterns of Foreign Assistance

The majority of foreign assistance comes from governments in the North. Table 13.2 lists the contributions of major donors toward the $60 billion in governmental foreign assistance provided in 1992. (Private donations provided an additional $10 billion.) Over 95 percent of government assistance comes from members of the **Development Assistance Committee (DAC),** consisting of states from Western Europe, North America, and Japan/Pacific. Several oil-exporting Arab countries provide some foreign development assistance as well.

The DAC countries have set themselves a goal to contribute 0.7 percent of their GDPs in foreign aid. But overall they give less than half this amount. Only Norway, Sweden, Denmark, and the Netherlands meet the target. France is close.

The United States gives the lowest percentage of GDP—one-seventh of 1 percent—of any of the 25 states of the industrialized West that make up the OECD. In total economic aid given ($10 billion), the United States had already slipped behind Japan ($11 billion) in 1993—a disparity heightened by the drop of the dollar relative to the yen in 1994–1995. In 1995, as the U.S. Congress was considering further cuts in foreign aid budgets, the OECD issued a report strongly criticizing the low level of U.S. foreign aid.

---

[33]Hook, Steven W. *National Interest and Foreign Aid.* Boulder, CO: Lynne Rienner, 1995. Krueger, Anne O., Constantine Michalopoulos, and Vernon W. Ruttan. *Aid and Development.* Baltimore: Johns Hopkins University Press, 1989. Smith, Brian H. *More Than Altruism: The Politics of Private Foreign Aid.* Princeton: Princeton University Press, 1990.

[34]Ensign, Margee M. *Doing Good or Doing Well? Japan's Foreign Aid Program.* New York: Columbia University Press, 1992. Orr, Robert M., Jr. *The Emergence of Japan's Foreign Aid Power.* New York: Columbia University Press, 1990.

TABLE 13.2 WHO'S HELPING?

Foreign Assistance, 1992

Donor	Assistance Given	
	Billion $	% of GDP
United States	11.7	0.2%
Japan	11.2	0.3%
France	8.3	0.6%
Germany	7.6	0.4%
Italy	4.1	0.3%
Britain	3.2	0.3%
Canada	2.5	0.5%
Total G7	48.6	0.3%
Netherlands	2.8	0.9%
Sweden	2.5	1.0%
Norway	1.3	1.2%
Denmark	1.4	1.0%
Other "North"	3.8	—
Saudi Arabia	0.8	1.4%
Other Arab	0.3	—
Other "South"	0.4	—
Total world	61.9	—

Source: Based on OECD data listed in United Nations. *World Economic Survey 1994.* New York: United Nations, p. 294.

Nearly 80 percent of the DAC countries' government assistance goes directly to governments in the third world as state-to-state **bilateral aid;** the rest goes through the UN or other agencies as **multilateral aid.** As of the late 1980s, Africa received about 35 percent of the total, South Asia 20 percent, the Middle East 20 percent, Latin America 15 percent, and China about 5 percent. Foreign aid made up a tiny fraction of GDP in Brazil, Mexico, and Nigeria, less than 1 percent of GDP in China and India, 4 percent in Pakistan, 8 percent in Bangladesh, and 20 percent in Indonesia. In an extreme case, 75 percent of Mozambique's GDP is foreign aid.[35]

Types of Aid Bilateral aid takes a variety of forms. *Grants* are funds given free to a recipient state, usually for some stated purpose. *Technical cooperation* refers to grants given in the form of expert assistance in some project rather than just money or goods. *Credits* are grants that can be used to buy certain products from the donor state. For instance, Japan might assist a state's agricultural development by giving credits that can be used to buy Japanese-built farm equipment. The United States regularly gives credits that can be used for purchases of U.S. grain. If people in a recipient country become accustomed to products from the donor state, they are likely to buy those same products in the future.

---

[35]1988 data from The Economist. *Book of Vital World Statistics.* New York: Random House, 1990.

Loans are funds given to help in economic development, which must be repaid in the future out of the surplus generated by the development process (they too are often tied to the purchase of products from the donor state). Unlike commercial loans, government-to-government development loans are often on subsidized terms, with long repayment times and low interest rates. Although still an obligation for the recipient country, such loans are relatively easy to service and thus do not hold back the country's accumulation of surplus in the short term.

Loan guarantees, which are used only occasionally, are promises by the donor state to back up commercial loans to the recipient. If the recipient state services such debts and ultimately repays them, there is no cost to the donor. But if the recipient cannot make the payments, the donor has to step in and cover the debts. The United States now puts aside money into a reserve fund, proportional to the loans it guarantees, to insure against potential defaults. A loan guarantee allows the recipient state to borrow money at lower interest rates from commercial banks (because the risk to the bank is much lower).

Military aid is not normally included in development assistance, but in a broad sense belongs there. It is money that flows from North to South, from government to government, and it does bring a certain amount of value into the third-world economy. For example, if a country is going to have a certain size army with certain weapons, then getting them free from a donor state frees up money that can be used elsewhere in the economy (not that it necessarily will be well spent; it might just buy more weapons). However, of all the forms of development assistance, military aid is certainly one of the least efficient and most prone to impede rather than help economic development. It is also geared almost exclusively to political alliances rather than the development needs of the recipient country.

The main agency dispensing U.S. foreign economic assistance (but not military aid) is the State Department's *Agency for International Development (USAID)*, which works mainly through the U.S. embassies in each recipient country. Major recipients of U.S. foreign aid include Israel, Egypt, and Turkey—all important strategic allies in the volatile Middle East. Like other great powers, the United States uses the promise of foreign aid, or the threat of cutting it off, as a leverage in political bargaining with recipients. For example, when Pakistan proceeded in the late 1980s with a nuclear weapons program, despite U.S. warnings, a sizable flow of U.S. aid was terminated. When Peru's president suspended democracy in 1992 (to fight the Shining Path rebellion), the United States cut off foreign aid to Peru; when the president agreed to schedule new elections and commit himself to a timetable for restoring democracy, the United States restored some of the aid. In Indonesia and elsewhere the United States has cut off foreign aid to protest human rights violations by the military. Thus foreign aid is used as a leverage to gain political influence in the third world.

The U.S. **Peace Corps** provides U.S. volunteers for technical development assistance in third-world states. They work at the request and under the direction of the host state but are paid an allowance by the U.S. government. Started by President Kennedy in 1961, the Peace Corps now sends about 5,000 volunteers to over sixty countries, where they participate in projects affecting about a million people. It is a small-scale program, but one that increases person-to-person contacts.

In foreign aid, the donor must have the permission of the recipient government to operate in the country. This goes back to the principle of national sovereignty and the history of colonialism. National governments have the right to control the distribution of

Governments provide $60 billion annually in foreign assistance, and private donors $10 billion more (1992 data). Of the G7 countries, the United States gives the least foreign aid as a percentage of GDP. Here, U.S. rice arrives in Somalia, December 1992.

aid and the presence of foreign workers on their soil. Only occasionally is this principle violated, as when the United States and its allies provided assistance to Iraqi Kurds against the wishes of the Iraqi government following the Gulf War. International norms may be starting to change in this regard, with short-term humanitarian assistance starting to be seen as a human right that should not be subject to government veto.

UN Programs Most of the multilateral development aid goes through UN *programs*. The place of these programs in the UN structure is described in Chapter 7 (see pp. 286–288). The overall flow of assistance through the UN is coordinated by the **UN Development Program (UNDP),** which manages 5000 projects at once around the world (focusing especially on technical development assistance). Other UN programs focus on concentrating capital, transferring technology, and developing workforce skills for manufacturing. UNIDO works on industrialization, UNITAR on training and research. But most UN programs focus on meeting basic needs. As we have seen, UNICEF works to help poor children, the UN Population Fund (UNFPA) spreads access to birth control, and the World Food Program (WFP) provides food aid for both disaster relief and long-term development. Other programs coordinate assistance in the areas of health (WHO), education (UNESCO), women's status (UNIFEM and INSTRAW), housing (Habitat), labor (ILO), and agriculture (FAO).

UN programs have three advantages in promoting economic development. One is that governments and citizens tend to perceive the UN as a friend of the third world, not a hostile or alien force, a threat to sovereignty, or a reminder of colonialism. The UN can sometimes mobilize technical experts and volunteers from other third-world countries so that people who arrive to help with development do not look like white European colonialists. For instance, a team of Egyptian medical workers under a UN program may be more easily accepted in an African country than French or British workers, however well-intentioned.

Second, UN workers may be more likely to make appropriate decisions because of their backgrounds and work in other third-world countries. UN workers who come from the third world or have worked in other poor countries in a region may be more sensitive to local conditions and to the pitfalls of development assistance than are aid workers from rich countries.

A third advantage is that the UN can organize its assistance on a global scale, giving priority to projects and avoiding duplication and the reinvention of the wheel in each state. For some issues—such as the fight against AIDS or the integration of development objectives with environmental preservation—there is no substitute for global organization.

A major disadvantage faced by the UN development programs is that they are funded largely through voluntary contributions by rich states. Each program has to solicit contributions in order to carry on its activities. As the UNFPA discovered in 1976, the contributions can be abruptly cut off if the program displeases a donor government (see p. 455). A second major disadvantage of UN programs is their reputation for operating in an inefficient, bureaucratic manner. These programs sometimes lack both the cohesion and the resources that governments and MNCs in the North take for granted.

The Disaster Relief Model

The remainder of this chapter discusses three models of development assistance, which are distinguished by the type of assistance provided rather than the type of donor (all three models encompass both government and private aid).

First is the disaster relief model. It is the kind of foreign assistance most likely to make the evening news when poor people are afflicted by famine, drought, earthquakes, flooding, or other such natural disasters. (War is also a disaster and can compound naturally occurring disasters.) When disaster strikes a poor state, many people are left with no means of subsistence and often without their homes. **Disaster relief** is the provision of short-term relief to such people in the form of food, water, shelter, clothing, and other essentials.

Disaster relief is very important because disasters can wipe out years of progress in economic development at a single blow. Generally the international community tries to respond with enough assistance to get people back on their feet. The costs of such assistance are relatively modest, the benefits visible and dramatic. Having a system of disaster relief in place provides the third world with a kind of insurance against sudden losses that could otherwise destabilize economic accumulation.

Disasters generally occur quickly and without much warning. Rapid response is difficult to coordinate. International disaster relief has become more organized and better coordinated in the past decade but is still a complex process that varies somewhat from one situation to the next. Contributions of governments, private charitable organizations, and other groups and agencies are coordinated through the *UN Office of the Disaster Relief Coordinator (UNDRO)* in Geneva. Typically, international contributions make up no more than about one-third of the total relief effort, the remainder coming from local communities and national governments in the affected states. The U.S. government's contributions are coordinated by the *Office of Foreign Disaster Assistance (OFDA)*, which is part of USAID.

Disaster relief is something of a collective good because the states of the North do not benefit individually by contributing, yet they benefit in the long run from greater stability in the South. Despite this problem and the large number of actors, disaster relief is generally a positive example of international cooperation to get a job done. Food donated by the World Council of Churches may be carried to the scene in U.S. military aircraft and then distributed by the International Committee of the Red Cross. Embarrassing failures in the past—of underresponse or overresponse, of duplication of efforts or agencies working at cross-purposes—have become rarer in the 1990s.[36]

The relationship of disasters with economic development is complex, and appropriate responses vary according to location, type and size of disaster, and phase of recovery. For instance, refugees displaced from their home communities have different needs (like tents) than earthquake or hurricane victims whose entire communities have been damaged (and who need help such as transport of supplies). Different resources are needed in the emergency phase (e.g., food and medical supplies) than in the reconstruction phase (e.g., earthquake-resistant housing designs). Responses that are too small in scale or too short-term may fail to meet critical needs, but those that are too large or prolonged can overwhelm the local economy and create dependency (reducing incentives for self-help). Thus, appropriate disaster relief can promote local economic development, whereas inappropriate responses can distort or impede such development and even create the conditions for future disasters.[37]

When the disaster is *war*, the lead role often falls to the **International Committee of the Red Cross (ICRC)**, based in Switzerland. International norms and traditions treat the ICRC as an agency with special protected status (see p. 299). Red Cross societies in each country are autonomous agencies that also participate in disaster relief efforts (they are called Red Crescent societies in Islamic countries and the Red Star of David in Israel).

International norms regarding states' legal obligations to assist others in time of natural disaster and to accept such assistance if needed are changing.[38] Perhaps by the end of

---

[36]*The Los Angeles Times*, October 22, 1989: A47.

[37]Anderson, Mary B., and Peter J. Woodrow. *Rising from the Ashes: Development Strategies in Times of Disaster.* Boulder, CO: Westview, 1989. Cuny, Frederick C. *Disasters and Development.* New York: Oxford University Press, 1983.

[38]Toman, Jiri. Towards a Disaster Relief Law: Legal Aspects of Disaster Relief Operations. In Frits Kalshoven, ed. *Assisting the Victims of Armed Conflict and Other Disasters.* Dordrecht, Netherlands: Martinus Nijhoff, 1989.

the 1990s—designated by the UN as the International Decade for Natural Disaster Reduction—a new international regime in this area will have solidified.

The Missionary Model

Beyond disaster relief, many governments and private organizations provide ongoing development assistance in the form of projects administered by agencies from the North in local communities in the South to help meet basic needs. Although such efforts vary, one could call the approach a *missionary* model because it resembles the charitable works performed by missionaries in poor countries in past centuries. In fact, many of these private programs are still funded by churches and carried out by missionaries. Often such assistance is considered "God's work."

Such charitable programs are helpful though not without problems. They are a useful means by which people in the North funnel resources to people in the South. Even during the colonial era, missionaries did much good despite sometimes perpetuating a stereotype of European superiority and native inferiority. Today's efforts to help poor people in third-world states gives individuals and communities some resources with which they may better contribute to national economic development.

The missionary model of foreign assistance contributes goods to third-world economies, but often with little understanding of local needs or long-term strategies. Here, free supplies are delivered by the U.S. ambassador and the captain of a U.S. Navy ship participating in Project Handclasp (January 1989). But is mouthwash really what Mauritania needs?

However, most handout programs are short-term and do not create sustained local economic development. They do not address the causes of poverty, the position of poor countries in the world economy, or local political conditions such as military rule or corruption.

One version of "missionary" assistance—advertised widely in the United States—lets citizens in rich countries "adopt" poor children in the third world. Photos of a hungry child stare at the reader from a magazine page while the accompanying text notes that a few cents a day can "save" the child. Although such programs raise awareness in the North of the extent of poverty in the South, at worst they tend to be exploitive and to reinforce racist and paternalistic stereotypes of the helplessness of third-world people.

The U.S. military operation to restore food relief in war-torn Somalia in 1992–1993 contained elements of the missionary model. President Bush called the mission "God's work" and it was often referred to as one to "save" Somalia. U.S. leaders tried to focus the mission narrowly on delivering food to hungry people despite appeals from the UN secretary-general and others that only disarming the warring factions could solve the Somali crisis. Later, political negotiation and some forceful disarming of factions quieted the civil war at least temporarily, and without doubt the U.S. intervention helped the situation in Somalia greatly. But in the end the United States and the UN pulled out without resolving the war and other political problems that had caused the famine and could do so again. The episode showed that helping starving people is often more complex than just sending in food shipments (even with military escorts to ensure their safe delivery).

There is a danger in the missionary model that people from the North may provide assistance inappropriate for a third-world state's local conditions and culture. This danger is illustrated by an experience in Kenya in the 1970s. Nomadic herders in the area of Lake Turkana near the Sahara desert—the Turkana tribe—were poor and vulnerable to periodic droughts. Western aid donors and the Kenyan government decided that the herders' traditional way of life was not environmentally sustainable and should be replaced by commercial fishing of the abundant tilapia fish in Lake Turkana. Norway, with long experience in fishing, was asked to teach fishing and boat-building methods to the Turkana. To create a commercially viable local economy, Norwegian consultants recommended marketing frozen fish fillets to Kenya and the world. Thus in 1981 Norway finished building a $2 million, state-of-the-art fish freezing plant on the shores of Lake Turkana and a $20 million road connecting the plant to Kenya's transportation system.

There were only three problems. First, with temperatures of 100 degrees outside (a contrast with Norway!), the cost of operating the freezers exceeded the income from the fillets. So after a few days the freezers were turned off and the facility became a dried-fish warehouse. Second, Turkana culture viewed fishing as the lowest-status profession, suitable only for those incompetent at herding. Third, every few decades Lake Turkana shrinks as drought reduces the inflow of water. Such a drought in 1984–1985 eliminated the gulf where the fishing operations were based. The Norwegians might have foreseen these problems by doing more homework instead of just transplanting what worked in Norway. When the drought hit, the 20,000 herders who had been brought to the lake to learn fishing were left in an overcrowded, overgrazed environment in which every tree was cut for firewood and most cattle died. Instead of becoming self-sufficient, the Turkana became totally dependent on outside aid.[39]

---

[39]Harden, Blaine. *Africa: Dispatches from a Fragile Continent*. New York: W. W. Norton, 1990.

The Oxfam Model

A third model of development assistance can be found in the approach taken by the private charitable group **Oxfam America** (one of seven groups worldwide descended from the Oxford Committee for Famine Relief, founded in 1942 in Britain). Originally devoted to short-term aid to famine victims, and still active in that effort, Oxfam America realized that over the longer term people needed not just handouts of food but the means to feed themselves—land, water, seed, tools, and technical training.

The distinctive aspect of the Oxfam model is that it relies on local communities to determine the needs of their own people and to carry out development projects. Oxfam does not operate projects itself but provides funding to local organizations. Nor does Oxfam call itself a donor and these organizations recipients. Rather, it calls both sides "project partners"—working together to accomplish a task. In this model, a little outside money can go a long way toward building sustained local economic development. Furthermore, projects help participants empower themselves by organizing to meet their own needs.

For example, Oxfam America helped the Ethiopian women's cooperative mentioned in Chapter 12 (see p. 494). Oxfam did not design or organize the project; women in Addis Ababa did. But when their garment-making workshop became profitable and was ready to expand and employ twice as many women, Oxfam gave the group a $15,000 grant to build a new building. This small grant helped to consolidate a new center of accumulation in one of the world's poorest neighborhoods.

After the Marxist-oriented military government of Ethiopia fell in 1991 following years of civil war, Oxfam America brought together the Addis Ababa women's leaders with a dozen other project partners in Ethiopia for a meeting. They agreed that the former government's centralized system of top-down economic development did not work, despite its socialist rhetoric, because it disempowered farm families (who make up the majority of the population). The full participation of poor people was seen as the key to successful foreign assistance. The relationship between North and South—groups like Oxfam and their project partners—was likened to a good marriage where decisions are made jointly and dependency does not develop.

In this model, third-world economic development is not charity; it is in the interests of people in the rich countries as well as the poor. A cooperative relationship between North and South is essential for a peaceful and prosperous world. Even in a narrow economic sense, development in the third world creates new markets and new products that will enrich the industrialized countries as well. In economics, the creation of wealth is a positive-sum game.

The Oxfam approach seeks to reconceptualize development assistance to focus on long-term development through a bottom-up basic needs strategy. "Genuine development," in Oxfam's view, "enables people to meet their essential needs; extends beyond food aid and emergency relief; reverses the process of impoverishment; enhances democracy; makes possible a balance between populations and resources; improves the well-being and status of women; respects local cultures; sustains the natural environment; measures progress in human, not just monetary terms; involves change, not just charity; requires the empowerment of the poor; and promotes the interests of the majority of people worldwide, in the global North as well as the South."[40]

---

[40]*Oxfam America News* [quarterly]. Boston: Oxfam America.

To promote its approach to North-South relations (and to raise funds for its project partners), Oxfam America carries on education and action programs in the United States. The most prominent is an annual Fast for a World Harvest, a week before Thanksgiving, that raises awareness among U.S. citizens about the extent and causes of third-world hunger. Thanks to the information revolution (see Chapter 10), information about third-world poverty and economic development is now more widely available to people in industrialized countries. Oxfam's 1991 Fast generated media coverage that reached about 100 million people in the United States.

Because of disappointment with the political uses of foreign aid in the past, Oxfam has tried to minimize the role in its projects of governments in both the North and South. For instance, Oxfam does not accept government funds nor does it make grants to governments.

The general goals of the Oxfam model of foreign aid are consistent with a broader movement in the global South toward grassroots **empowerment**. Efforts such as those of Oxfam partners are organized by poor people to gain some power over their situation and meet their basic needs—not by seizing control of the state in a revolution but by means that are more direct, more local, and less violent. The key to success is getting organized, finding information, gaining self-confidence, and obtaining needed resources to implement action plans.

For example, women in Bangladesh have a very low status in rural society (see "Women in Development" on pp. 493–494). Often they cannot own property, participate in politics, or even leave their houses without their husbands' permission. Now some women in rural Bangladesh have organized women's groups to raise women's self-esteem, promote their rights, and mobilize them to change conditions. One woman reported: "Our husbands used to beat us—now they don't. They used to not let us in the fields—now we go with them. They used to not help us at home—now they do. . . . We now can do all this thanks to the group and the support it has given us." In this example, economic development and the satisfaction of basic needs have been furthered not by violence or revolution, nor by the actions of the state, foreign governments, or international agencies, but directly at the community level.

In India, local women's groups using only the power of persuasion and logic have convinced some landowners to give them land for cooperative income-generating projects such as dairy farming, vegetable farming, and raising silkworms. Elsewhere in India, women working as gatherers of wood and other forest products got organized to win the legal minimum wage for 250,000 female forest workers—three times what they had been paid before. In this case, government action was necessary (by the provincial administration) but the pressure for such action came from local organizing. The women took their case to the public and the press, staging protest marches and getting an art exhibit relating to their cause displayed in the provincial capital.

Such examples do not mean that national and foreign governments are unimportant. On the contrary, government policies affect millions of people more quickly and more widely than do grassroots efforts. Indeed, grassroots organizing often has as an ultimate goal the restructuring of national political and social life so that policies reflect the needs of poor people. But the successes of grassroots empowerment show that poor communities can be more than victims of poverty waiting to be saved or passive bystanders in North-

The Oxfam model of foreign assistance emphasizes support for local groups that can stimulate self-sustaining economic development at a local level. A mutually beneficial North-South partnership is the global goal of such projects. This woman manages a cooperative store in San Salvador, El Salvador.

South relations. Nor do poor people need to place their hopes for change in violent revolutions aimed at toppling national governments—revolutions that lead to greater suffering more often than to stable economic development.

The Oxfam model has the advantage of promoting this trend toward grassroots empowerment, thereby overcoming the dangers of externally run programs under the disaster relief and missionary models. However, the Oxfam model to date has been tested only on a very small scale. Although the model may be effective in the local communities it reaches, it would have to be adopted widely and replicated on a much larger scale in order to influence the overall prospects for third-world development. It is unclear if the principles the model embodies, from the reliance on local community organizers to the avoidance of government involvement, would work on a massive scale.

Confronting the North-South Gap All three models of development assistance have contributions to make. Given the extent of poverty in the global South, it needs all the help from the North that it can get. Perhaps the most important point is for people in the North to be aware of the tremendous gap between North and South and to try to address the problem. Third-world poverty can seem so overwhelming that citizens in rich countries can easily turn their backs and just try to live their own lives.

But in today's interdependent world this really is not possible. North-South relations have become a part of everyday life. The integrated global economy brings to the North products and people from the South. The information revolution puts images of third-world poverty on TV sets in comfortable living rooms. The growing role of the UN brings North and South together in a worldwide community. Security relations and political economy alike have shifted in the post–Cold War era to give new prominence to the third world.

Ultimately the conflicts and dramas of North-South relations are little different from those of the rest of international relations or of other spheres of political and social life. The problems of IR are the problems of human society—struggles for power and wealth, efforts to cooperate despite differences, social dilemmas and collective goods problems, the balance between freedom and order, trade-offs of equity versus efficiency and of long-term versus short-term outcomes. These themes are inescapable in human society, from the smallest groups to the world community. The subject of international relations is in this sense an extension of everyday life and a reflection of the choices of individual human beings. IR belongs to all of us—North and South, women and men, citizens and leaders—who live together on this planet.

❖ CHAPTER SUMMARY

- Economic development in the third world has been uneven; per capita GDP increased in the 1970s but, except in Asia, decreased in the 1980s. Growth in the 1990s has been brisk in Asia but slow elsewhere.
- Evidence does not support a strong association of economic growth either with internal equality of wealth distribution or with internal inequality.
- The newly industrializing countries (NICs) in Asia—South Korea, Taiwan, Hong Kong, and Singapore—show that it is possible to rise out of poverty into sustained economic accumulation. Other third-world states are trying to emulate these successes, but it is unclear whether these experiences can apply elsewhere.
- China has registered strong economic growth in the past fifteen years of market-oriented economic reforms. Though still quite poor, China may be emerging as a leading success story in third-world economic development.
- Economic development in other large third-world countries such as India, Brazil, and Nigeria has been slowed by the inefficiency of state-owned enterprises, by corruption, and by debt.
- Import substitution has been largely rejected as a development strategy in favor of export-led growth. This reflects both the experiences of the NICs and the theory of comparative advantage.

◆   Most poor states want to develop a manufacturing base, but this is a difficult thing to do. Even when focused on low-capital industries, states have generally had to sharpen income disparities in the process of concentrating capital for manufacturing.

◆   The theory that democratization would accompany and strengthen economic development has not been supported by the actual experiences of third-world countries. But the opposite theory—that authoritarian government is necessary to maintain control while concentrating capital for industrialization—has also not been supported.

◆   Government corruption is a major obstacle to development throughout the third world.

◆   Given the shortage of local capital in most poor states, foreign investment by MNCs is often courted as a means of stimulating economic growth. MNCs look for favorable local conditions, including political and economic stability, in deciding where to invest.

◆   States in the global South seek the transfer of technology to support their future economic development. Technology transfer can be appropriate or inappropriate to local needs depending on the circumstances of each case.

◆   The "green revolution" of the 1960s was a massive North-South transfer of agricultural technology, which had both good and bad effects. Today's "green" technologies being transferred to the third world are techniques for environmentally sustainable development.

◆   Third-world debt, resulting largely from overborrowing in the 1970s and early 1980s, is a major problem. Through renegotiations and other debt management efforts, the North and South have improved the debt situation in recent years. However, the South remains over $1 trillion in debt to the North, and annual debt service consumes about one-sixth of all hard-currency earnings from exports of the South (much more in some regions and states).

◆   The IMF makes loans to states in the South conditional on economic and governmental reforms. These conditionality agreements often necessitate politically unpopular measures such as cutting food subsidies.

◆   The GATT trading regime works against the third world by allowing richer nations to protect sectors in which the third world has advantages—notably agriculture and textiles. The Generalized System of Preferences tries to compensate by lowering barriers to third-world exports.

◆   Efforts to improve the South's solidarity, cooperation, and bargaining position relative to the North—such as the New International Economic Order—have had little success.

◆   Foreign assistance, most of it from governments in the North, plays an important part in the economic development plans of the poorer states of the South.

◆   Only a few states in the North meet the goal of contributing 0.7 percent of their gross domestic product as foreign assistance to the South. The United States, at 0.15 percent of its GDP, contributes the smallest share of any industrialized state.

◆   Most foreign aid consists of bilateral grants and loans from governments in the North to specific governments in the South. Such aid is often used for political leverage, and promotes the export of products from the donor state.

◆ About one-fifth of foreign aid is not bilateral but is funneled through multilateral agencies—mostly UN programs.

◆ Disaster relief provides short-term aid to prevent a natural disaster from reversing a poor state's economic development efforts. Disaster relief generally involves cooperation by various donor governments, local governments, the UN, and private agencies.

◆ Handouts to poor communities to meet immediate needs for food and supplies outside times of disaster—here called the missionary model—can be helpful but also have several drawbacks. Such aid can be inappropriate to local needs and can encourage dependence.

◆ Efforts to support local organizations working to empower poor people and generate community economic development—here called the Oxfam model—are promising but have been tried only on a small scale.

❖ THINKING CRITICALLY

1. How might the strong economic growth of the Asian NICs and of China affect proposals for an Asian free-trade area similar to NAFTA and the EU? What would be the interests and worries of Japan, of China and the NICs, and of the poor states of the region, in such an arrangement?

2. Past successes in third-world economic development have depended heavily on developing a manufacturing base, which requires access to scarce capital. How do you think the information revolution and the increasing role of services in the world economy might change this pattern? Might any third-world countries find a niche in these growing sectors of the world economy and bypass manufacturing? What states or regions might be candidates for such an approach, and why?

3. How does the third-world debt problem compare with the U.S. debt, discussed in Chapter 9, in magnitude and effect? Do the two debt problems arise from similar causes? Which of them do you consider the more serious problem, and why?

4. Some scholars criticize the IMF for imposing harsh terms in its conditionality agreements with poor states. Others applaud the IMF for demanding serious reforms before providing financial resources. If you were a third-world leader negotiating with the IMF, what kinds of terms would you be willing to agree to and what terms would you resist? Why?

5. If the states in North America, Western Europe, and Japan/Pacific all met the target of providing 0.7 percent of GDP in foreign assistance, what might the effects be? How much additional aid would be made available? To whom would it likely go? What effects might it have on the recipient states and on third-world economic development overall?

❖ KEY TERMS

economic development
newly industrializing country (NIC)
four tigers/four dragons
free economic zone
import substitution vs. export-led growth
informal sector
brain drain
technology transfer
green revolution
debt service
default vs. renegotiation
Paris Club, London Club
IMF conditionality
New International Economic
  Order (NIEO)

UN Conference on Trade and
  Development (UNCTAD)
foreign assistance
Development Assistance Committee
  (DAC)
bilateral and multilateral aid
Peace Corps
UN Development Program
  (UNDP)
disaster relief
International Committee of the
  Red Cross (ICRC)
Oxfam America
empowerment

THE VIEW FROM 2046

INTERNATIONAL SECURITY

The New International
  System
Military Leverage

INTERNATIONAL POLITICAL ECONOMY

Global Integration
Environmental
  Adjustments
The South

YOUR WORLD

*Child in Sarajevo,
Bosnia, 1993.*

CHAPTER 14

POSTSCRIPT: IR IN 2046 A.D.

❖ THE VIEW FROM 2046

The author is honored to have been asked to write this postscript on the fiftieth anniversary of the publication of his textbook. From my perspective in the year 2046, the past fifty years trace the path that our world has followed since your generation first read this textbook. You are now, of course, 70-year-olds, and your choices have left their mark on history.

It is difficult to write something that will be read fifty years before it is written. This is especially true because there is no single future for the reader of 1996. My reality in 2046 is, for you, only one of many possible futures. I cannot tell you how your world will change in the next fifty years, but only how it might change. I invite you to think about your own future world and your role in making it the kind of future you want. And I encourage you, as you read about one future, to take exception where you find my world either unlikely or undesirable.

The following notes are my reflections on the textbook in light of the history of 1996 to 2046. I have organized these thoughts around a few of the book's major themes. They may therefore give you a chance to reflect back on what you have read—to review, to ponder, and to imagine.

❖ INTERNATIONAL SECURITY

International security still matters today, as it did in the 1990s. But the nature of security and the substantive situation have changed.

The New International System

One major theme of the book was the nature of the international system as a well-developed set of rules based on state sovereignty, territoriality, and "anarchy"—a lack of central government. Today, these principles are less important; the international system is more complex, more nuanced, and more interconnected with other aspects of planetary society.

State *sovereignty* still matters, but it is now counterbalanced by the principle of self-determination. No longer do international norms recognize the right of a government to rule a population by force against its will and to violate human rights. Through the judicious application of sanctions and rewards, the UN maintained the trend begun in the late twentieth century toward the spread of democracy and human rights.

Yes, the UN is alive and well; last year's hundredth anniversary celebration was a grand occasion. The UN has infringed on state sovereignty to the point that IR scholars rarely use the term *anarchy* any more. The UN has matured into a quasi government, less and less subject to the power of individual states. World Court rulings can be enforced by the UN's military and (much more often) nonmilitary means of leverage. The veto in the Security Council, useful in the UN's early decades, was eliminated. Representation in the General Assembly has been democratized: there is a formula for allocating voting power among the nearly four hundred member states.

In retrospect, a key turning point for the consolidation of the UN and the spread of democracy and human rights was the installation of democratic governments in Russia and China. The triumph of the Chinese democracy movement brought a unity of purpose to all the great powers. China's development this century into a new-technology economic and political giant shows the wisdom of the UN founders in foreseeing China's great-power status. (New technology now refers to the information-intensive technological style that replaced energy-intensive industrialization.)

The proliferation of destructive weapons in poor regions created great upheavals in which several cities were lost and many people suffered. Ultimately, these difficulties contributed to the realization that the flaws of an anarchic state system—collective goods problems and security dilemmas—had to be redressed by shifting much authority from states to the UN.

As for *territorial integrity*, it was probably becoming an obsolete concept back in the 1990s. As became all too clear in the difficult years of the early twenty-first century, national borders do not stop information, environmental changes, or missiles. States in 2046 still have a territorial basis, but their territory is now an administrative convenience. States now have less control of activities on their own territory and conversely have more chances to affect what happens outside their territory.

All these changes in the international system have been affected by the information revolution, which was still in its early stages in the 1990s. Information allows all the actors—state, substate, and supranational—to know what is going on everywhere in the world and to coordinate actions globally. Without it, how would the UN manage planetwide problems or operate the world political system? How would state leaders make rational decisions that achieve win-win outcomes? How would substate groups protect their human rights or defend against military attacks? Information has been the key to the diffusion of power, which in turn has reshaped the international system in many ways.

Military Leverage

Information and other new-technology developments have also profoundly changed the utility and role of military force. As targeting became more and more accurate, military forces gained increasing power of certain destruction. Wars, if you can call them that, became more widespread but at a lower level—a kind of ongoing skirmishing, especially in the global South, that colored the background of world politics well into the twenty-first century.

Paradoxically, the increasing power of destruction available to increasing numbers of actors eventually reduced the frequency of such skirmishing. The power of defensive weaponry made successful attacks more difficult, and the power of offensive weaponry made retaliation an extremely potent threat to deter an attack. The widespread skirmishing slowly gave way to a standoff in which opposing actors wielding military forces could not improve the situation by using those forces. Perhaps the no-win wars of the 1980s in Angola, Cambodia, and El Salvador were forerunners of this trend.

The global military standoff reproduced the essence of Cold War nuclear deterrence at a micro level throughout the world's pockets of conflict. The twentieth-century superpowers could not attack each other without destroying themselves, and the same now applies to the many military forces located around the world. A large force cannot reliably defeat a small one (or, to be more accurate, the costs of doing so are too high). This trend was already visible in the collapse of the European empires in the 1960s and 1970s as well as in the Vietnam and Afghanistan wars.

The increasing power of military leverage, then, actually made it less useful. Other forms of leverage, particularly economic rewards, became much more important power capabilities as world politics evolved in the twenty-first century. Yet the world has never been able to disarm entirely—because then a single actor wielding the tremendous destructive power of military force could again dominate other actors.

A partial disarmament has been accomplished, however. After a few decades of sporadic but intense military clashes, it became clear that a more stable and formal structure was needed to lock all parties' military forces in place and prevent outbreaks of violence. This was accomplished in the Global Cease-Fire Initiative, in conjunction with which more than two thousand outstanding conflicts with international ramifications were submitted to binding arbitration under a special agency of the World Court. During and after this process, multilateral military reductions left actors with defensive and minimal deterrent capabilities. This reduced the costs of maintaining military forces, and averted accidents and incidents.

Today, hundreds of actors retain military capabilities. But these capabilities, like the superpower nuclear forces of the late twentieth century, cannot be used productively. The highly intelligent weapons in these arsenals are based at home but are global in reach. Unlike nuclear weapons, today's weapons can be very selective in targeting, so an attack can reliably destroy a single building or vehicle rather than a whole city. But this does not make the weapons much more usable, because an attacked actor can reciprocate in kind—a response mandated by international norms. The norm of reciprocity thus ensures that an attack cannot pay.

The kinds of military forces that residents of the twentieth century would find familiar—ships, planes, trucks full of soldiers, and so forth—have undergone an interesting evolution. These mobile lower-technology forces still exist in today's world, but they are no longer armed. Rather, state leaders found that large military forces—with their tight discipline and centralized hierarchy—were more effective as positive than negative forms of leverage. Armies were incrementally stripped of weaponry and sent on new missions for disaster relief, development assistance, and related functions. The rich states of the North, in particular, modified their conventional forces for disarmed interventions in the South as part of the North-South assistance discussed shortly.

I personally believe that human survival and adaptation in these circumstances shows that we are, indeed, *rational* beings in a deep sense (not just a shortsighted, self-interested sense). We did not destroy our world; we did not allow the security dilemma to keep us from achieving favorable outcomes. We changed the rules of world politics when only such changes could further our well-being. However, philosophers are still debating the meaning of rationality.

Another question still being debated is the extent to which the integration of women into international politics contributed to the kinds of outcomes we have seen. Personally, I believe that the rising participation of women in recent decades has helped lead to the reduced reliance on military leverage, the increased effectiveness of conflict resolution, and the strengthening of human rights and democracy. It may be that the integration of women into conventional military forces contributed to those forces' redirection toward unarmed missions. But other IR scholars argue that these trends would all have developed with or without the increased participation of women.

❖ INTERNATIONAL POLITICAL ECONOMY

In IPE, as in international security, the developments of the past five decades reflect trends that were already becoming visible at the end of the twentieth century. The simultaneous trends toward integration and disintegration among states were among the most interesting then, and in many ways still are.

Global Integration

You are probably wondering whether the world in 2046 has a single language, a single currency, or a single culture. It does not. Today's integrated global economy operates efficiently without needing to impose such uniformity, because information technologies can provide simultaneous language translation, keep track of financial transactions, and carry hundreds of channels of culture at once on communication networks.

Each of the world's nearly four hundred states takes pride in its unique history and accomplishments. Its people have continued to speak their own language, to fly their own flag, to use their own currency with its pictures and emblems. Nationalism thus continues to be an important force despite the emergence of a quasi government in world political affairs. As many of the states of the late twentieth century broke up into smaller units, those units became more culturally and ethnically homogeneous, strengthening the "we" feeling on which nationalism rests.

At the same time, however, although people identify with their state, they also now hold an explicitly global identity. As the world's economic and cultural activities have become more integrated through telecommunications advances, and as humans have extended their perspective into outer space, people around the world have come to see their larger community as the whole world, even while maintaining ties to state-level and local communities. People do fly their state's flag, but they often fly the UN flag (unchanged since 1945) above it and their provincial or city flag below.

Likewise, each state continues to design its own currency with national symbols. But each bill now carries a World Bank certification stamp (encrypted against counterfeiting) in one corner. States are free to design their own currency but not to print as much as they want (this is another infringement of state sovereignty by supranational authority). The World Bank issues only the number of authorizations that will maintain the currency's exchange value relative to other states' currencies. All currencies are thus fixed at the same rate although they go by different names. Ukrainian money can be spent in Belarus without worrying about exchange rate fluctuations. There are no more hard currencies and no currency exchange markets. These changes generally resulted from the efforts of MNCs to create an international economic environment conducive to business.

In international trade, liberal economics has similarly prevailed because it has worked so well. Goods crossing international borders do not have to pay tariffs, just as the people buying and selling them do not need to worry about currency exchange fluctuations. States have learned that in order to survive they had to help, not impede, the creation of wealth by MNCs and other economic actors. States have survived, proliferated in number, and maintained their importance as *political* actors in part because of their willingness to give up many of their *economic* activities to private actors. International norms would not today condone the imposition of taxes on economic transactions just because they happened to cross state borders.

In the European Union as in the world as a whole, nationalism remained an important force. Contrary to some predictions, a United States of Europe never emerged. The European states remain separate members of the UN, with their own state governments, although the EU is an important administrative body on the regional level.

A regional level of governance developed in several other regions as well, following more or less in Europe's path. The most important of these was the Islamic Community, which encompassed most of the Middle East region. But regionalism there and elsewhere never gained the power that nationalism holds. Supranational authority has developed more at the global than the regional level.

Environmental Adjustments

Environmental degradation in the past fifty years turned out to be even worse than was expected in the 1990s. We have already experienced a rise of three degrees in the average world temperature, partly because of decisions made in the late twentieth century. (The degrees are in the Celsius scale; the United States finally adopted the metric system to facilitate exports.) Environmental damage emerged several decades ago as the single greatest obstacle to sustained economic growth in both the North and South (a trend presaged by Soviet-bloc environmental degradation, which contributed to that region's economic stagnation and collapse in the late twentieth century).

International response to environmental destruction centered around the UN—again infringing on the sovereignty of states over their own resource extraction, industrial activity, and pollution. Because of high costs, the large number of actors, and collective goods problems, international bargaining over the environment was difficult. An effective global environmental regime emerged only through the exertion of strong leadership by the United States, which at that time was still the world's only superpower, if not quite a hegemon.

By forcing the United States to act, the environmental problem created the conditions for the strengthening of the UN and the infringements on national sovereignty that eventually led to some solutions. We are not yet out of the woods, but at least the world can now respond to environmental problems coherently instead of being paralyzed by collective goods problems. The turbulent decades early in the twenty-first century saw much damage, but that spurred the world's great powers under U.S. leadership to take action to build a world order capable of restoring stability. Today's quasi-governmental UN is the result of that process.

The environmental problem also spurred the *new-technology* initiatives that shifted industrial activity into a less energy-intensive and more information-intensive technological style. This shift allowed growth in per capita incomes with lower strain on the environment and resources. The idea can be traced back to the call of the 1992 Earth Summit for sustainable economic growth that does not deplete resources and destroy ecosystems.

New technology moves information, instead of materials, to accomplish the same goals—with less strain on the environment. For example, in the 1980s and 1990s cars began using microcomputers to control fuel-injection systems in order to maximize energy efficiency and minimize pollution. Around the same time, MNCs began to hold international business conferences through telecommunications instead of sending people on fuel-burning, air-polluting planes. Workers began telecommuting instead of driving to company offices. Information (about genetic codes) was also harnessed in the biotechnology revolution that increased food supply, reduced the use of pesticides, reduced demand for water, and curtailed deforestation.

As a result of new-technology contributions, international relations are somewhat less conflict-ridden, because territory and natural resources are less often seen as scarce necessities to be fought over. Information technology has also made it harder to cheat on international agreements.

New technology has begun to shift some of our world's economic activities into outer space—notably the solar energy satellites that now provide almost half our energy. Just as the shift to oil as a leading energy source had political implications due to the geography of oil deposits, so too does the shift to space-solar energy have political implications. It means that our energy comes from a global commons, not from the territory of any state. Again this has forced us to strengthen our planetary governance through the UN to resolve conflicts.

New technology was forced into existence in large part by the economic growth of China and, to a lesser extent, India. It became clear that the traditional technological style of industrialization could not be sustained environmentally on the giant scale of these countries and that, through new technology, the North could contribute to a cleaner—and, as it turned out, cheaper—development path for the South (discussed shortly).

Population growth is one area in which there have been few surprises. Today's population of 10 billion is about what was projected toward the end of the twentieth century. Population has leveled out as poor countries in the South have moved through the demographic transition and birthrates have fallen.

Despite the continuing and serious problems we face in coping with global environmental damage, I feel that the international community is well on its way to adopting economic and political practices that will achieve a sustainable long-term relationship with the environment.

The South

In the troubled first decades of the twenty-first century, North-South relations moved to the center of world politics. At that time, demographic and economic trends sharpened the global North-South gap, with the North continuing to accumulate wealth while much of the South lingered in great poverty. The result was an upsurge in South-to-North migration and a wave of revolutionary violence in the South that increasingly spilled over into attacks against actors in the North. It became increasingly clear that the North would bear a high cost for failing to address the economic development of the South.

Taking advantage of their own fairly high degree of cooperation, the great powers managed to craft a global response to the North-South gap, a response that nearly all the world's states ultimately joined. This regime basically allocated the costs and benefits of a coherent world strategy for economic development. The adopted strategy essentially steered economies of poor states into new-technology long-term growth paths so that in future decades the development of the South would be environmentally sustainable.

It turned out that traditional European-style technological styles of industrialization were not only environmentally harmful but extremely inefficient. By using computerization and biotechnology innovations, poor states have been able to develop their economies much more efficiently than did Europe or North America. By the late twentieth century, scholars could already see the importance of education and literacy—the information base of a society—in economic development. Information technologies also contributed to economic efficiency by making corruption harder to conceal.

The world development initiatives have had success in eliminating the worst extremes of poverty in all but a handful of states. Much pain might have been spared had these initiatives come sooner, but perhaps it takes great pain to spur change. At any rate, stable accumulation is now taking place in most of the South. Once again, these recent successes have been made possible by the strengthening of international cooperation and coordination through the UN. With a weak UN such as existed at the turn of the century, it is doubtful that economic development in the South could have been addressed in the global and coherent manner necessary to succeed.

❖ YOUR WORLD

The world in which I live, in the year 2046, is not your future world. You are still living in the 1990s, and you have many possible futures. I would encourage you to think about three of those possible futures: the one you desire (the future world you would like to live in), the one you expect (the future you consider most likely), and the one that actually materializes. This third future is unknowable to you now, but as it unfolds you can compare it—at mileposts along the way—to the worlds that you desire and expect, and to the world that I have sketched in these pages.

The comparison of alternative futures may be facilitated by examining a variety of possible branch points where alternative paths diverge. For example, you could ask questions like the following (asking yourself, for each one, why you answer the way you do for your desired future and expected future):

1. Will state sovereignty be eroded by supranational authority?
2. Will norms of human rights and democracy become global?
3. Will the UN evolve into a quasi government for the world?
4. Will the UN be restructured?
5. Will World Court judgments become enforceable?
6. Will the number of states increase?
7. Will China become democratic? Will it become rich?
8. What effects will information technologies have on IR?
9. Will military leverage become obsolete?
10. Will weapons of mass destruction proliferate?
11. Will disarmament occur?
12. Will women participate more fully in IR? With what effect?
13. Will there be a single world currency?
14. Will there be a global free-trade regime?
15. Will nationalism fade out or continue to be strong?
16. Will many people develop a global identity?
17. Will world culture become more homogeneous or more pluralistic?
18. Will the EU or other regional IOs achieve political union?
19. Will global environmental destruction be severe? How soon?
20. Will new technologies avert environmental constraints?
21. Will global problems create stronger or weaker world order?
22. Will population growth level out? If so, when and at what level?
23. Will the poorest countries accumulate wealth? How soon?
24. What role will the North play in the South's development?

The choices you make and actions you take will ultimately affect, in some way, the world you live in. You cannot opt out of involvement in international relations. You are involved. And year by year, the information revolution and other aspects of interdependence are drawing you more closely into contact with the rest of the world. You can act in many ways, large and small, to bring the world you expect more into line with the world you desire. You can empower yourself by finding the actions and choices that define your place in international relations.

Now that you have completed the studies covered in this book, don't stop here. Keep learning about the world beyond your country's borders. Keep thinking about the world that might be in 2046 A.D. Be a part of the changes that will carry this world through the next fifty years. It's your world: study it, care for it, make it your own.

PHOTO CREDITS

AUTHOR INDEX

SUBJECT INDEX

Note: **Boldface** entries and page numbers indicate key terms. Entries for tables and figures are followed by (*table*) and (*fig.*), respectively.